HISTORY

OF THE

WAR IN THE PENINSULA

AND IN THE

SOUTH OF FRANCE

FROM THE YEAR 1807 TO THE YEAR 1814

VOLUME III

HISTORY

OF THE

WAR IN THE PENINSULA

AND IN THE

SOUTH OF FRANCE,

FROM THE YEAR 1807 TO THE YEAR 1814.

BY

W. F. P. NAPIER, C.B.

COLONEL H. P. FORTY-THIRD REGIMENT, MEMBER OF THE ROYAL SWEDISH
ACADEMY OF MILITARY SCIENCES.

VOL. III.

THE SECOND EDITION

CONSTABLE · LONDON

This edition first published in Great Britain 1993
by Constable and Company Limited
3 The Lanchesters, 162 Fulham Palace Road
London W6 9ER

Originally published in London in 1833
by Thomas and William Boone

ISBN 0 09 471860 1

Printed in Great Britain by
St Edmundsbury Press Ltd
Bury St Edmunds, Suffolk

TABLE OF CONTENTS.

BOOK IX.

CHAPTER I.

Inactivity of the Asturians and Gallicians—Guerilla system in Navarre and
Aragon—The Partidas surround the third corps—Blake abandons Aragon—
Suchet's operations against the Partidas—Combat of Tremendal—The ad-
vantages of Suchet's position—Troubles at Pampeluna—Suchet ordered by
Napoleon to repair there—Observations on the Guerilla system   .   .   1

CHAPTER II.

Continuation of the operations in Catalonia—St. Cyr sends Lecchi to the Ampurdan ; he returns with the intelligence of the Austrian war—Of Verdier's arrival
in the Ampurdan, and of Augereau's appointment to the command of the seventh
corps—Augereau's inflated proclamation—It is torn down by the Catalonians—
He remains sick at Perpignan—St. Cyr continues to command—Refuses to
obey Joseph's orders to remove into Aragon—Presses Verdier to commence
the siege of Gerona—Reinforces Verdier—Remains himself at Vich—Constancy of the Spaniards—St. Cyr marches from Vich, defeats three Spanish
battalions, and captures a convoy—Storms St. Felieu de Quixols—Takes a
position to cover Verdier's operations—Siege of Gerona—State of the contending parties—Assault of Monjouic fails—General Fontanes storms Palamos—Wimphen and the Milans make a vain attempt to throw succours into
Gerona—Monjouic abandoned   17

CHAPTER III.

Claros and Rovira attack Bascara and spread dismay along the French frontier
—Two Spanish officers pass the Ter and enter Gerona with succours—Alvarez
remonstrates with the junta of Catalonia—Bad conduct of the latter—Blake
advances to the aid of the city—Pestilence there—Affects the French army—
St. Cyr's firmness—Blake's timid operations—O'Donnel fights Souham, but
without success—St. Cyr takes a position of battle—Garcia Conde forces the
French lines and introduces a convoy into Gerona—Blake retires—Siege resumed—Garcia Conde comes out of the city—Ridiculous error of the French—
Conde forces the French lines and escapes—Assault on Gerona fails—Blake
advances a second time—Sends another convoy under the command of
O'Donnel to the city—O'Donnel with the head of the convoy succeeds, the
remainder is cut off—Blake's incapacity—He retires—St. Cyr goes to Perpignan
—Augereau takes the command of the siege—O'Donnel breaks through the
French lines—Blake advances a third time—Is beaten by Souham—Pino
takes Hostalrich—Admiral Martin intercepts a French squadron—Captain
Hollowell destroys a convoy in Rosas-bay—Distress in Gerona—Alvarez is
seized with delirium, and the city surrenders—Observations   .   .   31

CHAPTER IV.

Plot at Seville against the Supreme Junta defeated by lord Wellesley—Junta
propose a new form of government—Opposed by Romana—Junta announce the
convocation of the national Cortez, but endeavour to deceive the people—A
Spanish army assembled in the Morena under Eguia—Bassecour sends cavalry to reinforce Del Parque, who concentrates the Spanish army of the left
at Ciudad Rodrigo—He is joined by the Gallician divisions—Santocildes occupies Astorga—French endeavour to surprise him, but are repulsed—Ballasteros quits the Asturias, and marching by Astorga attempts to storm Zamora—
Enters Portugal—Del Parque demands the aid of the Portuguese army—Sir
A. Wellesley refuses, giving his reason in detail—Del Parque's operations—
Battle of Tamames—Del Parque occupies Salamanca, but hearing that
French troops were assembling at Valladolid retires to Bejar   .   .   55

CHAPTER V.

Areizaga takes the command of Eguia's army and is ordered to advance against
Madrid—Folly of the Supreme Junta—Operations in La Mancha—Combat of
Dos Barrios—Cavalry combat of Ocana—Battle of Ocana—Destruction of the
Spanish army   67

CHAPTER VI.

King Joseph's return to Madrid—Del Parque's operations—Battle of Alba de
Tormes—Dispersion of the Spanish troops—Their great sufferings and patience
—The Supreme Junta treat sir A. Wellesley's counsels with contempt—He
breaks up from the Guadiana and moves to the Mondego—Vindication of his
conduct for having remained so long on the Guadiana—French remain torpid
about Madrid—Observations   86

BOOK X.

CHAPTER I.

Joseph prepares to invade Andalusia—Distracted state of affairs in that province—
Military position and resources described—Invasion of Andalusia—Passes of the
Morena forced by the French—Foolish deceit of the Supreme Junta —Tumult
in Seville—Supreme Junta dissolved—Junta of Seville re-assembles, but
dispersed immediately after—The French take Jaen—Sebastiani enters Grenada—King Joseph enters Cordoba and afterwards marches against Seville—
Albuquerque's march to Cadiz—Seville surrenders—Insurrection at Malaga
put down by Sebastiani—Victor invests Cadiz—Faction in that city—Mortier
marches against Badajos—The visconde de Gand flies to Ayamonte—Inhos-
pitable conduct of the bishop of Algarve   101

CHAPTER II.

Operations in Navarre, Aragon, and Valencia—Pursuit of the student Mina—
Suchet's preparations—His incursion against Valencia—Returns to Aragon—
Difficulty of the war in Catalonia—Operations of the seventh corps—French
detachments surprised at Mollet and San Perpetua—Augereau enters Barcelona
—Sends Duhesme to France—Returns to Gerona—O'Donnel rallies the Spanish
army near Centellas—Combat of Vich—Spaniards make vain efforts to raise the
blockade of Hostalrich—Augereau again advances to Barcelona—Sends two
divisions to Reus—Occupies Manreza and Villa Franca—French troops de-

feated at Villa Franca and Esparaguera—Swartz abandons Manreza—Is defeated at Savadel—Colonel Villatte communicates with the third corps by
Falcet—Severolli retreats from Reus to Villa Franca—Is harassed on the
march—Augereau's unskilful conduct—Hostalrich falls—Gallant exploit of the
governor, Julian Estrada—Cruelty of Augereau 124

CHAPTER III.

Suchet marches against Lerida—Description of that fortress—Suchet marches
to Tarega—O'Donnel advances from Taragona—Suchet returns to Balaguer—
Combat of Margalef—Siege of Lerida—The city stormed—Suchet drives the
inhabitants into the citadel and thus forces it to surrender   .   .   . 144

CHAPTER IV.

Reflections on that act—Lazan enters Alcanitz, but is driven out by the French—
Colonel Petit taken with a convoy by Villa Campa, and assassinated after the
action—Siege of Mequinenza—Fall of that place—Morella taken—Suchet
prepares to enter Catalonia—Strength and resources of that province   . 158

CHAPTER V.

Operations in Andalusia—Blockade of Cadiz—Desertions in that city—Regency
formed—Albuquerque sent to England—Dies there—Regency consent to
admit British troops—General Colin Campbell obtains leave to put a garrison
in Ceuta, and to destroy the Spanish lines at San Roque—General William
Stewart arrives at Cadiz—Seizes Matagorda—Tempest destroys many vessels—
Mr. Henry Wellesley and general Graham arrive at Cadiz—Apathy of the
Spaniards—Gallant defence of Matagorda—Heroic conduct of a sergeant's
wife—General Campbell sends a detachment to occupy Tarifa—French prisoners cut the cables of the prison-hulks, and drift during a tempest—General
Lacey's expedition to the Ronda—His bad conduct—Returns to Cadiz—Re-
flections on the state of affairs   169

CHAPTER VI.

Continuation of the operations in Andalusia—Description of the Spanish and
Portuguese lines of position south of the Tagus—Situation of the armies in
Estremadura—Complex operations in that province—Soult's policy   . 188

CHAPTER VII.

Situation of the armies north of the Tagus—Operations in Old Castile and the
Asturias—Ney menaces Ciudad Rodrigo—Loison repulsed from Astorga—
Kellerman chases Carrera from the Gata mountains—Obscurity of the French
projects—Siege of Astorga—Mahi driven into Gallicia—Spaniards defeated at
Mombouey—Ney concentrates the sixth corps at Salamanca—The ninth corps
and the imperial guards enter Spain—Massena assumes the command of the
army of Portugal and of the northern provinces—Ney commences the first
siege of Ciudad Rodrigo—Julian Sanchez breaks out of the town—Massena
arrives and alters the plan of attack—Daring action of three French soldiers
—Place surrenders—Andreas Herrasti—His fine conduct—Reflections upon
the Spanish character   201

BOOK XI.

CHAPTER I.

Lord Wellington's policy—Change of administration in England—Duel between lord Castlereagh and Mr. Canning—Lord Wellesley joins the new ministry—Debates in Parliament—Factious violence on both sides—Lord Wellington's sagacity and firmness vindicated—His views for the defence of Portugal—Ministers accede to his demands—Grandeur of Napoleon's designs against the Peninsula—Lord Wellington enters into fresh explanation with the English ministers—Discusses the state of the war—Similarity of his views with those of sir John Moore—His reasons for not advancing into Spain explained and vindicated 215

CHAPTER II.

Greatness of lord Wellington's plans—Situation of the belligerents described—State of the French—Character of Joseph—Of his Ministers—Disputes with the Marshals—Napoleon's policy—Military governments—Almenara sent to Paris—Curious deception executed by the marquis of Romana, Mr. Stuart, and the historian Cabanes—Prodigious force of the French army—State of Spain—Inertness of Gallicia—Secret plan of the Regency for encouraging the Guerillas—Operations of those bands—Injustice and absurdity of the Regency, with respect to South America—England—State of parties—Factious injustice on both sides—Difficulty of raising money—Bullion committee—Wm. Cobbett —Lord King—Mr. Vansittart—Extravagance of the Ministers—State of Portugal—Parties in that country—Intrigues of the Patriarch and the Souza's—Mr. Stuart is appointed Plenipotentiary—His firmness—Princess Carlotta claims the regency of the whole Peninsula, and the succession to the throne of Spain 234

CHAPTER III.

Lord Wellington's scheme for the defence of Portugal—Vastness of his designs—Number of his troops—Description of the country—Plan of defence analysed—Difficulty of supplying the army—Resources of the belligerents compared—Character of the British soldier 254

CHAPTER IV.

Character of Miguel Alava—Portuguese government demand more English troops—Lord Wellington refuses, and reproaches the Regency—The factious conduct of the latter—Character of the light division—General Crawfurd passes the Coa—His activity and skilful arrangements—Is joined by Carrera —Skirmish at Barba del Puerco—Carrera invites Ney to desert—Romana arrives at head-quarters—Lord Wellington refuses to succour Ciudad Rodrigo —His decision vindicated—Crawfurd's ability and obstinacy—He maintains his position—Skirmish at Alameda—Captain Kraükenberg's gallantry—Skirmish at Villa de Puerco—Colonel Talbot killed—Gallantry of the French captain Guache—Combat of the Coa—Comparison between general Picton and general Crawfurd 273

CHAPTER V.

Slight operations in Gallicia, Castile, the Asturias, Estremadura, and Andalusia—Reynier passes the Tagus—Hill makes a parallel movement—Romana spreads his troops over Estremadura—Lord Wellington assembles a reserve at Thomar—Critical situation of Silveira—Captures a Swiss battalion at Puebla de Senabria—Romana's troops defeated at Benvenida—Lascy and captain Cockburne land troops at Moguer but are forced to reimbark—Lord Wellington's plan—How thwarted—Siege of Almeida—Allies advance to Frexadas—The magazine of Almeida explodes—Treachery of Bareiros—Town surrenders—The allies withdraw behind the Mondego—Fort of Albuquerque ruined by an explosion—Reynier marches on Sabugal, but returns to Zarza Mayor—Napoleon directs Massena to advance—Description of the country—Erroneous notions of lord Wellington's views entertained by both armies 297

CHAPTER VI.

Third Invasion of Portugal—Napoleon's prudence in military affairs vindicated—Massena concentrates his corps—Occupies Guarda—Passes the Mondego—Marches on Viseu—Lord Wellington falls back—Secures Coimbra, passes to the right bank of the Mondego, and is joined by the reserve from Thomar—General Hill anticipates his orders, and by a forced march reaches the Alva—The allied army is thus interposed between the French and Coimbra—Daring action of colonel Trant—Contemporaneous events in Estremadura, and the Condado de Niebla—Romana defeated—Gallantry of the Portuguese cavalry under general Madden—Dangerous crisis of affairs—Violence of the Souza faction—An indiscreet letter from an English officer, creates great confusion at Oporto—Lord Wellington rebukes the Portuguese Regency—He is forced to alter his plans, and resolves to offer battle—Chooses the position of Busaco 314

CHAPTER VII.

General Pack destroys the bridges on the Criz and Dao—Remarkable panic in the light division—The second and sixth corps arrive in front of Busaco—Ney and Regnier desire to attack, but Massena delays—The eighth corps and the cavalry arrive—Battle of Busaco—Massena turns the right of the allies—Lord Wellington falls back, and orders the northern militia to close on the French rear—Cavalry skirmish on the Mondego—Coimbra evacuated, dreadful scene there—Disorders in the army—Lord Wellington's firmness contrasted with Massena's indolence—Observations 327

CHAPTER VIII.

Massena resumes his march—The militia close upon his rear—Cavalry skirmish near Leiria—Allies retreat upon the lines—Colonel Trant surprises Coimbra—The French army continues its march—Cavalry skirmish at Rio Mayor—General Crawfurd is surprised at Alemquer and retreats by the wrong road—Dangerous results of this error—Description of the lines of Torres Vedras—Massena arrives in front of them—Romana reinforces lord Wellington with two Spanish divisions—Remarkable works executed by the light division at Aruda—The French skirmish at Sobral—General Harvey wounded—General St. Croix killed—Massena takes a permanent position in front of the Lines—He is harassed on the rear and flanks by the British cavalry and the Portuguese militia 348

CHAPTER IX.

State of Lisbon—Embargo on the vessels in the river—Factious conduct of the Patriarch—The desponding letters from the army—Base policy of ministers—

Alarm of lord Liverpool—Lord Wellington displays the greatest firmness, vigour, and dignity, of mind—He rebukes the Portuguese Regency, and exposes the duplicity and presumption of the Patriarch's faction—Violence of this faction—Curious revelation made by Baron Eben and the editor of the Braziliense—Lord Wellesley awes the Court of Rio Janeiro—Strengthens the authority of lord Wellington and Mr. Stuart—The French seize the Islands in the river—Foolish conduct of the governor of Setuval—General Fane sent to the left bank of the Tagus—Lord Wellington's embarrassments become more serious—The heights of Almada fortified—Violent altercation of the Regency upon this subject—The Patriarch insults Mr. Stuart and nearly ruins the common cause . . . - 366

CHAPTER X.

Massena's pertinacity—He collects boats on the Tagus, and establishes a depôt at Santarem—Sends general Foy to Paris—Casts a bridge over the Zezere—Abandons his position in front of the Lines—Is followed by lord Wellington—Exploit of serjeant Baxter—Massena assumes the position of Santarem—Lord Wellington sends general Hill across the Tagus—Prepares to attack the French—Abandons this design and assumes a permanent position—Policy of the hostile generals exposed—General Gardanne arrives at Cardigos with a convoy, but retreats again—The French marauders spread to the Mondego—Lord Wellington demands reinforcements—Beresford takes the command on the left of the Tagus—Operations of the militia in Beira—General Drouet enters Portugal with the ninth corps—Joins Massena at Espinhal—Occupies Leiria—Claparede defeats Silveira and takes Lamego—Returns to the Mondego—Seizes Guarda and Covilhoa—Foy returns from France—The duke of Abrantes wounded in a skirmish at Rio Mayor—General Pamplona organizes a secret communication with Lisbon—Observations 380

BOOK XII.

CHAPTER I.

General sketch of the state of the war—Lord Wellington objects to maritime operations—Expedition to Fuengirola—Minor operations in Andalusia—National Cortez assemble in the Isla de Leon—its proceedings—New regency chosen—Factions described—Violence of all parties—Unjust treatment of the colonies 405

CHAPTER II.

Soult assumes the direction of the blockade of Cadiz—His flotilla—Enters the Troccadero canal—Villantroys, or cannon mortars, employed by the French—Inactivity of the Spaniards—Napoleon directs Soult to aid Massena—Has some notion of evacuating Andalusia—Soult's first expedition to Estremadura—Carries the bridge of Merida—Besieges Olivenza—Ballasteros defeated at Castellejos—Flies into Portugal—Romana's divisions march from Cartaxo to the succour of Olivenza—That place surrenders—Romana dies—His character—Lord Wellington's counsels neglected by the Spanish generals—First siege of Badajos—Mendizabel arrives—Files the Spanish army into Badajos—Makes a grand sally—Is driven back with loss—Pitches his camp round San Christoval—Battle of the Gebora—Continuation of the blockade of Cadiz—Expedition of the allies under general Lapena—Battle of Barosa—Factions in Cadiz . 424

CHAPTER III.

Siege of Badajos continued—Imas surrenders—His cowardice and treachery—Albuquerque and Valencia de Alcantara taken by the French—Soult returns to Andalusia—Relative state of the armies at Santarem—Retreat of the French—Massena's able movement—Skirmish at Pombal—Combat of Redinha—Massena halts at Condeixa—Montbrun endeavours to seize Coimbra—Baffled by colonel Trant—Condeixa burnt by the French—Combat of Casal Nova—General Cole turns the French flank at Panella—Combat of Foz d'Aronce—Massena retires behind the Alva 453

CHAPTER IV.

Allies halt for provisions—State of the campaign—Passage of the Ceira—Passage of the Alva—Massena retires to Celerico—Resolves to march upon Coria—Is prevented by Ney, who is deprived of his command and sent to France—Massena abandons Celerico and takes post at Guarda—The allies oblige the French to quit that position, and Massena takes a new one behind the Coa—Combat of Sabugal—Trant crosses the Coa and cuts the communication between Almeida and Ciudad Rodrigo—His danger—He is released by the British cavalry and artillery—Massena abandons Portugal 477

CHAPTER V.

Estimate of the French loss—Anecdote of Colonel Waters—Lord Wellington's great conceptions explained—How impeded—Affairs in the south of Spain—Formation of the fourth and fifth Spanish armies—Siege of Campo Mayor—Place falls—Excellent conduct of major Tallaia—Beresford surprises Montbrun—Combat of Cavalry—Campo Mayor recovered—Beresford takes cantonments round Elvas—His difficulties—Reflections upon his proceedings—He throws a bridge near Jerumenha and passes the Guadiana—Outpost of cavalry cut off by the French—Castanos arrives at Elvas—Arrangements relative to the chief command—Beresford advances against Latour Maubourg, who returns to Llerena—General Cole takes Olivenza—Cavalry-skirmish near Usagre—Lord Wellington arrives at Elvas, examines Badajos—Skirmish there—Arranges the operations—Political difficulties—Lord Wellington returns to the Agueda—Operations in the north—Skirmishes on the Agueda—Massena advances to Ciudad Rodrigo—Lord Wellington reaches the army—Retires behind the Dos Casas—Combat of Fuentes Onoro—Battle of Fuentes Onoro—Evacuation of Almeida 494

CHAPTER VI.

Lord Wellington quits the army of Beira—Marshal Beresford's operations—Colonel Colborne beats up the French quarters in Estremadura, and intercepts their convoys—First English siege of Badajos—Captain Squire breaks ground before San Cristoval—His works overwhelmed by the French fire—Soult advances to relieve the place—Beresford raises the siege—Holds a conference with the Spanish generals, and resolves to fight—Colonel Colborne rejoins the army, which takes a position at Albuera—Allied cavalry driven in by the French—General Blake joins Beresford—General Cole arrives on the frontier—Battle of Albuera 529

CHAPTER VII.

Continuation of the battle of Albuera—Dreadful state of both armies—Soult retreats to Solano—General Hamilton resumes the investment of Badajos—Lord Wellington reaches the field of battle—Third and seventh divisions arrive—Beresford follows Soult—The latter abandons the castle of Villalba and retreats to Lerena—Cavalry action at Usagre—Beresford quits the army—General Hill reassumes the command of the second division, and lord Wellington renews the siege of Badajos—Observations 548

Papers relating to the former volumes.

I. Letter from major-general F. Ponsonby 567
II. Note upon the situation of Spain in 1808, dictated by Napoleon . . 568

APPENDIX.

No. I.

Returns of the French army in the Peninsula, extracted from the French muster-rolls 575

No. II.

Extracts of letters from lord Wellington to lord Liverpool, and one from sir John Moore to major-general M'Kenzie, commanding in Portugal . . 581

No. III.

Extracts from the correspondence of Mr. Vaughan, general Graham, colonel Nicholls, and from the official abstract of military reports by the British commanders at Cadiz 589

No. IV.

Extracts from king Joseph's correspondence 594

No. V.

Extracts of letters from lord Wellington 597

No. VI.

Extracts from a report made by the duke of Dalmatia to the prince of Wagram and Neufchatel 614
Intercepted letter from marshal Mortier to the emperor 618

No. VII.

Miscellaneous correspondence of the French marshals and others, and extracts from general Pelet's journal 618

No. VIII.

The French officers, prisoners of war at Oporto, to general Trant . . 634

No. IX.

A letter from lieutenant-general Graham to the right. hon. H. Wellesley, and state of the troops at Tarifa, under his command 635

Extract of a letter from general Frederick Ponsonby, and various other documents 640

No. X.

Extracts from the correspondence of captain Squire, of the engineers . 649

No. XI.

Extract of a letter from general Campbell to lord Liverpool . . . 651

LIST OF PLATES.

No. 1. Suchet's Operations, 1809-10 . . . *to face page* 10
2. Siege of Gerona . . . . . . *to face page* 48
3. Areizaga's Operations, 1809 . . . *to face page* 84
4. Invasion of Andalusia, 1810 . . . *to face page* 109
5. Defence of Portugal, 1810 . . . . *to face page* 266
6. Crawfurd's Operations, 1810 . . . *to face page* 292
7. Operations on the Mondego, 1810 . . *to face page* 336
8. Lines of Torres Vedras, 1810 . . . *to face page* 360
9. Battle of Barosa, March 5th, 1811 . . *to face page* 449
10. Massena's Retreat, Combat of Sabugal, 1811 *to face page* 490
11. Battle of Fuentes Onoro . . . . *to face page* 522
12. Battle of Albuera . . . . . *to face page* 546

NOTICE.

THE manuscript authorities consulted for this volume consist of original papers and correspondence of the duke of Wellington, marshal Soult, king Joseph, Mr. Stuart,* general Graham,† general Pelet,‡ general Campbell,§ captain Codrington,‖ and colonel Cox,¶ together with many private journals and letters of officers employed during the war.

Before the Appendix two papers are inserted, the one a letter from major-general Frederick Ponsonby relative to a passage in the description of the battle of Talavera; the other is an original note by the emperor Napoleon, which I had not seen when I published my first volume. The reader is referred to it as confirmatory of the arguments used by me when objecting to Joseph's retreat from Madrid.

* Lord Stuart de Rothesay.	† Lord Lynedoch.
‡ First aide-de-camp to marshal Massena.	§ Lieut.-gov. of Gibraltar.
‖ Admiral sir Edward Codrington.	¶ Governor of Almeida.

The reader is informed that, in the second volume, Book VI. & VII. should be Book VI., and Book IX. should be Book VIII.

HISTORY

OF THE

PENINSULAR WAR.

BOOK IX.

CHAPTER I.

WHEN Gallicia was delivered by the campaign of
Talavera, the Asturias became the head of a new
line of operation threatening the enemy's principal
communication with France. But this advantage
was feebly used. Kellerman's division at Valladolid, and Bonet's at San Andero, sufficed to hold
both Asturians and Gallicians in check; and the
sanguinary operations in the valley of the Tagus,
were collaterally, as well as directly, unprofitable to
the allies. In other parts, the war was steadily
progressive in favour of the French, yet their
career was one of pains and difficulties.

Hitherto Biscay had been tranquil, and Navarre
so submissive, that the artillery employed against
Zaragoza, was conveyed by the country people,
without an escort, from Pampeluna to Tudela. But
when the battle of Belchite terminated the regular
warfare in Aragon, the Guerilla system commenced
in those parts; and as the chiefs acquired reputa-

tion at the moment when Blake was losing credit
by defeats, the dispersed soldiers flocked to their
standards, hoping thus to cover past disgrace, and
to live with a greater license; because the regular
armies suffered under the restraints without en-
joying the benefits of discipline, while the irregulars purveyed for themselves. Thus, Zaragoza
being surrounded by rugged mountains, every
range became the mother of a Guerilla brood; nor
were the regular Partizan corps less numerous
than the Partidas.

On the left of the Ebro, the Catalonian colonels,
Baget, Perena, Pedroza, and the chief Theobaldo,
brought their Migueletes to the Sierra de Guara,
overhanging Huesca and Barbastro. In this position, commanding the sources of the Cinca and
operating on both sides of that river, they harassed
the communication between Zaragoza and the
French out-posts, and maintained an intercourse
with the governor of Lerida, who directed the
movements and supplied the wants of all the bands
in Aragon.

On the right of the Ebro, troops, raised in the
district of Molina, were united to the corps of
Gayan, and that officer, entering the mountains
of Montalvan, the valley of the Xiloca, and the
town of Daroca, pushed his advanced guards even
to the plain of Zaragoza, and occupied Nuestra
Senora del Aguilar; this convent, situated on the
top of a high rock near Carineña, he made his
depôt for provisions and ammunition, and surrounded the building with an entrenched camp.

On Gayan's left, general Villa Campa, a man of
talent and energy, established himself at Calatayud, with the regular regiments of Soria and La

Princessa, and making fresh levies, rapidly formed a large force, with which he cut the direct line between Zaragoza and Madrid.

Beyond Villa Campa's positions the circle of war was continued by other bands, which, descending from the Moncayo mountains, infested the districts of Taranzona and Borja, and intercepted the communications between Tudela and Zaragoza. The younger Mina, called the student, vexed the country between Tudela and Pampeluna; and the inhabitants of the high Pyrennean valleys of Roncal, Salazar, Anso, and Echo, were also in arms, under Renovalles. This officer, taken at Zaragoza, was, by the French, said to have broken his parole, but he pleaded a previous breach of the capitulation, and having escaped to Lerida passed from thence, with some regular officers, into the valleys, where he surprised several French detachments. His principal post was at the convent of San Juan de la Pena, which is built on a rock, remarkable in Spanish history as a place of refuge maintained with success against the Moorish conquerors; the bodies of twenty-two kings of Aragon rested in the church, and the whole rock was held in veneration by the Aragonese, and supposed to be invulnerable. From this post Saraza, acting under Renovalles, continually menaced Jaca, and communicating with Baget, Pedroza, and Father Theobaldo, completed, as it were, the investment of the third corps.

All these bands, amounting to, at least, twenty thousand armed men, commenced their operations at once, cutting off isolated men, intercepting convoys and couriers, and attacking the weakest parts of the French army. Meanwhile Blake having rallied his fugitives at Tortoza, abandoned Aragon, and proceeding to Taragona, endeavoured to keep the war alive in Catalonia.

Suchet, in following up his victory at Belchite, had sent detachments as far as Morella, on the borders of Valencia, and pushed his scouting parties close up to Tortoza. Finding the dispersion of Blake's troops complete, he posted Meusnier's division on the line of the Guadalupe, with orders to repair the castle of Alcanitz, so as to form a head of cantonments on the right bank of the Ebro; then crossing that river at Caspe with the rest of the army, he made demonstrations against Mequinenza, and even menaced Lerida, obliging the governor to draw in his detachments, and close the gates. After this he continued his march by Fraga, recrossed the Cinca, and leaving Habert's division to guard that line, returned himself in the latter end of June to Zaragoza by the road of Monzon.

Having thus dispersed the regular Spanish forces and given full effect to his victory, the French general sought to fix himself firmly in the positions he had gained. Sensible that arms may win battles, but cannot render conquest permanent, he projected a system of civil administration which might enable him to support his troops, and yet offer some security of property to those inhabitants who remained tranquil. But, as it was impossible for the people to trust to any system, or to avoid danger, while the mountains swarmed with the Partidas, Suchet resolved to pursue the latter without relaxation, and to put down all resistance in Aragon before he attempted to enlarge the circle

of his conquests; and he knew that while he CHAP.
thus laid a solid base for further operations, he
should also form an army capable of executing
any enterprize.

Commencing on the side of Jaca, he dislodged
the Spaniards from their positions near that castle,
in June, and supplied it with ten months' provisions. After this operation, Almunia and Carineña,
on the right of the Ebro, were occupied by his
detachments, and having suddenly drawn together
four battalions and a hundred cuirassiers at the latter point, he surrounded Nuestra Senora del Aguilar,
during the night of the 19th, destroyed the entrenched camp, and sent a detachment in pursuit of
Gayan. On the same day, Pedrosa was repulsed
on the other side of the Ebro, near Barbastro, and
general Habert also defeated Perena. The troops
sent in pursuit of Gayan dispersed his corps at
Uzed, Daroca was occupied by the French, and
the vicinity of Calatayud and the mountains of
Moncayo were then scoured by detachments from
Zaragoza, one of which took possession of the district of Cinco Villas. Meanwhile Jaca was continually menaced by the Spaniards of St. Juan de
la Pena, and Saraza, descending from thence by
the valley of the Gallego, on the 23d of August,
surprised and slew a detachment of seventy men
close to Zaragoza. On the 26th, however, five
French battalions stormed the sacred rock, and
penetrated up the valleys of Anso and Echo in
pursuit of Renovalles; nevertheless, that chief,
retiring to Roncal, obtained a capitulation for the
valley without surrendering himself.

These operations having, in a certain degree,
cleared Aragon of the bands on the side of Na-

varre and Castile, the French general turned against
those on the side of Catalonia. Baget, Perena, and
Pedrosa, were chased from the Sierra de Guarra, but
rallied between the Cinca and the Noguerra, and were
there joined by Renovalles, who assumed the chief
command; on the 23d of September, however, the
whole were routed by general Habert, the men dispersed, and the chiefs took refuge in Lerida and Mequinenza. Suchet then occupied Fraga, Candasnos,
and Monzon, established a flying bridge on the
Cinca, near the latter town, raised some field-works
to protect it, and that done, resolved to invade the
districts of Venasques and Benevarres, the subjection of which would have secured his left flank,
and opened a new line of communication with
France. The inhabitants, having notice of his project, assembled in arms, and being joined by the
dispersed soldiers of the defeated Partizans, menaced a French regiment posted at Graus. Colonel
La Peyrolerie, the commandant, marched the 17th
of October, by Roda, to meet them, but having
reached a certain distance up the valley, was surrounded, yet he broke through in the night, and
regained his post. During his absence the peasantry of the vicinity came down to kill his sick
men, the townsmen of Graus opposed this barbarity,
and marshal Suchet affirms that such humane conduct was not rare in Aragonese towns.

While this was passing in the valley of Venasque,
the governor of Lerida caused Caspe, Fraga, and
Candasnos to be attacked, and some sharp fighting
took place. The French maintained their posts,
but the whole circle of their cantonments being still
infested by the smaller bands, petty actions were
fought at Belchite, and on the side of Molino, at

Arnedo, and at Soria. Mina still intercepted the
communications with Pampeluna ; and Villa Campa,
quitting Calatayud, rallied Gayan's troops, and gathered others on the rocky mountain of Tremendal,
where a large convent and church once more furnished a citadel for an entrenched camp. Against
this place colonel Henriod marched from Daroca,
with from fifteen hundred to two thousand men and
three pieces of artillery, and driving back some
advanced posts from Ojos Negros and Origuela,
came in front of the main position at eleven o'clock
in the morning of the 25th of November.

COMBAT OF TREMENDAL.

The Spaniards were on a mountain, from the
centre of which a tongue of land shooting out,
overhung Origuela, and on the upper part of this
tongue stood the fortified convent of Tremendal.
To the right and left the rocks were nearly perpendicular, and Henriod, seeing that Villa Campa was
too strongly posted to be beaten by an open attack,
skirmished as if he would turn the right of the
position by the road of Albaracin. Villa Campa
was thus induced to mass his forces on that side,
and in the night, the fire of the bivouacs enabled
the Spaniards to see that the main body of the
French troops and the baggage were retiring, while
Henriod, with six chosen companies and two pieces
of artillery, coming against the centre, suddenly
drove the Spanish outposts into the fortified convent,
and opened a fire with his guns, as if to cover the
retreat. This cannonade, however, soon ceased, and
Villa Campa, satisfied that the French had retired,

was thrown completely off his guard; Henriod's six companies then secretly scaled the rocks of the position, rushed amongst the sleeping Spaniards, killed and wounded five hundred, and put the whole army to flight. Meanwhile, on the other side of the Ebro, a second attempt was made against the valley of Venasque, which being successful, that district was disarmed.

Petty combats still continued to be fought in other parts of Aragon, but the obstinacy of the Spaniards gradually gave way. In December, Suchet, (assisted by general Milhaud, with a moveable column from Madrid,) took the towns of Albaracin and Teruel, the insurgent junta fled to Valencia, and thus the subjection of Aragon was, in a manner, effected; for the interior was disarmed and quieted, and the Partidas, which still hung upon the frontiers, were obliged to recruit and be supplied from other provinces, and acted chiefly on the defensive. The Aragonese were indeed so vexed by the smaller bands, now dwindling into mere banditti, that a smuggler of Barbastro asked leave to raise a Spanish corps, with which he chased and suppressed many of them.

The reinforcements now pouring into Spain enabled the French general to prepare for extended operations. The original Spanish army of Aragon was reduced to about eight thousand men, of which, a part were wandering with Villa Campa, a part were in Tortoza, and the rest about Lerida and Mequinenza; those fortresses were, in fact, the only obstacles to a junction of the third with the seventh corps, and in them the Spanish troops who still kept the field took refuge, when closely pressed by the invaders.

The policy of the Supreme Junta was always to form fresh corps upon the remnants of their beaten armies. Hence Villa Campa, keeping in the mountains of Albaracin, recruited his ranks, and still infested the western frontier of Aragon: Garcia Novarro, making Tortoza his base of operations, lined the banks of the Algas, and menaced Alcanitz; and Perena, trusting to the neighbourhood of Lerida for support, posted himself between the Noguera and the Segre. However, the activity of the French gave little time to effect any considerable organization.

Suchet's positions formed a circle round Zaragoza. Tudela, Jaca, and the castle of Aljaferia were garrisoned, but his principal forces were on the Guadalupe and the Cinca, occupying Alcanitz, Caspe, Fraga, Monzon, Barbastro, Benevarres, and Venasque; of these, the first, third, and fourth were places of strength, and, whether his situation be regarded in a political, or a military light, it was become most important. One year had sufficed, not only to reduce the towns and break the armies, but in part to conciliate the feelings of the Aragonese—at that time, confessedly the most energetic portion of the nation—and to place the third corps, with reference to the general operations of the war, in a most formidable position.

1°. The fortified castle of Alcanitz formed a head of cantonments on the right bank of the Ebro, and being situated at the entrance of the passes leading into Valencia, furnished a base, from which Suchet could invade that rich province; and by which also, he could place the Catalonian army between two fires, whenever the seventh corps should again advance beyond the Llobregat.

2°. Caspe secured the communication between the wings of the third corps, while Fraga, with its wooden bridge over the Cinca, offered the means of passing that uncertain river at all seasons.

3°. Monzon, a regular fortification, in some measure balanced Lerida; and its flying bridge over the Cinca enabled the French to forage all the country between Lerida and Venasques; moreover a co-operation of the garrison of Monzon, the troops at Barbastro, and those at Benevarres, could always curb Perena.

4°. The possession of Venasques permitted Suchet to communicate with the moveable columns, (appointed to guard the French frontier,) while the castle of Jaca rendered the third corps in a manner independent of Pampeluna and St. Sebastian. In fine, the position on the Cinca and the Guadalupe, menacing alike Catalonia and Valencia, connected the operations of the third with the seventh corps, and henceforward we shall find these two armies gradually approximating until they formed but one force, acting upon a distinct system of invasion against the south.

Suchet's projects were, however, retarded by insurrections in Navarre, which, at this period, assumed a serious aspect. The student Mina, far from being quelled by the troops sent at different periods in chase of him, daily increased his forces, and, by hardy and sudden enterprizes, kept the Navarrese in commotion. The duke of Mahon, one of Joseph's Spanish adherents, appointed viceroy of Navarre, was at variance with the military authori-

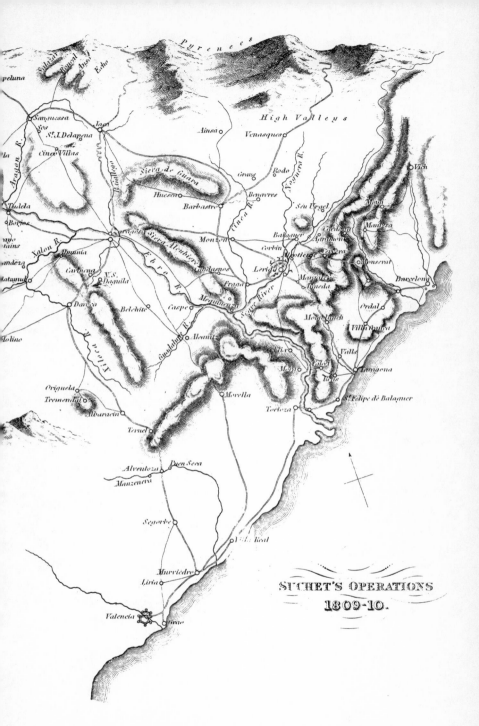

SUCHET'S OPERATIONS
1809-10.

Published by T. & W. Boone 1830.

ties, and all the disorders attendant on a divided administration, and a rapacious system, ensued. General D'Agoult, the governor of Pampeluna, was accused of being in Mina's pay, and his suicide during an investigation seems to confirm the suspicion, but it is certain that the whole administration of Navarre was oppressive, venal, and weak.

To avert the serious danger of an insurrection so close to France, the emperor directed Suchet to repair there with a part of the third corps, and that general soon restored order in Pampeluna, and eventually captured Mina himself; yet he was unable to suppress the system of the Partidas. " *Espoz y Mina*" took his nephew's place; and from that time to the end of the war, the communications of the French were troubled, and considerable losses inflicted upon their armies by this celebrated man—undoubtedly the most conspicuous person among the Partida chiefs. And here it may be observed how weak and inefficient this guerilla system was to deliver the country, and that, even as an auxiliary, its advantages were nearly balanced by the evils.

It was in the provinces lying between France and the Ebro that it commenced. It was in those provinces that it could effect the greatest injury to the French cause ; and it was precisely in those provinces that it was conducted with the greatest energy, although less assisted by the English than any other part of Spain : a fact leading to the conclusion, that ready and copious succours may be hurtful to a people situated as the Spaniards were. When so assisted, men are apt to rely more upon their allies than upon their own exertions.

But however this may be, it is certain that the Partidas of Biscay, Navarre, Aragon, and Catalonia, although they amounted at one time to above thirty thousand men, accustomed to arms, and often commanded by men of undoubted enterprize and courage, never occupied half their own number of French at one time; never absolutely defeated a single division; never prevented any considerable enterprize; never, with the exception of the surprise of Figueras, to be hereafter spoken of, performed any exploit seriously affecting the operations of a single " corps d'armée."

It is true, that if a whole nation will but persevere in such a system, it must in time destroy the most numerous armies. But no people will thus persevere, the aged, the sick, the timid, the helpless, are all hinderers of the bold and robust. There will, also, be a difficulty to procure arms, for it is not on every occasion that so rich and powerful a people as the English, will be found in alliance with insurrection; and when the invaders follow up their victories by a prudent conduct, as was the case with Suchet and some others of the French generals, the result is certain. The desire of ease natural to mankind, prevails against the suggestions of honour; and although the opportunity of covering personal ambition with the garb of patriotism may cause many attempts to throw off the yoke, the bulk of the invaded people will gradually become submissive and tranquil. It is a fact that, notwithstanding the violent measures resorted to by the Partida chiefs to fill their ranks, deserters from the French and even from the British formed one-third of their bands.

To raise a whole people against an invader may

be easy, but to direct the energy thus aroused, is a gigantic task, and, if misdirected, the result will be more injurious than advantageous. That it was misdirected in Spain was the opinion of many able men of all sides, and to represent it otherwise, is to make history give false lessons to posterity. Portugal was thrown completely into the hands of lord Wellington, but that great man, instead of following the example of the Supreme Junta, and encouraging independent bands, enforced a military organization upon totally different principles. The people were, indeed, called upon and obliged to resist the enemy, but it was under a regular system, by which all classes were kept in just bounds, and the whole physical and moral power of the nation rendered subservient to the plan of the general-in-chief. To act differently is to confess weakness: it is to say that the government being unequal to the direction of affairs permits anarchy.

The Partida system in Spain, was the offspring of disorder, and disorder in war is weakness accompanied by ills the least of which is sufficient to produce ruin. It is in such a warfare, that habits of unbridled license, of unprincipled violence, and disrespect for the rights of property are quickly contracted, and render men unfit for the duties of citizens; and yet it has with singular inconsistency been cited, as the best and surest mode of resisting an enemy, by politicians, who hold regular armies in abhorrence, although a high sense of honour, devotion to the cause of the country, temperance, regularity, and decent manners are of the very essence of the latter's discipline.

Regular armies have seldom failed to produce

great men, and one great man is sufficient to save
a nation : but when every person is permitted to
make war in the manner most agreeable to himself;
—for one that comes forward with patriotic intentions, there will be two to act from personal interest ; in short, there will be more robbers than

generals.   One of the first exploits of Espoz y Mina
was to slay the commander of a neighbouring band,
because, under the mask of patriotism, he was plundering his own countrymen : nay, this the most
fortunate of all the chiefs, would never suffer any
other Partida than his own to be in his district ;
he also, as I have before related, made a species of
commercial treaty with the French, and strove
earnestly and successfully to raise his band to the
dignity of a regular force.   Nor was this manner
of considering the guerilla system confined to the
one side.   The following observations of St. Cyr, a
man of acknowledged talents, show that, after considerable experience of this mode of warfare, he
also felt that the evil was greater than the benefit.

" Far from casting general blame on the efforts
" made by the Catalans, I admired them ; but, as
" they often exceeded the bounds of reason, their
" heroism was detrimental to their cause.   Many
" times it caused the destruction of whole popula-
" tions without necessity and without advantage.

" When a country is invaded by an army stronger
" than that which defends it, it is beyond question
" that the population should come to the assistance
" of the troops, and lend them every support ; but,
" without an absolute necessity, the former should
" not be brought on to the field of battle."—" It is
" inhuman to place their inexperience in opposition
" to hardened veterans.

" Instead of *exasperating* the people of Catalonia,
" the leaders should have endeavoured to *calm*
" them, and have directed their ardour so as to
" second the army on great occasions. But they
" excited them without cessation, led them day
" after day into fire, fatigued them, harassed them,
" forced them to abandon their habitations, to em-
" bark if they were on the coast, if inland to take
" to the mountains and perish of misery within
" sight of their own homes, thus abandoned to the
" mercy of a hungry and exasperated soldiery. The
" people's ardour was exhausted daily in partial
" operations, and hence, on great occasions, when
" they could have been eminently useful, they were
" not to be had.

" Their good will had been so often abused by
" the folly of their leaders, that many times their
" assistance was called for in vain. The peasantry,
" of whom so much had been demanded, began to
" demand in their turn. They insisted that the
" soldiers should fight always to the last gasp, were
" angry when the latter retreated, and robbed and
" ill-used them when broken by defeat.

" They had been so excited, so exasperated
" against the French, that they became habitually
" ferocious, and their ferocity was often as danger-
" ous to their own party, as to the enemy. The
" atrocities committed against their own chiefs dis-
" gusted the most patriotic, abated their zeal,
" caused the middle classes to desire peace as the
" only remedy of a system so replete with disorder.
" Numbers of distinguished men, even those who
" had vehemently opposed Joseph at first, began
" to abandon Ferdinand ; and it is certain that,
" but for the expedition to Russia, that branch of

" the Bourbons which reigns in Spain, would never
" have remounted the throne.

" The cruelties exercised upon the French mili-
" tary were as little conformable to the interest
" of the Spaniards. Those men were but the
" slaves of their duty, and of the state ; certain
" of death a little sooner or a little later, they,
" like the Spaniards, were victims of the same
" ambition. The soldier naturally becomes cruel
" in protracted warfare ; but the treatment expe-
" rienced from the Catalans brought out this dis-
" position prematurely ; and that unhappy people
" were themselves the victims of a cruelty, which
" either of their own will or excited by others,
" they had exercised upon those troops that fell
" into their power ; and this without any advantage
" to their cause, while a contrary system would, in
" a little time, have broken up the seventh corps,—
" seeing that the latter was composed of foreigners,
" naturally inclined to desert. But the murders
" of all wounded, and sick, and helpless men,
" created such horror, that the desertion, which at
" first menaced total destruction, ceased entirely."

Such were St. Cyr's opinions ; and, assuredly,
the struggle in Catalonia, of which it is now the
time to resume the relation, was not the least successful in Spain.

CHAPTER II.

OPERATIONS IN CATALONIA.

THE narrative of the Catalonian affairs was CHAP. II.
broken off at the moment, when St. Cyr having
established his quarters at Vich, received intel- 1809. SeeVol.II. p. 102.
ligence of the Austrian war, and that Barcelona
had been relieved by the squadron of admiral
Comaso. His whole attention was then directed
towards Gerona; and with a view to hastening
general Reille's preparation for the siege of that
place, a second detachment, under Lecchi, proceeded to the Ampurdan. During this time Conpigny continued at Taragona, and Blake made his
fatal march into Aragon; but those troops which,
under Milans and Wimphen, had composed Reding's left wing, were continually skirmishing with
the French posts in the valley of Vich, and the
Partizans, especially Claros and the doctor Rovira,
molested the communications in a more systematic
manner than before.

Lecchi returned about the 18th of May, with
intelligence that Napoleon had quitted Paris for
Germany, that general Verdier had replaced Reille
in the Ampurdan, and that marshal Augereau had
reached Perpignan in his way to supersede St. Cyr
himself in the command of the seventh corps. The
latter part of this information gave St. Cyr infinite
discontent. In his " Journal of Operations," he

asserts that his successor earnestly sought for the appointment, and his own observations on the occasion are sarcastic and contemptuous of his rival.

Augereau, who having served in Catalonia during the war of the revolution, imagined, that he had then acquired an influence which might be revived on the present occasion, framed a proclamation that vied with the most inflated of Spanish manifestoes; but the latter, although turgid, were in unison with the feelings of the people, whereas, Augereau's address, being at utter variance with those feelings, was a pure folly. This proclamation he sent into Catalonia, escorted by a battalion, but even on the frontier, the Miguelette colonel, Porta, defeated the escort, and tore down the few copies that had been posted. Augereau, afflicted with the gout, remained at Perpignan, and St. Cyr continued to command, but reluctantly, because (as he affirms) the officers and soldiers were neglected, and himself exposed to various indignities, the effects of Napoleon's ill-will. The most serious of these affronts was permitting Verdier to correspond directly with the minister of war in France, and the publishing of his reports in preference to St. Cyr's. For these reasons, the latter says he contented himself with a simple discharge of his duty. But, after the conspiracy in the second corps, Napoleon cannot be justly blamed for coldness towards an officer, who, however free himself from encouraging the malcontents in the French army, was certainly designed for their leader; it is rather to be admired that the emperor discovered so little jealousy. When a man has once raised himself to the highest power, he must inevitably give offence to his former comrades, for, as all honours and rewards, flowing from him, are taken as personal favours, so all checks and slights, or even the cessation of bene-fits, are regarded as personal injuries. Where the sanction of time is wanting to identify the sove-reign with the country, the discontented easily con-vince themselves that revenge is patriotism.

While St. Cyr was preparing for the siege of Gerona, Joseph, as we have seen, directed him to SeeVol.II. p. 358. march into Aragon, to repel Blake's movement against Suchet. This order he refused to obey, and with reason; for it would have been a great error to permit Blake's false movement to occupy two " corps d'armée," and so retard the siege of Gerona, to the infinite detriment of the French affairs in Catalonia. Barcelona was never safe while Hostalrich and Gerona were in the Spaniard's possession. St. Cyr was well aware of this, but the evils of a divided command are soon felt. He who had been successful in all his operations, was urgent, for many reasons, to commence the siege without delay; but Verdier, who had failed at Zara-goza, was cautious in attacking a town which had twice baffled Duhesme; and when pressed to begin, complained that he could not, after placing gar-risons in Rosas and Figueras, bring ten thousand men before Gerona, which, seeing the great extent of the works, were insufficient.

St. Cyr, disregarding the works, observed that the garrison did not exceed three thousand men, that it could not well be increased, and that ex-pedition was of more consequence than numbers. Nevertheless, considering that a depôt of provi-sions, established for the service of the siege at Figueras, and which it was unlikely Napoleon would replenish, must, by delay, be exhausted, as well as the supplies which he had himself collected at Vich, he sent all his own cannoniers, sappers, and artillery horses, two squadrons of cavalry, and six battalions of infantry to the Ampurdan, and having thus increased the number of troops there to eighteen thousand men, again urged Verdier to be expedite.

These reinforcements marched the 23d of May, and the covering army, diminished to about twelve thousand men under arms, continued to hold the valley of Vich until the middle of June. During this time, the Miguelettes often skirmished with the advanced posts, but without skill or profit; and the inhabitants of the town, always remained in the high mountains unsheltered and starving, yet still firm of resolution not to dwell with the invaders. This may be attributed partly to fear, but more to that susceptibility to grand sentiments, which distinguishes the Spanish peasants. Although little remarkable for hardihood in the field, their Moorish blood is attested by their fortitude; men and women alike, they endure calamity with a singular and unostentatious courage. In this they are truly admirable. But their virtues are passive, their faults active, and, continually instigated by a peculiar arrogance, they are perpetually projecting enterprises which they have not sufficient vigour to execute, although at all times they are confident and boasting more than becomes either wise or brave men.

Early in June, St. Cyr, having consumed nearly all his corn, resolved to approach Gerona, and secure the harvest which was almost ripe in that district; but, previous to quitting Vich, he sent his sick and wounded men, under a strong escort, to Barcelona, and disposed his reserves in such a manner that the operation was effected without loss. The army, loaded with as much grain as the men could carry, then commenced crossing the mountains which separate Vich from the districts of Gerona and Hostalrich. In two days it passed by Folgarolas, San Saturnino, Santa Hillario, and Santa Coloma de Farnes; the head-quarters were fixed at Caldas de Malavella on the 20th, the Fort of St. Felieu de Quixols was stormed on the 21st, and the Spanish privateers driven to seek another harbour. The French then occupied a half circle, extending from St. Felieu to the Oña river. Intermediate posts were established at St. Grace, Vidreras, Mallorquinas, Rieu de Arenas, Santa Coloma de Farnes, Castaña, and Bruñola, thus cutting off the communications between Gerona and the districts occupied by Coupigny, Wimphen, the Milans, and Claros.

During the march from Vich, the French defeated three Spanish battalions, and captured a convoy, coming from the side of Martorel, and destined for Gerona. St. Cyr calls them the forerunners of Blake's army, a curious error, for Blake was, on that very day, being defeated at Belchite, two hundred miles from Santa Coloma. Strictly speaking, there was, at this period, no Catalonian army, the few troops that kept the field were acting independently. Conpigny, the nominal commander-in-chief, remained at Taragona, where he and the other authorities, more occupied with personal quarrels and political intrigues than with military affairs, were thwarting each other. Thus the Spanish and French operations were alike weakened by internal divisions.

Verdier was slow, cautious, and more attentive to the facilities afforded for resistance than to the number of regular soldiers within the works ; he, or rather Reille, had appeared before Gerona on the 6th of May, but it was not till the 4th of June that, reinforced with Lecchi's division, he completed the investment of the place on both sides of the Ter. On the 8th, however, ground was broken ; and thus, at the very moment when Blake, with the main body of the army, was advancing against Zaragoza, in other words, seeking to wrest Aragon from the French, Catalonia was slipping from his own hands.

THIRD SIEGE OF GERONA.

When this memorable siege commenced, the relative situations of the contending parties were as follows :—Eighteen thousand French held the Ampurdan, and invested the place. Of this number about four thousand were in Figueras, Rosas, and the smaller posts of communication ; and it is remarkable that Verdier found the first-named place, notwithstanding its great importance, *destitute of a garrison*, when he arrived there from France. A fact consistent with Lord Collingwood's description of the Catalan warfare, but irreconcilable with the enterprise and vigour attributed to them by others.

St. Cyr, the distribution of whose forces has been already noticed, covered the siege with twelve thousand men, and Duhesme, having about ten Imperial Muster-Roll.MSS. thousand, including sick, continued to hold Barcelona. Forty thousand French were, therefore, disposed between that city and Figueras; while, on

the Spanish side, there was no preparation. Blake
was still in Aragon; Conpigny, with six thousand
of the worst troops, was at Taragona; the Milans
watched Duhesme; Wimphen, with a few thousand,
held the country about the Upper Llobregat; Juan
Claros and Rovira kept the mountains on the side
of Olat and Ripol; and, in the higher Catalonia,
small bands of Miguelettes were dispersed under
different chiefs. The Somatenes, however, continuing their own system of warfare, not only disregarded the generals, as in the time of Reding,
but fell upon and robbed the regular troops, whenever a favourable opportunity occurred. The
Spanish privateers, dislodged from St. Filieu, now
resorted to Palamos-bay, and the English fleet,
under Lord Collingwood, watched incessantly to
prevent any French squadron, or even single vessels,
from carrying provisions by the coast.

From Gerona, the governor did not fail to call
loudly on the generals, and even on the *Supreme
Central Junta*, for succours, but his cry was disregarded, and when the siege commenced, his
garrison did not exceed three thousand regular
troops, his magazines and hospitals were but scan-
tily provided, and he had no money. Alvarez
Mariano was, however, of a lofty spirit, great
fortitude, and in no manner daunted.

The works of Gerona, already described, were See Vol. I. p. 77.
little changed since the first siege; there, however,
as in Zaragoza, by a mixture of superstition,
patriotism, and military regulations, the moral as
well as physical force of the city had been called
forth. There, likewise, a sickness, common at a
particular season of the year, was looked for to

thin the ranks of the besiegers, and there also women were enrolled, under the title of the Company of Sta. Barbara, to carry off the wounded, and to wait upon the hospitals, and at every breath of air, says St. Cyr, their ribbons were seen to float amidst the bayonets of the soldiers! To evince his own resolution, the governor forbad the mention of a capitulation under pain of death; but severe punishments were only denounced, not inflicted. Alvarez, master of his actions, and capable of commanding without phrenzy, had recourse to no barbarous methods of enforcing authority; obstinate his defence was, and full of suffering to the besieged, yet free from the stain of cruelty, and rich in honour.

On the 4th of June the siege was begun, and, on the 12th, one mortar-battery, erected at Casen Rocca on the left of the Ter, and two breaching-batteries, established against Fort Monjouic, being ready to play, the town was summoned in form. The answer was an intimation that henceforth all flags of truce would be fired upon, which was the only proceeding indicative of the barbarian in the conduct of Alvarez.

The 13th the small suburb of Pedreto was taken possession of by the French, and early on the morning of the 14th, the batteries opened against Monjouic, while the town was bombarded from the Casen Rocca. The 17th the besieged drove the enemy from Pedreto, but were finally repulsed with the loss of above a hundred men.

The 19th the stone towers of St. Narcis and St. Louis, forming the outworks of Monjouic, being assaulted, the besieged, panic-stricken, abandoned them and the tower of St. Daniel also. The

French immediately erected breaching-batteries,
four hundred yards from the northern bastion of
Monjouic. Tempestuous weather retarded their
works, but they made a practicable opening by the
4th of July, and with a strange temerity resolved
to give the assault, although the flank fire of the
works was not silenced, nor the glacis crowned, nor
the covered way or counterscarp injured, and that
a half moon, in a perfect state, covered the approaches to the breach. The latter was proved by
the engineers, in a false attack, on the night of the
4th, and the resolution to assault was then adopted,
yet the storming-force drawn from the several
quarters of investment was only assembled in the
trenches on the night of the 7th; and during these
four days as the batteries ceased to play, the Spaniards retrenched, and barricadoed the opening.

At four o'clock in the morning of the 8th, the
French column, jumping out of the trenches, rapidly cleared the space between them and the fort,
descended the ditch, and mounted to the assault
with great resolution; but the Spaniards had so
strengthened the defences that no impression could
be made, and the assailants taken in flank and rear
by the fire from the half moon, the covered way,
and the eastern bastion, were driven back. Twice
they renewed the attempt, but their assault failed,
with a loss of a thousand men killed and wounded.
The success of the besieged was however mitigated
by an accidental explosion, which destroyed the
garrison of the small fort of St. Juan, situated
between Monjouic and the city.

About the period of this assault which was given
without St. Cyr's knowledge, the latter finding that
Claros and Rovira interrupted the convoys coming

from Figueras to Gerona, withdrew a brigade of Souham's division from Santa Coloma de Farnés, and posted it on the left of the Ter, at Bañolas. The troops on the side of Hostalrich were thus reduced to about eight thousand men under arms, although an effort to raise the siege was to be expected; for letters from Alvarez, urgently demanding succours of Blake, had been intercepted, and the latter, after his defeat in Aragon, was, as I have said, collecting men at Taragona.

Meanwhile, to secure the coast-line from Rosas to Quixols before Blake could reach the scene of action, St. Cyr resolved to take Palamos. To effect this, general Fontanes marched from St. Filieu, on the 5th of July, with an Italian brigade, six guns, and some squadrons of dragoons. Twice he summoned the place, and the bearer being each time treated with scorn, the troops moved on to the attack; but in passing a flat part of the coast near Torre Valenti, they were cannonaded by six gunboats so sharply, that they could not keep the road until the artillery had obliged the boats to sheer off.

STORMING OF PALAMOS.

This town having a good roadstead, and being only one march from Gerona, was necessarily a place of importance; and the works, although partly ruined, were so far repaired by the Catalans as to be capable of some defence. Twenty guns were mounted, and the town, built on a narrow rocky peninsula, had but one front, the approach to which was over an open plain completely commanded from the left by some very rugged hills, on which a

considerable number of Somatenes were assembled, with their line touching upon the walls of the town. Fontanes drove the Somatenes from this position, and a third time, summoned the place to surrender. The bearer was killed, and the Italians immediately stormed the works. The Spaniards flying towards the shore endeavoured to get on board their vessels, but the latter put off to sea, and some of Fontanes' troops having turned the town during the action, intercepted the fugitives, and put all to the sword.

Scarcely had Palamos fallen when Wimphen and the Milans, arriving near Hostalrich, began to harass Souham's outposts at Santa Coloma, hoping to draw St. Cyr's attention to that side, while a reinforcement for the garrison of Gerona should pass through the left of his line into the city. The French general was not deceived, but fifteen hundred chosen men, under the command of one Marshal, an Englishman, endeavoured to penetrate secretly through the enemy's posts at Llagostera; they were accompanied by an aide-de-camp of Alvarez, called Rich, apparently an Englishman also, and they succeeded on the 9th in passing general Pino's posts unobserved. Unfortunately a straggler was taken, and St. Cyr being thus informed of the march, and judging that the attempt to break the line of investment would be made in the night and by the road of Casa de Selva, immediately placed one body of men in ambush near that point, and sent another in pursuit of the succouring column.

As the French general had foreseen, the Spaniards continued their march through the hills at dusk, but being suddenly fired upon by the ambuscade, hastily retired, and the next day fell in with the other troops, and lost a thousand men; the rest dispersing, escaped the enemy, yet were ill used and robbed of their arms by the Somatenes. St. Cyr says that Mr. Marshal having offered to capitulate, fled during the negotiation, and thus abandoned his men; but the Spanish general Conpigny affirmed that the men abandoned Marshal, and refused to fight; that Rich run away before he had seen the enemy, and that both he and the troops merited severe punishment. It is also certain that Marshal's flight was to Gerona, where he afterwards fell fighting gallantly.

This disappointment was sensibly felt by Alvarez. Sickness and battle had already reduced his garrison to fifteen hundred men, and he was thus debarred the best of all defences, namely, frequent sallies as the enemy neared the walls; his resolution was unshaken, but he did not fail to remonstrate warmly with Conpigny, and even denounced his inactivity to the Supreme Junta. That general excused himself on the ground of Blake's absence, the want of provisions, and the danger of carrying the contagious sickness of Taragona into Gerona, and finally adduced colonel Marshal's unfortunate attempt, as proof that due exertion had been made. Yet he could not deny that Gerona had been invested two months, had sustained forty days of open trenches, a bombardment and an assault without any succour, and that during that time, he himself remained at Taragona, instead of being at Hostalrich with all the troops he could collect.

From the prisoners taken the French ascertained that neither Conpigny nor Blake had any intention of coming to the relief of Gerona, until sickness and famine, which pressed as heavily on the besiegers as on the besieged, should have weakened the ranks of the former; and this plan receives unqualified praise from St. Cyr, who seems to have forgotten, that with an open breach, a town, requiring six thousand men to man the works and having but fifteen hundred, might fall at any moment.

After the failure of the assault at Monjouic, Verdier recommenced his approaches in due form, opened galleries for a mine, and interrupted the communication with the city by posting men in the ruins of the little fort of St. Juan; his operations were, however, retarded by Claros and Rovira, who captured a convoy of powder close to the French frontier; and to prevent a recurrence of such events, the brigade from Souham's division was pushed from Bañolas to St. Lorenzo de la Muja.

The 2d of August, the fortified convent of St. Daniel, situated in the valley of the Galligan, between the Constable fort and Monjouic, was taken by the French, who thus entirely intercepted the communication between the latter place and the city. The 4th of August, the glacis of Monjouic being crowned, the counterscarp blown in and the flank defences ruined, the ditch was passed, and the half moon in front of the curtain carried by storm, but no lodgement was effected. During this day, Alvarez made an unsuccessful effort to retake the ruins of St. Juan, and at the same time, two hundred Spaniards who had come from the sea-coast with provisions, and penetrated to the

convent of St. Daniel, thinking that their countrymen still held it, were made prisoners.

On the 5th the engineers having ascertained
that the northern bastion being hollow, the troops
would, after storming it, be obliged to descend a
scarp of twelve or fourteen feet, changed the line
of attack, and commenced new approaches against
the eastern bastion. A second practical breach was
soon opened, and preparations made for storming
on the 12th, but in the night of the 11th, the
garrison blew up the magazines, spiked the guns,
and, without loss, regained Gerona. Thus the fort
fell, after thirty-seven days of open trenches and
one assault.

CHAPTER III.

VERDIER, elated by the capture of Monjouic, boasted, in his despatches, of the difficulties that he had overcome, and they were unquestionably great, for the rocky nature of the soil had obliged him to raise his trenches instead of sinking them, and his approaches had been chiefly carried on by the flying sap. But he likewise expressed his scorn of the garrison, held their future resistance cheap, and asserted that fifteen days would suffice to take the town, in which he was justified neither by past nor succeeding facts. The Spaniards, indignant at his undeserved contempt, redoubled their exertions and falsified all his predictions; and while these events were passing close to Gerona, Claros and Rovira, at the head of two thousand five hundred Migueletes, attacked Bascara a post between Figueras and Gerona at the moment when a convoy, escorted by a battalion, had arrived there from Belgarde. The commandant of Figueras, uniting some " *gens d'armes*" and convalescents to a detachment of his garrison, succoured the post on the 6th, but, meanwhile, the escort of the convoy had fallen back on France and spread such terror, that Augereau applied to St. Cyr for three thousand men to protect the frontier. That general refused this ill-timed demand, and, in his Memoirs, takes occasion to censure the system of moveable columns, as more likely to create than to suppress insurrections; as being harassing to the troops; weakening to the

CHAP. III.

1809. August.

main force, and yet ineffectual, seeing that the peasantry must always be more moveable than the columns, and better informed of their marches and strength. There is great force in these observations, and if an army is in such bad moral discipline that the officers commanding the columns cannot be trusted, it is unanswerable. It must also be conceded that this system, at all times requiring a nice judgement, great talents, and excellent arrangement, was totally inapplicable to the situation and composition of the seventh corps. Yet, with good officers and well combined plans, it is difficult to conceive any more simple or efficient mode of protecting the flanks and rear of an invading army, than that of moveable columns supported by small fortified posts; and it is sufficient that Napoleon was the creator of this system, to make a military man doubtful of the soundness of St. Cyr's objections. The emperor's views, opinions, and actions, will in defiance of all attempts to lessen them, go down, with a wonderful authority, to posterity.

A few days after the affair of Bascara, eight hundred volunteers, commanded by two officers, named Foxa and Cantera, quitted Olot, made a secret march through the mountains, arrived in the evening of the 10th, upon the Ter, in front of Angeles, and being baffled in an attempt to pass the river there, descended the left bank in the night, pierced the line of investment, and, crossing at a ford near St. Pons, entered Gerona at day-break. This hardy exploit gave fresh courage to the garrison; yet the enemy's approaches hourly advanced, pestilence wasted the besieged, and the Spanish generals outside the town still remained inactive. In this conjuncture, Alvarez and his council were not wanting to themselves; while defending the half ruined walls of Gerona with inflexible con- stancy, they failed not to remonstrate against the cold-blooded neglect of those who should have suc- coured them. The Supreme Junta of Catalonia, forwarded their complaints to the Central Junta at Seville, with a remarkable warmth and manliness of expression.

" The generals of our army," they said, " have " formed no efficient plan for the relief of Ge- " rona ; not one of the three lieutenant-generals " here has been charged to conduct an expedition " to its help ; they say that they act in confor- " mity to a plan approved by your Majesty. Can " it be true that your Majesty approves of aban- " doning Gerona to her own feeble resources ? If " so, her destruction is inevitable ; and should this " calamity befal, will the other places of Catalonia " and the Peninsula have the courage to imitate " her fidelity, when they see her temples and " houses ruined, her heroic defenders dead, or in " slavery ? And if such calamities should threaten " towns in other provinces, ought they to reckon " upon Catalonian assistance when this most in- " teresting place can obtain no help from them ?"— " Do you not see the consequences of this melan- " choly reflection, which is sufficient to freeze the " ardour, to desolate the hearts of the most zealous " defenders of our just cause ? Let this bulwark " of our frontier be taken, and the province is laid " open, our harvests, treasures, children, our- " selves, all fall to the enemy, and the country has " no longer any real existence."

In answer to this address, money was promised,

a decree was passed to lend Catalonia every succour, and Blake received orders to make an immediate effort to raise the siege. But how little did
the language of the Spaniards agree with their
actions ! Blake, indeed, as we shall find, made a
feeble effort to save the heroic and suffering city ;
but the Supreme Central Junta were only intent
upon thwarting and insulting the English general
after the battle of Talavera ; and this was the
moment that the Junta of Catalonia, so eloquent,
so patriotic with the pen, were selling, to foreign
merchants, the arms supplied by England for the
defence of their country !

Towards the end of August, when the French fire
had opened three breaches in Gerona, and the bombardment had reduced a great part of the city
to ashes, Blake commenced his march from Taragona with a force of eight or ten thousand regulars.
Proceeding by Martorel, El Valles, and Granollers,
he reached Vich, and from thence crossed the mountains to St. Hillario, where he was joined by Wimphen
and the Milans. As he had free communication
with Rovira and Claros, he could direct a body of not
less than twenty thousand men against the circle of
investment, and his arrival created considerable alarm
among the French. The pestilence which wasted
the besieged, was also among the besiegers, and
the hospitals of Figueras and Perpignan contained
many thousand patients, the battalions in the
field could scarcely muster a third of their nominal
strength. Even the generals were obliged to rise
from sick-beds to take the command of the brigades ;
and the covering army, inferior in number to the
Spanish force, was extended along more than thirty

miles of mountainous wooded country, intersected
by rivers, and every way favourable for Blake's
operations.
Verdier was filled with apprehension, lest a disastrous action should oblige him to raise the long-
protracted siege, notwithstanding his fore-boasts to
the contrary. But it was on such occasions that
St. Cyr's best qualities were developed. A most
learned and practised soldier, and of a clear methodical head, he was firm in execution, decided and
prompt in council; and, although, apparently wanting in those original and daring views, which mark
the man of superior genius, seems to have been perfectly fitted for struggling against difficulties. So
far from fearing an immediate battle, he observed,
" that it was to be desired, because his men were
now of confirmed courage, and Blake's inaction was
rather the thing to be dreaded; for, notwithstanding
every effort, not more than two days' provisions could
be procured, to supply the troops when together,
and it would be necessary after that period to scat-
ter them again in such a manner, that scarcely
two thousand would be disposable at any given
point. The Spaniards had already commenced
skirmishing in force on the side of Bruñola, and as
Blake expected no reinforcements, he would probably act immediately; hence it was necessary
to concentrate as many men as possible, in the
course of the night and next day, and deliver battle;
and there were still ten thousand good troops under
arms, without reckoning those that might be spared
from the investing corps."

On the other hand, Blake, with an army, numerous indeed but by no means spirited, was from
frequent defeat, become cautious without being

more skilful. He resolved to confine his efforts to
the throwing supplies of men and provisions into
the town ; forgetting that the business of a relieving
army is not to protract, but to raise a siege, and
that to save Gerona was to save Catalonia. He had
collected and loaded with flour, about two thousand
beasts of burthen, placed them in the mountains,
on the side of Olot, under an escort of four thousand infantry and five hundred cavalry ; and Garcia
Conde, an ambitious and fiery young man, undertook to conduct them to Gerona, by the flat ground
between the Ter and the Oña, precisely opposite
to that of the French attack. To facilitate this
attempt, Blake caused colonel Henry O'Donnel to
fall upon Souham's posts, near Bruñola, on the
evening of the 31st of August, supporting this
attack with another detachment under general
Logoyri. At the same time he directed colonel
Landen to collect the Miguelettes and Somatenes
on the side of Palamos, and take possession of
" *N. S. de los Angelos*," a convent, situated on a
high mountain behind Monjouic. Claros and Rovira
also received directions to attack the French on the
side of Casen Rocca. Thus the enemy were to be
assailed in every quarter, except that on which the
convoy was to pass.

O'Donnel, commencing the operations, attacked
and carried a part of the position occupied by one
of Souham's battalions at Bruñola, but the latter,
with an impetuous charge, again recovered the
ground. The Spanish general, being then joined
by Logoyri, renewed the skirmish, but could make
no further impression on the enemy. Meanwhile,
St. Cyr, having transferred his head-quarters to
Fornels, was earnestly advised to concentrate

his troops on the left of the Ter, partly, that it was thought Blake would attempt to penetrate on that side ; partly that, being so close to the Spanish army, the French divisions might, if ordered to assemble on their actual centre, be cut off in detail during their march. He however argued that his opponent must be exceedingly timid, or he would have attacked Souham with all his forces, and broken the covering line at once ; wherefore, seeing that such an opportunity was neglected, he did not fear to concentrate his own troops, on the Oña, by a flank march close under the beard of his unskilful adversary.

Souham's division, falling back in the night, took post the 1st of September, on the heights of San Dalmaz, reaching to Hostalnou, and at eight o'clock, the head of Pino's division entered this line, pro- longing it, by the left, in rear of the village of Rieudellot. At twelve o'clock, these two divisions were established in position, and at the distance of four miles in their rear, Verdier with a strong de- tachment of the besieging corps, was placed in re- serve on the main road to Gerona. Lecchi was sick, and his troops, commanded by Millosewitz, took post at Salt, guarding the bridge and the flat ground about St. Eugenio; having also instructions to cross the Ter and march against Rovira and Claros, if they should press the Westphalian divi- sion which remained at San Pons. The trenches under Monjouic were guarded. The mortar battery of Casa Rocca was disarmed, and the Westphalians had orders, if attacked, to retire to Sarria, and look to the security of the parc and the trenches.

A thick fog and heavy rain interrupted the view, and both armies remained apparently quiet until the middle of the day, when the weather clearing, St. Cyr rode to examine the Spanish positions; for the heads of Blake's columns were disposed as if he would have penetrated at once, by Bruñola, Coloma de Farnés, Vidreras, and Mallorquinas. Scarcely had the French general quitted Fornels, when Garcia Conde, who, under cover of the mist had been moving down the mountains, crossed the Ter at Amer, and descended the heights of Bañolas with his convoy. He was now on the flat ground; having two thousand men under Millosewitz, placed, as I have said, at Salt to watch the garrison and the movements of Rovira and Claros, and consequently, with their rear to the advancing convoy.

Verdier's reserve, the nearest support, was six miles distant, and separated from Millosewitz by considerable heights, and the Spanish columns, coming into the plain without meeting a single French post, advanced unperceived close to the main body, and, with one charge, put the whole to flight. The fugitives, in their panic, at first took the direction of the town, but being fired upon, turned towards the heights of Palau, made for Fornels, and would have gone straight into Blake's camp, if they had not met St. Cyr on his return from viewing that general's positions. Rallying and reinforcing them with a battalion from Pino's division, St. Cyr instantly directed them back again upon Salt, and at the same time sent Verdier orders to follow Garcia Conde with the reserve. It was too late, the latter had already entered the town, and Alvarez, sallying forth, destroyed the French works near St. Ugenio, and thinking the siege raised, had immediately sent five hundred sick men out of the town, into the convent of St. Daniel, which

place had been abandoned by the French two days CHAP.
before. Verdier, after causing some trifling loss to ———
Conde, passed the bridge of Salt, and marched 1809.
down the left of the Ter to Sarria, to save his parcs,
which were threatened by Rovira and Claros; for
when those two Partizans skirmished with the
Westphalian troops, the latter retired across the
Ter, abandoning their camp and two dismounted
mortars. Thus the place was succoured for a moment, but, as Blake made no further movement,
Alvarez was little benefitted by the success. The
provisions received, did not amount to. more than
seven or eight days' consumption, and the reinforcement, more than enough to devour this food, was
yet insufficient to raise the siege by sallies.

While Millosewitz's troops were flying on the
one side of the Ter, the reports of Claros and
Rovira, exaggerating their success on the other
side of that river, had caused Alvarez to believe
that Blake's army was victorious, and the French
in flight; hence, he refrained from destroying the
bridge of Salt, and Verdier, as we have seen, crossed it to recover his camp at Sarria. But for this
error, the garrison, reinforced by Conde's men,
might have filled the trenches, razed the batteries,
and even retaken Monjouic before Verdier could
have come to their support.

St. Cyr having now but one day's provisions left,
resolved to seek Blake, and deliver battle; but the
Spanish general retired up the mountains, when he
saw the French advancing, and his retreat enabled
St. Cyr again to disseminate the French troops.
Thus ended the first effort to relieve Gerona. It
was creditable to Garcia Conde, but so contemptible, with reference to the means at Blake's disposal,

that Alvarez believed himself betrayed, and, trusting thenceforth only to his own heroism, permitted
Conde's troops to go back, or to remain as they
pleased; exacting, however, from those who stopped, an oath not to surrender. Renewing the edict
against speaking of a capitulation, he reduced the
rations of the garrison first to one half, and afterwards to a fourth of the full allowance, a measure
which caused some desertions to the enemy; but
the great body of the soldiers and citizens were as
firm as their chief, and the townsmen freely sharing
their own scanty food with the garrison, made common cause in every thing.

Garcia Conde's success must be attributed partly
to the negligence of St. Cyr's subordinates; but
the extended cantonments, occupied in the evening
of the 31st, gave Blake, as the French general
himself acknowledges, an opportunity of raising
the siege without much danger or difficulty. Nor
were St. Cyr's dispositions for the next day perfectly combined; it is evident that giving Blake credit
for sound views, he was himself so expectant of
a great battle that he forgot to guard against
minor operations. The flat country between the
left of the Oña and the Ter was the natural line
for a convoy to penetrate to the town; hence it
was a fault to leave two thousand men in that
place, with their front to the garrison, and their
rear to the relieving army, when the latter could
steal through the mountains until close upon them.
Cavalry posts at least should have been established
at the different inlets to the hills, and beacons
raised on convenient eminences. The main body
of the army appears also to have been at too great
a distance from the town; the firing that took place

in the plain of Salt was disregarded by Verdier's
reserve, and the first information of the attack was
brought to Fornels by the fugitives themselves.

St. Cyr says that his generals of division were
negligent, and so weakened by sickness as to be
unable to look to their outposts; that he had
recommended to Verdier the raising of field-works
at the bridge of Salt and in the passes of the hills,
and, when his advice was disregarded, forbore,
from the peculiar situation in which he himself was
placed by the French government, to enforce his
undoubted authority. St. Cyr, however, acknowledges that his soldiers answered honestly to every
call he made, and he was bound, while he retained the command, to enforce every measure necessary for maintaining their honour. In other
respects, his prudence and vigilance were such as
beseemed his reputation. It was not so with Blake,
the whole of his operations proved that he had
lost confidence, and was incapable of any great
enterprize. He should have come up with a resolution to raise the siege or to perish. He contented
himself with a few slight skirmishes, and the intro-
duction of a small convoy of provisions, and then
notwithstanding the deep suffering of this noble
city, turned away, with a cold look, and a donation
that mocked its wants.

When the siege was resumed, St. Cyr withdrew
the French posts from Palau and Monte Livio,
leaving the way apparently open on that side, for
the return of Garcia Conde, who, deceived by this
wile, came out at daybreak on the 3d, with fifteen
hundred men and the beasts of burthen. He
halted for a little time, just beyond the gate, to
examine the country in front with his glass, and as

every thing appeared favourable, his troops were beginning to move forward, when the noise of drums beating to arms gave notice that an ambuscade was placed behind Palau. St. Cyr had, indeed, posted a brigade there in the hope of surprising the Spaniards, but the French forgetting the ambush, were performing the regular service of the camp at day-light, and a cry of astonishment burst from the Spanish column as it hastily retreated again into the town.

Baffled by this ridiculous mistake, and concluding that the next attempt would be by Castellar and La Bispal, St. Cyr placed Mazzuchelli's brigade (the same that had been behind Palau) in the valley of the Oña in such a manner that it could fall upon Conde's rear when the latter should again come forth. He likewise put a battalion on the hills in a position to head the Spanish column, and drive it back either upon Mazzuchelli's brigade, or upon La Bispal, where he also posted three battalions and a squadron of Pino's division.

The 4th, one thousand infantry, five hundred cavalry, and eleven hundred mules again came out of Gerona, and ascending the heights in which the fort of the Capuchin was situated, pushed in single files along a by-path, leading to Castellar da Selva. Mazzuchelli saw them plainly, but did not attack, waiting for the fire of the battalion ahead, and that battalion did not fire because Muzzuchelli did not attack, and it was supposed the Spaniards were part of his brigade. Garcia Conde quickly perceived their double error, and with great readiness filing off to his left, turned the right of the battalion in his front, and gained Castellar without hurt, although the French in Monjouic observing all that passed, plied their guns against the rear of his column. Being informed by the peasants at Castellar, that troops were also waiting for him at La Bispal, Conde made for Caza de Selva, and General Pino having notice of his approach, directed two battalions to seize the summit of a ridge which crossed the Spanish line of march; these battalions took a wrong direction, the Spaniards moved steadily on, and although their rear was attacked by Pino's personal escort, and that fifty men and some mules were captured, the main body escaped with honour.

There were now four open breaches in Gerona, Mazzuchelli's brigade and the troops at La Bispal were added to the investing corps, and the immediate fall of the city seemed inevitable, when the French store of powder failed, ten days elapsed before a fresh supply could be obtained, and Alvarez profited of this cessation, to retrench and barricade the breaches in the most formidable manner. Verdier had retaken the convent of St. Daniel in the valley of Galligan, and obliged the five hundred sick men to return to the town on the 4th; but Landen, the officer sent by Blake, on the 31st of August, to seize the convent of *Madonna de los Angeles*, had fortified that building, and introduced small supplies of provisions. This revived, in the mind of Alvarez, a plan for taking possession of the heights beyond those on which the Capuchin and Constable forts were situated, by which, in conjunction with the post at Madona de los Angeles, and with the assistance of Blake's army, he hoped to maintain an open communication with the country. But this bold and skilful conception he was unable to effect; because in a sally from the Capuchins on the 6th with eighteen hundred men, he was beaten by a single French regiment, and the same day Mazzuchelli's Italians stormed Madona de los Angeles, and put the garrison to the sword.

During these events, Verdier marched against Claros and Rovira who were posted at St. Gregorio, near Amer, but was repulsed with loss, and the French general Joba was killed. Meanwhile the batteries having recommenced their fire on the 13th, Alvarez made a general sally, by the gates of San Pedro, beat the guards from the trenches, and spiked the guns in one of the breaching batteries. The 18th, Verdier thinking the breaches practicable, proposed to give the assault, and required assistance from St. Cyr, but disputes between the generals of the covering and the investing forces were rife; the engineers of the latter declared the breaches practicable, those of the former asserted that they were not, and that while the fort of Calvary, outside the walls, although in ruins, was in possession of the Spaniards, no assault should be attempted.

Either from negligence, or the disputes between St. Cyr and Augereau, above five thousand convalescents capable of duty were retained in a body at Perpignan, and Verdier could not produce so many under arms for the assault, nor even for this number were there officers to lead, so wasting was the sickness. The covering army was scarcely better off, and Blake had again taken the position of St. Hilario. Howbeit, St. Cyr, seeing no better remedy, consented to try the storm provided Calvary were first taken.

Souham's division was appointed to watch Blake, Pino was directed to make a false attack on the opposite quarter to where the breaches were established, and, on the 19th, Verdier's troops, in three columns, advanced rapidly down the valley of Galligan to the assault; but the fort of Calvary had not been taken, and its fire swept the columns of attack along the whole line of march. Two hundred men fell before they reached the walls, and just as the summit of the largest breach was gained, the French batteries, which continued to play on the Spanish retrenchments, brought down a large mass of wall upon the head of the attacking column. The besieged resisted manfully, and the besiegers were completely repulsed from all the breaches with a loss of six hundred men. Verdier accused his soldiers of cowardice, and blamed St. Cyr for refusing to bring the covering troops to the assault; but that general asserted that the men had behaved perfectly well, and calling a council of war, proposed to continue the operations with as much vigour as the nature of the case would permit. His spirit was not however partaken by the council, and the siege was turned into a blockade.

St. Cyr's
Journal of
Operations

Blake now advanced with his army, and from the 20th to the 25th, made as if he would raise the blockade, yet his object was merely to introduce another convoy, and St. Cyr, divining his intention and judging that he would make the attempt on the 26th, resolved to let him penetrate the covering line, and then fall on him before he could reach the town. In this view, Souham's division was placed behind Palau and Pino's division at Casa de Selva, and Lecchi's division of the investing troops was directed to meet the Spaniards in front, while the two former came down upon their rear.

Blake assembled his troops on the side of Hostalrich, then made a circuitous route to La Bispal, and, taking post on the heights of St. Sadurni, detached ten thousand men, under Wimphen, to protect the passage of the convoy, of which Henry O'Donnel led the advanced guard. At day-break, on the 26th, O'Donnel fell upon the rear of the French troops at Castellar, broke through them, and reached the fort of the Constable with the head of the convoy; but the two French battalions which he had driven before him, rallying on the heights of San Miguel to the right of the Spanish column, returned to the combat, and at the same time St. Cyr in person, with a part of Souham's division came upon the left flank of the convoy, and, pressing it strongly, obliged the greater part to retrograde. Pino's division, then running up from Casa de Selva, attacked the rear-guard under Wimphen, the route was complete, and Blake made no effort to save the distressed troops. O'Donnel with a thousand men and about two hundred mules got safely into the town, the remainder of the convoy was taken, the Italians gave no quarter, and three thousand of the Spaniards were slain.

After this action, some troops being sent towards Vidreras, to menace Blake's communications with Hostalrich, he retired by the side of St. Filieu de Quixols, and Gerona was again abandoned to her sufferings which were become almost insupportable. Without money, without medicines, without food; pestilence within the walls, the breaches open. "If," said Alvarez, "the captain-general "be unable to make a vigorous effort, the whole of "Catalonia must rise to our aid, or Gerona will "soon be but a heap of carcases and ruins, the "memory of which will afflict posterity!"

St. Cyr having repaired, to Perpignan· to make arrangements for future supply, found Augereau in a good state of health, and obliged him to assume the command. Then, he says, every thing needful was bestowed with a free hand upon the seventh corps, because he himself was no longer in the way; but a better reason is to be found in the state of Napoleon's affairs. Peace had been concluded with Austria, the English expeditions to the Scheldt and against Naples had failed, and all the resources of the French government becoming disposable, not only the seventh, but every " corps d'armée" in Spain was reinforced.

Augereau, escorted by the five thousand convalescents from Perpignan, reached the camp before Gerona, the 12th of October. In the course of the following night, O'Donnel, issuing from the town on the side of the plain, broke through the guards, fell upon Souham's quarters, obliged that general to fly in his shirt, and finally effected a junction with Milans, at Santa Coloma; thus successfully executing as daring an enterprise as any performed during this memorable siege. Augereau, however, pressed the blockade, and thinking the spirit of the Spaniards reduced, offered an armistice for a month, with the free entry of provisions, if Alvarez would promise to surrender unless relieved before the expiration of that period. Such, however, was the steady virtue of this man and his followers, that, notwithstanding the grievous famine, the offer was refused.

Blake, on the 29th, took possession once more of the heights of Bruñola, but Souham with an inferior force put him to flight, and this enabled Augereau to detach Pino against the town of

Hostalrich. This place fortified with an old wall
and towers, was defended by two thousand men,
and supported by the fire of the castle; it was
however carried by storm, and the provisions and
stores laid up there captured, although Blake, with
his army, was only a few miles off. Meanwhile
rear-admiral Baudin, with a French squadron,
consisting of three ships of the line, two frigates,
and sixteen large store-ships, having sailed from
Toulon for Barcelona, about the 20th, was intercepted by admiral Martin on the 23d, who burnt
several of his smaller vessels and drove the rest on
shore at different places, when two of the line of
battle ships were set on fire by their own crews.
The store-ships and some of the armed vessels
took refuge at Rosas, put up boarding nettings,
and protecting their flanks by Rosas and the Tri-
nity-fort, presented a formidable front, having
above twenty guns on board disposed for defence,
besides the shore batteries. But on the 31st,
captain Hallowell appeared in the bay with a
squadron, and the same evening, sending his boats
in, destroyed the whole fleet, in despite of a very
vigorous resistance which cost the British seventy
men killed and wounded.

The distress of Gerona increased, desertions became frequent, and ten officers having failed in
a plot to oblige the governor to capitulate, went
over in a body to the enemy. During November,
famine and sickness tormented the city, and the
French were inactive for want of powder, but on
the 6th of December, ammunition having arrived,
the suburb of Marina, that of Girondella, the fort
of Calvary, and all the other towers beyond the
walls, were carried by the besiegers, and Alvarez,

SIEGE of GERONA
1810.

Belgarde

Lorenza La Muga

Figueres

Rosas

Castel Follit

Bescan

Bascara

Ripol

Olot

Banolas

Ter R.

Sarria

Casen Rocca

St Margarie

Amer

Ribes

Pong

Gerona

Ros Angelos

Saturni

Labispal

Roda

St Madurin

Brunola

Fornels

Vich

Hillario

St Coloma

Casa de Selva

Vidreros

Mona

Talabuti

Malorquinas

St Grau

St Guixols

Palamos

Berga

Manresa

Hostalrich

Montserrat

Tarasa

Perretna

Granoller

Arenys de Mur

Bruch

Sabadel

El Valles

Molet

Esparaguera

Ordal

Molins

Barcelona

Villa franca

Tarrasa

Rovera Claros

St Ser French

Sarria

St Gregorio

Ter River

Salt

Pong

Casen Rocca

Pedreto

Sugeto

St Louis

Losangeles

Amer

Garcia Conde's Convoy

Lechi 1st Sep.

Migenu

Condegan

Anales

Pinau

Castellar

St Sadurni

St Dalman

Brunola

Verdiers 1st Sep.

Oña

Bispal

St Cyrs 1st Sep.

Hostalnou

Fornels

St Coloma

Casa de Selva

Palama

Lagostera

Torre Valenti

Malorquinas

Blakes

Vidreres

Columns

Published by T. & W. Boone 1833.

thus confined to the circuit of the walls, was cut off from the Capuchin and Constable forts. He had been ill for some days, but rousing himself for a last effort, made a general sally on the 7th, retook the suburb of Girondella and the redoubts, and opening a way to the outworks of the Constable, carried off the garrison; the next day, overcome by suffering, he became delirious. A council of war then assembled, and after six months of open trenches, Gerona yielded on the 10th. The garrison marched out with the honours of war, the troops were to be exchanged in due course, the inhabitants were to be respected, and none but soldiers were to be considered prisoners. Such was the termination of a defence which eclipsed the glory of Zaragoza.

French and Spanish writers alike, affirm that Augereau treated Alvarez with a rigour and contumely that excited every person's indignation; and that, in violation of the capitulation, the monks were, by an especial order of Napoleon, sent to France. This last accusation admits, however, of dispute; the monks had during the siege, formed themselves into a regular corps, named the Crusaders; they were disciplined and clothed in a sort of uniform, and being to all intents soldiers, it can hardly be said, that to constitute them prisoners, was a violation, although it was undoubtedly a harsh interpretation of the terms.

Alvarez died at Figueras in his way to France; but so long as virtue and courage are esteemed in the world, his name will be held in veneration; and if Augereau forgot what was due to this gallant Spaniard's merit, posterity will not forget to do justice to both.

OBSERVATIONS.

1°. In this siege, the constancy with which the Geronans bore the most terrible sufferings accounts for the protracted resistance; yet constancy alone could not have enabled them to defy the regular progress of the engineer; the combinations of science are not to be defied with impunity; but the French combinations were not scientific, and this, saving the right of Gerona to the glory she earned so hardly, was the secret of the defence.

2°. General St. Cyr, after observing that the attack on Montjouic was ill judged and worse executed, says, " The principal approaches should have been conducted against the Marcadel, because the soil there, was easy to work in, full of natural hollows and clifts, and the defences open in flank and rear to batteries on the Monte Livio and the Casen Rocca; but on the side of Montjouic, the approaches, from the rocky nature of the soil, could only be carried forward by the flying sap, with great loss and difficulty." If, however, the Marcadel had fallen, the greatest part of the city would still have been covered by the Oña, and Montjouic, and the forts of the Constable and Capuchin, (regular places complete in themselves,) would have remained to be taken, unless it can be supposed, that a governor, who defended the feeble walls of the town after those outworks fell, would have surrendered all, because a lodgement was made in an isolated quarter. These things are, however, ordinarily doubtful, and certainly, it must always be a great matter with a general, to raise the moral confidence of his own army, and to sink that of his adversary, even though it should be by a momentary and illusive success.

3°. The faulty execution of the attack on Montjouic is less doubtful than the choice of direction. The cessation of the breaching fire for four days previous to the assault, and the disregard of the rules of art already noticed, amply account for failure; and it is to be observed, that this failure caused the delay of a whole month in the progress of the siege, that during that month disease invaded the army, and the soldiers, as they will be found to do in all protracted operations, became careless and disinclined to the labours of the trenches.

4°. The assault on the body of the place was not better conducted than that against Montjouic; and considering these facts, together with the jealousy and disputes between the generals, the mixture of Germans, Italians, and French in the army, and the maladministration of the hospitals, by which so many men were lost, and so many more kept from their duty, it is rather surprising that Gerona was taken at all.

5°. The foregoing conclusions in no wise affect the merits of the besieged, because the difficulties and errors of their adversaries only prolonged their misery. They fought bravely, they endured unheard-of sufferings with constancy, and their refusal to accept the armistice offered by Augereau, is as noble and affecting an instance of virtue as any that history has recorded. Yet how mixed are good and evil principles in man, how dependent upon accidental circumstances is the development of his noble or base qualities! Alvarez, so magnanimous, so firm, so brave, so patriotic at Gerona, was the same Alvarez who, one year before, surrendered the Barcelona Montjouic, on the insolent summons of Duhesme! At that period, the influence of a base court degraded public feeling, and what was weak in his character came to the surface, but in times more congenial to virtuous sentiments, all the nobility of the man's nature broke forth.

6°. When the siege of Gerona is contrasted with that of Zaragoza, it may shake the opinion of those who regard the wild hostility of the multitude as superior to the regulated warfare of soldiers. The number of enemies that came against the latter was rather less than those who came against the former city; the regular garrison of Zaragoza was above thirty thousand, that of Gerona about three thousand. The armed multitude, in the one, amounted to at least twenty-five thousand, in the other, they were less than six thousand. Cruelty and murder marked every step in the defence of Zaragoza, the most horrible crimes were necessary to prolong the resistance, above forty thousand persons perished miserably, and the town was taken within three months. In Gerona there was nothing to blush for; the fighting was more successful, the actual loss inflicted upon the enemy greater, the suffering within the walls neither wantonly produced nor useless; the period of its resistance doubled that of Zaragoza, and every proceeding tended to raise instead of sinking the dignity of human nature. There was less of brutal rule, more of reason, and consequently more real heroism, more success at the moment, and a better example given to excite the emulation of generous men.

7°. With reference to the general posture of

affairs, the fall of Gerona was a reproach to the Spanish and English cabinets. The latter having agents in Catalonia, and such a man as lord Collingwood in the Mediterranean, to refer to, were yet so ignorant, or so careless of what was essential to the success of the war, as to let Gerona struggle for six months, when half the troops employed by sir John Stuart to alarm Naples, if carried to the coast of Catalonia, and landed at Palamos, would have raised the siege. It was not necessary that this army should have been equipped for a campaign, a single march would have effected the object. An engineer and a few thousand pounds would have rendered Palamos a formidable post, and that place being occupied by English troops, and supported by a fleet, greater means than the French could have collected in 1809, would not have reduced Gerona. The Catalans, indeed, were not more tractable nor more disposed than others to act cordially with their allies; but the natural sterility of the country, the condensed manufacturing population, the number of strong posts and large fortified towns in their possession, and, above all, the long and difficult lines of communication which the French must have guarded for the passage of their convoys, would have rendered the invaders' task most difficult.

8°. From the commencement of the Spanish insurrection, the policy of the Valencians had been characterised by a singular indifference to the calamities that overwhelmed the other parts of Spain. The local Junta in that province, not content with asserting their own exclusive authority, imagined that it was possible to maintain Valencia independent, even though the rest of the Peninsula should be conquered; hence the siege of Zaragoza passed unheeded, and the suffering of Gerona made no impression on them. With a regular army of above ten thousand men, more than thirty thousand armed irregulars, and a large fleet at Carthagena, the governors of this rich province, so admirably situated for offensive operations, never even placed the fortified towns of their own frontier in a state of defence, and carelessly beheld the seventh and third corps gradually establishing, at the distance of a few days' march from Valencia itself, two solid bases for further invasion! But it is now time to revert to the operations of the " *Central Supreme Junta*," that it may be fully understood how the patriotism, the constancy, the lives, and the fortunes of the Spanish people, were sported with by those who had so unhappily acquired a momentary power in the Peninsula.

CHAP. IV.

WHEN sir Arthur Wellesley retired to the frontier of Portugal, the calumnies propagated in Andalusia, relative to the cause of that movement, were so far successful that no open revolt took place; but the public hatred being little diminished, a design was formed to establish a better government, as a preliminary to which, measures were secretly taken to seize the members of the Junta, and transport them to Manilla. The old Junta of Seville being the chief movers of this sedition, no good could be expected from the change, otherwise, such an explosion, although sure to be attended with slaughter and temporary confusion, was not unlikely to prove advantageous to the nation at large, it being quite obvious that some violent remedy was wanting to purge off the complicated disorders of the state.

" *Spain*," said lord Wellesley, " *has proved un-* " *true to our alliance, because she is untrue to* " *herself.*"—" *Until some great change shall be* " *effected in the conduct of the military resources of* " *Spain, and in the state of her armies, no British* " *army can attempt safely to co-operate with Spanish* " *troops in the territories of Spain.*"—" *No alliance* " *can protect her from the results of internal dis-* " *orders and national infirmity.*"

This evident discontent of the British ambassador led the conspirators to impart their designs to him, in the hopes of assistance; but he being accredited to the existing government, apprised it of the danger, concealing, however, with due regard to humanity, the names of those engaged in the plot. The Junta, in great alarm, immediately sought to mitigate the general hatred ; but still averse to sacrificing any power, projected a counter scheme. They had, for the public good according to some, for private emolument according to others, hitherto permitted trading, under licenses, with the towns occupied by the enemy. This regulation and some peculiarly-heavy exactions they now rescinded, and, as a final measure of conciliation, appointed, with many protestations of patriotism, commissioners to prepare a scheme of government which should serve until the fit period for convoking the Cortes arrived.

But the commissioners, principally chosen from amongst the members of the Junta, soon made manifest the real designs of that body. They proposed that five persons should form a supreme executive council, every member of the existing Junta, in rotation, to have a place; the colonies to be represented as an integral part of the empire ; and the council so composed, to rule until the Cortes should meet, and then to preside in that assembly. Thus under the pretence of resigning their power, by a simple change of form, the present and the future authority of the Junta were to be confirmed, and even the proposal, in favour of the colonies, was, following the opinion of lord Wellesley, a mere expedient to obtain a momentary popularity, and entirely unconnected with enlarged or liberal views of policy and government.

This project was foiled by Romana, who, being of the commission, dissented from his colleagues; and it was on this occasion that he drew up that

accusatory paper, quoted in another part of this
history, and the bad acts therein specified, although
sufficiently heinous, were not the only charges
made at this period. It was objected to some
amongst the Junta, that having as merchants,
contracted for supplying the army, they in their
public capacity, raised the price to be paid by the
treasury for the articles ; and that the members
generally were venal in their patronage, difficult
of access, and insolent of demeanour.

Romana proposed a council of regency, to be composed of five persons, not members of the Junta.
This council to be assisted by a fresh chosen Junta,
also composed of five members and a procurator-
general, and to be styled " *The Permanent Deputation of the Realm.*" One of this body to be a South
American, and the whole to represent the Cortes,
until the meeting of that assembly, which, he thought,
could not be too soon. His plan, introduced by
misplaced declarations in favour of arbitrary power,
and terminated by others equally strong in favour
of civil liberty, was not well considered. The
" *Permanent Deputation,*" being to represent the
Cortes, it was obvious that it must possess the right
of controlling the Regency ; but the numbers and
dignity of both being equal, and their interests
opposed, it was as obvious that a struggle would
commence, in which the latter, having the sole distribution of honours and emoluments, could not fail
to conquer, and no Cortes would be assembled.

Some time before this, when the terror caused by
sir Arthur Wellesley's retreat from Spain, was fresh,
Don Martin de Garay had applied to lord Wellesley for advice, as to the best form of government,
and that nobleman also recommended a " *Council*

of Regency," and, like Romana, proposed a second council; but with this essential difference, that the latter were only to arrange the details for electing the members of Cortes, a proclamation for the convocation of which was to be immediately published, together with a list of grievances, *" a Bill of Rights"* founded on an enlarged conciliatory policy, and having equal regard for the interests of the colonies as for those of the mother country. Garay approved of this advice while danger menaced the Junta; but when the arrangement for the command of the armies had been completed, and the first excitement had subsided, his solicitude for the improvement of the government ceased. It must, however, be acknowledged, that lord Wellesley condemned the existing system, as much for its democratic form as for its inefficiency; the English cabinet never forgot, that they were the champions of privilege, nor, that the war was essentially, less for the defence of Spain, than the upholding of the aristocratic system of Europe.

To evade Romana's proposition, the Junta, on the 28th of October, announced that the National Cortes should be convoked on the 1st of January, 1810, and assembled for business on the 1st of March following. Having thus, in some measure, met the public wishes, they joined to this announcement a virulent attack on the project of a Regency, affirming, and not without some foundation as regarded Romana's plan, that such a government would disgust the colonies, trample on the king's rights, and would never assemble the Cortes; moreover that it would soon be corrupted by the French. Then enlarging on their own merits in a turgid declamatory style, they defended their

past conduct by a tissue of misrepresentations,
which deceived nobody; for, to use the words of
lord Wellesley, " *no plan had been adopted for any*
" *effectual redress of grievances, correction of abuses*
" *or relief from exactions, and the administration*
" *of justice, the regulation of revenue, finance, com-*
" *merce, the security of persons and property, and*
" *every other great branch of government, were as*
" *defective as the military establishments.*"

However, the promise of assembling the Cortes
sufficed to lull the public wrath; and the Junta
resolved to recommence offensive military operations, which they fondly imagined would, at once,
crush the enemy, and firmly establish their own
popularity and power. They were encouraged by
a false, but general impression throughout Andalusia, that Austria had broken off negotiations
with France; and in September and October fresh
levies, raised in Estremadura and Andalusia, had
been incorporated with the remains of Cuesta's
old army; the whole forming a body of more than
sixty thousand soldiers, of which nearly ten thousand were cavalry. Nor was the assembling and
equipment of this force a matter of great difficulty;
for, owing to the feeble resistance made against
the invaders, the war had hitherto drawn so little
on the population, that the poorer sort never
evaded a call for personal service; and the enormous accumulation of English stores and money
at Cadiz and Seville, were sufficient for every
exigency.

In October Eguia advanced with this army a
short way into La Mancha; but when the French,
unwilling to lose the resources of that fertile province, made a movement towards him, he regained

the Sierra Morena on the 16th, taking post, first at St. Elena, and finally at La Carolina. The first and fourth corps then occupied the whole of La Mancha, with advanced posts at the foot of the mountains; the second and fifth corps were established in the valley of the Tagus and at Toledo; and the reserve at Madrid. During these movements, Bassecour, who commanded in Estremadura, detached eight hundred horsemen to reinforce the duke Del Parque, and quartered the rest of his forces behind the Guadiana. Thus in the latter end of October, there were sixty thousand men, under Eguia, covering Seville by the line of La Mancha; ten thousand under Bassecour on the line of Estremadura, and about six thousand employed as guards to the Junta and in the service of the depôts behind the Morena.

In the north, the Spanish army of the left was concentrated near Ciudad Rodrigo. For when Beresford marched down the Portuguese frontier to the Tagus, the duke Del Parque, reinforced with the eight hundred cavalry from Estremadura, and with the Gallician divisions of Mendizabel and Carrera, (amounting to thirteen thousand men, completely equipped from English stores, brought out to Coruña in July,) made a movement into the rugged country, about the Sierra de Francia, and sent his scouting parties as far as Baños. At the same time general Santocildes, marching from Lugo with two thousand men, took possession of Astorga, and menaced the rear of the sixth corps, which after forcing the pass of Baños, had been quartered between the Tormes and the Esla. In this situation, a French detachment attempted to surprise one of the gates of Astorga, on the 9th

SeeVol.II.
p. 427.

of October, and, being repulsed, returned to their
cantonments. Soon afterwards Ballasteros, having
again collected about eight thousand men in the
Asturias, armed and equipped them from English
stores, and, coming down to Astorga, crossed the
Esla, and attempted to storm Zamora. Failing in
this, he entered Portugal by the road of Miranda, and
from thence proceeded to join the duke Del Parque.
Thus the old armies of Gallicia and the Asturias
being broken up, those provinces were ordered to
raise fresh forces; but there was in Gallicia a general disposition to resist the authority of the Central Junta.

Del Parque, eager to act against the sixth corps,
had demanded, in September, through Perez Castro
the Spanish envoy at Lisbon, that the Portuguese
army should join him; this being referred to sir
Arthur Wellesley, he gave it a decided negative,
grounding his refusal upon reasons which I shall
insert at large, as giving a clear and interesting
view of the military state of affairs at this period.

" The enemy, he said, were superior to the allies, Letter from
Sir A. Wel-
including those which Beresford might bring into lesley, Spt.
23, 1809.
the field, not only in numbers, but (adverting to the MS.
composition of the Spanish armies, the want of
cavalry in some, of artillery in others, of clothing,
ammunition, and arms, and the deficiency of discipline in all) superior in efficiency even to a
greater degree than in numbers. These circumstances, and the absolute deficiency in means, were
the causes why, after a great victory at Talavera,
the armies had been obliged to recur to the defensive, and nothing had altered for the better
since.

" But, besides these considerations, the enemy

enjoyed peculiar advantages from his central position, which enabled him to frustrate the duke Del
Parque's intended operations. He could march a
part, or the whole of his forces to any quarter,
whereas the operation of the different corps of the
allies must necessarily be isolated, and each for a
time exposed to defeat. Thus there was nothing to
prevent the enemy from throwing himself upon the
duke Del Parque and Beresford, with the whole
corps of Ney, which was at Salamanca, of Soult,
which was at Plasencia, and with the force under
Kellerman, which was near Valladolid, in which
case, even if he, sir Arthur, had the inclination,
he had not the means of marching in time to save
them from destruction.

" In the same manner the British army, if it
took an advanced position, would be liable to a
fatal disaster ; so likewise would the Spanish army
of La Mancha. It followed, then, that if any one
of these armies made a forward movement, the
whole must co-operate, or the single force in activity
would be ruined ; but the relative efficiency and
strength of the hostile forces, as laid down in the
commencement of the argument, forbad a general
co-operation with any hopes of solid success ; and
the only consequence that could follow would be,
that, after a battle or two, some brilliant actions
performed by a part, and some defeats sustained by
others, and after the loss of many valuable officers
and soldiers, the allies would be forced again to
resume those defensive positions, which they ought
never to have quitted.

" Satisfied that this was the only just view of
affairs, he, although prepared to make an effort to
prevent Ciudad Rodrigo from falling into the

enemy's hands, was resolved not to give the duke
Del Parque any assistance to maintain his former
position, and he advised the Portuguese government,
not to risk Beresford's army in a situation which
could only lead to mischief. The proposed operation of the duke Del Parque was not the mode to
save Ciudad Rodrigo. The only effectual one was
to post himself in such a situation as that the
enemy could not attack and defeat him without a
long previous preparation, which would give time
for aid to arrive, and a march, in which the enemy
himself might be exposed to defeat. To expose
those troops to defeat which were ultimately to
co-operate in defence of Ciudad Rodrigo, was not
the way of preventing the success of an attempt
of that fortress. The best way was to place the
Spanish force in such a post that it could not be
attacked without risk to the enemy, and from
whence it could easily co-operate with the other
corps, which must be put in motion, if Ciudad was
to be saved; and although he would not take upon
himself to point out the exact position which the
duke Del Parque ought to occupy, he was certain
that, in his present forward one, although joined
by Beresford, he could not avoid defeat. Ciudad
Rodrigo would be lost, and other misfortunes would
follow, none of which could occur under any other
probable, or even possible concurrence of circumstances. In fine, that he had long been of opinion
that the war must necessarily be defensive on the
part of the allies, and that Portugal at least, if
not Spain, ought to avail herself of the short
period, which the enemy seemed disposed to leave
her in tranquillity, to organize, and equip, and
discipline her armies. Those objects could not be

BOOK
IX.
1809.
October.
accomplished, unless the troops were kept quiet, and yet they were much more important to all parties, than any desultory successful operations against the French troops about Salamanca; but any success was doubtful, and certain to be temporary, because the enemy would immediately collect in numbers sufficient to crush the allies, who must then return, having failed in their object, lost a number of men, and, what was worse, time, which would have been more usefully employed in preparing for a great and well combined effort."

This reasoning, solid, clear, convincing, made no impression upon the Spanish Junta or their general. Castro replied to it, by demanding a positive and definitive answer, as to when the Portuguese army would be in a condition to co-operate with the Spaniards in the Spanish territories.

Sir A. Wel-
lesley's
Correspon-
dence with
Don M.
Forgas,
October 19,
1809. MSS.
" *When there is a Spanish army with which the Portuguese can co-operate on some defined plan, which all parties will have the means, and will engage to carry into execution, as far as any person can engage to carry into execution a military operation.*" " *When means shall be pointed out, and fixed, for the subsistence of the Portuguese troops while they remain in Spain, so that they may not starve, and be obliged to retire for want of food, as was the case when lately in that country.*" " *When decided answers shall be given upon those points, I shall be enabled to tell the governors of Portugal that their excellencies have an army in a state to be sent into Spain.*" This was sir Arthur's reply, which ended the negotiation, and the duke Del Parque commenced operations by himself.

To favour the junction of Ballasteros, his first movement was towards Ledesma. General Mar-

chand immediately drew together, at Salamanca,
eleven thousand men and fourteen guns, and marched
to meet him. Thereupon, the duke, without having effected his junction, fell back to Tamames,
taking post half-way up a mountain of remarkable
strength ; where he awaited the enemy, with a
thousand cavalry and twenty thousand infantry, of
which the Gallicians only could be accounted experienced soldiers.

BATTLE OF TAMAMES.

General Losada commanded the Spanish right,
count Belvidere the reserve, Martin Carrera the
left, which being on the most accessible part of
the mountain was covered and flanked by the cavalry. Marchand, desirous of fighting before
Ballasteros could arrive, moved rapidly, reached
the foot of the mountain early on the 18th, and
immediately fell upon Del Parque's left. The
Spanish cavalry fled rather hastily, the French
horsemen followed closely, the infantry surprised
in the midst of an evolution were thrown into
disorder, and the artillery was taken. Carrera,
Mendizabel, and the duke, rallied the troops on
the higher ground, reinforced them from the reserve, and coming down with a fresh impetus, recovered the guns, and discomfited the French with
the loss of an eagle, one cannon, and several hundred men. During this brilliant combat on the
left, the right and centre were felt by the French
skirmishers, but the ground was too strong to make
any impression. Marchand, seeing his men repulsed in all quarters with loss, and fearing to be

enclosed by Ballasteros in that disordered state, retreated to Salamanca.

Del Parque did not venture to follow up his victory until the 21st, when, being joined by Ballasteros, he pushed with nearly thirty thousand men for Ledesma ; crossed the Tormes there on the 23d, turned Salamanca by a night march, and early in the morning of the 24th crowned the heights of San Cristoval in rear of that city, hoping to cut off Marchand's retreat, but that general had timely information, and was already at Toro, behind the Douro. Meanwhile, the news of the defeat at Tamames reached Madrid, Dessolle's division was detached through the Puerto Pico to reinforce the sixth corps, and Kellerman was directed to advance from Valladolid, and take the command of the whole.

When the duke Del Parque heard of this reinforcement, he fell back, not to Ciudad Rodrigo, but by the way of Alba de Tormes to Bejar, which latter place he reached on the 8th of November. And while these events were taking place in Castile, the Central Junta having finally concocted their schemes, were commencing an enterprise of unparalleled rashness on the side of La Mancha.

CHAPTER V.

In the arrangement of warlike affairs, difficulties being always overlooked by the Spaniards, they are carried on from one phantasy to another so swiftly, that the first conception of an enterprise is immediately followed by a confident anticipation of complete success, which continues until the hour of battle, and then when it might be of use, generally abandons them. Now the Central Junta having to deceive the people, affirmed that sir Arthur Wellesley had retreated to the frontiers of Portugal at the very moment when the French might have been driven to the Pyrenees, came very soon to believe this their own absurd calumny, and resolved to send the army at Carolina headlong against Madrid : nay, such was their pitch of confidence, that forenaming the civil and military authorities, they arranged a provisionary system for the future administration of the capital, with a care, that they denied to the army which was to put them in possession.

Eguia was considered unfit to conduct this enterprise, and Albuquerque was distasteful to the Junta; wherefore, casting their eyes upon general Areizaga, they chose him, whose only recommendation was, that, at the petty battle of Alcanitz, Blake had noticed his courage. He was then at Lerida, but reached La Carolina in the latter end of October; and being of a quick lively turn, and as confident as the Junta could desire, readily undertook to drive the French from Madrid.

This movement was to commence early in November, and at first, only Villa Campa, with the
bands from Aragon, were to assist. But when
Areizaga, after meeting the enemy, began to lose
confidence, the duke of Albuquerque, successor to
Bassecour in Estremadura, received instructions to
cause a diversion, by marching on Arzobispo and
Talavera de la Reyna. The duke Del Parque, coming by the pass of Baños, was to join him there;
and thus nearly ninety thousand men were to be
put in motion against Madrid, precisely on that
plan which sir Arthur Wellesley had just denounced
as certain to prove disastrous. Indeed, every
chance was so much in favour of the French, that
taking into consideration the solid reasons for remaining on the defensive, Areizaga's irruption may
be regarded as an extreme example of military
rashness, and the project of uniting Del Parque's
forces with Albuquerque's, at Talavera, was also
certain to fail; because, the enemy's masses were
already in possession of the point of junction, and
the sixth corps could fall on Del Parque's rear.

Partly to deceive the enemy, partly because they
would never admit of any opposition to a favourite
scheme, the Junta spread a report that the British
army was to co-operate, and permitted Areizaga to
march, under the impression that it was so. Nothing could be more untrue. Sir Arthur Wellesley
being at this period at Seville, held repeated con-
versations with the Spanish ministers and the members of the Junta, and reiterating all his former
objections to offensive operations, warned his audi-
tors that the project in question was peculiarly
ill-judged, and would end in the destruction of
their army. The Spanish ministers, far from at-

Appendix,
No. II.
Section 1.

tending to his advice, did not even *officially inform*
him of Areizaga's *march until the* 18*th of November*,
the very day before the fatal termination of the
campaign. Yet, on *the* 16*th they had repeated
their demand for assistance*, and with a vehemence,
deaf to reason, required that the British should
instantly co-operate with Albuquerque and Del
Parque's forces. Sir Arthur, firm to his first
views, never gave the slightest hopes that his
army would so act; and he assured the Junta
that the diversion proposed would have no effect
whatever.

OPERATIONS IN LA MANCHA.

Areizaga, after publishing an address to the
troops on the 3d of November, commenced his
march from La Carolina, with sixty pieces of artillery, and from fifty to sixty thousand men, of which
about eight thousand were cavalry. Several British
officers and private gentlemen, and the baron
Crossand, an Austrian military agent, attended the
head-quarters, which was a scene of gaiety and
boasting; for Areizaga, never dreaming of misfortune, gave a free scope to his social vivacity.
The army marched by the roads of Manzanares and
Damiel, with scarcely any commissariat preparation,
and without any military equipment save arms;
but the men were young, robust, full of life and
confidence, and being without impediments of any
kind, made nearly thirty miles each day. They
moved however in a straggling manner, quartering
and feeding as they could in the villages on their
route, and with so little propriety, that the peasantry

of La Mancha universally abandoned their dwellings, and carried off their effects.

Although the French could not at first give credit to the rumours of this strange incursion, they were aware that some great movement was in agitation, and only uncertain from what point and for what specific object the effort would be made. Jourdan had returned to France, Soult was major-general of the French armies, and under his advice, the king, who was inclined to abandon Madrid, prepared to meet the coming blow. But the army was principally posted towards Talavera, for the false reports had, in some measure, succeeded in deceiving the French as to the approach of the English; and it was impossible at once to conceive the full insanity of the Junta.

The second corps, commanded by general Heudelet, being withdrawn from Placentia, was, on the 5th, posted at Oropesa and Arzobispo, with an advanced guard at Calzada, and scouting parties watching Naval Moral, and the course of the Tietar.

The fifth corps, under Mortier, was concentrated at Talavera.

Of the fourth corps, half a division garrisoned Madrid in the absence of Dessolle's troops; the other half, under general Liger Belair, was behind the Tajuna, guarding the eastern approaches to the capital. The remaining divisions, commanded by Sebastiani, were, the one at Toledo, the other with Milhaud's cavalry at Ocaña.

The first corps, about twenty-one thousand strong, and commanded by marshal Victor, was at Mora and Yebenes, a day's march in advance of Toledo, but the cavalry of this corps under the command

of Latour Maubourg occupied Consuegra and Madrilejos, on the road to the Sierra Morena. The whole
army including the French and Spanish guards,
was above eighty thousand fighting men, without
reckoning Dessolle's division, which was on the
other side of the Guadarama mountains.

In the night of the 6th, information reached the
king, that six thousand Spanish horsemen, supported
by two thousand foot, had come down upon Consuegra from the side of Herencia, and that a second
column, likewise composed of cavalry and infantry,
had passed the Puerto de Piche, and fallen upon
the outposts at Madrilejos. All the prisoners taken
in the skirmishes agreed that the Spanish army
was above fifty thousand strong, and the duke of
Belluno immediately concentrated the first corps
at Yebenes, but kept his cavalry at Mora, by
which he covered the roads leading from Consuegra and Madrilejos upon Toledo. On the 8th,
there were no Spaniards in front of the first corps,
yet officers sent towards Ocaña, were chased back
by cavalry, hence Soult judged, what was indeed
the truth, that Areizaga continuing his reckless
march, had pushed by Tembleque towards Aranjuez,
leaving the first corps on his left flank. The division of the fourth corps was immediately moved
from Toledo by the right bank of the Tagus to
Aranjuez, from whence Sebastiani carried it to
Ocaña, thus concentrating about eight thousand
infantry, and fifteen hundred cavalry at that point
on the 9th; the same day Victor retired with the
first corps to Ajofrin.

On the 10th, Gazan's division of the fifth corps
was ordered to march from Talavera to Toledo, and
the first corps which had reached the latter town,

S.
Journal of
Opera-
tions,
MSS.

was directed to move up the right bank of the Tagus to Aranjuez to support Sebastiani, who holding fast at Ocaña, sent six squadrons to feel for the enemy towards Guardia. The Spaniards continuing their movement, met those squadrons and pursued them towards Ocaña.

COMBAT OF DOS BARRIOS.

Areizaga, ignorant of what was passing around him, and seeing only Sebastiani's cavalry on the table-land between the town of Dos Barrios and Ocaña, concluded that they were unsupported, and directed the Spanish horse to charge them without delay. The French thus pressed, drew back behind their infantry which was close. at hand, and unexpectedly opened a brisk fire on the Spanish squadrons which were thrown into confusion, and being charged in that state by the whole mass of the enemy's cavalry, were beaten, with the loss of two hundred prisoners and two pieces of cannon. Areizaga's main body was, however, coming up, Sebastiani fell back upon Ocaña, and the next morning took up a position on some heights lining the left bank of the Tagus and covering Aranjuez; the Spaniards entered Dos Barrios, but there their impetuous movement ceased. They had come down from the Morena like a stream of lava, and burst into La Mancha with a rapidity that scarcely gave time for rumour to precede them. This swiftness of execution, generally so valuable in war, was here but an outbreak of folly. Without any knowledge of the French numbers, or position, without any

plan of action, Areizaga had rushed like a maniac
into the midst of his foes, and then suddenly stood
still, trembling and bewildered.
From the 10th to the 13th he halted at Dos Barrios, and informed his government of Sebastiani's
stubborn resistance, and of the doubts which now
for the first time assailed his own mind. It was
then the Junta changing their plans, eagerly demanded the assistance of the British army, and
commanded the dukes of Albuquerque and Del
Parque to unite at Talavera. Albuquerque commenced his movement immediately, and the Junta
did not hesitate to assure both their generals and the
public, that sir Arthur was also coming on. Wherefore
Areizaga thus encouraged, and having had time to
recover from his first incertitude, made on the 14th
a flank march by his right to Santa Cruz la Zarza,
intending to cross the Tagus at Villa Maurique,
turn the French left, and penetrate to the capital by
the eastern side; but during his delay at Dos Barrios the French forces had been concentrated from
every quarter, and although to the south of Ocaña,
the ground is open and undulating; on the north,
the ramifications of the Cuença mountains, leading
down the left bank of the Tagus, presented, at
Santa Cruz, ridges which stretching strong and
rough towards Aranjuez, afforded good positions
for Sebastiani to cover that place.

Soult was awake to his adversary's projects, yet
could not believe that he would dare such a movement unless certain of support from the British
army, and therefore kept the different corps quiet
on the eleventh, waiting for Heudelet's report from
Oropesa. In the night it arrived, stating that rumours of a combined Spanish and English army

being on the march, were rife, but that the scouts
could not discover that the allied force was actually
within several marches. Soult, now judging, that
although the rumours should be true, his central
position would enable him to defeat Areizaga and
return by the way of Toledo in time to meet the
allies in the valley of the Tagus, put all his masses
again into activity. The first corps was directed to
hasten its march to Aranjuez; the fifth corps to
concentrate at Toledo; the second corps to abandon
Oropesa, Calzada and Arzobispo, and replacing the
fifth corps at Talavera, to be in readiness to close
upon the main body of the army. Finally, information being received of the duke Del Parque's
retreat from Salamanca to Bejar and of the re-occu-
pation of Salamanca by the sixth corps, Dessolle's
division was recalled to Madrid.

During the 12th, while the first, second, and fifth
corps were in march, general Liger Belair's brigade
continued to watch the banks of the Tajuna, and
the fourth corps preserved its offensive positions on
the height in the front of Aranjuez, having fifteen
hundred men in reserve at the bridge of Bayona.
The 14th the general movement was completed.
Two corps were concentrated at Aranjuez to assail
the Spaniards in front; one at Toledo to cross the
Tagus and fall upon their left flank, and the king's
guards at Madrid formed a reserve for the fourth
and first corps. The second corps was at Talavera,
and Dessolle's division was in the Guadarama on
its return to the capital. In fine, all was prepared
for the attack of Dos Barrios, when Areizaga's flank
march to Santa Cruz la Zarza occasioned new combinations.

In the evening of the 15th, it was known that

the Spaniards had made a bridge at Villa Maurique, and passed two divisions and some cavalry over the Tagus. The duke of Belluno was immediately ordered to carry the first and fourth corps (with the exception of a brigade left in Aranjuez) up the left bank of the Tagus, operating so as to fix Areizaga, and force him to deliver battle; and, with a view of tempting the Spaniard, by an appearance of timidity, the bridges of La Reyna and Aranjuez were broken down.

While these dispositions were making on the French side, the Spanish general commenced a second bridge over the Tagus; and part of his cavalry, spreading in small detachments, scoured the country, and skirmished on a line extending from Arganda to Aranjuez. The Partidas also, being aided by detachments from the army, obliged the French garrison to retire from Guardalaxara upon Arganda, and occupied the former town on the 12th. But, in the night of the 13th, eight French companies and some troops of light cavalry, by a sudden march, surprised them, killed and wounded two or three hundred men, and took eighty horses and a piece of artillery.

The 16th the infantry of the first and fourth corps was at Morata and Bayona, the cavalry at Perales and Chinchon, and, during this time, the fifth corps, leaving a brigade of foot and one of horse at Toledo, marched by Illescas towards Madrid, to act as a reserve to the duke of Belluno.

The 17th Areizaga continued his demonstrations on the side of the Tajuna, and hastened the construction of his second bridge; but on the approach of the duke of Belluno with the first corps, he stayed the work, withdrew his divisions from the

right bank of the Tagus, and on the 18th, (the
cavalry of the first corps having reached Villarejo
de Salvanes,) he destroyed his bridges, called in
his parties, and drew up for battle on the heights
of Santa Cruz de la Zarza.

Hitherto the continual movements of the Spanish
army, and the unsettled plans of the Spanish
general, rendered it difficult for the French to fix
a field of battle, but now Areizaga's march to
St. Cruz had laid his line of operations bare.
The French masses were close together, the
duke of Belluno could press on the Spanish front
with the first corps, and the king, calling the
fourth corps from Bayona, could throw twenty-five
or thirty thousand men on Areizaga's rear, by the
road of Aranjuez and Ocaña. It was calculated
that no danger could arise from this double line of
operations, because a single march would bring
both the king and Victor upon Areizaga, and if
the latter should suddenly assail either, each would
be strong enough to sustain the shock. Hence,
when Soult knew that the Spaniards were certainly
encamped at Santa Cruz, he caused the fifth corps,
then in march for Madrid, to move during the
night of the 17th upon Aranjuez, and the fourth
corps received a like order. The king, himself,
quitting Madrid, arrived there on the evening of
the 18th, with the Royal French Guards, two
Spanish battalions of the line, and a brigade of
Dessolle's division which had just arrived; in all
about ten thousand men. The same day, the duke
of Belluno concentrated the first corps at Villarejo de Salvanés, intending to cross the Tagus at
Villa Maurique, and attack the Spanish position on
the 19th.

A pontoon train, previously prepared at Madrid, enabled the French to repair the broken bridges, near Aranjuez, in two hours ; and about one o'clock on the 18th, a division of cavalry, two divisions of infantry of the fourth corps, and the advanced guard of the fifth corps, passed the Tagus, part at the bridge of La Reyna, and part at a ford. General Milhaud with the leading squadrons, immediately pursued a small body of Spanish horsemen, and was thus led to the table-land, between Antiguela and Ocaña, where he suddenly came upon a front of fifteen hundred cavalry supported by three thousand more in reserve. Having only twelve hundred dragoons, he prepared to retire, but at that moment general Paris arrived with another brigade, and was immediately followed by the light cavalry of the fifth corps ; the whole making a re-inforcement of about two thousand men. With these troops Sebastiani came in person, and took the command at the instant when the Spaniards, seeing the inferiority of the French, were advancing to the charge.

CAVALRY COMBAT AT OCANA.

The Spaniards came on at a trot, and Sebastiani directed Paris, with a regiment of light cavalry and the Polish lancers, to turn and fall upon the right flank of the approaching squadrons, which being executed with great vigour, especially by the Poles, caused considerable confusion, which the Spanish general endeavoured to remedy by closing to the assailed flank. But to effect this he formed his left centre in one vast column, whereupon

Sebastiani charged headlong into the midst of it with his reserves, and the enormous mass yielding to the shock, got into confusion, and finally gave way. Many were slain, several hundred wounded, and eighty troopers and above five hundred horses were taken. The loss of the French bore no proportion in men, but general Paris was killed, and several superior officers were wounded.

This unexpected encounter with such a force of cavalry, led Soult to believe that the Spanish general, aware of his error, was endeavouring to recover his line of operations. The examination of the prisoners confirmed this opinion, and in the night, information from the duke of Belluno and the reports of officers sent towards Villa Maurique arrived, all agreeing that only a rear-guard was to be seen at Santa Cruz de la Zarza. It then became clear that the Spaniards were on the march, and that a battle could be fought the next day. In fact Areizaga had retraced his steps by a flank movement through Villa Rubia and Noblejas, with the intention of falling upon the king's forces as they opened out from Aranjuez. He arrived on the morning of the 19th at Ocaña, but judging from the cavalry action, that the French could attack first, drew up his whole army on the same plain, in two lines, a quarter of a mile asunder.

Ocaña is covered on the north by a ravine, which commencing gently half a mile eastward of the town, runs deepening and with a curve, to the west, and finally connects itself with gullies and hollows, whose waters run off to the Tagus. Behind the deepest part of this ravine the Spanish left was posted, crossing the main road from

Aranjuez to Dos Barrios ; one flank rested on the gullies, the other on Ocaña. The centre was in front of the town, which was occupied by some infantry as a post of reserve, but the right wing stretched in the direction of Noblejas along the edge of a gentle ridge *in front* of the shallow part of the ravine. The cavalry was on the flank and rear of the right wing. Behind the army there was an immense plain, but closed in and fringed towards Noblejas with rich olive woods, which were occupied by infantry to protect the passage of the Spanish baggage, still filing by the road from Zarza. Such were Areizaga's dispositions.

Joseph passed the night of the 18th in reorganising his forces. The whole of the cavalry, consisting of nine regiments, was given to Sebastiani. Four divisions of infantry, with the exception of one regiment left at Aranjuez to guard the bridge, were placed under the command of marshal Mortier, who was also empowered, if necessary, to direct the movements of the cavalry. The artillery was commanded by general Senarmont. The Royal Guards remained with the King, and marshal Soult directed the whole of the movements.

Before day-break, on the 10th, the monarch marched with the intention of falling upon the Spaniards wherever he could meet with them. At Antiguela his troops quitting the high road, turned to their left, gained the table-land of Ocaña, somewhat beyond the centre of the Spanish position, and discovered Areizaga's army in order of battle. The French cavalry instantly forming to the front, covered the advance of the infantry, which drew up in successive lines as the divisions arrived on the plain. The Spanish out-posts fell

back, and were followed by the French skirmishers,
who spread along the hostile front and opened a
sharp fire.

About forty-five thousand Spanish infantry,
seven thousand cavalry, and sixty pieces of artillery were in line. The French force was only
twenty-four thousand infantry, five thousand sabres
and lances, and fifty guns, including the battery
of the Royal Guard. But Areizaga's position was
miserably defective. The whole of his left wing,
fifteen thousand strong, was paralyzed by the ravine; it could neither attack nor be attacked; the
centre was scarcely better situated, and the extremity of his right wing was uncovered, save by
the horsemen, who were, although superior in number, quite dispirited by the action of the preceding
evening. These circumstances dictated the order
of the attack.

BATTLE OF OCAÑA.

At ten o'clock, Sebastiani's cavalry gaining ground
to his left, turned the Spanish right. General Leval,
with two divisions of infantry in columns of regiments, each having a battalion displayed in front,
followed the cavalry, and drove general Zayas from
the olive-woods. General Girard, with his division
arranged in the same manner, followed Leval in
second line, and general Dessolles menaced the
centre with one portion of his troops, while another
portion lined the edge of the ravine to support the
skirmishers and awe the Spanish left wing. The
king remained in reserve with his guards. Thus
the French order of battle was in two columns :

the principal one, flanked by the cavalry, directed against and turning the Spanish right, the second keeping the Spanish centre in check, and each being supported by reserves.

These dispositions were completed at eleven o'clock, at which hour, Senarmont, massing thirty pieces of artillery, opened a shattering fire on Areizaga's centre. Six guns, detached to the right, played at the same time across the ravine against the left, and six others swept down the deep hollow, to clear it of the light troops. The Spaniards were undisciplined and badly commanded, but discovered no appearance of fear; their cries were loud and strong, their skirmishing fire brisk, and, from the centre of their line, sixteen guns opened with a murderous effect upon Leval's and Girard's columns, as the latter were pressing on towards the right. To mitigate the fire of this battery, a French battalion, rushing out at full speed, seized a small eminence close to the Spanish guns, and a counter battery was immediately planted there. Then the Spaniards gave back, their skirmishers were swept out of the ravine by a flanking fire of grape, and Senarmont immediately drawing the artillery from the French right, took Ocaña as his pivot, and, prolonging his fire to the left, raked Areizaga's right wing in its whole length.

During this cannonade, Leval, constantly pressing forward, obliged the Spaniards to change their front, by withdrawing the right wing *behind* the shallow part of the ravine, which, as I have before said, was in its rear when the action commenced. By this change, the whole army, still drawn up in two lines, at the distance of a quarter of a mile asunder, was pressed into somewhat of a convex form with the town of Ocaña in the centre, and hence Senarmont's artillery tore their ranks with a greater destruction than before. Nevertheless, encouraged by observing the comparatively feeble body of infantry approaching them, the Spaniards suddenly retook the offensive, and their fire, redoubling, dismounted two French guns; Mortier himself was wounded slightly, Leval severely, the line advanced, and the leading French divisions wavered and gave back.

The moment was critical, and the duke of Treviso lost no time in exhortations to Leval's troops, but, like a great commander, instantly brought up Girard's division through the intervals of the first line, and displayed a front of fresh troops, keeping one regiment in square on the left flank; for he expected that Areizaga's powerful cavalry, which still remained in the plain, would charge for the victory. Girard's fire soon threw the Spanish first line into disorder, and meanwhile, Dessolles, who had gained ground by an oblique movement, seeing the enemy's right thus shaken, seized Ocaña itself, and issued forth on the other side. The light cavalry of the king's guard, followed by the infantry, then poured through the town, and on the extreme left, Sebastiani, with a rapid charge, cut off six thousand infantry, and obliged them to surrender. The Spanish cavalry, which had only suffered a little from the cannonade, and had never made an effort to turn the tide of battle, now drew off entirely, and the second line of infantry gave ground as the front fell back upon it in confusion;

Areizaga, confounded and bewildered, ordered the left wing, which had scarcely fired a shot, to retreat, and then quitted the field himself.

For half an hour after this, the superior officers who remained, endeavoured to keep the troops together in the plain, and strove to reach the main road leading to Dos Barrios; but Girard and Dessolles' divisions being connected after passing Ocaña, pressed on with steady rapidity, while the Polish lancers and a regiment of chasseurs, out-flanking the Spanish right, continually increased the confusion : finally, Sebastiani, after securing his prisoners, came up again like a whirlwind, and charged full in the front with five regiments of cavalry. Then the whole mass broke, and fled each man for himself across the plain ; but, on the right of the routed multitude, a deep ravine leading from Yepes to Dos Barrios, in an oblique direction, continually contracted the space, and the pursuing cavalry arriving first at Barrios, headed nearly ten thousand bewildered men, and forced them to surrender. The remainder turned their faces to all quarters, and such was the rout, that the French were also obliged to disperse to take prisoners, for, to their credit, no rigorous execution was inflicted, and hundreds, merely deprived of their arms, were desired, in raillery, " to return to their homes, and abandon war as a trade they were unfit for." This fatal battle commenced at eleven o'clock ; before two thirty pieces of artillery, a hundred and twenty carriages, twenty-five stand of colours, three gene-rals, six hundred inferior officers, and eighteen thousand privates were taken, and the pursuit was still hot. Seven or eight thousand of the Spaniards contrived to make away towards the mountain of Tarancon, others followed the various routes through La Mancha to the Sierra Morena, and many saved themselves in Valencia and Murcia.

Meanwhile, the first corps, having passed the Tagus by a ford, re-established the bridge at Villa Maurique before ten o'clock in the morning, and finding Santa Cruz de la Zarza abandoned, followed Areizaga's traces; at Villatobas, the light cavalry captured twelve hundred carriages, and a little farther on, took a thousand of the fugitives who were making for Tarancon. The duke of Belluno, being thus apprized of the result of the battle, halted at Villatobas, but sent his cavalry forward to La Guardia, where they joined Sebastiani's horsemen, and the whole continuing the pursuit to Lillo, made five hundred more prisoners, together with three hundred horses. This finished the operations of the day, only eighteen hundred cannon-shot had been fired, and an army of more than fifty thousand men had been ruined. The French lost seventeen hundred men, killed and wounded; the Spaniards five thousand, and before nightfall, all the baggage and military carriages, three thousand animals, forty-five pieces of artillery, thirty thousand muskets, and twenty-six thousand captives were in the hands of the conquerors!

S.
Journal of
Operations
MSS.
Letter
from Lord
Wellington
to Lord Li-
verpool,
Nov. 30,
1809, MSS.

Areizaga reached Tembleque during the night, and La Carolina the third day after. On the road, he met general Benaz with a thousand dragoons that had been detached to the rear before the battle commenced; this body he directed on Madrilejos to cover the retreat of the fugitives, but so strongly did the panic spread that when Sebastiani ap-

Guadarama M.ts

Guadalaxara

MADRID

Arganda

Perales

Tajuna R.

Illesas

Bayona

Morata

Salvanes

Chinchon

Villa Maurique

Aranjuez

La Reyna

S.ta Cruz de
da Zarza

Villa Rubia

Talavera

Tagus R.

Toledo

Ontiqueta

Noblejas

Villa Tobas

To Tarancon

Ocaña

Yepes

Dosbarios

Guardia

Ajofrin

Trembleque

Lillo

Toledo M.ts

Mora

Yevenes

Consuegra

Madrilejos

Herencia

Puerto Piche

Guadiana R.

Villharta
de S.t Juan

Manzanares

EIZAGA'S
operations
1809.

Almagro

Morena M.ts

Despena Peros

La Carolina

▭ French before the Battle
▭ Spaniards d.º
▭ French in Battle
▭ Spaniards d.º

Published by T. & W. Boone.

proached that post on the 20th, Benaz's men fled,
without seeing an enemy, as fearfully as any who
came from the fight. Even so late as the 24th,
only four hundred cavalry, belonging to all regiments, could be assembled at Manzanares; and
still fewer at La Carolina.

CHAPTER VI.

BOOK
IX.

1809.
Nov.
JOSEPH halted at Dos Barrios, the night of the battle, and the next day directed Sebastiani, with all the light cavalry and a division of infantry, upon Madrilejos and Consuegra; the first corps, by St. Juan de Vilharta, upon the Sierra Morena, the fifth corps, by Tembleque and Mora, upon Toledo. One division of the fourth corps guarded the spoil and the prisoners at Ocaña. A second division, reinforced with a brigade of cavalry, was posted, by detachments, from Aranjuez to Consuegra. The monarch himself, with his guards and Dessolles' first brigade, returned, on the 20th, to Madrid.

Three days had sufficed to dissipate the storm on the side of La Mancha, but the duke Del Parque still menaced the sixth corps in Castile, and the reports from Talavera again spoke of Albuquerque and the English being in motion. The second brigade of Dessolles' division had returned from Old Castile on the 19th, and the uncertainty with respect to the British movements, obliged the king to keep all his troops in hand. Nevertheless, fearing that, if Del Parque gained upon the sixth corps, he might raise an insurrection in Leon, Gazan's division of the fifth corps was sent, from Toledo, through the Puerto Pico, to Marchand's assistance, and Kellerman was again directed to take the command of the whole.

During these events, the British army remained tranquil about Badajos; but Albuquerque, following his orders, had reached Peralada de Garbin, and seized the bridge of Arzobispo, in expectation of being joined by the duke Del Parque. That general, however, who had above thirty thousand men, thought, when Dessolles' division was recalled to Madrid, that he could crush the sixth corps, and, therefore, advanced from Bejar towards Alba de Tormes on the 17th, two days before the battle of Ocaña. Thus, when Albuquerque expected him on the Tagus, he was engaged in serious operations beyond the Tormes, and, having reached Alba the 21st, sent a division to take possession of Salamanca, which Marchand had again abandoned. The 22d he marched towards Valladolid, and his advanced guard and cavalry entered Fresno and Carpio. Meanwhile Kellerman, collecting all the troops of his government, and being joined by Marchand, moved upon Medina del Campo, and the 23d, fell with a body of horse upon the Spaniards at Fresno. The Spanish cavalry fled at once, but the infantry stood firm, and repulsed the assailants.

The 24th the duke carried his whole army to Fresno, intending to give battle; but on the 26th imperative orders to join Albuquerque having reached him, he commenced a retrograde movement. Kellerman, without waiting for the arrival of Gazan's division, instantly pursued, and his advanced guard of cavalry overtook and charged the Spanish army at the moment when a part of their infantry and all their horse had passed the bridge of Alba de Tormes; being repulsed, the French retired upon their supports, and the duke, seeing that an action was inevitable, brought the remainder of his troops,

Lord Wellington to Lord Liverpool. MSS.

with the exception of one division, back to the right bank.

BATTLE OF ALBA DE TORMES.

Scarcely was the line formed, when Kellerman came up with two divisions of dragoons and some artillery, and, without hesitating, sent one division to outflank the Spanish right, and, with the other, charged fiercely in upon the front. The Spanish horsemen, flying without a blow, rode straight over the bridge, and the infantry of the right being thus exposed, were broken and sabred, those on the left stood fast and repulsed the enemy. The duke rallied his cavalry on the other side of the river, and brought them back to the fight, but the French were also reinforced, and once more the Spanish horse fled without a blow. By this time it was dark, and the infantry of the left wing, under Mendizabel and Carrera, being unbroken, made good their retreat across the river, yet not without difficulty, and under the fire of some French infantry, which arrived just in the dusk. During the night the duke retreated upon Tamames unmolested, but at day-break when a French patrol came up with his rear, his whole army threw away their arms and fled outright. Kellerman, having meanwhile entered Salamanca, did not pursue, yet the dispersion was complete.

After this defeat, Del Parque rallied his army in the mountains behind Tamames, and, in ten or twelve days, again collected about twenty thousand men; they were however without artillery,

scarcely any had preserved their arms, and such
was their distress for provisions, that two months
afterwards, when the British arrived on the northern
frontier, the peasantry still spoke with horror of
the sufferings of those famished soldiers. Many
actually died of want, and every village was filled
with sick. Yet the mass neither dispersed nor
murmured! Spaniards, though hasty in revenge
and feeble in battle, are patient, to the last degree,
in suffering.

This result of the duke Del Parque's operation
had amply justified sir Arthur Wellesley's advice to
the Portuguese regency. In like manner the battle
of Ocaña, and the little effect produced by the duke
of Albuquerque's advance to Arzobispo, had justified that which he gave to the Central Junta. It
might therefore be imagined that the latter would
have received his after-counsels with deference;
but the course of that body was never affected by
either reason or experience. Just before the rout Lord Wellington to
Lord Li-
verpool,
Dec. 7.
1809.MSS.
of Alba de Tormes, sir Arthur Wellesley proposed
that ten thousand men, to be taken from the duke
Del Parque, should *reinforce Albuquerque, that the
latter might maintain the strong position of Meza
d'Ibor, and cover Estremadura for the winter.*
Meanwhile Del Parque's force, thus reduced one-
third, could, he said, be more easily fed, and might
keep aloof from the enemy until the British army
should arrive on the northern frontier of Portugal,
a movement long projected, and, as he informed
them, only delayed *to protect Estremadura until the
duke of Albuquerque had received the reinforcement.*
The only reply of the Junta was an order, directing Albuquerque *immediately to quit the line of the
Tagus, and take post at Llerena, behind the Gua-*

diana. Thus abandoning Estremadura to the enemy, and exposing his own front in a bad position to an army coming from Almarez, and his right flank and rear to an army coming from La Mancha.

This foolish and contemptuous proceeding, being followed by Del Parque's defeat, which endangered Ciudad Rodrigo, sir Arthur at once commenced his march for the north. He knew that twenty thousand Spanish infantry and six thousand mounted cavalry were again collected in La Carolina; and that the troops (eight thousand), who escaped from Ocaña, on the side of Tarancon, were at Cuença, under general Echevarria; and as the numbers reassembled in the Morena were (the inactivity of the French after the battle of Ocaña considered) sufficient to defend the passes and cover Seville for the moment, there was no reason why the British army should remain in unhealthy positions to aid people who would not aid themselves. Albuquerque's retrograde movement was probably a device of the Junta to oblige sir Arthur to undertake the defence of Estremadura, but it only hastened his departure. It did not comport with his plans to engage in serious operations on that side, yet to have retired when that province was actually attacked, would have been disreputable, wherefore, seizing this unhappily favourable moment to quit Badajos, he crossed the Tagus, and marched into the valley of the Mondego, leaving general Hill, with a mixed force of ten thousand men, at Abrantes.

The Guadiana pestilence had been so fatal that many officers blamed him for stopping so long, but it was his last hold on Spain, and the safety of the southern provinces was involved in his proceedings. It was not his battle of Talavera, but the position maintained by him on the frontier of Estremadura, which, in the latter part of 1809, saved Andalusia from subjection, and this is easy of demonstration; Joseph having rejected Soult's project against Portugal, dared not invade Andalusia, by Estremadura, with the English army on his right flank; neither could he hope to invade it by the way of La Mancha, without drawing sir Arthur into the contest. But Andalusia was, at this period, the last place where the intrusive king desired to meet a British army. He had many partisans in that province, who would necessarily be overawed if the course of the war carried sir Arthur beyond the Morena; nor could the Junta, in that case, have refused Cadiz, as a place of arms, to their ally. Then the whole force of Andalusia and Murcia would have rallied round the English army behind the Morena; and, as Areizaga had sixty thousand men, and Albuquerque ten thousand, it is no exaggeration to assume that a hundred thousand could have been organized for defence, and the whole of the troops, in the south of Portugal, would have been available to aid in the protection of Estremadura. Thus, including thirty thousand English, there would have been a mass of at least one hundred thousand soldiers, disposable for active operations, assembled in the Morena.

From La Carolina to Madrid is only ten marches, and while posted at the former, the allied army could have protected Lisbon as well as Seville, because a forward movement would oblige the French to concentrate round the Spanish capital. Andalusia would thus have become the principal object of the invaders; but the allied armies, holding the

BOOK
IX.

1809.
Nov.
passes of the Morena, their left flank protected by Estremadura and Portugal, their right by Murcia and Valencia, and having rich provinces and large cities behind them, and a free communication with the sea, and abundance of ports, could have fought a fair field for Spain.

Sir J.
Moore's
Correspon-
dence.
It was a perception of these advantages that caused sir John Moore to regret the ministers had not chosen the southern instead of the northern line for his operations. Lord Wellesley, also, impressed with the importance of Andalusia, urged his brother to adopt some plan of this nature, and the latter, sensible of its advantages, would have done so, but for the impossibility of dealing with Lord Wel-
lesley's
Correspon-
dence,
Parl. Pa-
pers, 1810. the Central Junta. Military possession of Cadiz and the uncontrolled command of a Spanish force were the only conditions upon which he would undertake the defence of Andalusia, conditions they would not accede to, but without which, he could not be secured against the caprices of men whose proceedings were one continued struggle against reason. This may seem inconsistent with a former assertion, that Portugal was the true base of operations for the English, but political as well as physical resources, and moral considerations weighed in that argument.

For the protection, then, of Andalusia and Estremadura, during a dangerous crisis of affairs, sir Arthur persisted, at such an enormous sacrifice of men, to hold his position on the Guadiana, yet it was reluctantly, and more in deference to his brother's wishes than his own judgement, that he remained after Areizaga's army was assembled. Having proved the Junta by experience, he was more clear-sighted, as to their perverseness, than lord

Wellesley, who, being in daily intercourse with the members, obliged to listen to their ready eloquence in excuse for past errors, and more ready promises of future exertion, clung longer to the notions that Spain could be put in the right path, and that England might war largely in conjunction with the united nations of the Peninsula, instead of restricting herself to the comparatively obscure operation of defending Lisbon. He was finally undeceived, and the march from Badajos for ever released the British general from a vexatious dependence on the Spanish government.

Meanwhile the French, in doubt of his intentions, appeared torpid. Kellerman remained at Salamanca, watching the movements of the duke Del Parque, and Gazan returned to Madrid. Milhaud, with a division of the fourth corps, and some cavalry, was detached against Echevarria, but on his arrival at Cuença, finding that the latter had retreated, by Toboado to Hellin in Murcia, combined his operations with general Suchet, and, as I have before related, assisted to reduce the towns of Albaracin and Teruel. Other movements there were none, but, as the Spanish regiments of the guard had fought freely against their countrymen, and many of the prisoners, taken at Ocaña, had offered to join the invaders' colours, the king conceived hopes of raising a national army. French writers assert that the captives at Ocaña made a marked distinction between Napoleon and Joseph. They were willing to serve the French emperor, but not the intrusive king of Spain. Spanish authors assume that none entered the enemy's ranks save by coercion and to escape; and that many did so with that view, and were successful, must be supposed, or the numbers said to have reassembled in the Morena, and at Cuença, cannot be reconciled with the loss sustained in the action. However the battles of Ocaña and Alba de Tormes terminated the series of offensive operations, which the Austrian war, and the reappearance of a British army in the Peninsula had enabled the allies to adopt, in 1809. Those operations had been unsuccessful, the enemy again took the lead, and the fourth epoch of the war commenced.

OBSERVATIONS.

1°. Although certain that the British army would not co-operate in this short campaign, the Junta openly asserted, that it would join Albuquerque in the valley of the Tagus. The improbability of Areizaga's acting, without such assistance, gave currency to the fiction, and an accredited fiction is, in war, often more useful than the truth ; in this, therefore, they are to be commended ; but, when deceiving their own general, they permitted Areizaga to act under the impression that he would be so assisted, they committed not an error, but an enormous crime. Nor was the general much less criminal for acting upon the mere assertion that other movements were combined with his, when no communication, no concerting of the marches, no understanding with the allied commander, as to their mutual resources and intentions, had taken place.

2°. A rushing wind, a blast from the mountains, tempestuous, momentary, such was Areizaga's movement on Dos Barrios, and assuredly it would be difficult to find its parallel. There is no post so strong, no town so guarded, that, by a fortunate stroke, may not be carried ; but who, even on the smallest scale, acts on this principle, unless aided by some accidental circumstance applicable to the moment ? Areizaga obeyed the orders of his government! no general is bound to obey orders (at least without remonstrance) which involve the safety of his army, to that he should sacrifice everything but victory; and many great commanders have sacrificed even victory, rather than appear to undervalue this vital principle.

3°. At Dos Barrios the Spanish general, having first met with opposition, halted for three days, evidently without a plan, and ignorant both of the situation of the first corps on his left flank, and of the real force in his front, yet this was the only moment in which he could hope for the slightest success. If, instead of a feeble skirmish of cavalry, he had borne forward, with his whole army, on the 11th, Sebastiani must have been overpowered and driven across the Tagus, and Areizaga, with fifty thousand infantry and a powerful cavalry, would, on the 12th, have been in the midst of the separated French corps, for their movement of concentration was not completely effected until the night of the 14th. But such a stroke was not for an undisciplined army, and this was another reason against moving from the Morena at all, seeing that the calculated chances were all against Areizaga, and his troops not such as could improve accidental advantages.

4°. The flank march, from Dos Barrios to Santa Cruz, although intended to turn the French left, and gain Madrid, was a circuitous route of at least a hundred miles, and, as there were three rivers to cross, namely, the Tagus, the Tajuña, and Henares, only great rapidity could give a chance of success; yet Areizaga was slow, so late as the 15th, he had passed the Tagus with only two divisions of infantry. Meanwhile the French moving on the inner circle, got between him and Madrid, and the moment one corps, out of the three opposed to him, approached, he recrossed the Tagus and concentrated again on the strong ground of Santa Cruz de la Zarza. The king by the way of Aranjuez had, however, already cut his line of retreat, and then Areizaga, who, on the 10th, had shrunk from an action with Sebastiani when the latter had only eight thousand men, sought a battle on the same ground with the king, who was at the head of thirty thousand, the first corps being also in full march upon the Spanish traces and distant only a few miles. Here it may be remarked that Victor, who was now to the eastward of the Spaniards, had been on the 9th to the westward at Yevenes and Mora, having moved in ten days, on a circle of a hundred and fifty miles, completely round this Spanish general, who pretended to treat his adversaries, as if they were blind men.

5°. Baron Crossand, it is said, urged Areizaga to entrench himself in the mountains, to raise the peasantry, and to wait the effect of Albuquerque's and Del Parque's operations. If so, his military ideas do not seem of a higher order than Areizaga's, and the proposal was but a repetition of Mr. Frere's former plan for Albuquerque; a plan founded on the supposition, that the rich plains of La Mancha were rugged mountains. In taking a permanent position at Santa Cruz or Tarancon, Areizaga must

have resigned all direct communication with Andalusia, and opened a fresh line of communication
with Valencia, which would have been exposed to
the third corps from Aragon. Yet without examining whether either the Spanish general or army
were capable of such a difficult operation, as adopting an accidental line of operations, the advice, if
given at all, was only given on the 18th, and on
the 16th, the first corps, the fourth, the greatest
part of the fifth, the reserve and the royal guards,
forming a mass of more than fifty thousand fighting
men, would have taught Areizaga that men and
not mountains decide the fate of a battle. But in
fact, there were no mountains to hold : between
Zarza and the borders of Valencia, the whole country is one vast plain, and on the 18th, there was
only the alternative of fighting the weakest of the
two French armies, or of retreating by forced
marches through La Mancha. The former was
chosen, Areizaga's army was destroyed, and in the
battle he discovered no redeeming quality. His
position was ill chosen, he made no use of his
cavalry, his left wing never fired a shot, and when
the men, undismayed by the defeat of the right, demanded to be led into action, he commanded a retreat, and quitted the field himself at the moment
when his presence was most wanted.

6°. The combinations of the French were methodical, well arranged, effectual, and it may seem
misplaced, to do ought but commend movements so
eminently successful; yet the chances of war are
manifold enough to justify the drawing attention to
some points of this short campaign. Areizaga's
rush from the mountains was so unexpected and
rapid, that it might well make his adversaries hesi-

tate, and hence perhaps the reason why the first corps circled round the Spanish army, and was singly to have attacked the latter in front at Zarza, on the 19th, whereas, reinforced with the division of the fourth corps from Toledo, it might have fallen on the rear and flank from Mora a week before ; that is, during the three days Areizaga remained at Dos Barrios, from whence Mora is only four hours march.

7°. The 11th, the king knew the English army had not approached the valley of the Tagus, Areizaga did not quit Dos Barrios until the 13th, and he remained at Zarza until the 18th. During eight days therefore, the Spanish general was permitted to lead, and had he been a man of real enterprise he would have crushed the troops between Dos Barrios and Aranjuez on the 10th or 11th. Indeed, the boldness with which Sebastiani maintained his offensive position beyond Aranjuez, from the 9th to the 14th, was a master-piece. It must, however, be acknowledged that Soult could not at once fix a general, who marched fifty thousand men about, like a patrole of cavalry, without the slightest regard to his adversary's positions or his own line of operations.

8°. In the battle, nothing could be more scientific than the mode in which the French closed upon and defeated the right and centre, while they paralyzed the left of the Spaniards ; the disparity of numbers engaged, and the enormous amount of prisoners, artillery, and other trophies of victory prove it to have been a fine display of talent. But Andalusia was laid prostrate by this sudden destruction of her troops ! why then was the fruit of victory neglected ? Did the king, unable to per-

ceive his advantages, controul the higher military
genius of his advising general? or was he distracted
by disputes amongst the different commanders? or,
did the British army at Badajos alarm him? An
accurate knowledge of these points is essential in
estimating the real share Spain had in her own deliverance.

9°. Sir Arthur Wellesley absolutely refused to co-
operate in this short and violent campaign. He remained a quiet spectator of events at the most critical period of the war; and yet on paper the Spanish
projects promised well. Areizaga's army exceeded
fifty thousand men, Albuquerque's ten thousand,
and thirty thousand were under Del Parque, who,
at Tamames had just overthrown the best troops in
the French army. Villa Campa also, and the Partida bands on the side of Cuença were estimated
at ten thousand; in fine, there were a hundred
thousand Spanish soldiers ready. The British army
at this period, although much reduced by sickness,
had still twenty thousand men fit to bear arms, and
the Portuguese under Beresford were near thirty
thousand, making a total of a hundred and fifty
thousand allies. Thirty thousand to guard the
passes of the Sierra de Gredos and watch the sixth
corps, a hundred and twenty thousand to attack the
seventy thousand French covering Madrid! Why,
then, was sir Arthur Wellesley, who only four
months before so eagerly undertook a like enterprise
with fewer forces, now absolutely deaf to the proposals of the Junta? " *Because moral force is to phy-
" sical force, as three to one in war.*" He had proved
the military qualities of Spaniards and French, and
he foresaw, to use his own expressions, " *that after*
" *one or two battles, and one or two brilliant actions by*

Letter to
Lord Li-
verpool.
MS.

" *some, and defeats sustained by others, all would have*
" *to retreat again :*" yet this man, so cautious, so
sensible of the enemy's superiority, was laying the
foundation of measures that finally carried him
triumphant through the Peninsula. False then
are the opinions of those, who, asserting Napoleon
might have been driven over the Ebro in 1808-9,
blame sir John Moore's conduct. Such reasoners
would as certainly have charged the ruin of Spain
on sir Arthur Wellesley, if at this period the
chances of war had sent him to his grave. But in
all times the wise and brave man's toil has been
the sport of fools!

Alba de Tormes ended the great military transactions of 1809. In the beginning, Napoleon broke
to atoms and dispersed the feeble structure of
the Spanish insurrection, after his departure the
invasion stagnated amidst the bickerings of his
lieutenants. Sir Arthur Wellesley turned the war
back upon the invaders for a moment, but the jealousy and folly of his ally soon obliged him to
retire to Portugal. The Spaniards then tried their
single strength, and were trampled under foot at
Ocaña, and notwithstanding the assistance of England, the offensive passed entirely from their hands.
In the next book we shall find them every where
acting on the defensive, and every where weak.

BOOK X.

CHAPTER I.

NAPOLEON, victorious in Germany, and ready
to turn his undivided strength once more against
the Peninsula, complained of the past inactivity of
the king, and Joseph prepared to commence the
campaign of 1810 with vigour. His first operations, however, indicated great infirmity of purpose. When Del Parque's defeat on one side
and Echevaria's on the other had freed his flanks,
and while the British army was still at Badajos,
he sent the fourth corps towards Valencia, but
immediately afterwards re-called it, and also the first
corps, which, since the battle of Ocaña, had been at
Santa Cruz de Mudela. The march of this last
corps through La Mancha had been marked by this
peculiarity, that, for the first time since the commencement of the war, the peasantry, indignant at
the flight of the soldiers, guided the pursuers to the
retreats of the fugitives.

Joseph's vacillation was partly occasioned by the
insurrection in Navarre, under Renovalles and
Mina ; partly because lord Wellington, previous to
quitting the Guadiana, had informed the Junta of
Badajos, as a matter of courtesy, that he was
about to evacuate their district, and his confi-

dential letter being published in the town Gazette,
and ostentatiously copied into the Seville papers,
made Joseph suspect it to be a cloak to some offensive project. However, the false movements of the
first and fourth corps distracted the Spaniards, and
emboldened the French partizans, who were very
numerous both in Valencia and Andalusia. When
the troubles in Navarre were quieted by Suchet, and
the distribution of the British army in the valley of
the Mondego known, Joseph seriously prepared
for the conquest of Andalusia. This enterprise,
less difficult than an invasion of Portugal, promised
immediate pecuniary advantages, which was no

slight consideration to a sovereign whose ministers
were reduced to want from the non-payment of their
salaries, and whose troops were thirteen months in
arrears of pay. Napoleon, a rigid stickler for the
Roman maxim, that " war should support war,"
paid only the corps near the frontiers of France, and
rarely recruited the military chest.

Both the military and political affairs of Andalusia were now at the lowest ebb. The calm produced by the promise to convoke the National
Cortes had been short-lived. The disaster of Ocaña
revived all the passions of the people, and afforded
the old Junta of Seville, the council of Castile, and
other enemies of the Central Junta, an opportunity
to pull down a government universally obnoxious,
and the general discontent was increased by the
measures adopted to meet the approaching crisis.
The marquis of Astorga had been succeeded by
the archbishop of Laodicea, under whose presi-
dency the Junta published a manifesto, assuring the
people that there was no danger,—that Areizaga
could defend the Morena against the whole power

of France,—that Albuquerque would, from the side of Estremadura, fall upon the enemy's rear,—and that a second Baylen might be expected. But, while thus attempting to delude the public, they openly sent property to Cadiz, and announced that they would transfer their sittings to that town on the 1st of February. Meanwhile, not to seem inactive, a decree was issued for a levy of a hundred thousand men, and for a forced loan of half the jewels, plate, and money belonging to individuals; sums left for pious purposes were also appropriated to the service of the state.

To weaken their adversaries, the Junta offered Romana the command of the army in the Morena and imprisoned the Conde de Montijo and Francisco Palafox. The marquis of Lazan, accused of being in league with his brother, was confined in Pensicola, and the Conde de Tilly, detected in a conspiracy to seize the public treasure and make for America, was thrown into a dungeon, where it is believed his infamous existence terminated. The celebrated Padre Gil was sent on a mission to Sicily. While on his passage he told an English gentleman, " *They have sent me on this embassy to get rid of my never ceasing remonstrances; and I have submitted to this banishment for fear I might be got rid of in another way!*" Romana refused to serve, and Blake, recalled from Catalonia, was appointed to command the troops re-assembled at La Carolina, most of the other generals kept aloof, and in Gallicia the Conde de Noronha, resigning his command, issued a manifesto against the Junta. The public hatred increased, and the partizans of Palafox and Montijo, certain that the people would be against the government under any circumstances, only waited for a favourable moment to commence violence. Andalusia generally, and Seville in particular, were but one remove from anarchy, when the intrusive monarch reached the foot of the Morena with a great and well organized army.

The military preparation of the Junta was in harmony with their political conduct. The decree for levying a hundred thousand men, issued when the enemy was but a few marches from the seat of government, was followed by an order to distribute a hundred thousand poinards, as if assassination were the mode in which a great nation could or ought to defend itself, especially when the regular forces at the disposal of the Junta, were still numerous enough, if well directed, to have made a stout resistance. Areizaga had twenty-five thousand men in the Morena; Echevaria, with eight thousand, was close by, at Hellin; five or six thousand were spread over Andalusia, and Albuquerque had fifteen thousand behind the Guadiana. The troops at Carolina were, however, dispirited and disorganized. Blake had not arrived, and Albuquerque, distracted with contradictory orders transmitted almost daily by the Junta, could contrive no reasonable plan of action, until the movements of the enemy enabled him to disregard all instructions. Thus, amidst a whirlpool of passions, intrigues, and absurdities, Andalusia, although a mighty vessel, and containing all the means of safety, was destined to sink.

This great province, composed of four kingdoms, namely, Jaen and Cordoba in the north, Grenada and Seville in the south, was protected on the right by Murcia and on the left by Portugal. The northern frontier only was accessible to the

French, who could attack it either by La Mancha or Estremadura; but, between those provinces, the Toledo and Guadalupe mountains forbad all military communication until near the Morena, where, abating somewhat of their surly grandeur, they leave a space through which troops could move from one province to the other in a direction parallel to the frontier of Andalusia.

Towards La Mancha, the Morena was so savage that only the royal road to Seville was practicable for artillery. This road entering the hills, a little in advance of Santa Cruz de Mudela, at a pass of wonderful strength, called the Despenas Perros, led by La Carolina and Baylen to Andujar. On the right, indeed, another route passed through the Puerto del Rey, but fell into the first at Navas Toloza, a little beyond the Despenas Perros, and there were other passes also, but all falling again into the main road, before reaching La Carolina. Santa Cruz de Mudela was therefore a position menacing the principal passes of the Morena from La Mancha.

To the eastward of Santa Cruz the town of Villa Nueva de los Infantes presented a second point of concentration for the invaders. From thence roads, practicable for cavalry and infantry, penetrated the hills by La Venta Quemada and the Puerto de San Esteban, conducting to Baeza, Ubeda, and Jaen.

In like manner, on the westward of Santa Cruz, roads, or, rather, paths, penetrated into the kingdom of Cordoba. One, entering the mountains, by Fuen Caliente, led upon Montoro; a second, called the La Plata, passed by La Conquista to Adamuz, and it is just beyond these roads that the ridges, separating La Mancha from Estremadura, begin to soften

down, permitting military ingress to the latter, by
the passes of Mochuello, Almaden de Azogues,
and Agudo.

If entering Estremadura by these passes an army
should then invade Andalusia, the Morena must still
be passed, and the only military communications
between those provinces were by three great roads,
namely, one from Medellin and Llerena to Guadalcanal; another from Badajos to Seville, by the
defiles of Monasterio and Ronquillo; a third by
Xeres de los Caballeros, Fregenal, and Araceña.
From Almaden, there was also a way, through
Belalcazar, to Guadalcanal; but all these routes,
except that of Araceña, whether from La Mancha
or Estremadura, after crossing the mountains, led
into the valley of the Guadalquivir, a river whose
waters, drawn from a multitude of sources, at first
roll westward, washing the foot of the Morena as
far as the city of Cordoba, then, bending gradually
towards the south, flow by Seville, and are finally
lost in the Atlantic.

To defend the passage of the Morena, Areizaga
posted his right in the defiles of San Esteban and
Montizon, covering the city of Jaen, the old walls
of which were armed. His left occupied the passes
of Fuen Caliente and Mochuello, covering Cordoba.
His centre was established at La Carolina and in
the defiles of the Despenas Perros and Puerto del
Rey, which were entrenched, but with so little
skill and labour as to excite the ridicule rather
than the circumspection of the enemy. And here
it may be well to notice an error relative to the
strength of mountain-defiles, common enough even
amongst men who, with some experience, have
taken a contracted view of their profession.

From such persons it is usual to hear of narrow passes, in which the greatest multitudes may be resisted. Now, without stopping to prove that local strength is nothing, if the flanks can be turned by other roads, we may be certain that there are few positions so difficult as to render superior numbers of no avail. Where one man can climb another can, and a good and numerous infantry, crowning the acclivities on the right and left of a disputed pass, will soon oblige the defenders to retreat, or to fight upon equal terms. If this takes place at any point of an extended front of defiles, such as those of the Sierra Morena, the dangerous consequences to the whole of the beaten army are obvious. Hence such passes should only be considered as fixed points, around which an army should operate freely in defence of more exposed positions, for defiles are doors, the keys of which are on the summits of the hills around them. A bridge is a defile, yet troops are posted, not in the middle, but behind a bridge, to defend the passage. By extending this principle, we shall draw the greatest advantages from the strength of mountain-passes. The practice of some great generals may, indeed, be quoted against this opinion; nevertheless, it seems more consonant to the true principles of war to place detachments in defiles, and keep the main body in some central point behind, ready to fall on the heads of the enemy's columns as they issue from the gorges of the hills.

Pierced by many roads, and defended by feeble dispirited troops, the Morena presented no great obstacle to the French; but, as they came up against it by the way of La Mancha only, there were means to render their passage difficult. If

Albuquerque, placing his army either at Almaden de Azogues, or Agudo, had operated against their right flank, he must have been beaten, or masked by a strong detachment, before Areizaga could have been safely attacked.

Nor was Andalusia itself deficient of interior local resources for an obstinate defence. Parallel to the Morena, and at the distance of about a hundred miles, the Sierra Nevada, the Apulxaras, and the Sierra Ronda, extend from the borders of Murcia to Gibraltar, cutting off a narrow tract of country along the coast of the Mediterranean, while the intermediate space between these sierras and the Morena is broken by less extensive ridges, forming valleys which, gradually descending and widening, are finally lost in the open country about Seville. Andalusia may therefore be considered as presenting three grand divisions of country:—1°. The upper, or rugged, between the Sierra Morena and the Sierra Nevada. 2°. The lower, or open country, about Seville. 3°. The coast-tract between the Nevada and Ronda, and the Mediterranean. This last is studded, in its whole length, with sea-port towns and castles, such as Malaga, Velez-Malaga, Motril, Ardra, Marbella, Estipona, and an infinity of smaller places.

No important line of defence is offered by the Guadalquivir. An army, after passing the Morena, would follow the course of its waters to gain the lower parts of Andalusia, and, thus descending, the advantage of position would be with the invaders. But, to reach the Mediterranean coast, not only the ridges of the Nevada or Ronda must be crossed, but most of the minor parallel ridges enclosing the valleys, whose waters run towards the

INVASION
of
ANDALUSIA
1810.

Published by T. & W. Boone 1833.

Atlantic. Now all those valleys contain great towns, such as Jaen and Cordoba, Ubeda, Grenada, and Alcala Real, most of which, formerly fortified, and still retaining their ancient walls, were capable of defence; wherefore the enemy could not have approached the Mediterranean, nor Grenada, nor the lower country about Seville, without first taking Jaen, or Cordoba, or both. The difficulty of besieging those places, while a Spanish army was stationed at Alcala Real, or Ecija, while the mountains, on both flanks and in the rear, were filled with insurgents, and while Albuquerque hung upon the rear at Almada, is apparent. Pompey's sons, acting upon this system, nearly baffled Cæsar, although that mighty man had friends in the province, and, with his accustomed celerity, fell upon his youthful adversaries before their arrangements were matured.

But in this, the third year of the war, the Junta were unprovided with any plan of defence beyond the mere occupation of the passes in the Morena. Those, once forced, Seville was open, and, from that great city, the French could penetrate into all parts and their communication with Madrid became of secondary importance, because Andalusia abounded in the materials of war, and Seville, the capital of the province, and, from its political position, the most important town in Spain, was furnished with arsenals, cannon-founderies, and all establishments necessary to a great military power.

INVASION OF ANDALUSIA.

The number of fighting-men destined for this

enterprise was about sixty-five thousand. Marshal Soult directed the movements, but the king was disposed to take a more prominent part, in the military arrangements than a due regard for his own interest would justify. To cover Madrid, and to watch the British army, the second corps was posted between Talavera and Toledo, with strong detachments pushed into the valley of the Tagus; two thousand men, drawn from the reserve, garrisoned the capital; as many were in Toledo, and two battalions occupied minor posts, such as Arganda and Guadalaxara. Gazan's division was recalled from Castile, Milhaud's from Aragon; the first, fourth, and fifth corps, the king's guards, and the reserve, increased by some reinforcements from France, were directed upon Andalusia.

During the early part of January, 1810, the troops, by easy marches, gained the foot of the Morena, and there Milhaud's division, coming by the way of Benillo, rejoined the fourth corps. A variety of menacing demonstrations, being then made along the front of the Spanish line of defence, between the 14th and 17th, caused Areizaga to abandon his advanced positions and confine himself to the passes of the Morena; on the 18th, the king arrived in person at Santa Cruz de Mudela, and the whole army was collected in three distinct masses.

In the centre, the artillery, the king's guards, the reserve, and the fifth corps, under marshal Mortier, were established at Santa Cruz and Elviso, close to the mouths of the Despenas Perros and the Puerto del Rey.

On the left, Sebastiani, with the fourth corps, occupied Villa Nueva de los Infantes, and prepared to penetrate, by Venta Quemada and Puerto San Esteban, into the kingdom of Jaen.

On the right, the duke of Belluno, placing a detachment in Agudo, to watch Albuquerque, occupied Almaden de Azogues, with the first corps, pushed an advanced guard into the pass of Mochuelo, and sent patrols through Benalcazar and Hinojosa towards Guadalcanal. By these dispositions, Areizaga's line of defence in the Morena, and Albuquerque's line of retreat from Estremadura, were alike threatened.

On the 20th, Sebastiani, after a slight skirmish, forced the defiles of Esteban, making a number of prisoners; and when the Spaniards rallied behind the Guadalen, one of the tributary torrents of the Guadalquiver, he again defeated them, and advancing into the plains of Ubeda, secured the bridges over the Guadalquiver.

In the centre Dessolles carried the Puerto del Rey without firing a shot, and Gazan's division crowning the heights right and left of the Despenas Perros, turned all the Spanish works in that pass, which was abandoned. Mortier, with the main body and the artillery, then poured through, reached La · Carolina in the night, and the next day took possession of Andujar, having passed in triumph over the fatal field of Baylen; more fatal to the Spaniards than to the French, for the foolish pride, engendered by that victory, was one of the principal causes of their subsequent losses.

Meanwhile the duke of Belluno pushed detachments to Montoro, Adamuz, and Pozzoblanco, and his patrols appeared close to Cordoba. His and Sebastiani's flanking parties communicated also with the fifth corps at Andujar, and thus, in two days, by skilful combinations upon an extent of fifty miles, the lofty barrier of the Morena was forced, and Andalusia beheld the French masses portentously gathered on the interior slopes of the mountains.

In Seville all was anarchy: Palafox and Montijo's partisans were secretly preparing to strike, and the Ancient Junta openly discovered a resolution to resume their former power. The timid, and those who had portable property, endeavoured to remove to Cadiz, but the populace opposed this, and the peasantry came into the city so fast that above a hundred thousand persons were within the walls, and the streets were crowded with multitudes that, scarcely knowing what to expect or wish, only wanted a signal to break out into violence. The Central Junta, fearing alike, the enemy, and their own people, prepared to fly, yet faithful to their system of delusion, while their packages were actually embarking for Cadiz, assured the people that the enemy had indeed forced the pass of Almaden, leading from La Mancha into Estremadura, but that no danger could thence arise; because the duke Del Parque was in full march to join Albuquerque, and those generals when united being stronger than the enemy would fall upon his flank, while Areizaga would co-operate from the Morena and gain a great victory!

It was on the 20th of January, and at the very moment when the Morena was being forced at all points, that this deluding address was published, and it was not until the day after that the Junta despatched orders for the duke Del Parque (who was then in the mountains beyond Ciudad Rodrigo) to effect that junction with Albuquerque from which such great things were expected ! Del Parque received the despatch on the 24th, and prepared to obey. Albuquerque, alive to all the danger of the crisis, had left general Contreras at Medellin with four thousand five hundred men, destined to form a garrison for Badajos, and marched himself on the 22d, with about nine thousand, towards Agudo, intending to fall upon the flank of the first corps ; he had scarcely commenced his movement, when he learned that Agudo and Almaden were occupied, and that the French patrols were already at Benalcazar and Hinojosa, within one march of his own line of retreat upon Seville. In this conjuncture, sending Contreras to Badajos, and his own artillery through the defile of Monasterio, he marched with his infantry to Guadalcanal. During the movement, he continued to receive contradictory and absurd orders from the Junta, some of which, he disregarded, and others he could not obey; wherefore, conforming to circumstances, when the Morena was forced, he descended into the basin of Seville, crossed the Guadalquivir a few leagues from that city, at the ferry of Cantillana, reached Carmona on the 24th, and immediately pushed with his cavalry for Ecija to observe the enemy's progress. Meanwhile the storm, so long impending over the Central Junta, burst at Seville.

Early on the 24th a great tumult arose. Mobs traversing all the quarters of the city, called out, some for the deposition of the Junta, others for the heads of the members. Francisco Palafox and Montijo were released, and the Junta of Seville being re-established by acclamation, the Central Junta, committed to their hands the defence of Andalusia, and endeavoured themselves to reach

Cadiz, each as he could ; yet with the full intention of reuniting and resuming their authority.
On the road however, some of them were cast into
prison by the people, some were like to be slain at
Xerez, and the Junta of Seville had no intention
that the Central Junta should ever revive. Saavedra, the President of the former, by judicious
measures calmed the tumult in the city, restored
Romana to the command of his old army, which
was now under the duke Del Parque, made some
other popular appointments, and in conjunction
with his colleagues sent a formal proposition to
the Junta at Badajos, inviting them to take into
consideration the necessity of constituting a Regency, which was readily acceded to. The events
of war crowding on, overlaid their schemes.
Three days after the flight of the Central Junta,
treason and faction being busy amongst the members of the Seville Junta, they also disbanded,
some remained in the town, others, amongst them
Saavedra, repaired to Cadiz. The tumults were then
renewed with greater violence, and Romana was
called upon to assume the command and defend the
city, but he evaded this dangerous honour, and
proceeded to Badajos.

Thus abandoned to themselves, the people of
Seville elected a military junta, and discovered the
same disposition, as the people of other towns in
the Peninsula had done upon like occasions. If men
like the Tios of Zaragoza, had then assumed command, they might have left a memorable tale and
a ruined city, but there were none so firm, or so
ferocious, and finally, a feeling of helplessness
producing fear in all, Seville was ready to submit
to the invaders.

When the passage of the mountains was completely effected, the French corps again received their artillery, the centre and right wing remained stationary, and a detachment of the first corps, which had approached Cordoba, returned to Montoro. Areizaga rallied his troops at Jaen, but Sebastiani marching from Ubeda, drove him upon Alcala Real, and Jaen surrendered with forty-six guns mounted on the walls. The Spanish general then made one more stand, and being again beaten, all his artillery was captured, and his army dispersed. Five thousand infantry and some squadrons of cavalry throwing away their arms escaped to Gibraltar, while Areizaga himself, with a remnant of horse, flying into the kingdom of Murcia, was there superseded by Blake. Meanwhile, Sebastiani having marched upon Grenada, entered it the 28th of January, and was received with apparent joy, so entirely had the government of the Central Junta extinguished the former enthusiasm of the people.

The capture of Jaen having secured the left flank of the French, the king with the centre and right, moved on Cordoba the 27th, and there also, as at Jaen and Grenada, the invaders were received without any mark of aversion,* and thus the upper

---

* Dupont's proceedings at Cordoba, as related in my first volume, have been commented upon in a recent publication, entitled " *Annals of the Peninsular Campaigns.*"
Upon the authority of general Foy, the author asserts that Cordoba was sacked, calls it " *a gratuitous atrocity,*" and " *an inhuman butchery,*" and no doubt, taking for fiction the stories of Agathocles, Marius, Sylla, and a thousand others, gravely affirms, that, *capacity and cruelty are rarely united ;* that *Dupont was a fool,* and that *Napoleon did not poison him in a dungeon,* but that he must have " *dragged on a miserable existence exposed to universal scorn and hatred.*"
Unfortunately for the application of this nursery philosophy, Dupont, although a bad officer, was a man of acknowledged talents, and became minister of war at the restoration of the Bourbons, a period fixed by the author of " *the Annals,*" *as the era of good government in France.*
I rejected Foy's authority, 1st, because his work, unfinished and posthumous, discovered more of the orator than the impartial historian, and he was politically opposed to Dupont. Secondly, because he was not an eye-witness, and his relation at variance with the " *official journal of Dupont's operations ;*" was also

country was conquered. But the projects of Joseph were not confined to Andalusia; he had opened a secret communication with Valencia, where his partisans undertook to raise a commotion whenever a French force should appear before that city ; hence, judging that no serious opposition would be made in Andalusia, he directed Sebastiani to cross the Sierra Nevada, and seize the Grenadan coast, an operation that would enable him with greater facility to act against Valencia. To ensure the success of the latter enterprise, he wrote from Cordoba to Suchet, urging him to make a combined movement from Aragon, and promising a powerful detachment from Andalusia, to meet him under the walls of Valencia.

Dessolles, with the reserve, occupied Cordoba and Jaen, and the first and fifth corps, followed by the king's guards, proceeded without delay towards Ecija, where it will be remembered, Albuquerque's cavalry had been posted since the night of the 24th. As the French approached, the duke fell back upon Carmona, from whence he could retreat either to Seville, or Cadiz, the way to the latter being through Utrera. But from Ecija there was a road through Moron to Utrera, shorter than that

contradicted by the testimony of a *British general of known talents and accuracy,* who obtained his information on the spot a few months subsequent to the event.

" Some time after the victory, *order was restored, pillage was forbidden under pain of death, and the chosen companies maintained the police.*"—Journal of Operations.

Cordoba was not pillaged, being one of the few places where the *French were well received.*—Letters from a British general to colonel Napier.

On this point, therefore, I am clear ; but the author of the " *Annals,*" after contrasting my account with Foy's, thus proceeds, " It is only necessary to add, that the preceding statement is given by colonel Napier *without any quotation of authority.*"

A less concise writer might have thought it right to add that, *six months* previous to the publication of the *Annals,* colonel Napier, hearing that some of his statements appeared inconclusive to the author of that work, *because there was no quotation of authority,* transmitted through a mutual friend, an assurance that he had authority for every *statement,* and that he would willingly *furnish the author with any or all of them :* no notice was taken of this offer .

leading through Carmona, and along this road
the cavalry of the first corps was pushed on the
27th. Albuquerque despairing for Seville, resolved
to make for Cadiz, and lest the enemy should reach
Utrera before him, gained that town with great
expedition, and thence moving through Lebrija
and Xeres, by long marches, journeying day and
night, reached Cadiz on the 3d of February. Some
French cavalry overtook and skirmished with his
rear at Utrera, but he was not pursued further,
save by scouting parties; for the king had altered
the original plan of operations, and ordered the
first corps which was then pushing for Cadiz, to
change its direction and march by Carmona against
Seville, and the 30th, the advanced guard came on
that city.

Some entrenchments and batteries had been
raised for defence, the mob still governing, fired
upon the bearer of the first French summons, and
announced in lofty terms a resolution to fight, and
besides the populace, there were about seven thousand troops, composed partly of fugitives from the
Morena, partly of the original garrison of the town.
Nevertheless, the city, after some negotiation, surrendered on the 31st, with all its stores, founderies,
and arsenals complete, and on the 1st of February
the king entered in triumph. The lower country
was thus conquered, and there remained only
Cadiz, and the coast tract lying between the Mediterranean and the Sierra de Nevada to subdue.

The first corps was immediately sent against
Cadiz, the fifth against Estremadura; and Sebas-
tiani, having placed fifteen hundred men in the
Alhambra, and incorporated among his troops, a
Swiss battalion, composed of those who had aban-

doned the French service in the battle of Baylen, seized Antequera.   He was desirous to establish himself firmly in those parts before he crossed the Nevada, but his measures were precipitated by unexpected events.   At Malaga, the people having imprisoned the members of the local Junta, were headed by a Capuchin friar, who resolved to fight the French, and collected a vast multitude armed in all manners above Antequera and Alhama, where the road from Grenada enters the hills.

As this insurrection was spreading, not only in the mountains, but through the plains of Grenada, Sebastiani resolved to fall on at once, lest the Grenadans having Gibraltar on the one flank, Murcia on the other, and in their own country, many sea-ports and fortified towns, should organize a regular system of resistance.   Wherefore, after a slight skirmish at Alhama, he penetrated the hills, driving the insurgents upon Malaga, near which place they rallied, and an engagement, with the advanced guard of the French, under general Milhaud, taking place, about five hundred Spaniards fell, and the conquerors entered the town fighting. A few of the vanquished took refuge on board some English ships of war, the rest submitted, and more than a hundred pieces of heavy, and about twenty pieces of field artillery with ammunition, stores, and a quantity of British merchandize, became the spoil of the conquerors.   Velez-Malaga opened its gates the next day, Motril was occupied, and thus the insurrection was quelled, for in every other part, both troops and peasantry, were terrified and submissive to the last degree.

General Campbell's Correspondence from Gibraltar. MSS.

Meanwhile, Victor followed the traces of Albuquerque with such diligence, as to reach Chiclana

on the 4th, and it is generally supposed, that he
might have rendered himself master of Leon, for
the defensive works at Cadiz, and the Isla were in
no way improved, but rather deteriorated since the
period of Sir George Smith's negotiation.   The
bridge of Zuazo was indeed broken, and the canal
of Santa Petri a great obstacle; but Albuquerque's
troops were harassed, dispirited, ill clothed, badly
armed, and in every way inefficient; the people of
Cadiz were apathetic, and the authorities, as usual,
occupied with intrigues and private interests.   In
this state, eight thousand Spanish soldiers could
scarcely have defended a line of ten miles against
twenty-five thousand French, if a sufficient number of boats could have been collected to cross
the canal.

Venegas was governor of Cadiz, but when it
was known that the Central Junta had been deposed at Seville, a Municipal Junta, chiefly composed of merchants, was elected by general ballot.
This body, as inflated and ambitious of power as
any that had preceded it, would not suffer the
fugitive members of the Central Junta to assume
any authority; and the latter, maugre their extreme
reluctance, were obliged to submit, but, by the advice of Jovellanos, they appointed a Regency, composed of men not taken from amongst themselves.
Although the Municipal Junta vehemently opposed
this proceeding, at first, the judicious intervention
of Mr. Bartholomew Frere induced them to acquiesce; and on the 29th of January, the bishop of
Orense, general Castaños, Antonio de Escaño,
Saavedra, and Fernandez de Leon, were appointed
Regents, until the Cortes could be assembled.

Leon was afterwards replaced by one Lardizabal, a native of New Spain.

The council of Castile, which had been reinstated before the fall of Seville, now charged the deposed Junta, and truly, with usurpation—the public voice added peculation and other crimes; and the Regency, which they had themselves appointed, seized their papers, sequestered their effects, threw some of the members into prison, and banished others to the provinces: thus completely extinguishing this at once odious, ridiculous, and unfortunate oligarchy. Amongst the persons composing it, there were undoubtedly some of unsullied honour and fine talents, ready and eloquent of speech, and dexterous in argument; but it is not in Spain only, that men possessing all the " grace and ornament" of words, have proved to be mean and contemptible statesmen.

Albuquerque, elected president of the Municipal Junta, and commander of the forces, endeavoured to place the Isla de Leon in a state to resist a sudden attack, and the French, deceived as to its real strength, after an ineffectual summons, proceeded to gird the whole bay with works. Meanwhile, Marshal Mortier, leaving a brigade of the fifth corps at Seville, pursued a body of four thousand men, that, under the command of the Visconde de Gand, had retired from that town towards the Morena; they evaded him, and fled to Ayamonte, yet were like to be destroyed, because the bishop of Algarve, from national jealousy, would not suffer them to pass the Portuguese frontier. Mortier, however, disregarding these fugitives, passed the Morena, by Ronquillos and Monasterio, and marching against Badajos, summoned it the 12th of February, but Contreras' detachment had arrived there on the 26th of January, and Mortier, finding, contrary to his expectation, that the place was in a state of defence, retired to Merida.

This terminated the first series of operations in the fourth epoch of the war; operations which, in three weeks, had put the French in possession of Andalusia and Southern Estremadura, with the exception of Gibraltar and Cadiz in the one, and of Badajoz, Olivenza, and Albuquerque in the other province. Yet, great as were the results of this memorable irruption, more might have been obtained, and the capture of Cadiz would have been a fatal blow to the Peninsula.

From Andujar to Seville is only a hundred miles, yet the French took ten days to traverse that space; a tardiness for which there appears no adequate cause. The king, apparently elated at the acclamations and seeming cordiality with which the towns, and even villages, greeted him, moved slowly. He imagined that Seville would open her gates at once; and thinking that the possession of that town, would produce the greatest moral effect, in Andalusia, and all over Spain, changed the first judicious plan of campaign, and marched thither in preference to Cadiz. The moral influence of Seville, was however transferred, along with the government, to Cadiz, and Joseph was deceived in his expectations of entering the former city as he had entered Cordoba. When he discovered his error there was still time to repair it by a rapid pursuit of Albuquerque, but fearing to leave a city with a hundred thousand people in a state of excitement upon his flank, he resolved to reduce

Seville, and met indeed with no formidable resistance, yet so much of opposition, as left him
only the alternative of storming the town or entering by negotiation. The first his humanity forbad;
the latter cost him time, which was worth his
crown, for Albuquerque's proceedings were only
secondary : the ephemeral resistance of Seville was
the primary cause of the safety of Cadiz.

The march by which the Spanish duke secured
the Isla de Leon, is only to be reckoned from Carmona. Previous to his arrival there, his movements, although judicious, were more the result of
necessity than of skill. After the battle of Ocaña,
he expected that Andalusia would be invaded;
yet, either fettered by his orders or ill-informed
of the enemy's movements, his march upon Agudo
was too late, and his after-march upon Guadalcanal, was the forced result of his position; he
could only do that, or abandon Andalusia and
retire to Badajos.

From Guadalcanal, he advanced towards Cordoba
on the 23d, and he might have thrown himself into
that town; yet the prudence of taking such a
decided part, was dependent upon the state of
public sentiment, of which he must have been a
good judge. Albuquerque, indeed, imagined that
the French were already in possession of the place,
whereas they did not reach it until four days later;
yet they could easily have entered it on the 24th,
and as he believed that they had done so, it is
apparent that he had no confidence in the people's
disposition; in this view, his determination to cross
the Guadalquivir, and take post at Carmona, was
the fittest for the occasion. It was at Carmona
he first appears to have considered Seville a lost

city; and when the French approached, we find CHAP. I.
him marching, with a surprising energy, towards
Cadiz, yet he was again late in deciding, for the 1810. February.
enemy's cavalry, moving by the shorter road to
Utrera, overtook his rear-guard; and the infantry
would assuredly have entered the Island of Leon
with him, if the king had not directed them upon
Seville. The ephemeral resistance of that city
therefore saved Albuquerque, and he, in return,
saved Cadiz.

CHAPTER II.

BOOK
X.
1810.
LORD WELLINGTON's plans were deeply affected by the invasion of Andalusia. But before treating of the stupendous campaign he was now meditating, it is necessary, once more to revert to the operations in the other parts of the Peninsula, tracing them up to a fixed point; because, although bearing strongly on the main action of the war, to recur to them chronologically, would totally destroy, the unity of narrative indispensable to a just handling of the subject.

OPERATIONS IN NAVARRE, ARAGON, AND VALENCIA.

January. Suchet, being ordered to quell the disorders in Navarre, repaired to Pampeluna, having previously directed an active pursuit of the student Mina, who, availing himself of the quarrel between the military governor and the viceroy, was actually master of the country between that fortress and Tudela, and was then at Sanguessa. General Harispe, with some battalions, marched straight against him from Zaragoza, while detachments from Tudela and Pampeluna endeavoured to surround him by the flanks, and a fourth body moving into the valleys of Ainsa and Medianoz, cut him off from the Cinca river.

Harispe quickly reached Sanguessa, but the
column from Pampeluna being retarded, Mina,
with surprising boldness, crossed its line of march,
and attacked Tafalla, thus cutting the great French
line of communication ; the garrison, however, made
a strong resistance, and Mina disappeared the
next day.   At this period, reinforcements from
France were pouring into Navarre, and a division, under Loison, was at Logroño, wherefore
Harispe having, in concert with that general and with
the garrison of Pampeluna, occupied Sanguessa,
Sos, Lodosa, Puenta de Reyna, and all the passages
of the Arga, Aragon, and Ebro rivers, launched
a number of moveable columns, that continually
pursued Mina, until chased into the high parts of
the Pyrenees, cold and hunger obliged his band to
disperse.   The enterprising chief himself escaped
with seven followers, and when the French were
tracking him from house to house, he, with a
romantic simplicity, truly Spanish, repaired to
Olite, that he might see Suchet pass on his way
from Zaragoza to Pampeluna.

But that general, while seemingly occupied with
the affairs of Pampeluna, was secretly preparing
guns and materials, for a methodical war of invasion, beyond the frontiers of Aragon, and when
general Reynier, coming soon afterwards from
France, with troops intended to form an eighth
corps, was appointed governor of Navarre, Suchet
returned to Zaragoza.   During his absence, although
some petty actions had taken place, his general
arrangements were not disturbed, and the emperor
having promised to increase the third corps to
thirty thousand men, with the intention of directing it at once against Valencia, all the stores befit-

ting such an enterprise were collected at Terruel in the course of January. The resistance of Gerona, and other events in Catalonia having, however, baffled Napoleon's calculations, this first destination of the third corps was changed. Suchet was ordered to besiege Tortoza or Lerida; the eighth corps, then forming at Logroño, was directed to cover his rear; the seventh corps to advance to the Lower Ebro and support the siege. But neither was this arrangement definitive; fresh orders sent the eighth corps towards Castile, and just at this moment Joseph's letter from Cordoba, calling upon Suchet to march against Valencia, arrived, and gave a new turn to the affairs of the French in Spain.

A decree of the emperor, dated the 8th of January, and constituting Aragon a particular government, rendered Suchet independent of the king's orders, civil or military. This decree, together with a renewed order to commence the siege of Lerida, had, however, been intercepted, and the French general, doubtful of Napoleon's real views, undertook the enterprise against Valencia; but wishing first to intimidate the partisans hanging on the borders of Aragon, he detached Laval against Villa Campa, who was defeated on the side of Cuenca, and his troops dispersed.

Suchet then fortified a post at Terruel, to serve as a temporary base of operations, and drew together at that place twelve battalions of infantry, a regiment of cuirassiers, several squadrons of light cavalry, and some field artillery, and, at the same time, caused six battalions and three squadrons of cavalry to be assembled at Alcanitz, under general Habert. The remainder of

the third corps was distributed on the line of the CHAP.
Cinca, and on the right bank of the Ebro. The II.
castles of Zaragoza, Alcanitz, Monzon, Venasque, 1810.
Jaca, Tudela, and other towns, were placed in a February.
state of defence, and four thousand men, newly
arrived from France, were pushed to Daroca, to
link the active columns to those left in Aragon.
These arrangements occupied the whole of February, and, on the 1st of March, a duplicate of the
order, directing Suchet to commence the siege of
Lerida, reached Terruel, yet as Habert's column
having marched on the 27th, by the road of Morella, was already committed in the province of
Valencia, the operation went on.

INCURSION TO VALENCIA.

The first day, brought Suchet's column, in presence of the Valencian army, for Ventura Caro,
captain-general of the province, was in march to
attack the French at Terruel, and his advanced
guard of five or six thousand regulars, accompanied
by armed peasants, was drawn up on some high
ground behind the river Mingares, the bed of which
is a deep ravine so suddenly sunk, as not to be
perceived until close upon it. The village and
castle of Alventoza, situated somewhat in advance
of the Spaniard's centre, were occupied, and commanded a bridge over the river. Their right rested
on the village and bridge of Puenseca, and their
left on the village of Manzanera, where the ground
was rather more practicable.

Suchet, judging that Caro would not fight so
far from Valencia, while Habert's column was turn-

ing his right, sent a division before daylight, on the 2d, to turn the left of the position, and cut off the retreat ; nevertheless, although the French, after a skirmish, crossed the ravine, the Spaniards retired with little loss upon Segorbe, and Caro fell back to the city of Valencia. Suchet then entered Segorbe, and on the 4th was at Murviedro, the ancient Saguntum, four leagues from Valencia. At the same time, Habert, who had defeated a small corps at Morella, arrived at Villa Real on the sea coast. The country between their lines of march was mountainous and impracticable, but after passing Saguntum, the columns united in the Huerta, or garden of Valencia, the richest and most delightful part of Spain.

Suchet arrived before the city on the 5th of March, and seized the suburb Seranos, and the harbour called the Grao. His spies at first confirmed the hopes of an insurrection within the walls, but the treason was detected, the leader, a baron Pozzo Blanco, publicly executed, and the archbishop and many others imprisoned ; in fine, the plan had failed, the populace were in arms, and there was no movement of French troops on the side of Murcia. Five days the French general remained before the city, vainly negotiating, and then, intrigue failing, and his army being inadequate to force the defences, he resolved to retire. In the night of the 10th he commenced his retreat in one column by Segorbe and Terruel. Meanwhile the Spanish partisans were gathering on his rear. Combats had already taken place at Liria and Castellon de la Plana, and general Villa Campa, who had reassembled his dispersed troops, captured four guns, with their ammunition and escort, between

Terruel and Daroca; cut off another detachment
of a hundred men left at Alventoza, and, having
invested the post at Terruel, on the 7th, by a
bold and ready witted attempt, nearly carried the
castle. The 12th, however, the head of Suchet's
column came in sight, Villa Campa retired, and
the 17th the French general reached Zaragoza.
During his absence, Pereña had invested Monzon,
and when the garrison of Fraga marched to its
relief, the Spaniards from Lerida, entered the latter
town, and destroyed the bridge and French entrenchments. Mina, also, was again become formidable, and, although several columns were sent
in chase of him, it is probable, that they would
have done no more than disperse his band for the
moment, but for an accident, which threw him into
their hands a prisoner.

Suchet's failure at Valencia was more hurtful to
the French than would at first sight appear. It
happened at the moment when the National Cortes,
so long desired, was at last directed to assemble;
and as it seemed to balance the misfortunes of
Andalusia, it was hailed by the Spaniards as the
commencement of a better era. The principal
military advantage was the delaying of the sieges
of Lerida and Mequinenza, whereby the subjection
of Catalonia was retarded; and although Suchet
labours, and successfully, to show that he was
drawn into this enterprise by the force of circumstances, Napoleon's avowed discontent was well
founded. The operations in Catalonia were so
hampered by the nature of the country, that it was
only at certain conjunctures, any progress could be
made, and one of the most favourable of those conjunctures, was lost, for want of the co-operation of

the third corps; but to understand this, the military topography of Catalonia must be well considered.

That province is divided in its whole length by shoots from the Pyrenees, which, with some interruptions, run to the Atlantic shores; for the sierras separating Valencia, Murcia, and Andalusia from the central parts of Spain, are but continuations of those shoots. The Ebro, forcing its way transversely through the ridges, parts Catalonia from Valencia, and the hills, thus broken by the river, push their rocky heads southward to the sea, cutting off Taragona from Tortoza, and enclosing what may be called the eastern region of Catalonia, which contains Rosas, Gerona, Hostalrich, Vich, Barcelona, Manreza, Taragona, Reus, and many more towns. The torrents, the defiles, and other, military features of this region have been before described. The western portion of Catalonia lying beyond the principal spine, is bounded partly by Aragon, partly by Valencia; and, like the eastern region, it is an assemblage of small plains and rugged valleys, each, the bed of a river, descending towards the Ebro from the Pyrenees. It contains the fortresses of Balaguer, Lerida, Mequinenza, Cervera, and, near the mouth of the Ebro, Tortoza, which, however, belongs in a military view rather to Valencia than Catalonia.

Vol. I.
Book I.
Chap. VI.

Now the mountain ridge, parting the eastern from the western region of Catalonia, could only be passed by certain routes, for the most part impracticable for artillery, and those practicable, leading upon walled towns at both sides of the defiles. Thus Cervera is situated on the principal and direct line from Lerida to Barcelona; Balaguer, Cardona, and Montserrat, on another and more circuitous road to the same city. Between Lerida and Taragona, stands Momblanch, and between Taragona, and Tortoza, the Fort St. Felippe blocks the Col de Balaguer. All these places were in the hands of the Spaniards, and a number of smaller fortresses, or castles, such as Urgel, Berga, and Solsona, served as rallying points, where the warlike Somatenes, of the higher valleys, took refuge from the moveable columns, and from whence, supplied with arms and ammunition, they sallied, to harass, the flanks and rear, of both the French corps.

In the eastern region, the line of operations for the seventh corps, was between the mountains and the sea-coast, and parallel with both; hence, the Spanish irregular forces, holding all the communications, and the high valleys on both sides of the great dividing spine, could at all times descend upon the rear and flanks of the French, while the regular troops, opposed to them on a narrow front, and supported by the fortresses of Gerona, Hostalrich, and Taragona, could advance or retire as circumstances dictated. And upon this principle, the defence of Catalonia was conducted.

Detachments and sometimes the main body of the Spanish army, passing by the mountains, or by sea from Taragona, harassed the French flanks, and when defeated, retired on Vich, Manresa, Montserrat, or Cervera, and finally to Taragona. From this last, the generals communicated with Tortoza, Valencia, Gibraltar, the Balearic Isles, and even Sicily, and drew succours of all kinds from those places, and meanwhile the bands in the mountains continued to vex the French communications; and it was only during the brief period of lassitude in

the Spanish army, following any great defeat, that
the seventh corps could chase those mountaineers.
Nor, until Gerona and Hostalrich fell, was it easy
to make any but sudden and short incursions towards Taragona, because the Miguelettes from the
higher valleys, and detachments from the army at
Taragona, again passing by the hills or by sea,
joined the garrisons, and interrupted the communication, and thus obliged the French to retire,
because the country beyond the Llobregat could
never feed them long.

But when Barcelona could not be succoured by
sea, it was indispensable to conduct convoys by
land, and to insure their arrival, the whole army
was obliged to make frequent movements in advance, retiring again when the object was effected;
this being often renewed, offered many opportunities for cutting off minor convoys, detachments,
and even considerable bodies isolated by the momentary absence of the army. Thus, during the
siege of Gerona, Blake passed through the mountains and harassed the besiegers. When the place
fell, he retired again to Taragona, and Augereau
took the occasion to attack the Miguelettes, and
Somatenes, in the high valleys; but in the midst of
this operation admiral Baudin's squadron, was
intercepted by admiral Martin, and the insatiable craving of Barcelona, obliged Augereau to
reassemble his army, and conduct a convoy there
by land; yet he was obliged to return immediately,
lest he should himself consume the provisions he
brought for the city. This retreat, as usual, drew
on the Spaniards, who were again defeated, and
Augereau once more advanced, in the intention of
co-operating with the third corps, which, he sup-

posed, would, following the Emperor's design, be before Lerida or Tortoza. But at this time, Suchet was on the march to Valencia; and Henry O'Donnel who had succeeded Blake in the command, recommenced the warfare on the French communications, and forced Augereau again to retire to Gerona, at the moment when Suchet, having returned to Aragon, was ready to besiege Lerida. Thus, like unruly horses in a chariot dragging different ways, the French impeded each other's movements. I shall now briefly narrate the events touched upon above.

OPERATIONS OF THE SEVENTH CORPS.

Gerona having fallen, general Souham with a division, scoured the high valleys, beat the Miguelettes of Claros and Rovira, at Besalu, Olot, Ribas, and Campredon, and at Ripoll destroyed a manufactory for arms. Being afterwards reinforced with Pino's division, he marched from Olot, by the road of Esteban and Manlieu, and although the Somatenes disputed the defiles near the last point, the French forced the passage, and took possession of Vich. Meanwhile Blake having been called to Andalusia, the Provincial Junta of Catalonia rejecting the duke Del Parque, took upon themselves to give the command to Henry O'Donnel, whose courage during the siege of Gerona had gained him a high reputation. He was now with the remains of Blake's army at Vich, and as the French approached that town he retired to the pass of Col de Sespina, from whence he had a free retreat upon Moya and Manresa. Souham's advanced

January.

guard, pursued, and at Tona, captured some baggage, but the Spaniard turned on finding his rear
pressed, and when the pursuers mounted the
heights of Sespina, charged with a shock, that sent
them headlong down again. Souham rallied the
beaten troops in the plain, and the next day offered
battle, but O'Donnel continued his retreat, and the
French general returned to Vich.

During these events, Augereau, leaving a detachment in Hostalrich to blockade the castle, marched
to Barcelona, by the road of Cardedieu; having
previously ordered Duhesme, to post three battalions
and five squadrons of cuirassiers, with some guns,
near the junction, of the roads of Cardedieu and
Manresa, to watch O'Donnel. Colonel Guery, commanding this detachment, placed one battalion at
Granollers, a second at Santa Perpetua, and with
the remainder occupied Mollet, taking no military
precautions, wherefore O'Donnel who had been
joined by Campo Verde, sent him to fall upon the
French posts. Campo Verde, passing by Tarrassa
and Sabadel, surprised and put to the sword or
captured all the troops at Santa Perpetua and
Mollet; those at Granollers, threw themselves into
a large building, and defended it for three days,
when by the approach of Augereau they were relieved. The marshal finding the streets of Mollet
strewed with French carcasses, ordered up the division of Souham from Vich, but passed on himself
to Barcelona; and when there, affecting to be convinced how oppressive Duhesme's conduct had
been, sent him to France in disgrace. After this
act of justice, or of personal malice, for it has been
called both names, Augereau, unable to procure
provisions without exhausting the magazines of Bar-

celona, resumed his former position at Gerona, and Souham returned to Vich.

All this time the blockade of Hostalrich continued; but the retreat of Augereau, and the success of Campo Verde's enterprise, produced extraordinary joy over all Catalonia. The prisoners taken, were marched from town to town, the action everywhere exaggerated, the decree for enrolling a fifth of the male population was enforced with vigour, and the execution entrusted to the Baron d'Erolles, a native of Talarn, who afterwards obtained considerable celebrity. The army, in which there was still a large body of Swiss troops, was thus reinforced, the confidence of the people increased hourly, and a Local Junta was established at Arenys de Mar, to organise the Somatenes on the coast, and to direct the application of succours from the sea. The Partisans, also re-assembling their dispersed bands in the higher valleys, again vexed the Ampurdan, and incommoded the troops blockading the citadel of Hostalrich.

O'Donnel himself, moving to Manresa, called the Miguelettes from the Lerida side, to his assistance; and soon formed a body of more than twelve thousand fighting-men, with which he took post at Moya, in the beginning of February, and harassed the French in front of Vich, while, in the rear of that town, Rovira occupied the heights above Roda. Souham, seeing the crests of the hills thus swarming with enemies, and, having but five thousand men of all arms to oppose to them, demanded reinforcements, but Augereau paid little attention to him, and O'Donnel, descending the mountain of Centellas, on the 20th, entered the plains in three columns. The French general had scarcely time to draw up his troops a little in front of the town, ere he was attacked with a vigour hitherto unusual with the Spaniards.

COMBAT OF VICH.

Rovira commenced the action, by driving the enemy's posts, on the side of Roda, back upon the town; O'Donnel, then, coming close up on the front of the French position, opened all his guns, and, throwing out skirmishers along the whole of the adverse line, filed his cavalry, under cover of their fire, to the right, intending to outflank Souham's left. The latter general, leaving a battalion to hold Rovira in check, encouraged his own infantry, and sent his dragoons against the Spanish horsemen, who, at the first charge, were driven back in confusion. The Spanish foot then fell in on the French centre, but failed to make any serious impression, wherefore O'Donnel, whose great superiority of numbers enabled him to keep heavy masses in reserve, endeavoured to turn both flanks of the enemy at the same time. Souham was now hard pressed, his infantry were few, his reserves all engaged, and himself severely wounded in the head. O'Donnel, who had rallied his cavalry, and brought up his Swiss regiments, was full of confidence, and in person fiercely led the whole mass once more against the left. At this critical period, the French infantry, far from wavering, firmly closed their ranks, and sent their volleys more rapidly into the hostile ranks, while the cavalry, sensible that the fate of all (for there was no retreat) hung upon the issue of their charge, met their adversaries with such a full career that horse and man went down before them, and the Swiss, being separated from the rest, surrendered. Rovira was afterwards driven away from the rear, and the Spanish army returned to the hills, having lost a full fourth of its own numbers, and killed or wounded twelve hundred of the enemy.

O'Donnel's advance, had been the signal, for all the irregular bands to act against the various quarters of the French; they were, however, with the exception of a slight succour thrown into Hostalrich, unsuccessful, and, being closely pursued by the moveable columns, dispersed. Thus the higher valleys were again subdued, the Junta fled from Arenys de Mar, Campo Verde returned to the country about Cervera, and O'Donnel, quitting the Upper Llobregat, retired by Taraza, Martorel, and Villa Franca to the camp of Taragona, leaving only an advanced guard at Ordal.

It was at this moment, when Upper Catalonia was in a manner abandoned by the Spanish general, that the emperor directed the seventh corps upon the Lower Ebro, to support Suchet's operations against Lerida and Mequinenza. Augereau, therefore, leaving a detachment under Verdier, in the Ampurdan, and two thousand men to blockade Hostalrich, ordered his brother and general Mazzucchelli (the one commanding Souham's, and the other Pino's division) to march upon Manreza, while he himself, with the Westphalian division, repaired once more to Barcelona, and from thence directed all the subsequent movements.

General Augereau, passing by Col de Sespina, entered Manreza, the 16th of March, and there

joined Mazzucchelli ; the inhabitants had abandoned
the place, and general Swartz was sent with a
brigade, from Moncada, to take possession, while the
two divisions continued their movement, by Montserrat upon Molino del Rey. The 21st they advanced to Villa Franca, and the Spaniards retired
from Ordal towards Taragona. The French, acting
under orders from Barcelona, left a thousand men
in Villa Franca, and, after scouring the country on
the right and left, passed the Col de San Cristina,
and established their quarters about Reus, by which
the Spanish army at Tarragona was placed between
them and the troops at Villa Franca.

O'Donnel, whose energy and military talents,
were superior to his predecessors, saw, and instantly
profited from this false position. By his orders,
general Juan Caro marched, with six thousand men,
against the French in Villa Franca, and, on the
28th, killed many and captured the rest, together
with some artillery and stores, but, being wounded
himself, resigned the command to general Gasca,
after the action. Augereau, alarmed for Manreza,
then detached columns, both by Olesa and Montserrat, to reinforce Swartz, and the first reached its destinations, but the other, twelve hundred strong, was
intercepted by Gasca, and totally defeated at Esparaguera on the 3d of April. Campo Verde immediately came down from the side of Cervera, took
the chief command, and proceeded against Manreza,
by Montserrat, while Milans de Boch, and Rovira,
hemmed in the French on the opposite side, and
the Somatenes gathered on the hills to aid the
operations. Swartz thus menaced evacuated the
town in the night, and thinking to baffle the Spaniards, by taking the road of Taraza and Sabadel,

was followed closely by Rovira and Milans, and so pressed, on the 5th of April, that with great difficulty and the loss of all his baggage, he reached Barcelona.

These operations having insulated the French divisions at Reus, an officer was despatched, by sea, with orders to recal them to Barcelona. Meanwhile count Severoli, who had taken the command of them, and whose first instructions were to cooperate with Suchet, feared to pass the mountains between Reus and the Ebro, lest he should expose his rear to an attack from Taragona, and perhaps fail of meeting the third corps at last. Keeping, therefore, on the defensive at Reus, he detached colonel Villatte, at the head of two battalions and some cavalry, across the hills, by Dos Aguas and Falcet, to open a communication with the third corps, a part of which had just seized Mora and Flix, on the Lower Ebro. Villatte having accomplished his object, returned with great celerity, fighting his way through the Somatenes, who were gathering round the defiles in his rear, and regaining Reus just as Severoli, having received the order of recal, was commencing his march for Barcelona.

In the night of the 6th, this movement took place, but in such confusion, that from Taragona, O'Donnel perceived the disorder, and sending a detachment, under colonel Orry, to harass the French, followed himself with the rest of his army. Nevertheless, Severoli's rear guard, covered the retreat successfully, until a position was attained near Villa Franca, where Orry, pressing on too closely, was wounded and taken, and his troops rejoined their main body. When these divisions arrived, Campo Verde fell back to Cervera, Severoli reached

Vacani.
Istoria
Militare
degl' Italiani in
Ispagna.

Barcelona, and Augereau retired to Gerona, having lost more than three thousand men, by a series of most unskilful movements ; the situation in which he had voluntarily placed himself, was precisely such as a great general would rejoice to see his adversary choose.

Barcelona, the centre of his operations, was encircled by mountains, to be passed only at certain defiles ; now Reus and Manresa, were beyond those defiles, and several days march from each other. Rovira and Milans being about San Culgat, cut the communication between Manresa and Barcelona ; O'Donnel at Taragona, was nearer to the defiles of Cristina, than the French divisions at Reus ; and his own communication with Campo Verde was open by Valls, Pla, and Santa Coloma de Querault ; and with Milans and Rovira, by Villa Franca, San Sadurni, and Igualada. Augereau indeed, had placed a battalion in Villa Franca, but this only rendered his situation worse ; for what could six hundred men effect in a mountainous country, against three considerable bodies of the enemy? The result was inevitable. The battalion, at Villa Franca, was put to the sword, Swartz only saved a remnant of his brigade by a timely flight, and the divisions at Reus with difficulty made good their retreat. O'Donnel, who, one month before, had retired from the battle of Vich, broken and discomfited by only five thousand French, now, with that very beaten army, baffled Augereau, and obliged him, although at the head of more than twenty thousand men, to abandon Lower Catalonia, and retire to Gerona with disgrace : a surprising change, yet one in which fortune had no share.

Augereau's talents for handling small corps in

a battle, have been recorded by a master hand. There is a vast difference between that and conducting a campaign. But the truth is, that Catalonia had, like Aragon, been declared a particular government, and Augereau, afflicted with gout, remained in the palace of Barcelona, affecting the state of a viceroy, when he should have been at the head of his troops in the field. On the other hand, his opponent, a hardy resolute man, excited by a sudden celebrity, was vigilant, indefatigable, and eager; he merited the success he obtained, and, with better and more experienced troops, that success would have been infinitely greater. Yet if the expedition to Valencia had not taken place, O'Donnel, distracted by a double attack, would have remained at Taragona, and neither the action of Vich, nor the disasters at Mollet, Villa Franca, and Esparaguera, would have taken place.

Napoleon, discontented, as he well might be, with these operations, sent M'Donald, duke of Tarentum, to supersede Augereau; meantime, the latter, having reached Gerona, disposed his troops in the most commodious manner to cover the blockade of Hostalrich, giving Severoli the command.

FALL OF HOSTALRICH CASTLE.

This citadel had been invested early in January. Situated on a high rock, armed with forty guns, well garrisoned, and commanded by a brave man, it was nearly impregnable, and the French at first endeavoured to reduce it by a simple blockade, but towards the middle of February, they commenced the erection of mortar batteries.   Severoli also pressed the place more vigorously than before, and although O'Donnel, collecting convoys on the side of Vich and Mattaro, caused the blockading troops to be attacked at several points by the Miguelettes, every attempt to introduce supplies failed.   The garrison was reduced to extremity, and honourable terms were offered, but the governor, Julian Estrada, rejected them, and prepared to break through the enemy's line; an exploit always expected from a good garrison in Turenne's days, and, as Napoleon has shewn by numerous examples, generally successful.

Napoleon's
Memoirs.

May.

O'Donnel, who could always communicate with the garrison, being aware of their intention, sent some vessels to Arenys de Mar, and made demonstrations from thence, and from the side of St. Celoni, to favour the enterprise; and in the night of the 12th, Estrada, leaving his sick behind, came forth with about fourteen hundred men.   He first made as if for St. Celoni, afterwards turning to his right, he broke through on the side of St. Felieu de Buxalieu and pushed for Vich; but the French closing rapidly from the right and left, pursued so closely, that Estrada himself was wounded, and taken, together with about three hundred men, many were killed, the rest dispersed in the mountains, and eight hundred reached Vich in safety; this courageous action was therefore successful.   Thus, after four months of blockade and ten weeks of bombardment, the castle fell, the line of communication with Barcelona was completed, and the errors committed by Duhesme were partly remedied, after two years of field operations, many battles, and four sieges.

Two small islands, called Las Medas, situated at the mouth of the Ter, and affording a safe anchorage, were next seized. This event which facilitated the passage of the French vessels, stealing from port to port with provisions, or despatches, finished Augereau's career. It had been the very reverse of St. Cyr's. The latter, victorious in the field, was humane afterwards; but Augereau, endeavouring to frighten those people into submission, whom he had failed to beat, erected gibbets along the high-roads, upon which every man taken in arms was hung up without remorse, which cruelty produced precisely the effect that might be expected. The Catalans more animated by their successes, than daunted by this barbarous severity, became incredibly savage in their revenge, and thus all human feeling lost, both parties were alike steeped in blood and loaded with crimes.

Victoires
et Conquêtes des
Française.

CHAPTER III.

WHILE Augereau lost, in Barcelona, the fruits of his success at Gerona, Suchet, sensible how injurious the expedition to Valencia had proved, was diligently repairing that error. Reinforcements from France, had raised his fighting men to about twenty-three thousand, and of these, he drew out thirteen thousand to form the siege of Lerida; the remainder, were required to maintain the forts in Aragon, and to hold in check the Partisans, principally in the higher valleys of the Pyrenees. Villa Campa however, with from three to four thousand men, still kept about the lordship of Molina, and the mountains of Albaracin.

Two lines of operation were open to Suchet, the one, short and direct, by the high road leading from Zaragoza through Fraga to Lerida; the other circuitous, over the Sierra de Alcubierre, to Monzon, and from thence to Lerida. The first was inconvenient, because the Spaniards, when they took Fraga, destroyed the bridge over the Cinca. Moreover, the fortress of Mequinenza, the Octogesa of Cæsar, situated at the confluence of the Segre and the Ebro, was close on the right flank, and might seriously incommode the commnications with Zaragoza, whereas the second route, although longer, was safer, and less exhausted of forage and provisions.

Monzon was already a considerable military establishment, the battering train consisting of forty pieces, with seven hundred rounds of ammunition attached to each, was directed there, and placed under the guard of Habert's division, which occupied the line of the Cinca. Leval leaving general Chlopiski with a brigade at Daroca, to observe Villa Campa, drew nearer to Zaragoza with the rest of his division. Musnier marched with one brigade to Alcanitz, and was there joined by his second brigade, which had been conducted to that point, from Terruel, across the Sierra de Gudar. And while these movements were executing, the castles of Barbastro, Huesca, Ayerbe, Zuera, Pina, Bujarola, and other points on the left of the Ebro, were occupied by detachments.

The right bank of that river, being guarded by Leval's division, and the country on the left bank, secured by a number of fortified posts, there remained two divisions of infantry, and about nine hundred cavalry, disposable for the operations against Lerida. On the Spanish side, Campo Verde was with O'Donnel at Manreza, Garcia Novaro was at Taragona, having small detachments on the right bank of the Ebro to cover Tortoza; Perenna with five battalions occupied Balaguer on the Upper Segre.

Such were the relative situations of both parties, when general Musnier quitting Alcanitz towards the end of March, crossed the Guadalupe, drove Novarro's detachments within the walls of Tortoza, and then remounting the Ebro, seized some boats, and passing that river at Mora and at Flix, communicated, as I have before related, with colonel Villatte of the seventh corps. While this was passing on the Ebro, general Habert crossed the Cinca in two columns, one of which moved straight upon Balaguer, while the other passed the Segre at Camarasa. Perenna, fearing to be attacked on both sides of that river, and not wishing to defend Balaguer, retired down the left bank, and using the Lerida bridge, remounted the right bank to Corbins, where he took post behind the Noguerra, at its confluence with the Segre.

Suchet himself having repaired to Monzon the 10th of April, placed a detachment at Candasnos to cover his establishments from the garrison of Mequinenza, and the 13th advanced with a brigade of infantry, and all his cavalry, by Almacellas, against Lerida ; meanwhile Habert, descending the right bank of the Segre, forced the passage of the Noguerra, and obliged Perenna to retire within the place. The same day Musnier came up from Flix, and the town being thus encompassed, the operations of the seventh and third corps were connected. Suchet's line of operations from Aragon, was short, direct, and easy to supply, because the produce of that province was greater than the consumption. Augereau's line was long and unsafe, and the produce of Catalonia was at no time equal to the consumption.

Lerida contained about eighteen thousand inhabitants. Situated upon the high road from Zaragoza to Barcelona, and about sixty-five miles from each, it possessed a stone bridge over the Segre, and was only a short distance from the Ebro, and the Cinca rivers ; its strategic importance was therefore great, and the more so, that it in a manner commanded the plain of Urgel, called the granary of Catalonia. The regular governor was named Gonsalez, but Garcia Conde had been appointed chief commandant, to appease his discontent at O'Donnel's elevation ; and the troops he

brought with him had encreased the garrison
to nine thousand regulars, besides the armed inhabitants.

The river Segre covered the town on the south
east, and the head of the bridge was protected on
the left bank, by a rampart and ditch enclosing a
square stone building. The body of the place on
the north side, was defended by a wall, without
either ditch or covered way, but strengthened and
flanked by bastions, and by towers. This wall on the
east, was joined to a rocky hill more than two hundred and fifty feet high, the top of which sustained
the citadel, which was an assemblage of huge solid
edifices, clustered about a castle of great height, and
surrounded by an irregular work flanked by good
bastions with ramparts from forty to fifty feet high.

The descent from the citadel into the town, was
gentle, and the works were there strengthened
by ditches; on the other parts, the walls could
be seen to their base; yet the great height of the
rock rendered it impossible to breach them, and
the approaches were nearly inaccessible. Between
the citadel-rock and the river, the town was
squeezed out, about two or three hundred yards,
and the salient part was secured by an entrenchment, and by two bastions called the Carmen and
the Magdalen.

To the westward of the town, at the distance of
seven or eight hundred yards, the hill, on which
Afranius and Petreius encamped to oppose Cæsar,
was crowned, on the end next to Lerida, by Fort
Garden, which was again covered by a large horn-
work with ditches above twenty feet deep; and at
the farthest extremity of the Afranian hill, two large
redoubts called the Pilar and San Fernando, secured

the whole of the flat summit. All the works of
Lerida were in good condition, and armed with more
than one hundred pieces of artillery, the magazines
were full, and the people enthusiastic. A local
Junta also had been formed to excite public feeling,
and two officers of artillery had already been murdered and their heads nailed to the gates of the town.

The siege was to be a joint operation by the
third and seventh corps, but the information derived from colonel Villatte, and the appearance of
Spanish Partisans on the lower Ebro, led Suchet
to suspect that the seventh corps had already retired, and that the burthen would rest on him alone,
wherefore he still kept his battering train at Monzon, intending to wait until O'Donnel's plans should
be clearly indicated, before he commenced the
siege. Meanwhile, he established a communication
across the Segre, by means of a rope ferry, one
league above Lerida, and after closely examining
the defences, prepared materials for the construction of batteries. Two battalions of the investing troops had been left at Monzon and
Balaguer, the remainder were thus distributed.
On the left bank of the Segre, at Alcoteletge,
four thousand men, including the cavalry, which
was composed of a regiment of cuirassiers and
one of hussars, were stationed as a corps of observation; Harispe, with three battalions, invested
the bridge-head of Lerida. By this disposition,
the ferry-boat was protected, and all danger from
the sudden rising of the Segre obviated, because the
stone bridge of Balaguer furnished a certain communication. The rest of the troops occupied different positions, on the roads to Monzon, Fraga, and
Corbins, but as the number was insufficient to com-

plete the circle of investment round Fort Garden,
that part was continually scoured by patrols.

Scarcely were these arrangements completed when a Spanish officer, pretending to bear propositions for an exchange of prisoners, was stopped on the left bank of the Segre, and the French general detained him, suspecting his real object was to gain information; for there were rumours, that O'Donnel was collecting troops at Momblanch, that Campo Verde was at Cervera, and that the Somatenes of the high valleys were in arms on the upper Segre. Suchet anxious to ascertain the truth of these reports, reinforced Harispe with three hundred hussars on the 19th of April, and carried the corps of observation to Balaguer. The governor of Lerida took that opportunity to make a sally, but was repulsed, and the 21st, the French general, to strengthen his position at Balaguer, caused the bridge of Camarasa, above that town, to be broken, and then advanced as far as Tarrega, forty miles on the road to Barcelona, to obtain intelligence; for he was still uncertain of Augereau's movements, and like every other general, French or English, found it extremely difficult to procure authentic information. On this occasion, however, by a happy fortune, he ascertained that O'Donnel, with two divisions, was at Momblanch, ready to descend the mountains and succour Lerida; wherefore returning by one forced march to Balaguer, he directed Musnier to resume his former position at Alcoleletge.

This rapidity was well-timed, for O'Donnel had passed the defiles of Momblanch, with eight thousand chosen infantry, and six hundred cavalry, and was encamped at Vinaxa, about twenty-five miles

from Lerida, on the 22d, when a note from
Garcia Conde, saying that, the French reserve
being drawn off, the investing force was weak,
reached him.   Being willing to seize the favourable moment, he immediately pushed forward,
reached Juneda, fourteen miles from Lerida, by
ten o'clock in the morning of the 23d, and, after a
halt of two hours, resumed his march with the
cavalry and one division of infantry, leaving the
other to follow more leisurely.

COMBAT OF MARGALEF.

Four miles from Juneda, stood the ruined village
of Margalef, and from thence to Lerida was an
open country, on which O'Donnel could perceive
no covering force; hence, trusting implicitly to
Conde's information (already falsified by Suchet's
activity), the Spanish general descended the hills,
and crossed the plain in three columns, one following the high road and the other two marching on
the right and left.   The centre outstripping the
flankers, soon beat back the advanced posts of
Harispe; but that general, charged with his three
hundred hussars, upon the centre Spanish column,
so suddenly, that it was thrown into confusion, and
fled towards Margalef, to which place, the flank
columns also retreated, yet in good order.   During
this skirmish, the garrison sallied over the bridge,
but as the French infantry stood firm, the besieged, seeing the rout of O'Donnel's people,
returned to the town.

Meanwhile, Musnier, hearing the firing, guessed
the real state of affairs, and marched at once with

his infantry and four hundred cuirassiers from Alcoteletge across the plain towards Margalef, hoping to cut off the Spaniards' retreat. O'Donnel who had rallied his troops, was already in line of battle, having the artillery on the right and the cavalry on the left, but his second division was still in the rear. The French cuirassiers and a battery of light artillery, came up at a quick pace, a cannonade commenced, and the Spanish cavalry rode forward, when the French cuirassiers, commanded by general Boussard, charged hotly, and forced them back on the line of battle in such a manner that the latter wavered, and Boussard, observing the confusion, came with a rude shock upon the flank of the infantry. The Walloon guards made a vain effort to form square, but the confusion was extreme, and finally nearly all the Spanish infantry threw down their arms or were sabred. The cuirassiers, elated with their success, then met and overthrew a Swiss regiment, forming the advanced guard of the second Spanish division; yet the main body of the latter checked their fury, and O'Donnel retreated in good order, and without further loss to the defile of Momblanch. This action, although not discreditable to O'Donnel, was very unfortunate. The plain was strewed with carcasses; three Spanish guns, one general, eight colonels, and above five thousand men were captured; and the next day the prisoners, being first ostentatiously marched under the walls of the town, were shown to the Spanish officer who had been detained on the 19th, after which he was dismissed by the road of Cervera, that he might spread the news of the defeat.

Suchet wishing to profit from the effect of this

victory upon the besieged, attempted the night after the battle, to storm the redoubts of San Fernando and Pilar.   He was successful with the latter, and the assailants descended into the ditch of San Fernando, and as the Spaniards, only fifty in number and unprovided with hand grenades, could not drive them away, a parley ensued, when it was agreed that the French should retire without being molested.   Thus the Pilar was also saved, for being commanded by San Fernando, it was necessarily evacuated.   Previous to this attempt, Suchet had summoned the city to surrender, offering safe conduct for commissioners to count the dead on the field of Margalef, and to review the prisoners ; but Garcia Conde replied, " *that Lerida had never looked for external succour in her defences.*"

SIEGE OF LERIDA.

The absolute retreat of Augereau, was now fully ascertained, yet the victory of Margalef, and the apathy of the Valencians, encouraged Suchet to commence the siege in form.   The prisoners were sent to France by the way of Jaca, the battering train was brought up from Monzon, and all the other necessary preparations being completed, the Spanish out-posts were driven within the walls between the 26th and 27th.   The following night, under the direction . of general Haxo, ground was broken three hundred yards from the bastions of the Carmen and Magdalen; the Spaniards threw some fireballs, and opened a few guns, without interrupting the workmen, and when day broke, the besiegers were well covered in the trenches.

In the night of the 30th the first parallel was completed. Breaching and counter batteries were commenced, six sixteen-pounders were destined to batter the left face of the Carmen, four long twelve-pounders, to ruin the defences of the Magdalen, and four mortars of eight inches to throw shells into the citadel. The weather was rainy and the labour heavy, yet the works advanced rapidly, and on the 2d of May, a fourth battery, armed with two mortars and two sixteen-pounders, was raised against the Carmen. Meanwhile the Spanish musqueteers, incommoded the trenches from the left bank of the Segre, which obliged the French to contract the circle of investment on that side.

In the evening of the 4th, six hundred Spaniards, sallying from the Carmen, carried the fourth battery and all the left of the trenches, while another body, coming from the Magdalen, menaced the right of the French works. The French guards held the latter in check, and the reserves finally drove the former back into the town; but after this attack, a ditch and rampart, to serve as a place of arms, was carried from the battery which had been taken, down to the river; and as the light troops still continued to ply the trenches from the other side of the Segre, ground was broken there, close to the water, and a battery of two guns was constructed to answer six Spanish field-pieces, posted on the bridge itself. The parallel of the main attack was also extended on the right, embracing a part of the northern front of the citadel, and two mortars were placed at this extremity.

All the French batteries opened at day-break on the 7th, the mortars played into the town and citadel, and four Spanish guns were dismounted in the Carmen. Nevertheless, the counter fire silenced three French batteries, the dismounted guns were replaced, and three hundred men, stealing out at dusk by the Puerta Nueva, fell upon the right of the parallels, took the two mortars, and penetrated as far as the approaches against the Magdalen. This sally was repulsed by the French reserves, but they suffered from the Spanish guns in the pursuit, and in the night a violent storm, with rain, damaged the batteries and overflowed the trenches. From the 8th to the 11th the besiegers laboured at their works, and opened a second parallel one hundred and fifty yards in advance of the first, with the intention of forming fresh batteries ; that being closer under the citadel-rock, would be less exposed to its plunging fire. More guns, and of a larger size, were also mounted ; three new batteries were constructed, and marksmen were planted to harass the Spanish cannoneers.

On the 12th the fire recommenced from eight batteries, containing fifteen guns and nineteen mortars. The besieged replied at first sharply, but in a little time stammered in their answers, the French artillery took the ascendent, the walls of the Carmen and Magdalen crumbled under their salvos, and a portable magazine blew up in the citadel. Towards evening two breaches in the Carmen, and one in the Magdalen, appeared practicable, and after dark, some Swiss deserters coming out through the openings, brought intelligence, that the streets of the town behind the breaches, were retrenched and defended by batteries.

Suchet's hopes of an early termination to the

siege now rose high. He had from the first supposed, that the vehemence of the citizens, and of the armed peasantry who had entered the place, would oblige the governor to fight the town to the last, instead of reserving his efforts for the defence of the citadel. He knew that armed mobs, easily excited, are as easily discouraged, and he projected to carry the breaches briskly, and, with one sweep, to force all the inhabitants into the citadel, being well assured that they would hamper, if not entirely mar, the defence of that formidable fortress: but he resolved first, to carry the forts of San Fernando and the Pilar and the horn-work of Fort Garden, lest the citizens, flying from the assault of the breaches, should take refuge on that side. To effect this, three columns, provided with ladders and other necessary implements, simultaneously mounted the hill of Afranius that night; one marched against the redoubts, and the others were ordered to storm the horn-work on two sides. The Pilar was carried without difficulty, and the garrison flying towards Fort Garden, fell in with the second French column, which arrived with the fugitives at the ditch of the horn-work, and being there joined by the third column, which had taken a wrong direction, the whole mass entered the place fighting. The Spaniards saved themselves in Fort Garden, but meanwhile the people in Fernando resisted desperately, and that redoubt was not taken until two-thirds of the defendants were put to the sword. Thus the French effected their object with the loss of a hundred men.

During this operation the great batteries played into the citadel only, but, at daybreak, renewed their fire on the breaches; steps were also cut in

the parallel, to facilitate the advance of the troops
to the assault; and all the materials, necessary to
effect a solid lodgement on the walls, were conveyed into the trenches. These arrangements being
completed at seven o'clock in the evening of the
13th, the signal was made, and four storming
parties jumped out of the trenches; two made for
the Carmen, one against the Magdalen, and one
moved close by the river, and the Spaniards being
at this moment preparing a sally to retake the
horn-work of Fort Garden, did so little expect this
assault, that they suffered the French to mount the
breaches without opposition; but then rallying,
found such a fire of musquetry and artillery upon
the heads of the principal columns, that the latter
staggered and would have yielded if Habert had
not revived their courage, and led them into the
town, at the very moment that the troops on the right
and left having also forced their way, turned all the
retrenchments in the streets. On the other side of
the river, general Harispe carried the bridge, and
Suchet himself, with the reserve, followed close
upon the steps of the storming-parties; the Spaniards were thus overpowered, and the regular
troops commenced a retreat into the citadel.

Suchet's
Memoirs.
It was now that the French general put his design in execution. Harispe's brigade passing the
bridge, made for the gate of St. Anthony, looking
towards Fort Garden, and thus cut off all egress
from the town; this done, the French columns advanced from every side, in a concentric direction,
upon the citadel, and, with shouts, and stabs, and
musquetry, drove men, women, and children before
them, while the guns of the castle smote friends
and foes alike. Then, flying up the ascent, the

shrieking and terrified crowds rushed into the fortress with the retiring garrison, and crowded on the summit of the rock; but, all that night, the French shells fell amongst the hapless multitude, and, at daylight, the fire was redoubled, and the carnage swelled, until Garcia Conde, overpowered by the cries and sufferings of the miserable people, hoisted the white flag. At twelve o'clock, the horrible scene terminated. The capitulation that followed was honourable in terms to the besieged, but Fort Garden being included, Suchet became master of Lerida, with its immense stores and near eight thousand prisoners, for the whole loss of the garrison had been only twelve hundred men.

Thus suddenly was this powerful fortress reduced, by a proceeding, politic indeed, but scarcely to be admitted within the pale of civilized warfare. For, though a town, taken by assault, be considered the lawful prey of a licentious soldiery, this remnant of barbarism, disgracing the military profession, does not warrant the driving of unarmed helpless people, into a situation, where they must perish from the fire of the enemy, unless the governor fail in his duty. Suchet justifies it, on the ground, that he thus spared a great effusion of blood which must necessarily have attended a protracted siege, and the fact is true. But this is to spare soldiers' blood at the expense of women's and children's, and, had Garcia Conde's nature been stern, he, too, might have pleaded expediency, and the victory would have fallen to him who could longest have sustained the sight of mangled infants and despairing mothers.

CHAP. IV.

WHEN Lerida fell, Conde was accused of treachery, but there seems no foundation for the charge; the cause stated by Suchet was sufficient for the effect; yet the defence was very unskilful. The walls, on the side of the attack, could not be expected, and scarcely did, offer an impediment to the French general; hence the citadel should have been the better prepared, and, as the besiegers' force, the corps of observation being deducted, did not exceed the garrison in number, it might have baffled Suchet's utmost efforts. Engineers require that the relative strength of besiegers and besieged, should not be less than four to one; yet here the French invested a force equal to themselves, and in a short time reduced a great fortress in the midst of succouring armies; for Lerida had communications, 1°. With the armed population of the high valleys; 2°. With O'Donnel's corps of fourteen thousand; 3°. With Cervera, where Campo Verde was posted with four thousand men; 4°. With Tortoza, where the marquis of Lazan, now released from his imprisonment, commanded from five to six thousand; 5°. With Valencia, in which province there was a disposable army of fifteen thousand regular and more than thirty thousand irregular soldiers.

It is evident that, if all these forces had been directed with skill and concert upon Lerida, not only the siege would have been raised, but the very safety of the third corps endangered; and it was to obviate this danger that Napoleon directed the seventh corps to take such a position on the Lower Ebro as would keep both O'Donnel and the Valencians in check. Augereau, as we have seen, failed to do this; and St. Cyr asserts that the seventh corps could never safely venture to pass the mountains, and enter the valley of the Ebro. On the other hand, Souchet affirms that Napoleon's instructions could have been obeyed without difficulty. St. Cyr himself, under somewhat similar circumstances, blockaded Taragona for a month; Augereau, who had more troops and fewer enemies, might have done the same, and yet spared six thousand men to pass the mountains. Suchet would then have been tranquil with respect to O'Donnel, would have had a covering-army to protect the siege, and the succours, fed from the resources of Aragon, would have relieved Catalonia.

Augereau has been justified, on the ground, that the blockade of Hostalrich would have been raised while he was on the Ebro. The danger of this could not have escaped the emperor, yet his military judgement, unerring in principle, was often false in application, because men measure difficulties by the standard of their own capacity, and Napoleon's standard only suited the heroic proportions. One thing is, however, certain, that Catalonia presented the most extraordinary difficulties to the invaders. The powerful military organization of the Miguelettes and Somatenes,—the well-arranged system of fortresses, — the ruggedness and sterility of the country,—the ingenuity and readiness of a manufacturing population thrown out of work, — and, finally, the aid of an English fleet, combined to render the conquest of this province a gigantic task. Nevertheless, the French made progress, each step planted slowly indeed and with pain, but firmly, and insuring the power of making another.

Hostalrich and Lerida fell on the same day. The acquisition of the first consolidated the French line of communication with Barcelona ; and, by the capture of the second, Suchet obtained large magazines, stores of powder, ten thousand muskets, the command of several dangerous rivers, easy access to the higher valleys, and a firm footing in the midst of the Catalonian strong-holds ; and he had taken or killed fifteen thousand Spanish soldiers. Yet this was but the prelude to greater struggles. The Miguelettes supplied O'Donnel with abundance of men, and neither his courage nor his abilities were at fault. Urgel, Cardona, Berga, Cervera, Mequinenza, Taragona, San Felippe Balaguer, and Tortoza the link of connexion between Valencia and Catalonia, were still to be subdued, and, during every great operation, the Partisans, being unmolested, recovered strength. Thus during the siege of Lerida, the marquis of Lazan entered the town of Alcanitz with five thousand men, and would have carried the castle, but that general Laval despatched two thousand men, from Zaragoza, to its succour, when the Spaniards, after a skirmish in the streets, retired ; and, while this was passing at Alcanitz, Villa Campa intercepted four hundred men conducting a convoy of provisions from Calatayud to Zaragoza. Colonel Petit, the commander, being attacked in the defile of Frasno, was forced to abandon his convoy, and, under a continued fire, to fight his way for ten miles, until his detachment, reduced to one hundred and eighty wounded men, passed the Xalon river, and, at the village of Arandiza, finally repulsed the assailants. The remainder of this desperate band were taken or killed, and Petit himself, wounded, a prisoner, and sitting in the midst of several Spanish officers, was basely murdered the evening after the action. Villa Campa put the assassin to death, but at the same time, suffered the troops to burn alive an old man, the Alcade of Frasno, who was taken among the French.

This action happened the day Lerida fell, and the next day, Chlopiski, following Villa Campa's march from Daroca, reached Frasno, but the Spaniards were no longer there; Chlopiski, then dividing his forces, pursued them, by the routes Calatayud and Xarava, to Molina, where he destroyed a manufactory for arms, and so pressed the Spanish general, that his troops disbanded, and several hundred retired to their homes. At the same time, an attack, made from the side of Navarre, on the garrison of Ayerbe, was repulsed.

These petty events, while they evinced the perseverance of the Spaniards, proved also the stability of Suchet's power in Aragon. His system was gradually sapping the spirit of resistance in that province. In Lerida his conduct was as gentle and moderate as the nature of this unjust war would permit; and, however questionable the morality of the proceeding by which he reduced the citadel, it must be acknowledged that his situation required most decided measures, for the retreat of the seventh corps set free not only O'Donnel's army, but Campo Verde's and all the irregular bands. The

Somatenes of the high valleys appeared in force, on the Upper Segre the very day of the assault; eight hundred Miguelettes attacked Venasque three days after: and Campo Verde, marching from Cervera, by Aramunt, took post in the mountains of Lliniana, above Talarn and Tremp, where great bodies of the Somatenes also assembled.

Their plans were disconcerted by the sudden fall of Lerida; the Miguelettes were repulsed from Venasque; the Somatenes defeated at Tremp; and general Habert, marching from Balaguer, cut off Campo Verde from Cervera, and forced him to retreat upon Cardona. If the citadel of Lerida had held out, and O'Donnel, less hasty, had combined his march, at a later period, with these Somatenes and with Campo Verde, the third corps could scarcely have escaped a disaster; whereas, now the plain of Urgel and all the fertile valleys opening upon Lerida fell to the French, and Suchet, after taking measures to secure them, turned his arms against Mequinenza. This place situated at the confluence of the Segre and the Ebro, just where the latter begins to be navigable, was the key to further operations. The French general could not advance in force against Tortoza, nor avail himself of the water-carriage, until Mequinenza should fall; and such was his activity that one detachment, sent the day after the assault of Lerida, by the left bank of the Segre, was already before the place; and Musnier's division, descending the right bank of that river, drove in some of the outposts and commenced the investment on the 20th of May.

Mequinenza, built on an elbow of land formed by the meeting of the Segre and Ebro, was fortified

by an old Moorish wall, and strengthened by modern batteries, especially on the Fraga road, the
only route by which artillery could approach. A
shoot from the Sierra de Alcubierre filled the space
between the two rivers, and narrowing as they
closed, ended in a craggy rock, seven hundred feet
high and overhanging the town, which was built
between its base and the water. This rock was
crowned by a castle, with a rampart, which being
inaccessible on two sides from the steepness, and
covered, on a third by the town, could only be assailed, on the fourth, along a high neck of land,
three hundred yards wide, that joined the rock to
the parent hills : and the rampart on that side, was
bastioned, lined with masonry, and protected by a
ditch, counterscarp, and covered way with palisades.
No guns could be brought against the castle,
until the country people, employed by Suchet, had
opened a way from Torriente, over the hills, and
this occupied the engineers until the 1st of June, and
meanwhile the brigade, which had defeated Lazan
at Alcanitz, arrived on the right bank of the Ebro,
and completed the investment. The 30th of May,
general Rogniat, coming from France, with a reinforcement of engineer-officers, and several companies of sappers and miners, also reached the camp,
when, taking the direction of the works, he contracted the circle of investment, and commenced
active operations.

CHAP.
IV.

1810.
May.

SIEGE OF MEQUINENZA.

The Spaniards made an ineffectual sally the 31st ;

and, the 2d of June, the French artillery, consisting
of eighteen pieces, of which six were twenty-four
pounders, being brought over the hills, the advanced posts of the Spaniards were driven into the
castle.   During the night, ground was broken two
hundred yards from the place, under a destructive
fire of grape,, and while this was passing on the
height, approaches were made against the town, in
the narrow space between the Ebro and the foot of
the rock.   Strong infantry posts were also entrenched, close to the water, on the right bank of
that river, to prevent the navigation, but of eleven
boats freighted with inhabitants and their property
nine effected their escape.

In the night of the 3d the parallels on the rock were
perfected, the breaching-batteries were commenced,
and parapets of sand-bags were raised, from behind
which the French infantry plied the embrasures of
the castle with musketry ; the works against the
town were also advanced, but in both places, the
nature of the ground greatly impeded the operations.   The trenches above, being in a rocky soil,
were opened chiefly by blasting ; those below were
in a space too narrow for batteries, and, moreover,
searched by a plunging fire, both from the castle,
and from a gun mounted on a high tower in the
town wall.   The troops on the right bank of the
Ebro, however, opened their musketry with such
effect on the wall, that the garrison could not
stop, and both the wall and tower were then esca-
laded without difficulty, the Spaniards all retiring
to the castle.   The French placed a battalion in
the houses, and put those next the rock in a state
of defence; and although the garrison of the

castle rolled down large stones from above, they killed more of the inhabitants than of the enemy.

The 6th the French batteries on the rock, three in number, were completed; and, in the night, forty grenadiers carried by storm a small outwork called the horse-shoe. The 7th, Suchet, who had been at Zaragoza, arrived in the camp and, on the 8th, sixteen pieces of artillery, of which four were mortars, opened on the castle. The Spaniards answered with such vigour, that three French guns were dismounted, yet the besiegers acquired the superiority, and at nine o'clock in the morning, the place was nearly silenced, and the rampart broken in two places. The Spaniards endeavoured to keep up the defence with musketry, while they mounted fresh guns, but the interior of the castle was so severely searched by the bombardment, that, at ten o'clock, the governor capitulated. Fourteen hundred men became prisoners of war; forty-five guns, and large stores of powder and of cast iron were captured, and provisions for three months were found in the magazines.

Two hours after the fall of Mequinenza, general Mont-Marie, commanding the troops on the right bank of the Ebro, marched, against Morella, in the kingdom of Valencia, and took it on the 13th of June; for the Spaniards, with a wonderful negligence, had left that important fort, commanding one of the principal entrances into the kingdom of Valencia, without arms or a garrison. When it was lost, general O'Donoju, with a division of the Valencian army, advanced to retake it, but Mont-Marie defeated him. The works were then repaired, and Morella became a strong and important place of arms.

By these rapid and successful operations Suchet secured, 1°. A fortified frontier against the regular armies of Catalonia and Valencia; 2°. Solid bases for offensive operations, and free entrance to those provinces; 3°. The command of several fertile tracts of country and of the navigation of the Ebro; 4°. The co-operation of the seventh corps, which, by the fall of Lerida, could safely engage beyond the Llobregat. But, to effect the complete subjugation of Catalonia, it was necessary to cut off its communications by land with Valencia, and to destroy O'Donnel's base. The first could only be effected, by taking Tortoza, the second by capturing Taragona. Hence the immediate sieges of those two great places, the one by the third, and the other by the seventh corps, were ordered by the emperor.

Suchet was ready to commence his part, but many and great obstacles arose: the difficulty of obtaining provisions, in the eastern region of Catalonia, was increased by O'Donnel's measures, and that general, still commanding above twenty thousand men, was neither daunted by past defeats, nor insensible to the advantages of his position. His harsh manners and stern sway, rendered him hateful to the people; but he was watchful to confirm the courage, and excite the enthusiasm of his troops by conferring rewards and honours on the field of battle, and, being of singular intrepidity himself, his exhortations had more effect. Two years of incessant warfare had also formed several good officers, and the full strength and importance

of every position and town were, by dint of
experience, becoming known. With these helps
O'Donnel long prevented the siege of Tortoza,
and found full employment for the enemy during
the remainder of the year. Nevertheless, the conquest of Catalonia advanced, and the fortified
places fell one after another, each serving, by its
fall, to strengthen the hold of the French, in the
same proportion that it had before impeded their
progress.

The foundations of military power were, however, deeply cast in Catalonia. There the greatest
efforts were made by the Spaniards, and ten thousand British soldiers, hovering on the coast, ready
to land on the rear of the French, or to join
the Catalans in an action, could at any period of
1809 and 1810, have paralyzed the operations of
the seventh corps, and saved Gerona, Hostalrich,
Tortoza, Taragona, and even Lerida. While those
places were in the hands of the Spaniards and
their hopes were high, English troops from
Sicily were reducing the Ionian islands or loiter-
ing on the coast of Italy ; but when all the fortresses of Catalonia had fallen, when the regular
armies were nearly destroyed, and when the people
were worn out with suffering, a British army
which could have been beneficially employed elsewhere, appeared, as if in scorn of common sense,
on the eastern coast of Spain. Notwithstanding
the many years of hostility with France, the
English ministers were still ignorant of every
military principle ; and yet too arrogant to ask
advice of professional men ; for it was not until
after the death of Mr. Perceval, and when the

decisive victory of Salamanca shewed the giant in his full proportions, that even Wellington himself was permitted the free exercise of his judgement, although he was more than once reminded by Mr. Perceval, whose narrow views continually clogged the operations, that the whole responsibility of failure would rest on his head.

CHAPTER V.

SUCHET's preparations equally menaced Valencia, and Catalonia, and the authorities in the former province, perceiving, although too late, that an exclusive and selfish policy would finally bring the enemy to their own doors, resolved to co-operate with the Catalonians, while the Murcians, now under the direction of Blake, waged war on the side of Grenada, and made excursions against the fourth corps. The acts of the Valencians shall be treated of when the course of the history leads me back to Catalonia, those of the Murcian army belong to the

OPERATIONS IN ANDALUSIA.

During the month of February, the first corps was before Cadiz, the fourth in Grenada, Dessolles' division at Cordoba, Jaen, and Ubeda, and the fifth corps (with the exception of six battalions and some horse left at Seville) in Estremadura. The king, accompanied by marshal Soult, moved with his guards and a brigade of cavalry, to different points, and received from all the great towns assurances of their adhesion to his cause. But as the necessities of the army demanded immediate and heavy contributions, both of money and provisions, moveable columns were employed to collect them, especially for the fourth corps, and with so little attention to

BOOK
X.

1810.
March.
King Jo-
seph's Cor-
respon-
dence, cap-
tured at
Victoria.
MSS.

discipline as soon to verify the observations of St. Cyr, that they were better calculated to create than to suppress insurrections. The people exasperated by disorders, and violence, and at the same time excited by the agents of their own and the British government, suddenly rose in arms, and Andalusia, like other parts of Spain, became the theatre of a petty and harassing warfare.

The Grenadans of the Alpujarras, were the first to resist, and this insurrection spreading on the one hand through the Sierra de Ronda, and on the other, towards Murcia, received succours from Gibraltar, and was aided by the troops and armed peasantry under the command of Blake. The communication between the first and fourth corps across the Sierra de Ronda, was maintained by a division of the former, posted at Medina Sidonia, and by some infantry and hussars of the latter quartered in the town of Ronda. From the latter place, the insurgents, principally smugglers, drove the French, while at the other extremity Blake marching from Almeira, took Ardra and Motril, and at the same time the mountaineers of Jaen and Cordoba interrupted Dessolles' communications with La Mancha.

These movements took place in the beginning of March, and the king and Soult being then in the city of Grenada, sent one column across the mountain by Orgiva to fall upon the flank of Blake at Motril, while a second moving by Guadix and Ohanes upon Almeria, cut off his retreat. This obliged the Murcians to disperse, and at the same time, Dessolles defeated the insurgents on the side of Ubeda; and the garrison of Malaga, consisting of three battalions, marched to restore the communications with the first corps. Being joined by the detachment

beaten at Ronda, they retook that post on the 21st CHAP.
of March; but during their absence the people from V.
the Alpuxaras entered Malaga, killed some of the 1810.
March.
inhabitants as favourers of the enemy, and would
have done more, but that another column from
Grenada came down on them, and the insurrection
was thus strangled in its birth. It had however,
sufficed to prevent the march of the troops designed
to co-operate with Suchet at Valencia, and it was
of so threatening a character, that the fifth corps
was recalled from Estremadura, and all the French
troops at Madrid, consisting of the garrison, and a
part of the second corps, were directed upon Almagro in La Mancha, the capital itself being left in MrStuart's
charge of some Spanish battalions in the invader's Correspondence.
service. The king who feared the Valencian and MSS.
Murcian armies would invade La Mancha, repaired
thither, and after a time returned to Madrid. The
duke of Dalmatia then remained chief commander
of Andalusia, aud proceeded to organize a system
of administration so efficacious, that neither the
efforts of the Spanish government, nor of the army
in Cadiz, nor the perpetual incursions of Spanish
troops issuing from Portugal, and supported by
British corps on that frontier, could seriously shake
his hold, but this will be better shewn hereafter;
at present, it is more convenient to notice

THE BLOCKADE OF CADIZ.

Marshal Victor having declined an assault on Feb.
the Isla, spread his army round the margin of
the bay, and commenced works of contravallation
on an extent of not less than twenty-five miles.

The towns, the islands, castles, harbours, and rivers,
he thus enclosed are too numerous, and in their relative bearings, too intricate for minute description ;
yet, looking as it were from the French camps, I shall
endeavour to point out the leading features.

The blockade was maintained in three grand divisions or entrenched positions, namely, Chiclana,
Puerto Real, and Santa Maria. The first, having its
left on the sea-coast near the Torre Bermeja, was
from thence carried across the Almanza, and the
Chiclana rivers, to the Zuraque ; on a line of eight
miles, traced along a range of thickly wooded hills,
and bordering a marsh from one to three miles
broad. This marsh, traversed in its breadth by the
above-mentioned rivers, and by a number of navigable water-courses or creeks, was also cut in its whole
length by the Santi Petri, a natural channel connecting the upper harbour of Cadiz with the open sea.
The Santi Petri, nine miles long, from two to three
hundred yards wide, and of depth to float a seventy-
four, received the waters of all the creeks crossing
the marsh and was the first Spanish line of defence.
In the centre, the bridge of Zuaro, by which the
only road to Cadiz passes, was broken and defended
by batteries on both sides. On the right hand, the
Caraccas, or Royal Arsenal, situated on an island
just in the harbour mouth of the channel, and on
account of the marsh inattackable, save by water or
by bombardment, was covered with strong batteries
and served as an advanced post. On the left hand
the castle of Santi Petri, also built on an island, defended the sea mouth of the channel.

Beyond the Santi Petri was the Isla de Leon,
in form a triangle, the base of which rested on
that channel, the right side on the harbour, the left

on the open sea, and the apex pointing towards Cadiz. All this island was a salt-marsh, except one high and strong ridge in the centre, about four miles long, upon which the large town of La Isla stands, and which being within cannon shot of the Santi Petri, offered the second line of defence.

From the apex, called the Torre Gardo, a low and narrow isthmus about five miles long, connected the island with the rocks upon which Cadiz stood, and across the centre of this narrow isthmus, a cut called the Cortadura, defended by the large unfinished fort of Fernando, offered a third line of defence. The fourth and final line, was the land front of the city itself, regularly and completely fortified.

On the Chiclana side therefore, the hostile forces were only separated by the marsh ; and although the Spaniards commanded the Santi Petri, the French having their chief depôts in the town of Chiclana, could always acquire the mastery in the marsh and might force the passage of the channel ; because the Chiclana, Zuraque, and Almanza creeks, were navigable above the lines of contravallation. The thick woods behind, afforded the means of constructing an armed flotilla ; and such was the nature of the ground bordering the Santi Petri itself, on both sides, that off the high road, it could only be approached by water, or by narrow footpaths, leading between the salt-pans of the marsh.

The central French or Puerto Real division, extending from the Zuraque on the left, to the San Pedro a navigable branch of the Guadalete on the right, measured about seven miles. From the Zuraque to the town of Puerto Real, the line was traced along a ridge skirting the marsh, so as to

form with the position of Chiclana a half circle.
Puerto Real itself was entrenched, but a tongue of
land four miles long projected from thence perpen-
dicularly on to the narrow isthmus of Cadiz. This
tongue, cloven in its whole length by the creek or
canal of Troccadero, separated the inner from the
outward harbour, and at its extreme points stood
the village of Troccadero, and the fort of Matagorda, opposed to which there was on the isthmus
of Cadiz a powerful battery called the Puntales.
From Matagorda to the city was above four thousand yards, but across the channel to Puntales was
only twelve hundred; it was therefore the nearest
point to Cadiz and to the isthmus, and was infinitely
the most important post of offence. From thence the
French could search the upper harbour with their
fire and throw shells into the Caraccas and the fort
of Fernando, while their flotilla safely moored in
the Troccadero creek, could make a descent upon the
isthmus, and thus turn the Isla, and all the works
between it and the city. Nevertheless, the Spaniards
dismantled and abandoned Matagorda.

The third or Santa Maria division of blockade,
followed the sweep of the bay, and reckoning from
the San Pedro, on the left, to the castle of Santa
Catalina the extreme point of the outer harbour, on
the right, was about five miles. The town of Santa
Maria, built at the mouth of the Guadalete in the
centre of this line, was entrenched and the ground
about Santa Catalina was extremely rugged.

Besides these lines of blockade which were connected by a covered way, concealed by thick woods,
and, when finished, armed with three hundred guns,
the towns of Rota and San Lucar de Barameda were
occupied. The first, situated on a cape of land

opposite to Cadiz, was the northern point of the great bay or roadstead, the second commanded the mouth of the Guadalquivir. Behind the line of blockade, Latour Maubourg, with a covering division, took post at Medina Sidonia, his left being upon the upper Guadalete, and his advanced posts watching the passes of the Sierra de Ronda. Such was the position of the first corps. I shall now relate the progress of events within the blockaded city.

The fall of the Central Junta, the appointment of the regency and the proclamation for convoking the national Cortes have been already touched upon. Albuquerque, hailed as a deliverer, elected governor, commander in chief, and president of the Junta, appeared to have unlimited power, but in reality, possessed no authority, except over his own soldiers, and did not meddle with administration. The regency appointed provisionally and composed of men without personal energy or local influence, was obliged to bend and truckle to the Junta of Cadiz; and that imperious body without honour, talents, or patriotism, sought only to obtain the command of the public revenue for dishonest purposes, and meanwhile privately trafficked with the public stores.

Albuquerque's troops were in a deplorable state; the whole had been long without pay, and the greater part were without arms, accoutrements, ammunition, or clothes. When he demanded supplies, the Junta declared that they could not furnish them; but the duke affirming this to be untrue, addressed a memorial to the Regency, and the latter, anxious to render the Junta odious, yet fearing openly to attack them, persuaded Albuquerque to publish his memorial. The Junta replied by an

CHAP.
V.

1810.
Feb.

Albu-
querque's
Manifesto.

Private
Correspon-
dence of
Officers
from Ca-
diz. 1810.
MSS.

BOOK
X.
___
1810.
Feb.
exposition, false as to facts, base and ridiculous in reasoning; for although they had elected the duke president of their own body, they accused him amongst other things, with retreating from Carmona too quickly; and they finished with a menacing intimation, that, supported by the populace of Cadiz, they were able and ready to wreak their vengeance on all enemies. Matters being thus brought to a crisis, both Albuquerque and the Regency gave way, and the former being sent ambassador to England, it was thought he meant to go to South America, but he died in London, some months after, of a phrenzy brought on, as it is said, by grief and passion at the unworthy treatment he received. He was judged to be a brave and generous man, but weak and hasty, and easy to be duped.

Appendix,
No. 3,
Sec. 2.

The misery of the troops, the great extent of the positions, the discontent of the seamen, the venal spirit of the Junta, the apathy of the people, the feebleness of the Regency, the scarcity of provisions, and the machinations of the French, who had many favourers and those amongst the men in power all combined to place Cadiz in the greatest jeopardy; and this state of affairs would have led to a surrender, if England had not again filled the Spanish storehouses, and if the Regency had not consented to receive British troops into the city. Their entrance saved it, and at the same time, general Colin Campbell (who had succeeded sir John Cradock as governor of Gibraltar) performed a great service to his country, for, by persevering negotiation, he obtained that an English garrison should likewise enter Ceuta, and that the Spanish lines of San Roque, and the forts round the harbour of Algesiras should be demolished. Both measures were very essential to

General
Campbell's
Correspon-
dence.
MSS.

the present and permanent interests of England, and

the last especially so, because it cleared the neighbourhood of the fortress, and gave it a secure harbour. Gibraltar, at this time, contained a mixed and disaffected population of more than twelve thousand persons, and merchandize to the value of two millions sterling, which could have been easily destroyed by bombardment Ceuta which was chiefly garrisoned by condemned troops, and filled with galley-slaves, and its works miserably neglected, had only six days' provisions, was at the mercy of the first thousand French that could cross the streights; and the possession of it would have availed the enemy in many ways, especially in obtaining provisions from Barbary, where his emissaries were exceedingly active.

General William Stewart arrived in Cadiz, on the 11th of February, with two thousand men, a thousand more joined him from Gibraltar, and the whole were received with an enthusiasm, that proved sir George Smith's perception to have been just, and that Mr. Frere's unskilful management of the Central Junta, had alone prevented a similar measure the year before. The 17th a Portuguese regiment, thirteen hundred strong, was also admitted into the city, Spanish troops came in daily in small bodies; two ships of war, the Euthalion and Undaunted, arrived from Mexico with six millions of dollars; and another British battalion, a detachment of artillery, and more native troops, having joined the garrison, the whole Official
Abstract of
Operations
at Cadiz.
1810.
MSS. force assembled behind the Santi Petri, was not less than four thousand Anglo-Portuguese, and fourteen thousand Spaniards. Yet there was little of enthusiasm amongst the latter; and in all this time, not a

man among the citizens had been enrolled or armed, or had volunteered, either to labour or to fight. The ships recovered at Ferrol, had been transferred to Cadiz, so there were in the bay, twenty-three men of war, of which four of the line, and three frigates were British; and thus, money, troops, and a fleet, in fine, all things necessary to render Cadiz formidable, were collected, yet to little purpose, because procrastination, jealousy, ostentation, and a thousand absurdities, were the invariable attendants of Spanish armies and governments.

General Stewart's first measure, was to recover Matagorda, the error of abandoning which was to be attributed as much to admiral Purvis as to the Spaniards. In the night of the 22d, a detachment consisting of fifty seamen and marines, twenty-five artillery-men, and sixty-seven of the ninety-fourth regiment, the whole under the command of captain M'Lean, pushed across the channel during a storm, and taking possession of the dismantled fort, before morning effected a solid lodgement, and although the French cannonaded the work with field-artillery all the next day, the garrison, supported by the fire of Puntales, was immoveable.

The remainder of February passed without any event of importance, yet the people suffered from the want of provisions, especially fresh meat; and from the 7th to the 10th of March, a continued tempest, beating upon the coast, drove three Spanish and one Portuguese sail of the line, and a frigate and from thirty to forty merchantmen, on shore, between San Lucar and St. Mary's. One ship of the line was taken, the others burnt and part of the crews brought off by boats from the fleet; but many men, and amongst others a part of the fourth English regiment fell into the hands of the enemy, together with an immense booty.

Early in March, Mr. Henry Wellesley, minister plenipotentiary, arrived, and on the 24th of that month, general Graham coming from England assumed the chief command of the British, and immediately caused an exact military survey of the Isla to be made. It then appeared, that the force hitherto assigned for its defence, was quite inadequate, and that to secure it against the utmost efforts of the enemy, twenty thousand soldiers, and a system of redoubts, and batteries, requiring the labour of four thousand men for three months, Appendix,
No. 3,
Sect. 1. were absolutely necessary. Now, the Spaniards had only worked beyond the Santi Petri, and that without judgement; their batteries in the marsh were ill placed, their entrenchments on the tongue of land at the sea mouth of that channel, were of contemptible strength, and the Caraccas which they had armed with one hundred and fifty guns, being full of dry timber could be easily burned by carcasses. The interior defences of the Isla were quite neglected, and while they had abandoned the important posts of Matagorda, and the Troccadero, they had pushed their advanced batteries, to the junction of the Chiclana road with the Royal-causeway, in the marsh; that is to say, one mile and a half beyond the bridge of Zuazo, and consequently exposed, without support, to flank attacks both by water and land.

It was in vain that the English engineers presented plans, and offered to construct the works; the Spaniards would never consent to pull down a house, or destroy a garden; their procrastination paralyzed their allies, and would have lost the place, had the French been prepared to press it vigorously. They were indifferent to the progress of the enemy, and to use general Graham's expression, they wished the English would drive away the French, *that they might go and eat strawberries at Chiclana*. Nor were the British works (when the Spaniards would permit any to be constructed) well and rapidly completed, for the Junta furnished bad materials, there was a paucity of engineer-officers, and, from the habitual negligence of the ministerial departments at home, neither the proper stores, nor implements had been sent out. Indeed, an exact history, drawn from the private journals of commanders of British expeditions, during the war with France, would show an incredible carelessness of preparation on the part of the different cabinets. The generals were always expected to " make bricks without straw," and thus the laurels of the British army were for many years blighted. Even in Egypt, the success of the venerable hero, Abercrombie, was due, more to his perseverance and unconquerable energy before the descent, than to his daring operations afterwards.

Additional reinforcements reached Cadiz the 31st, and both sides continued to labour, but the allies slowly and without harmony, and, the supplies being interrupted, scarcity increased; many persons were forced to quit Cadiz, two thousand men were sent to Ayamonte to collect provisions on the Guadiana; and notwithstanding this, so strange a people were the Junta that they deceived Mr. Wellesley by assurances that the magazines were full, and thus induced him to suffer them to send wheat and flour away from the city, which was actually done, at the very time they were thus pressed by want!

General
Graham's
Correspon-
dence,
MSS.

But now Matagorda, which, though frequently cannonaded, had been held fifty-five days, impeded the completion of the enemy's works at the Troccadero point. This small fort, of a square form, with one angle projecting towards the land, without a ditch, and without bomb-proofs sufficient for the garrison, was little calculated for resistance; and, as it could only bring seven guns to bear, a Spanish seventy-four and an armed flotilla were moored on the flanks, to co-operate in the defence. The French had however raised great batteries behind some houses on the Troccadero, and, as daylight broke, on the 21st of April, a hissing shower of heated shot, falling on the seventy-four, and in the midst of the flotilla, obliged them to cut their cables and take shelter under the works of Cadiz. Then the fire of forty-eight guns and mortars, of the largest size, was concentrated upon the little fort of Matagorda, and the feeble parapet disappeared in a moment before this crashing flight of metal. The naked rampart and the undaunted hearts of the garrison remained, but the troops fell fast, the enemy shot quick and close, a staff, bearing the Spanish flag, was broken six times in an hour, and the colours were at last fastened to the angle of the work itself, while the men, especially the sailors, besought the officers to hoist the British ensign, attributing the slaughter to their fighting under a foreign flag. Thirty hours this tempest lasted, and sixty-four men out of one hundred and forty were down, when general Graham, finding a diversion he had projected impracticable, sent boats to carry off the survivors. The bastion was then blown up, under the direction of major Lefebre, an engineer of great promise, but he also fell,

BOOK
X.

1810.
April.

the last man whose blood wetted the ruins thus abandoned. Here I must record an action of which it is difficult to say whether it were most feminine or heroic. A sergeant's wife, named Retson, was in a casemate with the wounded men, when a very young drummer was ordered to fetch water from the well of the fort; seeing the child hesitate, she snatched the vessel from his hand, braved the terrible cannonade herself, and, although a shot cut the bucket-cord from her hand, she recovered it, and fulfilled her mission.*

After the evacuation of Matagorda, the war languished at Cadiz; but Sebastiani's cavalry infested the neighbourhood of Gibraltar, and he himself entered the capital of Murcia, on the 23d, when Blake retired upon Alicant and Carthagena. Meanwhile the French covered Matagorda point with batteries; but they were pressed for provisions, and general Campbell, throwing a detachment into Tarifa, drove their foragers from that vicinity, which abounds with cattle. The Spaniards at San Roque promised to reinforce this detachment, yet by their tardiness enabled the enemy to return with four hundred foot and some cavalry, and although the former were repulsed, the horse foraged the country, and drove off several herds of cattle during the action. General Campbell then increased the detachment to five hundred men, with some guns, and placed the whole under the command of major Brown of the 28th.

In May the French prisoners, cutting the cables of two hulks, drifted in a heavy gale to the French

General
Camp-
bell's Cor-
respon-
dence.
MSS.

---

* An interesting account of this noble-minded woman, is to be found in a small volume, entitled, " *Sketches of a Soldier's Life, in Ireland,*" by the author of " *The Eventful Life of a Soldier.*" This last work was erroneously designated, in my first volume, as " *The Life of a Sergeant.*"

CHAP.
V.

1810.
May.
Appendix,
No. III.
Section 1.

side of the bay; and the boats sent against them
being beat off, by throwing cold shot from the decks,
above fifteen hundred men saved themselves in
despite of the fire from the boats of the allied fleet,
and from the batteries, which was continued after the
vessels had grounded; although the miserable creatures, thus struggling for life, had been treated with
horrible cruelty, and, being all of Dupont's or Vedel's
corps, were prisoners only by a dishonourable breach
of faith! Meanwhile, in Cadiz, disorder was daily
increasing. The Regency having recalled Cuesta
to their military councils, he published an attack
on the deposed Central Junta, and was answered so
as to convince the world, that the course of all
parties had been equally detrimental to the state.
Thus fresh troubles were excited. The English
general was hampered by the perverse spirit of the
authorities, and the Spanish troops were daily
getting more inefficient from neglect, when the
departure of Albuquerque enabled Blake to take
the chief command in the Isla, and his presence
produced some amelioration in the condition and
discipline of the troops. At his instance, also, the
Municipal Junta consented, although reluctantly,
that the British engineers should commence a
regular system of redoubts for the defence of the
Isla.

English reinforcements continued to arrive, and
four thousand Spaniards, from Murcia, joined the
garrison, or rather army, now within the lines;
yet such was the state of the native troops, and
the difficulty of arranging plans, that hitherto the
taking of Matagorda had been the only check
given to the enemy's works. It was, however,
necessary to do something; and, after some ill-

BOOK
X.

1810.
June.
General
Graham's
Des-
patches.
MSS.

judged plans of the Regency had been rejected by Graham, general Lacy was embarked, with three thousand infantry and two hundred cavalry, to aid the armed peasants, or Serranos, of the Ronda. These people had been excited to arms, and their operations successfully directed by captain Cowley and Mr. Mitchel, two British artillery-officers, sent from Gibraltar. General Campbell also offered to reinforce Lacy, from Gibraltar, if he would attack Malaga, where there were twenty thousand males fit to carry arms, and the French were only two thousand, and cooped in the citadel, a Moorish castle, containing but twelve guns, and dependent for water on the town, which was itself only supplied by aqueducts from without. Lacy rejected this enterprise, and demanded that eight hundred men, from Gibraltar, should make a diversion to the eastward, while he, landing at Algesiras, moved on Ronda; this being assented to, the English armament sailed under the command of general Bowes.

Lacy made good his movement upon Ronda the 18th of June; but the French, having fortified it, were too strong at that point, or, rather, Lacy, a man of no enterprise, durst not act, and, when he was joined by many thousand mountaineers, he arrested their leaders for some offence, which so disgusted the men that they disbanded. The enemy, alarmed by these operations, which were seconded from the side of Murcia, and by an insurrection at Baeza, put all their disposable troops in motion; the insurrection at Baeza was quickly crushed, and general Rey, marching from Seville, against Lacy, entirely defeated and cut him off from Gibraltar, so that he was forced to re-embark with a few men at Estipona, and returned to Cadiz in July.

Here it is impossible not to reflect on the little use made of the naval power, and the misapplication of the military strength in the southern parts of Spain. The British, Portuguese, and Spanish soldiers, at Cadiz, were, in round numbers, 30,000, the British in Gibraltar 5000, in Sicily 16,000, forming a total of more than fifty thousand effective troops, aided by a great navy, and favourably placed for harassing that immense, and, with the exception of the Valencian and Murcian coasts, uninterrupted French line of operations, which extended from the south of Italy to Cadiz; for, even from the bottom of Calabria, troops and stores were brought to Spain. Yet a Neapolitan rabble, under Murat, in Calabria, and from fifteen to twenty thousand French around Cadiz, were allowed to paralyze this mighty power.

It is true that vigilance, temper, and arrangement, and favourable localities, are all required, in the combined operations of a fleet and army, and troops disembarking, also require time to equip for service. But Minorca offered a central station, and a place of arms for the army, and a spacious port for the fleet; the coast of Catalonia and Valencia is so pacific and safe, that seldom or never does a gale blow on shore; the operations would always have been short, and independent of the Spanish authorities, and lord Collingwood was fitted, by his talents, discretion, zeal, experience, and accurate knowledge of those coasts, successfully to direct such a floating armament. What coast-siege, undertaken by the seventh or third corps, could have been successfully prosecuted, if the garrison had been suddenly augmented with fifteen or twenty thousand men from the ocean? After one or two successful descents, the very appearance of a ship of war would have checked the operations of a siege, and obliged the enemy to concentrate : whereas, the slight expeditions of this period, were generally disconcerted by the presence of a few French companies.

In July the British force, in Cadiz, was increased to eight thousand five hundred men, and Sir Richard Keats arrived to take the command of the fleet. The enemy, intent upon completing his lines, and constructing flotillas at Chiclana, Santa Maria, and San Lucar de Barameda, made no attacks, and his works have been much censured, as ostentatiously extended, and leading to nothing. This is however a rash criticism ; for the Chiclana camp was necessary to blocade the Isla, and, as the true point for offensive operations, was at the Troccadero, the lines of Puerto Real and Santa Maria, were necessary to protect that position, to harass the fleet, to deprive the citizens of good water, which in ordinary times, was fetched from Puerto Maria, and finally to enable the flotilla, constructing at San Lucar, to creep round the coast. The chances from storms, as experience proved, almost repaid the labour, and it is to be considered that Soult contemplated a serious attack upon Cadiz, not with a single corps, generally weaker than the blockaded troops, but, when time should ripen, with a powerful army. Events in other parts of the Peninsula first impeded, and finally frustrated this intention, yet the lines were, in this view, not unnecessary or ostentatious.

Neither was it a slight political advantage, that the duke of Dalmatia should hold sway in Seville for the usurper's government, while the National

Cortes, and the Regency, were cooped up in a narrow corner of the province. Moreover, the preparations at Matagorda constantly and seriously menaced Cadiz, and a British division was necessarily kept there, for the English generals were well assured, that otherwise, some fatal disaster would befall the Spaniards. Now if a single camp of observation at Chiclana had constituted all the French works, no mischief could have been apprehended, and Graham's division, consisting of excellent soldiers, would have been set free, instead of being cooped up, without any counterbalance in the number of French troops at the blockade; for the latter aided indirectly, and at times directly, in securing the submission of Andalusia, and if not at Cadiz, they must have been covering Seville as long as there was an army in the Isla.

CHAPTER VI.

WHILE the blockade of Cadiz proceeded, Seville was guarded by a few thousand men of the fifth corps, left by Mortier when he advanced against Badajos ; and even from this small body six hundred infantry, under general Remond, and two hundred cavalry, were sent to attack the viscount De Gand, who was still at Ayamonte, vainly demanding a refuge in Portugal. The latter had four thousand troops, but declining an engagement, passed by his left through Gibraleon into the Sierra de Aroche, bordering on the Condado de Niebla, and the French immediately occupied Moguer and Huelva, towns situated at the mouths of the Odiel and Tinto rivers, from whence Cadiz had hitherto drawn supplies. Meanwhile the viscount returning to Ayamonte, sailed with his troops to Cadiz, and was replaced by general Copons, who came with two thousand men to gather provisions on the lower Guadiana, and in the Tinto and Odiel districts.

On the other side of Seville, Sebastiani had an uneasy task. The vicinity of Gibraltar and of the Murcian army, the continued descents on the coast, and the fierceness of the Moorish blood, rendered Grenada the most disturbed portion of Andalusia ; a great part of that fine province, visited by the horrors of insurrectional war, was ravaged and laid waste.

In the northern parts of Andalusia, about Jaen and Cordoba, Dessolles reduced the struggle to a trifling Guerilla warfare; but it was different in La Mancha, where the Partidas became so numerous and the war so onerous, that one of Joseph's ministers, writing to a friend, described that province as peopled with beggars and brigands. It remains to speak of Estremadura which was become the scene of various complicated movements and combats, producing no great results, indeed, but important as being connected with and bearing on the defence of Portugal.

The Spanish and Portuguese line of frontier, south of the Tagus, may be divided into three parts.

1°. From the Tagus to Badajos, on the Guadiana. 2°. From Badajos to the Morena. 3°. From the Morena to the sea. Each of these divisions is about sixty miles. Along the first, two-thirds of which is mountainous and one-third undulating plains and thick woods, a double chain of fortresses guard the respective frontiers. Alcantara, Valencia de Alcantara, Albuquerque, and Badajos are the Spanish; Montalvao, Castello de Vide, Marvao, Aronches, Campo Mayor, and Elvas, the principal Portuguese places. The three first on either side are in the mountains, the others in the open country, which spreads from the Guadiana to Portalegre, a central point, from whence roads lead to all the above-named fortresses.

From Badajos to the Morena, forms the second division of the country, it is rugged and the chain of fortresses continued. On the Portuguese side, Juramenha, Mourao and Moura; on the Spanish, Olivenza (formerly Portuguese), Xeres de los Cavalleros, and Aroche.

From the Morena to the sea, the lower Guadiana

separates the two kingdoms. The Spanish side, extremely rugged, contained the fortresses of San Lucar de Guadiana, Lepe, and Ayamonte. The Portuguese frontier, Serpa, Mertola, Alcontin, and Castro Marin, and, although the greater number of these places were dismantled, the walls of all were standing, some in good repair, and those of Portugal for the most part garrisoned by militia and ordenanza.

When Mortier attempted Badajos, on the 12th of February, Romana was near Truxillo, and the place was so ill provided, that a fortnight's blockade would have reduced it; but the French general, who had only brought up eight thousand infantry and a brigade of cavalry, could not invest it in face of the troops assembling in the vicinity, and therefore retired to Zafra, leaving his horsemen near Olivenza. In this position he remained until the 19th of February, when his cavalry was surprised at Valverde, and the commander Beauregard slain. Romana then returned to Badajos the 20th; and the 27th, Mortier leaving some troops in Zafra, marched to Merida, to connect himself with the second corps, which had arrived at Montijo, on the Guadiana.

It will be remembered that this corps, commanded by general Mermet, occupied the valley of the Tagus in its whole length during the invasion of Andalusia, and communicating with the sixth corps through the pass of Baños, formed an intermediate reserve between Mortier and Kellerman. The latter was at Bejar, and Miranda de Castanar, watching the duke Del Parque, in the early part of January, but withdrew to Salamanca, when the British army arrived in the valley of the Mondego.

The duke Del Parque then left Martin Carrera with a weak division in the Sierra de Gata, marched, with thirteen thousand men, through the pass of Perales, crossed the Tagus at Barca de Alconete on the 10th of February, and on the 12th, the day Mortier summoned Badajos, was in position with his right at Albuquerque and his left on the Guadiana.

When Mermet, whose advanced guard was at Placentia, knew of this movement, he first detached three thousand men across the Tagus, by Seradillo, to observe Del Parque, and soon afterwards Soult's brother, with four thousand men from Talavera, crossed the bridge of Arzobispo, advanced by Caceres, surprised some Spanish troops at Villa del Rey and reaching Montijo, pushed patrols close to Badajos. The remainder of the second corps arrived at Caceres by degrees; general Reynier took the command, and, as I have said, was joined by Mortier, who immediately commenced defensive works at Merida, and prepared gabions and facines as if to besiege Badajos.

These demonstrations attracted the notice of general Hill, who advanced with ten thousand men from Abrantes to Portalegre; and then Romana, finding himself, by the junction of the duke Del Parque's army, at the head of twenty-five thousand men, resolved to act against the communications of the French. His first division, commanded by Charles O'Donnel, brother to the Catalan general, occupied Albuquerque. The second, under Mendizabel, was posted near Castello de Vide. The third, consisting of five thousand Asturians, was sent, under Ballasteros, to Olivenza, and the fourth remained at Badajos. The fifth, under Contreras, was detached to Monasterio, with orders to interrupt Mortier's communication with Seville.

Contreras reached Xeres de los Cavalleros the 1st of March, but a detachment from Zafra soon drove him thence, and Romana retired to Campo Mayor with three divisions, leaving Ballasteros with the fourth at Olivenza. On the other hand, Mortier, uneasy about Contreras' movements, repaired to Zafra, leaving the second corps at Merida. The 10th, Romana, advanced again towards Albuquerque, and having pushed a detachment beyond the Salor river, it was surprised by general Foy. The 14th O'Donnel endeavoured to surprise Foy in return, but the latter, with very inferior numbers, fought his way through the Puerto de Trasquillon, and the Spaniards took possession of Caceres.

At this period the insurrections in Grenada, the movements of the Murcian army, and the general excitement of Valencia, in consequence of Suchet's retreat, caused Joseph to recal Mortier for the defence of Andalusia ; wherefore the latter, after holding a council of war with Reynier, destroyed the works at Merida, on the 19th, and retired to Seville, leaving Gazan's division at Monasterio. Reynier having sent his stores to Truxillo drove the Spaniards out of Caceres the 20th, and followed them to the Salor, but afterwards took post at Torremacho, and O'Donnel returned to Caceres.

There are two routes leading from Merida and Badajos to Seville : 1°. The Royal Causeway, which passes the Morena by Zafra, Los Santos, Monasterio, and Ronquillo. 2°. A shorter, but more difficult, road, which, running westward of

the causeway, passes the mountains by Xeres de
los Cavalleros, Fregenal, and Araceña. These
parallel routes, have no cross communications in
the Morena, but on the Estremaduran side, a road
runs from Xeres de los Cavalleros to Zafra, and
on the Andalusian side, there is one from Araceña to
Ronquillo. Now when Mortier retired, Ballasteros
marched from Olivenza to Xeres de los Cavalleros,
and being joined by Contreras, their united corps,
amounting to ten thousand men, gained the Royal
Causeway by Zafra, and, on the evening of the 29th,
coming up with Gazan, fought an undecided action ;
the next day it was renewed, and the Spaniards
having the worst, Ballasteros retired to Araceña and
Contreras to the high mountains above Ronquillo.
From Araceña, Ballasteros marched to Huerva,
within a few leagues of Seville, but Girard drove
him back again to Araceña, yet again entering
the Condado de Neibla, he established himself at
Zalamea de Real on the Tinto river.

Meanwhile, Romana detached a force to seize
Merida, and cut the communication of the fifth
corps with Reynier ; but that general, marching
with eight thousand men from Torremocha, passed
through to Medellin before the Spaniards arrived,
and pushed troops, the 2d of April, into the Morena,
intending to take Contreras in rear, while Gazan
attacked him in front ; and this would have happened, but that O'Donnel, immediately threatened
Merida, and so drew Reynier back. Nevertheless,
Contreras was attacked by Gazan, at Pedroche,
and so completely defeated, that he regained Zafra
in the night of the 14th, with only two thousand
men ; Ballasteros also, assailed by a detachment
from Seville, retired to Araceña.

The 20th, Reynier marched to Montijo, and
O'Donnel retired from Caceres, but his rear guard
was defeated at La Rocca the 21st, and his division
would have been lost, if Mendizabel, and Hill also,
had not come to his aid, whereupon Reynier declining a general action, retired to Merida. The
insurrection in the Alpuxaras was now quelled, the
Valencians remained inactive, Joseph re-entered
Madrid, Soult assumed the government of Andalusia, and Mortier returned to Estremadura. On
the Spanish side, Contreras was displaced, and
Imas, his successor, advanced to Ronquillo, in
Mortier's rear; Ballasteros remained at Aroche;
Hill returned to Portalegre, and Romana encamped,
with fourteen thousand men, near Badajos, where
a Spanish plot was formed to assassinate him. It
was discovered, but the villain who was to have
executed the atrocious deed escaped.

MrStuart's
Correspon-
dence.
MSS.

Notwithstanding Romana's presence, Reynier and
the younger Soult, passed the Guadiana below Badajos, with only four hundred cavalry, and closely
examined the works of that fortress, in despite of
the whole Spanish army; at the same time, Mortier's advanced guards arrived on the Guadiana,
and a reinforcement of four thousand men joined the
second corps from Toledo; however the want of provisions would not permit the French to remain con-
contrated, and Mortier returned to the Morena, to
watch Imas. The 14th of May, a French detachment again came close up to Badajos, then took
the road to Olivenza, and would have cut off Ballasteros, if Hill had not by a sudden march to
Elvas, arrested its movement. Meanwhile, Ballasteros again menaced Seville, and was again driven
back upon Aroche, with a loss of three hundred men.

To check these frequent incursions, the French threatened the frontier of Portugal, by the Lower Guadiana; sometimes appearing at Gibraleon, and Villa Blanca, sometimes towards Serpa, the possession of which would have lamed Ballasteros' movements, yet the advantages were still chequered. A Portuguese flotilla intercepted, at the mouth of the Guadiana, a convoy of provisions going to the first corps; and O'Donnel having made an attempt, during Reynier's absence, to surprise Truxillo, was repulsed, and regained Albuquerque with great difficulty. It would be perplexing, to trace farther and in detail all the movements, on the line from Badajos to Ayamonte, yet two circumstances there were, of historical importance. In the beginning of July, Lacy being in the Sierra de Ronda, Ballasteros near Aroche, and Copons in the Condado Neibla, the French marched against Lacy, leaving Seville garrisoned solely by Spaniards in Joseph's service; and while this example was furnished by the enemy, the Portuguese and Spanish troops on the frontier, complaining, the one of inhospitality, the other of robbery and violence, would, but for the mediation of the British authorities, have commenced a regular war, and their mutual jealousy and hatred was extended to the governments on both sides.

Hitherto, Hill had not meddled in the Spanish operations, save, when Romana was hardly pressed, but the latter's demands for aid were continual, and most of his projects were ill judged, and contrary to lord Wellington's advice. On the 26th of June however, Reynier passing the Guadiana, foraged all the country about Campo Mayor, and then turned by Montijo to Merida; it was known also

that his corps belonged to the army assembling in
Castile for the invasion of Portugal, that he had collected mules and other means of transport in Estremadura ; and the spies asserted, that he was going
to cross the Tagus. Hill, therefore, gathered his
divisions well in hand, ready to move as Reynier
moved, to cross the Tagus if he crossed it, and by
parallel operations to guard the frontier of Beira.
The march of the second corps was, however, post-
poned, and the after operations belonging to greater
combinations, will be treated of in another place.

OBSERVATIONS.

1°. Although, apparently complicated, the movements in Estremadura were simple in principle.
The valley of the Guadiana as far as Badajos, is
separated from the valley of the Tagus, by a range
of heights, connecting the Guadalupe mountains
with those of Albuquerque ; and the country between
those hills and the Tagus, contained fertile valleys,
and considerable towns, such as Valencia de Alcantara and Caceres. To profit from their resources
was an object to both parties. Reynier, whose base
was at Truxillo, could easily make incursions as far
as Caceres, but beyond that town, the Salor, presented a barrier, from behind which, the Spaniards
supported by the fort of Albuquerque, could observe whether the incursion was made in force, and
act accordingly ; hence O'Donnel's frequent advances and retreats.

2°. Reynier could not operate seriously, unless
in unison with the fifth corps, and by the valley
of the Guadiana, and Merida, on account of its

stone-bridge, was the key of his movements. But Mortier's base of operations, being in Andalusia, his front, was spread, from Zafra to Merida, to cover his line of retreat, and to draw provisions from about Lerena; now the road of Xeres de los Cavalleros was always open to the Spaniards, and the frequent advances of Ballasteros and Contreras, were to harass Mortier's line of communication. Wherefore the clue of affairs was this; Romana, holding Badajos, and being supported by Hill, acted on both flanks of the French, and the Portuguese frontier furnished a retreat from every part of his lines of operation; but, as his projects were generally vague and injudicious, lord Wellington forbad Hill to assist, except for definite and approved objects.

3°. To stop Romana's movements, Mortier had only to unite the 2d and 5th corps and give battle, or, if that was refused, to besiege Badajos, which, from its influence, situation, and the advantage of its stone bridge, was the key to the Alemtejo; and this he ardently desired. Soult, however, would not permit him to undertake any decisive operation while Andalusia was exposed to sudden insurrections and descents from Cadiz; and to say that either marshal was wrong would be rash, because two great interests clashed. Mortier and Reynier united, could have furnished twenty thousand infantry, fifty guns, and more than three thousand cavalry, all excellent troops. Romana having garrisoned Badajos, Olivenza, and Albuquerque, could not bring more than fifteen thousand men into line, and must have joined Hill. But with a mixed force and divided command, the latter could not have ventured a battle in the plain country beyond Portalegre. A defeat would have opened Lisbon to the

Appendix,
No. V. Section 1.

victor, and lord Wellington must then have detached
largely from the north; the king and Soult could
have reinforced Mortier, and the ultimate consequences are not to be assumed.

On the other hand, Soult, judging, that ere
further conquests were attempted, the great province of Andalusia, should be rendered a strong hold,
and independent of extraneous events, bent all his
attention to that object.   An exact and economical
arrangement provided for the current consumption
of his troops, and vast reserve magazines were filled
without overwhelming the people.   The native
municipal authorities, recognized and supported
in matters of police and supply, acted zealously,
yet without any imputation upon their patriotism;
for those who see and feel the miseries, flowing from
disorderly and wasting armies, may honestly assist a
general labouring to preserve regularity.   All this
could not be the work of a day, and meanwhile the
marshals under Soult's orders, being employed only
in a military capacity, desired the entire controul of
their own corps, and to be engaged in great field
operations, because, thus only could they be distinguished.   But the duke of Dalmatia while con-
tributing to the final subjugation of Spain, by concentrating the elements of permanent strength in
Andalusia, was also well assured, that, in fixing a
solid foundation for future military operations, he
should obtain reputation as an able administrator
and pacificator of a conquered country.

4°. Soult's views, however, clashed, not more
with those of the generals, than with the wishes of
the king, whose poverty forced him to grasp at all
the revenues of Andalusia, and who having led
the army, in person across the Morena, claimed

both as monarch and conqueror. He who wields
the sword will always be first served. Soult,
guided by the secret orders of Napoleon, resisted
the king's demands, and thus excited the monarch's
hatred to an incredible degree; nevertheless, the
duke of Dalmatia, never lost the emperor's confidence, and his province, reference being had to the
nature of the war, was admirably well governed.
The people were gradually tranquillized ; the military resources of the country drawn forth, and considerable bodies of native troops raised, and even
successfully employed, to repress the efforts of the
Partisan chiefs.   The arsenal of construction at
Seville was put into full activity ; the mines of
lead at Linares were worked ; the copper of the
river Tinto gathered for the supply of the founderies, and every provision for the use of a large
army collected ; privateers also were fitted out, a
commerce was commenced with neutral nations in
the ports of Grenada ; and finally, a secret, but con- Mr. Stu-
siderable, traffic carried on with Lisbon itself, de- art's Cor-
respon-
monstrated the administrative talents of Soult.   An- dence,
MSS.
dalusia soon became the most powerful establishment of the French in Spain.

5°. Both marshals appear to have entertained
sound views, and the advantages of either plan being
considered, leads to the reflection that they might
have been reconciled.   A reinforcement of twenty-
five thousand men in Estremadura, during the
months of June and July, would have left scarcely
a shadow of defence for Portugal ; and it would seem
that Napoleon had an eye to this, as we find him directing Suchet, in July, to co-operate with fifteen
thousand men in Massena's invasion, whenever
Tortoza should fall.   The application of this reason-

ing will, however, be better understood as the narrative advances; and whether Napoleon's recent
marriage with the Austrian princess drew him away
from business, or that, absorbed by the other
many and great interests of his empire, he neglected Spanish affairs; or whether deceived by exaggerated accounts of successes, he thought the
necessity for more troops less than it really was, I
have not been able to ascertain. Neither can I find
any good reason, why the king, whose army was
increased to twenty thousand men before the end of
June, made no movement to favour the attack on
Portugal. It is, however, scarcely necessary to
seek any other cause, than the inevitable errors, that
mar all great military combinations not directed by
a single hand.

CHAPTER VII.

THE operations, south of the Tagus, having been described, those which occurred, north of that river, shall now be traced; for previous to the invasion of Portugal, the French stretched in one great line across the Peninsula, from Cadiz to Gihon, and eagerly discussed the remnants of the Spanish armies.

It will be remembered, that the duke Del Parque left Martin Carrera in the Gata mountains, to interrupt the communication, between the Salamanca country and the valley of the Tagus. Julian Sanchez also, issuing from time to time out of Ciudad Rodrigo, cut off the French foragers in the open country between the Agueda and the Douro; and beyond the Douro, the Gallician army, under Garcia (in number about ten thousand), occupied Puebla de Senabria, Puente Ferrada, Villa Franca, and Astorga, menacing the right flank, and rear, of the sixth corps. Mahy was organising a second army at Lugo, and in the Asturias, the captain-general D'Arco, commanded seven thousand men, three thousand of which were posted at Cornellana, under general Ponte. Thus an irregular line of defence, six hundred miles long, was offered to the invaders, but without depth or substance, save at Badajos and Ciudad Rodrigo, behind which the British and Portuguese troops were lying.

On the other hand, the French, holding the in-

terior line, kept their masses only on the principal
routes, communicating by moveable columns, and
thus menaced all the important points without
scattering their forces. The influx of fresh troops
from France, continually added to their solidity,
especially in Old Castile, where Ney had resumed
the command, being supported by Kellerman with
the force of his government, and by an eighth
corps under the duke of Abrantes.

The invasion of Andalusia was the signal for a
general movement of all the French in Spain ; and
while Victor and Mortier, menaced Cadiz and
Badajos, Ney summoned Ciudad Rodrigo, and
Bonet, entering the Asturias, threatened Gallicia
by the Concija d'Ibas. At the same time, Loison,
with eight thousand fresh men, occupied Leon and
Medina del Campo, and the advanced guard of
the eighth corps passed Valladolid. Loison gave
out that he would invade Gallicia by Puebla de
Senabria, and on the 15th of February, his cavalry
cut to pieces five hundred Spanish troops at Alca-
nizas, but he finally marched against Astorga, and,
at the same time, Bonet destroyed Ponte's force at
Potes de Sierra, and advanced to Nava de Suarna.
These movements alarmed the Spaniards. Garcia,
menaced at once by Bonet and by Loison, and
fearing equally for Astorga and Lugo, threw two-
thirds of his army into the former, and carried the
remainder to Villa Franca, to support Mahi.

Ney, however, made only a feint of escalading
Ciudad Rodrigo, and Loison, although supported by
the men from Leon, who advanced to Puente
Orbijo, was repulsed from Astorga. Junot then concentrated the eighth corps at Benevente, intending
to besiege Astorga in form ; but he was suddenly

called towards Madrid, lest disorders should arise in
the capital during the king's absence. Mahi and
Garcia being apprised of this, immediately brought
up the new levies to the edge of the mountains,
thinking to relieve the Asturians by threatening an
irruption into the plains of Leon; but as Loison still
remained at Benevente, they were unable to effect
their object, and, after drawing off five thousand
men from Astorga, retired to Villa Franca.

Bonet did not pass Nava de Suarna, and when
general Arco had rallied the Asturian fugitives at
Louarca, Garcia, leaving Mahi to command in
Gallicia, marched himself with the remnant of the
old army of the left, to join Romana at Badajos.
Meanwhile Kellerman advanced to Alba de Tormes,
and detachments from his and Ney's force chased
Carrera from the Gata and Bejar mountains, driving him sometimes over the Alagon, sometimes
into Portugal. It is unnecessary to trace all these
movements, because the French, while preparing for
greater operations, were continually spreading false
reports, and making demonstrations in various
directions to mislead the allies, and to cover their
own projects.

Those projects were at first obscure. It is certain that the invasion of Portugal by the northern
line, was not finally arranged, until a later period;
yet it seems probable, that while Bonet drew the
attention of the Gallician army towards Lugo, the
duke of Abrantes designed to penetrate by Puebla
Senabria; not as Loison announced, for the invasion of Gallicia, but to turn the Tras os Montes
and descend by the route of Chaves upon Oporto, while Ney, calling the second corps to the
aid of the sixth, should invest Ciudad Rodrigo.

BOOK
X.

1810.
March.

Whatever designs might have been contemplated, they were frustrated, partly by the insurrection in Grenada and the failure of Suchet against Valencia, partly by disunion amongst the generals, for here also Ney and Junot complained reciprocally; and every where it was plainly seen that the French corps d'armée, however formidable in themselves, would not, in the absence of Napoleon, act cordially in the general system.

When the commotions in the south subsided, Junot returned to Old Castile; Loison joined the sixth corps on the Tormes; Kellerman retired to Valladolid; detachments, placed on the Douro, maintained the communications between Ney and Junot; and the latter, having drawn a reinforcement from Bonet, invested Astorga with ten thousand infantry, two thousand cavalry, eighteen field-guns, six twenty-four pounders, and two mortars. His covering-divisions were placed, one at Benevente, to watch the road of Mombuey, one near Puebla de Senabria, and one at Puente Ferrada. Mahi immediately concentrated the Gallician army at Villa Franca and Fonceabadon, and detached fifteen hundred men, under Echevarria, to Mombuey and Puebla, to harass the flank and rear of the investing army; yet his force was weak, the Gallician authorities had frequently assured lord Wellington that it amounted to twenty thousand well-organized troops; it now appeared that only eight thousand were in the field, and those ill provided, and prone to desertion.

Mr. Stu-
art's Cor-
respon-
dence,
MSS.

SIEGE OF ASTORGA.

Santocildes, the governor, was an officer of

courage; his garrison consisted of two thousand five hundred infantry, besides cannoneers and armed peasantry, and the Moorish ramparts had been strengthened by fresh works; but there was little ammunition, scarcely twenty days' rations, and nothing outside the walls, capable of seriously disturbing the enemy. The town stood in an open plain, and had three suburbs; Puerto de Hierro to the north, St. Andreas to the east, and Retebia to the west. On the two last Junot made false attacks, and conducted his real approaches, against the front between Puerto de Hierro and Retebia.

The place was invested the 22d, and Puerto de Hierro was carried by storm, two sallies were repulsed, and the trenches opened, before the end of the month. A breach was then commenced, but the battering-guns soon became unserviceable, and the line of approach was flanked by the houses of Retebia, which were filled with Spanish infantry. Nevertheless, the town suffered from shells, the wall was broken on the 20th of April, an assault was ordered, and although a previous attack on Retebia had failed Santocildes was so distressed for ammunition, that he offered to capitulate.

Junot refused the terms demanded, and, at five o'clock in the evening of the 21st, some picked troops ran up to the breach, which was well retrenched and stockaded, and defended with great obstinacy, while the flank fire from Retebia stopped the supporting columns. The storming-party, thus abandoned to its own exertions, was held at bay on the summit of the breach; and being plied on both flanks, and in front, with shot from the houses of the town, and in rear by the musketry from Retebia, it would have been totally destroyed, but for the scarcity of ammunition, which paralyzed the Spanish defence. Three hundred French are said to have fallen on the breach itself, but the remainder finally effected a lodgement in the ruins. During the night, a second attack on Retebia proving successful, a communication was opened from the parallels to the lodgement, and strong working-parties were sent forward, who cut through the stockade into the town, when the governor surrendered.

Mahi, who had advanced to the edge of the mountains, as if he would have succoured the place, hearing of this event, retired to Bembibre, where his rear was overtaken and defeated by general Clausel on the 24th. He then fell back to Lugo, and recalled his detachment from Mombuey ; but the French from Benevente were already in that quarter, and, on the 25th, totally defeated Echevaria at Castro Contrijo. Meanwhile, Junot placed garrisons in Astorga and Leon, and restored Bonet his division. That general, who had retired to Santander during the siege, then re-occupied Oviedo and Gihon, defeated the Asturians, and once more menaced Gallicia by the road of Concija, and by that of Sales ; several slight actions ensued ; the French penetrated no farther, and the Junta of Gallicia reinforced the Asturians with three thousand men.

During the siege of Astorga, the sixth corps was concentrated at Salamanca ; a strong detachment of Kellerman's troops seized the pass of Baños ; and Martin Carrera, quitting the hills, joined the English light division near Almeida. In fine, the great operations were commencing, and the line of communication with France, was encumbered with the advancing reinforcements. A large battering-train, collected from Segovia, Burgos, and Pampeluna, arrived at Salamanca; general Martineau, with ten thousand men for the eighth corps, reached Valladolid; general Drouet passed the Pyrennees with a ninth corps, composed of the fourth battalions of regiments already in Spain; and these were followed by seventeen thousand of the imperial guards, whose presence gave force to the rumour, that the emperor himself was coming to take the chief command.

Fortunately for the allies, this report, although rife amongst all parties, and credited both by Joseph's ministers, and the French ambassador at Madrid, proved groundless; a leader for the projected operations was still to be named. I have been informed that marshal Ney resumed the command of the sixth corps, under the im-pression that he was to conduct the enterprise against Portugal; that the intrigues of marshal Berthier, to whom he was obnoxious, frustrated his hopes; that Napoleon, fatigued with the disputes of his lieutenants, had resolved to repair in person to the Peninsula; that his marriage, and some important political affairs, diverted him from that object, and that Massena, prince of Esling, was finally chosen; partly for his great name in arms, partly that he was of higher rank than the other marshals, and a stranger to all the jealousies and disputes in the Peninsula. His arrival was known in May amongst the allies, and lord Wellington had no longer to dread the formidable presence of the French emperor.

That Massena's base of operations might not be

exposed to the interference of any other authority in Spain, the four military governments of Salamanca, Valladolid, Asturias, and St. Andero were placed under his temporary authority, which thus became absolute in the northern provinces. But previous to taking the command of the troops, he repaired to Madrid, to confer with the king, and it would seem that some hesitation as to the line of invasion still prevailed in the French councils ; because in the imperial muster-rolls, the head-quarters of the army of Portugal are marked as being at Caceres in Estremadura, and the imperial guards are returned as part of that army, yet during the month of April only ; a circumstance strongly indicating Napoleon's intention to assume the command himself. The northern line was, however, definitively adopted, and, while the prince of Esling was still in the capital, the eighth corps passed the Tormes, and Ney commenced the

FIRST SIEGE OF CIUDAD RODRIGO.

Lord Wellington's
Correspondence.
MSS.

The conduct of the governor of this fortress had in the beginning of the year appeared so suspicious, that lord Wellington demanded his removal. Don Andreas Herrasti, the actual governor, was a veteran of fifty years' service, whose silver hairs, dignified countenance, and courteous manners excited respect ; and whose courage, talents, and honour were worthy of his venerable appearance. His garrison amounted to six thousand fighting men, besides the citizens ; and the place, built on a height overhanging the northern bank of the Agueda river, was amply supplied with artillery and stores of all kinds.

The works were, however, weak, consisting of an old rampart, nearly circular, about thirty feet in height, and without other flanks than a few projections containing some light guns: a second wall, about twelve feet high, called a " *fausse braie*," with a ditch and covered way, surrounded the first, yet was placed so low on the hill, as scarcely to offer any cover to the upper rampart. There were no bomb-proofs, even for the magazine, and Herrasti was forced to place his powder in the church, which he secured as he might.

Beyond the walls, and totally severed from the town, the suburb of Francisco, defended by an earthern entrenchment, and strengthened by two large convents, formed an outwork to the north-east of the place. The convent of Santa Cruz served a like purpose on the north-west; and between these posts there was a ridge called the Little Teson, which, somewhat inferior in height to the town, was only a hundred and fifty yards from the body of the place. There was also a Greater Teson, which, rising behind the lesser at the distance of six hundred yards from the walls, overlooked the ramparts, and saw into the bottom of the ditch.

The country immediately about Ciudad Rodrigo, although wooded, was easy for troops; especially on the left bank of the Agueda, to which the garrison had access by a stone bridge within pistol-shot of the castle-gate. The Agueda itself, rising in the Sierra de Francia, and running into the Douro, is subject to great and sudden floods; and six or seven miles below the town, near San Felices, the channel deepens into one continued and frightful chasm, many hundred feet deep, and overhung with huge desolate rocks.

During February and March, the French departed as lightly as they had advanced against Ciudad Rodrigo; but, on the 25th of April, a camp was pitched upon a lofty ridge five miles eastward of the city; and, in a few days, a second, and then a third, arose: and these portentous clouds continued to gather on the hills until June, when fifty thousand fighting men came down into the plain, and throwing two bridges over the Agueda, begirt the fortress.

This multitude, composed of the sixth and eighth corps, and a reserve of cavalry, was led by Ney, Junot, and Montbrun. The sixth corps invested the place, the eighth occupied San Felices Grande, and other points, the cavalry swarmed on both sides of the river, but the battering train with a great escort was still two days' march in the rear, for the rains inundating the flat country between the Agueda and the Tormes, rendered the roads impassable. The bridges were established on the 2d and 7th of June, the one above, the other below the town, and on the 13th, ground was broken on the Greater Teson. The 22d, the artillery arrived, and preparations were made to contract the circle of investment on the left bank of the Agueda, which had hitherto been but slightly watched. That night, Julian Sanchez, with two hundred horsemen, passed silently out of the castle-gate, and, crossing the river, fell upon the nearest French posts, pierced their line in a moment, and reached the English light division, then behind the Azava, six miles from Ciudad Rodrigo. This event, induced Ney, to reinforce his troops on the left bank, and a movement, to be hereafter noticed, was directed against general Crawfurd the 25th, on which day, also, the French batteries opened.

Ney's plan was to breach the body of the place without attending to the Spanish fire, and salvos, from forty-six guns, constantly directed on one point, soon broke the old masonry of the ramparts; nevertheless the besieged, who could bring twenty-four guns to bear on the Teson, shot so well that three magazines blew up at once in the trenches, and killed above a hundred of the assailants. On the 27th, the prince of Esling arriving in the camp, summoned the governor to surrender, and Herrasti answered in the manner to be expected from so good a soldier. The fire was then resumed until the 1st of July, when Massena, sensible that the mode of attack was faulty, directed the engineers to raise counter-batteries, to push their parallels to the Lesser Teson, work regularly forward, blow in the counterscarp, and pass the ditch in form. Meanwhile, to facilitate the progress of the new works, the convent of Santa Cruz, on the right flank, was carried after a fierce resistance; and, on the left, the suburb was attacked, taken, and retaken by a sally, in which great loss was inflicted on the French. Howbeit, the latter remained masters of every thing beyond the walls.

During the cessation of fire, consequent upon the change in the French dispositions, Herrasti removed the ruins from the foot of the breach, and strengthened his flank defences. On the 9th of July, the besieger's batteries, being established on the Lesser Teson, re-opened with a terrible effect. In twenty-four hours, the fire of the

Intercepted French Correspondence, MSS.

Spanish guns was nearly silenced, part of the town was in flames, a reserve magazine exploded on the walls, the counterscarp was blown in by a mine, on an extent of thirty-six feet, the ditch was filled by the ruins, and a broad way made into the place. Three French soldiers, of heroic courage, then rushed out of the ranks, mounted the breach, looked into the town, and having thus, in broad daylight, proved the state of affairs, discharged their muskets, and, with matchless fortune, retired unhurt to their comrades.

The columns of assault immediately assembled. The troops, animated by the presence of Ney, and excited by the example of the three men who had so gallantly proved the breach, were impatient for the signal, and a few moments would have sent them raging into the midst of the city, when the white flag suddenly waved on the rampart, and the venerable governor was seen standing alone on the ruins, and signifying, by his gestures, that he desired to capitulate. He had stricken manfully, while reason warranted hope, and it was no dishonour to his silver hairs, that he surrendered when resistance could only lead to massacre and devastation.

Six months had now elapsed, since the French resuming the plan of conquest interrupted by the Austrian war and by the operations of sir Arthur Wellesley, had retaken the offensive. Battle after battle they had gained, fortress after fortress they had taken, and sent the Spanish forces, broken and scattered, to seek for refuge in the most obscure parts: solid resistance there was none, and the only hope of deliverance for the Peninsula rested upon the British general. How he realized that hope shall be related in the next book. Meanwhile, the reader should bear in mind that the multifarious actions related in the foregoing chapters, were contemporaneous, and that he has been led, as it were, round the margin of a lake, whose turbulent waters spread on every side. Tedious to read, and trifling many of the circumstances must appear, yet, as a whole, they form what has been called the Spanish military policy: and, without accurate notions on that head, it would be impossible to appreciate the capacity of the man who, like Milton's phantom, paved a broad way through their chaotic warfare.

I have been charged with incompetence to understand, and, most unjustly, with a desire to underrate the Spanish resistance; but it is the province of history to record, foolish as well as glorious deeds, that posterity may profit from all, and neither will I mislead those who read my work, nor sacrifice the reputation of my country's arms to shallow declamation upon the unconquerable spirit of independence. To expose the errors is not to undervalue the fortitude of a noble people. In their constancy, in the unexampled patience, with which they bore the ills inflicted alike by a ruthless enemy, and by their own sordid governments, the Spaniards were truly noble: but shall I say that they were victorious in their battles, or faithful in their compacts; that they treated their prisoners with humanity; that their Juntas were honest or wise; their generals skilful; their soldiers firm? I speak but the bare truth, when I assert, that they were incapable of defending their own cause! Every action, every correspondence, every proceeding of the six years that the war

lasted, rise up in support of this fact; and to
assume that an insurrection so conducted did, or
could possibly baffle the prodigious power of
Napoleon is an illusion. Spain baffle him! Her
efforts were amongst the very smallest causes of
his failure. Portugal has far greater claims to
that glory. Spain furnished the opportunity; but
it was England, Austria, Russia, or rather fortune,
that struck down that wonderful man.   The
English, more powerful, more rich, more profuse,
perhaps more brave than the ancient Romans; the
English, with a fleet, for grandeur and real force,
never matched; with a general equal to any emergency; fought as if for their own existence. The
Austrians brought four hundred thousand good
troops to arrest the conqueror's progress; the
snows of Russia destroyed three hundred thousand
of his best soldiers; and finally, when he had lost
half a million of veterans, not one of whom died
on Spanish ground, Europe, in one vast combination, could only tear the Peninsula from him, by
tearing France along with it. What weakness, then,
what incredible delusion to point to Spain, with all
her follies, and her never-ending defeats, as a proof
that a people fighting for independence must be
victorious. She was invaded, because she adhered
to the great European aristocracy; she was delivered, because England, enabled that aristocracy
to triumph, for a moment, over the principles of the
French revolution.

BOOK XI.

CHAPTER I.

THE defence of Portugal, was not the result of any fortuitous combination of circumstances, nor was lord Wellington moved thereunto, by any hasty ambition to magnify his own reputation, but calmly and deliberately, formed his resolution, after a laborious and cautious estimate of the difficulties and chances of success. Reverting then to the period, when, by retreating upon Badajos, he divorced his operations from the folly of Spain, I shall succinctly trace his military and political proceedings up to the moment, when, confident in the soundness of his calculations, he commenced his project, unmoved by the power of his enemy, the timidity of his friends, the imprudence of his subordinates, or the intrigues of discontented men, who secretly, and with malignant perseverance, laboured to thwart his measures and to ruin his designs.

CHAP. I.

1810.

After the retreat from Spain in 1809, he repaired to Seville, partly to negotiate with the Central Junta, upon matters touching the war, but principally to confer with his brother, ere the latter quitted the Peninsula. Lord Wellesley's departure was caused by the state of politics in England, where a change in the administration

was about to take place; a change, sudden indeed,
but not unexpected, because the ineptitude of the
government, was, in private, acknowledged by many
of its members, and the failure of the Walcheren
expedition, was only the signal, for a public avowal
of jealousies and wretched personal intrigues,
which had rendered the Cabinet of St. James's the
most inefficient, Spain excepted, of any in Europe.
Mr. Canning, the principal mover of those in-
Lord Cas-
tlereagh's
statement. trigues, had secretly denounced lord Castlereagh
to his colleagues, as a man incapable of conducting
the public affairs, and exacted from them a pro-
Mr. Can-
ning's
statement. mise to dismiss him. Nevertheless, he permitted
that nobleman, ignorant of the imputation on his
abilities, to plan, and conduct the fitting out, of the
most powerful armament that ever quitted England.
When it became evident that loss and ruin waited
on this unhappy expedition, Mr. Canning claimed
the fulfilment of the promise, and the intrigue
thus becoming known to lord Castlereagh, was
by him characterised as " *a breach of every prin-*
" *ciple of good faith, both public and private.*"
This was followed by a duel; and by the dissolution
of the administration. Mr. Perceval and lord Liverpool being then empowered to form another Cabinet, after a fruitless negotiation with lord Grey,
and lord Grenville, assumed the lead themselves,
and offered the department of foreign affairs to lord
Wellesley.

Contrary to the general expectation, he accepted
it. His brother had opened to him those great
views for the defence of Portugal, which were
afterwards so gloriously realized; but which could
never have been undertaken with confidence by that
general, unless secure of some powerful friend in

the administration, embued with the same sentiments, bound by common interest, and resolute,
to support him when the crisis of danger arrived.
It was therefore wise, and commendable, in lord
Wellesley, to sacrifice something of his own personal pretensions, to be enabled to forward projects,
promising so much glory to the country and his
own family, and the first proceedings in parliament
justified his policy.

Previous to the change in the Cabinet, sir Arthur
Wellesley had been created baron Douro, and viscount Wellington ; but those honours, although
well deserved, were undoubtedly conferred as much
from party as from patriotic feeling, and greatly
excited the anger of the opposition members, who
with few exceptions, assailed the general, personally,
and with an acrimony not to be justified. His See Par-
liamentary
Debates.
merits, they said, were nought ; his actions silly,
presumptuous, rash ; his campaign one deserving
not reward, but punishment. Yet he had delivered
Portugal, cleared Gallicia and Estremadura, and
obliged one hundred thousand French veterans to
abandon the offensive and concentrate about Madrid!

Lord Grey opposing his own crude military notions, to the practised skill of sir Arthur. petu-
lantly censured the latter's dispositions at Talavera;
others denied that he was successful in that action ;
and some, forgetting that they were amenable to
history, even proposed to leave his name out of
the vote of thanks to the army ! That battle, so
sternly fought, so hardly won, they would have set
aside with respect to the commander, as not war-
ranting admission to a peerage always open to venal
orators ; and the passage of the Douro, so promptly, so daringly, so skilfully, so successfully exe-

cuted, that it seemed rather the result of inspiration than of natural judgement, they would have cast away as a thing of no worth !

This spirit of faction was, however, not confined to one side : there was a ministerial person, at this time, who in his dread of the opposition, wrote to lord Wellington complaining of his inaction, and calling upon him to do something that would excite a public sensation : *any thing provided blood were spilt !*　A calm but severe rebuke, and the cessation of all friendly intercourse with the writer, discovered the general's abhorrence of this detestable policy.　When such passions were abroad, it is evident that lord Wellesley's accession to the government, was essential to the success of lord Wellington's projects.

Those projects delivered the Peninsula and changed the fate of Europe, and every step made towards their accomplishment merits attention, as much from the intrinsic interest of the subject, as that it has been common to attribute his success to good fortune and to the strenuous support he received from the Cabinet at home.　Now it is far from my intention to deny the great influence of fortune in war, or that the duke of Wellington has always been one of her peculiar favourites; but I will make it clearly appear, that if he met with great success, he had previously anticipated it, and upon solid grounds; that the Cabinet did not so much support him as it was supported by him; and finally, that his prudence, foresight, and firmness were at least as efficient causes as any others that can be adduced.

Immediately after the retreat from Jaraceijo, and while the ministers were yet unchanged, lord Castlereagh, brought, by continual reverses, to a more sober method of planning military affairs, had demanded lord Wellington's opinion upon the expediency, the chance of success, and the expense of defending Portugal. This letter reached the general on the 14th of September, 1809; but the subject required many previous inquiries and a careful examination of the country; and at that period, any plan for the defence of Portugal, was necessarily to be modified, according to the energy or feebleness of the Spaniards in Andalusia. Hence it was not until after his return from Seville, a few days previous to the defeat at Ocaña, that lord Wellington replied to lord Liverpool, who, during the interval, had succeeded lord Castlereagh in the war department.

Adverting to the actual state of the French troops in the Peninsula, he observed, that unless the Spanish armies met with some great disaster, the former *could not then make an attack upon Portugal;* yet, if events should enable them to do so, that the forces at that moment in the latter might defend it. " But the peace in Germany," he said, " might " enable France to reinforce her armies in Spain " largely, when the means of invading Portugal " would be increased ; not only in proportion to the " additional troops then poured in, but also in pro- " portion to the effect which such a display of " additional strength would necessarily have upon " the spirit of the Spaniards. Even in that case, " *until Spain should have been conquered and ren-* " *dered submissive*, the French would find it diffi- " cult, if not impossible, to obtain possession of " Portugal, *provided England employed her armies* " *in defence of that country, and that the Portu-*

" *guese military service was organised to the full ex-*
" *tent of which it was capable.*   But the number of
" British forces employed should not be less than
" thirty thousand effective men, although the Por-
" tuguese regular force, actually enrolled, consist-
" ed of thirty-nine thousand infantry, three thou-
" sand artillery, and three thousand cavalry ; and
" the militia amounted to forty-five thousand, ex-
" clusive of the ordenanças."

The next point of consideration was the probable
expense.   " The actual yearly cost of the British
" army in Portugal, exclusive of the hire of tran-
" sport-vessls, was about £1,800,000, being only
" half a million sterling more than they would cost
" if employed in England.   Hence the most im-
" portant consideration was the expense of renova-
" ting, and supporting the Portuguese military, and
" civil services.   The British government, had al-
" ready subsidised the Portuguese Regency, at the
" rate of six hundred thousand pounds yearly,
" being the expense of twenty thousand men, which
" the latter were bound by treaty to place at the
" service of the English commander-in-chief.

" But this was far from sufficient to render the
" Portuguese army efficient for the impending
" contest.   The revenue of Portugal was between
" eight and nine millions of dollars, the expenses
" between fourteen and fifteen millions, leaving a
" deficiency of more than six millions of dollars.
" Hence, for that year, the most pressing only of
" the civil and military demands had been paid,
" and the public debt and the salaries of the public
" servants were in arrear.   The advances already
" made by Great Britain amounted to two millions
" of dollars ; there remained a deficiency of four

" millions of dollars, which, after a careful inquiry,
" it appeared could not be made good by Portugal;
" and it was obvious that the administration would,
" when distressed, gradually appropriate the sub-
" sidy to support the civil authorities to the detri-
" ment of the military service. Nay, already money
" from the English military chest had been ad-
" vanced to prevent the Portuguese army from
" disbanding from want of food.

" It was impossible to diminish the expenses of
" the Regency, and yet the French invasion and
" the emigration to the Brazils had so impoverished
" the country that it was impossible to raise the
" revenue or to obtain money by loans. The people
" were unable to pay the taxes already imposed,
" and the customs, which formed the principal
" branch of Portuguese revenue, were reduced to
" nothing by the transfer of the Brazilian trade
" from the mother-country to Great Britain. This
" transfer, so profitable to the latter, was ruinous to
" Portugal, and, therefore, justice as well as policy
" required that England should afford pecuniary
" assistance to the Regency.

" Without it, nothing could be expected from
" the Portuguese army. The officers of that army
" had, for many years, done no duty, partly that
" their country having been, with some trifling
" exceptions, at peace nearly half a century, they
" had continued in the same garrisons, and lived
" with their families; and, to these advantages,
" added others arising from abuses in the service.
" Now the severe but necessary discipline intro-
" duced by marshal Beresford, had placed the Por-
" tuguese officers in a miserable situation. All
" abuses had been extirpated, additional expenses

" had been inflicted, and the regular pay was not
" only insufficient to support them in a country
" where all the necessaries of life were enormously
" dear, but it was far below the pay of the English,
" Spanish, and French officers, with whom, or
" against whom, they were to fight.

" If, therefore, the war was to be carried on, it
" was advisable to grant a subsidy of one hundred
" and thirty thousand pounds yearly, to enable the
" Regency to increase the pay of the Portuguese
" officers ; and to this sum, for the reasons before-
" mentioned, should be added a further subsidy of
" about three hundred thousand pounds, to supply
" the actual deficiency in the Portuguese revenues.
" Or, if the English cabinet preferred it, they might
" take ten thousand more Portuguese troops into
" pay, which could be done at an expense of two
" hundred and fifty thousand pounds. With such
" assistance, the difficulties of the moment might
" be overcome ; but, without it, he lord Wellington,
" felt assured, that the whole financial and military
" system of the Portuguese would break down at
" once ; all the expense, hitherto incurred, would
" be cast away, and all hopes of defending the
" country extinguished. It was for the ministers
" to decide.

" There remained two other points to consider—
" the re-embarkation of the British army, in the
" event of failure, and the chances of the Portu-
" guese nation continuing the contest alone. As
" to the first, he could carry off everything safely,
" except the horses of the cavalry and artillery,
" those could not be carried off, if the embarkation
" took place after a lost battle ; and, if under other
" circumstances, the expense of horse-transports

" would be more than the worth of the animals.
" As to the second point, if the British army
" evacuated Portugal, under any circumstances, he
" could not give hopes that the contest could be
" prolonged effectually by the natives. Although
" I," he said, " *consider the Portuguese government*
" *and army as the principals in the contest for their*
" *own independence, and that their success or failure*
" *must depend principally upon their own exertions*
" *and the bravery of their army, and that I am*
" *sanguine in my expectations of both, when excited*
" *by the example of British officers and troops, I*
" *have no hope of either, if his Majesty should now*
" *withdraw the army from the Peninsula, or if it*
" *should be obliged to evacuate it by defeat. There*
" *is no doubt that the immediate consequences will be*
" *the possession of Lisbon by the enemy, probably*
" *without a contest; and other consequences will*
" *follow, affecting the state of the war, not only in*
" *Portugal but Spain.* If, therefore, it should be
" thought advisable now to withdraw, or if, even-
" tually the British army should be obliged to with-
" draw from Portugal, I would recommend a con-
" sideration of the means of carrying away such of
" the Portuguese military as should be desirous of
" emigrating, rather than continue, by their means,
" the contest in this country."

Peniche and Setuval offered secure points of
embarkation in the event of failure, but neither
were likely to come within the scope of the operations, and lord Wellington's opinion as to the
facility of carrying off the army from Lisbon was
founded chiefly upon admiral Berkeley's assurances
that the embarkation would not take longer than
four hours, during which time, even though the

left bank of that river should be occupied by the enemy, the ships of war could sustain the fire and at the same time sweep with their own guns all the ground above Passo d'Arcos, which, from the circumstance of its having no surf, was thought preferable to St. Julian's for an embarkation. But the admiral's views, as I shall have occasion to observe hereafter, were erroneous; the fleet could not remain in the Tagus, for the purpose of an embarkation, if the enemy were in possession of the left bank.

Although alarmed at the number of men demanded, a number which, from the recent loss sustained on the Walcheren expedition, they truly observed, would, in case of disaster, endanger the safety of England, the ministers assented to lord Wellington's proposals; they undertook to pay ten thousand additional Portuguese troops, and to advance money for the increased stipends to the officers; and being now pledged to an annual subsidy of nearly one million, they with justice required that the Portuguese Regency, under pain of the subsidy being stopped, should keep all that part of the military establishment which remained under their own direction in a state of complete efficiency.

Thus supported, lord Wellington proceeded with vigorous intelligence to meet the impending contest. His troops removed from the Guadiana, took healthy cantonments on the north-eastern frontier of Portugal. He expected a reinforcement of five thousand infantry and a regiment of cavalry from England, smaller detachments had already reached him, and the army when it commenced its march from the Guadiana was

numerically thirty thousand strong; but those
actually under arms scarcely amounted to twenty
thousand, for nine thousand were in hospital, and
many in the ranks were still tottering from the
effects of past illness.

The 20th of January, the head-quarters, and
the artillery parc, were established at Viseu, in
Upper Beira. The cavalry was quartered, by
single regiments, at Golegao, Punhete, Torres Novas, Celerico, and Santarem. General Hill was
left with five thousand British, and a like number
of Portuguese at Abrantes; and the remainder of
the infantry (one regiment, forming the garrison of
Lisbon, excepted) was distributed along the valley
of the Mondego.

The plans of the English general were, at first,
grounded upon the supposition, that the French
would follow the right or northern line, in preference to the centre or southern line of operations,
against the Peninsula, that is, *attack Portugal from
the side of Old Castile*, rather than *Andalusia from
the side of La Mancha*. In this he was mistaken.
The movements were again directed by Napoleon,
his views were as usual gigantic, and not Andalusia
alone, but every part of the Peninsula, was destined
to feel the weight of his arms. Fresh troops, flushed
with their recent German victories, were crowding
into Spain, reinforcing the corps to their right and
left, scouring the main communications, and following the footsteps of the old bands, as the latter
were impelled forward in the career of invasion.
Hence, the operations against Andalusia so deeply
affected the defence of Portugal, that, on the 31st
of January, at the moment Seville was opening
her gates, lord Wellington demanded fresh instruc-

tions, reiterating the question, whether *Portugal should be defended at all;* but at the same time transmitting one of those clear and powerful statements, which he invariably drew up for the ministers' information previous to undertaking any great enterprise; statements, in which, showing the bearings of past and present events, and drawing conclusions as to the future with a wonderful accuracy, he has given irrefragable proofs, that envious folly has attributed to fortune, and the favour of the cabinet, successes, which were the result of his own sagacity and unalterable firmness.

" The enemy," he said, "aimed at conquering the south; he would no doubt obtain Seville with all its resources; and the defeat and dispersion of the Spanish armies would be the consequences of any action, in which either their imprudence or necessity, or even expediency, might engage them. The armies might, however, be lost and the authorities dispersed, but the war of Partisans would continue; Cadiz might possibly hold out, and the Central Junta even exist within its walls, but it would be without authority, because the French would possess all the provinces. This state of affairs, left Portugal untouched; yet it was chiefly to that country he wished to draw the ministers' attention.

" They already knew its military situation and resources. If arms could be supplied to the militia, a gross force of ninety thousand men, regularly organized, could be calculated upon, exclusive of the armed population and of the British army. Much had been done within the last nine months, for the enrolment, organization, and equipment of this great force; but much remained to be done, and with very insufficient means, before the fifty thousand men, composing the militia, could possibly contend with the enemy; and although this should be effected, the whole army would still want that confidence in themselves and in their officers, which is only to be acquired by military experience.

" When the affairs of Spain should, as before supposed, be brought to that pass, *that a regular resistance would cease, no possibility existed of the contest in that country being renewed on such a scale as to afford a chance of success, although the possession of each part might be precarious, depending upon the strength of the French force holding it, and that the whole might prove a burthen rather than an advantage to the French government.* Thence arose this question, ' Will the continuation of the contest in Portugal, afford any reasonable prospect of advantage against the common enemy, or of benefit to the allies?'

" It was impossible to calculate upon any certain grounds the degree of assistance to be expected from the Portuguese troops. For the regulars every thing that discipline could effect had been done, and they had been armed and equipped as far as the means of the country would go. The militia also had been improved to the extent which the expense of keeping them embodied would permit. The Portuguese had confidence in the British nation and army; they were loyal to their Prince; detested the French government, and were individually determined to do every thing for the cause. Still they were not to be certainly calculated upon until inured to war, because the

BOOK
IX.

1810.
January.

majority of their officers were of an inferior description and inexperienced in military affairs."

Under these circumstances, and *adverting to the
approaching subjection of Spain*, he demanded to
know whether " *the enemy, bending the greatest
part of his force against Portugal, that country
should be defended, or measures taken to evacuate
it, carrying of all persons, military and others, for
whose conveyance means could be found.* But under
any circumstances, (he said) the British army could
always be embarked in despite of the enemy."

Such being the view taken of this important
subject by lord Wellington, it may seem proper
here to notice an argument which, with equal ignorance and malice, has often been thrust forward
in disparagement of sir John Moore, namely, that
he declared Portugal could not be defended,
whereas lord Wellington did defend that country.
The former general premising that he was not prepared to answer a question of such magnitude,
observed, that the frontier, being, although rugged,
open, could not be defended against a superior
force ; yet that Almeida, Guarda, Belmonte, Baracal, Celerico, and Viseu, might be occupied as temporary positions to check the advance of an enemy,
and cover the embarkation of stores, &c., which
could only be made at Lisbon. That the Portuguese in their own mountains would be of much
use, and that he hoped that they could alone defend
the Tras os Montes. That, if the French succeeded
in Spain, it would be vain to resist them in Portugal " *because the latter was without a military
" force,*" and if it were otherwise, from the experience of Roriça and Vimiero, no reliance was

Mr. James
Moore's
Narrative.

Appendix,
No. II.
Section 12.

to be placed on their troops. This opinion, hastily given, had reference only to the *state of affairs existing at that moment*, being expressly founded, *on the miserable condition and unpromising character of the Portuguese military, Spain also being supposed conquered.*

Now lord Wellington, after two campaigns in the country; after the termination of the anarchy, which prevailed during sir John Cradock's time; after immense subsidies had been granted to Portugal, her whole military force reorganized, and her regular troops disciplined, paid, and officered by England; after the war in Germany had cost Napoleon fifty thousand men, the campaign in the Peninsula at least fifty thousand more; in fine, after mature consideration, and when Spain was still fighting; when Andalusia, Catalonia, Murcia, Valencia, Gallicia, and the Asturias, were still uninvaded; when Ciudad Rodrigo and Badajos, most important posts with reference to this question, were still in possession of the Spaniards, and prepared for defence; lord Wellington, I say, came to the conclusion, that Portugal might be defended against the enemy then in the Peninsula, provided *an enormous additional subsidy and a powerful auxiliary army were furnished by England, and that one earnest and devoted effort was made by the whole Portuguese nation.* And when Andalusia fell, he warned his government, that, *although success could only be expected from the devotion and ardour of the Portuguese, their army could not even then be implicitly trusted.* Lisbon also, he considered as the only secure point of resistance, and he occupied Viseu, Guarda, Almeida, Belmonte, and Celerico, as temporary posts.

Letter to lord Liverpool, Nov. 14, 1809.MSS.

Ibid. Jan. 31, 1810. MSS.

BOOK
XI.
1810.

But, in all things concerning this war, there was between those generals, a remarkable similarity of opinion and plan of action.

"*The French,*" said sir John Moore, "*will find the Spaniards troublesome subjects, but in the first*
Mr. James
Moore's
Narrative.
instance they will have little more than a march to subdue the country."

"*The defeat and dispersion of the Spanish armies will be,*" said lord Wellington, "*the probable consequence of any action in which either imprudence,*
Letter to
lord Liver-
pool, Jan.
31, 1810.
MSS.
necessity, or even expediency, may lead them to engage. The armies may be lost, the authorities dispersed, but the war of Partisans will probably continue."

And when the edge of the sword was, in 1810, as in 1808, descending on the unguarded front of Andalusia, lord Wellington, on the first indication of Joseph's march, designed to make a movement similar in principle to that executed by sir John
Appendix,
No. II.
Section 3.
Moore on a like occasion; that is, by an irruption into Castile, to threaten the enemy's rear, in such sort that he should be obliged to return from Andalusia or suffer his forces in Castile to be beaten. Nor was he at first deterred from this project, by the knowledge, that fresh troops were entering Spain. The Junta, indeed, assured him that only eight thousand men had reinforced the French; but, although circumstances led him to doubt this assertion, he was not without hopes to effect his purpose before the reinforcements, whatever they might be, could come into line. He had even matured his plan, as far as regarded the direction of the march, when other considerations obliged him to relinquish it, and these shall be here examined, because French and Spanish writers then,

and since, have accused him of looking on with indifference, if not with satisfaction, at the ruin of the Central Junta's operation, as if it only depended upon him to render them successful.

Why he refused to join in the Spanish projects has been already explained. He abandoned his own,—

1°. Because the five thousand men promised from England had not arrived, and his hospitals being full, he could not, including Hill's division, bring more than twenty thousand British soldiers into the field. Hill's division, however, could not be moved without leaving the rear of the army exposed to the French in the south,—a danger, which success in Castile, by recalling the latter from Andalusia, would only increase.

2°. The Portuguese had suffered cruelly during the winter from hunger and nakedness, the result of the scarcity of money before-mentioned. To bring them into line, was to risk a total disorganization, destructive alike of present and future advantages. On the other hand, the French in Castile, consisting of the sixth corps and the troops of Kellerman's government, lord Wellington knew to be at least thirty thousand strong, of which twenty thousand were in one mass; and, although the rest were dispersed from Burgos to Avila, from Zamora to Valladolid, they could easily have concentrated in time to give battle, and would have proved too powerful. That this reasoning was sound shall now be shewn.

Mortier's march from Seville would not have terminated at Badajos, if the British force at Abrantes, instead of advancing to Portalegre, had been employed in Castile. The invasion of Andalusia, was only part of a general movement through-

Lord Wellington's Correspondence. MSS.

out Spain; and when the king placed himself at the head of the army, to force the Morena, Kellerman marched from Salamanca to Miranda del Castanar and Bejar, with the sixth corps, and thus secured the defiles leading into the valley of the Tagus; at the same time, the second corps coming down that valley, communicated with the sixth by the pass of Banos, and with the fifth by Seradillo and Caceres. Hence, without losing hold of Andalusia, three *corps d'armée*, namely, the sixth, second, and fifth, amounting to fifty thousand men, could, on an emergency, be brought together to oppose any offensive movement of lord Wellington's. Nor was this the whole of the French combinations; in rear of all these forces, Napoleon was crowding the Peninsula with fresh armies, and not eight thousand, as the Central Junta

asserted, but one hundred thousand men, rendered disposable by the peace with Austria and the evacuation of Walcheren, were crossing, or to cross, the western Pyrennees.

Of these, the first detachments reinforced the divisions in the field, but the succeeding troops formed an eighth and ninth corps, and the former, under the command of the duke of Abrantes, advancing gradually through Old Castile, was actually in the plains of Valladolid, and would, in conjunction with Kellerman, have overwhelmed the British army, but for that sagacity, which the French, with derisive but natural anger, and the Spaniards, with ingratitude, have termed " *The selfish caution of the English system.*"

Truly, it would be a strange thing, to use so noble and costly a machine, as a British army, with all its national reputation to support, as lightly as those Spanish multitudes, collected in a day, dispersed in an hour, reassembled again without difficulty, and incapable of attaining, and consequently, incapable of losing, any military reputation.

CHAPTER II.

THE greatness of the French reinforcements having dispelled the idea of offensive operations, lord Wellington turned his whole attention to Portugal, and notwithstanding the unfavourable change of circumstances, the ministers consented that he should undertake its defence; yet, the majority yielded to the influence of his brother, rather than to their own conviction of its practicability, and threw the responsibility entirely on the shoulders of the general. The deep designs, the vast combinations, the mighty efforts, by which he worked out the deliverance of that country, were beyond the compass of their policy; and even now, it is easier to admire than to comprehend, the moral intrepidity which sustained him under so many difficulties, and the sagacity which enabled him to overcome them; for he had an enemy with a sharp sword to fight, the follies and fears of several weak cabinets to correct, the snares of unprincipled politicians to guard against, and finally to oppose public opinion. Failure was every where anticipated, and there were but few who even thought him serious in his undertaking.

But having now brought the story of the war down to that period, when England setting Portugal and Spain as it were aside undertook the contest with France, it will be well to take a survey of the respective conditions and plans of the belligerents; and to shew how great the preparations, how pro-

digious the forces on both sides, and with what a
power each was impelled forward to the shock.

State of the French.—France victorious, and in
a state of the highest prosperity, could with ease,
furnish the number of men, required to maintain the struggle in the Peninsula for many years.
The utmost strength of the Spaniards had been
proved, and it was evident that if the French could
crush the British armies, disorder and confusion
might indeed be prolonged for a few years, yet no
effectual resistance made, and as in the war of succession, the people would gradually have accommo-
dated themselves to the change of dynasty; especially as the little worth of Ferdinand was now fully
demonstrated, by an effort to effect his release.
For when baron Kolli, the agent employed on this
occasion, was detected, and his place supplied by
one of the French police, to ascertain the intentions
of the captive king, the latter, *influenced by personal fears alone*, not only refused to make the attempt, but dishonourably denounced Kolli to the
French government. The only real obstacles then
to the entire conquest of the Peninsula were Cadiz
and Portugal. The strength of the former was
precarious, and the enormous forces assembled to
subdue the latter appeared to be equal to the task.
Yet in war, there are always circumstances, which,
though extraneous to the military movements, influence them as much as the wind influences the
sailing of a ship, and amongst the most important
of these, must be reckoned the conduct of the intrusive king.

Joseph was a man of so amiable a nature, that
even the Spaniards never accused him of any thing
worse than being too convivial; but it is evident

BOOK
XI.

1810.

that he was unequal to his task and mistook his true situation, when, resisting Napoleon's policy, he claimed the treatment of an independent king. He should have known that he was a tool, and in Spain, could only be a tool of the emperor's. To have refused a crown, like his brother Lucien, would have been heroic firmness, but like his brother Louis, first to accept, and then to resist the hand that conferred it, was a folly that, without ameliorating the condition of the Spaniards, threw fatal obstacles in Napoleon's path. Joseph's object was to create a Spanish party for himself by gentle and just means, but the scales fell from the hands of justice when the French first entered the Peninsula, and while the English supported Spain, it was absurd to expect even a sullen submission, much less attachment, from a nation so abused; neither was it possible to recast public feeling, until the people had passed through the furnace of war. The French soldiers were in Spain for conquest, and without them the intrusive monarch could not keep his throne.

Now Joseph's Spanish ministers, were men who joined him upon principle, and who, far from shewing a renegado zeal in favour of the French, were as ardently attached to their own country, as any of those who shouted for Ferdinand VII.; and whenever Spanish interests clashed (and that was constantly) with those of the French armies, they as

Appendix,
No. IV.
Sec. 1.

well as the king invariably supported the former; and so strenuously, that in Paris it was even supposed that they intended to fall on the emperor's troops. Thus civil contention weakened the military operations, and obliged Napoleon either to take the command in person, or to adopt a policy which however defective, will perhaps be found to have been the best adapted to the actual state of affairs.

He suffered, or as some eager to lower a great man's genius to their own level, have asserted, he fomented disputes between the marshals and the king; but the true question is, could he prevent those disputes? A wise policy, does not consist in pushing any one point to the utmost perfection of which it may be susceptible, but in regulating and balancing opposing interests, in such a manner, that the greatest benefit shall arise from the working of the whole. To arrive at a sound judgement of Napoleon's measures, therefore, it would be necessary to weigh all the various interests of his political position, and there are not sufficient materials yet before the world, to do this correctly; yet we may be certain, that his situation with respect both to foreign and domestic policy, required extraordinary management. It must always be remembered, that, he was not merely a conqueror; he was also the founder, of a political structure too much exposed to storms from without, to bear any tampering with its internal supports. If money be the sinew of war, it is also the vital stream of peace, and there is nothing more remarkable in Napoleon's policy, than the care with which he handled financial matters, avoiding as he would the plague, that fictitious system of public credit, so fatuitously cherished in England. He could not without hurting France, transmit large quantities of gold to Spain, and the only resource left was to make " *the war maintain the war.*" Now Joseph's desire of popularity, and the feelings of his ministers, were opposed to this system; nor were the proceeds of the contributions always applied for the benefit of the troops. This demanded a remedy; yet openly to declare the king of no consideration would have been impolitic in the highest degree. The emperor adopted an intermediate course, and formed what were called " *particular military governments*," such as Navarre, Aragon, Catalonia, and Andalusia, in which the marshal, or general, named governor possessed both the civil and military power: in short, he created

See Vol. I.
p. 420.
viceroys as he had threatened to do when at Madrid, and, though many disadvantages attended this arrangement, it appears to have been wise and consistent with the long reach which distinguishes all Napoleon's measures.

The principal disadvantages were, that it mortally offended the king, by thwarting his plans for

Appendix,
No. IV.
Sections 2
and 3.
establishing a national party; that many of the governors were wantonly oppressive, and attentive only to their own situation, without regarding the general objects of the war; that both the Spanish ministers and the people regarded it as a step towards dismembering Spain, and especially with respect to the provinces beyond the Ebro; and, indeed, the annexing those parts to France, if not resolved upon, was at one time contemplated by the emperor. On the other hand, experience proved, that Joseph was not a general equal to the times.

Mémoires
de St. Hé-
lène.
Napoleon himself admits, that, at this period, the marauding system necessary to obtain supplies, joined to the Guerilla warfare, had relaxed the discipline of the French armies, and introduced a horrible license, while the military movements were feebly pushed. Hence, perhaps, the only effectual means to obtain the resources of Spain for the troops, with least devastation, was to make the

success of each "*corps d'armée*," and the reputation of its commander, dependent upon the wel-
fare of the province in which it was fighting.
And, although some of the governors, had neither
the sense nor the justice to fulfil this expectation,
others, such as Soult and Suchet, did tranquillize
the people, and yet provided all necessary things
for their own troops; results which would certainly
not have been attained under the supreme government of the king, because he knew little of war,
loved pleasure, was of an easy, obliging disposition,
and had a court to form and maintain.

I am aware that the first-named generals, especially Soult, were included by Joseph amongst
those who, by oppressing the people, extended the
spirit of resistance; but this accusation was the
result of personal enmity, and facts, derived from
less interested quarters, as well as the final results,
prove that those officers had a longer reach in their
policy than the king could understand.

There is yet another view in which the matter
may be considered. Napoleon says he left many
provinces of Italy under the harsh government
of Austria, that the spirit of jealousy, common to
the small states of that country, might be broken,
and the whole rendered amenable and ready to
assimilate, when he judged the time ripe to re-form
one great kingdom. Now the same policy may
be traced in the military governments of Spain.
The marshal's sway, however, wisely adapted to
circumstances, being still the offspring of war and
violence, was, of necessity, onerous and harsh;
but the Peninsula once subdued, this system would
have been replaced by the peaceful government
of the king, who would then have been regarded

as a deliverer. Something of this nature was also necessary to sweep away the peculiar privileges which many provinces possessed, and of which they were extremely tenacious; and the iron hand of war, only, could introduce that equality which was the principal aim and scope of the constitution of Bayonne.

Nevertheless, the first effects of the decree establishing this system, were injurious to the French cause. Fresh contributions were exacted to supply the deficiency occasioned by the cessation of succours from France; and, to avoid these, men, who would otherwise have submitted tranquilly, fled from the military governments. The Partidas also suddenly and greatly increased, and a fresh difficulty arose about their treatment when prisoners. These bodies, although regardless of the laws of war themselves, claimed all the rights of soldiers from their adversaries, and their claim was supported by the Spanish government. Thus, when Soult, as major-general for the king, proclaimed that military execution would be done on the bands in Andalusia, as assassins, and beyond the pale of military law, the Regency answered, by a retaliatory declaration; and both parties had strong grounds for what they did. The Junta, because the defence of the country now rested chiefly on the Partidas. Joseph, because the latter, while claiming the usages of war, did not act upon them, and were, by the Junta, encouraged in assassination. Mina, and, indeed, all the chiefs, put their prisoners to death whenever it became inconvenient to keep them; and Saraza publicly announced his hope of being able to capture Madame Suchet when she was pregnant, that he might destroy the mother and the infant together! And such things were common during this terrible war. The difficulties occurring in argument were, however, overcome in practice; the question of the treatment of the prisoners was generally decided by granting no quarter on either side.

Joseph, incensed at the edict establishing the governments, sent the marquis of Almenara to Paris, to remonstrate with his brother, and to complain of the violence and the injustice of the French generals, especially Ney and Kellerman; and he denounced one act of the latter, which betrayed the most wanton contempt of justice and propriety; namely, the seizure of the national archives at Simancas, by which infinite confusion was produced, and the utmost indignation excited, without obtaining the slightest benefit, political or military. Another object of Almenara's mission was to ascertain if there was really any intention of seizing the provinces beyond the Ebro; and this gave rise to a curious intrigue; for his correspondence, being intercepted, was brought to Mr. Stuart, the British envoy, and he, in concert with Romana, and Cabanes the Spanish historian, simulating the style and manner of Napoleon's state-papers, composed a counterfeit " *senatus consultum*" and decree for annexing the provinces beyond the Ebro to France, and transmitted them to Joseph, whose discontent and fears were thereby greatly increased. Meanwhile, his distress for money was extreme, that his ministers were at times actually destitute of food.

These political affairs impeded the action of the armies, but the intrinsic strength of the latter was truly formidable; for, reckoning the king's French guards, the force in the Peninsula was not less

CHAP. II.

1810.

Appendix, No. IV. Section 2.

Appendix, No. IV. Section 5.

BOOK
XI.

1810.

Appendix,
No. I.
Section 1.
than *three hundred and seventy thousand men, and eighty thousand horses*. Of these, forty-eight thousand men were in hospital, four thousand prisoners, and twenty-nine thousand detached; leaving nearly two hundred and eighty thousand fighting men actually under arms, ready either for battle or siege: and moreover, a fresh reserve, eighteen thousand strong, was in march to enter Spain. In May, this prodigious force had been re-organized; and in July was thus distributed :—

Governments or Armies in the 2d Line.

			Total Strength.
1. Catalonia	Seventh corps......	Duke of Tarento .	55,647
2. Aragon	Third corps........	Gen. Suchet	33,007
3. Navarre..........	Detachments and a division of the Imperial Guards....	Gen. Reille	21,887
4. Biscay	Detachments	Gen. Caffarelli ..	6,570
5. Old Castile, comprising Burgos, Aranda, and Soria	Divisions of the Imperial Guards and Cavalry	Gen. Dorsenne ..	10,303
6. Valladolid, &c....	Detachments	Gen. Kellerman..	6,474
7. Asturias..........	One division	Gen. Bonet......	9,898

Total for the governments....143,786

Armies in the 1st Line.

Army of the South, composed of the first, fourth, and fifth corps, under the command of Soult 72,769

Army of the Centre, composed of the Royal Guards, two divisions of infantry, and two of cavalry, under the personal command of the king 24,187

Army of Portugal, composed of a reserve of cavalry and the second, sixth, and eighth corps, under the command of Massena 86,896

The ninth corps, commanded by general Drouet, distributed, by divisions, along the great line of communication from Vittoria to Valladolid 23,815

A division under general Serras, employed as a moveable column to protect the rear of the army of Portugal 10,605

218,272

Thus the plan of invasion was determined in three distinct lines, namely, the third and seventh corps on the left; the army of the south in the centre;

the army of Portugal on the right. But the interior circle was still held by the French, and their lines of communication were crowded with troops.

State of Spain.—On the right, the armies of Valencia and Catalonia, were opposed to the third and seventh corps; and their utmost efforts could only retard, not prevent the sieges of Taragona and Tortoza. In the centre, the Murcian troops and those assembled at Cadiz, were only formidable by the assistance of the British force under general Graham. On the left, Romana, supported by the frontier fortresses, maintained a partizan warfare from Albuquerque to Ayamonte, but looked to Hill for safety, and to Portugal for refuge. In the north, the united forces of Gallicia and Asturia, did not exceed fifteen thousand men; and Mahi declared his intention of retiring to Coruña if Bonet advanced beyond the frontiers. Indeed, the Gallicians were so backward to join the armies, that, at a later period, Contreras was used to send through the country moveable columns, attended by an executioner, to oblige the villages to furnish their quota of men. Yet, with all this severity, and with money and arms continually furnished by England, Gallicia never was of any signal service to the British operations.

Memoirs
of Contre-
ras, pub-
lished by
himself.

But, as in the human body livid spots and blotches appear as the vital strength decays, so, in Spain, the Partidas suddenly and surprisingly increased as the regular armies disappeared. Many persons joined these bands, as a refuge from starvation; others from a desire to revenge the licentious conduct of the marauding French columns; and, finally, the Regency, desirous of pushing the system to its utmost extent, established secret Guerilla Juntas, in each province, enjoining them, diligently to collect stores and provisions in secure places. District inspectors and paymasters, selected by the nearest general officer in command of regular troops, were also appointed, as superintendents of details relative to the discipline and payment of the Partidas, and particular tracts were charged with the supplies, each according to its means. Lastly, every province was divided into three parts, each part, following its population, being to furnish seven, eight, or nine squadrons of this irregular force ; and the whole, whenever circumstances required it, to unite and act in mass.

The first burst of these bands, occasioned the French considerable loss, impeded their communications, and created great alarm. It was a second insurrection of the whole country. The Murcians, in concert with the peasants of Grenada and Jaen, waged war in the mountains of Andalusia. Franquisetto and Palarea beset the neighbourhood of Ciudad Real and Toledo in La Mancha. El Principe, Saornil, Temprano, and Juan Abril, keeping the circuit of the Carpentino mountains, from the Somosierra to Avila, and descending sometimes on the side of New, sometimes on the side of Old Castile, sometimes in Estremadura, carried off small French posts even close to the capital, and slew the governor of Segovia at the very gates of that town. On the other side of Madrid, Duran with two thousand men, and the Empecinado, with twelve hundred cavalry and infantry, kept the hills above Guadalaxara, as far as Cuenca, and ventured sometimes to give battle in the plain. Espoz y Mina was formidable in Navarre. Longa

and Campillo, at the head of more than two thousand men, harassed Biscay and the neighbourhood
of Vittoria, and the chain of communication, between these great bands and the Empecinado, was
maintained by Amor, Merino, and the Friar Sapia;
the two first acting about Burgos, and the third
holding the mountains above Soria. In the Asturias, Escaidron, continually hanging upon the
flanks and rear of Bonet, between St. Andero and
Oviedo, acted in concert with Campillo on one
side, and with Porlier on the other, and this last
chief, sometimes throwing himself into the mountains on the borders of Gallicia, and sometimes
sailing from Coruña, constantly troubled the Asturias by his enterprises. To curb these bands, the
French fortified all their own posts of communication and correspondence, and slew numbers of the
Guerillas, many of whom were robbers that, under
pretence of acting against the enemy, merely harassed their own countrymen; few were really
formidable, though all were vexatious. Enough
has been said upon this point.

But, while reduced to this irregular warfare, for
preventing the entire submission of Old Spain, the
Regency, with inconceivable folly and injustice,
were alienating the affections of their colonies, and
provoking civil war, as if the terrible struggle in
the Peninsula were not sufficient for the ruin of
their country. The independence of Spain was,
with them, of subordinate interest to the continuance of oppression in South America. Money,
arms, and troops, were withdrawn from the Peninsula, to subdue the so-called rebellious colonists;
nor was any reflection made on the inconsistency,
of expecting Napoleon's innumerable hosts to be

beaten close to their own doors, by Guerilla operations, and yet attempting, with a few divisions,
to crush whole nations, acting in the same manner,
at three thousand miles distance. Such being the
state of French and Spanish affairs, it remains to
examine the condition of England and Portugal, as
affecting the war in the Peninsula.

England.—The contentions of party were vehement, and the ministers' policy resolved itself into
three principal points: 1°. The fostering the public
inclination for the war ; 2°. The furnishing money for the expenses ; 3°. The recruiting of the
armies. The last was provided for by an act passed
in the early part of 1809, which offered eleven
guineas bounty to men passing from the militia to
the line, and ten guineas bounty to recruits for the
militia ; this was found to furnish about twenty-
four thousand men in the year ; but the other
points were not so easily disposed of. The opposition, in parliament, was powerful, eloquent, and
not very scrupulous. The desperate shifts which
formed the system of the ministers, were, indeed,
justly attacked, but when particulars, touching the
contest in Portugal, were discussed, faction was
apparent. The accuracy of Beresford's report of
the numbers and efficiency of the native forces, was
most unjustly questioned, and the notion of successful resistance assailed by arguments and by
ridicule, until gloom and doubt were widely spread
in England, and disaffection wonderfully encouraged
in Portugal ; nor was the mischief thus caused, one
of the smallest difficulties encountered by the
English general.

On the other side, the ministers, trusting to their
majorities in parliament, reasoned feebly and igno-

rantly, yet wilfully, and like men expecting that
fortune would befriend them, they knew not why or
wherefore; and they dealt also more largely than
their adversaries in misrepresentations to mislead the
public mind. Every treasury newspaper teemed
with accounts of battles which were never fought,
plans which were never arranged, places taken
which were never attacked, and victories gained
where no armies were. The plains of the Peninsula
could scarcely contain the innumerable forces of
the Spaniards and Portuguese; cowardice, weakness, treachery, and violence were the only attri-
butes of the enemy; if a battle was expected, his
numbers were contemptible, if a victory was gained,
his host was countless. Members of parliament
related stories of the enemy which had no foundation in truth, and nothing, that consummate art of
intrigue could bring to aid party spirit, and to stifle
reason, was neglected.

But the great and permanent difficulty was to
raise money. The country, inundated with bank-
notes, was destitute of gold. Napoleon's continental
system burthened commerce, the exchanges were
continually rising against England; and all the evils
which sooner or later are the inevitable result of a
factitious currency, were too perceptible to be longer
disregarded in parliament. A committee appointed
to investigate the matter, made early in the session
of 1810, a report in which the evils of the existing
system, and the causes of the depreciation were
elaborately treated, and the necessity of returning
to cash payments enforced : but the authors did not
perceive, or at least did not touch upon the injustice,
and the ruin, attending a full payment in coin of
sterling value, of debts contracted in a depreciated

BOOK
XI.

1810.
Paper
against
Gold.

paper currency. The celebrated writer, William Cobbett, did not fail, however, to point out this very clearly, and subsequent experience has confirmed his views. The government at first endeavoured to stave off the bullion question; but finding that they must either abandon the prosecution of the war in the Peninsula, or deny the facts adduced by the committee, adopted the latter. On the motion of Mr. Vansittart, the house voted in substance that a pound note and a shilling were equal in value to a golden guinea of full weight, although light guineas were then openly sold at twenty-eight shillings each. Lord King, by demanding gold from those of his tenants, whose leases were drawn before the depreciation of bank-notes, exposed all the fraud and the hollowness of the minister's system; and the vote of the Commons, although well calculated to convince the minister's opponents, that no proposition could be too base, or absurd, to meet with support in the existing parliament, did not remove the difficulties of raising money; hence no resource remained, but that of the desperate spendthrift, who never intending to pay, cares not on what terms he supplies his present necessities. The peculiar circumstances of the war, had, however, given England a monopoly of the world's commerce by sea, and the ministers affirming, that the country was in a state of unexampled prosperity, began a career of expense, the like of which no age or nation had ever seen; yet without one sound or reasonable ground for expecting ultimate success, save the genius of their general, which they but half appreciated, and which the first bullet might have extinguished for ever.

State of Portugal.—In this country, three parties

were apparent. That of the *people* ready to peril
body and goods for independence. That of the
fidalgos, who thought to profit from the nation's
energy without any diminution of ancient abuses.
That of the *disaffected*, who desired the success of
the French; some as thinking that an ameliorated
government must follow, some from mere baseness
of nature. This party, looked to have Alorna, Pamplona, and Gomez Freire, as chiefs if the enemy
triumphed. Those noblemen, in common with many
others, had entered the French service in Junot's
time, under the authority of the prince regent's
edict to that effect; Freire more honourable than
his companions, refused to bear arms against his
country; the two others had no scruples, and Pamplona even sketched a plan of invasion, which is at
this day in the military archives at Paris.

The great body of the people, despising both
their civil governors and military chiefs, relied on
the British general and army; but the fidalgos, or
cast of nobles, working in unison with, and supported by the regency, were a powerful body, and
their political proceedings after the departure of
sir John Cradock, demand notice. The patriarch,
formerly bishop of Oporto, the marquis de Olhào
Monteiro Mor, and the marquess of Das Minas, these
composed the regency, and they and every other
member of the government were jealous of each
other, exceedingly afraid of their superiors in the
Brazils, and, with the exception of the secretary,
Miguel Forjas, unanimous in support of abuses.
As the military organization carried on by Beresford, was only a restoration of the ancient institutions of the country, it was necessarily hateful
to the regency, and to the fidalgos, who profited

by its degeneracy. The opposition of these people joined to unavoidable difficulties in finance, and other matters, retarded the progress of the regular army towards efficiency during 1809, and rendered the efforts to organize the militia, and ordenança, nearly nugatory. Nevertheless, the energy of lord Wellington and of Beresford, and the comparatively zealous proceedings of Forjas, proved so disagreeable to Das Minas, who was in bad health, that he resigned, and immediately became a centre, round which all discontented persons, and they were neither few nor inactive, gathered. As the times, obliged the government, to permit an unusual freedom of discussion in Lisbon, it naturally followed that the opinions of designing persons were most obtruded, and those opinions being repeated in the British parliament, were printed in the English newspapers, and re-echoed in Lisbon. Thus a picture of affairs was painted in the most glaring colours of misrepresentation, at the moment when the safety of the country depended upon the devoted submission of the people.

After Das Minas' resignation, Mr. Stuart and three Portuguese, namely, Antonio, called Principal Souza, the Conde de Redondo, and doctor Noguiera, were added to the regency by an intrigue which shall be hereafter noticed. The last was a man of honesty, talent, and discretion, but Souza daring, restless, irritable, indefatigable, and a consummate intriguer, created the utmost disorder. Seeking constantly to thwart the proceedings of the British generals, he was strenuously assisted by the patriarch, whose violence and ambition were no way diminished, and whose influence amongst the people was still very considerable. An exceedingly powerful cabal, was thus formed, whose object was to obtain the supreme direction of the civil and military affairs, and to control both Wellington and Beresford. The Conde Linhares, head of the Souza family, was prime minister in the Brazils; the Principal was in the regency at Lisbon; the chevalier Souza was envoy at the British court, and a fourth of the family, don Pedro de Souza, was in a like situation near the Spanish regency; playing into each others' hands, and guided by the subtle Principal, they concocted very dangerous intrigues, and their proceedings, as might be expected, were at first supported with a high hand by the cabinet of Rio Janeiro. Lord Wellesley's energetic interference reduced the latter, indeed, to a reasonable disposition, yet the cabal secretly continued their machinations, and what they durst not attempt by force, they sought to attain by artifice.

In the latter end of the year 1809, Mr. Villiers had, fortunately for the cause, been replaced as envoy, by Mr. Charles Stuart, and this gentleman, well experienced in the affairs of the Peninsula, and disdaining the petty jealousies which had hitherto marked the intercourse of the principal political agents with the generals, immediately applied his masculine understanding, and resolute temper, to forward the views of lord Wellington. It is undoubted, that the dangerous political crisis which followed his arrival, could not have been sustained, if a diplomatist less firm, less able, or less willing to support the plans of the commander had been employed.

To resist the French was the desire of two of the three parties in Portugal, but with the fidalgos, it was a question of interest more than of patriotism.

Yet less sagacious than the clergy, the great body
of which, perceiving at once that they must stand
or fall with the English army heartily aided the
cause, the fidalgos clung rather to the regency.
Now the caballers in that body, who were the same
people that had opposed sir Hew Dalrymple, hoped
not only to beat the enemy, but to establish the
supremacy of the northern provinces (of which
they themselves were the lords) in the administration of the country, and would therefore consent
to no operations militating against this design.
Moreover the natural indolence of the people being
fostered by the negligence and fears of the regency
rendered it most difficult to obtain the execution of
any works or the fulfilment of any agreement in
which the Portuguese government or the civil
authorities were concerned.

Another spring of political action, was the hatred
and jealousy of Spain common to the whole Portuguese nation. It created difficulties during the
military operations, but it had a visibly advantageous effect upon the people, in their intercourse
with the British. For when the Spaniards shewed
a distrust of their allies, the Portuguese were more
minded to rely implicitly on the latter, to prove
that they had no feeling in common with their
neighbours. Yet, notwithstanding this mutual dislike, the princess Carlotta, wife to the Prince Regent,
and sister to Ferdinand, claimed, not only the succession to the throne of Spain in the event of her
brother's death or perpetual captivity, but the immediate government of the whole Peninsula as
hereditary Regent; and to persuade the Spanish
tribunals to acknowledge her claims, was the object
of Pedro Souza's mission to Cadiz.

Although the council of Castile, always ready to overthrow the Spanish Regency, readily recognized Carlotta's pretensions in virtue of the decision of the secret Cortes of 1789 which abolished the Salique law of Philip the Fifth, the regents would pay no attention to them; yet Souza, renewing his intrigues when the Cortes assembled, by corruption obtained from the majority of the members a secret acknowledgement of the princess's claim. His further progress was, however, promptly arrested by lord Wellington, who foresaw that his success would affect, not only the military operations in Portugal, by placing them under the control of the Spanish government, but the policy of England afterwards, if power over the whole Peninsula was suffered thus to centre in one family. Moreover, although at first he thought it might prove beneficial in the event of the Peninsula being conquered, he soon judged it a scheme, concocted at Rio Janeiro, to embarrass himself and Beresford; for it was at first kept secret from the British Cabinet, and it was proposed that the princess should reside at Madeira, where, surrounded by the contrivers of this plan, she could only have acted under their directions. Thus it is plain that arrogance, deceit, negligence in business, and personal intrigues, were common to the Portuguese and Spanish governments; and why they did not produce the same fatal effects in the one as in the other country, will be shewn in the succeeding chapters.

CHAPTER III.

BOOK
XI.
_____
1810.

WHEN lord Wellington required thirty thousand British troops to defend Portugal, he considered the number that could be fed and managed with such an inexperienced staff and civil administration as that of the English army, rather than what was necessary to fight the enemy; and hence it was, that he declared success would depend upon the exertions and devotion of the native forces. Yet knowing, from his experience in Spain, how passions, prejudices, and abuses would meet him at every turn, he would trust neither the simple enthusiasm of the people, nor the free promises of their governors, and insisted that his own authority as *marshal-general of Portugal* should be independent of the local government, and absolute over all arrangements concerning the English and Portuguese forces, whether regulars, militia, or " ordenanças ;" for his designs were vast, and such as could only be effected by extraordinary means.

Appendix
No.V. Sec-
tion 9.

Armed with this power, and with the influence derived from the money supplied by England, he first called upon the Regency, to revive and enforce the ancient military laws of the realm, by which all men were to be enrolled, and bear arms. That effected, he demanded that the people should be warned and commanded to destroy their mills, to remove their boats, break down their bridges, lay waste their fields, abandon their dwellings, and carry off their property, on whatever line the

invaders should penetrate: and that this might be
deliberately and effectually performed, he designed
at the head of all the allied regular forces, to front
the enemy, in such sort, that, without bringing on
a decisive battle, the latter should yet be obliged
to keep constantly in a mass; while the whole population, converted into soldiers, and closing on
the rear and flanks, should cut off all resources,
save those carried in the midst of the troops.

But it was evident, that if the French could find,
or carry, supplies, sufficient to maintain themselves
until the British commander, forced back upon the
sea, should embark, or giving battle be defeated,
the whole of this system must necessarily fall to
pieces, and the miserable ruined people submit
without further struggle. To avoid such a cala-
mitous termination, it was necessary to find a position, covering Lisbon, where the allied forces could
neither be turned by the flanks, nor forced in front
by numbers, nor reduced by famine, and from
which a free communication could be kept up with
the irregular troops closing round the enemy.
The mountains filling the tongue of land upon
which Lisbon is situated, furnished this key-stone
to the arch of defence. Accurate plans of all the
positions, had been made under the directions of
sir Charles Stuart in 1799, and, together with the
French colonel Vincent's minutes, shewing how
they covered Lisbon, were in lord Wellington's
possession. From those documents the original
notion of the celebrated lines of Torres Vedras are
said to have been derived; but the above-named
officers only contemplated such a defence as might
be made by an army in movement, before an equal
or a greater force. It was lord Wellington, who first

conceived the design, of turning those vast mountains into one stupendous and impregnable citadel,
wherein to deposit the independence of the whole
Peninsula.

Hereafter the lines shall be described more mi-
nutely ; at present it must suffice to observe, that
intrenchments, inundations, and redoubts secured
more than five hundred square miles of mountainous country lying between the Tagus and the
ocean.　Nor was this the most gigantic part of the
English general's undertaking.　He was a foreigner,
ill supported by his own government, and holding
power under that of Portugal by a precarious
tenure, and he was vehemently opposed by the local
authorities, by the ministers, and by the nobility
of that country ; yet, in this apparently weak
position, he undertook at one and the same time, to
overcome the abuses engendered by centuries of
misgovernment, and to oblige a whole people, sunk
in sloth, to arise in arms, to devastate their own
lands, and to follow him to battle against the most
formidable power of modern times.

Notwithstanding the secret opposition of the
Regency, and of the *fidalgos*, the ancient military
laws were revived, and so effectually, that the returns for the month of May gave a gross number
of more than four hundred and thirty thousand
men in arms, of which about fifty thousand were
regular troops, fifty-five thousand militia, and the
remainder " ordenanças ;" but this multitude was
necessarily subject to many deductions.　The
" *capitans mor*," or chiefs of districts, were at first
exceedingly remiss in their duty, the fidalgos evaded
service by the connivance of the government, and the
total number of " ordenanças" really assembled, fell

far short of the returns, and all were ill-armed. This also was the case with the militia, only thirty-two thousand of which had muskets and bayonets; and deserters were so numerous, and the native authorities connived at absence under false pretences, to such an extent, that scarcely twenty-six thousand men ever remained with their colours. Of the regular troops the whole were in good condition; thirty thousand being in the pay of England, were completely equipped, clothed, disciplined, and for the most part commanded by British officers; but, deduction being made for sick men and recruits, the actual number under arms did not exceed twenty-four thousand infantry, three thousand five hundred cavalry, and three thousand artillery. Thus the disposable native force was about fifty-six thousand men, one-half of which were militia.

At this period, the British troops employed in the Peninsula, exclusive of the garrison of Gibraltar, somewhat exceeded thirty-eight thousand men of all arms, of which six thousand were in hospital or detached, and above seven thousand were in Cadiz. The latter city was protected by an allied force of nearly thirty thousand men, while the army, on whose exertions the fate of the Peninsula rested, was reduced to twenty-five thousand British, such was the policy of the English cabinet; for this was the ministers' and not the general's arrangement. The ordenanças being set aside, the actual force at the disposition of lord Wellington, cannot be estimated higher than eighty thousand men, and the frontier to defend, reckoning from Braganza to Ayamonte, four hundred miles long. The great military features, and the arrangements made to take advantage of them in conformity with the general plan of defence, shall now be described.

The Portuguese land frontier presents four great divisions open to invasion:—

1°. The northern line of the Entre Minho and the Tras os Montes, extending from the mouth of the Minho, to Miranda on the Douro.

2°. The eastern line of the Tras os Montes following the course of the Douro from Miranda to Castel Rodrigo.

3°. The frontier of Beira from Castel Rodrigo to Rosaminhal on the Tagus.

4°. The Alemtejo and the Algarve frontiers, stretching, in one line from the Tagus to the mouth of the Guadiana.

But these divisions may be simplified with respect to the military aspect of the country; for Lisbon taken as the centre, and the distance from thence to Oporto as the radius, a sweep of the compass to Rosaminhal will trace the frontier of Beira; and the space lying between this arc, the Tagus, and the sea-coast, furnished the main body of the defence. The southern and northern provinces being considered as the wings, were rendered subservient to the defence of the whole; but each had a separate system for itself, based on the one general principle, that the country should be wasted, and the best troops opposed to the enemy without risking a decisive action, while the irregular forces closed round the flanks and rear of the invaders.

The northern and southern provinces have been already described, Beira remains to be noticed. Separated by the Douro from the Entre Minho and Tras os Montes, it cannot well be invaded on that line, except one or both of those provinces be first subdued; but from Castel Rodrigo to Rosaminhal, that is from the Douro to the Tagus, the frontier touches upon Spain, and perhaps the clearest method to describe the conformation of the country will be to enter the camp of the enemy.

An invading army then, would assemble at Ciudad Rodrigo, or at Coria, or at both those places. In the latter case, the communications could be maintained, directly over the Gata mountains by the pass of Perales, or circuitously, by Placentia and the pass of Baños; and the distance being by Perales not more than two marches, the corps could either advance simultaneously, or unite and force their way at one point only. In this situation, the frontier of Beira between the Douro and the Tagus, would offer them an opening of ninety miles against which to operate. But in the centre, the Sierra de Estrella, lifting its snowy peaks to the clouds and stretching out its gigantic arms, would seem to grasp and claim the whole space; the summit is impassable, and streaming down on either hand, numerous rivers cleaving deeply, amidst ravines and bristled ridges, continually oppose the progress of an army. Nevertheless, the invaders could penetrate to the right and left of this mountain in the following directions :—

From Ciudad Rodrigo.—1°. By the valley of the Douro.—2°. By the valley of the Mondego.—3°. By the valley of the Zezere.

From Coria.—1°. By Castello Branco and the valley of the Tagus; and, 2°. By the mountains of Sobreira Formosa.

To advance by the valley of the Douro, would

be a flank movement through an extremely difficult
country, and would belong rather to an invasion
of the northern provinces than of Beira, because
a fresh base must be established at Lamego or
Oporto, before the movement could be prosecuted
against Lisbon.

To gain the valley of the Mondego there are
three routes. The first passing by Almeida and
Celerico, the second by Trancoso and Viseu, the
third by Alfayates and Guarda over the high
ridges of the Estrella. To gain the valley of the
Zezere, the march is by Alfayates, Sabugal, and
Belmonte, and whether to the Zezere or the Mondego, these routes, although rugged, are practicable
for artillery; but between Guarda and Belmonte
some high table-land offers a position where a large
army (for a small one it is dangerous) could seal the
passage on either side of the mountain, except by
the Trancoso road. In fact, the position of Guarda
may be called the breast-plate of the Estrella.

On the side of Coria, an invading army must first
force or turn the passages of the Elga and Ponçul
rivers, to reach Castello Branco, and that done,
proceed to Abrantes by the valley of the Tagus
or over the savage mountain of Sobreira Formosa.
But the latter is impracticable for heavy artillery,
even in summer, the ways broken and tormented
by the deep channels of the winter torrents, the
country desert, and the positions if defended,
nearly impregnable. Nor is the valley of the
Tagus to be followed, save by light corps, for the
villages are few, the ridges not less steep than
those of Sobreira, and the road quite impracticable
for artillery of any calibre.

Such, and so difficult, being the lines of invasion through Beira, it would seem that a superior enemy might be met with advantage on the threshold of the kingdom ; but it is not so. For, first, the defending army must occupy all the positions on this line of ninety miles, while the enemy, posted at Ciudad Rodrigo and Coria, could, in two marches, unite and attack on the centre, or at either extremity, with an overwhelming force. Secondly, the weakness of the Beira frontier consists in this, *the Tagus along its whole course is, from June to December, fordable as low down as Salvatierra, close under the lines.* A march through the Alemtejo and the passage of the river at any place below Abrantes would, therefore, render all the frontier positions useless ; and although there were no enemy on the borders of the Alemtejo itself, the march from Ciudad Rodrigo by Perales, Coria, and Alcantara, and thence by the southern bank to the lowest ford in the river, would be little longer than the route by the valley of the Mondego or that of the Zezere. For these reasons *the frontier of Portugal must be always yielded to superior numbers.*

Both the conformation of the country, and the actual situation of the French corps, led lord Wellington to expect, that the principal attacks would be by the north of Beira and by the Alemtejo, while an intermedeate connecting corps would move by Castello Branco upon Abrantes, and, under this impression, he made the following dispositions. Elvas, Almeida, and Valença, in the first, and Peniche, Abrantes, and Setuval, in the second line of fortresses, were garrisoned with native troops, part regulars, part militia.

General Baccellar, having Silviera and the

British colonels, Trant, Miller, and J. Wilson, under his orders, occupied the provinces beyond the Douro, with twenty-one regiments of militia, including the garrison of Valença, on the Minho.

The country between Penamacor and the Tagus, that is to say, the lines of the Elga and the Ponçul, was guarded by ten regiments of militia, a regiment of native cavalry, and the Lusitanian legion. In the Alemtejo, including the garrisons, four regiments of militia were stationed, and three regiments held the fortresses of the Algarves. There remained in reserve, twelve regiments of the fifty composing the whole militia force, and these were distributed in Estremadura on both sides of the Tagus, but principally about Setuval. The regular Portuguese troops, deducting those in garrison at Almeida Elvas and Cadiz, were at Thomar and Abrantes.

The British, organized in five divisions of infantry and one of calalry, were distributed as follows :—

		Men.	
1st Division	General Spencer, about	6000	Viseu.
2d Division, including the 13th Dragoons .	General Hill,·· ,,	5000	Abrantes & Portalegre.
3d Division	General Picton, ,,	3000	Celerico.
4th Division	General Cole,·· ,,	4000	Guarda.
Light Division	Robert Crawfurd, ,,	2400	Pinhel.
The Cavalry	General Cotton, ,,	3000	Valley of Mondego.

Total······23,400 under arms.

Thus the wings of the defence were composed solely of militia and ordenança, and the whole of the regular force was in the centre. The Portuguese at Thomar, and the four British divisions of infantry posted at Viseu, Guarda, Pinhel, and Celerico, formed a body of thirty-eight thousand men, the greater part of which could, in two marches, be united either at Guarda or between that position and the Douro. On the other side Beresford and Hill could, in as short a period, unite by the boat-bridge of Abrantes, and thus thirty-two thousand men would be concentrated on that line. If the enemy should attempt the passage of the Elga either direct from Coria, or by a flank movement of the second corps from Estremadura, across the Tagus, Beresford could succour the militia by moving over the Sobreira Formosa to Castello Branco, while Hill could reach that place much quicker than general Reynier, in consequence of an arrangement which merits particular attention.

It has been already said that the march from Abrantes to Castello Branco is over difficult mountains, and to have repaired the roads between these places would have been more useful to the enemy than to the allies, as facilitating a passage for superior numbers to penetrate by the shortest line to Lisbon. But lord Wellington, after throwing boat-bridges over the Tagus and the Zezere, and fortifying Abrantes, established between the latter and Castello Branco a line of communication by the left bank of the Tagus, through Niza, to the pass of Vilha Velha, where, by a flying bridge, the river was re-crossed, and from thence a good road led to Castello Branco. Now the pass of Vilha Velha is prodigiously strong for defence, and the distance from Abrantes to Castello Branco being nearly the same by Niza as by the other bank of the river, the march of troops was yet much accelerated, for the road near Vilha Velha being reconstructed by the engineers, was excellent.

Thus all the obstacles to an enemy's march by the north bank were preserved. The line by Vilha Velha, enabled Hill to pass from Portalegre, or Abrantes, to Castello Branco by a flank movement in less time than Reynier; and also provided a lateral communication for the whole army, which we shall hereafter find of vital importance in the combinations of the English general; supplying the loss of the road by Alcantara and the pass of Perales, which otherwise would have been adopted. The French, also, in default of a direct line of communication between Estremadura and the Ciudad Rodrigo country, were finally forced to adopt the circuitous road of Almaraz and the pass of Baños, and it was in allusion to this inconvenience that I said both parties sighed over the ruins of Alcantara.

Notwithstanding this facility of movement and of concentration, the allies could not deliver a decisive battle near the frontier, because the enemy could unite an overwhelming force in the Alemtejo, before the troops from the north could reach that province, and a battle lost there, would, in the dry season, decide the fate of Lisbon. To have concentrated the whole army in the south, would have been to resign half the kingdom and all its resources to the enemy; but to save those resources for himself, or to destroy them, was the very basis of lord Wellington's defence, and all his dispositions were made to oblige *the French to move in masses*, and to *gain time himself;* time to secure the harvests, time to complete his lines, time to perfect the discipline of the native troops, and to give full effect to the arming and organization of the ordenança; above all things, time to consolidate that moral ascendancy over the public mind which he was daily acquiring. A closer examination of his combinations will shew, that they were well adapted to effect these objects.

1°. The enemy dared not advance, except with *concentrated masses*, because, on the weakest line of resistance, he was sure to encounter above twenty thousand men.

2°. If, choosing the Alemtejo, he suddenly dispersed Romana's troops and even forced back Hill's, the latter passing the Tagus at Abrantes, and uniting with Beresford, could dispute the passage of the Tagus until the arrival of the army from the north; and no regular and sustained attempt could be made on that side without first besieging Badajos or Elvas to form a place of arms.

3°. A principal attack on the central line could not be made without sufficient notice being given by the collection of magazines at Coria, and by the passage of the Elga and Ponçul, Beresford and Hill could then occupy the Sobreira Formosa. But an invasion on this line, save by a light corps in connexion with other attacks, was not to be expected; for, although the enemy should force the Sobreira and reach Abrantes, he could not besiege the latter, in default of heavy artillery. The Zezere, a large and exceedingly rapid river, with rugged banks, would be in his front, the Tagus on his left, the mountains of Sobreira in his rear, and the troops from Guarda and the valley of the Mondego would have time to fall back.

4°. An attack on Guarda could always be resisted long enough to gain time for the orderly retreat of the troops near Almeida, to the valley of the Mondego, the road from Belmonte towards

Thomar by the valley of the Zezere was purposely broken and obstructed, and that from Thomar by Espinal to the Ponte de Murcella was repaired and widened; thus the inner and shorter line was rendered easy for the allies, while the outward and longer line was rendered difficult for the enemy, and to secure quick reports telegraphs were established from Lisbon to Elvas, to Abrantes and to Almeida.

The space between Guarda and the Douro, an opening of about thirty miles leading into the valley of the Mondego, remains to be examined. Across this line of invasion, the Agueda, the Coa, and the Pinel, run, in almost parallel directions from the Sierra de Francia and Sierra de Estrella, into the Douro, all having this peculiarity, that as they approach the Douro their channels invariably deepen into profound and gloomy chasms; and there are few bridges. But the principal obstacles were the fortresses of Ciudad Rodrigo and Almeida, both of which it was necessary to take before an invading army could establish a solid base of invasion. After this the lines of the Douro and of the Mondego would be open. If the French adopted the second, they could reach it by Guarda, by Alverca, and by Trancoso, concentrating at Celerico, where they would have to choose between the right and the left bank. In the latter case, they must march between the Mondego and the Estrella mountains, until they reached the Alva, a river falling at right angles into the Mondego, behind which they would find the allied army in a position of surprising strength. If, to avoid that, they marched by the right of the Mondego upon Coimbra, there were other obstacles to be hereafter noticed; but, in either case, the allied forces,

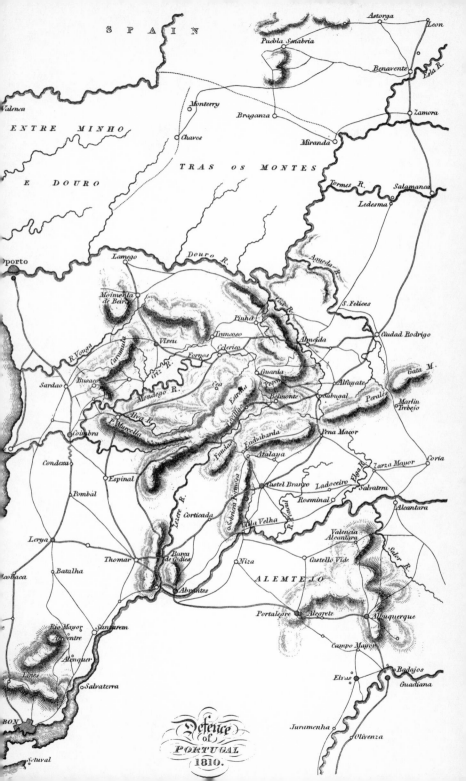

Defence of
PORTUGAL
1810.

having *interior lines of communication*, could, as
long as the Belmonte road was sealed, concentrate
in time behind the Alva, or in front of Coimbra.
Hence it was on the side of the Alemtejo that
danger was most to be apprehended, and it behoved general Hill to watch vigilantly and act
decisively in opposition to general Reynier. For the
latter having necessarily the lead in the movements, might, by skilful evolutions and rapid
marches, either join the sixth and eighth corps
before Hill was aware of his design, and thus overwhelm the allied divisions on the Mondego; or
drawing him across the Tagus, furnish an opportunity for a corps from Andalusia to penetrate by
the southern bank of that river.

In these dispositions the English general had
regard only to the enemy's actual situation, and
expecting the invasion to be in summer, but in the
winter season the rivers and torrents being full,
and the roads deteriorated, the defence would have
been different; fewer troops would then suffice to
guard the Tagus, and the Zezere, the Sobreira
Formosa would be nearly impassable, a greater
number of the allied troops, could be collected
about Guarda, and a more stubborn resistance made
on the northern line.

Every probable movement being thus previously
well considered, lord Wellington trusted that his
own military quickness, and the valour of the
British soldiers, could baffle any unforeseen strokes
during the retreat, and once within the Lines, (the
Portuguese people and the government doing their
part) he looked confidently to the final result. He
judged that, in a wasted country, and with thirty
regiments of militia, in the mountains on the flank

BOOK
XI.

1810.
and rear of the enemy, the latter could not long
remain before the Lines, and his retreat would be
equivalent to a victory for the allies. There were
however many hazards. The English commander,
sanguine and confident as he was, knew well how
many counter-combinations were to be expected;
in fine, how much fortune was to be dreaded in a
contest with eighty thousand French veterans
having a competent general at their head. Hence,
to secure embarkation in the event of disaster, a
third line of entrenchments was prepared, and
twenty-four thousand tons of shipping were constantly kept in the river to receive the British
forces; measures were also taken to procure a like
quantity for the reception of the Portuguese troops,
and such of the citizens as might wish to emigrate.
It only remained to feed the army.

Lord Wel-
lington's
Correspon-
dence.
MSS.

In the Peninsula generally, the supplies were
at all times a source of infinite trouble on both
sides, and this, not as some have supposed, because
Spain is incapable of supplying large armies; there
was throughout the war an abundance of food in
that country, but it was unevenly distributed, difficult to get at, and the people are of a nature to
render it impossible to depend upon contracts even
where they are friendly; some places were exhausted,
others overflowing, the difficulty was to transport
provisions, and in this the allies enjoyed a great
advantage; their convoys could pass unmolested,
whereas the French always required strong guards
first to collect food and then to bring it up to their
armies. In Portugal there was however a real
deficiency, even for the consumption of the people;
after a time scarcely any food for man or beast,
(some cattle and straw from the northern pro-

vinces excepted,) was to be obtained in that country : nay, the whole nation was at last in a manner fed by England. Every part of the world accessible to ships and money was rendered subservient to the cravings of this insatiable war, and yet it was often a doubtful and a painful struggle against famine, even near the sea ; but at a distance from that nurse of British armies, the means of transport necessarily regulated the extent of the supply. Now wheel-carriage was scarce and bad in Portugal, and for the most part the roads forbade its use; hence the only resource, for the conveyance of stores, was water-carriage, to a certain distance, and afterwards beasts of burthen.

Lisbon, Abrantes, and Belem Castle, on the Tagus; Figueras and Raiva de Pena Cova, on the Mondego, and, finally, Oporto and Lamego, on the Douro, were the principal depôts formed by lord Wellington, and his magazines of consumption were established at Viseu, Celerico, Condeixa, Leiria, Thomar, and Almeida. From those points four hundred miserable bullock-cars and about twelve thousand hired mules, organized in brigades of sixty each, conveyed the necessary warlike stores and provisions to the armies ; when additional succours could be obtained, it was eagerly seized, but this was the ordinary amount of transport, and all his magazines in advance of Lisbon were so limited and arranged that he could easily carry them off or destroy them before the enemy.

With such means and with such preparations was the defence of Portugal undertaken, and it must be evident to the most superficial observer, that, amidst so many difficulties, and with such a number of intricate combinations, lord Wellington's situation was not one in which a general could sleep; and that, due allowance being made for fortune, it is puerile to attribute the success to aught but his talents and steel-hardened resolution.

In the foregoing exposition of the political and military force of the powers brought into hostile contact, I have only touched, and lightly, upon the points of most importance, designing no more than to indicate the sound and the diseased parts of each. The unfavourable circumstances for France would appear to be the absence of the emperor,— the erroneous views of the king,—the rivalry of the marshals,—the impediments to correspondence,— the necessity of frequently dispersing from the want of magazines,—the iniquity of the cause, and the disgust of the French officers, who, for the most part, spoiled by a rapid course of victories on the continent, could not patiently endure a service, replete with personal dangers over and above the ordinary mishaps of war, and promising little ultimate reward.

For the English, the quicksands were—the memory of former failures on the continent,—the financial drain,—a powerful and eloquent opposition, pressing a cabinet, so timid and selfish that the general dared not risk a single brigade, lest an accident should lead to a panic amongst the ministers which all lord Wellesley's vigour would be unable to stem,—the intrigues of the Souza party,— and the necessity of persuading the Portuguese to devastate their country for the sake of defending a *European cause*. Finally, the babbling of the English newspapers, from whose columns the enemy constantly drew the most certain information of the strength and situation of the army. On the other

side, France had possession of nearly all the fortified towns of the Peninsula, and, while her enormous army threatened to crush every opponent, she
offered a constitution, and recalled to the recollec-
tion of the people that it was but a change of one
French dynasty for another. The church started
from her touch, but the educated classes did not
shrink less from the British government's known
hostility to all free institutions. What, then, remained for England to calculate upon? The extreme hatred of the people to the invaders, arising
from the excesses and oppressions of the armies,—
the chances of another continental war,—the complete dominion of the ocean with all its attendant
advantages,—the recruiting through the militia,
which was, in fact, a conscription with two links in
the chain instead of one; lastly, the ardour of the
troops to measure themselves with the conquerors
of Europe, and to raise a rival to the French emperor. And here, as general Foy has been at some
pains to misrepresent the character of the British
soldiers, I will set down what many years' experience gives me the right to say is nearer the truth
than his dreams.

That the British infantry soldier is more robust
than the soldier of any other nation, can scarcely be
doubted by those who, in 1815, observed his powerful frame, distinguished amidst the united armies
of Europe; and, notwithstanding his habitual excess
in drinking, he sustains fatigue, and wet, and the
extremes of cold and heat with incredible vigour.
When completely disciplined, and three years are
required to accomplish this, his port is lofty, and
his movements free; the whole world cannot produce
a nobler specimen of military bearing, nor is the

mind unworthy of the outward man. He does not, indeed, possess that presumptuous vivacity which would lead him to dictate to his commanders, or even to censure real errors, although he may perceive them; but he is observant, and quick to comprehend his orders, full of resources under difficulties, calm and resolute in danger, and more than usually obedient and careful of his officers in moments of imminent peril.

It has been asserted that his undeniable firmness in battle, is the result of a phlegmatic constitution uninspired by moral feeling. Never was a more stupid calumny uttered! Napoleon's troops fought in bright fields, where every helmet caught some beams of glory, but the British soldier conquered under the cold shade of aristocracy; no honours awaited his daring, no despatch gave his name to the applauses of his countrymen, his life of danger and hardship was uncheered by hope, his death unnoticed. Did his heart sink therefore! Did he not endure with surpassing fortitude the sorest of ills, sustain the most terrible assaults in battle unmoved, overthrow, with incredible energy, every opponent, and at all times prove that, while no physical military qualification was wanting, the fount of honour was also full and fresh within him!

The result of a hundred battles and the united testimony of impartial writers of different nations have given the first place, amongst the European infantry, to the British; but, in a comparison between the troops of France and England, it would be unjust not to admit that the cavalry of the former stands higher in the estimation of the world.

CHAPTER IV.

IN resuming the thread of military events, it is necessary to refer back to the commencement of the year, because the British operations on the frontier of Beira were connected, although not conducted in actual concert, with those of the Spaniards; and here I deem it right to notice the conduct of Miguel Alava, that brave, generous, and disinterested Spaniard, through whom this connexion was kept up. Attached to the British head-quarters, as the military correspondent of the Junta, he was too sagacious not to perceive the necessity of zealously seconding the English general. But in the manner of doing it, he never forgot the dignity of his own country, and, as he was too frank and honest for intrigues, his intercourse was always honourable to himself and advantageous to both nations.

It will be remembered that in February, Ney threatened Ciudad Rodrigo at the same time that Mortier menaced Badajos and that Hill advanced from Abrantes to Portalegre. Lord Wellington immediately reinforced the line between Pinhel and Guarda, and sent the light division across the Coa, to observe the enemy's proceedings. The Portuguese Regency were alarmed, and demanded more British troops; but lord Wellington replied that the numbers already fixed would be as great as he could feed, and he took that occasion to point out, that the measures agreed upon, with respect to the native forces, were neither executed with vigour nor im-

CHAP. IV.

1810. February.

Appendix, No. V. Section 1.

partiality; and that the carriages and other assistance, required for the support of the British soldiers then in the country were not supplied. These
matters he urgently advised them to amend before
they asked for more troops; and, at the same time,
as the Regency in the hope of rendering him unpopular with the natives, intimated a wish that he
should take the punishment of the offenders into his
own hands, he informed them that, although he
advised the adoption of severe measures, he would
not be made the despotic punisher of the people,
while the actual laws were sufficient for the purpose.

When Ney first appeared before Ciudad Rodrigo,
and the second corps under Mermet was at Placentia,
Lord Wellington was considerably embarrassed;
the French might have passed from Placentia across
the Tagus, and pushed between Hill and the
army in Beira, or even between the latter and Lisbon, seeing that the Portuguese government had
with their usual apathy neglected the works projected for opening the road from Thomar to
Espinal; and thus, instead of being within three or
four marches of the Tagus, Lord Wellington was
nine marches distant. He was, therefore, forced
to keep a keen watch upon the motions of the
second corps, and to have his own troops in hand
to withdraw from the frontier, lest the French
should suddenly cross the Tagus, for the want of
good information was now and for a long time after
severely felt. This was in February; but when Del
Parque's movement from Gata to Badajos occupied
the attention of Mermet, and that Junot commenced
the siege of Astorga, the repairs of the road to
Espinal being also in a forward state, his situation

See pages
191-2.

was different : the Portuguese army was brought up to Cea and Viseu, and the militia in the northern provinces were ordered to concentrate at Braga to guard the Tras os Montes.

Ciudad Rodrigo being soon after seriously menaced, Lord Wellington sent a brigade of heavy cavalry to Belmonte, and transferred his own quarters to Celerico; for he contemplated a sudden incursion into Castile with his whole army, intending .to strike at the French magazines in Salamanca. But when he considered the force they had in his front, which could be also reinforced by Kellerman's and Junot's corps, and would therefore be strong enough to defend the Tormes, he relinquished this project, and confined his views to the succour of Ciudad Rodrigo, if occasion should offer, without detriment to the general plan of defending Portugal in the lines. The conduct of both the British and the Portuguese governments cramped his exertions. The resources of the country were not brought forward, and the English general could scarcely maintain his actual position, much less advance; yet the Regency treated his remonstrances lightly, exactly following the system of the Spanish Central Junta during the campaign of Talavera.

Indignant at their conduct, he told them that "their proceedings were evasive and frivolous; that the army could neither move forward nor remain without food; that the time was one which would not admit of idle or hollow proceedings, or partiality, or neglect of public for private interests; that the resources were in the country, could be drawn forth, and must be so if the assistance of England

Appendix,
No. V.
Section 1.

was desired; finally, that punishment should follow disobedience, and, to be effectual, must begin with the higher classes." Then, issuing a proclamation, he pointed out the duties and the omission of both magistrates and people, and by this vigorous interference procured some immediate relief for his troops.

Meanwhile general Crawfurd had commenced a series of remarkable operations with the light division. His three regiments of infantry were singularly fitted for any difficult service; they had been for several years under sir John Moore, and, being carefully disciplined in the peculiar school of that great man, came to the field with such a knowledge of arms, that, in six years of real warfare, no weakness could be detected in their system.

As the enemy's posts on the Agueda rendered it impossible for the light division to remain, without cavalry, beyond the Coa, unless some support was at hand, nearer than Guarda or Celerico; Crawfurd proposed that, while he advanced to the Agueda, Cole, with the fourth division, should take up the line of the Coa. But that general would not quit his own position at Guarda; and lord Wellington approving, and yet desirous to secure the line of the Coa with a view to succour Ciudad Rodrigo, brought up the third division to Pinhel; and then reinforcing Crawfurd with the first German hussars, (four hundred excellent and experienced soldiers,) and with a superb troop of horse-artillery, commanded by captain Ross, gave him the command of all the outposts, and ordered Picton and Cole to support him, if called upon.

In the middle of March, Crawfurd lined the bank of the Agueda with his hussars, from Escalhon

on the left, to Navas Frias on the right, a distance
of twenty-five miles, following the course of the
river. The infantry were disposed in small parties
in the villages between Almeida and the Lower
Agueda; the artillery was at Fort Conception,
and two battalions of Portuguese caçadores which
soon afterwards arrived, were placed in reserve,
making a total of four thousand men, and six guns.

The French at this period were extended
in divisions from San Felices to Ledesma and
Salamanca, but as they did not occupy the
pass of Perales, Carrera's Spanish division being
at Coria, was in communication with Crawfurd,
whose line, although extended, was very advantageous. For from Navas Frias to the Douro,
the Agueda was rendered unfordable by heavy
rain, and only four bridges crossed it on that whole
extent, namely, one at Navas Frias; one at Villar,
about a league below the first; one at Ciudad
Rodrigo; and one at San Felices, called the bridge
of Barba del Puerco. While therefore, the hussars
kept a good watch at the two first bridges which were
distant, the troops could always concentrate under
Almeida before the enemy could reach them from that
side; and on the side of Barba del Puerco, the ravine
was so profound that a few companies of the ninety-
fifth were considered capable of opposing any numbers. This arrangement sufficed while the Agueda
was swollen; but that river was capricious, often falling many feet in a night without apparent reason.
When it was fordable, Crawfurd always withdrew
his outposts, and concentrated his division, and
his situation demanded a quickness and intelligence
in the troops, the like of which has seldom been
known. Seven minutes sufficed for the division

to get under arms in the middle of the night, and a quarter of an hour, night or day, to bring it in order of battle to the alarm-posts, with the baggage loaded and assembled at a convenieut distance in the rear. And this not upon a concerted signal, or as a trial, but at all times and certain.

The 19th, general Ferey, a bold officer, desiring either to create a fear of French enterprise at the commencement of the campaign, or thinking to surprise the division, collected six hundred grenadiers close to the bridge of San Felices; and, just as the moon, rising behind him, cast long shadows from the rocks, and rendered the bottom of the chasm dark, he silently passed the bridge, and, with incredible speed, ascending the opposite side, bayoneted the sentries, and fell upon the piquet so fiercely, that friends and enemies went fighting into the village of Barba del Puerco while the first shout was still echoing in the gulf below. So sudden was the attack, and so great the confusion, that the British companies could not form, but each soldier encountering the nearest enemy, fought hand to hand, and their colonel, Sydney Beckwith, conspicuous by his lofty stature and daring actions, a man capable of rallying a whole army in flight, urged the contest with such vigour that, in a quarter of an hour, the French column was borne back, and pushed over the edge of the descent.

This skirmish proved, that, while the Agueda was swollen, the enemy could gain nothing by slight operations; but it was difficult to keep in advance of the Coa, because the want of money had reduced the whole army to straits, and Crawfurd, notwithstanding his prodigious activity, was unable to feed his division, wherefore giving the reins to his fiery temper, he seized some church-plate, with a view to the purchasing of corn. For this rash act he was rebuked, and such redress granted that no mischief followed, and fortunately the proceeding itself had some effect in procuring supplies, as it convinced the priests that the distress was not feigned.

When the sixth corps again approached Ciudad Rodrigo in the latter end of April, lord Wellington, as I have before said, moved his head-quarters to Celerico, and Carrera took post at St. Martin Trebeja, occupying the pass of Perales; but being there menaced by Kellerman's troops, he came down, in May, from the hills to Ituero on the Azava river, and connected his left with the light division, which was then posted at Gallegos Espeja and Barba del Puerco. Crawfurd and he then agreed that, if attacked, the British should concentrate in the wood behind Espeja, and if unable to maintain themselves there, should unite with the Spaniards at Nava d'Aver, and finally retire to Villa Mayor, a village covering the passage of the Coa by the bridge of Seceira, from whence there was a sure retreat to Guarda.

It was at this period that Massena's arrival in Spain became known to the allies; the deserters, for the first time, ceased to speak of the emperor's commanding in person, and all agreed that serious operations would soon commence. No good information could be obtained; but, as the river continued unfordable, Crawfurd maintained his position, until the end of May, when certain advice of the march of the French battering-train was received through Andreas Herrasti: and, the

1st of June, Ney, descending upon Ciudad Rodrigo, threw a bridge, on trestles, over the Agueda at the convent of Caridad, two miles above, and, a few days afterwards, a second at Carboneras, four miles below the fortress. This concentration of the French troops relieved the northern provinces of Portugal from danger, sixteen regiments of militia were immediately brought down from Braganza to the Lower Douro, provisions came by water to Lamego, the army was enabled to subsist, and the military horizon began to clear.

The 8th, four thousand French cavalry having crossed the Agueda, Crawfurd concentrated his forces at Gallegos and Espeja, and the Spaniards occupied the wood behind the last-named village, and it was at this moment, when Spain was overwhelmed, and when the eye could scarcely command the interminable lines of French in his immediate front, that Martin Carrera thought fit to invite marshal Ney to desert!

Nothing could be more critical than Crawfurd's position. From the Agueda to the Coa the whole country, although studded with woods and scooped into hollows, was free for cavalry and artillery, and there were at least six thousand horsemen and fifty guns within an hour's march of his position. His right was at Espeja, where thick woods in front rendered it impossible to discover an enemy until close upon the village, while wide plains behind, almost precluded hope, in a retreat before the multitude of French cavalry and artillery. The confluence of the Azava with the Agueda offered indeed some security to his left; because the channel of the former river there became a chasm, and the ground rose high and rugged at each side of the bridge of

Marialva, two miles in front of Gallegos. Nevertheless, the bank on the enemy's side was highest,
and, to obtain a good prospect, it was necessary to
keep posts beyond the Azava; moreover the bridge
of Marialva could be turned by a ford, below the
confluence of the streams.

The 10th, the Agueda became fordable in all
parts, but, as the enemy occupied himself with the
raising of redoubts, to secure his bridge at Carboneras, and with other preparations for the siege
of Rodrigo, Crawfurd, trusting to his own admirable arrangements, and to the surprising discipline
of his troops, still maintained his dangerous position. He thus encouraged the garrison of Ciudad
Rodrigo, and protected the villages in the plain
between the Azava and the Coa from the enemy's
foraging parties.

On the 18th, the eighth corps was seen to take
post at San Felices, and other points, and all the
villages, from the Sierra de Francia to the Douro,
were occupied by the French army. The 23d,
Julian Sanchez, breaking out of Ciudad, came
into Gallegos. The 25th, the French batteries
opened against the fortress, their cavalry closed
upon the Azava, and Crawfurd withdrew his outposts to the left bank. The 26th, it was known
that Herrasti had lost one hundred and fifty killed,
and five hundred wounded; and, the 29th, a
Spaniard, passing the French posts, brought Carrera a note, containing these words: " *O venir
luego! luego! luego! a secorrer esta plaza.*" (" Oh!
come, now! now! now! to the succour of this
place." On the 1st of July the gallant old man repeated his " *Luego, luego, luego, por ultimo vez.*"

Meanwhile, lord Wellington, still hoping that the
enemy, by detaching troops, would furnish an oppor-

tunity of relieving Ciudad Rodrigo, reinforced Crawfurd with the 14th and 16th light dragoons, and transferred his own quarters to Alverca, a village half-way
between Almeida and Celerico. The Spaniards supposed he would attack, and Romana, quitting Badajos, came to propose a combined movement for carrying off the garrison. This was a trying moment! The
English general had come from the Guadiana with
the avowed purpose of securing Rodrigo; he had,
in a manner, pledged himself to make it a point in
his operations; his army was close at hand, the
garrison brave and distressed, the governor honour-
ably fulfilling his part. To permit such a place to
fall without a stroke struck, would be a grievous
disaster, and a more grievous dishonour to the
British arms; the troops desired the enterprise;
the Spaniards demanded it, as a proof of good faith;
the Portuguese to keep the war away from their
own country : finally, policy seemed to call for this
effort, lest the world might deem the promised defence of Portugal a heartless and a hollow boast.
Nevertheless, Romana returned without his object.
Lord Wellington absolutely refused to venture even
a brigade, and thus proved himself a truly great
commander, and of a steadfast mind.

It was not a single campaign but a terrible war
that he had undertaken. If he lost but five thousand men, his own government would abandon the
contest ; if he lost fifteen, he must abandon it himself. His whole disposable force did not exceed
fifty-six thousand men, of these, twelve thousand
were with Hill, and one-half of the remainder were
untried and raw. But this included all, even to
the Portuguese cavalry and garrisons. All could
not, however, be brought into line, because Reynier,
acting in concert with Massena, had, at this period,

collected boats, and made demonstrations to pass
the Tagus and move upon Coria; French troops
were also crossing the Morena, in march towards
Estremadura, which obliged lord Wellington to
detach eight thousand Portuguese to Thomar, as a
reserve; and these and Hill's corps being deducted,
not quite twenty-five thousand men were available
to carry off the garrison in the face of sixty thousand
French veterans. This enterprise would also have
taken the army two marches from Guarda, and Coria
was scarcely more distant from that place; hence,
a division must have been left at Guarda, lest
Reynier, deceiving Hill, should reach it first.

Twenty thousand men of all arms remained, and
there were two modes of using them. 1°. In an
open advance and battle. 2°. In a secret movement
and surprise. To effect the last, the army might
have assembled in the night upon the Azava, and
filed over the single bridge of Ciudad Rodrigo,
with a view of capturing the battering train, by a
sally, or of bringing off the garrison. But, without dwelling on the fact that Massena's information
was so good that he knew, in two days after it occurred, the object of Romana's visit, such a movement could scarcely have been made unobserved,
even in the early part of the siege, and, certainly,
not towards the end, when the enemy were on the
Azava.

Appendix,
No. VII.
Section I.

An open battle a madman only would have ventured. The army, passing over a plain, in the face
of nearly three times its own numbers, must have
exposed its flanks to the enemy's bridges on the
Agueda, because the fortress was situated in the
bottom of a deep bend of the river, and the
French were on the convex side. What hope then

for twenty thousand mixed soldiers cooped up between two rivers, when eight thousand cavalry and
eighty guns should come pouring over the bridges
on their flanks, and fifty thousand infantry would have
followed to the attack ? What would even a momentary success' have availed ? Five thousand undisciplined men brought off from Ciudad Rodrigo,
would have ill supplied the ten or twelve thousand
good troops lost in the battle, and the temporary
relief of the fortress would have been a poor com-
pensation for the loss of Portugal. For what was
the actual state of affairs in that country ?—The
militia deserting in crowds to the harvest, the
Regency in full opposition to the general, the measures for laying waste the country not perfected,
and the public mind desponding ! The enemy
would soon have united his whole force and advanced to retrieve his honour, and who was to have
withstood him ?

Massena, sagacious and well understanding his
business, only desired that the attempt should be
made. He held back his troops, appeared careless, and in his proclamations taunted the English
general, that he was afraid !—that the sails were
flapping on the ships prepared to carry him away—
that he was a man, who, insensible to military
honour, permitted his ally's towns to fall without
risking a shot to save them, or to redeem his
plighted word ! But all this subtlety failed, lord
Wellington was unmoved, and abided his own
time. " If thou art a great general, Marius, come
down and fight ! If thou art a great general, Silo,
make me come down and fight !"

Ciudad Rodrigo left to its fate, held out yet a
little longer, and meanwhile the enemy pushed

infantry on to the Azava; Carrera retired to the
Dos Casas river; and Crawfurd, reinforced with
the sixteenth and fourteenth light dragoons, placed
his cavalry at Gallegos, and concentrated his infantry in the wood of Alameda, two miles in rear,
from whence he could fall back, either to the
bridge of Almeida by San Pedro, or to the bridge
of Castello Bom by Villa Formosa. Obstinate
however not to relinquish a foot of ground that he
could keep either by art or force, he disposed his
troops in single ranks on the rising grounds, in the
evening of the 2d of July, and then sending some
horsemen to the rear to raise the dust, marched the
ranks of infantry in succession, and slowly, within
sight of the enemy, hoping that the latter would
imagine the whole army was come up to succour
Ciudad Rodrigo. He thus gained two days, but,
on the 4th of July, a strong body of the enemy
assembled at Marialva, and a squadron of horse,
crossing the ford below the bridge, pushed at full
speed towards Gallegos driving back the picquets;
the enemy then passed the river, and the British
retired skirmishing upon Alameda, leaving two
guns, a troop of the 16th and a troop of German
hussars to cover the movement. This rear-guard
was scarcely drawn up on a hill half-cannon shot
from a streamlet with marshy banks, which crossed
the road to Alameda, when a column of French horsemen was observed coming on at a charging pace,
diminishing its front as it approached the bridge,
but resolute to pass, and preserving the most perfect
order, notwithstanding some well-directed shots
from the guns. Captain Kraüchenberg, of the
hussars, proposed to charge those who first came
over, but the English officer did not conceive his

orders warranted it, and the gallant German riding
full speed against the head of the advancing columns
with his single troop, killed the leading officers, overthrew the front ranks, and drove the
whole back. Meanwhile the enemy crossed the
stream at other points, and a squadron coming close
up to Alameda was driven off by a volley from the
third caçadores.

This skirmish not being followed up by the
enemy, Crawfurd took a fresh post with his infantry and guns in a wood near Fort Conception ;
his cavalry, reinforced by Julian Sanchez and Carrera's divisions, were disposed higher up on the
Duas Casas, and the French withdrew behind the
Azava, leaving only a piquet at Gallegos. Their
marauding parties however entered the villages of
Barquillo and Villa de Puerco for three nights successively, and Crawfurd, thinking to cut them
off, formed two ambuscades, one near Villa de
Puerco with six squadrons, another of three squadrons near Barquillo ; he also placed his artillery,
five companies of the ninety-fifth and the third
caçadores in reserve, for the enemy were again in
force at Gallegos and even in advance of it.

A little after day-break, on the 11th, two French
parties were observed, the one of infantry near Villa
de Puerco, the other of cavalry at Barquillo, and
the open country on the right would have enabled
the six squadrons to get between the infantry in
Villa de Puerco and their point of retreat ; but this
was circuitous, and Crawfurd preferred pushing
straight through a stone enclosure as the shortest
road. The enclosure proved difficult, the squadrons were separated, and the French, two hundred
strong, had time to draw up in square on a rather

steep rise of land, yet so far from the edge, as not to be seen until the ascent was gained. The two squadrons which first arrived, galloped in upon them, and the charge was rough and pushed home, but failed; the troopers received the fire of the square in front and on both sides, and in passing saw and heard the French captain, Guache, and his serjeant-major exhorting the men to shoot carefully. Scarcely was this charge over when the enemy's cavalry came out of Barquillos, and the two British squadrons having re-formed, rode against it, and made twenty-nine men and two officers prisoners, a few being also wounded. Meanwhile colonel Talbot mounting the hill with four squadrons of the fourteenth dragoons, bore gallantly in upon captain Guache; but the latter again opened such a fire, that Talbot himself and fourteen men went down close to the bayonets, and the stout Frenchman made good his retreat. Crawfurd then returned to the camp, having had thirty-two troopers, besides the colonel, killed or wounded in this unfortunate affair.

That day Ciudad Rodrigo surrendered, and the Spanish troops, grieved and irritated, separated from the light division, and marching by the pass of Perales, rejoined Romana; Crawfurd then assumed a fresh position, a mile and a half from Almeida, and demanded a reinforcement of two battalions. Lord Wellington replied that he would give him two divisions, if he could hold his ground, but that he could not do so, and, knowing the temper of the man, he repeated his former orders *not to fight beyond the Coa.*

On the 21st, the enemy's cavalry again advanced, Fort Conception was blown up, and Crawfurd fell back to Almeida, apparently disposed to cross the

Coa, but nothing was further from his thoughts. Braving the whole French army, he had kept with a weak division, for three months, within two hours march, of sixty thousand men, appropriating the resources of the plains entirely to himself, and this exploit, only to be appreciated by military men, did not satisfy his feverish thirst of distinction. Hitherto he had safely affronted a superior power, and forgetting that his stay beyond the Coa was a matter of sufferance, not real strength, with head-strong ambition, he resolved, in defiance of reason and of the reiterated orders of his general, to fight on the right bank.

The British force under arms now consisted of four thousand infantry, eleven hundred cavalry, and six guns, and his position, one mile and a half in length, extended in an oblique line towards the Coa. The cavalry piquets were upon the plain in his front, his right was on some broken ground, and his left resting on an unfinished tower, eight hundred yards from Almeida, was defended by the guns of that fortress ; but his back was on the edge of the ravine forming the channel of the Coa, and the bridge was more than a mile distant, in the bottom of the chasm.

COMBAT OF THE COA.

A stormy night ushered in the 24th of July. The troops, drenched with rain, were under arms before day-light, expecting to retire, when a few pistol shots in front, followed by an order for the cavalry reserves and the guns to advance, gave notice of the enemy's approach ; and as the morning cleared, twenty-four thousand French infantry, five thousand cavalry, and thirty pieces of artillery were observed in march beyond the Turones. The British line was immediately contracted and brought under the edge of the ravine ; but meanwhile Ney, who had observed Crawfurd's false disposition, came down with the stoop of an eagle. Four thousand horsemen and a powerful artillery swept the plain, the allied cavalry gave back, and Loison's division coming up at a charging pace, made towards the centre and left of the position.

While the French were thus pouring onward, several ill-judged changes were made on the English side ; part of the troops were advanced, others drawn back, and the forty-third regiment most unaccountably placed within an enclosure of solid masonry, at least ten feet high, situated on the left of the road, about half-musket shot down the ravine, and having but one narrow outlet. While thus imprisoned, the firing in front redoubled, the cavalry, the artillery, and the caçadores successively passed by in retreat, and the sharp clang of the ninety-fifth rifle was heard along the edge of the plain above. A few moments later, and the forty-third would have been surrounded, if here, as in every other part of this field, the quickness and knowledge of the battalion officers had not remedied the faults of the general. One minute sufficed to loosen some large stones, a powerful effort burst the enclosure, and the regiment, re-formed in column of companies, was the next instant up with the riflemen. There was no room to array the line, no time for any thing but battle, every captain carried off his company as an independent body, and joining as he could with the ninety-fifth or fifty-second, the whole presented a mass of skirmishers, acting in small parties and under no regular command, yet each confident in the courage and discipline of those on his right and left; and all regulating their movements by a common discretion and keeping together with surprising vigour.

It is unnecessary to describe the first burst of French soldiers. It is well known with what gallantry the officers lead, with what vehemence the troops follow, and with what a storm of fire they waste a field of battle. At this moment, with the advantage of ground and numbers, they were breaking over the edge of the ravine, their guns ranged along the summit, played hotly with grape, and their hussars, galloping over the glacis of Almeida, poured down the road, sabring every thing in their way. Ney, desirous that Montbrun should follow this movement with the whole of the French cavalry, and so cut off the troops from the bridge, sent five officers in succession to urge him on ; and, indeed, so mixed were friends and enemies at the moment, that only a few guns of the fortress durst open, and no courage could have availed against such overwhelming numbers. But Montbrun enjoyed an independent command, and, as the attack was made without Massena's knowledge, he would not stir. Then the British regiments, with singular intelligence and discipline, extricated themselves from their perilous situation. Falling back slowly, and yet stopping and fighting whenever opportunity offered, they made their way through a rugged country tangled with vineyards, in despite of their enemies, who were so fierce and eager, that even the horsemen rode in amongst the enclosures, striking at the soldiers as they mounted the walls or scrambled over the rocks.

As the retreating troops approached the river, they came upon a more open space; but the left wing being harder pressed, and having the shortest distance, arrived while the bridge was still crowded and some of the right wing distant. Major M'Leod, of the forty-third, seeing this, rallied four companies on a hill just in front of the passage, and was immediately joined by a party of the ninety-fifth; and at the same time, two other companies were posted by brigade-major Rowan, on another hill flanking the road. These posts were maintained until the enemy, gathering in great numbers, made a second burst, when the companies fell back; but at that moment the right wing of the fifty-second was seen marching towards the bridge, which was still crowded with the passing troops. M'Leod, a very young man, but with a natural genius for war, immediately turned his horse round, called to the troops to follow, and, taking off his cap, rode with a shout towards the enemy. The suddenness of the thing, and the distinguished action of the man, produced the effect he designed; a mob of soldiers rushed after him, cheering and charging as if a whole army had been at their backs, and the enemy's skir-mishers, astonished at this unexpected movement, stopped short. Before they could recover from their surprise, the fifty-second crossed the river, and M'Leod, following at full speed, also gained the other side without a disaster.

As the regiments passed the bridge, they planted themselves in loose order on the side of the moun-tain. The artillery drew up on the summit and the cavalry were disposed in parties on the roads to the right, because two miles higher up the stream there were fords, and beyond them the bridge of Castello Bom; and it was to be apprehended that, while the sixth corps was in front, the reserves, and a division of the eighth corps, then on the Agueda, might pass at those places and get between the division and Celerico. The river was, however, rising fast from the rains, and it was impossible to retreat farther.

The French skirmishers, swarming on the right bank, opened a biting fire, which was returned as bitterly; the artillery on both sides played across the ravine, the sounds were repeated by numberless echoes, and the smoke, rising slowly, resolved itself into an immense arch, spanning the whole chasm, and sparkling with the whirling fuzes of the flying shells. The enemy gathered fast and thickly, his columns were discovered forming behind the high rocks, and a dragoon was seen to try the depth of the stream above, but two shots from the fifty-second killed horse and man, and the carcasses, floating between the hostile bands, showed that the river was impassable. The monotonous tones of a French drum were then heard. The next instant, the head of a noble column darkened the long narrow bridge, a drummer and an officer in a splendid uniform, leaped forward together, and the whole rushed on with loud cries. The depth of the ravine at first deceived the English soldiers' aim, and two-thirds of the passage was won ere a shot had brought down an enemy; yet a few paces onwards the line of death was traced, and the whole of the leading French section fell as one man! Still the gallant column

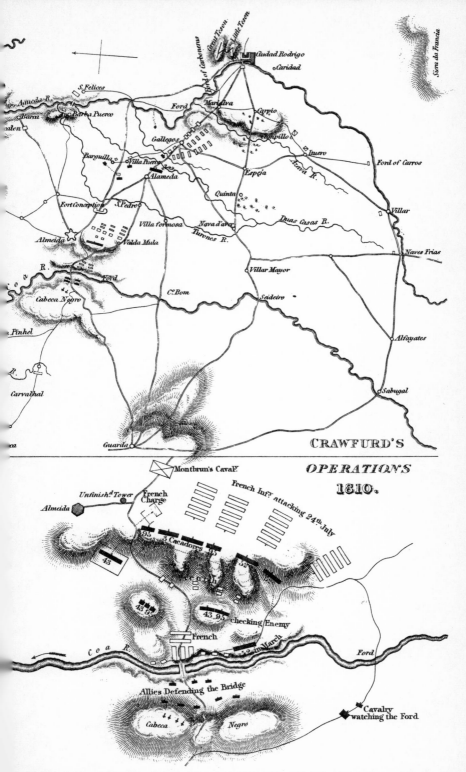

CRAWFURD'S

OPERATIONS
1810.

Sierra da Francia

Ciudad Rodrigo
Caridad
Great Teson
Little Teson
Ford of Carboneras
Ford
Marialva
Carpio
Pompillo
Inuero
Ford of Carros
S. Felices
Barba Puerco
Gallegos
Espeja
Agua R.
Almeda R.
Barra
Galen
Barguilla
Villa Puerco
Alameda
Quinta
Villar
Fort Conception
S. Pedro
Villa formosa
Nava d'aver
Turones R.
Duas Casas R.
Naves Frias
Almeida
Valde Mula
Villar Mayor
Coa R.
Ford
Co. Bom
Seideiro
Cabeca Negro
Alfayates
Pinhel
R.
Carvalhal
Sabugal
Guarda

Montbrun's Caval.
Unfinish.d Tower
French Charge
French Infy attacking 24th July
Almeida
95
3 Cacadores
95
43
52
43.95
43.95
checking Enemy
French
52 in March
Coa R.
Ford
Allies Defending the Bridge
Cabeca
Negro
Cavalry watching the Ford.

Published by T & W Boone 1830

pressed forward, but no foot could pass that terrible line; the killed and wounded rolled together, until the heap rose nearly even with the parapet, and the living mass behind melted away rather than gave back.

The shouts of the British now rose loudly, but they were confidently answered, and, in half an hour, a second column, more numerous than the first, again crowded the bridge. This time, however, the range was better judged, and ere half the distance was won, the multitude was again torn, shattered, dispersed, and slain; ten or twelve men only succeeded in crossing, and took shelter under the rocks at the brink of the river. The skirmishing was then renewed, and a French surgeon coming down to the very foot of the bridge, merely waved his handkerchief and commenced dressing the wounded under the hottest fire; nor was this touching appeal unheeded, every musket turned from him, although his still undaunted countrymen were preparing for a third attempt. The impossibility of forcing the passage was, however, become too apparent, and this last effort, made with feebler numbers and less energy, failed almost as soon as it commenced.

Nevertheless, the combat was unnecessarily continued. By the French, as a point of honour, to cover the escape of those who had passed the bridge. By the English, from ignorance of their object. One of the enemy's guns was dismantled, a powder-magazine blew up, and many continued to fall on both sides until about four o'clock, when a heavy rain causing a momentary cessation of fire, the men amongst the rocks returned, unmolested, to their own party, the fight ceased, and Craw-furd retired behind the Pinhel river. Forty-four Portuguese, two hundred and seventy-two British, including twenty-eight officers, were killed, wound-ed, or taken, and it was at first supposed that lieutenant Dawson and half a company of the fifty-second, which had been posted in the unfinished tower, were also captured ; but that officer kept close until the evening, and then, with great intel-ligence, passed all the enemy's posts, and, crossing the Coa at a ford, rejoined his regiment.

In this action the French lost above a thousand men, the slaughter at the bridge was fearful to behold ; but Massena claimed to have taken two pieces of artillery, and it was true, for the guns intended to arm the unfinished tower, near Almeida, were lying dismounted at the foot of the building. They, however, belonged to the garrison of Almeida, not to the light division. That they were not mount-ed and the tower garrisoned was certainly a great negligence; the enemy's cavalry could not otherwise have fallen so dangerously on the left of the posi-tion, and the after-investment of Almeida would have been retarded. In other respects, the governor, severely censured by Crawfurd, at the time, for not opening his fire sooner and more vigorously, was un-blameable; the whole affair had been so mis-managed by the general himself, that friends and enemies were mingled together from the first, and the shots from the fortress would have killed both.

During the fight, general Picton came up alone from Pinhel, Crawfurd desired the support of the third division, it was refused, and, excited by some previous disputes, the generals separated after a sharp altercation. Picton was decidedly wrong, because Crawfurd's situation was one of extreme danger; he could not retire, and Massena might undoubtedly have thrown his reserves, by the bridge of Castello Bom, upon the right flank of the division, and destroyed it between the Coa and the Pinhel rivers. Picton and Crawfurd were, however, not formed by nature to act cordially together. The stern countenance, robust frame, saturnine complexion, caustic speech, and austere demeanour of the first, promised little sympathy with the short thick figure, dark flashing eyes, quick movements, and fiery temper of the second; nor, did they often meet without a quarrel. Nevertheless, they had many points of resemblance in their characters and fortunes. Both were inclined to harshness, and rigid in command; both prone to disobedience, yet exacting entire submission from inferiors; and they were alike ambitious and craving of glory. They both possessed decided military talents, were enterprising and intrepid; yet neither were remarkable for skill in handling troops under fire. This, also, they had in common, that both, after distinguished services, perished in arms, fighting gallantly, and being celebrated as generals of division while living, have, since their death, been injudiciously spoken of, as rivalling their great leader in war.

That they were officers of mark and pretension is unquestionable, and Crawfurd more so than Picton, because the latter never had a separate command, and his opportunities were necessarily more circumscribed; but to compare either to the duke of Wellington displays ignorance of the men and of

the art they professed. If they had even compre-
hended the profound military and political combinations he was then conducting, the one would have
carefully avoided fighting on the Coa, and the
other, far from refusing, would have eagerly prof-
fered his support.

CHAPTER V.

DURING the siege of Ciudad Rodrigo, an expedition sailing from Coruña, under Porlier, seized Santona, and dismantled that and other points on the coast. At the same time Mahi, coming down from the Gallician mountains, menaced Astorga, and a detachment of his army, under Toboado Gil, occupied Puebla de Senabria, acting in concert with Silveira. Mahi's movements could not be well opposed by either Kellerman or Serras, during the siege, because the former had a strong detachment in Baños, and the troops of the latter were spread over too great an extent of ground; but, when the place fell, the eighth corps, being detached beyond the Tormes, to gather provisions, enabled Serras to act against the Gallicians. The latter were then driven into the mountains, and Toboado Gil, removing his stores from Puebla Senabria, drew closer to Silveira, in expectation of an attack; but Serras, only placing a Swiss battalion and sixty dragoons at Puebla, fell back to Zamora, and the eighth corps reoccupied the country between the Tormes and the Agueda.

Meanwhile Bonet defeated the Spaniards at Sales, and entered Castropol, on the frontier of Gallicia, but returned to Oviedo, on hearing of the expedition to Santona. The Spaniards then re-embarked for Coruña, the project of a larger armament, to be directed against Santander itself, was adopted, and

Mahi affirmed that, if more arms and ammunition were sent to him from England, he would clear the plains of Leon, as far as the Esla river. His demands were complied with; sir Home Popham was appointed to superintend the naval expeditions against the coast of the Asturias and Biscay, and a serious interruption of the French communications was planned, but never realised.

General Reynier now passed the Tagus with the second corps, but it appears that this movement should have been executed in June, for boats were collected at Barca de Alconete, in the middle of that month; and the French only waited for a detachment from Andalusia, when Mendizabel, taking the road of Zafra, attacked that detachment, at Los Santos, on the 23d, and Reynier immediately moved to its succour with one division of infantry and all his cavalry. At this period the insurrection caused by Lascy's expedition to the Ronda, had drawn all the troops of the fifth corps from Seville to that side, the duke of Aremberg and general Remond had fallen back behind the river Tinto, and Copons had advanced to collect provisions on the Odiel. In this threatening state of affairs, instead of returning to Merida, Reynier endeavoured to surprise Imas, at Xeres de los Cavalleros, and failing in that, pushed across the Morena against Ballasteros, and the latter being at Campo Frio, beyond Aracena, and, ignorant that Imas had retreated, could only save himself by a hasty flight across the frontier of Portugal. Meanwhile, Lascy being beaten in the Ronda, the fifth corps retired to Seville, D'Aremberg and Remond re-occupied Huelva and Moguer, and Reynier, going back to Merida, resumed his design of passing the Tagus. His boats were still at Alconete, for the Spaniards had neglected this opportunity of destroying them; but, as it was necessary to cover the operations both from Hill's division which was concentrated at Campo Mayor, and from the Portuguese troops behind the Elga river, a strong rear guard was placed on the Salor to watch the former, and the French division at Banos advanced to Coria to awe the latter. Reynier then quitting Merida the 10th of July, marched, by Truxillo and Caceres, upon Alconete and Almaraz, and effected the passage, his rear guard following on the 16th. This cautious operation saved him from an attack meditated by Hill, who had received orders to unite with Romana, and drive the second corps back, with a view to gather the harvest for the victualling of Badajos and the other frontier fortresses. The passage of the Tagus being thus effected by the French, general Hill made a parallel movement, which, on his part, only required thirty-six hours; and meanwhile, lord Wellington assembled a reserve at Thomar, under the command of general Leith, consisting of eight thousand Portuguese and two thousand British infantry, just arrived from England.

Reynier having reached Coria, detached a force, by Perales, upon Sabugal, but recalled it when he found that Hill, having crossed the Tagus by Vilha Velha, was at Castello Branco on the 21st. The two generals then faced each other. Hill, joined by a strong body of Portuguese cavalry, under general Fane, encamped, with sixteen thousand men and eighteen guns, at Sarzedas, just in front of the Sobreira Formosa; his advanced guard was in Castello Branco, his horsemen on the line of the

Ponçul; and a brigade of Portuguese infantry was posted at Fundao, to keep up the communication with Guarda, and to cover the Estrada Nova. Behind Hill, Leith occupied the line of the Zezere, and thus twenty-six thousand men, besides the militia, were in observation between the Estrella and the Tagus.

Reynier first made demonstrations on the side of Salvatierra, but being repulsed by some Portuguese cavalry, divided his forces between Penamacor and Zarza Mayor; he also established a post of one hundred and fifty men on the left bank of the Tagus, near the mouth of the Rio Del Monte; and, by continual movements, rendered it doubtful, whether he meant to repass the Tagus, or to advance upon Sarzedas, or to join Massena. Meanwhile, Ballasteros returned to Aracena; Imas to Xeres de los Cavalleros; O'Donnel entered Truxillo, and Carlos d'España cut off the French post on the Rio del Monte. Romana was, however, soon obliged to concentrate his troops again, for Mortier was on the Guadalquivir, with a view to re-enter Estremadura. Such was the situation of the armies in the beginning of August; but Massena, when assured that Reynier had crossed the Tagus, directed the sixth corps and the cavalry upon Almeida, which led, as we have seen, to the combat on the Coa, during which, Loison, imagining the governor to be a native, pressed him to desert the cause of the English: "*that vile people, whose object was to enslave the Portuguese.*"

Lord Wellington's situation was now critical. Ciudad Rodrigo furnished the French with a place of arms; they might disregard Almeida, and their tardy investment of it, viewed in conjunction with the great magazines collecting at Ciudad Rodrigo, indicated an intention of so doing. Massena's dispositions were such as rendered his true designs difficult to be discovered. The sixth corps and the reserve cavalry were, indeed, around Almeida, but, by telegraphic intercourse with the garrison, it was known that the investment was not real, and the heads of the columns pointed towards Celerico. Loison's advanced guard was in Pinhel the day after Crawfurd's action; the second corps, divided between Zarza Mayor and Penamacor, and with boats, near Alcantara, on the Tagus, menaced equally the line of that river and the line of the Zezere; and it was as likely that Massena would join Reynier as that Reynier would join Massena. It was known by an intercepted letter, that Napoleon had ordered Reynier to invade by the line of Abrantes while the 5th corps entered the Alemtejo, and Massena acted by the valley of the Mondego; but as Reynier was by the same letter placed under Massena's command and that the 5th corps was not then in a condition to move against the Alemtejo, no certain notion of the enemy's intention could be formed. The eighth corps and the divisions of Serras and Kellerman being between the Tormes and the Esla, might break into the northern provinces of Portugal, while the sixth and second corps should hold the allies in check, and this was undoubtedly the surest course; because the taking of Oporto would have furnished many resources, stricken the natives with terror, dispersed the northern militia, opened the great coast-road to Lisbon, and enabled Massena to avoid all the difficult country about the Mondego. The English general must then have retired before the second and sixth corps, unless he attacked Ney; an unpromising measure, because of the enemy's

strength in horse: in fine, although Massena was
dilatory, he had one hundred and sixteen thousand
men and the initial operations in his power, and
lord Wellington was obliged to wait upon his movements.

The actual position of the allies was too extended and too forward, yet to retire at once would
have seemed timid; hence lord Wellington remained
quiet during the 25th, 26th, and 27th of July,
although the enemy's posts were thickening on
the Pinhel river. The 28th, the British cavalry
advanced to Frexadas, and the infantry withdrew
behind the Mondego, except the fourth division,
which remained at Guarda. The light division
occupied Celerico; the other divisions were posted
at Penhancos, Carapichina, and Fornos; the Portuguese troops were a day's march behind. The
sick and wounded men were transferred daily to the
rear, and the line of retreat kept free from encumbrance. The enemy then made a demonstration towards St. Joa de Pesquera, and defeated
some militia at Fosboa, on the Douro, but finally
retired across the Coa, and, after a few skirmishes
with the garrison on the 3rd of August, left the
communication with Almeida again free. At the
same time, a detachment of Reynier's horse was
encountered at Atalaya, near Fundao, and beaten
by the Portuguese cavalry and ordenança, with a
loss of fifty killed or taken, after which the French
withdrew from Penamacor.

On the side of Gallicia, Kellerman advanced
from Benevente to Castro Contrijo, and detachments from Serras's division penetrated towards
Monterey, ordering provisions for ten thousand
men on the road to Braganza. Silveira then marched

on Senabria, defeated a few of the enemy's cavalry there on the 6th; invested the Swiss on the 7th; and, on the 10th, obliged them to capitulate at the moment when Serras, who had foolishly left them there and neglected to succour them in time, was tardily coming to their relief. Five hundred men and an eagle were taken, and Silveira, who did not lose a man, thought of giving battle to Serras, but Beresford alarmed at such rashness sent him imperative orders to retreat; an operation he performed by abandoning his rear guard, which was under the command of colonel J. Wilson, and which, being closely pressed, was saved by that officer under circumstances of such difficulty that he received the public thanks of the marshal.

This advantage in the north was balanced by a disaster in Estremadura. The Spanish generals, never much disposed to respect lord Wellington's counsels, were now less so than before, from the discontent engendered by the fall of Ciudad Rodrigo. He had pressed upon Romana the policy of avoiding battles; had procured permission that Campo Mayor should be given to him as a place of arms, with leave to retire into Portugal when overmatched by the enemy; and he had shewn him that Hill's departure greatly augmented the necessity of caution. Nevertheless, Romana joined Ballasteros, and, as their united force amounted to eighteen thousand infantry and two thousand cavalry beside Partidas, the English general immediately foresaw that they would offer battle, be defeated, and lay open the whole frontier of the Alemtejo; he, therefore, directed Hill to send Madden's brigade of Portuguese cavalry to their assistance.

Madden reached Campo Mayor the 14th, but Romana's advanced guard under Mendizabel had been defeated on the 11th at Benvenida, and having lost six hundred men, was going to lay down its arms, when fortunately Carrera arrived with the Spanish cavalry and disengaged it; the whole then retreated across the Morena to Monte Molin and Fregenal, but the French pursued and slew or took four hundred more. The following day Mortier entered Zafra, and Romana retired to Almendralejos. The enemy did not, however, press this advantage, because Lascy with three thousand men from Cadiz convoyed by Capt. Cockburn of the British navy, had landed near Moguer and driven the duke of Aremberg towards Seville, while Copons drove Remond upon Zalamea; and although the French soon rallied and obliged Lascy to re-embark, Mortier was withdrawn towards the Morena, and Romana again advanced to Zafra. This affair at Moguer was very contemptible, but the tumid nature of Cockburn's despatches on the occasion obtained for it a momentary celebrity.

It would appear that Massena had been waiting for Mortier's movements to develope his own plans, for on the day that the latter entered Zafra, the sixth corps formally invested Almeida, and lord Wellington immediately bringing up the Portuguese, recrossed the Mondego; the British being at Pinhel, Frexadas, and Guarda, and the Portuguese at Celerico, Govea, Melho, and Trancoso. In this situation, expecting a vigorous defence from Almeida, he had good hopes to delay the enemy for six weeks or two months, when the rains setting in would give him additional advantages in the defence of the country. He had intended to keep

the light division on the Cabeça Negro overhanging the bridge of the Coa, and thus secure a communication with the garrison, or force the French
to invest the place with their whole army. Crawfurd's rashness marred this plan, and he himself
was so dispirited by the action on the 24th, that
the commander-in-chief did not think it prudent to
renew the project. Yet Massena's tardiness and
the small force with which he finally invested the
place, led lord Wellington to think of assembling
secretly a large and chosen body of men behind
the Cabeça Negro, with the view of suddenly
forcing the bridge and the fords and taking the
French battering train, or at least bringing off the
garrison ; but while revolving this great stroke in
his mind, an unexpected and terrible disaster broke
his measures.

SIEGE OF ALMEIDA.

This fortress, although regularly constructed with
six bastions, ravelins, an excellent ditch, and covered
way, was extremely defective. The ramparts were
too high for the glacis, and from some near ground,
on the side of the attack, the bottom of the ditch
might be seen. An old square castle, built on a
mound in the centre of the town, contained three
bomb proofs, the doors of which were not secure ;
and with the exception of some damp casements in
one bastion, there was no other magazine for the
powder. Colonel Cox was governor, and his gar- Colonel
Cox's Nar-
rison composed of one regular and two militia rative.
regiments, a body of artillery and a squadron of
cavalry, amounted to about four thousand men.

On the 18th, the trenches were begun under cover of a false attack, and in the morning of the 26th (the second parallel being commenced) sixty-five pieces of artillery mounted in ten batteries opened at once. Many houses were soon in flames and the garrison was unable to extinguish them; the counter fire was, however, briskly maintained, and little military damage was sustained. Towards evening the cannonade slackened on both sides; but just after dark the ground suddenly trembled, the castle bursting into a thousand pieces, gave vent to a column of smoke and fire, and with a prodigious noise the whole town sunk into a shapeless ruin! Treason or accident had caused the magazines to explode, and the devastation was incredible. The ramparts were breached, the greatest part of the guns thrown into the ditch, five hundred people were struck dead on the instant, and only six houses left standing; the stones thrown out hurt forty of the besiegers in the trenches, and the surviving garrison, aghast at the horrid commotion, disregarded all exhortations to rally. Fearing that the enemy would take the opportunity to storm the ramparts, the governor beat to arms, and, running to the walls, with the help of an artillery officer, fired off the few guns that remained; but the French shells fell thickly all the night, and in the morning of the 27th, two officers appeared at the gates, with a letter from Massena, offering terms.

Cox, sensible that further resistance was impossible, still hoped that the army would make a movement to relieve him, if he could impose upon the enemy for two or three days; and he was in act of refusing the prince of Esling's offer, when a mu-

tiny, headed openly by the lieutenant-governor, one
Bernardo Costa, and secretly by José Bareiros, the
chief of artillery, who had been for some time in
secret correspondence with the French, obliged him
to yield. The remainder of the native officers disturbed by fear, or swayed by the influence of those
two, were more willing to follow than to oppose their
dishonourable proceedings, and Costa expressed
his resolution to hoist the white flag. The governor
seeing no remedy by force, endeavoured to procras-
tinate, and, being ignorant of Bareiros' treason, sent
him to the enemy with counter propositions. Bareiros immediately informed Massena of the true
state of garrison, and never returned ; and the final
result was a surrender upon agreement that the
militia should retire to their homes, and the regulars remain prisoners of war.

While the treaty was pending and even after
the signature of the articles, in the night of the
27th, the French bombarded the place. This act,
unjustifiable, and strange because Massena's aide-
de-camp, colonel Pelet, was actually within the
walls when the firing commenced, was excused, on
the ground of an error in the transmission of orders;
it, however, lasted during the whole night, and Cox
also asserts that the terms of the capitulation with
respect to the militia were violated. Pelet indignantly denies this, affirming that when the garrison
still amounting to three thousand men perceived
the marquis d'Alorna amongst the French generals,
the greatest part immediately demanded service,
and formed a brigade under general Pamplona, and
the truth of this account is confirmed by two facts ;
namely, that the arganil militia were sent in by

Justifica-
tion of Co-
lonel
W. Cox.

Note by
Gen. Pelet.
Appendix
to Vol. XII.
Victoires et
Conquêtes
des Fran-
cais.

MrStuart's
Correspon-
dence.
MSS.

Massena the next day, and the 24th Portuguese regiment did certainly take service with the enemy in a body. Yet, so easily are men's minds moved by present circumstances, that the greater number deserted again, when they afterwards saw the allied armies.

Bareiros, having joined the enemy, escaped punishment, but De Costa, being tried, was afterwards shot as a traitor, by the orders of marshal Beresford. His cowardice and mutiny merited this chastisement, yet the evidence on which he was condemned was an explanatory letter, written to lord Liverpool by ·Cox, while a prisoner at Verdun.

The explosion, the disappearance of the steeple, and cessation of fire, proclaimed the misfortune of Almeida in the allied camp, but the surrender was first ascertained by lord Wellington on the 29th, when, with a telescope, he observed many French officers on the glacis of the place. The army then withdrew to its former position behind the Mondego ; and while these things were passing on the Coa, the powder magazine in Albuquerque, being struck with lightning, also exploded and killed four hundred men. Reynier, after several demonstrations towards Castello Branco, in one of which he lost a squadron of horse, now suddenly reached Sabugal the 1st of September; and as the British piquets on the Pinhel were attacked the following day by the horsemen of the sixth corps, the enemy's plans seemed to be ripe for execution. Lord Wellington therefore transferred his quarters to Govea, withdrew his infantry behind Celerico, and fixed his cavalry at that place with posts of observation at Guarda and at

Trancoso.   Reynier, however, suddenly returned to
Zarza Mayor, and, throwing a bridge over the
Tagus at Alcantara, again involved the French pro-
jects in obscurity.

Massena experienced considerable difficulty in
feeding his forces, and he seemed at first, either
disinclined to commence the invasion or undecided
as to the mode.   Two months had elapsed since the
surrender of Ciudad Rodrigo, Almeida had only
resisted for ten days, the French army was still
behind the Coa, and it would seem, by a second intercepted letter, dictated by Napoleon, in September, that he expected further inaction: " Lord Wellington," he observed to Massena, " has only
eighteen thousand men, Hill has only six thousand;
and it would be ridiculous to suppose that twenty-
five thousand English can balance sixty thousand
French, if the latter do not trifle, but fall boldly
on after having *well observed where the blow may be
given*.   You have twelve thousand cavalry, and
four times as much artillery as is necessary for
Portugal.   Leave six thousand cavalry and a proportion of guns between Ciudad Rodrigo, Alcantara,
and Salamanca, and with the rest commence operations.   The emperor is too distant, and the positions
of the enemy change too often, to direct how you
should attack; but it is certain that the utmost
force the English can muster, including the troops
at Cadiz, will be twenty-eight thousand men."
This letter was accurate as to the numbers of the
English army, but Napoleon was ignorant how
strongly lord Wellington was thrusting Portugal
forward in the press.

Massena had commenced the invasion before

these instructions reached him; and to understand his operations it is essential to have a clear idea of the country in which they were conducted. The advanced positions of the allies extended from Almeida over the Sierra de Estrella, by Guarda to Fundao, Sarzedas, and Castello Branco; no enemy could penetrate that line unless by force, and a serious attack on any one point was to be the signal for a gradual retreat of the whole, in concentric directions towards the Lines. But, if Guarda were evacuated, the enemy while menacing Celerico, could move either by Belmonte or Covilhao and separate general Hill from lord Wellington, the distance between those generals being twice as great as the enemy's perpendicular line of march would be. To balance this disadvantage, the road from Covilhao was broken up, a Portuguese brigade was placed in Fundao, and general Leith's corps was stationed at Thomar, between two entrenched positions, which formed the second temporary line of resistance. The first of those positions was behind the Zezere, extending from the Barca de Codies to the confluence of that river with the Tagus. The second behind the Alva, a strong and swift stream descending from the Estrella and falling into the Mondego some miles above Coimbra. Both were strong, the rivers deep and difficult of access, and the Sierra de Murcella closely hugs the left bank of the Alva.

During the spring and summer the Portuguese militia, now forming the second line on the Zezere under Leith, had been kept in winter quarters, although with danger to the defence of the country; but the destitute state, with respect to money, in which the English ministers kept lord Wellington, prevented him from being able to bring these troops into the field until the last moment.

Hill's line of retreat from Sarzedas to the Zezere, has been already noticed, and from that river to the Alva, there was a military road constructed through the mountains to Espinhal. But the country from Celerico to the Murcella, a distance of about sixty miles, is one long defile, lying between the Sierra Estrella and the Mondego; and the ridge upon which Celerico stands, being a shoot from the Estrella, and encircled by a sweep of the Mondego, closes this defile in front. In like manner the Sierra Murcella, covered by the Alva river, closes it in the rear, and the intermediate parts are but a succession of smaller streams and lower ridges. The principal road was repaired and joined to the road of Espinhal, and a branch was also carried across the Mondego to Coimbra. Thus an internal communication was established for the junction of all the corps. Nevertheless, between Celerico and the Alva, the country was not permanently tenable; because, from Guarda and Covilhao, there were roads over the Estrella to Gouvea, Cea, and Gallices, towns in rear of Celerico;· and the enemy could also turn the whole tract by moving through Trancoso and Viseu, and so down the right bank of the Mondego to Coimbra.

Lord Wellington keeping the head of his army one march behind Celerico, in observation of the routes over the Estrella, and his rear close to the Alva, was master of this line of retreat; and as the Mondego was fordable in summer and bridged at several points, he could pass it by a flank move-

ment in a few hours.   Now the right bank was
also one great defile, lying between the river and
the Sierra de Alcoba or Caramula.   This mountain
stretching with some breaks from the Douro to
Coimbra, separates the valley of the Mondego
from the coast line ; and in approaching Coimbra it
sends out a lofty transverse shoot, called the Sierra
de Busaco, exactly in a line with the Sierra de
Murcella, and barring the way on the right bank
of the Mondego in the same manner that the latter
Sierra bars it on the left bank.   Moreover this
route to Coimbra was the worst in Portugal, and
crossed by several deep tributaries of the Mondego,
the most considerable of which were the Criz and
Dao.   The Vouga, however, opened a passage
through the Alcoba near Viseu, and that way the
French could gain the great road from Oporto, and
so continue their movement upon Coimbra.

Such being the ground on both sides of the
Mondego, the weakest point was obviously towards
the Estrella, and lord Wellington kept the mass of
his forces there.   Massena was ill-acquainted with
the military features, and absolutely ignorant of
the lines of Torres Vedras ; indeed, so secretly
and circumspectly had those works been carried on,
that only vague rumours of their existence reached
the bulk of the English army.   Nay, the Portuguese government and the British envoy, although
aware defensive works were constructing, knew not
their nature, and imagined, until the last moment, that
the entrenchments immediately round Lisbon were
the lines ! Many British officers laughed at the notion
of remaining in Portugal, and the major part supposed
the campaign on the frontier to be only a decent cloak
to cover the shame of an embarkation.   In England

the opposition asserted that lord Wellington would embark; the Portuguese dreaded it; the French army universally believed it; and the British ministers seem to have entertained the same opinion, for at this time an officer of engineers arrived at Lisbon, whose instructions, received personally from lord Liverpool, were unknown to lord Wellington, and commenced thus:—" *As it is probable that the army will embark in September.*"

CHAPTER VI.

THIRD INVASION OF PORTUGAL.

MASSENA's command, extended from the banks of the Tagus to the Bay of Biscay, from Almeida to Burgos; and the number of his troops present under arms exceeded one hundred and ten thousand men. From these however must be deducted thirteen thousand in the Asturias and province of Santander, four thousand in the government of Valladolid, eight thousand under Serras at Zamora and Benevente, and lastly, the reserve of Bayonne under general Drouet, nineteen thousand strong, which, organized as a ninth corps entered Spain in August, and was replaced at Bayonne by a fresh reserve under general Caffarelli. Thus, the active army of invasion did not much exceed seventy thousand; and as every man, combatant or non-combatant, is borne on the strength of a French army, not more than fifty-five thousand infantry and about eight thousand horsemen were with the eagles. The ninth corps had, however, orders to follow the traces of the prince of Esling, and the void thus left at Burgos and Valladolid was supplied by sixteen thousand of the young guard.

This arrangement shows how absurdly Napoleon has been called a rash warrior, and one never thinking of retreat. No man ever made bolder marches, but no man ever secured his base with more care. Here, he would not suffer any advance to fresh conquests until his line of communication had been strengthened with three additional fortresses,—namely, Astorga, Ciudad, and Almeida; and while he employed sixty-five thousand men in the invasion of Portugal, he kept more than eighty thousand in reserve. Thus, even the total loss of the army destined to make what is technically termed "a point" upon Lisbon, would, as a mere military disaster, have scarcely shaken his hold of Spain.

Massena's instructions were to convert Ciudad Rodrigo and Almeida into places of arms for the conquest of Portugal, and to move on both sides of the Tagus against Lisbon in the beginning of September. But either thinking his force too weak to act upon two lines at the same time, or trusting to the co-operation of Soult's army from Andalusia, he relinquished the Alemtejo, looking only to the northern bank of the Tagus; and hence, as the experience of Junot's march in 1807, warned him off the Sobreira mountains, his views were confined to the three roads of Belmonte, Celerico, and Viseu.

The strength of the positions about the Alva was known to him, as were also the measures taken to impede a descent from Covilhao to Espinhal; but Alorna, Pamplona, and the other Portuguese in the French camp, with a singular ignorance, asserted that the road by Viseu and Coimbra was easy, and that no important position covered the latter town. The French general thus deceived resolved suddenly to assemble all his forces, distribute thirteen days' bread to the soldiers, and pour in one solid mass down the right bank of the Mondego, not doubting to reach Coimbra before general Hill could join lord Wellington.

Note by
General
Pelet.
Vide Victoires et
Conquêtes
des Francais, vol.
xi.

In pursuance of this project the three corps were
directed to concentrate on the 16th of September;
Reynier's at Guarda, Ney's, and the heavy cavalry,
at Maçal da Chao, and Junot's at Pinhel. By this
disposition all three roads were alike menaced, and
the allies being kept in suspense as to the ultimate
object, Massena hoped to gain one march; a great
thing, seeing that from Coimbra he was not more
than a hundred miles, whereas Hill's distance from
that town was longer. To cover the real object
with more care, and to keep Hill as long as possible at Sarzedas, the French general caused
Guarda to be seized on the 12th, by a detachment,
which withdrew again immediately, as if it were
only a continuation of the former feints; and meanwhile Reynier, having first ascertained that Mortier
was at Monasterio, threatening Estremadura, suddenly destroyed the boat-bridge at Alcantara, and
marched towards Sabugal.

On the 13th the allies re-established their post
at Guarda; on the 15th, it was again driven away
by a considerable mass of the enemy, and retired
up the side of the Estrella; at the same time the
cavalry in front of Celerico was forced back in the
centre, and the post at Trancoso chased towards
Mongualde on the left. Lord Wellington then felt
assured that the invasion was at last in serious
progress; and having ascertained, beyond a doubt,
that the troops in Guarda were of Reynier's corps,
despatched his final orders for Hill and Leith to
concentrate on the Alva.

On the 16th, Reynier descended from Guarda
to the plains bordering the Mondego, and being
there joined by the sixth corps and Montbrun's horsemen, the whole passed the river, and, pushing

through Celerico, drove back the cavalry posts of
the allies to the village of Cortiço; but there the
first German hussars turning, overthrew the leading squadrons, and made some prisoners. Near
Cortiço, the road branched off to the bridge of
Fornos and to Gouvea, and a French brigade took
the latter to cover the march of the main body
which made for Fornos. This feint was however
closely watched, for there is a custom, peculiar to the
British army, of sending mounted officers, singly
to observe the enemy's motions; and, such is their
habit, they will penetrate through the midst of his
cantonments, cross the line of his movement, and
hover, just out of musket-shot, for whole days, on
the skirts of his columns, until they obtain a clear
notion of the numbers and the true direction of his
march. Colonel Waters, one of these exploring
officers, being close on the left of Reynier's troops
during this day, reported their movements, and in
the evening, leading some of the German cavalry
behind the enemy, took several prisoners and the
baggage of a general.

As the French movements were now decided,
Lord Wellington directed the first, third, and fourth
divisions upon the Alva; withdrew his heavy cavalry
from the front; and placed the light division at St.
Romao, in the Estrella, to cover the head-quarters,
which were transferred, that night, to Cea.

The 17th, the whole of the second and sixth corps
were observed to pass the bridge of Fornos, and
the advanced guard approached Mongualde. But
the eighth corps still kept the road leading towards
Oporto, for ten thousand militia of the northern
provinces, forming the brigades of Trant, T. Wilson,

and Miller, had been collected upon the Douro to
harass the enemy's right flank and rear; and Trant,
with about three thousand, was already at Moimenta
de Beira, in the defiles leading through the hills
to Lamego. The country between the Coa and
Coimbra, on both sides of the Mondego, had been
before laid waste, the mills were destroyed, the
ordenança were in arms, and the helpless population hidden amongst the highest mountains.

On the 18th, the French advanced guard reached
the deserted city of Viseu. Pack's Portuguese
brigade immediately passed the Mondego at
Fosdao, and took post beyond the Criz; and general Pakenham, with a brigade of the first division, entered Coimbra, to protect it from the
enemy's scouting parties. On the 19th, captain
Somers Cocks, a very gallant and zealous officer,
commanding the cavalry post which had been
driven from Guarda, came down from the Estrella,
and following the enemy through Celerico, ascertained that neither sick men nor stores were left
behind: hence it was evident that Massena, re-
linquishing his communications, had thrown his
cavalry, infantry, artillery, parcs, baggage and
hospital waggons, in one mass, upon the worst road
in Portugal.

The allies were now in motion to cross the
Mondego, when a false report, that the enemy
was again on the left bank, arrested the general
movement. The next day, the truth being known,
the third, fourth, and light divisions, and the British cavalry passed the river at Pena Cova, Olivarez,
and other places; the light division moved to Mortagao in support of Pack; the third and fourth

entered the villages between the Sierra de Busaco and Mortagao, and the horsemen occupied a plain between the light division and Pack's brigade.

But the eighth corps pointed towards the valley of the Vouga, and it was still doubtful whether Massena would not that way gain the main road from Oporto to Coimbra; general Spencer, with the first division, therefore, marched upon Milheada, and Trant was directed to join him by a march through San Pedro de Sul to Sardao. Meanwhile Leith arrived on the Alva, and general Hill was only one march behind; for having discovered Reynier's movements on the 12th, and at the same time, getting intelligence that all the French boats on the Tagus had been destroyed; he, with a ready decision, anticipating lord Wellington's orders, directed his artillery by Thomar, and putting his troops in motion that evening, reached Espisnal on the 20th. There he was joined by general Lecor, who, with equal vigour and judgement, had brought the Portuguese brigade, by long marches, from Fundao. On the 21st, Hill arrived on the Alva, and pushed his cavalry in observation beyond that river. Thus the two corps of the allied army were united on the same day that the main body of the enemy entered Viseu; and, although the French horsemen were on the Criz, the bridges had been destroyed by Pack; and the project of surprising Coimbra was baffled.

Neither had Massena failed to experience other evil consequences from his false movement. He had been obliged to repair the road from day to day for his artillery, and it was still twenty miles from Viseu on the 19th. Trant, aware of this, formed the hardy project of destroying it. Quit-

ting Moimenta de Beira in the night, with a
squadron of cavalry, two thousand militia, and five
guns, on the 20th, he surprised a patrole of ten men,
from whom he learnt that the convoy was at hand,
and that Montbrun's cavalry was close in the rear.
Nevertheless, as the defiles were narrow, he charged
the head of the escort, and took a hundred prisoners and some baggage. The convoy then fell
back, and Trant followed, the ways being so
narrow that Montbrun could never come up to the
front. At this time, a resolute attack would have
thrown the French into utter confusion, but the militia were unmanageable ; and the enemy, having
at last rallied a few men, and repulsed the Portuguese cavalry, with a loss of twelve troopers, the
whole got into disorder, wherefore Trant, seeing nothing more was to be effected, returned to Moimenta
de Beira, and from thence marched to Lamego with
his prisoners. The French, ignorant of the number
and quality of their assailants, still fell back, and
did not finally reach Viseu until the 23d, by which,
Massena lost two most important days.

While these events were passing in the valley of
Mondego, a small expedition from Cadiz again
landed at Moguer, to aid Copons in collecting
provisions on the Tinto. It was, however, quickly
obliged to reimbark, and Copons was defeated by
general Remond, with the loss of three hundred
men on the 15th. Meanwhile, Romana attacked the
French posts near Monasterio, pushing his cavalry
towards Seville, whereupon Soult sent the fifth corps
against him, and he retired, but was beaten at Fuente
de Canto on the same day that Copons had been
defeated on the Tinto. The pursuit was continued
to Fuente del Maestre ; and the whole army was

like to disperse in flight, when Madden's Portuguese cavalry came up, and, charging the pursuers
with signal gallantry, overthrew the leading
squadrons, recovered some prisoners, and gained
time for the Spaniards to rally. Nevertheless, the
French entered Zafra, and Romana retreated, by
Almendralejo and Merida, to Montijo, on the 18th,
throwing a garrison into Olivenza, and three battalions into Badajos. Being, however, sensible that the
latter place was in no condition to resist a serious
attack, he directed the Junta to repair to Valencia
d'Alcantara, and took refuge himself at Elvas.

Lord Wellington's anticipations were thus realized
and the Alemtejo laid open. Fortunately for the
allies, Sebastiani was at this moment near Carthagena in pursuit of the Murcian army ; a fresh insurrection had broken out in the mountains of Grenada, and the castles of Motril and Almunecar were
taken. Copons also advanced to the Tinto, and all
these calls upon Soult taking place at one time, he
was unable to bring quite twelve thousand men to
Zafra, a number inadequate to the invasion of
the Alemtejo ; because several British regiments
withdrawn from Cadiz, and others coming from
England, had reached Lisbon about this period,
and formed a reserve for the allies, of more than
five thousand good troops. Wherefore the French
returned to Ronquillo, the Spaniards again advanced
to Xeres de los Cavalleros, and Araceña, and this
dangerous crisis glided gently away. To understand its importance, it is necessary to shew how
increasing political embarrassments had thwarted
the original plan of the English general.

The first vexatious interference of the Souza
faction had been checked, but the loss of Almeida

furnished a favourable opportunity to renew their clamorous hostility to the military proceedings. Falsely asserting, that the provisions of that fortress had been carried away by the English commissaries, and as falsely pretending that lord Wellington had promised to raise the siege, this party hypocritically assumed, that his expressions of sorrow for its fall were indications of an intention to remove by a splendid victory the public despondency. They vehemently insisted, also, on a defence of the frontier, inveighed against the destruction of the mills, endeavoured to force their own friends of the fidalgo faction on to the staff of marshal Beresford, that they might the more readily embarrass the operations ; and even proposed to have the fleet and transports sent away from the Tagus ! Meanwhile, neglecting or delaying the measures agreed upon for laying waste the country, they protected the minor authorities when disobedient, refrained from punishing delinquents, and took every occasion to mislead the public mind at the very moment when the enemy commenced the invasion. Nor was there wanting either accident or indiscretion to increase the growing confusion.

Mr. Stu-
art's Pa-
pers. MSS.

Appendix,
No. II.
Section II.

When Almeida fell, an officer of the guards writing to a friend at Oporto, indiscreetly asserted, that Massena was advancing in front with a hundred thousand French ; and that eighty thousand more were moving in rear of the allies upon Lisbon. This letter being made public, created such a panic amongst the English merchants, that one and all they applied for ships to carry their families and property away, and there arose such a tumult that Trant was obliged to quit his command for the purpose of suppressing the commotion. To dry this

source of mischief lord Wellington issued proclamations; and, in the orders of the day, declared that
he would not seek to ascertain the author of this
and similar letters, being assured that the feelings
and sense of the officers would prevent any repetition, of such hurtful conduct.

To the regency he addressed himself in a
more peremptory and severe manner; he reproved
them for the false colouring given to his communications; and informed them that he would never
" *permit public clamour and panic to induce him to
change, in the smallest degree, a system and plan of
operation which he had adopted after mature consideration, and which daily experience proved to be
the only one likely to produce a good end.*" This remonstrance only increased the virulence of his opponents; and such was their conduct, that, before
lord Wellington reached Busaco, he was obliged
to tell them, " *their miserable intrigues must
cease or he would advise his own government to withdraw the British army.*"

Meanwhile their proceedings had been so mischievously successful, that the country between the
Mondego, the Tagus, and the Lines, still contained
provisions sufficient for the French during the ensu-
ing winter; and the people were alike unprepared to
expect an enemy or to attempt a removal of their
property.

Lord Wellington could but choose then, between
stopping the invaders on the Mondego, or wasting
the country by force as he retreated. But what
an act the last! His hopes depended upon the
degree of moral strength he was enabled to call
forth; and he would have had to retire with a mixed
force before a powerful army and an eminent com-

mander, his rear guard engaged, and his advance driving miserable multitudes before it to the capital, where nothing was prepared to save them from famine; but where the violent and powerful faction in the regency was ready to misrepresent every proceeding, and inflame the people's minds: and this, when the court of Rio Janeiro was discontented, and the English ministers, as I shall have occasion to shew, panic-stricken by the desponding letters of some general officers about the commander-in-chief! It was evidently necessary to fight, although Massena had seventy thousand veterans, and lord Wellington could only bring about fifty thousand men into line, more than half of which were untried soldiers.

The consequences of such a battle were not, however, to be estimated by the result on the field. The French general might indeed gain every thing by a victory; but, if defeated, his powerful cavalry and the superior composition and experience of his army would prevent it from being very injurious; or a serious check might induce him to turn his attention from Coimbra towards Oporto, contenting himself with the capture of that city, and the reduction of the northern provinces, until more formidable preparations should enable him to renew his first design. Nor could the time thus gained by the allies be as profitably employed in the defence. The French could be reinforced to any amount, whereas the English general's resources could not be much improved; and it was very doubtful if either England or Portugal would longer endure the war, without some palpable advantage to balance the misery and the expense.

Such was the state of affairs, when the allies

passed to the right bank of the Mondego with a view to fight the battle thus forced upon their general. While the French remained concentrated at Viseu, the first division, under Spencer, was held at Milheada in observation of the great road from Oporto; the light division at Mortagao watching the road from Viseu; and the remainder of the army was in reserve ready to move to either side. But when the French advanced guard had repaired the bridges over the Criz, and passed that river, lord Wellington recalled the first division, and fixed upon the Sierra de Busaco for his position of battle.

This mountain, about eight miles in length, abuts to the right on the Mondego, and on the left is connected with the Sierra de Caramula by a hilly rugged country, impervious to the march of an army. A road along the crest of Busaco afforded an easy communication; and at Pena Cova, just behind the right hand extremity, a ford in the Mondego permitted the troops to pass in a few hours to the Murcella ridge, behind the Alva. The face of Busaco was steep, rough, and fit for defence. The artillery of the allies fixed on certain points, could play along the front freely, and there was some ground on the summit suitable for a small body of cavalry. But neither guns nor horsemen of the enemy had a fair field, their infantry were to contend with every difficulty, and the approach to the position was also unfavourable to an attacking army.

After passing the Criz, a table-land permitted Massena to march, in a wide order of battle, to Mortagao, but then a succession of ascending ridges led to the Sierra Busaco, which was separated from the last by a chasm, so profound, that the naked eye could hardly distinguish the movement of troops in the bottom, yet in parts so narrow that twelve-pounders could range to the salient points on the opposite side. From Mortagao four roads conducted to Coimbra. The first, unfrequented and narrow, crossed the Caramula to Boyalva, a village situated on the western slope of that sierra, and from thence led to Sardao and Milheada. The other roads, penetrating through the rough ground in front, passed over the Sierra de Busaco ; one by a large convent on the right hand of the highest point of the ridge ; a second on the left hand of this culminating point, by a village called St. Antonio de Cantara ; and a third, which was a branch from the second, followed the Mondego to Pena Cova.

When this formidable position was chosen, some officers expressed their fears that Massena would not assail it. *" But, if he does, I shall beat him,"* was the reply of the English general. He was well assured that the prince would attack ; for his advanced guard was already over the Criz, the second and sixth corps were in mass on the other side of that river ; and it was improbable that so celebrated a commander would, at the mere sight of a strong position, make a retrograde movement, change all his dispositions, and adopt a new line of operations by the Vouga, which would be exposed also to the militia under Baccellar. Massena was, indeed, only anxious for a battle, and, being still under the influence of Alorna's and Pamplona's false reports, as to the nature of the country in his front, never doubted that the allies would retire before him.

CHAPTER VII.

GENERAL PACK, on the 22d, destroyed the bridges over the Criz, and fell back upon the light division; but, the 23d, the enemy re-established the communications, passed the river, and obliged the British horse to quit the plain, and take to the hills behind Mortagao. Three squadrons of light and one regiment of heavy cavalry were retained there by lord Wellington; but the rest he sent over the Sierra de Busaco to the low country about Milheada, whence he recalled Spencer, and at the same time caused the third and fourth divisions to take their ground on the position, the former at St. Antonio de Cantara, the latter at the convent. The light division falling back only a league, then encamped in a pine wood, where happened one of those extraordinary panics that, in ancient times, were attributed to the influence of a hostile god. No enemy was near, no alarm was given, yet suddenly the troops, as if seized with a phrenzy, started from sleep and dispersed in every direction: nor was there any possibility of allaying this strange terror, until some persons called out that the enemy's cavalry were amongst them, when the soldiers mechanically run together in masses, and the illusion was instantly dissipated.

The 24th, the enemy skirmished with the picquets in front of Mortagao, the light division, retiring four miles, occupied very strong ground, and, in the evening, some of the enemy's cavalry approaching too close, were charged by a squadron of the fourteenth dragoons, and overthrown, with the loss of twenty or thirty men.

Early on the 25th, Crawfurd moved down from his strong post to the front, and appeared somewhat disposed to renew the scene at the Coa. The enemy's cavalry were gathering in front, and the heads of three infantry columns were plainly descried on the table-land above Mortagao, coming on a-breast, and with a most impetuous pace, while heavy clouds of dust, rising and loading the atmosphere for miles behind, showed that the whole French army had passed the Criz, and was in full march to attack. The cavalry skirmishers were already exchanging pistol-shots, when lord Wellington, arriving, ordered the division to retire, and, taking the personal direction, covered the retreat with the fifty-second and ninety-fifth, the cavalry, and Ross's troop of horse-artillery. Nor was there a moment to lose, for the enemy, with incredible rapidity, brought up both infantry and guns, and fell on so briskly, that all the skill of the general and the readiness of the excellent troops composing the rear guard, could scarcely prevent the division from being dangerously engaged. Howbeit, a series of rapid and beautiful movements, a sharp cannonade, and an hour's march, brought everything back, in good order, to the great position; but, almost at the same moment, the opposite ridge was crowned by the masses of the sixth corps, the French batteries opened as the English troops mounted the steep ascent on which the convent was situated, and Reynier, taking the left hand route, along which a Portuguese battalion had retired, also arrived at St. Antonio de Cantara, in front of the third division. Before three

o'clock, forty thousand French infantry were em-
battled on the two points, and the sharp musketry
of the skirmishers arose from the dark-wooded
chasms beneath.

Ney, whose military glance was magical, perceived in an instant that the position, a crested not
a table mountain, could not hide any strong reserve,
that it was scarcely half occupied, and that great
part of the allied troops were moving from one
place to another, with that sort of confusion which
generally attends the first taking up of unknown
ground. He therefore desired to make an early and
powerful attack; but the prince of Esling was at
Mortagao, ten miles in the rear, and an aide-de-
camp, despatched to inform him of the state of
affairs, after attending two hours for an audience,
was (as I have been informed) told, that everything
must await Massena's arrival. Thus a most favourable opportunity was lost; for the first division of
the allies, although close at hand, was not upon the
ridge, Leith's troops, now called the fifth division,
were in the act of passing the Mondego, and Hill
was still behind the Alva. Scarcely twenty-five
thousand men were actually in line, and there were
great intervals between the divisions.

Reynier coincided with Ney, and they wrote in
concert to Massena, on the 26th, intimating their
joint desire to attack. The prince of Esling, however, did not reach the field until twelve o'clock.
He brought with him the eighth corps, with which,
and the cavalry, he formed a reserve connecting the
sixth and second corps, and then sending out his
skirmishers along the whole front, proceeded carefully to examine the position from left to right.

But the situation of the allies was now greatly

Appendix,
No. V.

changed. Hill's corps, having crossed the Mondego, was posted athwart the road leading over the Sierra to Pena Cova; on his left Leith prolonged the line of defence, having the Lusitanian legion in reserve; Picton, with the third division, supported by Champlemond's Portuguese brigade, was next to Leith; and Spencer, with the first division, occupied the highest part of the ridge, being between Picton and the convent. The fourth division closed the extreme left, covering a path leading to Milheada, where the cavalry held the flat country, one heavy regiment only being kept in reserve on the summit of the Sierra. Pack's brigade and some other Portuguese troops formed a sort of advanced guard to the first division, being posted half way down the mountain. On their left, the light division, supported by a German brigade, occupied a tongue of land jutting out nearly half a mile in front of, and lower than the convent, the space between being scooped like the hollow of a wave before it breaks. Along the whole of the front, skirmishers were thrown out on the mountain side, and about fifty pieces of artillery were disposed upon the salient points.

Ney was averse to attack after the delay which had taken place, but Massena resolved to attempt carrying the position. Reynier thought that he had only to deal with a rear-guard of the allies; and the prince, whether partaking of this error, or confident in the valour of his army, directed the second and sixth corps to fall on the next day, each to its own front, while the eighth corps, the cavalry, and the artillery remained in reserve. To facilitate the attack, the light troops, dropping, by twos and threes, into the lowest parts of the valley, endea-

voured, in the evening, to steal up the wooded
dells and hollows, and to establish themselves unseen close to the picquets of the light division.
Some companies of rifle corps and caçadores checked this proceeding, but similar attempts made with
more or less success at different points of the position,
seemed to indicate a night attack, and excited all the
vigilance of the troops. Yet, were it otherwise,
none but veterans, tired of war, could have slept,
for the weather was calm and fine, and the dark
mountain masses, rising on either side, were crowned with innumerable fires, around which more than
a hundred thousand brave men were gathered.

BATTLE OF BUSACO.

Before day-break on the 27th, the French formed
five columns of attack; three under Ney, opposite
to the convent, and two under Reynier, at St.
Antonio de Cantara these points being about three
miles asunder. Reynier's troops had comparatively
easier ground before them, and were in the midst of
the picquets and skirmishers of the third division
almost as soon as they could be perceived to be
in movement. The allies resisted vigorously, and
six guns played along the ascent with grape, but
in less than half an hour the French were close
upon the summit; so swiftly and with such astonishing power and resolution did they scale the mountain, overthrowing every thing that opposed their
progress. The right of the third division was
forced back; the eighth Portuguese regiment was
broken to pieces, and the hostile masses gained
the highest part of the crest, just between the third

See notice
at the be-
gining of
this vol.

and the fifth divisions. The leading battalions immediately established themselves amongst the crowning rocks, and a confused mass wheeled to the right, intending to sweep the summit of the sierra; but at that moment lord Wellington caused two guns to open with grape upon their flank, a heavy musketry was still poured into their front, and in a little time, the forty-fifth and the eighty-eighth regiments charged so furiously that even fresh men could not have withstood them. The French, quite spent with their previous efforts, only opened a straggling fire, and both parties, mingling together, went down the mountain side with a mighty clamour and confusion. The dead and dying strewed the way even to the bottom of the valley.

Meanwhile the French who first gained the crest had re-formed their ranks with the right resting upon a precipice overhanging the reverse side of the Sierra; thus the position was in fact gained, if any reserve had been at hand, for the greatest part of the third division, British and Portuguese, were fully engaged, and a misty cloud capped the summit, so that the enemy, thus ensconced amongst the rocks, could not be seen, except by general Leith. That officer had put his first brigade in motion to his own left as soon as he perceived the vigorous impression made on the third division, and he was now coming on rapidly; but he had two miles of rugged ground to pass in a narrow column before he could mingle in the fight. Keeping the royals in reserve, he directed the thirty-eighth to turn the right of the French, and as the precipice prevented this, colonel Cameron, of the ninth, who had been informed by a staff-officer

of the critical state of affairs, formed his regiment
in line under a violent fire, and, without returning
a single shot, ran in upon and drove the grenadiers
from the rocks with irresistible bravery, plying
them with a destructive musketry as long as they
could be reached ; and yet with excellent discipline
refraining from pursuit, lest the crest of the position
should be again lost, for the mountain was so rugged that it was impossible to judge clearly of the
general state of the action. The victory was, however, secure. Hill's corps edged in towards the
scene of action ; Leith's second brigade joined the
first, and a great mass of fresh troops was thus
concentrated, while Reynier had neither reserves
nor guns to restore the fight.

Ney's attack had as little success. From the
abutment of the mountain upon which the light
division was stationed, the lowest parts of the
valley could be discerned. The ascent was steeper
and more difficult than where Reynier had attacked,
and Crawfurd, in a happy mood of command, had
made masterly dispositions. The table-land between him and the convent was sufficiently scooped
to conceal the forty-third and fifty-second regiments, drawn up in line ; and a quarter of a mile
behind them, but on higher ground and close to
the convent, a brigade of German infantry appeared to be the only solid line of resistance on
this part of the position. In front of the two
British regiments, some rocks, overhanging the
descent, furnished natural embrasures, in which the
guns of the division were placed, and the whole
face of the hill was planted with the skirmishers
of the rifle corps and of the two Portuguese caça-
dore battalions.

While it was yet dark, a straggling musketry was heard in the deep hollows separating the armies, and when the light broke, three divisions of the sixth corps were observed entering the woods below and throwing forward a profusion of skirmishers; soon afterwards Marchand's division emerging from the hollow, took the main road, as if to turn the right of the light division, Loison's made straight up the face of the mountain in front, and the third remained in reserve.

General Simon's brigade, which led Loison's attack, ascended with a wonderful alacrity, and though the light troops plied it unceasingly with musketry, and the artillery bullets swept through it from the first to the last section, its order was never disturbed, nor its speed in the least abated. Ross's guns were worked with incredible quickness, yet their range was palpably contracted every round, and the enemy's shot came singing up in a sharper key, until the skirmishers, breathless and begrimed with powder, rushed over the edge of the ascent, the artillery suddenly drew back, and the victorious cries of the French were heard within a few yards of the summit. Crawfurd, who standing alone on one of the rocks, had been intently watching the progress of this attack, then turned, and in a quick shrill tone desired the two regiments in reserve to charge! the next moment a horrid shout startled the French column, and eighteen hundred British bayonets went sparkling over the brow of the hill. Yet so truly brave and hardy were the leaders of the enemy, that each man of the first section raised his musket, and two officers and ten soldiers fell before them. Not a Frenchman had missed his mark! They could do no more! The head of their column was violently overturned and driven upon the rear, both flanks were lapped over by the English wings, and three terrible discharges at five yards' distance completed the rout. In a few minutes a long trail of carcasses and broken arms indicated the line of retreat. The main body of the British stood fast; but several companies followed the pursuit down the mountain, until Ney moving forward his reserve, and opening his guns from the opposite height killed some men, and thus warned the rest to recover their own ground. The German brigade then spread over the hill, and the light division resumed its original position.

Loison shewed no disposition to renew the attack, but Marchand's people, who had followed the main road, broke into several masses, gained a pine wood half-way up the mountain, and sent a cloud of their skirmishers against the highest part, at the very moment that Simon was defeated. Such, however, was the difficulty of ascending, that the Portuguese troops alone held the enemy in check, and half a mile higher up, Spencer shewed a line of the royal guards, which forbade any hope of success. From the salient point of land occupied by the light division, Crawfurd's artillery also took the main body of the French in the wood, in flank; and Ney, who was there in person, after sustaining this murderous fire for an hour, relinquished the attack. The desultory fighting of the light troops then ceased, and before two o'clock Crawfurd having assented to a momentary truce, parties of both armies were mixed amicably together searching for the wounded men.

Towards evening, however, a French company

See Notice at the beginning of this Vol.

having, with signal audacity, seized a village within half-musket shot of the light division, refused to retire, which so incensed Crawfurd that, turning twelve guns on the village, he overwhelmed it with bullets for half an hour. After paying the French captain this distinguished honour, the English general, recovering his temper, sent a company of the forty-third down, which cleared the village in a few minutes. Meanwhile an affecting incident, contrasting strongly with the savage character of the preceding events, added to the interest of the day. A poor orphan Portuguese girl, about seventeen years of age, and very handsome, was seen coming down the mountain and driving an ass, loaded with all her property, through the midst of the French army. She had abandoned her dwelling in obedience to the proclamation, and now passed over the field of battle with a childish simplicity, totally unconscious of her perilous situation, and scarcely understanding which were the hostile and which the friendly troops, for no man on either side was so brutal as to molest her.

In this battle of Busaco, the French after astonishing efforts of valour, were repulsed, in the manner to be expected from the strength of the ground, and the goodness of the soldiers opposed to them ; and their loss, although prodigiously exaggerated at the time, was great. General Graind'orge and about eight hundred men were slain ; generals Foy and Merle wounded ; general Simon was made prisoner. The whole loss sustained may be estimated at four thousand five hundred men, while that of the allies did not exceed thirteen hundred, because the musketry and artillery of the latter were brought into full activity, whereas the

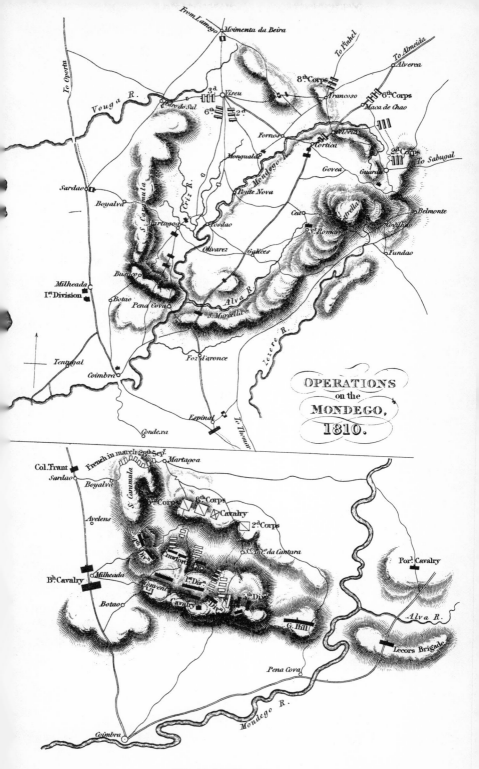

OPERATIONS on the MONDEGO, 1810.

Published by T. & W. Boone 1830.

French sought to gain the day by resolution and audacity rather than by fire.

Massena now judged the position of Busaco impregnable, and to turn it by the Mondego impossible, as the allies could pass that river quicker than himself; but a peasant informed him of the road leading from Mortagao over the Caramula to Boyalva, and he resolved to turn lord Wellington's left. To cover this movement the skirmishing was renewed with such vigour on the 28th, that a general battle was for some time expected. Yet an ostentatious display of men, the disappearance of baggage, and the throwing up of entrenchments on the hill covering the roads to Mortagao plainly indicated some other design. Howbeit, it was not until evening when the enemy's masses in front being sensibly diminished, and his cavalry descried winding over the distant mountains, that the project became quite apparent. Hill then crossed the Mondego, and retired by Espinal upon Thomar, while the centre and left of the army defiled in the night by the other roads upon Milheada. In this manner Busaco was evacuated before the 29th; the guns followed the convent road, and the light division furnished the rear-guard until they passed Fornos, where the open country enabled the cavalry to relieve them.

Massena's scouts reached Boyalva in the evening of the 28th, and it has been erroneously asserted, that Trant's absence from Sardao alone enabled the French general to execute his design. Trant was however at Sardao, four miles from Boyalva, before one o'clock on the 28th; but having, through a mistake of Baccellar's, marched from Lamego, by the circuitous route of Oporto, instead of the di-

rect road through San Pedro do Sul, he lost men
from fatigue and desertion, and could bring only
fifteen hundred militia into line. Hence his absence
or presence could have produced no effect whatever,
even though he had, as lord Wellington intended,
been at Boyalva itself. Accordingly, the French
cavalry, pushing between him and the British
horse, on the 29th cut off one of his patroles, and
the next morning drove him, with the loss of twenty
men, behind the Vouga.

When Massena's main body had cleared the defiles of Boyalva, it marched upon Coimbra, and
the allies, crossing the Mondego at that city, commenced the passage of the defiles leading upon
Condexa and Pombal. The commissariat stores,
which had been previously removed from Raiva de
Pena Cova to Figueras, were then embarked at
Peniché; the light division and the cavalry remained
on the right bank of the Mondego; and Baccellar
was directed to bring down all the militia of the
northern provinces upon the Vouga. The foolish
policy of the native government now became evident,
notwithstanding the proclamations, and the urgent,
and even menacing remonstrances of the English
general, the Portuguese Regency had not wasted
the country behind the Mondego. During the few
days that the enemy was stopped at Busaco, only
the richest inhabitants had quitted Coimbra, when
the allied army retreated, that city was still popu-
lous; and when the approach of the enemy left no
choice but to fly or to risk the punishment of death
and infamy announced in the proclamation, so
direful a scene of distress ensued that the most
hardened of men could not behold it without emo-
tion. Mothers, with children of all ages, the sick,

the old, the bedridden, and even lunatics, went or were carried forth, the most part, with little hope and less help, to journey for days in company with contending armies. Fortunately for this unhappy multitude, the weather was fine, and the roads firm, or the greatest number must have perished in the most deplorable manner. And, notwithstanding all this misery, the object was not gained : the people fled, but the provisions were left, and the mills were but partially and imperfectly ruined.

On the 1st of October, the outposts were attacked, and driven from the hills bounding the plain of Coimbra to the north. The French, on entering this plain, suffered some loss from a cannonade, and the British cavalry was drawn up in line, but with no serious intention of fighting ; and was soon after withdrawn across the Mondego, yet somewhat un-skilfully, for the French following briskly, cut down some men even in the middle of the river, and were only prevented from forcing the passage by a strong skirmish, in which fifty or sixty men fell.

This scrambling affair obliged the light division to march hastily through the city, to gain the defiles of Condeixa, which commence at the end of the bridge ; all the inhabitants who had not before quitted the place then rushed out, each with what could be caught up in the hand, and driving before them a number of animals loaded with sick people or children. At the entrance to the bridge, the press was so great that the troops halted for a few moments, just under the prison ; the jailor had fled with the keys ; the prisoners, crowding to the win-dows, were endeavouring to tear down the bars with their hands, and even with their teeth, and bellowing in the most frantic manner, while the bitter lamentations of the multitude increased, and the pistol shots of the cavalry engaged at the ford below, were distinctly heard.

Captain William Campbell, an officer of Crawfurd's staff, burst the prison-doors, and released the wretched inmates, and the troops forced their way over the bridge; but at the other end, the up-hill road, passing between high rocks, was so crowded that no effort, even of the artillery, could make way. A troop of French dragoons crossed a ford, and hovering close upon the flank, increased the confusion; and a single regiment of foot would have sufficed to destroy the division, wedged in, as it was, in a hollow way, and totally incapable of advancing, retreating, or breaking out on either side. At last, some of the infantry opened a passage to the right, and, by great exertions, the road was cleared for the guns; but it was not until after dusk that the division reached Condeixa, although the distance was less than eight miles. Head-quarters were that night at Redinha, and the next day at Leiria.

Hitherto the marches had been easy, the weather fine, and provisions abundant, nevertheless, the usual disorders of a retreat had already commenced. In Coimbra, a quantity of harness and intrenching tools were scattered in the streets; at Leiria, the magazines were plundered by the troops and camp-followers; at Condeixa, a magazine of tents, shoes, spirits, and salt meat was destroyed, or abandoned to the enemy: and, while the streets were flowing, ancle deep, with rum, the light division and Pack's Portuguese brigade, at the distance of a

quarter of a mile, were obliged to slaughter their
own bullocks, and received only half rations of
liquor!

Lord Wellington arrested this growing disorder
with a strong hand. Three men, taken in the fact
at Leiria, were hanged on the spot, and some
regiments, whose discipline was more tainted than
others, were forbidden to enter a village. This
vigorous exercise of command, aided by the fine
weather and the enemy's inactivity, restored order
amongst the allies, while Massena's conduct, the
reverse of the English general's, introduced the
confusion of a retreat in the pursuing army. In
Coimbra, the French general permitted such waste
that in a few days, resources were dissipated which
under good arrangements, would have supplied his
troops for two months; and, during this licentious
delay the advantage gained by his dangerous flank
march to Boyalva was lost.

OBSERVATIONS.

1°. " *Attack vigorously, after having observed well
where to strike.*" This simple, but profound expression in Napoleon's letter of service, forms the
test by which the prince of Esling's operations
should be judged.

2°. The design of turning the strong ground
behind Celerico, by the route of Viseu, required
close and rapid movements; yet the French general
did not quit Viseu, to march against Coimbra, until
the tenth day after passing the Pinhel. This was
not a " *a vigorous attack.*"

3°. Massena should have brought the allies to

action in a forward position; and he might have done so either when Almeida fell, or before that event, because the complement of mules for the service of the army not being then full, the commissariat was dependent upon the country carts, and when the first retrograde movement took place from Alverca, the drivers fled with their animals, producing infinite confusion in the rear. The commissary-general Kennedy contrived, indeed, to procure fifteen hundred additional mules; but, intermediately, a brisk advance of the enemy would have forced the English general to fight, or retire more hastily than would have beseemed his reputation, or suited his political position.

4°. If the prince of Esling had not been misled by Alorna and Pamplona, and the more readily that the estates of the latter were situated about Coimbra, he would have judged that the line his adversary had studied for eight months, and now so carefully and jealously guarded, was more likely to afford advantages, than the circuitous route by Viseu, which was comparatively neglected. The French general, ill acquainted with the scene of action, but having the stronger and more moveable army, should have followed closely.

A rapid pursuit, through Celerico, would have brought the French army on to the Alva before Hill or even Leith could have joined lord Wellington. The latter must then have fought with half his own army, or he must have retreated to the Lines. If he offered battle with so few troops, his position could be turned either by the right or left; on the left, by the slopes of the Estrella; on the right by crossing the Mondego, for Busaco was too extensive to be occupied before Hill and Leith arrived. Now, the road by Viseu being the longest and least practicable, demanded great diligence to compensate for the difficulties of the way ; and to gain Coimbra and force the allies to a battle before Hill arrived, were objects more readily to be attained by the left bank of the Mondego. The point where to strike was therefore not " *well considered,*" and it is clear that Massena did not rightly estimate the greatness of his enterprise.

5°. When the rocks of Busaco glittering with bayonets first rose on the prince of Esling's view, two fresh questions were to be solved. Was he to attack or to turn that formidable post? Or, availing himself of his numerical strength and central situation, was he to keep the allies in check, seize Oporto, and neglect Lisbon until better combinations could be made? The last question has been already discussed ; but, contrary to the general opinion, the attack upon Busaco appears to me faulty in the execution rather than in the conception ; and the march by which that position was finally turned, a violation of the soundest principles of war. In a purely military view, the English general may be censured for not punishing his adversary's rashness.

With respect to the attack, sixty-five thousand French veterans had no reason to believe that fifty thousand mixed and inexperienced troops, distributed on a mountain more than eight miles long, were impregnably posted. It would have been no overweening presumption in the French general to expect, that three corps well disposed, supported by a numerous artillery, and led on the first day, (as Ney desired,) might carry some part of the position, and it is an error, also, to suppose that guns could not

have been used : the light division were constantly
within range, and thirty pieces of artillery employed
on that point would have wonderfully aided the
attack by the sixth corps.   But when a general in
chief remains ten miles from a field of battle, gives
his adversary two days to settle in a position, makes
his attacks without connection, and without artillery, and brings forward no reserves, success is impossible even with the valiant soldiers Massena
commanded.

6°. " *An army should always be in condition to
fight.*"

" *A general should never abandon one line of communication without establishing another.*"

" *Flank marches within reach of an enemy are
rash and injudicious.*"

These maxims of Napoleon, the greatest of all
generals, have been illustrated by many examples ;
Senef, Kollin, Rosbach, the valley of the Brenta,
Salamanca, attest their value.   Now, Massena violated all three, by his march to Boyalva, and some
peculiar circumstances, or desperate crisis of affairs
should be shewn, to warrant such a departure from
general principles.   Sir Joshua Reynolds, treating
of another art says, " *genius begins where rules end.*"
But here genius was dormant, and rules disregarded.
Massena was not driven to a desperate game.
The conquest of Oporto was open to him so was a
march by Viseu upon the Vouga, which, though
demanding time, was safe ; in going by Boyalva,
he threw his whole army into a single and narrow
defile, within ten miles of an enemy in position ;
and that also (as I have been informed by an
officer of marshal Ney's staff) with much disorder :
the baggage and commissariat, the wounded and

sick, the artillery, cavalry, and infantry, mixed together; discord raging amongst the generals, confusion amongst the soldiers, and in the night season when every difficulty is doubled. His *" army was not, then, in a condition to fight."* He was making *" a flank march within reach of an enemy in position,"* and he was *" abandoning his line of communication without having established another."*

7°. Lord Wellington was within four hours march of either end of the defile, through which the French army was moving. He might have sent the first division and the cavalry (forming with Portuguese regular troops, and Trant's militia, a mass of twelve or fourteen thousand men) to Sardao, to head the French in the defile; while the second, third, fourth, fifth, and light divisions, advancing by Martagao, assailed their rear. That he did not do so, is to be attributed to his political position. His mixed and inexperienced army was not easily handled; war is full of mischances, and the loss of a single brigade might have caused the English government to abandon the contest altogether. Nevertheless, his retreat was more critically dangerous than such an attack would have been, and in a military view the battle of Busaco should not have been fought: it was extraneous to his original plan, it was forced upon him by events, and was in fine a political battle.

8°. Massena's march, being unopposed, was successful. The allied army could not cope with him in the open country between Busaco and the sea, where his cavalry would have had a fair field; hence lord Wellington, reverting to his original plan, retreated by the Coimbra and Espinhal roads. But the prince of Esling was at Avelans de Cima and Milheada on the 30th; the allied cavalry and the light division being still on the right bank of the Mondego, which was fordable in many places below Coimbra. Had the French general, directing his march through Tentugal, crossed at those fords, and pushed rapidly on to Leiria, by the route sir Arthur Wellesley followed, in 1808, against Junot, the communication with Lisbon would have been cut : terror and confusion would then have raged in the capital, the patriarch's faction would have triumphed, and a dangerous battle must have been risked before the Lines could be reached.

9°. When the allies had gained Leiria, and secured their line of retreat, the fate of Portugal was still in the French general's hands. If he had established a fresh base at Coimbra ; employed the ninth corps to seize Oporto ; secured his line of communication with that city and with Almeida by fortified posts ; and afterwards, extending his position by the left, attacked Abrantes, and given his hand to a corps sent by Soult from the south, not only would the campaign have been so far a successful one, but in no other manner could he have so effectually frustrated his adversary's political and military projects. Lord Wellington dreaded such a proceeding, and hailed the renewed advance of the French army, which like the rising of a heavy cloud discovered a clear horizon beneath.

Even at Coimbra, the prince was unacquainted with the existence of the Lines, and believed that, beyond Santarem, the country was open for the usage of all arms. It is strange that, when Junot, Loison, Foy, and many other officers, who had served in Portugal, were present, better information was not obtained ; but every part of this campaign illustrated Massena's character, as drawn by Napoleon:—" Brave, decided, and intrepid; dull in conversation, but in danger acquiring clearness and force of thought; ambitious, filled with self-love, neglectful of discipline, regardless of good administration, and, consequently, disliked by the troops; his dispositions for battle bad, but his temper pertinacious to the last degree; he was never discouraged!"

10°. It appears that the French reached Coimbra at the moment when the fourteen days' bread, carried by the soldiers, was exhausted, and it is worthy of consideration that French soldiers are accustomed to carry so much bread. Other nations, especially the English, would not husband it; yet it was a practice of the ancient Romans, and it ought to be the practice of all armies. It requires a long previous discipline and well-confirmed military habits; but, without it, men are only half efficient, especially for offensive warfare. The secret of making perfect soldiers is only to be found in national customs and institutions; men should come to the ranks fitted, by previous habits, for military service, instead of being stretched as it were upon the bed of Procrustes, by a discipline which has no resource but fear.

CHAPTER VIII.

From the 1st until the 3d, the French army was in disorder. The 4th, Massena resumed his march by Condeixa and Leiria, leaving his sick and wounded, with a slender guard, (in all about four thousand seven hundred men,) at Coimbra. His hospital was established at the convent of Santa Clara, on the left bank of the river, and all the inhabitants, who were averse or unable to reach the Lines, came down from their hiding-places in the mountains. But scarcely had the prince left the city, when Trant, Miller, and Wilson, with nearly ten thousand militia, closed upon his rear, occupying the sierras on both sides of the Mondego, and cutting off all communication with Almeida.

On the evening of the 4th, the French drove the English picquets from Pombal, and, the next morning, pushed so suddenly upon Leiria, as to create some confusion. The road was however crossed at right angles, by a succession of parallel ravines, and captain Somers Cocks taking advantage of one, charged the head of the enemy, and checked him until general Anson's brigade of cavalry, and captain Bull's troop of artillery, arrived to his support. The French then, forming three columns, endeavoured to bear down the British with the centre, while the others turned the flanks. The ravines were difficult to pass; Bull's artillery played well into the principal body, and Anson, charging as it emerged from every defile, slew a great number. The British lost three officers and about fifty men, the enemy considerably more, and, in five hours, he did not gain as many miles of ground, although he had thirty-six squadrons opposed to ten. During this delay, Leiria was cleared, and the army retreated; the right by Thomar and Santarem; the centre by Batalha and Rio Mayor; the left by Alcobaça and Obidos, and at the same time a native force, under colonel Blunt, was thrown into Peniché. Massena followed, in one column, by the way of Rio Mayor; but, meanwhile, an exploit, as daring and hardy as any performed by a Partizan officer during the war, convicted him of bad generalship, and shook his plan of invasion to its base.

SURPRISE OF COIMBRA.

Colonel Trant reached Milheada, intending to unite with Miller and J. Wilson, the latter having made a forced march for that purpose, but they were still distant, his own arrival was unknown at Coimbra, and he resolved to attack the French in that city without waiting for assistance. Having surprised a small post at Fornos early in the morning of the 7th, he sent his cavalry, at full gallop, through the streets of Coimbra, with orders to pass the bridge, and cut off all communication with the French army, of whose progress he was ignorant. Meanwhile, his infantry penetrated at different points into the principal parts of the town, the enemy, astounded, made little or no resistance and the convent of Santa Clara surrendered at discretion; thus, on the third day after the prince of

Esling had quitted the Mondego, his depôts and hospitals, and nearly five thousand prisoners wounded and unwounded, amongst which there was a company of the marines of the imperial guards, fell into the hands of a small militia force! The next day, Miller and Wilson, arriving, spread their men on all the lines of communication, and picked up above three hundred more prisoners, while Trant conducted his to Oporto.

During the first confusion, the Portuguese committed some violence on the prisoners, and the Abbé du Pradt and other French writers have not hesitated to accuse Trant of disgracing his country and his uniform by encouraging this conduct, whereas, his exertions repressed it ; and if the fact, that not more than ten men lost their lives under such critical circumstances, was not sufficient refutation, Appendix, No. VIII. the falsehood is placed beyond dispute in a letter of thanks, written to colonel Trant, by the French officers who fell into his hands.

This disaster made no change in Massena's dispositions. He continued his march, and, on the 8th, his advanced guard drove the cavalry piquets out See Notice at the beginning of this Vol. of Rio Mayor. General Slade, who commanded the brigade, took no heed of this; and the enemy, pushing rapidly on, was like to have taken the battery of artillery in Alcoentre ; a good deal of confusion ensued, but the royals and the sixteenth drove the French out of the town, sabred many, and made twelve prisoners. The next day the skirmish was renewed with various turns of fortune, and, finally, the British retreated.

Meanwhile the allied army was entering the Lines. The first, fourth, and fifth divisions in the centre by Sobral, the third division on the left by

Torres Vedras, and Hill's corps on the right by Alhandra. The light division and Pack's brigade should also have entered by Aruda. But Crawfurd, who had reached Alemquer on the 9th, was still there, at three o'clock, p. m. on the 10th; and the weather being stormy, the men were placed under cover, and no indication of marching was given by the general. He knew that all the cavalry had already filed into the lines, yet he posted no guards, sent no patroles forward, and took no precaution against a surprise, although the town situated in a deep ravine was peculiarly exposed to such a disaster.

Some officers, uneasy at this state of affairs, anxiously watched the height in front, and, about four o'clock, observed some French dragoons on the summit, which was within cannon shot. The alarm was instantly given, and the regiments got under arms; but the principal post of assembly had been marked on an open space, very much exposed to an enemy's guns, and from whence the road led through an ancient gateway to the top of the mountain behind. The numbers of French increased every moment, they endeavoured to create a belief that their artillery was come up, and although this feint was easily seen through, the general desired the regiments to break and reform on the other side of the archway, out of gun range. In a moment all was disorder. The baggage animals were still loading, the streets were crowded with the followers of the division, and the whole in one confused mass rushed or were driven headlong to the archway. Several were crushed, and with worse troops, a general panic must have ensued; but the greatest number of the soldiers, ashamed of the order, stood firm in their ranks until the first confusion had abated.

Nevertheless the mischief was sufficiently great, and the enemy's infantry descending the heights, endeavoured some to turn the town on the left, while others pushed directly through the streets in pursuit, and thus with his front in disorder, and his rear skirmishing, and night falling, Crawfurd commenced a retreat. The weather was, however, so boisterous that the fire soon ceased, and a few men wounded and the loss of some baggage was all the hurt sustained ; yet so uncertain is every thing in war, that this affair had like to have produced the most terrible results in another quarter.

The division, instead of marching by Caregada and Cadafaes, followed the route of Sobral, and was obliged in the dark to make a flank march of several miles along the foot of the Lines to gain Aruda, which was meanwhile left open to the enemy. In this state, the cavalry patroles from Villa Franca, meeting some stragglers and followers of the camp near Caregada, were by them told that the light division was cut off; a report confirmed in some measure by the unguarded state of Aruda, and by the presence of the enemy's scouts on that side. This information alarmed general Hill for the safety of the second line, and the more so that the weakest part was in the vicinity of Aruda ; he therefore made a retrograde movement towards Alverca with a view to watch the valley of Calandrix, or to gain the pass of Bucellas according to circumstances. Hence, when the enemy was in full march against the Lines, the front from Alhandra to the forts above Sobral, a distance of eight

or nine miles, was quite disgarnished of troops.
The true state of affairs was, however, quickly
ascertained, and Hill regained Alhandra before
day-light on the 11th.

During this time the second and the eighth corps
passed Alemquer, the former marching upon Villa
Franca, the latter upon Sobral. Reynier's movements
on the French left were languid, he did not discover
the unguarded state of Alhandra, and his picquets
did not enter Villa Franca until late the next day.
But on the right general Clausel, one of the most
distinguished officers in the French army, coming
upon Sobral, in the dusk, with the head of the
eighth corps dislodged the troops of the first division, occupied the ridge on which the town is built,
and in the night threw up some entrenchments
close under the centre of the allies' position.

It is however time to give a more detailed description of those celebrated works, improperly
called

THE LINES OF TORRES VEDRAS.

It has been already said, that they consisted of Memoran-
three distinct ranges of defence. da of the
lines, &c.
The first, extending from Alhandra on the Tagus by Col. J.
T. Jones,
to the mouth of the Zizandre on the sea-coast, Royal Engineers,
was, following the inflections of the hills, twenty- printed for
private cir-
nine miles long. culation.

The second, traced at a distance varying from
six to ten miles in rear of the first, stretched from
Quintella on the Tagus to the mouth of the St.
Lorenza, being twenty-four miles in length.

The third, intended to cover a forced embarkation,

extended from Passo d'Arcos on the Tagus to the tower of Junquera on the coast. Here an outer line, constructed on an opening of three thousand yards, enclosed an entrenched camp designed to cover the embarkation with fewer troops, should the operation be delayed by bad weather; within this second camp, Fort St. Julian's (whose high ramparts and deep ditches defied an escalade) was armed and strengthened to enable a rear-guard to protect both itself and the army.

The nearest part of the second line was twenty-four miles from these works at Passo d'Arcos, and some parts of the first line were two long marches distant; but the principal routes led through Lisbon, where measures were taken to retard the enemy and give time for the embarkation.

Of these stupendous Lines, the second, whether regarded for its strength or importance, was undoubtedly the principal; the others were only appendages, the one as a final place of refuge, the other as an advanced work to stem the first violence of the enemy, and to enable the army to take up its ground on the second line without hurry or pressure. Massena having, however, wasted the summer season on the frontiers, the first line acquired such strength, both from labour and from the fall of rain, that lord Wellington resolved to abide his opponent's charge there.

The ground presented to the French being, as it were, divided into five parts or positions, shall be described in succession from right to left.

1°. *From Alhandra to the head of the valley of Calandrix.* This distance, of about five miles, was a continuous and lofty ridge, defended by thirteen redoubts, and for two miles rendered inaccessible by a scarp fifteen to twenty feet high, executed along the brow. It was guarded by the British and Portuguese divisions under general Hill, and flanked from the Tagus by a strong flotilla of gun-boats, manned by British seamen.

2°. *From the head of the vale of Calandrix to the Pé de Monte.* This position, also five miles in length, consisted of two salient mountains forming the valley of Aruda, that town being exactly in the mouth of the pass. Only three feeble redoubts, totally incapable of stopping an enemy for an in-stant, were constructed here, and the defence of the ground was entrusted to general Crawfurd and the light division.

3°. *The Monte Agraça.* This lofty mountain overtopped the adjacent country in such a manner, that from its summit the whole of the first line could be distinctly observed. The right was sepa-rated from the Aruda position, by a deep ravine which led to nothing; the left overlooked the vil-lage and valley of Zibreira; the centre overhung the town of Sobral. The summit of this moun-tain was crowned by an immense redoubt, mount-ing twenty-five guns, and having three smaller works, containing nineteen guns, clustered around it. The garrisons, amounting to two thousand men, were supplied by Pack's brigade; and on the reverse of the position, which might be about four miles in length, the fifth division, under general Leith, was posted in reserve.

4°. *From the valley of Zibreira to Torres Vedras.* This position, seven miles long, was at first without works; because it was only when the rains had set in, that the resolution to defend the first line permanently, was adopted. But the ground being rough and well defined, the valley in front, deep, and watered by the Zizandre, now become a considerable river, it presented a fine field of battle for a small army. The first and fourth, and a sixth division formed of troops just arrived from England and from Cadiz, were there posted, under the immediate command of lord Wellington himself, whose head-quarters were fixed at Pero Negro, near the Secorra, a rock, on which a telegraph was erected, communicating with every part of the Lines.

5°. *From the heights of Torres Vedras to the mouth of the Zizandre.* The right flank of this position and the pass in front of the town of Torres Vedras were secured, first, by one great redoubt, mounting forty guns; secondly, by several smaller forts, judiciously planted so as to command all the approaches. From these works to the sea a range of moderate heights were crowned with small forts; but the chief defence there, after the rains had set in, was to be found in the Zizandre, which was not only unfordable, but overflowed its banks, and formed an impassable marsh. A paved road, parallel to the foot of the hills, ran along the whole front; that is, from Torres Vedras, by Runa Sobral and Aruda, to Alhandra. This was the nature of the *first* line of defence; the *second* was still more formidable.

1°. *From the mouth of the St. Lourença to Mafra.* In this distance of seven miles, there was a range of hills naturally steep, artificially scarped, and covered by a deep, and in many parts impracticable ravine. The salient points were secured by forts, which flanked and commanded the few accessible points; but as this line was extensive, a secondary post was fortified a few miles in the rear, to secure a road leading from Ereceira to Cintra.

2°. *On the right of the above line the Tapada, or royal park of Mafra.* Here there was some open ground for an attack. Yet it was strong, and, together with the pass of Mafra, was defended by a system of fourteen redoubts, constructed with great labour and care, well considered with respect to the natural disposition of the ground, and, in some degree, connected with the secondary post spoken of above: in front, the Sierra de Chypre, covered with redoubts, obstructed all approaches to Mafra itself.

3°. *From the Tapada to the pass of Bucellas.* In this space of ten or twelve miles, which formed the middle of the second line, the country is choked by the Monte Chique, the Cabeça, or head of which is in the centre of, and overtopping all the other, mountain masses. A road, conducted along a chain of hills, high and salient, but less bold than any other parts of the line, connected Mafra with the Cabeça, and was secured by a number of forts. The country in front was extremely difficult, and a second and stronger range of heights, parallel to and behind the first, offered a good fighting position, which could only be approached with artillery by the connecting road in front; and to reach that, either the Sierra de Chypre, on the left, or the pass of the Cabeça de Monte Chique, on the right, must have been carried. Now the works covering the latter consisted of a cluster of redoubts constructed on the inferior rocky heads in advance of the Cabeça, and completely commanding all the approaches, and both from their artificial and natural strength, nearly impregnable to open force. The Cabeça and its immediate flanks were considered secure in their natural precipitous strength; and, in like manner, the ridges connecting the Cabeça with the pass of Bucellas, being impregnable, were left untouched, save the blocking of one bad mule road that led over them.

3°. *From Bucellas to the low ground about the Tagus.* The pass of Bucellas was difficult, and strongly defended by redoubts on each side. A ridge, or rather a collection of impassable rocks, called the Sierra de Serves, stretched to the right for two miles without a break, and then died away by gradual slopes in the low ground about the Tagus. These declivities and the flat banks of the river offered an opening two miles and a half wide, which was laboriously and carefully strengthened by redoubts, water-cuts, and retrenchments, and connected by a system of forts with the heights of Alhandra; but it was the weakest part of the whole line in itself, and the most dangerous from its proximity to the valleys of Calandrix and Aruda.

There were five roads practicable for artillery piercing the *first line* of defence, namely, two at Torres Vedras, two at Sobral, and one at Alhandra; but as two of these united again at the Cabeça, there were, in fact, only four points of passage through the *second line*, that is to say, at Mafra, Monte Chique, Bucellas, and Quintella in the flat ground. The aim and scope of all the works was to bar those passes and to strengthen the favourable fighting positions between them, without impeding the movements of the army. Those objects were at-

tained, and it is certain that the loss of the *first*
line would not have been injurious, save in reputation, because the retreat was secure upon the *second*
and stronger line; and the guns of the first were
all of inferior calibre, mounted on common truck
carriages, and consequently immoveable and useless
to the enemy.

The movements of the allies were free and unfettered by the works. The movements of the
French army were impeded and cramped by the
great Monte Junta, which, rising opposite the centre
of the first line, sent forth a spur called the Sierra
de Baragueda in a slanting direction, so close up
to the heights of Torres Vedras that the narrow
pass of Ruña alone separated them. As this pass
was commanded by heavy redoubts, Massena was
of necessity obliged to dispose his forces on one or
other side of the Baragueda, and he could not
transfer his army to either without danger; because
the sierra, although not impassable, was difficult;
and the movement, which would require time and
arrangement, could always be overlooked from the
Monte Agraça, whence, in a few hours, the allied
forces could pour down upon the head, flank, or
rear of the French while in march. And this
could be done with the utmost rapidity, because
communications had been cut by the engineers to
all important points of the Lines, and a system of
signals was established, by which orders were
transmitted from the centre to the extremities in a
few minutes.

Thus much I have thought fit to say respecting
the Lines; too little for the professional reader, too
much, perhaps, for a general history. But I was
desirous to notice, somewhat in detail, works, more

in keeping with ancient than modern military labours ; partly that a just idea might be formed of the talents of the British engineers who constructed them, and partly to show that lord Wellington's measures of defence were not, as some French military writers have supposed, dependent upon the first line. Had that been stormed, the standard of Portuguese independence could still have been securely planted amidst the rocks of the second position.

To occupy fifty miles of fortification, to man one hundred and fifty forts, and to work six hundred pieces of artillery, required a number of men ; but a great fleet in the Tagus, a superb body of marines sent out from England, the civic guards of Lisbon, the Portuguese heavy artillery corps, and the militia and ordenança of Estremadura furnished, altogether, a powerful reserve. The native artillery and the militia supplied all the garrisons of the forts on the second, and most of those on the first line. The British marines occupied the third line ; the navy manned the gun-boats on the river, and aided, in various ways, the operation in the field. The recruits from the depôts, and all the men on furlough, being called in, rendered the Portuguese army stronger than it had yet been; and the British army, reinforced, as I have said, both from Cadiz and England, and remarkably healthy, presented such a front as a general would desire to see in a dangerous crisis.

It was, however, necessary not only to have strength, but the appearance of strength ; and lord Wellington had so dealt with Romana that, without much attention to the wishes of his own government, the latter joined the allies with two divisions. Yet the English general did not act thus, until he was

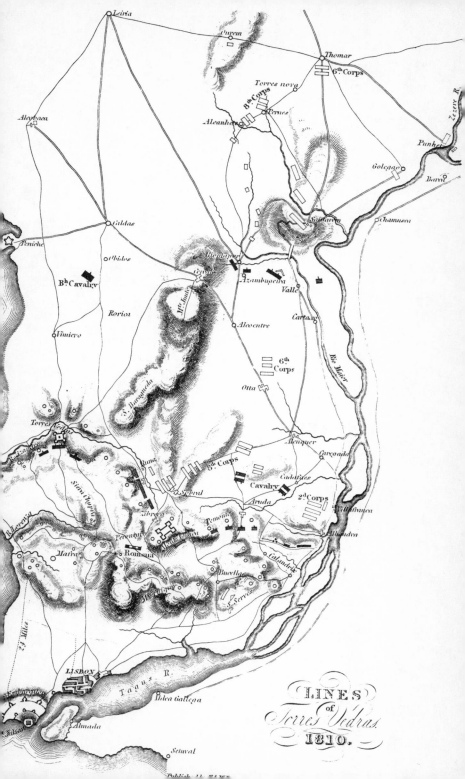

LINES of Torres Vedras 1810.

assured that Massena's force was insufficient to drive the British from Lisbon. He felt that it would have been dishonest to draw Romana's troops into a corner, where they could not (from want of shipping) have escaped in the event of failure. The first division of Spaniards, led by Romana himself, crossed the Tagus at Aldea Gallega the 19th, and the 24th was posted at Enxara de los Cavalleros, just behind the Monte Agraça ; the other followed in a few days; and thus before the end of October, not less than one hundred and thirty thousand fighting men received rations within the Lines; more than seventy thousand being regular troops, completely disposable and unfettered by the works.

Meanwhile, Mendizabel, with the remainder of the Spanish army, reinforced by Madden's Portuguese dragoons, advanced towards Zafra. Ballasteros, at the same time, moved upon Aracena ; and Mortier, ignorant of Romana's absence, retired across the Morena on the 8th, to be near Soult who was then seriously menacing Cadiz. Thus fortune combined, with the dispositions of the English general, to widen the distance, and to diversify the objects of the French armies, at the moment when the allies were concentrating the greatest force on the most important point.

Massena, surprised at the extent and strength of works, the existence of which had only become known to him five days before he came upon them, employed several days to examine their nature. The heights of Alhandra he judged inattackable ; but the valleys of Calandrix and Aruda attracted his attention. Through the former he could turn Hill's position, and come at once upon the weakest part of the second line ; yet the abattis and re-

doubts erected, and hourly strengthening, gave
him little encouragement to attack there; the
nature of the ground about Aruda also was such
that he could not ascertain what number of troops
guarded it, although he made several demonstrations, and frequently skirmished with the light
division, to oblige Crawfurd to shew his force.

That general, by making the town of Aruda an
advanced post, had rendered it impossible to discover
his true situation without a serious affair; and, in
an incredible short space of time, the division,
with prodigious labour, had secured the position
in a manner really worthy of admiration. For
across the ravine on the left, a loose stone wall,
sixteen feet thick and forty feet high, was raised;
and across the great valley of Aruda, a double line
of abattis was drawn; not composed, as is usual,
of the limbs of trees, but of full-grown oaks and
chestnuts, dug up with all their roots and branches,
dragged, by main force, for several hundred yards,
and then reset and crossed, so that no human
strength could break through. Breast-works, at
convenient distances, to defend this line of trees,
were then cast up; and along the summits of the
mountain, for a space of nearly three miles, including the salient points, other stone walls, six
feet high and four in thickness, with banquettes,
were built; so that a good defence could easily
have been made against the attacks of twenty thousand men.

The next points that drew Massena's attention
were the Monte Agraca and the vale of the Upper
Zizandre, where, from the recent period at which
lord Wellington had resolved to offer battle on
the first line, no outworks had been constructed;

neither the valley of Zibreira, nor the hills above Runa, had been fortified. Here it was possible to join battle on more equal terms, but the position of the allies was still very formidable ; the flanks and rear were protected by great forts, and not only was a powerful mass of troops permanently posted there, but six battalions, drawn from Hill's corps, and placed at Bucellas, could, in a very short time, have come into action.

Beyond Runa, the Baragueda ridge and the forts of Torres Vedras forbad any flank movement by the French general ; and it only remained for him to dispose his troops in such a manner between Villa Franca and Sobral that, while the heads of the columns menaced the weakest points of the Lines, a few hours would suffice to concentrate the whole army at any part between the Tagus and the Baragueda ridge. The second corps, still holding the hills opposite Alhandra, extended its right along some open ground as far as Aruda ; and being covered, at that point, by a force of cavalry, was connected with the eighth corps, the head of which was pushed forward on Sobral, occupying the lower ridges of the Baragueda, and lining the banks of the Zizandre as far as Duas Portas on the road to Runa : the outposts of each army being there nearly in contact.

Massena did not bring the sixth corps beyond Otta, and his dispositions were not made without several skirmishes, especially near Sobral, on the morning of the 14th, where, attempting to dislodge the seventy-first regiment from a field-work, his troops were repulsed, pursued, and driven from their own retrenchments, which were held until evening ; and only evacuated because the whole of the eighth corps was advancing for the purpose of permanently establishing its position. The loss of the allies in these petty affairs amounted to one hundred and fifty, of which, the greatest part fell at Sobral ; that of the enemy was estimated higher. The English general Harvey was wounded, and at Villa Franca the fire of the gun-boats killed the French general St. Croix, a young man of signal ability and promise.

The war was now reduced to a species of blockade. Massena's object was to feed his army until reinforcements reached it ; lord Wellington's to starve the French before succour could arrive. The former spread his moveable columns in the rear to seek for provisions, and commenced forming magazines at Santarem, where his principal depôt was established ; but the latter drew down all the militia and ordenança of the north on Massena's rear, putting them in communication with the garrison of Peniché on one side, and on the other with the militia of Lower Beira. Carlos d'España also, crossing the Tagus acted between Castello Branco and Abrantes. Thus, the French were completely enclosed without any weakening of the regular army.

To aid the communication between Peniché and the militia of the North, Obidos surrounded by old walls had been put in a state of defence ; but the Portuguese government having neglected to furnish it with provisions, it had been evacuated. Nevertheless, major Fenwick again occupied it temporarily with three hundred militia, and being supported by a Spanish battalion and by a strong detachment of British cavalry posted at Ramalhal, hemmed in the French on that side ; and a move-

able column, under colonel Waters, issuing from
Torres Vedras, made incursions against the enemy's
marauding detachments, capturing many prisoners,
and part of a considerable convoy which was passing the Baragueda. The French were thus continually harassed, yet their detachments scoured
the whole country, even beyond Leiria, and obtained
provisions in considerable quantities.

Meanwhile, the main bodies of the hostile forces
remained quiet, although Massena's right was
greatly exposed. Lord Wellington had four British
divisions and Romana's corps, forming a mass of
twenty-five thousand men, close round Sobral ;
and, by directing the greatest part of his cavalry
and the six battalions at Bucellas, upon Aruda,
he could have assembled from eight to ten thousand men there also ; these last advancing a short
distance into the plain, could, in conjunction with
Hill, have kept the second corps in check, while
the twenty-five thousand, pouring down at daylight
from the Monte Agraça, from the valley of Zibreira,
and from the side of Ruña, could have enveloped
and crushed the head of the eighth corps long
before the sixth could have reached the scene of
action. But war is a curious and complicated web!
and while the purely military part was thus happily
situated and strong, the political part was one of
weakness and alarm. Scarcely could the English
general maintain a defensive attitude, struggling
as he was against the intrigues and follies of men
who have, nevertheless, been praised for their
" earnest and manly co-operation."

See An-
nals of the
Peninsu-
lar War,
Vol. II.
p. 331.

CHAPTER IX.

BOOK
XI.

1810.
October.
Mr. Stu-
art's Pa-
pers. MSS.
THE presence of the enemy, in the heart of the country, embarrassed the finances, and the Regency applied to England for an additional subsidy. Mr. Stuart, seeing the extreme distress, took upon himself to direct the house of Sampayo to furnish provisions to the troops on the credit of the first subsidy; he also made the greatest exertions to feed the fugitive inhabitants forty thousand of whom arrived before the 13th of October, and others were hourly coming in, destitute and starving. Corn, to be purchased at any price, was sought for in all countries; from Ireland, America, and Egypt; and one thousand tons of government shipping were lent to merchants to fetch grain from Algiers. One commission of citizens was formed to facilitate the obtaining cattle and corn from the northern provinces; another to regulate the transport of provisions to the army, and to push a trade with Spain through the Alemtejo. Small craft were sent up the Tagus to carry off both the inhabitants and their stock, from the islands and from the left bank; and post-vessels were established along the coast to Oporto. Bullion and jewels were put on board the men of war; a proclamation was issued, calling upon the people to be tranquil, and a strong police was established to enforce this object. Finally, to supply the deficiency of tonnage created by the sending off the transports in search of corn, an

embargo was laid upon the port of Lisbon ; it was strongly protested against by the Americans, but an imperious necessity ruled.

All these measures were vehemently opposed by the Patriarch and his faction; and that nothing might be wanting to shew how entirely the fate of the Peninsula depended, in that hour, upon lord Wellington's firmness, the fears of the British cabinet, which had been increasing as the crisis approached, were now plainly disclosed. Their private letters contained hints at variance with their public despatches. They evidently wished their general to abandon the country, but threw the responsibility upon him ; they were unable to comprehend his genius ; they thought him rash, and were themselves unequal to the crisis. They had not the manliness either to resign the contest or to carry it on with vigour, and cast their base policy with a view only to their own escape in case of failure. During the retreat from the north, affairs seemed so gloomy to the eyes of some officers of rank, that their correspondence bore evidence of their feelings ; the letters of general Spencer and general Charles Stewart appeared so desponding to lord Liverpool, that he transmitted them to lord Wellington, and by earnestly demanding an opinion upon their contents, showed how deeply they had disturbed his own mind.

Thus beset on every side, the English general rose like a giant. Without noticing either the arguments or the forebodings in these letters, he took a calm historical review of the circumstances which had induced him to defend Portugal, and which he had before explained to the very minister he was addressing ; then shewing that, up to that period his opinions had been in every instance justified by the results, he assumed that it was reasonable to confide in his judgement for the future. Having thus vindicated his prudence and foresight, he traced out the probable course of coming events, discussing both his own and the enemy's designs, and that with such sagacity that the subsequent course of the war never belied his anticipations. This remarkable letter exists, and, were all other records of lord Wellington's genius to be lost, it would alone suffice to vindicate his great reputation to posterity.

Having with conscious superiority replied to his own government, he, with a fierceness rendered necessary by the crisis, turned upon the patriarch and his coadjutors. Reproaching them for their unpatriotic, foolish, and deceitful conduct, he told
them plainly that they were unfaithful servants of their country and their prince ; and threatened *to withdraw the British army altogether*, if the practices of which he complained were not amended.

" The king of England and the prince regent of Portugal had," he said, " entrusted him with the conduct of the military operations, and he would not suffer any person to interfere. He knew what to do, and he would not alter his plans to meet the *senseless suggestions of the Regency*. Let the latter look to their own duties ! Let them provide food for the army and the people, and keep the capital tranquil." " With principal Souza," he said, " it was not possible to act, and, if that person continued in power, the country would be lost. Either the principal or himself must quit their employments ; if himself, he would take care that the world should know the reasons ; meanwhile he

would address the prince upon the conduct of the
Regency.

"He had hoped," he resumed in another letter,
"that the Portuguese government was satisfied with
his acts, and that instead of endeavouring to render
all defence useless by disturbing the minds of the
populace at Lisbon, they would have adopted
measures to secure the tranquillity of that capital.
But, like other weak individuals, they added duplicity to weakness, and their past expressions of approbation and gratitude he supposed were intended
to convey censure. All he asked from them was to
preserve tranquillity, to provide food for their own
troops while employed in the Lines, and to be prepared, in case of disaster, to save those persons and
their families who were obnoxious to the enemy."
"I have," he said, "little doubt of final success,
but *I have fought a sufficient number of battles to
know, that the result of any is not certain, even with
the best arrangements.*"

These reproaches were neither too severe nor ill-
timed, for the war had been hanging in even balance, and the weight of interested folly thus thrown
in by the Regency, was beginning to sink the scale.
Yet to shew the justice of lord Wellington's complaints, it is necessary to resume the thread of those
intrigues which have been before touched upon.
Instead of performing their own duties, the government assumed, that the struggle could be maintained on the frontier, and when they should have
been removing the people and the provisions from
the line of retreat, they were discussing the expediency of military operations which were quite impracticable. When convinced of their error by
facts, they threw the burthen of driving the coun-

try upon the general, although they knew that he was ignorant even of the names and places of abode of those officers and magistrates who were to execute it, and that there was but one Portuguese agent at head-quarters to give assistance in translating the necessary orders.

When this was remarked to them, they issued the orders themselves, but made the execution referable to the general, without his knowledge, and well knowing that he had no means of communicating with the country people, and this at the very moment of the enemy's advance. The battle of Busaco, by delaying the French army, had alone enabled the orders, even to reach the persons to whom they were addressed. But it was the object of the Regency, by nourishing and soothing the national indolence, to throw the odium of harsh and rigorous measures upon the British authorities. Lord Wellington, however, while he reproached them for this conduct, never shrunk from the odium; he avowed, in his proclamations, that he was the author of the plan for wasting the country, and he was willing the Regency should shelter themselves under his name, but he was not willing to lose the fruit of his responsibility, nor content that those whose courage did shrink from the trial, " should seek popularity with the populace at the expense of the best interests of the country."

After the disputes which followed the fall of Almeida, the English government convinced that a more secure and powerful grasp must be taken of Portugal, permitted their envoy, Mr. Stuart, to have a seat in the Regency, and influenced by lord Wellington, insisted that the subsidy should be placed under the control of the British instead of the native authorities. Lord Wellesley also gave assurances that if the army was forced to quit Lisbon, the Portuguese troops should be carried to Oporto, and the war recommenced in that quarter; but Mr. Stuart very prudently reserved this information until the necessity should arrive, well knowing that the Patriarch and Souza, who had already proposed to go there themselves, would eagerly seize the occasion to urge the evacuation of Lisbon. The 2d of October, Mr. Stuart took his seat, and together with doctor Noguera, the Conde de Redondo, and the marquis Olhao (the former of whom was decidedly averse to the Souzas' faction, and the two latter moderate in their conduct) proceeded to control the intrigues and violence of the Patriarch and principal Souza. It was full time, for both were formally protesting against the destruction of the mills in Beira, and vigorously opposing every measure proposed by lord Wellington.

They were deeply offended by the suppression of the Lusitanian legion, which about this time was incorporated with the regular forces; they had openly declared, that the Portuguese troops should not retreat from the frontiers; and that if the enemy obliged the British army to embark, not a native, whether soldier or citizen, should go with it. When the allies, notwithstanding this, fell back to the Lines, Souza proposed that the Regency should fly to the Algarves, which being indignantly protested against by Mr. Stuart, Souza threatened to quit the government. The dispute was then referred to lord Wellington, and, on the 6th of October, drew from him those severe expressions of which an abstract has been given above. When the army approached the lines Souza proposed that the

Portuguese troops should remain outside while the British took shelter within! a notion so preposterous as almost to justify marshal Beresford's observation that he knew not whether the proposer were more fool, rogue, or madman.

The restless Principal however pursued his designs with activity, and, in conjunction with his brothers and the Patriarch, established a regular and systematic opposition to lord Wellington's plans of defence. Factious in council, they were also clamorous out of doors, where many echoed their sentiments, from anger at some wanton ravages, that, in despite of the general's utmost efforts, had marked the retreat. They courted the mob of Lisbon servilely and grossly; and Antonio Souza getting the superintendence of the succours for the fugitive population, became the avowed patron of all persons preferring complaints. He took pains to stimulate and exasperate the public griefs, and to exaggerate the causes of them, frequently hinting that the Portuguese people and not the British army had formerly driven out the French. All these calumnies being echoed by the numerous friends and partisans of the caballers, and by the fidalgos, who endeavoured to spread discontent as widely as possible, there wanted but slight encouragement from the Brazils, to form a national party, and openly attack the conduct of the war.

To obtain this encouragement, Raymundo, the old tool of the party in the Oporto violences, was sent to the court of Rio Janeiro, to excite the prince regent against lord Wellington; and the Patriarch himself wrote to the prince of Wales and to the duke of Sussex, thinking to incense them also against the English general. But the extent and nature of the intrigues may be estimated from a revelation made at the time by baron Eben, and by the editor of a Lisbon newspaper, called the *Braziliense*.

Those persons abandoning the faction, asserted that the Patriarch, the Souzas, and (while he remained in Portugal) the ex-plenipotentiary, Mr. Villiers, were personally opposed to lord Wellington, marshal Beresford, and Mr. de Forjas, and were then seeking to remove them from their situations, and to get the duke of Brunswick appointed generallissimo in place of Beresford. This part of the project was very naturally aided by the Princess of Wales; and the caballers in London had also sounded the Duke of Sussex, but he repulsed them at the outset. Part of their plan was to engage a newspaper to be their organ in London as the " *Braziliense*" was in Lisbon; and in their correspondence they designated lord Wellington by the name of *Alberoni*, lord Wellesley *Lama*, Beresford *Ferugem*, Mr. Stuart *Labre*, the Patriarch *Saxe*, Antonio Souza *Lamberti*, colonel Bunbury and Mr. Peel, the under-secretaries of state, *Thin* and *Bythin*, sir Robert Wilson *De Camp*, lord Liverpool *Husband*, Mr. Villiers *Fatut*, Mr. Casamajor *Parvénu*, and so on of many others. After Mr. Villiers' departure the intrigue was continued by the Patriarch and the Souzas, but upon a different plan; for, overborne by Mr. Stuart's vigour in the council, they agreed to refrain from openly opposing either him or Forjas, but resolved to write down what either might utter, and transmit, that which suited their purpose, to the Conde de Linhares and the chevalier Souza, who undertook to represent. the information so received, after their own fashion, to the cabinets of St. James' and Rio Janeiro.

Mr. Stuart having thus obtained their secret, was
resolute to suppress their intrigues; but first endeavoured to put them from their mischievous designs,
by the very humourous expedient of writing a letter to Domingo Souza, in his own cypher, warning
him and his coadjutors not to proceed, as their
party was insecure, while Mr. Stuart, lord Wellington, Beresford, and Forjas being united and resolved
to crush all opposition, might be made friends but
would prove dangerous enemies! This had apparently some effect at first, but Principal Souza
would not take any hint, and the violent temper of
the Patriarch soon broke forth again. He made
open display of his hostility to the English general;
and it is worthy of observation, that, while thus
thwarting every measure necessary to resist the
enemy, his faction did not hesitate to exercise the
most odious injustice and cruelty against those
whom they denominated well-wishers to the French,
provided they were not of the Fidalgo faction. By
a decree of the prince regent's, dated the 20th of
March, 1809, private denunciations in cases of
disaffection, were permitted, the informer's name
to be kept secret; and in September, 1810, this
infamous system, although strenuously opposed by
Mr. Stuart, was acted upon, and many persons
suddenly sent to the islands, and others thrown
into dungeons. Some might have been guilty; and
the government pretended that a traitorous correspondence with the enemy was carried on through
a London house, which they indicated; but it does
not appear that a direct crime was brought home to
any, and it is certain that many innocent persons
were oppressed.

All these things shewing that vigorous measures

were necessary to prevent the ruin of the general cause, lord Wellesley dealt so with the Brazilian court, that every intrigue there was soon crushed, lord Wellington's power in Portugal was confirmed, and his proceedings approved of. Authority was also given him to dismiss or to retain Antonio Souza and even to remove lord Strangford, the British envoy at Rio Janeiro, who had been the contriver of the obnoxious change in the members of the Regency, and whose proceedings generally were in unison with the malcontents and mischievously opposed to lord Wellington's and Mr. Stuart's policy in Portugal. The subsidies were placed under lord Wellington's and Mr. Stuart's control, and admiral Berkeley was appointed to a seat in the Regency; in fine, Portugal was reduced to the condition of a vassal state; a policy which could never have been attempted, however necessary, if the people at large had not been willing to acquiesce. But firm in their attachment to independence and abhorring the invaders, they submitted cheerfully to this temporary assumption of command; and fully justified the sagacity of the man, who thus dared to grasp at the whole power of Portugal with one hand, while he kept the power of France at bay with the other.

Although so strongly armed, lord Wellington removed no person, but with equal prudence and moderation reserved the exercise of this great authority until further provocation should render it absolutely necessary. This remedy for the disorders above related was however not perfected for a long time, nor until after a most alarming crisis of affairs had been brought on by the conduct of the Lisbon cabal, of which notice shall be taken hereafter.

From the strength of the Lines, it was plain that offensive operations were more to be dreaded on the left, than on the right bank of the Tagus. In the Alemtejo, the enemy could more easily subsist, more effectually operate to the injury of Lisbon, and more securely retreat upon his own resources. Lord Wellington had therefore repeatedly urged the Regency to oblige the inhabitants to carry off their herds and grain from that side, and from the numerous islands in the river and above all things to destroy or remove every boat. To effect this a commission had been appointed; but so many delays and obstacles were interposed by the Patriarch and his coadjutors, that the commissioners did not leave Lisbon until the enemy was close upon the river, both banks being still stocked with cattle and corn, and what was worse, forty large boats being on the right side. This enabled the French to seize the islands especially Lizirias, where they obtained abundance of provisions; and while the Regency thus provided for the enemy, they left the fortresses of Palmella, St. Felippe de Setuval, and Abrantes with empty magazines.

Lord Wellington thinking that the ordenança on the left bank, of whom five hundred were, contrary to his wishes, armed with English muskets and furnished with two pieces of artillery, would be sufficient to repel any plundering parties attempting to cross the Tagus, was unwilling to spare men from the Lines : he wanted numbers there, and he also judged that the ordenança would, if once assisted by a regular force, leave the war to their allies. Meanwhile Antonio Souza was continually urging the planting of ambuscades, and other like frivolities, upon the left bank of the Tagus, and as his opinions were spread abroad by his party, the governor of Setuval adopted the idea, and suddenly advanced with his garrison to Salvatierra on the river side.

This ridiculous movement attracted the enemy's attention, and lord Wellington fearing they would pass over a detachment, disperse the Portuguese troops, and seize Setuval before it could be succoured, peremptorily ordered the governor to return to that fortress. This retrograde movement caused the dispersion of the ordenança, and consternation reigned in the Alemtejo; the supply of grain coming from Spain was stopped, the chain of communications broken, and, the alarm spreading to Lisbon, there was no remedy but to send general Fane, with some guns and Portuguese cavalry, that could be ill spared from the Lines, to that side. Fane immediately destroyed all the boats he could find, hastened the removal of provisions and patrolling the banks of the river as high as the mouth of the Zezere, kept a strict watch upon the enemy's movements.

Other embarrassments were however continually arising. The number of prisoners in Lisbon had accumulated so as to become a serious inconvevience; for the Admiralty, pretending to be alarmed at a fever generated by the infamous treatment the prisoners received at the hands of the Portuguese government, refused permission to have them transported to England, in vessels of war, and other ships could not be had. Thus the rights of humanity, and the good of the service, were alike disregarded, for had there been real danger, lord Wellington would not have continually urged the measure. About this time also admiral Berkeley,

whose elaborate report the year before, stated that,
although the enemy should seize the heights of
Almada, he could not injure the fleet in the river,
admitted that he was in error; and the engineers
were directed to construct secondary lines on that
side.

Another formidable evil, arising from the conduct
of the Regency, was the state of the Portuguese
army. The troops were so ill supplied that more
than once they would have disbanded, had they not
been relieved from the British magazines. Ten
thousand soldiers of the line deserted between
April and December, and of the militia two thirds
were absent from their colours; for, as no
remonstrance could induce the Regency to put the
laws in force against the delinquents, that which
was at first the effect of want became a habit; so
that even when regularly fed from the British stores
within the Lines, the desertion was alarmingly
great.

Notwithstanding the mischiefs thus daily growing up, neither the Patriarch nor the Principal
ceased their opposition. The order to fortify the
heights of Almada caused a violent altercation in
the Regency, lord Wellington, greatly incensed,
denounced them to the Prince Regent, and his
letter produced such a paroxysm of anger in
the Patriarch, that he personally insulted Mr.
Stuart, and vented his passion in the most indecent
language against the general. Soon after this, the
deplorable state of the finances obliged the government to resort to the dangerous expedient of requisitions in kind for the feeding of the troops:
and in that critical moment the Patriarch, whose
influence was, from various causes, very great, took

CHAP.
IX.

1810.

Appendix,
No. V.
Section 10.

occasion to declare that " he would not suffer bur-thens to be laid upon the people which were evidently for no other purpose than *to nourish the war in the heart of the kingdom.*"

But it was his and his coadjutors' criminal conduct that really nourished the war, for there were ample means to have carried off in time, ten-fold the quantity of provisions left for the enemy. Massena could not then have remained a week before the Lines, and his retreat would have been attended with famine and disaster, if the measures previously agreed to by the Regency had been duly executed. Whereas now, the country about Thomar, Torres Novas, Gollegao, and Santarem was absolutely untouched; the inhabitants remained, the mills, but little injured, were quickly repaired, and lord Wellington had the deep mortification to find, that his well considered design was frustrated by the very persons from whom he had a right to expect the most zealous support. There was, indeed, every reason to believe that the prince of Esling would be enabled to maintain his positions until an overwhelming force should arrive from Spain to aid him. " *It is heart-breaking,*" was the bitter reflection of the British general, " *to contemplate the chance of failure from such obstinacy and folly.*"

CHAPTER X.

THE increasing strength of the works, and the report of British deserters (unhappily very numerous at this period), soon convinced Massena that it was impracticable to force the Lines without great reinforcements. His army suffered from sickness, from the irregular forces in the rear, and from the vengeance of individuals, driven to despair by the excesses which many French soldiers, taking advantage of the times, committed in their foraging courses. Nevertheless, with an obstinate pertinacity, only to be appreciated by those who have long made war, the French general maintained his forward position, until the country for many leagues behind him was a desert; and then, reluctantly yielding to necessity, he sought for a fresh camp in which to make head against the allies, while his foragers searched more distant countries for food.

Early in October artillery officers had been directed to collect boats for crossing both the Tagus and the Zezere. Montbrun's cavalry, stretching along the right bank of the former, gathered provisions, and stored them at Santarem; and both there and at Barquina (a creek in the Tagus, below the mouth of the Zezere), rafts were formed and boats constructed with wheels, to move from one place to another, but, from the extreme paucity of materials and tools, the progress was necessarily slow. Meanwhile Fane, reinforced by some infantry, watched them closely from the left bank; Carlos d'España came down from Castello Branco to Abrantes; Trant acted sharply on the side of Ourem, and Wilson's Portuguese militia so infested the country from Espinhal to the Zezere, that Loison's division was detached upon Thomar to hold him in check.

Towards the end of October, however, all the hospitals, stores, and other incumbrances of the French army were removed to Santarem; and, on the 31st, two thousand men forded the Zezere above Punhete to cover the construction of a bridge. From this body, four hundred infantry and two hundred dragoons, under general Foy, moved against Abrantes, and, after skirmishing with the garrison, made towards Sobreira Formosa, when the allies' bridge at Villa Velha was foolishly burnt; but Foy, with a smaller escort, immediately pushed for Pena Macor, and the 8th had gained Ciudad Rodrigo, on his way to France, having undertaken to carry information of the state of affairs to Napoleon; a task which he performed with singular rapidity, courage, and address. The remainder of his escort retiring down the Zezere, were attacked by Wilson, and suffered some loss.

The bridge on the Zezere was destroyed by floods, the 6th of November, but the enemy having entrenched the height over Punhete, restored it, and cast a second at Martinchel, higher up the river. Massena then commenced his retrograde march, but with great caution, because his position was overlooked from the Monte Agraça, and the defile of Alemquer being in the rear of the eighth corps, it was an operation of some danger to withdraw from before the Lines. To cover the movement from the knowledge of the Partizans in the rear, Montbrun's cavalry marched upon Leiria, and his detachments scoured the roads to Pombal, on the one side, and towards the Zezere, on the other. Meanwhile the sixth corps marched from Otta and Alemquer to Thomar, and Loison removed to Golegao with his division, reinforced by a brigade of dragoons.

These dispositions being made, general Clausel withdrew from Sobral during the night of the 14th, and the whole of the eighth corps passed the defile in the morning of the 15th, under the protection of some cavalry, left in front of Aruda, and of a strong rear-guard on the height covering Alemquer. The second corps then retreated from Alhandra by the royal causeway upon Santarem, while the eighth corps marched by Alcoentre upon Alcanhede and Torres Novas.

This movement was not interrupted by lord Wellington. The morning of the 15th proved foggy, and it was some hours after day-break ere he perceived the void space in his front which disclosed the ability of the French general's operations. Fane had reported on the 14th that boats were collecting at Santarem, and information arrived at the same time that reinforcements for Massena were on the march from Ciudad Rodrigo. The enemy's intention was not clearly developed. It might be a retreat to Spain; it might be to pass round the Monte Junta, and so push the head of his army on Torres Vedras, while the allies were following the rear. Lord Wellington, therefore, kept the principal part of the army stationary, but directed the second and light divisions to follow the enemy, the former along the causeway to Villa Franca, the latter to

Alemquer; at the same time he called up his cavalry,
and requested admiral Berkeley to send all the
boats of the fleet up the Tagus, to enable the allies
to pass rapidly to the other bank, if necessary.

Early on the 16th the enemy was tracked, marching in two columns, the one upon Rio Mayor, the
other upon Santarem. Having passed Alcoentre,
it was clear that he had no views on Torres Vedras;
but whether he was in retreat to cross the Zezere
by the bridges at Punhete and Martinchel, or
making for the Mondego, was still uncertain. In
either case, it was important to strike a blow at the
rear, before the reinforcements and convoy, said to
be on the road from Ciudad Rodrigo, could be met
with. The first division was immediately brought
up to Alemquer, the fifth entered Sobral, the light
division and cavalry marched in pursuit, and four
hundred prisoners were made, principally marauders. A remarkable exploit was performed by one
Baxter, a serjeant of the sixteenth dragoons. This Private
man, having only five troopers with him, came sud- Journal of
the Hon.
denly upon a piquet of fifty men, who were cooking, Captain
Somers
but instantly running to their arms, killed one of Cocks, 16th
Dragoons.
the dragoons; nevertheless Baxter broke in amongst
them so strongly, that, with the assistance of
some countrymen, he made forty-two captives.

The 17th, the eighth corps marched upon Alcanhede and Pernes, and the head of the second corps
reached Santarem, when Fane, deceived by some
false movements, reported that they were in full
retreat, and the troops at Santarem only a rear-
guard. This information seeming to be confirmed
by the state of the immense plains skirting the
Tagus, which were left covered with straw-ricks,
it was concluded that Massena intended to pass the

Zezere, over which it was known that he had cast a second bridge. Hill was immediately ordered to cross the Tagus with the second division and thirteenth dragoons, and move upon Abrantes, either to succour that fortress or to head the march of the French. Meanwhile, the fourth, fifth, and sixth divisions were directed upon Alemquer, the first division and Pack's brigades upon Cartaxo, and the light division reached El Valle on the Rio Mayor. At this village there was a considerable rear guard formed, and as general Crawfurd had not profited from the lesson on the Coa, an unequal engagement would have ensued, but for the opportune arrival of the commander-in-chief. In the evening the enemy joined their main body on the heights of Santarem.

Hitherto, lord Wellington, regarding the security of the Lines with a jealous eye, had acted very cautiously. On the 15th and 16th, while the French were still hampered by the defiles, his pursuit was even slack, although it would in no degree have risked the safety of the Lines, or of the pursuing troops, to have pushed the first, second, and light divisions and Pack's brigade vigorously against the enemy's rear. On the 18th, however, when Hill had passed the Tagus at Villada, and Fane was opposite to Abrantes, the English general, whether deceived by false reports, or elated at this retrograde movement, this proof of his own superior sagacity, prepared, with a small force, to assail what he then thought the rear guard of an army in full retreat. But the French general had no intention of falling back any farther, his great qualities were roused by the difficulty of his situation, he had carried off his army with admirable arrangement, and his new position was chosen with equal sagacity and resolution.

Santarem is situated on a mountain, which, rising almost precipitously from the Tagus, extends about three miles inland. In front, a secondary range of hills formed an outwork, covered by the Rio Mayor, which is composed of two streams, running side by side to within a mile of the Tagus, where they unite and flow in a direction parallel with that river for many miles; the ground between being an immense flat, called the plain of Santarem. In advancing by the royal road from Lisbon, the allies ascended the Rio Mayor, until they reached the Ponte Seca, a raised causeway, eight hundred yards long, leading to the foot of the French position. On the right hand of this causeway as far as the Tagus, a flat sedgy marsh, not impassable, but difficult from deep water-cuts, covered the French left. On the left, the two streams of the Rio Mayor overflowing, presented a vast impassable sheet of water and marsh, covering the French right, and, in the centre, the causeway offered only a narrow line of approach, barred at the enemy's end, by an abattis, and by a gentle eminence, with a battery looking down the whole length. To force this dangerous passage was only a preliminary step, the secondary range of hills was then to be carried before the great height of Santarem could be reached; finally, the town, with its old walls, offered a fourth point of resistance.

In this formidable position, the second corps covered the rich plain of Golegao, which was occupied by Loison's division of the sixth corps, placed there to watch the Tagus, and keep up the chain of communication with Punhete. On Reynier's right, in a rugged country, which separated Santarem from the Monte Junta and the Sierra de Alcoberte,

the eighth corps was posted ; not in a continuous
line with the second, but having the right pushed
forward to Alcanhete, the centre at Pernes, and the
left thrown back to Torres Novas, where Massena's
head-quarters were fixed.   On the right of Alcanhete, the cavalry were disposed as far as Leiria, and
the sixth corps was at Thomar, in reserve, having
previously obliged Wilson's militia to retire from
the Zezere upon Espinhal.

Massena thus enclosed an immense tract of fertile
country, the plain of Golegao supplied him with
maize and vegetables, and the Sierra de Alcoberte
with cattle.   He presented a formidable head to
the allies at Santarem ; commanded the road, by
Leiria, to Coimbra, with the eighth corps and the
cavalry ; that from Thomar, by Ourem, to Coimbra,
with the sixth corps ; and, by his bridges over the
Zezere, opened a line of operations towards the
Spanish frontier, either through Castello Branco, or
by the Estrada Nova and Belmonte. He also preserved
the power of offensive operations, by crossing the
Tagus on his left, or of turning the Monte Junta by
his right, and thus paralyzing a great part of the
allied force, appeared, even in retreating, to take
the offensive.

His first dispositions were, however, faulty in
detail.   Between Santarem and the nearest division
of the eighth corps there was a distance of ten or
twelve miles, where the British general might penetrate, turn the right of the second corps, and cut
it off from the rest of the army.   Reynier, fearing
such an attempt, hurried off his baggage and hospitals to Golegao, despatched a regiment up the
Rio Mayor to watch two bridges on his right, by
which he expected the allies to penetrate between

him and the eighth corps, and then calling upon Junot for succour, and upon Massena for orders, proceeded to strengthen his own position. It was this march of Reynier's baggage, that led Fane to think the enemy was retreating to the Zezere, which, corresponding with lord Wellington's high-raised expectations, induced him to make dispositions, not for a general attack, by separating the second corps from the rest of the army; but, as I have before said, for assaulting Santarem in front with a small force, • thinking he had only to deal with a rear guard.

On the 19th, the light division entering the plain between the Rio Mayor and the Tagus advanced against the heights by the sedgy marsh. The first division under Spencer, was destined to attack the causeway, and Pack's Portuguese brigade and the cavalry were ordered to cross the Rio Mayor, at the bridges of Saliero and Subajeira, to turn the right of the French. The columns were formed for the attack, and the skirmishers of the light division were exchanging shots with the enemy in the sedgy marsh, when it was found that the guns belonging to Pack's brigade had not arrived, wherefore lord Wellington, not quite satisfied with the appearance of his adversary's force, after three hours' demonstrations, ordered the troops to retire to their former ground. It was, indeed, become evident, that the French were determined to maintain the position. Every advantageous spot of ground was fully occupied, the most advanced centinels boldly returned the fire of the skirmishers, large bodies of reserve were descried, some in arms, others cooking; the strokes of the hatchet, and the fall of trees, resounded from the woods clothing the hills, and the commencement of a triple line of abattis, and the fresh earth of entrenchments were discernible in many places.

On the 20th the demonstrations were renewed; but, as the enemy's intention to fight was no longer doubtful, they soon ceased, and orders were sent to general Hill to halt at Chamusca, on the left bank of the Tagus. General Crawfurd, however, still thought it was but a rear-guard at Santarem, his eager spirit was chafed, he seized a musket, and, followed only by a serjeant, advanced ·in the night along the causeway; thus commencing a personal skirmish with the French piquets, from whose fire he escaped by miracle, convinced at last that the enemy were not yet in flight.

Meanwhile Clausel brought his division from Alcanhete close up to Santarem, and Massena carefully examining the dispositions of the allies, satisfied himself, that no great movement was in agitation; wherefore, recalling the baggage of the second corps, he directed Clausel to advance towards Rio Mayor; a feint which instantly obliged lord Wellington to withdraw the first division and Pack's brigade to Cartaxo, the light division being also held in readiness to retreat. In truth, Massena was only to be assailed by holding the second corps in check at the Ponte Seca, while a powerful mass of troops penetrated in the direction of Tremes and Pernes; but heavy rains rendered all the roads impracticable, and as the position of Santarem was maintained for several months, and many writers have rashly censured the conduct of both generals, it may be well to shew here that they acted wisely and like great captains.

It has been already seen how, without any extreme dissemination of his force, the French general contrived to menace a variety of points and thus to command two distinct lines of retreat; but there were other circumstances that equally weighed with him. He expected momentarily to be joined by the ninth corps, which had been added to his command, and by a variety of detachments; his position, touching upon Leiria and upon the Zezere, enabled him to give his hand to these reinforcements and convoys, either by the line of the Mondego or that of Belmonte and the Estrada Nova; at the same time he was ready to communicate with any troops coming from Andalusia to his assistance. He was undoubtedly open to a dangerous attack, between Santarem and Alcanhete; but he judged, that his adversary would not venture on such a decisive operation, requiring rapid well-timed movements, with an army composed of three different nations, and unpractised in great evolutions. In this, guided by his long experience of war, he calculated upon moral considerations with confidence, and he that does not understand this part of war is but half a general.

Like a great commander, he calculated likewise upon the military and political effect, that his menacing attitude would have. While he maintained Santarem, he appeared, as it were, to besiege Lisbon; he prolonged the sufferings of that city; and it has been estimated that forty thousand persons died from privations within the Lines during the winter of 1810: moreover he encouraged the disaffected, and shook the power which the English had assumed in Portugal, thus rendering their final success so doubtful in appearance, that few men had sagacity enough to judge rightly upon the subject.

At this period also, as the illness of George the Third, by reviving the question of a Regency in England, had greatly strengthened the opposition in parliament, it was most important that the arguments of the latter against the war should seem to be enforced by the position of the French army. It is plain therefore that, while any food was to be obtained, there were abundant reasons to justify Massena in holding his ground; and it must be admitted that, if he committed great errors in the early part of his campaign, in the latter part he proved himself a daring, able, and most pertinacious commander.

On the side of the British general, such were the political difficulties, that a battle was equally to be desired and dreaded. Desirable, because a victory would have silenced his opponents both in England and Portugal, and placed him in a situation to dictate the measures of war to the ministers instead of having to struggle incessantly against their fears. Desirable, to relieve the misery of the Portuguese people, who were in a state of horrible suffering; but, above all things desirable, lest a second and a third army, now gathering in Castile and in Andalusia, should reach Massena, and again shut up the allies in their works.

Dreaded, because a defeat or even a repulse would have been tantamount to the ruin of the cause; for it was at this period that the disputes in the Regency, relative to the Lines, at Almada, were most violent, and the slightest disaster would have placed the Patriarch at the head of a national party. Dreaded, because of the discussions relative to the appointment of a Regency in England, seeing, that any serious military check would have caused the opposition to triumph, and the troops to be withdrawn from Portugal. So powerful, indeed, were the opposition, and so much did the ministers dread their cry for economy, that forgetting the safety of the army in their keen love of place, they had actually ordered lord Wellington to send home the transports to save expence! In fine, Mr. Percival with that narrow cunning that distinguished his public career, was, to use an expression attributed to him, " *Starving the war in Portugal,*" in despite of lord Wellesley's indignation and of lord Wellington's remonstrances. In this balanced state it was essential that a battle, upon which so many great interests hung, should not be fought, except on terms of advantage. Now those terms were not to be had. Lord Wellington, who had received some reinforcements from Halifax and England, had indeed more than seventy thousand fighting men under arms, and the enemy at this time was not more than fifty thousand: nevertheless, if we analyze the composition and situation of both, it will be found that the latter, from the advantage of position, could actually bring more soldiers into the fight.

In the Portuguese army, since the month of April, the deaths had been four thousand, the disbanded four thousand, the deserters ten thousand, the recruits thirty thousand; the numbers were therefore increased, but the efficiency for grand evolutions rather decreased; and every department under Beresford, was at its last gasp from the negligence of the government, which neither paid the troops nor provided them with food. The Spanish auxiliaries also, ill-governed and turbulent, were at open discord with the Portuguese; and their general was neither able in war himself nor amendable to those who were.

While the heights of Almada were naked, the left bank of the Tagus required twelve thousand men ; and two British divisions were kept in the Lines, because the French at Alcanhete were nearer to Torres Vedras than the allies were at Cartaxo. During an attack on Pernes, Reynier might break out from Santarem, and ten thousand men were therefore necessary to hold him in check ; thus the disposable troops, comprehending soldiers of three nations, and many recruits, would have fallen short of forty-five thousand, while Massena could bring nearly all his force together on one point ; because a few men would have sufficed to watch the British division on the left of the Tagus and at Santarem.

Lord Wellington's experience in the movement of great armies was not at this period equal to his adversary's, and the attack was to be made in a difficult country, with deep roads, where the Alviella, the Almonda, and other rivers, greatly swelled by incessant rain, furnished a succession of defensive lines to the enemy, and in case of defeat the means of carrying off two-thirds of his army. Victory might crown the attempt, but the stakes were unequal. If Massena lost even a third of his force, the ninth corps could have replaced it. If lord Wellington failed, the Lines were gone, and with them the whole Peninsula. He judged it better to remain on the defensive, to strengthen the Lines, and to get the works at Almada sufficiently forward ; meanwhile to perfect the discipline of the Portuguese troops, improve the organization of the militia in rear of the enemy, and above all to quiet the troubles and remedy the evils occasioned by the Patriarch's faction. Amongst these evils the destitute state of the fortresses, especially Abrantes, was prominent. Lord Wellington at one moment seriously thought of withdrawing the garrison from thence to prevent the men from starving.

In this view, the light division, supported by a brigade of cavalry, occupied Valle and the heights overlooking the marsh and inundation; the bridge at the English end of the causeway was mined, and a sugar-loaf hill, looking straight down the approach, was crowned with embrasures for artillery and laced in front with a zigzag covered way, capable of containing five hundred infantry : the causeway being thus blocked, the French could not, while the inundation kept up, make any sudden irruption from Santarem.

On the left of the light division, posts were extended along the inundation to Malhorquija ; thence, by a range of heights to Rio Mayor ; and behind the latter place, Anson's cavalry was stationed in observation of the roads leading from Pernes and Alcanhede. In rear of Anson, a position was entrenched at Alcoentre, and occupied by a division of infantry. Thus all the routes leading upon the Lines between the Tagus and the Monte Junta, were secured by what are technically called heads of cantonments, under cover of which, the other divisions were disposed in succession. The first and the head-quarters were at Cartaxo, a few miles in the rear of Valle, the remainder at Alemquer and Sobral. Torres Vedras was, however, always occupied in force, lest the enemy should make a sudden march round the Monte Junta.

Massena, satisfied that his front was safe, continued to build boats, fortified a post at Tancos, on the Tagus, and expected, with impatience, the arrival of a convoy escorted by five thousand men, with which general Gardanne was coming from Ciudad Rodrigo. This reinforcement, consisting of detachments and convalescents left in Castile when the army entered Portugal, had marched by Belmonte and the Estrada Nova, and the 27th, was at Cardijos, within a few leagues of the French bridges on the Zezere. The advance of a cavalry patrol on either side would have opened the communications, and secured the junction; but, at that moment, Gardanne, harassed by the ordenança, and deceived by a false rumour that general Hill was in Abrantes, ready to move against him, suddenly retreated upon Sabugal, with such haste and blindness, that he sacrificed a part of his convoy, and lost many men.

Notwithstanding this event, Massena, expecting to be joined by the ninth corps, greatly strengthened his position at Santarem, which enabled him to draw the bulk of his forces to his right, and to continue his marauding excursions in the most daring manner. General Ferey, with a strong detachment of the sixth corps, crossing the Zezere, foraged the country as far as Castello Branco without difficulty, and returned without loss; Junot occupied Leiria and Ourem with detachments of the eighth corps; and on the 9th of December a battalion endeavoured to surprise Coimbra: Trant, however, baffled that project. Meanwhile, Drouet avowed a design to invade the Tras os Montes, but the 22d of December occupied the line of the Coa with the ninth corps, while Massena's patroles appeared again on the Mondego above Coimbra, making inquiries about the fords: all the spies likewise reported that a great reunion of forces from the south was to take place near Madrid.

These things gave reason to fear, either that Massena intended to file behind the Mondego and seize Oporto; or that the reinforcements coming to him were so large that he meant to establish bridges over the Mondego, and occupy the northern country without quitting his present position. It was known that a tenth corps was forming at Burgos, and the head of the fifth corps was again in Estremadura; the French boats at Punhete and Barquiña were numerous and large; and in all parts there was evidence of great forces assembling for a mighty effort on both sides of the Tagus.

It was calculated that, before the end of January, more than forty thousand fresh troops would co-operate with Massena, and preparations were made accordingly. An outward line of defence, from Aldea Gallega to Setuval, was already in a forward state; Abrantes, Palmella, and St. Felippe de Setuval had been at last provisioned; and a chain of forts parallel to the Tagus were constructing on the hills lining the left bank from Almada to Traffaria. Labourers had also been continually employed in strengthening the works of Alhandra, Aruda, and Monte Agraça, which were now nearly impregnable, soldiers only being wanting to defy the utmost force that could be brought against them. To procure these, lord Wellington wrote earnestly to lord Liverpool on the 29th of December, demonstrating the absolute necessity of reinforcing the army, wherefore five thousand British troops were ordered to embark for Lisbon, and three regiments were drafted from Sicily.

Sickness having obliged general Hill to go home in

December, but, it being known that Soult was collecting a disposable force behind the Morena, the troops on the left bank of the Tagus were augmented, and marshal Beresford assumed the command, for the Portuguese army was now generally incorporated with the British divisions. His force, composed of eighteen guns, two divisions of infantry, and five regiments of cavalry, Portuguese and British, was about fourteen thousand men, exclusive of Carlos d'Espana's brigade, which, being at Abrantes, was also under his orders.

To prevent the passage of the Tagus; to intercept all communication between Massena and Soult; to join the main body of the army, by Vellada if in retreat, and by Abrantes if in advance; were the instructions given to Beresford. He fixed his quarters at Chamusca, disposed his troops along the Tagus, from Almeyrim by Chamusca, as high as the mouth of the Zezere, established signals between his different quarters, and scouring the roads leading towards Spanish Estremadura, established a sure and rapid intercourse with Elvas and the other frontier fortresses. He also organized good sources of intelligence at Golegao, at Santarem, and at Thomar, and, in addition to these general precautions, erected batteries opposite the mouth of the Zezere; but, against the advice of the engineers, he placed them at too great distance from the river, and in other respects unsuitably, and offering nothing threatening to the enemy: the French craft dropped down frequently towards Santarem, without hindrance, until colonel Colborne, of the sixty-sixth regiment, moored a guard-boat close to the mouth of the Zezere, and disposed fires in such a manner on the banks

Appendix,
No. I.
Section 1.

of the Tagus that nothing could pass without being observed.

Meanwhile on the side of Santarem, as all the country between Alcanhete and the Ponte Seca continued impracticable from the rain, the main bodies of both armies were, of necessity, tranquil. Anson's cavalry, however, acting in concert with major Fenwick, who came down from Obidos towards Rio Mayor, harassed the enemy's foraging parties; and in the Upper Beira several actions of importance had taken place with the militia, which it is time to notice as forming an essential part of lord Wellington's combinations.

It will be remembered that the ninth corps, being ordered to scour Biscay and Upper Castile in its progress towards the frontier of Portugal, was so long delayed that, instead of keeping the communications of Massena free, and securing his base, Drouet lost all connexion with the army of Portugal. Meanwhile the Partidas of Leon and Salamanca gave such employment to Serras' division that the Tras os Montes were unmolested, and Silveira, falling down to the Lower Douro, appeared, on the 29th of October, before Almeida. Its former garrison had entered the French service, yet immediately deserted to their countrymen, and Silveira then blockaded the place closely, and made an attempt to surprise a French post at San Felices, but failed.

In November, however, the head of the ninth corps reached Ciudad Rodrigo, bringing a large convoy of provisions, collected in Castile, for Massena. Lord Wellington, anxious to prevent this from reaching its destination, directed Silveira to intercept it if possible, and ordered Miller on the

16th to Viseu, in support.   On the 13th, general Gardanne, with four thousand infantry and three squadrons of cavalry, raised the blockade of Almeida, took possession of Pinhel, and supported by the ninth corps, conducted the convoy towards Sabugal and Penamacor.   The 16th, he was between Valverde and Pereiro Gavillos, but Silveira falling upon him killed some of his men, took many prisoners, and then retiring to Trancoso on the 17th, united with Miller, who took post at Guarda. Nevertheless, Gardanne pursued his march, but finally, as we have seen, retreated from Cardigos in a panic.

Drouet had not yet received the orders to put himself under Massena's command, but, at the representation of Foy, moved forward into Portugal, and to hide his object, spread the report, already noticed, of his intention to penetrate the Tras os Montes.   The 17th December, he passed the Coa with fourteen thousand infantry and two thousand cavalry, and crossing the Mondego the 18th, encamped near Gouvea, the 22d.   Thence the cavalry and one division under general Claparede, marched against Silveira, and after a skirmish occupied Trancoso; while Drouet with eleven battalions, and the troops under Gardanne, which he had rallied, made for the Alva and reached Ponte Murcella the 24th.

Hitherto lord Wellington's communications with Baccellar, had been carried on, through Trant on the side of Coimbra, and through Wilson on that of Espinhal and Abrantes.   But this sudden advance of the ninth corps obliged Wilson to cross the Mondego to avoid being enclosed; and Drouet effecting his junction with Massena by Espinhal, established his division at Leiria, and spreading towards the sea cut off all communication between the allies and the northern provinces. On the 2d of January, however, Trant intercepted a letter from Drouet to Claparede, giving an account of his own arrival, and of the state of Massena's army; intimating, also, that a great operation was in contemplation, and that the fifth corps was daily expected in the Alemtejo; he directed Claparede to seize Guarda, to forage the neighbouring villages, to watch the road of Belmonte, and if Silveira should be troublesome, to defeat him.

Silveira, an insufficient man, naturally vain, and inflated with his former successes, had already attacked Claparede, and was defeated with the loss of two hundred men at Ponte Abad, on the side of Trancoso, and Baccellar, alarmed for the safety of Oporto, recalled Miller and Wilson. The first immediately moved upon Viseu, and the last who had already repassed the Mondego and taken a hundred stragglers of Drouet's division, marched hastily towards the same point. Meanwhile, Silveira had again provoked Claparede, who pressed him so closely, from the 10th to the 13th of January, that he drove him with loss over the Douro at Pezo de Ragoa, seized Lamego, and menaced Oporto before any troops could concentrate to oppose him. However, when Baccellar brought up his reserve to the Pavia, and Miller's and Wilson's corps reached Castro d'Airo, Claparede returned to Moimenta de Beira, closely followed by Wilson. Meanwhile, the arrival of the ninth corps having relieved the French troops in Leon, the latter again menaced Tras os Montes, which obliged Silveira to march to Braganza, and

BOOK
XI.

1810.

as Miller died at Viseu, only Wilson and Trant continued to harass the enemy's parties.

Claparede taking post at Guarda, according to his instructions, seized Covilhao, while Foy, who in returning from France had collected about three thousand infantry and cavalry, convalescents, was marching by the road of Belmonte. Foy had escaped innumerable perils. At Pancorbo he was fain to fly from the Partidas, with the loss of his despatches and half his escort; and now at Enxabarda entering the Estrada Nova, notwithstanding Claparede's vicinity, he was harassed by colonel Grant with a corps of ordenança from the Lower Beira, and although he suffered nothing by the sword, three hundred of his men died on the mountain from cold. On the 2d of February he reached Santarem, where affairs were coming to a crisis.

During December and January, the country being always more or less flooded, the armies had continued in observation; but Massena's positions were much strengthened, his outposts were reinforced, and his marauding excursions extended in proportion to his increasing necessities. The weak point on either side was towards Rio Mayor, any movement there created great jealousy, especially as the season advanced and the roads became firmer. Hence, on the 19th of January (some reinforcements having landed at Lisbon a few days before) a fear lest the allies should be concentrating at Alcoentre, had induced Junot to drive the outposts from Rio Mayor to probe the state of affairs, and a general attack was expected; but after a skirmish, he returned with a wound, which disabled him for the rest of the campaign.

Early in February, a column of six thousand CHAP.
X. French again scouring all the country beyond the ——— Zezere, got much concealed food near Pedragoa, 1810.
February. while other detachments arriving on the Mondego below Coimbra, carried off four hundred oxen and two thousand sheep intended for the allies. These excursions gave rise to horrible excesses, which broke down the discipline of the French army, and were not always executed with impunity; the British cavalry at various times redeemed many cattle, and brought in a considerable number of prisoners, amongst them an aide-de-camp of general Clausel's.

Meanwhile, Massena organized a secret communication with Lisbon, through the Portuguese general Pamplona, who effected it by the help of the fidalgos in that capital : their agents, under the pretence of selling sugar to the inhabitants of Thomar and Torres Novas, passed by the road of Caldas and thence through the mountains of Pedragoa. Lord Wellington, on the other hand, was understood to have gained a French officer of rank, and it is certain that both generals had excellent information.

In this manner hostilities were carried on, each commander impatiently waiting for reinforcements which should enable him to act offensively. How both were disappointed, and how other events hitherto unnoticed, bore upon the plans of each, must be the subject of another book.

OBSERVATIONS.

1°. " *War is not a conjectural art.*" Massena forgetting this, assumed that the allies would not

make a stand in front of Lisbon, and that the militia
would not venture to attack Coimbra; but the battle
of Busaco and the capture of his hospitals evinced
the soundness of the maxim. Again, he conjec-
tured that the English would re-embark if pressed;
the Lines put an end to that dream: yet once awake,
he made war like a great man, proving more formidable with reduced means and in difficulties,
than he had been when opportunity was rife and
his numbers untouched. His stay at Santarem
shews what thirty thousand additional men acting
on the left bank of the Tagus could have done.
Had they arrived on the heights of Almada before
admiral Berkeley's error was discovered, the supply
of provisions, from Alemtejo and from Spain, would
then have been transferred from Lisbon to the French
armies; the fleet would have been driven from the
Tagus, and the misery of the inhabitants, the fears
of the British cabinet, the machinations of the Patriarch, and the little chance of final success, would
probably have induced the British general to embark.

2°. It has been observed, that Massena, in the
first week might have easily passed the Tagus,
secured the resources of the Alemtejo, and driven the
British fleet out of the port. This was not so practicable as it might at first sight appear. The rains
were heavy; the fords impassable; the French had
not boats sufficient for a bridge; a weak detachment would have been useless, a strong detachment
would have been dangerous: to collect boats, cast a
bridge, and raise the entrenchments necessary to
defend it, in the face of the allied forces, would
have been neither a safe nor sure operation; moreover, Massena would then have relinquished the

certain aid of the ninth for the uncertain assistance of the fifth corps.

3°. Lord Wellington conjecturing the French to be in full retreat, had like to have received a severe check at Santarem; he recovered himself in time, and with this exception, it would be difficult to support essential objections to his operations: yet, many have been urged, as that, he might have straightened the enemy's quarters more effectually at Santarem; that Hill's corps, passing through Abrantes, could have destroyed the bridges at Punhete, and lining the Zezere, have cut off Massena's reinforcements, and obliged him to abandon his positions or even to capitulate. This last idea, advanced at the time by colonel Squires, an engineer of great zeal and ability, perfectly acquainted with the localities, merits examination.

As a simple operation it was feasible, but the results were not so certain; the Lines of Almada being unfinished, the rashness of leaving the Tagus unguarded, before an enemy who possessed eighty large boats, exclusive of those forming the bridges on the Zezere, is apparent; Hill's corps must then have been replaced, and the army before Santarem would have been so weak as to invite a concentrated attack, to the great danger of the Torres Vedras Lines. Nor was the forcing of the French works at Punhete a matter of certainty; the ground was strong, there were two bridges over the Zezere, and the sixth corps, being within a short march, might, by passing at Martinchel, have taken Hill in flank.

4°. The same officer, at a later period, miscalculating the enemy's numbers at thirty thousand men, and the allies at more than seventy thousand regulars, proposed that Beresford should cross the Tagus at Azingha, behind the Almonda, and march upon Golegao, while lord Wellington, concentrating at Rio Mayor, pushed upon Torres Novas. It was no common head that conceived this project, by which seventy thousand men would, in a single march, have been placed in the midst of the enemy's extended quarters; but the hand of Napoleon could scarcely have launched such a thunder-bolt. Massena had still fifty thousand fighting-men; the boats from Abrantes must have been brought down, to pass the Tagus; the concentration of troops at Rio Mayor would scarcely have escaped the enemy's notice, an exact concert, in point of time, was essential. But the eighth corps could have held the allies in check on the Alviella, while Reynier, from Santarem, and Ney, from Thomar, crushed Beresford between the Almonda and the Tagus: moreover the roads about Tremes were nearly impassable from rain during December, and in January, Soult, of whose operations I shall speak in the next book, was menacing the Alemtejo. Any disaster happening to the allies would have relieved the enemy's difficulties, when nothing else could. A campaign is like other works of art ; accessaries, however splendid, must be rejected when not conducive to the main object. That judgement, which duly classes the value of every feasible operation, is the best quality of a general, and lord Wellington possessed it in a remarkable degree ; to it, his genius and his courage were both subservient; without it he might have performed many brilliant exploits in the Peninsula, but he could never have conducted the war to a successful end.

BOOK XII.

CHAPTER I.

In the preceding book, Spanish affairs have been little noticed, although lord Wellington's combinations were deeply affected by them. The general position of the allies, extending from Coruña to Cadiz, presented a great crescent, in the convex of which the French armies were operating; and it was clear that, when checked at Lisbon, the most important point, their wings, could reinforce the centre; unless the allied forces, at the horns of the crescent, acted vigorously on a system which the harbours and fortresses, at either extremity, pointed out as suitable to those who possessed the absolute command of the sea. A British army and fleet were therefore established at Cadiz, and a squadron of frigates at Coruña, and how far this warfare relieved the pressure on lord Wellington I shall now show.

The Gallician troops, under Mahi, usually hanging on the borders of Leon, were always reported to be above twenty thousand men, when arms or stores were demanded from England, but there were never more than ten or twelve thousand in line; and, although Serras' division, of only eight thousand, was spread over the plains, from Benevente to the Agueda, during Massena's advance, no stroke of importance was effected against it. The arrival of the ninth corps, in October, put an end to all hopes from the Gallicians in that quarter, although the Partidas often surprised both posts and convoys. Behind Mahi there was, however, a second army, from four to six thousand strong, embodied to defend the coast line towards the Asturias; and, in the latter province, about eight thousand men, including the irregular bands of Porlier and other chiefs, constantly watched Bonet's movements.

That general frequently mastered the Asturias, but could never maintain himself there; because the country is a long defile, lying between the great mountains and the sea, and being crossed by a succession of parallel ridges and rivers, is admirably calculated for partizan warfare in connexion with a fleet. If he penetrated towards Gallicia, British and Spanish frigates, from Coruña, landing troops at the ports of Gihon, Santander, or Santona, could always form a junction with the great bands of Longa, Mina, and Amor, and excite insurrections on his rear. In this manner Porlier, as before related, forced him to withdraw from Castropol, after he had defeated general Ponte at Sales, about the period of Almeida being invested. The advantages of such operations being evident, the British government sent sir Home Popham to direct the naval, and general Walker the military affairs at Coruña. Preparations were then made to embark a considerable force, under Renovales, to renew the attack at Santona and Santander; the Partidas of the interior were to move at the same time; a battalion of marines was assembled, in England, to

garrison Santona, when taken, and Mahi promised
to co-operate by an incursion. Serras, however,
threatened the frontier of Gallicia, Mahi remained in suspense, and this, together with the
usual procrastination of the Spaniards, and the late
arrival of sir Home Popham, delayed the expedition until October, although Porlier, Escadron, and
other chiefs had commenced an isolated attack in the
beginning of September. Finally, Serras returned
to Zamora, Mahi sent a division into Leon, and
Bonet, aware of the preparations at Coruña, first
concentrated at Oviedo, and then fell back towards
Santander, leaving a post at Gihon.

On the 16th of October Renovales sailed, but
with only thirteen hundred men; accompanied,
however, by general Walker, who carried ten thousand stand of arms and ammunition. The 19th,
entering the harbour of Gihon, they captured some
French vessels, and Porlier, coming up on the land
side, took some treasure and eighty prisoners. The
next day, Renovales proceeded to Santona, but
tempests impeded his landing, and he returned to
Coruña the 2d of November, with only eight hundred and fifty men: a frigate and a brig had foun-
dered, with the remainder of his troops, in a dreadful gale, which destroyed all the Spanish naval
force along the coast, twelve vessels being wrecked
even in the harbour of Coruña. Meanwhile, Mahi,
leaving Toboado Gil's division to watch Serras,
entered the Asturias with the rest of the Gallicians,
and being joined first by the troops of that province,
and soon after by Renovales, was very superior to
the French; yet he effected nothing, and Bonet
maintained his line from Gihon, through Oviedo,
to the borders of Leon.

BOOK
XII.

1810.
Nov.

Abstract
of General
Walker's
Military
Reports
from Gal-
licia.MSS.

In this manner hostilities wore feebly on; the Junta of the Asturias continued, as from the first, distinguished by their venality and indifference to the public good, their province was in a miserable and exhausted state; and the powers of the British naval officers on the coast not being defined, occasioned some dispute between them and general Walker, and gave opportunity to the Junta to interfere improperly with the distribution of the English stores. Gallicia was comparatively rich, but its Junta culpably inactive in the discharge of duties and oppressive in government, disgusted the whole province, and a general desire to end their power was prevalent. In the course of the winter a combination of the clergy was formed to oppose both the Local Junta and the General Cortes, and assumed so threatening an aspect, that Mahi, who was then on the coast, applied to be taken in an English vessel to Coruña, to ensure his personal safety. One Acuña was soon after arrested at Ponferrada, the discontent spread, and the army was more employed to overawe these factions than to oppose the enemy. Little advantage, therefore, was derived from the Spanish operations in the north; and general Walker, despairing to effect any thing useful, desired either that a British force should be placed at his disposal or that he might join the army in Portugal.

These expeditions from Coruña naturally increased the audacity of the inland partidas, who could only become really dangerous, by having a sea-port where they could receive supplies and reinforcements; or embarking save themselves in extremity, and change the theatre of operations.

To prevent this, the emperor employed considerable numbers of men in the military governments touching on the Bay of Biscay, and had directed, as we have seen, the "*corps d'armée*," in their progress towards Portugal, to scour all the disturbed countries to the right and left. The ninth corps had been thus employed during the months of August and September, but when it passed onward, the partidas resumed their activity. Mina, Longa, Campillo, and Amor, frequently united about Villar Caya and Espinosa in numbers sufficient to attack large French detachments with success; and to aid them, general Walker repeatedly recommended the taking possession of Santona with a corps of British troops. That town, having the best winter harbour along the coast, and being built on a mountain promontory joined to the main by a narrow sandy neck, could have been made very strong. It would have cut off Bonet's communication with France by sea, have given the British squadron a secure post from whence to vex the French coasts, and it offered a point of connexion with the partidas of the Rioja, Biscay, and Navarre.

Lord Liverpool, swayed by these considerations, desired to employ a corps of four thousand men to secure it; but, having first demanded lord Wellington's opinion, the latter " earnestly recommended that no such maritime operations should be undertaken. For," said he, " unless a very large force was sent, it would scarcely be able to effect a landing, and maintain the situation of which it might take possession. Then that large force would be unable to move or effect any object at all adequate to the expence, or to the expectations which would be formed from its strength,

Letter to
Lord Li-
verpool,
7th May,
1811. MSS.

owing to the want of those equipments and supplies in which an army landed from its ships must
be deficient. It was vain to hope for any assistance, even in this way, much less military assistance from the Spaniards; the first thing they
would require uniformly would be money; then
arms, ammunition, clothing of all descriptions,
provisions, forage, horses, means of transport, and
every thing which the expedition would have a
right to require from them; and, after all, *this
extraordinary and perverse people would scarcely
allow the commander of the expedition to have a voice
in the plan of operations, to be followed when the
whole should be ready to undertake any, if indeed
they ever should be ready.*"

Napoleon now caused Caffarelli's reserve to
enter Spain, ordered Santona to be fortified, directed other reinforcements from France upon the
northern provinces, and finally sent marshal Bessieres to command the young guard, the third and
fourth governments, and that of the Asturias, including Bonet's division, the whole forming a distinct force, called the army of the north, which on
the 1st of January, 1811, exceeded seventy thousand, fifty-nine thousand men and eight thousand
horses being present under arms; and Bessieres,
who had received unusual powers, was especially
ordered to support and furnish all necessary assistance to the army of Portugal. This was the state
of the northern parts of Spain.

Appendix,
No. I. Sec-
tion 6.

In the middle parts, the army of the centre, or
that immediately under the king, at first about
twenty thousand, was, before the end of the year,
carried up to twenty-seven thousand, exclusive of
French and Spanish guards and juramentados, or

native troops, who had taken the oath of allegiance: with this power he protected his court, watched the movements of the Valencians, and chased the Guerillas of the interior.

The summer and autumn of 1810 were, however, for reasons before-mentioned, a period of great activity with these irregulars; numerous petty actions were constantly fought around the capital, many small French posts, and numbers of isolated men and officers, were cut off, and few despatches reached their destinations without a considerable escort. To remedy this, the lines of correspondence were maintained by small fortified posts which run from Madrid; through Guadarama and Segovia to the provinces of Valladolid and Salamanca; through Buitrago and Somosierra to the army of the north; through Guadalaxara and Calatayud to the army of Aragon; through La Mancha to the army of the south; and by the valley of the Tagus, Arzobispo, and Truxillo, to the fifth corps during its incursions into Estremadura; a brigade of cavalry, was also generally stationed at Truxillo.

As the warfare of the Partidas was merely a succession of surprises and massacres, little instruction, and no pleasure, can be derived from the details; but in the course of the summer and autumn, not less than twelve considerable, and an infinite number of trifling affairs, took place between the moveable columns and these bands: the latter were however almost always beaten, and at the close of the year, only the Empecinado, Duran, Sanchez, Longa, Campillo, Porlier, and Mina retained any great reputation; and the country people were so harassed,

1810.

that counter Partidas, in many places assisted the French.

The situation of the army of the centre enabled the king to aid Massena, either by an advance upon the Elga, or by reinforcing, or, at least, supporting the fifth corps in Estremadura. But Joseph, troubled by the Partidas, and having many convoys to protect, was also averse to join any of the marshals, with all of whom, except Massena, he was on ill terms ; neither were his relations with Napoleon such as to induce him to take an interest in any military operations, save those which affected the immediate security of his court. His poverty was extreme; he was surrounded by French and Spanish intriguers ; his plan of organizing a national party was thwarted by his brother's regulations; plots were formed, .or supposed to be formed, against his person ; and, in this uneasy posture, the secondary part he was forced to sustain, combined with his natural gentleness, which shrunk from the terrible scenes of bloodshed and devastation continually before his eyes, rendered his situation so irksome, that he resolved to vacate the throne and retire to France, a resolution which he soon afterwards partially executed. Such being the course of affairs in the northern and central provinces, it remains to trace the more important military operations at the southern horn of the crescent, where the allies were most favourably situated to press the left flank of the invaders.

Sebastiani was peculiarly exposed to a harassing warfare, because of the city of Grenada and other towns in the interior, which he was obliged to hold at the same time with those on the coast,

Appendix,
No. IV.
Section 4.

although the two districts were completely separated by the mountains. Hence a large body of troops were necessarily kept in the strip of country bordering the Mediterranean, although they were menaced, on the one flank, by Gibraltar and the Spanish troops at San Roque; on the other by the Murcian army; and in front, by continual descents from the sea; while, from the shallowness and length of their position, they were unable to concentrate in time to avoid being cut off in detail. Now the Murcian army, nominally twenty thousand, was based upon the cities of Murcia and Carthagena, and menaced alike the coast-line and that of Grenada by the route of Baza and Guadix; and any movement towards the latter, was sure to attract the French, while troops landing from Cadiz or Gibraltar fell upon their disseminated posts along the coast.

To meet this system, Sebastiani, keeping his reserves about Grenada, where he had entrenched a permanent camp, made sudden incursions, sometimes against the Murcians, sometimes against the Spanish forces on the side of Gibraltar; but that fortress afforded a refuge to the patriots on one side, and Carthagena, surrounded by arid lands, where, for two marches, no water is to be found, always offered a sure retreat on the other. Meanwhile the French general endeavoured to gain the important castles on the coast, and to put them into a state of defence; Estipona and Marbella were defended, and the latter sustained many attacks, nor was it finally reduced until the 9th of December, when the garrison, of one hundred men, took refuge on board the Topaze frigate. But Sebastiani's hold of these towns, and even the security of the French troops along the coast, depended upon the communications across the mountains with Grenada, Chiclana, and Seville; and to impede these, general Campbell sent British officers into the Ronda, who successfully directed the wild mountaineers of that district, until their operations were marred by Lascy's misconduct.

The various movements and insurrections in Grenada during the summer of 1810 have been already noted; and, in October, general Campbell and admiral Penrose, conjointly with the governor of Ceuta, renewed the design of surprising Malaga, where were many privateers and a flotilla of gunboats, supposed to be destined against the islands near Ceuta. The French depot for the siege of Marbella was at Fuengirola, which is only thirty miles from Malaga, and it was judged that an attack there would draw the troops from the latter place; and the more surely, as general Valdemoro, commanding the Spanish force at San Roque, engaged to co-operate on the side of Ronda.

EXPEDITION OF FUENGIROLA.

General C.
Campbell's
Correspon-
dence,
MSS.

On the 13th of October, captain Hope, in the Topaze, sailed from Ceuta, with a division of gunboats and a convoy, containing a brigade of twelve-pounders, sixty-five gunners, a battalion of the eighty-ninth regiment, a detachment of foreign deserters, and the Spanish imperial regiment of Toledo; in all fifteen hundred men, including serjeants. Lord Blayney, commanding this force, was directed to make a false attack on Fuengirola, and should the enemy come out from Malaga, he was to sail against that place. A landing was effected the same day, and Sebastiani instantly marched, leaving only three hundred men in Malaga: lord Blayney was as instantly apprised of the success of the demonstration, yet he remained two days cannonading the castle with twelve-pounders, although the heavier metal of the gun-boats and of the frigate, had before failed to make any impression on the walls; and during this time his dispositions betrayed the utmost contempt of military rules. On the second day, while he was on board a gun-boat himself, the garrison, which did not exceed two hundred men, having first descried Sebastiani's column, made a sally, took the battery, and drove the British part of the investing force headlong towards the boats. Lord Blayney landed, rallied his men, and re-took the artillery; but at this moment two squadrons of French cavalry came up, and his lordship, mistaking them for Spaniards, ordered the firing to cease. He was immediately made prisoner; his troops again fled to the beach, and would have been sabred but for the opportune arrival of the Rodney with the eighty-second regiment, the flank companies of which were immediately disembarked and first checked the enemy. The Spanish regiment, untouched by the panic, regained the ships regularly and without loss; of the British, two officers and thirty men were killed or wounded, and one general, seven inferior officers, and nearly two hundred serjeants and privates taken. Thus an expedition, well contrived and adequate to its object, was ruined by misconduct, and terminated in disaster and disgrace.

Scarcely was this affair finished, when Valdemoro and the marquis of Portasgo appeared in

Appendix,
No. XI.

BOOK
XII.

1810.
October.

General
Camp-
bell's Cor-
respon-
dence.
MSS.

the Ronda; an insurrection commenced at Velez Malaga and in the neighbouring villages; and Blake, who had returned from Cadiz to the army in Murcia, advanced, with eight thousand men, towards Cullar on the side of Baza. General Campbell immediately furnished money to Portasgo, and embarked a thousand stand of arms for the people of Valez Malaga. An English frigate was also sent to cruize along the coast. Sebastiani, however, being relieved from the fear of a descent, soon quelled this insurrection; and then sending Milhaud on before with some cavalry, followed himself with reinforcements for general Rey, who was opposed to Blake. The latter, retiring behind the Almanzora river, was overtaken by Milhaud, and defeated on the 4th of November, when his army dispersed: at the same time, a contagious fever, breaking out at Carthagena, spread along the coast to Gibraltar and Cadiz, and the Spanish operations on the side of Murcia ceased.

In the kingdom of Seville, the war turned chiefly upon the blockade of the Isla, and the movements of the Spanish armies in Estremadura. Provisions for Cadiz were principally drawn from the Condado de Neibla, and it has been seen that Copons, aided by descents from the ocean, endeavoured to secure this important resource; but neither his efforts, nor the descents, would have availed, if Ballasteros had not co-operated by constantly menacing Seville from Araceña and the Aroche mountains. Neither could Ballasteros have maintained the war there, were it not for the support of Badajos and Olivenza; under cover of which, Romana's army protected his line of operation, and sent military supplies and reinforcements. On the possession of Badajos, therefore, the supply of Cadiz chiefly depended.

Seville was the French point of defence; Cadiz Estremadura and the Condado de Neibla their points of offence. The want of provisions, the desire to cut off the Spanish convoys, or the sudden irruption of troops from Cadiz, threatening their posts at Moguer and Heulva, always drew them towards the coast; the enterprises of Ballasteros brought them towards Araceña, and, in like manner, the advance of Romana towards the Morena brought them to Estremadura. But Romana had wasted the greater part of the latter province, and as the fifth corps alone was disposable, either for offensive movements, or for the defence of the country around Seville, Soult contented himself with such advantages as could be gained by sudden strokes; frequently, however, crossing the mountains to prevent the Spaniards from permanently establishing themselves on the frontier of Andalusia.

In October, Romana, as we have seen, entered the Lines of Torres Vedras, and Mendizabal, who remained with two divisions, finding that Mortier, unconscious of Romana's absence, had retired across the mountains, occupied Merida. He wished to establish himself in the yet unwasted country about Llerena, but the appearance of a moveable column on the frontier of La Mancha, sent him back to Badajos, and, on the 20th of November, he united with Ballasteros. The French then fortified Gibraleon and other posts in the Condado de Neibla, while Girard's division re-appeared at Guadalcanal, and being joined by the column from La Mancha, foraged the country towards Llerena.

Mendizabel then took post at Zafra with nine thousand infantry and two thousand cavalry, including Madden's Portuguese brigade, but meanwhile, Copons, who had four thousand men, was totally defeated at Castillejos by D'Aremberg, and retired to Puebla de Gusman.

At Cadiz, no change or military event had occurred after the affair of Matagorda, save the expeditions against Moguer, already noticed, and a slight attempt of the Spaniards against the Chiclana works in September; but all men's hopes and expectations had been wonderfully raised by political events which it was fondly hoped would secure both independence and a good constitution to Spain. After two years of intrigues and delay, the National Cortes assembled, and the long suppressed voice of the people was at last to be heard. Nevertheless, as the members of the Cortes could not be duly and legally chosen in the provinces possessed by the enemy; and as some members were captured by the French on their journey to Cadiz, many persons unknown, even by name, to their supposed constituents, were chosen; and a new principle of election was also adopted; for all persons twenty-five years old, not holding office or pension under the government, nor incapacitated by crime, nor by debts to the state, nor by bodily infirmity, were eligible to sit if chosen, which had never before been the rule. A supplement of sixty-eight members was likewise provided to supply accidental vacancies; and it was agreed that twenty-six persons then in Spain, natives of the colonies, should represent those dependencies.

Towards the latter end of September this great assembly met, and immediately took the title of

Majesty : it afterwards declared the press free in respect of political, but not of religious matters, abolished some of the provincial juntas, re-appointed captains-general, and proceeded to form a constitution worded in the very spirit of democracy. These things, aided by a vehement eloquence, drew much attention to the proceedings of the Cortes, and a fresh impulse seemed given to the war : but men brought up under despotism do not readily attain the fashions of liberty.

The Provincial Junta, the Central Junta, the Junta of Cadiz, the Regency, had all been, in succession, violent and tyrannical in act, while claiming only to be popular leaders, and this spirit did not desert the Cortes. Abstract principles of liberty were freely promulgated, yet tyrannical and partial proceedings were of common occurrence; and the reformations, by outstripping the feelings and understandings of the nation, weakened the main springs of its resistance to the French. It was not for freedom, but from national pride and from religious influence, that the people struck. Liberty had no attractions for the nobles, nor for the monastics, nor even for the merchants; and the Cortes, in suppressing old establishments and violating old forms and customs, wounded powerful interests, created active enemies, and shocked those very prejudices which had produced resistance to Napoleon.

In the administration of the armies, in the conduct of the war, in the execution of the laws, and the treatment of the colonies, there was as much of vanity, of intrigue, of procrastination, negligence, folly, and violence as before. Hence the people were soon discontented; and when the power of the religious orders was openly attacked by a proposition to abolish the inquisition, the clergy became active enemies of the Cortes. The great cause of feudal privileges being once given up, the natural tendency of the Cortes was towards the enemy. A broad line of distinction was thus drawn between the objects of the Spanish and English governments in the prosecution of the war; and, ere the contest was finished, there was a schism between the British cabinet and the Spanish government, which would inevitably have thrown the latter into Napoleon's hands, if fortune had not, at the moment, betrayed him in Russia.

The Regency, jealous of the Cortes, and little pleased with the inferior title of highness accorded them, were far from partaking of the republican spirit; and so anxious to check any tendency towards innovation, that early in the year they had invited the duke of Orleans to command the provinces bordering on France, permitted him to issue proclamations, and received him at Cadiz with the honours of a royal prince; intending to oppose his authority to that of the Local Juntas, at the moment, and finally, to that of the Cortes. He had touched at Taragona and had been well received, but at Cadiz the people regarded him with indifference. Mr. Wellesley opposed his stay because lord Wellington judged that his reception in Spain would tend to render the Spanish war popular in the South of France, and the English ministers wishing to prevent any future embarrasments from his intrigues in Spain, sent him a verbal invitation to reside in England. This he did not accept, but the Cortes aware of the cause of his arrival, obliged him to quit Spain, and soon after displacing the Regency of

Five, appointed Joachim Blake, Gabriel Cisgar, and Pedro Agar in their stead. During the absence of the two first, substitutes were provided, but one of them (Palacios) making some difficulty about taking the oath, was immediately declared to have forfeited the confidence of the nation; so peremptorily did the Cortes proceed.

Nevertheless, the new regents, not more pleased with the democratic spirit than their predecessors, and yet wishing to retain the power in their own hands, refused to listen to the princess of Brazils' claim, and thus factions sprang up on every side; for the republicans were not paramount in the Cortes at first, and the majority of that assembly were so subtilely dealt with by Pedro Souza, that they privately admitted Carlotta's claims both to the succession and the immediate control of the whole Peninsula.

Don Manuel Lapeña being declared captain-general of Andalusia, and commander of the forces in the Isla, was subservient to the views of the Cortes; but the new Regency, anxious to have a counterbalancing force, and being instigated also by persons from Badajos, enemies to Romana, re-moved that officer in December, and ordered his divisions to separate from the British army and come to Cadiz. The conduct of those divisions had, indeed, given little satisfaction either to the British or Portuguese, but numbers were so abso-lutely necessary to lord Wellington, that colonel O'Neal was sent to remonstrate with the Regency; and, by shewing that the fall of Estremadura, and the total loss of communication with the interior of Spain would ensue, obtained a momentary re-spite.

MrStuart's Papers, MSS.

In matters relating to the war against the French, or to the administration of the country, the Spanish leaders were incapable of acting cordially on any mature plan; but with respect to the colonies, all parties agreed to push violence, injustice, cruelty, and impolicy to their utmost bounds. To please the British government, the first Regency had published, in May, a decree, permitting the South Americans to export their own products, under certain conditions. This legalizing of a trade, which could not be suppressed, and which was but a decent return to England for her assistance, gave offence to the Municipal Junta of Cadiz; and its resentment was so much dreaded that the Regency, in June, disowned their own decree of the previous month and even punished the printers, as having given birth to a forged instrument. Exasperated at this treatment, the colonies, who had resisted all the intrigues of the French, with a firmness and singleness of purpose very displeasing to the government in Old Spain, openly discovered their discontent, and then the authorities in the Mother Country, throwing off the mask of liberality and patriotism, exposed their own secret views. " It is not enough that Americans should be Spanish subjects now, but that in all cases they should belong to Spain," was the proclamation of the Regency, in answer to a declaration from the Caraccas, avowing attachment to the cause of Ferdinand: meaning that, if Spain should pass under the power of the usurper America must follow, as having no right to decide in any case for herself.

When the Cortes met, America expected more justice; she had contributed ninety millions of dollars for the support of the war, and many of her sons had served zealously in person; she had also been declared an integral part of the empire by the Central Junta, and her deputies were now permitted to sit in the Great National Assembly. She was however soon made to understand, that the first of these privileges meant eternal slavery, and that the second was a mere form. " The Americans complain of having been tyrannized over for three hundred years! they shall now suffer for three thousand years," and " I know not to what class of beasts the Americans belong:" such were the expressions heard and applauded in the Cortes, when the rights of the colonists were agitated in that assembly. Better to lose Spain to Joseph, if America be retained, than to save Spain if America be separated from her, was a feeling deeply rooted in every Spanish heart, a sentiment covertly expressed in many public documents, and openly acted upon; for, when repeated insults, treachery, and continued violence, had driven the colonists to defend their rights in arms, the money and stores, supplied by England for the support of the war against the French, were applied to the fitting out of expeditions against America. Thus the convocation of the National Cortes, far from improving the posture of affairs, dried up the chief sources of revenue, weakened the army in the field, offended many powerful bodies in the state, involved the nation in a colonial war, and struck at the root of the alliance with England.

CHAPTER II.

WHILE the Spaniards in the Isla were occupied with the debates of the Cortes, the French works were laboured with care. The chain of forts was perfected, each being complete in itself with ditch and palisades and a week's provisions; the batteries at the Trocadero were powerful, and the flotillas at San Lucar de Barameda, Santa Maria, Puerto Real, and Chiclana, were ready for action. Soult repaired in person to San Lucar, and in the last night of October, thirty pinnaces and gun-boats slipping out of the Guadalquivir eluded the allied fleet, passed along the coast to Rota, and from thence, aided by shore batteries, fought their way to Santa Maria and the San Pedro. But, to avoid the fire of the fleet and forts in doubling Matagorda, the duke of Dalmatia, remembering what he had formerly effected at Campo Saucos on the Minho, transported his flotilla on rollers, overland; in November, one hundred and thirty armed vessels and transports were assembled in the Trocadero canal. This success was, however, alloyed by the death of general Senarmont, an artillery officer of the highest reputation.

At the Trocadero point there were immense batteries, and some notable pieces of ordnance called cannon-mortars, or Villantroys, after the inventor. These huge engines were cast in Seville, and, being placed in slings, threw shells with such prodigious force as to range over Cadiz, a distance of more than five thousand yards. But to obtain this flight the shells were partly filled with lead, and their charge of powder was too small for an effective explosion. Nevertheless, they produced some alarm in the city, and were troublesome to the shipping. But Soult's real design was first to ruin, by a superior fire, the opposite fort of the Puntales, then pass the straits with his flotilla, and establish his army between the Isla and the city; nor was this plan chimerical, for on the side of the besieged there was neither concert nor industry.

Two drafts, made, in August and September, by lord Wellington, had reduced Graham's force to five thousand men, and in October the fever broke out in Cadiz; but as Soult's preparations became formidable, reinforcements were drawn from Gibraltar and Sicily, and, at the end of the year, seven thousand British, Germans, and Portuguese, were still behind the Santi Petri. Hence Graham felt confident, 1°. That, with due preparation, he could maintain the Puntales even though its fire should be silenced. 2°. That Soult must establish a stronger flotilla than the allies, or his communication with Matagorda could not be maintained. 3°. That the intercourse between the army in Isla and the garrison of Cadiz could not be interrupted, unless the great redoubt of the Cortadura was lost.

To ensure the superiority of naval means, admiral Keats drew all the armed craft from Gibraltar. To secure the land defence, general Graham perseveringly urged the Regency to adopt certain plans, and he was warmly seconded by sir Henry Wellesley, but neither their entreaties, nor the imminence of the danger, could overcome the apathy of the Spaniards. Their army, reinforced by a small body from Ceuta, was wanting in discipline, clothing, and

Graham's
Despatches
MSS.

equipments, and only sixteen thousand men of all arms were effective on a muster-roll of twenty-three thousand. The labour of the British troops, far from being assisted, was vexatiously impeded; it was the end of December, and after many sharp altercations, ere Graham could even obtain leave to put the interior line of the Cortadura in a state of defence; although, by a sudden disembarkation, the enemy might enter it from the rear, and cut off the army of the Isla from the city. But while the duke of Dalmatia was collecting means of attack, the events in Portugal prevented the execution of his design.

Appendix,
No. III.
Sections 1,
2, 3, 4.

When Massena had passed the frontier, his communications with France became so uncertain, that the emperor's principal source of information was through the English newspapers. Foy brought the first exact intelligence of the posture of affairs. It was then that the army of the north was directed to support the army of Portugal; that the ninth corps was made a component part of the latter; that the prince of Esling was enjoined to hold fast between Santarem and the Zezere; to besiege Abrantes; and to expect the duke of Dalmatia, who had been already several times commanded to move through the Alemtejo, to his assistance. The emperor seems even to have contemplated the evacuation of Andalusia and the concentration of the whole army of the south on the Tagus, a project that would have strengthened rather than weakened the French in the Peninsula, because it was more important to crush the regular warfare in Portugal, than to hold any particular province.

The King's
Correspon-
dence, cap-
tured at
Vittoria.

Massena's instructions reached him in due time, Soult's were intercepted by the Guerillas, and the duplicates did not arrive before the end of December:

a delay affording proof, that thirty thousand men would scarcely have compensated for the uncertainty of the French communications. Postponing his design against Cadiz, the Duke of Dalmatia then repaired to Seville, carrying with him Latour Maubourg's cavalry and five thousand infantry from the first corps. His instructions neither prescribed a line of movement nor enjoined any specific operation; the prince of Esling was to communicate his plan, to which Soult's was to be subordinate. But no certain intelligence even of Massena's early proceedings had reached Seville, and such were the precautions of lord Wellington, such the activity of the Partidas, that from the time Soult quitted Cadiz, until his operation terminated, no communication could be effected between the two marshals, and each acted in perfect ignorance of the plans and situation of the other.

The duke of Dalmatia considering that Sebastiani had his hands full; and that the blockade of Cadiz, and the protection of Seville on the side of Neibla and of Araceña, would not permit the drawing off more than twenty thousand men from Andalusia; represented to the Emperor that with such a force, he durst not penetrate the Alemtejo, leaving Olivenza and Badajos, and Ballasteros, (who would certainly join Mendizabel) on his rear; and that Romana alone, without reckoning British troops, could bring ten thousand men against his front; hence he demanded leave to besiege those places, and Napoleon consented. Meanwhile, order was taken to secure Andalusia during the operations. Dessolles' division had been recalled to form the army of the centre, and general Godinot took his place at Cordoba; a column of ob-

Marshal Soult's Correspondence. MSS.

BOOK
XII.

1811.
January.

King Jo-
seph's Cor-
respon-
dence.
MSS.

servation was posted under general Digeon at Ecija ;
Seville entrenched on the side of Neibla, was given
over to general Daricau ; and a detachment under
Remond was posted at Gibraleon. The expedi-
tionary army, consisting of sixteen thousand infantry, artillery, sappers and miners, and about four
thousand cavalry and fifty-four guns, was assembled
on the 2d January. An equipage of siege, a light
pontoon train, and seventeen hundred carts, for
stores and provisions, were also prepared ; and
Soult's administration was now so efficient, that he
ordered a levy of five thousand young Spaniards,
called " *escopeteros*" (fuzileers) to maintain the police
of the province.

SOULT'S FIRST EXPEDITION TO ESTREMADURA.

Mortier moving from Guadalcanal, entered Zafra
on the 5th January, Mendizabal retired to Merida,
and Ballasteros, in consequence of orders from the
Regency, passed over the mountains to Frejenal.
But winter tempests raged, the French convoy which
moved on Araceña, overwhelmed by storms, was
detained at the foot of the mountains, and to protect it, Gazan marching from Zafra, drove Ballasteros out of Frejenal.   Meanwhile, the Spanish
leaders, as well those in Estremadura, as in Cadiz,
were quite ignorant of Soult's intentions, some asserting that he was going to pass the Tagus at
Almaraz, others, that his object was only to crush
Ballasteros. Lord Wellington alone divined the
truth, and it was he who first gave Mendizabal
notice, that the French were assembling at
Seville at all, so destitute of intelligence and of

Appendix,
No. II.
Sec. 5, 6.

military knowledge were the Spaniards.   Now when
the French were breaking into Estremadura, terror
and confusion spread far and wide ; Badajos was
ill provisioned, Albuquerque in ruins, Olivenza
nearly dismantled ; and, in the midst of this disorder, Ballasteros was drawn off towards the Condada de Neibla by the Regency, who thus deprived
Estremadura of half its defenders at the moment
of invasion.

Lord Wellington had advised that the troops
should be concentrated, the bridges over the Guadiana mined for destruction, and the passage of that
river disputed to gain time ; but these things being
neglected, an advanced guard of cavalry alone carried the bridge of Merida on the 6th.   Soult then
turned upon Olivenza with the infantry, and while
Latour Maubourg's dragoons held Mendizabal in
check on the side of Badajos, Briche's light horsemen collected cattle on the side of Estremadura.
Gazan's division, still posted near Frejenal, protected the march of the artillery and convoy, and La
Houssaye's brigade, belonging to the army of the
centre, quitting Truxillo, marched against the Partidas and scoured the banks of the Tagus from
Arzobispo to Alcantara.

FIRST SIEGE OF OLIVENZA.

This place, although regularly fortified with nine
bastions, a covered way, and some unfinished ravelins, was incapable of a good defence.   With an old
breach slightly repaired, very few guns mounted,
and commanding no passage of the Guadiana, it
was of little importance to the French ; yet, as con-

taining four thousand troops, it was of some consequence to reduce it.   Lord Wellington had pressed
Romana to destroy the defences entirely, or to
supply it with the means of resistance, and the
marquis decided on the former ; but Mendizabel
slighting his orders, had thrown his best division
into the place.

It was invested the 11th ; an abandoned outwork,
three hundred and forty yards south of the town,
was taken possession of the first night, and breaching batteries of eight guns, and counter batteries of
six guns were then marked out.   The trenches were
opened on the west, and approaches carried on by
the flying sap against the old breach ; but the rains
were heavy and continual, the scarcity of entrench-
ing-tools great, and it was not until the 18th, when
the head of the convoy had passed the mountains,
that the works could be properly advanced.

On the 19th the covered way was crowned, and
the 20th the breaching batteries opened their fire ;
two mortars also threw shells into the town, and a
globe of compression was prepared to blow in the
counterscarp.   In the evening, Mendizabel skirmished unsuccessfully with Latour Maubourg's
horsemen, and, on the 21st, the mine was completed and preparations made for the passage of the
ditch.   The Spanish general, unable from the absence of Ballasteros' division to relieve Olivenza,
now demanded succour from Romana, who sent
Carlos D'España's brigade from Abrantes the 18th,
and general Virues, with his own Spanish division,
from Cartaxo on the 20th.   The 21st, the governor
of Olivenza was informed of this, and replied that
he would maintain the place to the last moment ;
but the next day he capitulated, having still pro-

visions, ammunition, eighteen guns, and four thousand one hundred effective soldiers. The 26th Soult marched against Badajos.

Meanwhile Ballasteros advanced upon Neibla, but being followed by Gazan, was overtaken at Castillejos on the 28th, and, after a sharp battle, driven with the loss of fifteen hundred prisoners besides killed and wounded over the Guadiana; the Spanish artillery was saved in the castle of Paymigo, and the infantry took refuge at Alcontin and Mertola. Ballasteros' force was thus in a few days reduced by three thousand men, and, that nothing might be left to alarm the French in that quarter, the Regency re-called Copon's force to Cadiz. In this manner a fortress was taken, and twelve thousand men, who, well employed, might have frustrated the French designs against Badajos, were all dispersed, withdrawn, or made prisoners in twenty days after the commencement of Soult's expedition.

For many months previous to these events lord Wellington had striven to teach the Spanish commander that there was but one safe mode of proceeding in Estremadura, and Romana had just yielded to his counsels, when the sudden arrival of the French threw every thing into confusion. The defence of the Guadiana, the dismantling of Olivenza, the concentration of the forces were all neglected. Romana, however, had sent his divisions towards the frontier; they reached Montemor the 22d; the 23d they received Mendizabel's orders to halt as Olivenza had surrendered; the 24th Romana died of an aneurism in the heart. He was a worthy man and of quick parts, although deficient in military talent. His death was a great loss, yet his influence was on the wane; he had many enemies, and his authority was chiefly sustained by the attachment of his troops, and by his riches, for his estates being in the Balearic Isles, his revenues did not suffer by the war.

Mendizabal now commanded in Estremadura. He had received Romana's orders to adopt lord Wellington's plan; which was to concentrate all the Spanish troops, amounting to at least ten thousand men, on the frontier, and, before the enemy appeared on the right bank of the Guadiana, to occupy a certain position of great natural strength close to Badajos; the right touching the fort of St. Christoval, the front covered by the Gebora river and by the Guadiana, the fortress of Campo Mayor immediately in rear of the left, and Elvas behind the centre. When Mendizabal should be entrenched on this position, and a strong garrison in Badajos, the English general thought Soult could not invest or even straighten the communications of the town; yet, knowing well the people he dealt with, he

prophetically observed, " *with soldiers of any other nation success is certain, but no calculation can be made of any operation in which Spanish troops are engaged.*"

When Olivenza fell, a small garrison was in Albuquerque, another in Valencia d'Alcantara; Carlos d'España was in Campo Mayor, and Virues, with Romana's divisions, was at Montemor. When Soult drove back the out-posts of Badajos on the 26th, Mendizabal shut himself up with six thousand men in that fortress; but, although a siege had been expected for a year, the place was unprovisioned. It was, however, still possible to execute the English general's plan, yet no Spaniard moved, and, on the 27th, Latour Maubourg, crossing the Guadiana at Merida, forded the Gebora, and cut off the communications with Campo Mayor and Elvas.

FRENCH SIEGE OF BADAJOS.

This city stands on a tongue of land at the confluence of the Guadiana with the Rivillas. The first is a noble river five hundred yards broad, the second a trifling stream. A rock, one hundred feet high, and crowned by an old castle, overhangs the meeting of the waters ; and the town, spreading out like a fan as the land opens between the rivers, is protected by eight regular curtains and bastions, from twenty-three to thirty feet in height, with good counterscarps, covered way, and glacis. On the left bank of the Guadiana the out-works were, 1°. the Lunette of San Roque, covering a dam and sluice on the Rivillas, by which an inundation could be commanded ; 2°. an isolated redoubt, called the Picurina, situated beyond the Rivillas, and four hundred yards from the town ; 3°. the Pardaleras, a defective crown-work, central between the Lower Guadiana and the Rivillas, and two hundred yards from the ramparts.

On the right bank of the Guadiana a hill, crowned by a regular fort three hundred feet square, called San Christoval, overlooked the interior of the castle ; and a quarter of a mile farther down the stream, the bridge, six hundred yards in length, was protected by a bridge-head, slightly connected with San Christoval, but commanded on every side.

Soult constructed a ferry on the Guadiana, above the confluence of the Gebora, and three attacks were opened against the town the 28th, two on the side of Picurina and one on that of the Pardaleras. The 29th and 30th slight sallies were repulsed, but tempestuous weather spoiled the works. Gazan's division was distant, the infantry before the place were few, and, on the 30th, the garrison making a vigorous sally from the Pardaleras, killed or wounded sixty men and cleared the trenches. Meanwhile some Spanish cavalry, gliding round the left of the French, sabred several engineers and sappers, and then retired.

Conquête
de l'Anda-
lusie, par
Edouard
Lapéne.

Siège de
Badajos,
par le Col.
Lamare.

In the night of the 2d of February a violent tempest flooded the Rivillas, carried away the French bridges, drowned men and horses, damaged the depôts, and reduced the besiegers to the greatest distress. The cavalry employed in the investment could no longer forage; scarcity was felt in the camp; the convoys could only arrive by detachments; the rigour of winter bivouacs caused sickness; and, on the 3d, the Spaniards, making a second sally from Pardaleras, killed or wounded eighty men and ruined a part of the parallel. The same day Gazan arrived in camp, but the French cavalry being withdrawn from the right bank of the Guadiana, in consequence of rigorous weather, the communication was re-established with Elvas, and Mendizabal called the divisions in Portugal to his assistance. Virues immediately marched upon Elvas, Carlo d'España, and Madden united at Campo Mayor, and Julian Sanchez brought down his Partida from Upper Estremadura.

Lord Wel-
lington's
Correspon-
dence.
MSS.

Mr. Stu-
art's Pa-
pers.MSS.

In the night of the 5th, Mendizabal repaired to

Elvas in person, passed the Caya the next day, and being joined on the road by the troops from Campo Mayor, pushed the few French horsemen still on the right of the Guadiana over the Gebora. The Portuguese brigade crossed that river in pursuit, and captured some baggage; but the infantry entered Badajos, for Mendizabal again neglecting lord Wellington's counsel, designed not to take up a position behind the Gebora, but to raise the siege by a sally; yet he delayed this until the next day, thus risking to have his whole army shut up in an ill-provided fortress; for Latour Maubourg, seeing that Madden was unsupported, turned and drove him back over the Gebora with loss.

Badajos now contained sixteen thousand men, and, early on the 7th, Carrera and Carlos d'España, at the head of five thousand infantry and three hundred cavalry, breaking out at the Picurina side, with one burst carried the trenches and the batteries; the soldiers fought with surprising ardour, but the entire want of arrangement on the part of the generals (unworthy to command the brave men under them) ruined all. They had not even provided the means to spike the guns; and when Mortier brought his reserves against the front and flank of the attack, the whole driven back in disorder, re-entered the city, having eighty-five officers and near six hundred soldiers killed and wounded; the enemy also lost several engineers and four hundred men.

While this action took place on the left bank, Latour Maubourg occupied the ground between the Gebora and the Caya, and again cut off the communication with Elvas and Campo Mayor; but his forces were too weak to maintain themselves there, and Mendizabal, leaving the defence of the town entirely to the governor, Rafael Menacho, pitched his own camp round San Christoval. Some days previous to this, the French had bombarded Badajos, a proceeding only mischievous to themselves; for the inhabitants, terrified by the shells, fled in great numbers while the communication was open, but left behind their provisions, which enabled Menacho to feed his garrison without difficulty.

Soult observing the numbers, and awake to all the real resources of the Spanish succouring army, feared lest delay should produce a change of commanders, or of system, and resolved to bring matters to a crisis. On the 11th he stormed the Pardaleras; on the 12th, he sent fifteen hundred cavalry across the Guadiana to Montijo; and, on the 14th, he threw shells into the camp about Christoval, which obliged Mendizabal to remove from the heights in front of that fort. Meanwhile, intelligence that Castaños was appointed captain-general of the Estremadura created the greatest anger amongst Romana's soldiers: they had long considered themselves independent of the central government, and in this mood, although the position behind the Gebora, recommended by lord Wellington, was at last occupied, little attention was paid to military discipline. The English general had expressly advised Mendizabal to increase the great natural strength of this position with entrenchments; for his design was that the Spaniards, whom he thought quite unequal to open field-operations, should have an impregnable post, whence they could safely aid in the defence of the town, and yet preserve a free communication with the

Appendix,
No.X.Section 2.

Lord Wellington to
Lord Liverpool.
MSS.

Alemtejo, until the arrival of his own reinforcements CHAP. (which he expected in the latter end of January) II. should enable him to raise the siege. Mendizabal, 1811. with that arrogance which is peculiar to his nation, February. rejected this counsel, and hung twelve days on the heights of Christoval in a torpid state; and when driven thence, by the French shells, he merely destroyed a small bridge over the Gebora, neither casting up entrenchments, nor keeping a guard in his front, nor disposing his men with care. Soult observing these things, suddenly leaped upon him.

BATTLE OF THE GEBORA.

The Guadiana and the Gebora rivers covered the Spanish position, but this did not deter the duke of Dalmatia from attempting to pass both and surprise the camp. And first to deprive Mendizabal of the aid of San Christoval, and to create a diversion, the French mortar-batteries again threw shells on the 17th; yet the swell of the rivers would not permit the main operation to be commenced before the evening of the 18th : but on that day the cavalry drew down the right bank of the Guadiana from Montijo, and the artillery and infantry crossed at the French ferry, four miles above the confluence of the Gebora. These combinations were so exactly executed, that, at daybreak, on the 19th, six thousand infantry and three thousand cavalry were in order of battle on the right bank of the Guadiana.

The Gebora was still to be forded, and, behind it, the Spaniards had ten thousand infantry, a considerable artillery, and fifteen hundred cavalry, besides many armed followers of the camp ; the whole number not being less than fifteen thousand. But a thick mist covered the country, no Spanish posts were in advance, and Soult, riding through the French ranks, and exhorting the soldiers to fight manfully, commenced the passage of the Gebora. His cavalry forded five miles up the stream, and his infantry passed in two columns, on the right and left of the ruined bridge : a few shots, near the latter, first alarmed the Spaniards, and, as the instant clamour amongst the multitude indicated that the surprise was complete, Mortier, who directed the movements, rapidly formed the line of battle.

At eight o'clock the fog cleared away, and the first beams of the sun and the certainty of victory flashed together on the French soldiers. Their horsemen were already around the Spanish left, iinfantry, cavalry, and guns, heaped together in the centre, were waving to and fro in disorder, and the right having fallen away from San Cristoval was unsupported. In a few moments, general Girard placed three battalions between the Spanish army and that fort, the artillery roared and the French bore forward, as one man, to the attack. Six battalions pressed the centre, Girard moved against the right, Latour Maubourg's cavalry charged the left. Thus surrounded, Mendizabel's troops instinctively crowded on the centre, and for some time resisted by their inert weight. But the French infantry soon closed on the mass with a destroying musketry, the horsemen rode in with loose bridles, and the Spaniards were shaken, divided, and slaughtered. Their cavalry fled out-

right, and even Madden's Portuguese, disregarding
alike his exhortations and example, shamefully
turned their backs. At ten o'clock the fight was
over; Virues was taken, Mendizabel and Carrera
escaped with difficulty; España alone made good
his retreat to Campo Mayor with two thousand
men. A few reached Elvas, three thousand got
into Badajos, by the bridge, and nine hundred
bodies strewed the field. Eight thousand, including
armed followers, were made prisoners, and guns,
colours, muskets, ammunition, baggage, all fell
into the enemy's hands. It was a disastrous and a
shameful defeat. In the depth of winter, Soult,
with a small force, had passed two difficult rivers,
carried a strong position, and annihilated an army
which had been two years in constant service.
Mendizabel, instead of destroying the bridge over
the Gebora, should have cast others, that he might
freely issue to attack the French while crossing the
Guadiana; he should have opposed them again in
passing the Gebora; or he might have passed
through Badajos, and fallen on the troops in the
trenches, with his whole army, while Soult was
still entangled between the rivers.

In the evening after the action the French cast
up entrenchments, posting three battalions and
the heavy cavalry on the important position they
had gained, and the next day the works of the
siege were renewed with greater activity; yet
the difficulty of Soult's undertaking was rendered
apparent by his victories. The continual rains, interrupting the arrival of his convoys, obliged him
to employ a number of men at a great distance to
gather provisions; nearly two thousand French had
been killed or wounded in the two sieges and in

this battle, many also were sick, and Badajos was
still powerful. The body of the place was entire,
the garrison nine thousand strong, was, by the
flight of the inhabitants, well provided with food ;
and there was no want of other stores : the governor was resolute and confident ; the season rigorous
for the besiegers ; no communication had been yet
opened with Massena ; and lord Wellington, in
momentary expectation that his reinforcements would
arrive, was impatient to bring on a crisis. Meanwhile, the duke of Dalmatia's power, in Andalusia,
was menaced in the most serious manner.

CONTINUATION OF THE BLOCKADE OF CADIZ.

When general Graham was aware of Soult's departure, and knew, also, that the fifth corps had
quitted Seville, he undertook, in concert with the
Spaniards, to drive Victor out of his lines. A
force, sailing from Cadiz the 29th of January, was
to have been joined, in rear of the enemy, by the
troops from Tarifa under major Brown, and by
three thousand Spaniards, from Algesiras and San
Roque under general Beguines ; contrary winds detained both the troops and the vessels carrying
counter orders to Beguines and Brown, who advanced, the first to Medina, the other to Casa Vieja.
Victor, having notice of this project, at first kept
close, but afterwards sent troops to retake Medina
and Casa Vieja ; and, in the course of February,
twelve thousand men, drawn from the northern governments, were directed upon Andalusia, to reinforce the different corps. The first corps was thus
increased to twenty thousand men, of which fifteen

thousand were before Cadiz, and the remainder at San Lucar, Medina Sidonia, and other quarters. Nevertheless, on the 21st of February, ten thousand infantry and near six hundred cavalry, of the allies, were again embarked at Cadiz, being to land at Tarifa, and march upon the rear of the enemy's camp at Chiclana. General Zayas commanding the Spanish forces left in the Isla was directed to cast a bridge over the San Petri near the sea mouth; Ballasteros, with the remains of his army was to menace Seville; the Partizans were to act against the fourth corps; insurrections were expected in all quarters, and many took place in Sebastiani's district.

The British troops passed their port in a gale, the 22d, but, landing at Algesiras, marched to Tarifa the next day, when they were joined by the twenty-eighth, and the flank companies of the ninth and eighty-second regiments. Thus somewhat more than four thousand effective troops (including two companies of the twentieth Portuguese and one hundred and eighty German hussars) were assembled under general Graham; all good and hardy troops, and himself a daring old man and of a ready temper for battle.

Appendix,
No. IX.
Section 2.

General La Peña arrived on the 27th, with seven thousand Spaniards, and Graham, for the sake of unanimity, ceded the chief command, although it was contrary to his instructions. The next day, the whole moved forward about twelve miles, and passed the mountain ridges that, descending from Ronda to the sea, separate the plains of San Roque from those of Medina and Chiclana. Being now within four leagues of the enemy's posts, the troops were re-organized. The vanguard was given to Lardizabal ; the centre to the prince of Anglona ; the reserve, composed of two Spanish regiments and the British were confided to Graham ; and the cavalry of both nations, formed in one body, was commanded by colonel Whittingham, then in the Spanish service.

The French covering division, under general Cassagne, consisted of three battalions and a regiment of horse placed at Medina, with outposts at Vejer de la Frontera and Casa Viejas. Before La Peñas arrival, the irregulars had attacked Casa Viejas, and general Beguines had even taken Medina ; but Cassagne, reinforced by a battalion of infantry from Arcos, retook and entrenched it the 29th ; and the signal of action being thus given, the French generals in the higher provinces, perceiving that the people were ready for commotion, gathered in their respective forces at Seville, Ecija, and Cordoba, following the orders left by Soult. In Grenada the insurgents were especially active, and Sebastiani, doubtful if the storm would not break on his head, concentrated a column at Estipona, which was a good covering point to the coast line, and one whence he could easily gain Ronda. Victor manned his works at Rota, Santa Maria, Puerto Real, and the Troccadero with a mixed force, of refugee French, juramentados, and regular troops ; but he assembled eleven thousand good soldiers near Chiclana, between the roads of Conil and Medina, to await the unfolding of the allies' project.

At first, La Peña's march pointed to Medina Sidonia ; his vanguard stormed Casa Viejas on the 2d of March, and the troops from Algesiras, amounting to sixteen hundred infantry besides several hundreds of irregular cavalry, coming in, en-

Intercepted Letter of General Werle to Sebastiani, Alhama, March 12.

Appendix, No. I. Section 6.

creased his force to twelve thousand infantry, eight
hundred horsemen, and twenty-four guns. The 3d
he resumed his march, but hearing that Medina
Sidonia was entrenched, turned towards the coast,
and drove the French from Vejer de la Frontera.
The following evening he continued his movement,
and at nine o'clock on the morning of the 5th, after
a skirmish, in which his advanced guard of cavalry
was routed by a French squadron, he reached the
Cerro de Puerco, called by the English the heights
of Barosa; being then only four miles from the
sea mouth of the Santi Petri.

The hill of Barosa is a low ridge creeping in from
the coast about one mile and a half, and overlooking
a high broken plain of small extent. This plain
was bounded on one side by the coast cliffs; on the
other by the forest of Chiclana, and in front by a
pine-wood, beyond which rose a long narrow height
called the Bermeja, which filled the space between
the Almanza creek and the sea; and which could
be reached by moving either through the pine-wood
in front or by the beach under the cliffs.

At Tarifa, Graham, judging that Victor would
surely come out of his lines to fight, had obtained
from La Peña a promise to make short marches;
to keep the troops fresh for battle; and not to
approach the enemy except in a concentrated mass.
Nevertheless, the day's march from Casa Vieja,
being made through bad roads, with ignorant
guides, had occupied fifteen hours, and the night
march to Barosa had been still more fatiguing.
The troops came up in a straggling manner, and
ere they had all arrived, La Peña, as if in contempt
of his colleague, without either disclosing his own
plans, or communicating by signal or otherwise

Appendix,
No. IX.
Section 1.

with Zayas, sent the vanguard, reinforced by a squadron and three guns, straight against the mouth of the Santi Petri. Zayas had cast his bridge there on the 2d, and commenced an entrenchment, but, in the following night, being surprised by the French, was driven again into the Isla; hence this movement of the vanguard was exceedingly dangerous: Lardizabal, however, after a sharp skirmish, in which he lost nearly three hundred men, forced the enemy's posts between the Almanza creek and the sea, and effected a junction with Zayas.

Graham was now extremely desirous of holding the Barosa height in force, as the key both to offensive and defensive movements; and he argued that no general in his senses would lend his flank to an enemy, by attacking the Bermeja while Barosa was thus occupied. Lascy, the chief of the Spanish staff, opposed this reasoning, and La Peña, without ceremony, commanded Graham to march the British troops through the wood to Bermeja. With great temper, he obeyed this uncourteous order, leaving the flank companies of the ninth and eighty-second, under major Brown, as a guard for the baggage; he marched, however, in the full persuasion that La Peña would remain with Anglona's division and the cavalry at Barosa, and the more so, as a Spanish detachment was still on the side of Medina. But scarcely had the British entered the wood, when La Peña, without any notice, carried off the corps of battle, directed the cavalry to follow by the sea-road, and repaired himself to Santi Petri, leaving Barosa crowded with baggage, and protected only by a rear-guard of four guns and five battalions.

During these movements, Victor had remained close in the forest of Chiclana, and as the patrols of the allied cavalry reported that they could see no enemy, Graham's march being only of two miles, seemed secure. The French marshal was, however, keenly watching the allies' progress. Having recalled his infantry from Medina Sidonia as soon as La Peña had reached Barosa, he momentarily expected their arrival; and he felt so sure of success, that his cavalry then at Medina and Arcos were directed upon Vejer and other places, to cut off the fugitives after the battle. Appendix, No. I. Section 7. The duke of Belluno had in hand fourteen pieces of artillery and nine thousand excellent troops, of the divisions of Laval, Ruffin, and Villatte. From these he drew three grenadier battalions as reserves, and attached two of them and three squadrons of cavalry to the division of Ruffin, which formed his left wing; the other he joined to the division of Laval, which formed his centre. Villatte's troops, about two thousand five hundred in number, after retiring from Bermeja, were posted close to a bridge on the Almanza creek, to cover the works of the camp, and to watch the Spanish forces at Santi Petri and Bermeja.

BATTLE OF BAROSA.

When Victor observed that Graham's corps was in the wood, that a strong body of Spaniards was on the Bermeja, a third body, with all the baggage, at Barosa, and a fourth still in march from Vejer, he took Villatte's division as his pivot, and came with a rapid pace into the plain, and began the

battle.   Laval was directed against the English,
but Victor himself, with Ruffin's brigade, ascending
the reverse side of Barosa, cut off the Spanish detachment on the road to Medina, drove the whole
of the rear-guard off the height towards the sea,
dispersed the baggage and followers of the army
in all directions, and took three Spanish guns.

Major Brown, seeing the general confusion, and
being unable to stem the torrent, slowly retired
into the plain, and sending notice of this attack
to Graham, demanded orders.   That general,
being then near Bermeja, answered, that he was
to fight; and instantly facing about himself, regained the plain with the greatest celerity, expecting to find La Peña, with the corps of battle and
the cavalry, on the height.   But when the view
opened, he beheld Ruffin's brigade flanked by the
chosen battalions, near the top of Barosa at the
one side, the Spanish rear-guard and baggage flying
in confusion on the other, the French cavalry between the summit and the sea, and Laval close on
his own left flank; but La Peña he could see no
where.   In this desperate situation, he felt that to
retreat upon Bermeja, and thus bring the enemy,
pell-mell with the allies on to that narrow ridge,
must be disastrous, wherefore, without a moment's
hesitation, he resolved to attack, although the key
of the field of battle was already in the enemy's
possession.

Ten guns, under major Duncan, instantly opened
a terrific fire against Laval's column, while colonel
Andrew Barnard, with the riflemen and the Portuguese companies, running vehemently out on the
left, commenced the fight: the remainder of the
British troops, without any attention to regiments

or brigades, so sudden was the affair, formed two masses, one of which under general Dilkes marched hastily against Ruffin, and the other under colonel Wheately against Laval. Duncan's guns ravaged the French ranks, Laval's artillery replied vigorously, Ruffin's batteries took Wheately's column in flank, and the infantry on both sides pressed forward eagerly, and with a pealing musketry. When near together, a fierce, rapid, prolonged charge of the British overthrew the first line of the French, and, notwithstanding its extreme valour, drove it in confusion, over a narrow dip of ground upon the second, which was almost immediately broken in the same manner, and only the chosen battalion, hitherto posted on the right, remained to cover the retreat.

Meanwhile Brown had marched headlong against Ruffin. Nearly half of his detachment went down under the enemy's first fire; yet he maintained the fight, until Dilkes' column, which had crossed a deep hollow and never stopt even to reform the regiments, came up, with little order indeed, but in a fierce mood, and then the whole ran up towards the summit; there was no slackness on any side, and at the very edge of the ascent their gallant opponents met them. A dreadful, and for some time a doubtful, fight ensued; but Ruffin and Chaudron Rousseau, commanding the chosen grenadiers, both fell mortally wounded, the English bore strongly onward, and their incessant slaughtering fire forced the French from the hill with the loss of three guns and many brave soldiers.

The discomfitted divisions, retiring concentrically, soon met, and with infinite spirit endeavoured to reform and renew the action. The play of Duncan's guns, close, rapid, and murderous, rendered the attempt vain. Victor quitted the field of battle, and the British having been twenty-four hours under arms, without food, were too exhausted to pursue.

While these terrible combats of infantry were fighting, La Peña looked idly on, neither sending his cavalry, nor his horse-artillery, nor any part of his army, to the assistance of his ally ; nor yet menacing the right of the enemy, which was close to him and weak. The Spanish Walloon guards, the regiment of Ciudad Real, and some Guerilla cavalry, indeed turned without orders, coming up just as the action ceased ; and it was expected that colonel Whittingham, an Englishman commanding a powerful body of horse, would have done as much ; but no stroke in aid of the British was struck by a Spanish sabre that day, although the French cavalry did not exceed two hundred and fifty men, and it is evident that the eight hundred under Whittingham might, by sweeping round the left of Ruffin's division, have rendered the defeat ruinous. So certain, indeed, was this, that colonel Frederick Ponsonby, drawing off the hundred and eighty German hussars belonging to the English army, reached the field of battle, and charging the French squadrons just as their retreating divisions met, overthrew them, took two guns, and even attempted, though vainly, to sabre Rousseau's chosen battalions.

Such was the fight of Barosa. Short, for it lasted only one hour and a half, but most violent and bloody ; for fifty officers, sixty serjeants, and above eleven hundred British soldiers, and more than two

From Chiclana

Point of union in retreat

Spa Cut

Lagoon

Isla

Villate

Cavalry Charge

To Medin

Grenadeers

Laval

Wheatly

Almanza Creek

Lardizabal

Zayas

Lapeña

Brown

Ruffin

Dilkes

Grenadeers

Bermeja

Ger.ⁿ Hussars

French Cavalry

Whittingham

Spanish Bat.ⁿ

Fugitives & Baggage

Tory Barosa

Sand beach

1 Mile

BATTLE of BAROSA
5ᵗʰ March 1811.

Xerez

Ronc

R. San Pedro

Isla

Medina Sidonia

Chiclana

Barosa

Casa Vieja

San Roque

Es

Vijar la frontera

Algeiseras

Tarifa

Gibralte

thousand Frenchmen were killed and wounded; six guns, an eagle, two generals (both mortally wounded), together with four hundred other pri- soners, fell into the hands of the victors.

After the action, Graham remained some hours on the height, still hoping that La Peña would awake to the prospect of success and glory, which the extreme valour of the British had opened. Four thousand men and a powerful artillery had come over the Santi Petri, and thus the Spanish general was at the head of twelve thousand infantry and eight hundred cavalry, all fresh troops; while before him were only the remains of the French line of battle retreating in the greatest disorder upon Chiclana. But all military feeling was extinct in Appendix, La Peña, and as Graham could no longer endure Section 1. such command, the morning of the 6th saw the British filing over the bridge into the Isla.

On the French side, Cassagne's reserve came up from Medina, and a council of war being held in the night of the 5th, Victor, although of a des- ponding nature, proposed another attack, but the suggestion being ill received, nothing was done. On the 6th, Admiral Keats, landing his seamen and marines, dismantled, with exception of Cata- lina, every fort from Rota to Santa Maria, and even obtained momentary possession of the latter place. This caused such confusion and alarm in the French camp, that the duke of Belluno, leaving garrisons at the great points of his lines, and a rear guard at Chiclana, retreated behind the San Pedro, Official where he expected to be immediately attacked. If of Military La Peña had even then pushed to Chiclana, Graham MSS. and Keats were willing to make a simultaneous at- tack upon the Trocadero; yet the 6th and 7th pass-

ed, without even a Spanish patrole following the
French.   On the 8th Victor returned to Chiclana,
whereupon La Peña recrossed the Santi Petri, and
destroyed the bridge; and his detachment on the
side of Medina being thus cut off from the Isla,
was soon afterwards obliged to retire to Algesiras.

All the passages in this extraordinary battle were
so broadly marked, that observations would be useless.   The contemptible feebleness of La Peña furnished a surprising contrast to the heroic vigour of
Graham, whose attack was an inspiration rather
than a resolution, so wise, so sudden was the decision, so swift, so conclusive was the execution.
The original plan of the enterprise having been
however rather rashly censured, some remarks on
that head may be useful.   " Sebastiani," it is said,
" might, by moving on the rear of the allies, have
crushed them, and they had no right to calculate
upon his inactivity."   This is a shallow criticism.
Graham, weighing the natural dislike of one general to serve under another, judged, that Sebastiani,
harassed by insurrections in Grenada, would not
hastily abandon his own district, menaced as it was
by insurrection, to succour Victor, before it was
clear where the blow was to be struck.   The distance from Tarifa to Chiclana was about fifty miles,
whereas, from Sebastiani's nearest post to Chiclana
was above a hundred, and the real object of the
allies could not be known until they had passed the
mountains separating Tarifa from Medina.   Com-
bining these moral and physical considerations,
Graham had reason to expect several days of free
action ; and thus indeed it happened, and with a
worthy colleague he would have raised the blockade :
more than that could scarcely have been hoped, as

Appendix,
No. IX.
Section 5.

the French forces would have concentrated either
before Cadiz or about Seville or Ecija; and they
had still fifty thousand men in Andalusia.

Victor's attack on the 5th, was well-judged, well-
timed, and vigorous; with a few thousand more
troops he, alone, would have crushed the allies.
The unconquerable spirit of the English prevented
this disaster, but if Graham or his troops had
given way, or even hesitated, the whole army must
have been driven like sheep into an enclosure; the
Almanza creek on one side, the sea on the other,
the San Petri to bar their flight, and the enemy
hanging on their rear in all the fierceness of victory.
Indeed, such was La Peña's misconduct, that the
French, although defeated, gained their main point;
the blockade was renewed, and it is remarkable that,
during the action, a French detachment passed near
the bridge of Zuazo without difficulty, and brought
back prisoners; thus proving that with a few more
troops Victor might have seized the Isla. Meanwhile Ballasteros, who had gone against Seville,
was chased, in a miserable condition, to the Aroche
hills, by Daricau.

In Cadiz violent disputes arose. La Peña, in an
address to the Cortes, claimed the victory for himself. He affirmed that all the previous arrangements were made with the knowledge and approbation of the English general, and the latter's retreat
into the Isla he indicated as the real cause of failure:
Lascy and general Cruz-Murgeon also published
inaccurate accounts of the action, and even had
deceptive plans engraved to uphold their statements. Graham, stung by these unworthy proceedings, exposed the conduct of La Peña in a
letter to the British envoy; refused with disdain

the title of grandee of the first class voted to him by the Cortes; and when Lascy used some expressions relative to the action personally offensive, he enforced an apology with his sword. But having thus shewn himself superior to his opponents at all points, the gallant old man soon afterwards relinquished his command to general Cooke, and joined lord Wellington's army.

CHAPTER III.

WHILE discord prevailed at Cadiz, nearly the
whole of Andalusia was disturbed by insurrections of
the peasantry, nevertheless, such was Soult's resolution, the siege of Badajos continued. Early in
March, the second parallel being completed and the
Pardaleras taken into the works, the approaches were
carried by sap to the covered way, and mines were
prepared to blow in the counterscarp. However
Rafael Menacho, the governor, was in no manner
dismayed; his sallies were frequent and vigorous,
his activity and courage inspired his troops with
confidence, he had begun to retrench in the streets
behind the part attacked, the fire of the besiegers
was inferior to that of the besieged, and every thing
seemed to promise favourably, when on the evening
of the 2d, during a sally, in which the nearest French
batteries were carried, the guns spiked, and trenches
partly ruined, Menacho was killed, and the command fell to Imas, a man so unworthy that a
worse could not any where be found. The spirit
of the garrison then died away, the besiegers'
works advanced rapidly, the ditch was passed, a
lodgement was made on one of the ravelins, the
rampart was breached, and the fire of the besieged
being nearly extinguished, on the 10th of March
the place was summoned in a peremptory manner.

At this time the great crisis of the campaign
having passed, a strong body of British and Portuguese troops were ready to raise the siege of

Badajos. In three different ways, by telegraph, by a letter, and by a confidential messenger, the governor was informed, that Massena was in full retreat and that the relieving army was actually in march. The breach was still impracticable, provisions were plentiful, the garrison above eight thousand strong, the French army reduced, by

sickness, by detachments and the previous operations, to less than fourteen thousand men. Imas read the letter, and instantly surrendered, handing over at the same moment the intelligence thus obtained to the enemy. He also demanded that his grenadiers should march out of the breach; it was granted, and he was obliged to enlarge the opening himself ere they could do so! Yet this man so covered with opprobrium, and who had secured his own liberty while consigning his fellow soldiers to a prison, and his own character to infamy, was never punished by the Spanish rulers: lord Wellington's indignant remonstrances forced them, indeed, to bring him to trial, but they made the process last during the whole war.

When the place fell, Mortier marched against Campo Mayor, and Latour Maubourg seizing Albuquerque and Valencia d'Alcantara, made six hundred prisoners, but Soult, alarmed by the effects of the battle of Barosa, returned to Andalusia. He had, in fifty days, mastered four fortresses and invested a fifth; he had killed or dispersed ten thousand men, and taken twenty thousand with a force which, at no time, exceeded the number of his prisoners. Yet great and daring and successful as his operations had been, the principal object of his expedition was frustrated, for Massena was in retreat! lord Wellington's

combinations had palsied the hand of the conqueror!

While the siege of Badajos was proceeding, no
change took place in the main positions of either
army at Santarem. The French general had been
encouraged to maintain his ground by the state
of the Portuguese army, which he hoped would
break up the alliance; for such had been the
conduct of the Regency, that the native troops
were starving in their own country, while the
British were well fed, and the deserters from the
former, without knowing the cause, had a story,
as true as it was pitiable, to tell of their miseries.
The English general, certain that the French, who
were greatly reduced by sickness, must soon quit
their ground if he could relieve Badajos, only waited
for his reinforcements to send Beresford with
fourteen thousand men against Soult; but the
battle of the Gebora ruined this plan and changed
his situation. The arrival of the reinforcements
could not then enable him to detach a sufficient
number of men to relieve Badajos, and it was no
longer a question of starving Massena, but of
beating him before Soult could take Badajos
and the two armies be joined. Wherefore he
resolved to post ten thousand men before the hill
of Santarem to hold Reynier in check; to make
Beresford cross the Tagus at Abrantes, and fall on
Massena's rear; and meanwhile moving himself
with the rest of the army by Rio Mayor and
Tremes, to force back the French centre and right,
and cutting off their left, to drive it into the Tagus.
But nothing could be attempted until the troops
from England arrived, and day after day passed in
vain expectation of their coming. Being embarked

in January, they would have reached Lisbon before the end of that month, if sir Joseph Yorke, the admiral, had taken advantage of a favourable wind, which blew when the troops were first put on board; he however neglected this opportunity, contrary gales followed, and the ordinary voyage of ten days was prolonged for six weeks.

On the other hand, the French general's situation was becoming very perilous. To besiege Abrantes was above his means, and although that fortress was an important strategic point for the allies who had a moveable bridge, it would not have been so for the French. Massena could only choose then, to force the passage of the Tagus alone, or to wait until Soult appeared on the left bank, or to retreat. For sometime he seemed inclined to the first, shewing great jealousy of the works opposite the mouth of the Zezere, and carrying his boats on wheel-carriages along the banks of the Tagus, as if to alarm Beresford and oblige him to concentrate to his left: yet that general relaxed nothing of his vigilance, neither spy nor officer passed his lines of observation, and Massena knew, generally, that Soult was before Badajos, but nothing more. However, time wore away, sickness wasted the army, food became daily scarcer, the organization of the troops was seriously loosened, the leading generals were at variance, and SecVol.II. the conspiracy to put St. Cyr at the head of the army in Spain was by no means relinquished.

Under these accumulating difficulties even Massena's obstinacy gave way; he promised to retreat when he had no more provisions left than would serve his army for the march. A tardy resolution, yet adopted at the moment, when to maintain his position was more important than ever, as ten days

longer at Santarem would have insured the co-operation of Soult. General Pelet says, that the latter
marshal, by engaging in the siege of Badajos and
Olivenza, instead of coming directly down upon the
Tagus, was the cause of Massena's failure. This can
hardly be sustained. Before those sieges and the
battle of the Gebora, Mendizabal could have assembled twenty thousand men on Soult's rear, and there
was a large body of militia on the Ponçul and the
Elga ; Beresford had fourteen thousand British and
Portuguese regulars, besides ordenanca ; and the
infinite number of boats at lord Wellington's command would have enabled him to throw troops upon
the left bank of the Tagus, with a celerity that
would have baffled any effort of Massena to assist
the duke of Dalmatia. Now, if the latter had been
defeated, with what argument could he have defended his reputation as a general, after having left
three or four garrisoned fortresses and thirty-five
thousand men upon his flank and rear ; to say nothing of the results threatened by the battle of
Barosa. The true cause of Massena's failure was the
insufficiency of his means to oppose the English
general's combinations. The French army reduced
by sickness to forty thousand fighting men, exclusive of Drouet's troops at Leiria, would have been
unable to maintain its extended position against the
attack meditated by lord Wellington ; and when
Massena, through the means of the fidalgos, knew
that the English reinforcements were come, he prepared to retreat. Those troops landed the 2d of
March, and, the 6th, the French had evacuated the
position of Santarem.

At this time Napoleon directed the armies of
Spain to be remodelled. The king's force was dimi-

nished, the army of the south increased ; general
Drouet was ordered to march with eleven thousand
men to the fifth corps, which he was appointed
to command, in place of Mortier ; the remainder
of the ninth corps was to compose two divisions,
under the command of Clausel and Foy, and to be
incorporated with the army of Portugal.   Marmont
was appointed to relieve Ney in the command of
the sixth corps ; Loison was removed to the second
corps ; Bessieres was ordered to post six thousand
men at Ciudad Rodrigo, to watch the frontiers
of Portugal and support Claparede.   Of the imperial guards ; seven thousand were to assemble at
Zamora, to hold the Gallicians in check, and the
Appendix,
No. VII. remainder at Valladolid, with strong parties of
cavalry in the space between those places, that
intelligence of what was passing in Portugal might
be daily received.   Thus Massena was enabled to
adopt any operation that might seem good to him,
without reference to his original base ; but the
order for the execution of these measures did not
reach the armies until a later period.

RETREAT OF THE FRENCH FROM SANTAREM.

Several lines of operation were open to the prince
of Esling.   1°. He could pass the Tagus, between
Punhete and Abrantes, by boats, or by fords which
were often practicable after a week of dry weather.
2°. He could retire, by the Sobreira Formosa, upon
Castello Branco, and open a communication with
the king by Placentia, and with the duke of Dalmatia by Alcantara.   3°. He could march, by the
Estrada Nova and Belmonte, to Sabugal, and

afterwards act according to circumstances. 4°. He

could gain the Mondego, and ascend the left bank of that river towards Guarda and Almeida ; or, crossing it, march upon Oporto through an untouched country. Of these four plans, the first was perilous, and the weather too unsettled to be sure of the fords. The second and third were difficult, from the ruggedness of the Sobreira, and exposed, because the allies could break out by Abrantes upon the flank of the army while in retreat. Massena decided on the last, although his actual position being to the left of the line of retreat, he was necessarily forced to make a flank movement, with more than ten thousand sick men and all his stores, under the beard of an adversary, before he could begin his retreat. Yet this he executed, and in a manner befitting a great commander.

Commencing his preparations by destroying munition, and all guns that could not be horsed, he passed his sick and baggage, by degrees, upon Thomar, keeping only his fighting-men in the front, and at the same time indicating an intention of passing the Zezere. But when the impediments of the army had gained two marches, Ney suddenly assembled the sixth corps and the cavalry on the Lys, near Leiria, as if with the intention of advancing against Torres Vedras, a movement that necessarily kept lord Wellington in suspense. Meanwhile, the second and eighth corps, quitting Santarem, Tremes, and Alcanhete, in the night of the 5th, fell back, by Pernes, upon Torres Novas and Thomar, destroying the bridges on the Alviella behind them. The next morning the boats were burnt at Punhete, and Loison retreated by the road of Espinal to cover the flank of the main line of retreat, while the remainder of the army, by rapid concentric marches, made for a position in front of Pombal. The line of movement to the Mondego was thus secured, and four days gained; for lord Wellington, although aware that a retreat was in progress of execution, was quite unable to take any decided step, lest he should open the Lines to his adversary. Nevertheless he had caused Beresford to close to his right on the 5th, and at daylight, on the 6th, discovering the empty camps of Santarem, followed the enemy closely with his own army.

Thomar seemed to be the French point of concentration; but as their boats were still maintained at Punhete, general William Stewart crossed the Tagus, at Abrantes, with the greatest part of Beresford's corps, while the first, fourth, and sixth divisions, and two brigades of cavalry, marched to Golegao; the light division also reached Pernes, where the bridge was rapidly repaired by captain Tod, of the royal staff-corps. The 7th, as the enemy had burnt his boats on the Zezere, the Abrantes bridge was brought down to that river, and Stewart, crossing, moved to Thomar, on which place the divisions at Golegao were likewise directed. But the retreat being now decidedly pronounced for the Mondego, the troops at Thomar were ordered to halt, while the light division, German hussars, and royal dragoons followed the eighth corps, and took two hundred prisoners.

This day's march disclosed a horrible calamity. A large house, situated in an obscure part of the mountains, was discovered, filled with starving persons. Above thirty women and children had sunk; and, sitting by the bodies, were fifteen or sixteen survivors, of whom one only was a man, but all so enfeebled as to be unable to eat the little food we had to offer them. The youngest had fallen first, all the children were dead. None were emaciated, but the muscles of the face were invariably drawn transversely, giving an appearance of laughing, and presenting the most ghastly sight imaginable. The man seemed most eager for life, the women appeared patient and resigned; and, even in this distress, had covered and arranged the bodies of those who first died, with decency and care.

While one part of the army was thus in pursuit, the third and fifth divisions moved from the Lines, upon Leiria, the Abrantes' boats fell down the river to Tancos, where a bridge was fixed, and the second and fourth divisions, and some cavalry, were then directed to return from Thomar to the left bank of the Tagus, to relieve Badajos. Beresford, who had remained with a part of his corps near Barca, likewise sent a brigade of cavalry to Portalegre for that purpose.

Lord Wellington, misled partly by a letter of general Trant's, partly by information obtained in Santarem, and partly by Massena's feigned movement, at first thought the retreat would be by the Puente de Murcella; but on the 8th he was convinced it was directed towards Coimbra, and on the 9th, the enemy, instead of continuing his retreat, concentrated the sixth and eighth corps and Montbrun's cavalry on a table-land, in front of Pombal, where the light division skirmished with his advanced posts, and the German horse charged his cavalry with success, taking some prisoners. Here, finding the French disposed to accept battle, the English general was compelled to alter his plans. To fight with advantage, it was necessary to bring up, from Thomar, the troops destined to relieve Badajos. Not to fight, was to give up to the enemy Coimbra, and the untouched country behind, as far as Oporto: Massena would thus retire with the advantages of a conqueror. In this state of affairs, intelligence received from Badajos, described that place as being in a sufficient state to hold out for a month. This decided the question.

The fourth division and the heavy cavalry, already on the march for the Alemtejo, were countermanded; general Nightingale, with a brigade of the first division and some horse, was directed by the road of Espinal, to observe the second corps; and the rest of the army was concentrically directed upon Pombal. How dangerous a captain Massena could be, was here proved. His first movement began the 4th, it was the 11th before a sufficient number of troops could be assembled to fight him at Pombal, and, during these seven days, he had executed one of the most difficult operations in war, gained three or four marches, and completely organized his system of retreat. Had any rain fallen on the first day, the allies could not have followed him with artillery, such was the state of the roads, and he having before sent off or destroyed all his guns except a few light pieces would thus have had another great advantage.

SKIRMISH AT POMBAL.

Pack's brigade and the cavalry, the first, third, fourth, fifth, sixth, and light divisions, and the Portuguese troops, which were attached, like the

Latin auxiliaries of the Roman legion, to each British division, were assembling in front of the enemy on the 10th; when Massena, who had sent his baggage over the Soure river in the night by the bridge of Pombal, suddenly retired through that town. He was closely followed by the light division, the streets were still encumbered, and Ney drawing up a rear-guard on a height behind the town, threw a detachment into the old castle of Pombal. He had, however, waited too long. The French army was moving in some confusion and in a very extended column of march, by a narrow defile, between the mountains and the Soure river, which was fordable, and the British divisions were in rapid motion along the left bank, with the design of crossing lower down, and cutting Massena's line of retreat. The fall of night prevented this operation, but a sharp skirmish took place at Pombal, where the ninety-fifth and the third caçadores of the light division, after some changes of fortune, drove the French from the castle and town with such vigour, that they could not destroy the bridge, although it was mined. About forty of the allies were hurt, and the loss of the enemy was somewhat greater.

In the night Massena continued his retreat, which now assumed a regular and concentrated form. The baggage and sick, protected by the reserve cavalry, marched first; they were followed by the eighth corps, while the sixth, with some light cavalry, and the best horsed of the artillery, were destined to stem the pursuit. Ney had been ordered to detach Marcognet's brigade on the 10th, from the Lys, to seize Coimbra; but some delay

having taken place, Montbrun was now appointed
for that service, which was very important; for lord
Wellington's immediate object was to save Coimbra,
and he designed, by skilful, rather than daring, operations, to oblige Massena to quit the Portuguese ter-
ritory. The moral effect of such an event, he judged,
would be sufficient for the general cause; but as his
reinforcements were still distant, he was obliged to
keep the fourth division and the heavy cavalry from
the relief of Badajos, and was therefore willing to
strike a sudden stroke also, if a fair occasion offered.
Howbeit the country was full of strong positions, the
roads hollow and confined by mountains on either
hand; every village formed a defile; the weather
was moderate, and favourable to the enemy, and
Ney, with a wonderfully happy mixture of courage,
readiness, and skill, illustrated every league of
ground by some signal combination of war.

Day-break, on the 12th, saw both armies in
movement, and eight miles of march, and some slight
skirmishing, brought the head of the British into a
hollow way, leading to a high table-land on which
Ney had disposed five thousand infantry, a few
squadrons of cavalry, and some light guns. His
centre was opposite the hollow road, his wings
were covered by wooded heights, which he occupied with light troops; his right rested on the
ravine of the Soure; his left on the Redinha,
which circling round his rear fell into the Soure.
Behind him the village of Redinha, situated in a
hollow, covered a narrow bridge and a long and
dangerous defile; and, beyond the stream, some
very rugged heights, commanding a view of the
position in front of the village, were occupied by

a division of infantry, a regiment of cavalry, and a battery of heavy guns, all so skilfully disposed as to give the appearance of a very considerable force.

COMBAT OF REDINHA.

After examining the enemy's position for a short time, lord Wellington directed the light division, now commanded by sir William Erskine, to attack the wooded slopes covering Ney's right, and in less than an hour these orders were executed. The fifty-second, the ninety-fifth, and the caçadores, assisted by a company of the forty-third, carried the ascent and cleared the woods, and their skirmishers even advanced on to the open plain; but the French battalions, supported by four guns, immediately opened a heavy rolling fire, and at the same moment, colonel Ferriere, of the third French hussars, charged and took fourteen prisoners. This officer, during the whole campaign, never failed to break in upon the skirmishers in the most critical moments, sometimes with a squadron, sometimes with only a few men; he was always sure to be found in the right place, and was continually proving how much may be done, even in the most rugged mountains, by a small body of good cavalry.

Erskine's line, consisting of five battalions of infantry and six guns, being formed in such a manner that it outflanked the French right, tending towards the ford of the Redinha, was now reinforced with two regiments of dragoons, and meanwhile Picton seized the wooded heights protecting the French left.　Thus Ney's position was laid bare.　Nevertheless, that marshal observing that lord Wellington, deceived as to his real numbers, was bringing the mass of the allied troops into line, far from retreating, even charged Picton's skirmishers, and continued to hold his ground with an astonishing confidence if we consider his position; for the third division was nearer to the village and bridge than his right, and there were already cavalry and guns enough on the plain to overwhelm him.　In this posture both sides remained for about an hour, when three shots were fired from the British centre as a signal for a forward movement, and suddenly a most splendid spectacle of war was exhibited.　The woods seemed alive with troops, and in a few moments thirty thousand men, forming three gorgeous lines of battle, were stretched across the plain, bending on a gentle curve, and moving majestically onwards, while horsemen and guns, springing forward simultaneously from the centre and from the left wing, charged under a general volley from the French battalions: the latter were instantly hidden by the smoke, and when that cleared away no enemy was to be seen !

Ney keenly watching the progress of this grand formation, had opposed Picton's foremost skirmishers with his left, and, at the same moment, withdrew the rest of his people with such rapidity, that he gained the village ere the cavalry could touch him: the utmost efforts of Picton's skirmishers and of the horse-artillery scarcely enabled them to gall the hindmost of the French with their fire.　One howitzer was, indeed, dismounted close to the bridge, but the village of Redinha was in flames behind it, and the marshal wishing to confirm the courage of his soldiers at the commencement of the retreat, in person superintended the carrying it off, which he effected ; yet with the loss of fifteen or twenty men, and with great danger to himself, for the British guns were thundering on his rear, and the light troops of the third division, chasing like heated blood hounds, passed the river almost at the same time with the French. The reserves of the latter then cannonaded the bridge from the heights beyond, but a fresh disposition of attack being made by lord Wellington, while the third division continued to press the left, Ney fell back upon the main body which was at Condeixa, ten miles in the rear.

The British had twelve officers and two hundred men killed and wounded in this combat, and the enemy lost as many ; but he might have been utterly destroyed ; for there is no doubt, that the duke of Elchingen remained a quarter of an hour too long upon his first position, and that, deceived by the skilful arrangement of his reserve, lord Wellington paid him too much respect. Nevertheless the extraordinary facility and precision with which the English general handled so large a force, was a warning to the French commander, and produced a palpable effect upon the after operations.

On the 13th, the allies renewed the pursuit, and before ten o'clock discovered the French army, the second corps, which was at Espinhal, excepted, in order of battle. The crisis of Massena's retreat had arrived, the defiles of Condeixa, leading upon Coimbra, were behind him ; those of Miranda de Corvo, leading to the Puente de Murcella, were on his left ; and in the fork of these two roads Ney was

seated on a strong range of heights covered by a
marsh, his position being only to be approached
by the highway leading through a deep hollow
against his right.   Trees were felled to obstruct the
passage, a palisado was constructed across the hollow, and breast-works were thrown up on each side.
Massena here intended to stop the pursuit, while
Montbrun seized Coimbra.   His design was to pass
the Mondego, and either capture Oporto or maintain a position between the Douro and the Mondego,
until the operations of Soult should draw the
British away, or until the advance of Bessieres
with the army of the north, should enable himself
again to act offensively.

Hitherto the French general had appeared the
abler tactician, but now his adversary assumed the
superiority. When at Thomar, lord Wellington,
in expectation that Massena would cross the Mondego, had directed Baccellar to look to the security of Oporto, intending himself to follow the
French with the utmost rapidity. He had also
ordered Trant and Wilson to abandon the Mondego
and Vouga rivers, the moment the fords should
become passable and retire across the Douro. They
were also to break up the roads as they retreated,
to remove all boats and means of transport, and to
defend that river to extremity, that the army might
have time to close upon the enemy's rear.

Wilson had been in observation of the Ponte
Murcella road, but hearing that the enemy were
menacing an attack on Coimbra, he crossed the
Mondego at Pena Cova, and thus, passing between the French parties, effected a junction with
Trant.   Then in pursuance of the orders above
mentioned, both fell back, Wilson upon Busaco,

and Trant towards the Vouga. But the latter who had destroyed an arch of the bridge at Coimbra, and placed guards at the fords as far down as Figueras, soon returned with a part of his force, for the sound of guns had reached his outposts, the river was rising, and he felt assured that the allied army was close upon the heels of the enemy.

As early as the evening of the 11th, the French appeared at the suburb of Santa Clara, and a small party of their dragoons actually forded the Mondego at Pereiras that day. On the 12th, some French officers examined the bridge of Coimbra, but a cannon-shot from the other side wounded one of them, and a general skirmish took place along the banks of the river, during which a party attempting to feel their way along the bridge, were scattered by a round of grape. The fords were, however, actually practicable for cavalry, and there were not more than two or three hundred militia and a few guns at the bridge, for Baccellar had obliged Trant again to withdraw the greatest part of his force on the 11th; nevertheless the latter opposed the enemy with the remainder, and it would appear that the French imagined the reinforcement, which reached Lisbon the 2d of March, had been sent by sea to the Mondego and was in Coimbra. This was an error. Coimbra was saved by the same man and the same militia that had captured it during the advance.

Montbrun sent his report to Massena early on the 13th, and the latter too readily crediting his opinion of Trant's strength, relinquished the idea of passing the Mondego, and determined to retire by the Puente de Murcella. To ensure the power of changing his front, and to secure his communication with Reynier and Loison, he had carried

Campagne des Fran-cais en Portugal.

Clausel's division to Fonte Coberta, a village about five miles on his left, situated at the point where the Anciao road falls into that leading to Murcella. There Loison re-joined him, and being thus pivotted on the Anciao Sierra, and covering the line of communication with the second corps, while Ney held Condeixa, he considered his position secure. The baggage was, however, observed filing off by the Murcella road when the allies first came upon Ney, and lord Wellington instantly comprehending the state of affairs, as instantly detached the third division by a very difficult path over the Sierra de Anciao to turn the enemy's left.

For some time all appeared quiet in the French lines. Massena, in repairing to Fonte Coberta, had left Ney orders, it is said, to set fire to Condeixa at a certain hour, when all the divisions were simultaneously to concentrate at Casal Nova, in a second position, perpendicular to the first, and covering the road to Puente Murcella. Towards three o'clock, however, Picton was descried winding round the bluff end of a mountain, about eight miles distant, and as he was already beyond the French left, instant confusion pervaded their camp; a thick smoke arose from Condeixa, the columns were seen hurrying towards Casal Nova, and the British immediately pushed forward. The felled trees and other obstacles impeded their advance at first, and a number of fires, simultaneously kindled, covered the retreating troops with smoke, while the flames of Condeixa stopped the artillery; hence the skirmishers and some cavalry only could close with the rear of the enemy, but so rapidly, as to penetrate between the division at Fonte Coberta and the rest of the French, and it is affirmed that the prince of Esling, who was on the road, only escaped capture by taking the feathers out of his hat and riding through some of the light troops.

Condeixa being thus evacuated, the British cavalry pushed towards Coimbra, opened the communication with Trant, and cutting off Montbrun, took some of his horsemen. The rest of the army kindled their fires, and the light division planted piquets close up to the enemy, but the night was dark, and about ten o'clock, the French divisions, whose presence at Fonte Coberta was unknown to lord Wellington, stole out, and passing close along the front of the British posts, made for Miranda de Corvo. The noise of their march being heard, was imagined to be the moving of the French baggage to the rear, and was so reported to sir William Erskine, whereupon that officer, concluding that their army was in full retreat, without any further inquiry, put the light division in march at day-light on the 14th.

COMBAT OF CASAL NOVA.

The morning was so obscured that nothing could be descried at the distance of a hundred feet, but the sound of a great multitude was heard on the hills in front, and it being evident that the French were there in force, many officers represented the rashness of thus advancing without orders and in such a fog; nevertheless Erskine, with an astounding negligence, sent the fifty-second forward in a simple column of sections, without a vanguard or other precaution, and even before the piquets had come in from their posts. As the road dipped sud-

denly, descending into a valley, the regiment was
immediately lost in the mist, which was so thick,
that the troops, unconsciously passing the enemy's
out-posts, had like to have captured Ney himself,
whose bivouac was close to the piquets.   The riflemen followed in a few moments, and the rest of the
division was about to plunge into the same gulf,
when the rattling of musketry and the booming of
round shot were heard, and the vapour slowly rising,
discovered the fifty-second on the slopes of the
opposite mountain, engaged, without support, in
the midst of the enemy's army.

At this moment lord Wellington arrived.   His
design had been to turn the left of the French, for
their front position was very strong; and behind it
they occupied the mountain ridges, in succession, to
the Deuca river and the defiles of Miranda de Corvo.
There was, however, a road leading from Condeixa
to Espinhal, and the fourth division was already in
march by it for Panella, having orders, to communicate with Nightingale, to attack Reynier, and to gain
the sources of the Deuca and Ceira rivers.   Between
the fourth division and Casal Nova the third division
was more directly turning the enemy's left flank; and
meanwhile the main body was coming up to the front,
but as it marched in one column, it required time to
reach the field.   Howbeit Erskine's error forced on
this action, and the whole of the light division were
pushed forward to succour the fifty-second.

The enemy's ground was so extensive, and his
skirmishers so thick and so easily supported, that,
in a little time, the division was necessarily stretched out in one thin thread, and closely engaged in
every part, without any reserve ; nor could it even
thus present an equal front, until Picton sent the

riflemen, of the sixtieth, to prolong the line. Nevertheless, the fight was vigorously maintained amidst the numerous stone enclosures on the mountain side, some advantages were even gained, and the right of the enemy was partially turned; yet the main position could not be shaken, until Picton near, and Cole further off, had turned it by the left. Then, the first, fifth, and sixth divisions, the heavy cavalry, and the artillery, came up on the centre, and Ney commenced his retreat, covering his rear with guns and light troops, and retiring from ridge to ridge with admirable precision, and, for a long time, without confusion and with very little loss. Towards the middle of the day, however, the British guns and the skirmishers got within range of his masses, and the retreat became more rapid and less orderly; yet he finally gained the strong pass of Miranda de Corvo, which had been secured by the main body of the French. Here Montbrun rejoined the army. He had summoned Coimbra on the 13th at noon, and, without waiting for an answer, passed over the mountain and gained the right bank of the Deuca by a very difficult march.

The loss of the light division this day was eleven officers and a hundred and fifty men; that of the enemy was greater, and about a hundred prisoners were taken.

During the action of the 14th, Reynier, seeing the approach of the fourth division, hastily abandoned Panella, whereupon Cole having effected a junction with Nightingale, passed the Deuca, and Massena fearing lest they should gain his rear, set fire to the town of Miranda, and passed the Ceira that night. His whole army was now compressed and crowded in one narrow line,

between the higher sierras and the Mondego, and
to lighten the march, he destroyed a greater quantity of ammunition and baggage. His encumbrances were, however, still so heavy, and the confusion in his army so great, that he directed Ney
to cover the passage with a few battalions, charging
him not to risk an action; but Ney, little regarding his orders, kept, on the left bank, ten or
twelve battalions, a brigade of cavalry, and some
guns, which produced the

COMBAT OF FOZ D'ARONCE.

The French right rested on some wooded and
rugged ground, and their left upon the village
of Foz d'Aronce, and the 15th, the weather was
so obscure that the allies could not reach the Ceira,
before four o'clock in the evening; wherefore the
troops, as they came up, proceeded to kindle fires
for the night, thinking that as Ney's position was
strong, nothing would be done. But lord Wellington,
having cast a rapid glance over it, directed the
light division, and Pack's brigade, to hold the right
in play, ordered the third division against the left,
and at the same moment the horse-artillery, galloping forward to a rising ground, opened with a
great and sudden effect. Ney's left wing being
surprised and overthrown by the first charge of the
third division, dispersed in a panic, and fled in
such confusion towards the river, that some, mis-
sing the fords, rushed into the deeps and were
drowned, and others crowding on the bridge were
crushed to death. On the right the ground was
so rugged and close that the action resolved itself

into a skirmish, and thus Ney was enabled to use some battalions to check the pursuit of his left, but meanwhile darkness came on and the French troops in their disorder fired on each other. Only four officers and sixty men fell on the side of the British. The enemy's loss was not less than five hundred, of which one-half were drowned, and an eagle was afterwards found in the bed of the river when the waters subsided. In the night Massena retired behind the Alva; yet Ney, notwithstanding this disastrous combat, maintained the left bank of the Ceira, until every encumbrance had passed, and then blowing up seventy feet of the bridge, sent his corps on, remaining himself, with a weak rear-guard, on the right bank.

Thus terminated the first part of the retreat from Santarem, during which the French commander, if we except his errors with regard to Coimbra, displayed infinite ability, but withal a harsh and ruthless spirit. I pass over the destruction of Redinha, Condeixa, Miranda de Corvo, and many villages on the route; the burning of those towns covered the retrograde movements of the army, and something must be attributed to the disorder, which usually attends a forced retreat: but the town of Leiria, and the convent of Alcobaça, were given to the flames by express orders from the French head-quarters; and, although the laws of war rigorously interpreted, authorize such examples when the inhabitants take arms, it can only be justly done, for the purpose of overawing the people, and not from a spirit of vengeance when abandoning the country. But every horror that could make war hideous attended this dreadful march! Distress, conflagrations, death,

Lord Wellington's Despatches

in all modes! from wounds, from fatigue, from water, from the flames, from starvation! On every side unlimited violence, unlimited vengeance! I myself saw a peasant hounding on his dog, to devour the dead and dying, and the spirit of cruelty once unchained smote even the brute creation. On the 15th the French general, to diminish the encumbrances of his march, had ordered a number of beasts of burthen to be destroyed; the inhuman fellow, charged with the execution, hamstringed five hundred asses and left them to starve, and thus they were found by the British army on that day. The mute but deep expression of pain and grief, visible in these poor creatures' looks, wonderfully roused the fury of the soldiers, and so little weight has reason with the multitude, when opposed by a momentary sensation, that no quarter would have been given to any prisoner at that moment. A humane feeling would thus have led to direct cruelty. This shows how dangerous it is in war to listen to the passions at all, since the most praiseworthy could be thus perverted by an accidental combination of circumstances.

The French have, however, been accused of many crimes, which they did not and could not commit: such as the driving of all women above ten years of age into their camp at Redinha, near which there were neither men nor women to be driven. The country was a desert! They have also been charged by the same writer with the mutilating John the First's body in the convent of Batalha, during Massena's retreat; but the body of that monarch had been wantonly pulled to pieces, and carried off by British officers, during the retreat of the allies!

Southey,
Peninsular
War,
Vol. III.

CHAPTER IV.

On the 16th the allies halted, partly because the Ceira was swollen and unfordable, partly from the extreme exhaustion of the troops who had suffered far greater privations than the enemy. The latter, following his custom, carried fifteen days' bread; the allies depended upon a commissariat, which broke down under the difficulties, not from any deficiency in Mr. Kennedy, the chief of the department, who was distinguished alike for zeal, probity, and talent; but from the ill conduct of the Portuguese government, who, deaf to the repeated representations of lord Wellington and Beresford, would neither feed the Portuguese troops regularly while at Santarem, nor fill their magazines, nor collect the means of transport for the march. Hence, after passing Pombal, the greater part of the native force had been unable to continue the pursuit, and the brigades under general Pack and colonel Ashworth, which did keep up and engaged daily with the enemy, were actually four days without food of any sort. Numbers died of inanition on the roads, and to save the whole from destruction, the British supplies were shared with them. The commissary-general's means were thus overlaid, the whole army suffered, and necessity obliged lord Wellington to halt. Nevertheless he had saved Coimbra, forced the enemy into a narrow, intricate, and ravaged country, and, with an inferior force, turned him out of every strong position; and this, by a series of movements, based on the soundest principles of war. Noting the skill and tenacity with which Massena and Ney clung to every league of ground and every ridge defensible against superior numbers, he had seized the higher slopes of the mountains by Picton's flank march on the 13th, and again by Cole's on the 14th; and thus, continually menacing the passes in rear of the French, obliged them to abandon positions which could scarcely have been forced. This method of turning the strength of the country to profit is the true key to mountain warfare; he who receives battle in the hills has always the advantage, and he who first seizes the important points chooses his own field of battle.

In saying an inferior force, I advert to the state of the Portuguese army and to Badajos; for when lord Wellington had saved Coimbra, and seen that the French would not accept a general battle, except on very advantageous terms, he detached a brigade of cavalry, some guns, and a division of native infantry, from Condeixa, to the Alemtejo. And again in the night of the 13th, having received intelligence that Badajos had surrendered, and feeling all the importance of this event, he had detached the fourth division to the Alemtejo, for he designed that Beresford should immediately retake the lost fortress. Thus lord Wellington had less than twenty-five thousand men in hand during the subsequent operations, but, as the road of Espinhal was the shortest line to the Tagus, general Cole, as we have seen, moved into it by Panella, thus threatening Massena's flank and rear at the same moment that he gained a march towards his ultimate destination. Meanwhile, Trant and Wilson, with the militia, moving up the right bank of the Mondego, parallel to the enemy's line of retreat, forbad his foragers to pass that river, and were at hand either to interfere between him and Oporto, or to act against his flank and rear.

Such were the dispositions of the English general; but the military horizon was still clouded. Intelligence came from the north that Bessieres, after providing for his government, had been able to draw together, at Zamora, above seven thousand men, and menaced an invasion of Gallicia, and, although Mahi had an army of sixteen thousand men, lord Wellington anticipated no resistance. In the south, affairs were even more gloomy. The battle of Barosa, the disputes which followed, and the conduct of Imas and Mendizabal, proved that, from Spain, no useful co-operation was ever to be expected. Mortier, also, had invested Campo Mayor, and it was hardly expected to hold out until Beresford arrived. The Spaniards, to whom it had been delivered, under an engagement of honour, entered into by Romana, to keep it against the enemy, had disloyally neglected and abandoned it at the very moment when Badajos fell, hence two hundred Portuguese militia, thrown in at the moment, had to defend this fortress, which required a garrison of five thousand regulars. Nor was the enemy, immediately in the British front, the last to be considered.

Appendix,
No. II.
Section 9.

Ibid.

Ney withdrew from the Ceira in the evening of the 16th, and on the 17th the light division forded that river with great difficulty, while the rest of the army passed over a trestle bridge, made in the night by the staff-corps. The French were, however, again in position immediately behind the

Alva, and on the Sierra de Moita, and they had
destroyed the Ponte Murcella and the bridge near
Pombeira; the second corps had moved towards
the upper part of the river, and Massena had spread
his foraging parties to a considerable distance, designing to halt for several days. He was disturbed
sooner than he expected; for the 1st, 3d, and 5th
British divisions being directed on the 18th by the
Sierre de Guiteria, made way over that rugged
mountain with a wonderful perseverance and
strength, and thus menaced the French left, while
the 6th and the light divisions cannonaded their
right on the Lower Alva.

As the upper course of the river, now threatened
by lord Wellington's right, was parallel to the
French line of retreat, Massena recalled the second
corps, and, quitting the Lower Alva also, concentrated on the Sierra de Moita, lest the divisions,
moving up the river, should cross, and fall on
his troops while separated and in march. It then
behoved the allies to concentrate also, lest the
heads of their columns should be crushed by the
enemy's masses. The Alva was deep, wide, and
rapid, yet the staff-corps succeeded in forming a
most ingenious raft-bridge, and the light division
immediately passed between Ponte Murcella and
Pombeira, and at the same time the right wing
of the army entered Arganil, while Trant and Wilson
closed on the other side of the Mondego. Massena then recommenced his retreat with great rapidity, and being desirous to gain Celerico and the defiles leading upon Guarda betimes, again destroyed
baggage and ammunition, and abandoned even his
more distant foraging-parties, who were thus intercepted and taken, to the number of eight hundred,

in returning to the Alva; for lord Wellington, seeing the success of his combinations, had immediately directed all his columns upon Moita, and the whole army was assembled there on the 19th. The pursuit was renewed the 20th, through Penhancos, but only with the light division and the cavalry; the communication was, however again opened with Wilson and Trant who had reached the bridge of Fornos, and with Silveira, who was about Trancoso. The third and sixth divisions followed in reserve, but the remainder of the army halted at Moita, until provisions, sent by sea from Lisbon to the Mondego, could come up to them. The French having reached Celerico the 21st, with two corps and the cavalry, immediately opened the communication with Almeida, by posting detachments of horse on the Pinhel; and at the same time Reynier, who had retired through Govea, occupied Guarda with the second corps.

Massena had now regained his original base of operations, and his retreat may be said to have terminated; yet he was far from wishing to re-enter Spain, where he could only appear as a baffled general, and shorn of half his authority, because Bessieres commanded the northern provinces, which, at the commencement of the invasion, had been under himself. Hence, anxious to hold on to Portugal, and that his previous retreat might appear only a change of position, he formed the design of throwing all his sick men and other incumbrances into Almeida, then, passing the Estrella at Guarda, to make a countermarch, through Sabugal and Pena Macor, to the Elga, and so establish a communication across the Tagus with Soult, and by the valley of the Tagus with the king.

BOOK
XII.

1811.
March.

But now the factions in his army had risen to such a height that he could no longer command the obedience of his lieutenants; Montbrun, Junot, Drouet, Reynier, and Ney were all at variance with each other and with him. The first had, in the beginning of the retreat, been requested to secure Coimbra, instead of which he quitted Portugal, carrying with him Claparede's division. Marcognet's brigade was then ordered for that operation, but it did not move, and finally, Montbrun undertook it, and failed as we have seen in default of vigour. Junot was disabled by his wound, but his faction did not the less shew their discontent. Reynier's dislike to the prince was so strong, that the officers carrying flags of truce, from his corps, never failed to speak of it to the British, and Ney, more fierce than all of them, defied Masssena's authority. To Ney the dangerous delay at Pombal, the tardiness of Marcognet's brigade, and, finally, the too-sudden evacuation of the position at Condeixa, have been at-

General
Pelet's
Notes. See
Vol. xxi.
Victoires
et Con-
quêtes des
Francais.

tributed : and it is alleged by his censurers that, far from being ordered to set fire to that town on the 13th, as the signal for a preconcerted retreat, he had promised Massena to maintain the position for twenty-four hours longer. The personal risk of the latter, in consequence of the hasty change of position, would seem to confirm this ; but it is certain that, when Picton was observed passing the Sierra de Anciao by a road before unknown to the French, and by which the second corps could have been separated from the army, and the passes of Miranda de Corvo seized, Ney would have been frantic to have delayed his movement.

At Miranda, the long gathering anger broke out in a violent altercation between the prince and the marshal, and at Celerico, Ney, wishing to fall back on Almeida, to shorten the term of the retreat, absolutely refused to concur in the projected march to Coria, and even moved his troops in a contrary direction. Massena, a man not to be opposed with impunity, then deprived him of his command, and gave the sixth corps to Loison. Each marshal sent confidential officers to Paris to justify their conduct to the emperor, and from both of those officers I have derived information, but as each thinks that the conduct of his general was approved by Napoleon, their opinions are irreconcilable upon many points; I have, therefore, set down in the narrative the leading sentiments of each, without drawing any other conclusions than those deducible from the acknowledged principles of art and from unquestioned facts. Thus judging, it appears that Massena's general views were as superior to Ney's as the latter's readiness and genius in the handling of troops in action were superior to the prince's. Yet the duke of Elchingen often played too near the flame, whereas nothing could be grander than the conceptions of Massena : nor was the project now meditated by him the least important.

From Guarda to Zarza Mayor and Coria was only two days march longer than to Ciudad Rodrigo, but the army of Portugal must have gone to the latter place a beaten army, seeking for refuge and succour in its fortresses and reserves, and being separated from the central line of invasion : whereas, by gaining Coria, a great movement of war, wiping out the notion of a forced retreat, would have been accomplished. A close and concentric direction would thus have been given to the armies of the south, of the centre, and of Portugal ; and then a powerful demonstration against Lisbon would inevitably have brought lord Wellington back to the Tagus. Thus the conquests of the campaign, namely, Ciudad Rodrigo, Almeida, Badajos, and Olivenza, would have been preserved, and meanwhile the army of the north could have protected Castile and menaced the frontier of Portugal. Massena, having maturely considered this plan, gave orders, on the 23d, for the execution, but Ney, as we have seen, thwarted him. Meanwhile the English horse and the militia, hovering round Celerico, made in different skirmishes a hundred prisoners and killed as many more, and the French cavalry posts withdrew from the Pinhel. The sixth corps then took a position at Guarda; the second corps at Belmonte; the eighth corps and the cavalry in the eastern valleys of the Estrella.

Ney's insubordination had rendered null the plan of marching upon the Elga; but Massena expected still to maintain himself at Guarda with the aid of the army of the south, and to hold open the communications with the king and with Soult. His foragers had gathered provisions in the western valleys of the Estrella, and he calculated upon being able to keep his position for eight days with his own force alone. And independent of the general advantage, it was essential to hold Guarda for some time, because Drouet had permitted Julian Sanchez to cut off a large convoy destined for Ciudad Rodrigo, and had left Almeida with only ten days' provisions. Lord Wellington's ready boldness, however, disarranged all the prince's calculations.

The troops had come up from Moita on the 28th, and with them the reinforcements, which were organized as a seventh division. The light division and the cavalry then passed the Mondego at Celerico, and, driving the French out of Frexadas, occupied the villages beyond that place: at the same time, the militia took post on the Pinhel river, cutting the communication with Almeida, while the third division was established at Porca de Misarella, half way up the mountain, to secure the bridges over the higher Mondego. Early on 29th the third, sixth, and light divisions, and two regiments of light cavalry, disposed in five columns of attack on a half circle round the foot of the Guarda mountain, ascended by as many paths, all leading upon the town of Guarda, and outflanking both the right and left of the enemy. They were supported on one wing by the militia, on the other by the fifth division, and in the centre by the first and seventh divisions. A battle was expected, but the absence of Ney was at once felt by both armies; the appearance of the allied columns for the first time threw the French into the greatest confusion, and, without firing a shot, this great and nearly impregnable position was abandoned. Had the pursuit been as vigorous as the attack, it is not easy to see how the second corps could have rejoined Massena; Reynier, however, quitted Belmonte in the night, and recovered his communication with a loss of only three hundred prisoners, although the horse-artillery and cavalry had been launched against him at daylight on the 30th, and much more could have been done, if general Slade had pushed his cavalry forward with the celerity and vigour the occasion required.

On the 1st of April, the allied army descended the mountains, and reached the Coa; but the French general, still anxious to maintain at once his hold of Portugal and the power of operating either on the side of Coria or of Ciudad Rodrigo and Almeida, was in position on the right bank of that river. The sixth corps was at Rovina, with detachments guarding the bridge of Seceiras and the ford of Atalayon, and the communication with Almeida was maintained by a brigade of the ninth corps, which was posted near the ford of Junça. The second corps was on the hills behind Sabugal, stretching towards Alfayates, and having strong detachments at the bridge of Sabugal and the ford of Rapoulha de Coa. The eighth corps was at Alfayates; and a post was established at Rendo to maintain the communication between the second and the sixth corps. In this situation, the French army was disposed on two sides of a triangle, the apex of which was at Sabugal, and both fronts were covered by the Coa, because Sabugal was situated in a sharp bend of the stream. By holding Alfayates, Massena commanded the passes leading through St. Martin Trebeja to Coria; and in the French camp a notion prevailed, that the allied divisions were scattered and might be beaten in detail by a sudden attack; the disputes amongst the generals prevented this enterprize, which was founded on false information, from being attempted.

During the first two days of April lord Wellington occupied a line parallel to the enemy's right, which could not be attacked because the Coa, which is in itself a considerable river, runs along its whole course in a rugged channel, which continually deepens as the stream flows. Trant and Wilson were, however, directed to pass below Almeida, and penetrate between that fortress and Ciudad Rodrigo, thus menacing the enemy's right, flank, and rear, and meanwhile lord Wellington, leaving the sixth division opposite Ney's corps at Rovina, and a battalion of the seventh corps at the bridge of Seceiras to cover the left flank and rear of the allies, prepared with the remainder of the army to turn and attack the left of the French position. For this purpose at daylight on the 3d general Slade's cavalry was directed to cross the Upper Coa where the bed was most practicable, the light division ordered to ford the river a little below, the third division still lower, and the fifth division, with the artillery, to force the bridge of Sabugal; but the first and seventh divisions, with the exception of the battalion at Seceiras, were held in reserve. Thus ten thousand men being pivotted upon the fifth division at Sabugal were destined to turn Reynier's left, to separate him from the eighth corps, and to surround and crush him before the sixth corps could come from Rovina to his succour. One of those accidents which are frequent in war marred this well-concerted plan.

COMBAT OF SABUGAL.

The morning was so foggy, that the troops could not gain their respective posts of attack with that simultaneous regularity which is so essential to success, and in the light division no measures were taken by sir William Erskine to put the columns in a right direction, the brigades were not even held together; he carried off the cavalry without communicating with colonel Beckwith, and this officer, who commanded the first brigade, being without any instructions, halted at a ford in expectation of further orders. While thus waiting a staff officer rode up, and somewhat hastily asked, why he did not attack? The thing appeared rash, but with an enemy in his front he could make no reply, wherefore passing the river, which was deep and rapid, he mounted a very steep wooded hill on the other side. Four companies of the ninety-fifth led up in skirmishing order, followed by the forty-third regiment, and meanwhile the caçadores and the other brigade having passed the river, were moving independently to the right, but upon the true point of direction, and they were now distant. A dark heavy rain rendered it impossible for some time to distinguish friends or foes, and the attack was made too soon, for owing to the obscurity, none of the divisions of the army had yet reached their respective posts. It was made also in a partial, scattered, and dangerous manner, and on the wrong point; for Reynier's whole corps was directly in front, and Beckwith, having only one bayonet regiment and four companies of riflemen, was advancing against more than twelve thousand infantry, supported by cavalry and artillery.

Scarcely had the riflemen reached the top of the hill, when a compact and strong body of French drove them back upon the forty-third, the weather cleared at the instant, and Beckwith at once saw and felt all the danger, but his heart was too big to quail at it. With one fierce charge he beat back the enemy, gained and kept the summit of the hill, although two French howitzers poured showers of grape into his ranks, and a fresh force came against his front, while considerable bodies advanced on either flank. Fortunately Reynier, little

expecting to be assailed, had, for the convenience
of water, placed his main body in the low ground
behind the height on which the action commenced.
His renewed attack was, therefore, up hill, yet his
musketry, heavy from the beginning, soon increased
to a storm, and his men sprung up the acclivity
with such violence and clamour, that it was evident
nothing but the most desperate fighting could save
the British from destruction.

Captain Hopkins, commanding a flank company
of the forty-third, running out to the right, with admirable presence of mind seized a small eminence,
close to the French guns and commanding the ascent
up which the French troops who had turned the right
flank were approaching.   His first fire was so sharp,
that the assailants were thrown into confusion ; they
rallied, but were again disordered by the volleys of
this company, and when a third time they endeavoured to form a head of attack, Hopkins with a sudden charge increased their disorder, and at the same
moment the two battalions of the fifty second regiment, which had been attracted by the fire, entered
the line.   Meanwhile, the centre and left of the
forty-third were furiously engaged, and wonderfully
excited ; for Beckwith wounded in the head, and
with the blood streaming down his face, rode
amongst the foremost of the skirmishers, directing
all with ability, and praising the men, in a loud
cheerful tone.   The musket bullets flew thicker and
closer every instant, and the fight became very
dangerous ; but the French fell fast, and a second
charge again cleared the hill.   One howitzer was
taken by the 43d and the skirmishers were even
descending towards the enemy's ground below,
when small bodies of cavalry came galloping in

from all parts, and obliged them to take refuge with the main body, which instantly reformed its line behind a low stone wall. In this state of affairs, a French squadron of dragoons having surmounted the ascent, rode with incredible daring up to the wall and were in the act of firing over it with pistols, when a rolling volley laid nearly the whole of them lifeless on the ground. By this time however a very strong column of infantry having rushed up the face of the hill, endeavoured to break in and retake the howitzer, which was on the edge of the descent and only fifty yards from the wall ; but no man could reach it and live, so deadly was the forty-third's fire. Meanwhile two English guns came into action, and the 52d charging violently upon the flank of the enemy's infantry, again vindicated the possession of the height ; nevertheless fresh squadrons of cavalry which had followed the infantry in the last attack, seeing the 52d men scattered by their charge, flew upon them with great briskness, and caused some disorder amongst the foremost skirmishers, but they were soon repulsed.

Reynier, convinced at last that he had acted unskilfully in sending up his troops piece-meal, now put all his reserves, amounting to nearly six thousand infantry with artillery and cavalry, in motion, and outflanking the division on its left, appeared resolute to storm the contested height. But at this critical period, the fifth division passed the bridge of Sabugal, the British cavalry appeared on the hills beyond the enemy's left, and general Colville with the leading brigade of the third division issuing out of the woods on Reynier's right, opened a fire on that flank, which instantly decided the fate of the day. The French general fearing to be sur-

MASSENA'S RETREAT
Combat of Sabugal
1811.

Sedeiras
6th Div.
Rovina
6th Corps
Cavalry
Rendo
2nd Corps
Guarda
Rapoulha
5th Div.
Sabugal
3rd Div.
95
43
Coa R.

Tran
Almeida
Trant
Alverca
Celerico
Fornos
Gouvea
Guarda
Mondego R.
Iva R.
Estrella
Sabugal
Moita
Belmonte
Marcella
Arganil
S. Quiteria
Pena Macor
Foz d'Aronce
Deuca R.
Ceira R.
Coimbra
Miranda
Cazal Nova
Espinhal
Pereiras
Panella
Condeixa
Ponte Coberte
4th Div.
Nightingale
Zezere R.
Fol. Div.
S. Amao
Redinha
Soure R.
Pombal
Castello Branco
Lys R.
Elga R.
Leria
Vilha Velha
Tagus R.
Thomar
Alcanhede
Torre Novas
Niza
Rio Maior
Pernes
Punhete
Abiella R.
Golegao
Tancos
Abrantes
Santarem

rounded then hastily retreated upon Rendo, where
the sixth corps, which had been put in march when
the first shots were heard, met him, and together
they fell back upon Alfayates, pursued by the
English cavalry. The loss of the allies in this
bloody encounter, which did not last quite an hour,
was nearly two hundred killed and wounded, that
of the enemy was enormous; three hundred dead
bodies were heaped together on the hill, the greatest
part round the captured howitzer, and more than
twelve hundred were wounded! so unwisely had
Reynier handled his masses and so true and constant was the English fire. The principal causes of
this disproportion were, first, the heavy rain which
gave the French only a partial view of the British,
and secondly, the thick wood which ending near the
top of the hill, left only an open and exposed space
for the enemy to mount after the first attack; yet it
was no exaggeration in lord Wellington to say, Official
" that this was one of the most glorious actions that Despatch.
British troops were ever engaged in."

The next day, the light division took the route
of Valdespina, to feel for the enemy on the side of
the passes leading upon Coria; Massena was, however, in full retreat for Ciudad Rodrigo, and on the
5th crossed the frontier of Portugal, when the vigour
of the French discipline on sudden occasions was
surprisingly manifested. Those men who had for
months been living by rapine, whose retreat had
been one continued course of violence and devastation, having now passed an imaginary line of frontier, became the most orderly of soldiers; not the
slightest rudeness was offered to any Spaniard, and
every thing demanded was scrupulously paid for, Appendix,
although bread was sold at two shillings a pound! No. IV.
Section 2.

Massena himself also, fierce and terrible as he was
in Portugal, always treated the Spaniards with gentleness and moderation.

While these events were passing at Sabugal,
Trant after crossing the Lower Coa with four thousand militia, had taken post two miles from Almeida.
But the river suddenly flooded behind him, all the
bridges had been broken by Massena, and near
fort Conception, there was a brigade of the ninth
corps, which had been employed to cover the march
of the battering train from Almeida to Ciudad Rodrigo. In this dangerous situation, Trant constructed a
temporary bridge with great difficulty and was going
to retire on the 6th, when he received a letter from
the British head-quarters, desiring him to be vigilant
in cutting the communication with Almeida, and
fearless, because the next morning a British force
would be up to his assistance. Marching then to Val
de Mula, he boldly interposed between the fortress
and the brigade of the ninth corps; but the promised
succours did not appear, and the still advancing
French were within half a mile of his position!
His destruction appeared inevitable when suddenly
two cannon shots were heard to the southward, the
enemy's troops formed squares in retreat, and in
a few moments six squadrons of British cavalry and captain Bull's troop of horse artillery,
came sweeping up the plain in their rear. Military order and coolness, marked the French retreat
across the Turones, yet the cannon shots ploughed
with a fearful effect through their dense masses, and
the horsemen continually flanked their line of march:
they however gained the rough ground, and finally
escaped over the Agueda by Barba del Puerco,
but with the loss of three hundred men killed,

wounded, and prisoners. Trant was thus saved as
it were by a miracle; for some unexpected accident
having prevented the English infantry from marching in the morning, according to lord Wellington's
promise, he had pushed on this cavalry, which would
have been useless an hour later.

The prince of Esling had reached Ciudad Rodrigo
two days before this event, and lord Wellington now
stood victorious on the confines of Portugal, having
executed what to others appeared incredibly rash
and vain even to attempt.

CHAPTER V.

MASSENA entered Portugal with sixty-five thousand men, his reinforcements while at Santarem were about ten thousand, and he repassed the frontier with forty-five thousand; hence the invasion of Portugal cost him about thirty thousand men, of which fourteen thousand might have fallen by the sword or been taken. Not more than six thousand were lost during the retreat; but had lord Wellington, unrestrained by political considerations, attacked him vigorously at Redinha, Condeixa, Casal Nova, and Miranda de Corvo, half the French army would have been lost. It is unquestionable that a retreating army should fight as little as possible.

When the French reached the Agueda, their cavalry detachments, heavy artillery, and convalescents, again augmented the army to more than fifty thousand men, but the fatigues of the retreat and the want of provisions, would not suffer them to shew a front to the allies; wherefore, drawing two hundred thousand rations from Ciudad, they fell back to Salamanca, and lord Wellington invested Almeida. The light division occupied Gallegos and Espeja, the rest of the army were disposed in villages on both sides of the Coa, and the head-quarters were transferred to Villa Formosa. Here colonel Waters, who had been taken near Belmonte during the retreat, rejoined the army. Con-

fident in his own resources, he had refused his
parole, and, when carried to Ciudad Rodrigo,
rashly mentioned his intention of escaping to the
Spaniard in whose house he was lodged. This
man betrayed him, but a servant, detesting his
master's treachery, secretly offered his aid; Waters
only desired him to get the rowels of his spurs
sharpened, and when the French army was near
Salamanca, he being in the custody of *gens d'armes*,
waited until their chief, who rode the only good
horse in the party, had alighted, then giving the
spur to his own beast, galloped off! an act of
incredible resolution and hardihood, for he was on
a large plain, and before him, and for miles behind
him, the road was covered with the French columns. His hat fell off, and, thus distinguished,
he rode along the flank of the troops, some encouraging him, others firing at him, and the *gens
d'armes*, sword in hand, close at his heels; nevertheless he broke at full speed, between two columns,
gained a wooded hollow, and, having baffled his
pursuers, evaded the rear of the enemy's army.
The third day he reached head-quarters, where lord
Wellington had caused his baggage to be brought,
observing that he would not be long absent!

Massena, having occupied Salamanca, and com- Appendix,
No. VII.
municated with Bessieres, sent a convoy to Ciudad
Rodrigo, and lord Wellington was unable to prevent its entrance. He had sent the militia to their
homes, disposed his army between the Coa and the
Agueda, and blockaded Almeida; he also caused two
temporary bridges to be laid (where the road from
Cinco Villas to Pinhel crosses the Coa) to secure
a retreat for the troops on that side, if pressed,
which might easily happen; for the Portuguese

BOOK
XII.

1811.
April.
army was in a dreadful state, and the continued misconduct of the Regency, and the absolute want of money, gave little hope of amelioration. It was therefore impossible to take a position beyond the Agueda.

The depots were now re-established at Lamego on the Douro, and at Raiva on the Mondego, and magazines of consumption were formed at Celerico, from whence the mule-brigades brought up the provisions by the way of Castello Bom. Measures were also taken at Guarda, Pena Macor, and Castello Branco, to form commissariat establishments which were to be supplied from Abrantes; but the transport of stores was difficult, and this consideration, combined with the capricious nature of the Agueda and Coa, rendered it dangerous to blockade both Ciudad Rodrigo and Almeida; seeing that the troops would have those rivers behind them, while the position itself would be weak and extended. The blockade of Almeida was undertaken because, from intercepted letters and other sources, it was known to have provisions only for a fortnight, but lord Wellington was prepared to relinquish it if pressed, because it formed no part of the plan which he contemplated.

The success in Portugal had given stability to the English ministers, and it would appear that they were satisfied, and at first meant to limit their future efforts to the defence of that country, for lord Liverpool now required the return of many battalions. But offensive warfare in Spain, occupied the general's thoughts, and two lines of operation had presented themselves to his mind.—1°. Under the supposition that it would be long ere Massena could again make any serious attempt on Portugal, to remain

Lord Wellington to lord Liverpool, May 7th, 1810. MSS.

on the defensive in Beira, and march against the
army of the South to raise the siege of Cadiz.—
2°. If Almeida fell to the blockade, to besiege
Ciudad Rodrigo; if Almeida did not so fall, to
besiege both together; if they were taken, to
march at once into the heart of Spain, and
open a communication with Valencia and with the
army of Sicily. This great and lofty conception
would have delivered Andalusia as certainly as any
direct operation; for thus Madrid, the great depôt
of the French, would have been taken, the northern
and southern armies cut asunder, and the English
base momentarily fixed on the Mediterranean coast:
then the whole of the Spanish and British force
could have been concentrated, and one or two great
battles must have decided the fate of Spain.

Filled with this grand project lord Wellington
demanded reinforcements from England, and leave
to carry his designs into execution, if occasion offered: yet he checked his secret aspirations, when
reflecting upon the national pride and perverseness
of the Spaniards, on their uncertain proceedings,
and the great difficulty, if not impossibility, of en-
suring any reasonable concert and assistance. When
to this he added the bad disposition of the Portuguese Regency, and the timid temper of the English ministers, so many jarring elements were presented that he could make no fixed combinations.
Nevertheless, maturing the leading points of action
in his own mind, he resolved to keep them in view,
adapting his proceedings to circumstances as they
should arise.

His projects were however necessarily conditional,
because if Napoleon reinforced his armies again,
new combinations would be created ; and before

any other measure, it was essential to recapture Badajos. The loss of that place had affected the safety of Cadiz, and it interfered with the execution of both the above mentioned plans, and with the safety of Portugal, by enabling the enemy to besiege Elvas. So deeply and sagaciously, however, had the English general probed the nature of the contest, that we shall find his after operations strictly conformable to these his first conceptions, and always successful.

Judging now that Massena would be unable to interrupt the blockade of Almeida lord Wellington left the command of the northern army to general Spencer, and departed for the Alemtejo, where Beresford was operating : but, as this was one of the most critical periods of the war, it is essential to have a clear notion of the true state of affairs in the South, at the moment when Beresford commenced his memorable campaign.

Soult returned to Andalusia immediately after the fall of Badajos, leaving Mortier to besiege Campo Mayor. His arrival at Seville and the fame of his successes restored tranquillity in that province, and confidence amongst the troops.

Intercepted Letter from Chief of Engineers, Garbe, Mar. 25th. Both had been so grievously shaken by the battle of Barosa, that the works of Arcos, Lucar, Medina, and Alcalade Gazules, intended to defend the rear of the first corps, had been stopped, and the utmost despondency prevailed. However discontent

Official Abstract of Military Reports, from Cadiz, 1811. MSS. and gloom also prevailed in Cadiz. The government had for some days pretended to make a fresh effort against Victor, but as the fall of Badajos menaced the city with famine, Zayas was finally detached with six thousand infantry and four hundred cavalry to Huelva. His object was to gather provisions in the Conda de Neibla, where Ballasteros had, on the 10th of March, surprised and dispersed Remond's detachment. The French were however soon reinforced, Zayas was checked by D'Aremberg, and, as many of his men deserted to Ballasteros, he withdrew the rest. Blake then assumed the command, Ballasteros and Copons were placed under his orders, and the united corps, amounting to eleven thousand infantry and twelve hundred cavalry, were called the *fourth army.* Meanwhile Mendizabal rallying the fugitives from the battle of the Gebora, at Villa Viciosa, reorganized a weak corps, called the *fifth army.* During these proceedings, Mortier had occupied Albuquerque and Valencia d'Alcantara, and carried on the siege of Campo Mayor. This fortress being commanded, at four hundred yards distance, by a hill, on which there was an abandoned horn-work, would have fallen at once, but for the courage and talents of major Tallaia, a Portuguese engineer. With only two hundred men, and five mounted guns, he made such skilful dispositions, that the French opened regular trenches, battered the wall in breach with six guns, bombarded the palace with eleven mortars, and pushed a sap to the crest of the glacis. At the end of five days a breach was made, but Tallaia, although ill seconded by the garrison, repulsed one partial assault, and, being summoned for the second time, demanded and obtained twenty-four hours to wait for succour. None arrived, and this brave man surrendered the 21st of March. Mortier then returned to the Guadiana, leaving Latour Maubourg to dismantle the works and remove the artillery and stores to Badajos.

Such was the posture of affairs when Beresford,

who had quitted the northern army after the combat of Foz d'Aronce, arrived at Portalagre with twenty thousand infantry, two thousand cavalry, and eighteen guns. His instructions were to relieve Campo Mayor, and to besiege Olivenza and Badajos. The first had already surrendered, but the marshal, being within two marches of it, judged that he might surprise the besieging corps, and, with this view, put his troops in motion.

COMBAT OF CAMPO MAYOR.

In the morning of the 25th the advanced guard of cavalry, supported at some distance by a detachment of infantry under colonel Colborne, came suddenly upon Campo Mayor. Latour Maubourg was marching out in confusion, with nearly nine hundred cavalry, three battalions of infantry, some horse artillery and the battering train of sixteen guns. The English cavalry under general Long immediately turned the town by the left, and the French retreated by the Badajos road. The allies following along some gentle slopes, then formed a half circle round their enemy, who was now on a fine plain, and colonel Colborne, although still at a considerable distance, was coming up at a running pace, followed by the rest of the second division. In this state of affairs, the French infantry halted in square, with their cavalry both before and behind them. General Long, who had brought up the thirteenth dragoons, and some Portuguese squadrons, the heavy cavalry being in reserve, then ordered the former to attack.

Colonel Head immediately led the thirteenth for-

ward, the French hussars as readily rode out from their
infantry and with loose reins the two bodies came
fiercely together. Many men were dismounted by
the shock, but the combatants pierced clear through
on both sides, then re-formed and again charged in See notice
at the
the same fearful manner! The fighting now be- commencement of
came desperate, until Head's troopers riding this volume.
closely together, overthrew horse and man, and
finally forced the enemy to fly. The French
square fired upon the victorious squadrons, but
the latter without flinching, galloped past the
long line of the convoy, hewed down the gunners, and being joined by the Portuguese, the
hussars still fighting here and there in small
bodies, continued the pursuit. They thought with
reason that the heavy dragoons, the artillery, and
the infantry, some of which were close up, would
be sufficient to dispose of whatever part of the
enemy's force was thus passed. But marshal
Beresford would not suffer the heavy dragoons
to charge; he would not suffer more than two
guns to be brought up when he might have had
six; he would not suffer those two guns to fire
more than a few rounds ; and the French marching
steadily onward, recovered their battering train,
and effected their retreat in safety! Meanwhile,
the thirteenth and the Portuguese, having pushed
on even to the bridge of Badajos, were repulsed
by the guns of that fortress, and being followed
by Mortier in person, and met by the retiring
square, and by all of the beaten cavalry who
could find refuge with it, lost some prisoners.
Of the allies one hundred men were killed or hurt,
and above seventy taken. Of the enemy about

three hundred suffered, one howitzer was captured, and the French colonel Chamorin was slain in single combat by a trooper of the thirteenth.

To profit from sudden opportunities, a general must be constantly with his advanced guard in an offensive movement. When this combat commenced, Beresford was with the main body, and baron Trip, a staff-officer, deceived by appearances, informed him, that the thirteenth had been cut off. Hence the marshal, anxious to save his cavalry, which he knew could not be reinforced, would not follow up the first blow, observing that the loss of one regiment was enough. But the regiment was not lost, the country was open and plain, the enemy's force and the exact posture of affairs easy to be discerned ; and although the thirteenth were severely reprimanded, for having pursued so eagerly without orders, the unsparing admiration of the whole army consoled them.

Campo Mayor was thus recovered so suddenly, that the French left eight thousand rations of bread in the magazines ; and they also evacuated Albuquerque and Valencia d'Alcantara, being infinitely dismayed by the appearance of so powerful an army in the south : indeed, so secretly and promptly had lord Wellington assembled it, that its existence was only known to the enemy by the blow at Campo Mayor. But, to profit from such able dispositions, it was necessary to be as rapid in execution, giving the enemy no time to recover from his first surprise ; and this was the more essential, because the breach of Badajos was not closed, nor the trenches obliterated, nor the exhausted magazines and stores replenished. Soult had carried

away six battalions and a regiment of cavalry, four
hundred men had been thrown into Olivenza, three
thousand into Badajos; and thus, including the losses
sustained during the operations, Mortier's numbers were reduced to less than ten thousand men.
He could not therefore have maintained the line
of the Guadiana and collected provisions also.
Beresford should have instantly marched upon
Merida, driven back the fifth corps, and opened
a fresh communication by Jerumenha with Elvas;
the fall of Badajos would then have been in-
evitable. The confusion occasioned by the sudden See Notice at the com-
appearance of the army at Campo Mayor and the mence-
moral impression produced by the charge of the ment of this vol.
thirteenth dragoons, guaranteed the success of this
march; the English general might even have passed
the river at Merida before Mortier could have ascertained his object.

Beresford, neglecting this happy opportunity,
put his troops into quarters round Elvas, induced
thereto by the fatigue and wants of the soldiers,
especially those of the fourth division, who had
been marching incessantly since the 6th of the
month, and were bare-footed and exhausted.

He had been instructed, by lord Wellington, to
throw a bridge over the Guadiana at Jerumenha,
to push back the fifth corps, and to invest Olivenza
and Badajos. The Portuguese government were to
have provided some of the means for these operations, and a report had been made, to the effect, that
all things necessary, that is to say, that provisions,
shoes, battering-guns, ammunition, and transport
were actually collected; that the Guadiana abounded
in serviceable craft; that twenty large boats,
formerly belonging to Cuesta, which had been

brought away from Badajos before the siege, were at Elvas; and that all other necessaries would be sent from Lisbon. It now appeared that no magazines of provisions or stores were prepared; that very little transport was provided; that only five of Cuesta's boats had been brought from Badajos; that there was no serviceable craft on the river, and that some small pontoons, sent from Lisbon, were unfit to bear the force of the current, or to sustain the passage of guns. The country, also, was so deficient in provisions, that the garrison stores of Elvas were taken to feed the army.

All these circumstances combined to point out Merida as the true line of operations; moreover, plenty of food was to be had on the left bank of the Guadiana, and the measures necessary to remedy the evil state of affairs on the right bank, did not require the presence of an army to protect them. The great distress of the fourth division for shoes, alone offered any serious obstacle; but, under the circumstances, it would not have been too much to expect a momentary effort from such an excellent division, and it might without danger even have been left behind.

Marshal Beresford preferred halting until he could procure the means of passing at Jerumenha, an error that may be considered as the principal cause of those long and bloody operations which afterwards detained lord Wellington more than a year on the frontiers of Portugal. For, during Beresford's delay, general Phillipon, one of the ablest governors that ever defended a fortress, levelled the trenches, restored the glacis, and stopped the breach; and Latour Maubourg, who had succeeded Mortier in command of the troops, covered the country with foraging parties, and filled the magazines.

Captain Squire, of the engineers, undertook to bridge the Guadiana under Jerumenha. He fixed trestle-piers on each side in the shallows, and connected them with the five Spanish boats and a squadron of cavalry was secretly passed over, by a ford, to protect the workmen from surprise. The 3d of April, the bridge was finished, and the troops assembled during the night in the woods near Jerumenha, intending to cross at daylight, but the river suddenly swelling, swept away the trestles, rendered the ford impassable, and stopped the operations. No more materials could be immediately procured, the Spanish boats were therefore converted into flying bridges for the cavalry and artillery, and Squire constructed a slight narrow bridge for infantry with the pontoons and with casks taken from the neighbouring villages. To cover this operation a battalion was added to the squadron already on the left bank, and the army commenced passing the 5th of April; but it was late in the night of the 6th, ere the whole had crossed and taken up their position, which was on a strong range of hills, covered by a swampy rivulet.

During this time, Latour Maubourg was so entirely occupied in securing and provisioning Badajos, that his foragers were extended fifty miles to the rear, and he took no notice whatever of Beresford's proceedings. This error savoured rather of the Spanish than of the French method of making war; for it is evident that a moveable column of five thousand infantry, with guns and cavalry, could, notwithstanding the guns of Jerumenha, have easily cut off the small detachment of the British on the left bank, and thus have completely frustrated the operations. The allied troops, being so numerous, should have been carried over in the boats, and entrenched on the other side in sufficient force to resist any attack before the construction of the bridge was attempted. It is not easy to say which general acted with most imprudence ; Latour Maubourg in neglecting, or Beresford in unnecessarily tempting fortune.

When the British were in possession of the left bank, the French general awaking, collected three thousand infantry, five hundred cavalry, and four guns at Olivenza, whence he marched, at daylight on the 7th, to oppose a passage which had been completed the day before. He, however, surprised a squadron of the thirteenth, which was in front, and then came so close up to the main body as to exchange shots ; yet he was permitted to retire unmolested, in the face of more than twenty thousand men !

During these proceedings, the fifth Spanish army re-occupied Valencia d'Alcantara and Albuquerque, and pushed cavalry posts to La Rocca and Montijo, Ballasteros entered Fregenal, and Castaños, who was appointed to command in Gallicia as well as Estremadura, arrived at Elvas. This general was in friendly intercourse with Beresford, but had a grudge against Blake. At first, he pretended to the chief authority, as the elder captain-general ; Blake demanded a like power over Beresford, who was not disposed to admit the claim. Now Castaños, having little liking for a command under such difficult circumstances, and being desirous to thwart Blake, and fearful lest Beresford should, under these circumstances, refuse to pass the Guadiana, arranged, that he who brought the greatest force in the field should be generalissimo. Thus the inferior officer commanded in chief.

To cover his bridges, which he reconstructed in a more substantial manner, Beresford directed extensive entrenchments to be executed by the militia from Elvas, and then leaving a strong detachment for their protection, advanced with the remainder of the army. Latour Maubourg retired upon Albuera, and the allies, who had been joined by Madden's cavalry, summoned Olivenza on the 9th. Beresford apparently expected no defence ; for it was not until after the governor had rejected the summons that he sent major Dickson to Elvas to prepare a battery train for the siege. Meanwhile the army encamped round the place, the communication with Ballasteros was opened, and Castaños advancing with the fifth army to Merida pushed his cavalry to Almendralejos. The French then fell back to Llerena, and Beresford, leaving general Cole with the fourth division and Madden's cavalry to besiege Olivenza, took post himself at Albuera on the 11th. In this position he communicated by his left with Castaños, and by spreading his horsemen in front cut off all communication with Badajos. The army now lived on the resources of the country, and a brigade was sent to Talavera Real to collect supplies.

The 14th, six twenty-four pounders reached Olivenza, and, being placed in a battery constructed on an abandoned horn-work formerly noticed, played with such success, that the breach became practicable before the morning of the 15th. Some riflemen posted in the vineyards kept down the fire of the place, and the garrison, consisting of three hundred and eighty men, with fifteen guns, surrendered at discretion.

Cole was immediately directed upon Zafra by the road of Almendral. Beresford, who had recalled the brigade from Talavera, was already in motion for the same place by the royal causeway. His object was to drive Latour Maubourg over the Morena, and cut off general Maransin. The latter general, who had been in pursuit of Ballasteros ever since the retreat of Zayas, and had defeated him at Fregenal on the 12th, was following up his victory towards Salvatierra. The allies were therefore close upon him, but an alcalde gave him notice of their approach, and he retreated in safety. Meanwhile two French regiments of cavalry, advancing from Llerena to collect contributions, reached Los Santos, between which place and Usagre they were charged by the thirteenth dragoons, and followed for six miles so vigorously that one hundred and fifty were killed or taken, without the loss of a man on the part of the pursuers.

On the 16th general Cole arrived from Olivenza, and the whole army being thus concentrated about Zafra, Latour Maubourg retired on the 18th to Guadalcanal; the Spanish cavalry then occupied Llerena, and the resources of Estremadura were wholly at the service of the allies. During these operations, general Charles Alten, coming from Lisbon with a brigade of German light infantry, reached Olivenza, and lord Wellington also arrived at Elvas, where Beresford, after drawing his infantry nearer to Badajos, went to meet him. The presence of the general-in-chief was very agreeable to the troops; they had seen, with surprise, great masses put in motion without any adequate results, and thought the operations had been slow, without being prudent. The whole army was over the Guadiana on the 7th, and, including the Spaniards from Montijo, Beresford commanded at least twenty-five thousand men, whereas Latour Maubourg never had more than ten thousand, many of whom were dispersed foraging, far and wide: yet the French general, without displaying much skill, had maintained himself in Estremadura for ten days; and during this time, no corps being employed to constrain the garrison of Badajos, the governor continued to bring in timber and other materials for the defence, at his pleasure.

Lord Wellington arrived the 21st. The 22d, he forded the Guadiana just below the mouth of the Caya with Madden's cavalry and Alten's Germans, and pushed close up to Badajos. A convoy, escorted by some infantry and cavalry, was coming in from the country, and an effort was made to cut it off; but the governor sallied, the allies lost a hundred men, and the convoy reached the town.

Lord Wellington, now considering that Soult would certainly endeavour to disturb the siege with a considerable force, demanded the assent of the Spanish generals to the following plan of combined operations, before he would commence the investment of the place. 1°. That Blake, marching up from Ayamonte, should take post at Xeres de los Cavalleros. 2°. That Ballasteros should occupy Burquillo on his left. 3°. That the cavalry of the fifth army, stationed at Llerena, should observe the road of Guadalcanal, and communicate through

Zafra, by the right, with Ballasteros. These dispositions were to watch the passes of the Morena.
4°. That Castaños should furnish three battalions
for the siege, and keep the rest of his corps at
Merida, to support the Spanish cavalry. 5°. That
the British army should be in second line, and, in
the event of a battle, Albuera, centrically situated
with respect to the roads leading from Andalusia to
Badajos, should be the point of concentration for
all the allied forces.

The whole of the train and stores, for the attack
on Badajos, being taken from the ramparts and
magazines of Elvas, the utmost prudence was required to secure the safety of the guns, lest that
fortress, half dismantled, should be exposed to a
siege. Wherefore as the Guadiana, by rising ten
feet, had again carried away the bridges at Jerumenha, on the 24th lord Wellington directed the
line of communication with Portugal to be established by Merida, until more settled weather
should admit of fresh arrangements. Howbeit,
political difficulties intervening obliged him to
delay the siege. The troops under Mendizabal
had committed many excesses in Portugal; the
disputes between them and the inhabitants were
pushed so far, that the Spanish general had pillaged
the town of Fernando, and the Portuguese government, in reprisal, meant to seize Olivenza, which
had formerly belonged to them. The Spanish Regency indeed publicly disavowed Mendizabal's conduct, and Mr. Stuart's strenuous representations
deterred the Portuguese from plunging the two
countries into a war; but this affair, joined to the
natural slowness and arrogance of the Spaniards,

prevented both Castaños and Blake from giving an immediate assent to the English general's plans. Meanwhile, intelligence reached the latter that Massena was in force on the Agueda; wherefore, reluctantly directing Beresford to postpone the siege until the Spanish generals should give in their assent, or until the fall of Almeida should enable a British reinforcement to arrive, he ordered the militia of the northern provinces again to take the field, and repaired with the utmost speed to the Coa.

OPERATIONS IN THE NORTH.

During his absence, the blockade of Almeida had been closely pressed, while the army was so disposed as to cut off all communication. The allied forces were, however, distressed for provisions, and great part of their corn came from the side of Ledesma, being smuggled by the peasants through the French posts, and passed over the Agueda by ropes, which were easily hidden amongst the deep chasms of that river, near its confluence with the Douro.

Massena was intent upon relieving the place. His retreat upon Salamanca had been to restore the organization and equipments of his army, which he could not do at Ciudad Rodrigo, without consuming the stores of that fortress. His cantonments extended from San Felices by Ledesma to Toro, his cavalry was in bad condition, and his artillery nearly unhorsed. But from Bessieres he expected, with reason, aid, both of men and provisions, and in that expectation was prepared to renew the cam-

paign immediately.   Discord, that bane of military
operations,   interfered.   Bessieres had neglected
and continued to neglect the army of Portugal.
Symptoms of hostilities with Russia were so apparent, even at this period, that he looked rather
to that quarter than to what was passing before
him, and his opinion that a war in the north was
inevitable was so openly expressed as to reach
the English army.   Meanwhile, Massena vainly
demanded the aid, which was necessary to save the
only acquisition of his campaign.   A convoy of
provisions had, however, entered Ciudad Rodrigo
on the 13th of April, and on the 16th a reinforcement and a second convoy also succeeded in gaining
that fortress, although general Spencer crossed the
Agueda, with eight thousand men, to intercept
them ; a rear-guard of two hundred men was indeed, overtaken, and surrounded by the cavalry in
in an open plain, but it was not prevented from
reaching the place.

Towards the end of the month, the new organization, decreed by Napoleon, was put in execution.
Two divisions of the ninth corps joined Massena ;
and Drouet was preparing to march with the remaining eleven thousand infantry and cavalry, to
reinforce and take the command of the fifth corps,
when Massena, having collected all his own detachments, and received a promise of assistance from
Bessieres, prevailed upon him to defer his march
until an effort had been made to relieve Almeida.
With this view the French army was put in motion
towards the frontier of Portugal.   The light division immediately resumed its former positions, the
left at Gallegos and Marialva, the right at Espeja ;
the cavalry were dispersed, partly towards the

sources of the Azava, and partly behind Gallegos.
While in this situation, colonel O'Meara and
eighty men of the Irish brigade were taken by
Julian Sanchez, the affair having been, it was
said, preconcerted, to enable the former to quit the
French service.

On the 23d, two thousand French infantry and
a squadron of cavalry marching out of Ciudad Rodrigo, made a sudden effort to seize the bridge of
Marialva, but the passage was bravely maintained
by captain Dobbs, with one company of the fifty-
second and some riflemen. On the 25th, Massena
reached Ciudad Rodrigo, and the 27th, his advanced guards felt all the line of the light division
from Espeja to Marialva. Lord Wellington arrived
on the 28th, and immediately concentrated the
main body of the allies behind the Dos Casas river.
The Azava being swollen and difficult to ford, the
enemy continued to feel the line of the outposts, until
the 2d of May, when the waters having subsided,
the whole French army was observed coming out
of Ciudad Rodrigo. The light division, after a
slight skirmish of horse at Gallegos, then commenced a retrograde movement, from that place and
from Espeja, upon Fuentes Onoro. The country immediately in rear of those villages was wooded as
far as the Dos Casas, but an open plain between
the two lines of march offered the enemy's powerful
cavalry an opportunity of cutting off the retreat.
The French appeared regardless of this advantage,
and the division remained in the woods bordering
the right and left of the plain until the middle of
the night, when the march was renewed, and the
Dos Casas was crossed at Fuentes Onoro.

This beautiful village had escaped all injury du-

ring the previous warfare, although occupied alter-
nately, for above a year, by both sides. Every family
in it was well known to the light division, and it was
therefore a subject of deep regret, to find, that the
preceding troops had pillaged it, leaving only the
shells of houses where, three days before, a friendly
population had been living in comfort. This wanton act was so warmly felt by the whole army, that
eight thousand dollars were afterwards collected by
general subscription for the poor inhabitants, but
the injury sunk deeper than the atonement.

Lord Wellington had determined not to risk
much to maintain his blockade, and he was well
aware that Massena, reinforced by the army of the
north and by the ninth corps, could bring down
superior numbers; for so culpably negligent had
the Portuguese government been, that their troops
were actually starving. The infantry had quitted
their colours, or had fallen sick, from extenuation, by
thousands, the cavalry were rendered quite useless,
and it was even feared that the whole would dis-
band. Nevertheless, when the moment of trial
arrived, the English general trusting to the valour
of his soldiers, and the ascendancy over the enemy
which they had acquired during the pursuit from
Santarem, would not retreat, although his army,
reduced to thirty-two thousand infantry, twelve
hundred cavalry in bad condition, and forty-two
guns, was unable, seeing the superiority of the
French horse, to oppose the enemy's march in the
plain.

The allies occupied a fine table-land, lying between the Turones and the Dos Casas. The left was
at Fort Conception, the centre opposite to the village
of Alameda, the right at Fuentes Onoro, the whole

distance being five miles. The Dos Casas, flowing in a deep ravine, protected the front of this line, and the French general could not, with any prudence, venture to march, by his own right, against Almeida, lest the allies, crossing the ravine at the villages of Alameda and Fuentes Onoro, should fall on his flank, and drive him into the Agueda. Hence, to cover the blockade, which was maintained by Pack's brigade and an English regiment, it was sufficient to leave the fifth division near Fort Conception, and the sixth division opposite Alameda. The first and third were then concentrated on a gentle rise, about a cannon-shot behind Fuentes Onoro, where the steppe of land, which the army occupied, turned back, and ended on the Turones, becoming rocky and difficult as it approached that river.

FIRST COMBAT OF FUENTES ONORO.

The French came up in three columns abreast. The cavalry, the sixth corps, and Drouet's division appeared at Fuentes Onoro, but the eighth and second corps, moving against Alameda and Fort Conception, seemed to menace the left of the position, wherefore, the light division, after passing the Dos Casas, reinforced the sixth division. General Loison however, without waiting for Massena's orders, fell upon Fuentes Onoro, which was occupied by five battalions of chosen troops, detached from the first and third divisions.

Most of the houses of this village were quite in the bottom of the ravine, and an old chapel and some buildings on a craggy eminence, over-

hung one end.   The low parts were vigorously defended, yet the violence of the attack was so great,
and the cannonade so heavy, that the British
abandoned the streets, and could scarcely maintain
the upper ground about the chapel.   Colonel Wil-
liams, the commanding officer, fell badly wounded,
and the fight was becoming very dangerous, when
the twenty-fourth, the seventy-first, and the seventy-
ninth regiments, marching down from the main
position, charged so roughly, that the French
were forced back, and, after a severe contest,
driven over the stream of the Dos Casas.   During
the night the detachments were withdrawn ; but
the twenty-fourth, the seventy-first, and seventy-
ninth regiments were left in the village, where two
hundred and sixty of the allies and somewhat more
of the French had fallen.

On the 4th Massena arrived, and, being joined
by Bessieres with twelve hundred cavalry and a
battery of the imperial guard, examined all the
line, and made dispositions for the next day.   His
design was to hold the left of the allies in check
with the second corps, and to turn the right with
the remainder of the army.   Forty thousand
French infantry, and five thousand horse, with
thirty pieces of artillery, were under arms, and
they had shewn in the action of the 3d that
their courage was not abated ; it was, therefore, a
very audacious resolution in the English general
to receive battle on such dangerous ground.   His
position, as far as Fuentes Onoro, was indeed
strong and free for the use of all arms, and it
covered his communication by the bridge of Castello Bom ; but, on his right flank, the plain was
continued in a second steppe to Nava d'Aver, where

See Note,
Appendix,
No. I.
Section II.

a considerable hill overlooking all the country, commanded the roads leading to the bridges of Seceiras and Sabugal. The enemy could, therefore, by a direct march from Ciudad Rodrigo, place his army at once in line of battle upon the right flank of the allies, and attack them while entangled between the Dos Casas, the Turones, the Coa, and the fortress of Almeida; the bridge of Castello Bom alone would have been open for retreat. To prevent this stroke, and to cover his communications with Sabugal and Seceiras, lord Wellington, yielding to general Spencer's earnest suggestions, stretched his right wing out to Nava d'Aver, the hill of which he caused Julian Sanchez to occupy, supporting him by the seventh division, under general Houston. Thus the line of battle was above seven miles in length, besides the circuit of blockade. The Dos Casas, indeed, still covered the front; but above Fuentes Onoro, the ravine became gradually obliterated, resolving itself into a swampy wood, which extended to Poço Velho, a village half way between Fuentes and Nava d'Aver. The left wing of the seventh division occupied this wood and the village of Poço Velho, but the right wing was refused.

BATTLE OF FUENTES ONORO.

It was Massena's intention to have made his dispositions in the night, in such a manner as to commence the attack at day-break on the 5th; but a delay of two hours occurring, the whole of his movements were plainly descried. The eighth corps withdrawn from Alameda, and supported by all the French cavalry, was seen marching above the village

of Poco Velho, and at the same time the sixth corps
and Drouet's division took ground to their own left,
yet still keeping a division in front of Fuentes.
At this sight the light division and the English
horse hastened to the support of general Houston,
while the first and third divisions made a movement
parallel to that of the sixth corps. The latter,
however, drove the left wing of the seventh division,
consisting of Portuguese and British, from the village of Poço Velho with loss, and was gaining
ground in the wood also, when the riflemen of the
light division arriving at that point, restored the
fight. The French cavalry, then passing Poço
Velho, commenced forming in order of battle on
the plain, between the wood and the hill of Nava
d'Aver. Julian Sanchez immediately retired across
the Turones, partly in fear, but more in anger, at
the death of his lieutenant, who, having foolishly
ridden close up to the enemy, making many violent
gestures, was mistaken for a French officer, and
shot by a soldier of the guards, before the action
commenced.

Montbrun occupied himself with this weak partida for an hour, but when the Guerilla chief had entirely fallen back, he turned the right of the seventh
division, and charged the British cavalry, which
had moved up to its support. The combat was very
unequal, for, by an abuse too common, so many men
had been drawn from the ranks as orderlies to general
officers, and for other purposes, that not more than
a thousand English troopers were in the field. The
French therefore with one shock drove in all the cavalry outguards, and cutting off captain Ramsay's
battery, came sweeping in upon the reserves of horse
and upon the seventh division. But their leading

squadrons approaching in a disorderly manner, were partially checked by the British, and at the same time a great commotion was observed in their main body. Men and horses there closed with confusion and tumult towards one point, a thick dust arose, and loud cries, and the sparkling of blades and the flashing of pistols, indicated some extraordinary occurrence. Suddenly the multitude became violently agitated, an English shout pealed high and clear, the mass was rent asunder, and Norman Ramsay burst forth at the head of his battery, his horses breathing fire, stretched like greyhounds along the plain, the guns bounded behind them like things of no weight, and the mounted gunners followed in close career. Captain Brotherton of the 14th dragoons, seeing this, instantly rode forth with a squadron, and overturned the head of the pursuing troops, and general Charles Stewart joining in the charge, took the French general Lamotte, fighting hand to hand. The enemy, however, came in strongly, and the British cavalry retired behind the light division, which was immediately thrown into squares, but ere the seventh division, which was more advanced, could do the same, the horsemen were upon them, and some were cut down. Nevertheless the men stood firm, and the Chasseurs Brittaniques ranging behind a loose stone wall, poured in such a fire that their foes recoiled and seemed bewildered.

But while these brilliant actions were passing at this point, the French were making progress in the wood of Pozzo Velho, and as the English divisions were separated, and the right wing turned, it was abundantly evident that the battle would soon be lost, if the original concentrated position above

Fuentes Onoro was not quickly regained. Lord
Wellington, therefore, ordered the seventh division
to cross the Turones and move down the left bank to
Frenada—the light division to retire over the plain
and the cavalry to cover the rear. He also withdrew the first and third divisions, placing them
and the Portuguese, in line, on the steppe before
described as running perpendicular to the ravine
of Fuentes Onoro.

General Crawfurd, who had resumed the command of the light division, first covered the passage of the seventh division over the Turones, and
then retired slowly over the plain in squares,
having the British cavalry principally on his right
flank. He was followed by the enemy's horse,
which continually outflanked him, and near the
wood surprised and sabred an advanced post of the
guards, making colonel Hill and fourteen men prisoners, but then continuing their charge against the
forty-second regiment, the French were repulsed.
Many times Montbrun made as if he would storm the
light division squares, and although the latter were
too formidable to be meddled with, there was not,
during the war, a more dangerous hour for England.
The whole of that vast plain as far as the Turones
was covered with a confused multitude, amidst
which the squares appeared but as specks, for
there was a great concourse, composed of commissariat followers of the camp, servants, baggage,
led horses, and peasants attracted by curiosity,
and finally, the broken piquets and parties coming
out of the woods. The seventh division was separated from the army by the Turones, five thousand
French cavalry, with fifteen pieces of artillery,
were close at hand impatient to charge, the in-

fantry of the eighth corps was in order of battle
behind the horsemen, and the wood was filled with
the skirmishers of the sixth corps. If the latter
body, pivoting upon Fuentes, had issued forth,
while Drouet's divisions fell on that village;
if the eighth corps had attacked the light division,
while the whole of the cavalry made a general
charge, the loose multitude encumbering the plain
would have been driven violently in upon the first
division, in such a manner as to have intercepted
the latter's fire and broken its ranks.

No such effort was made. Montbrun's horsemen
merely hovered about Crawfurd's squares, the
plain was soon cleared, the cavalry took post behind
the centre, and the light division formed a reserve
to the right of the first division, sending the riflemen amongst the rocks to connect it with the
seventh division, which had arrived at Frenada
and was there joined by Julian Sanchez.

At sight of this new front, so deeply lined with
troops, the French stopped short, and commenced
a heavy cannonade, which did great execution from
the closeness of the allied masses; but twelve
British guns replied with vigour and the violence
of the enemy's fire abated. Their cavalry then
drew out of range, and a body of infantry attempting to glide down the ravine of the Turones
was repulsed by the riflemen and the light companies of the guards.

All this time a fierce battle was going on
at Fuentes Onoro. Massena had directed Drouet
to carry this village at the very moment
when Montbrun's cavalry should turn the right
wing; it was, however, two hours later ere the
attack commenced. The three British regiments

made a desperate resistance, but overmatched in number, and little accustomed to the desultory fighting of light troops, were pierced and divided. Two companies of the seventy-ninth were taken, colonel Cameron was mortally wounded, and the lower part of the town was carried; the upper part was, however, stiffly held, and the rolling of the musketry was incessant.

Had the attack been made earlier, and the whole of Drouet's division thrown frankly into the fight, while the sixth corps moving through the wood closely turned the village, the passage must have been forced and the left of the new position outflanked; but now lord Wellington having all his reserves in hand, detached considerable masses to the support of the regiments in Fuentes. The French continued also to reinforce their troops, the whole of the sixth corps and a part of Drouet's division were finally engaged, and several turns of fortune occurred. At one time the fighting was on the banks of the stream and amongst the lower houses; at another upon the rugged heights and round the chapel, and some of the enemy's skirmishers even penetrated completely through towards the main position; but the village was never entirely abandoned by the defenders, and, in a charge of the seventy-first, seventy-ninth, and eighty-eighth regiments, led by colonel M'Kinnon against a heavy mass which had gained the chapel eminence, a great number of the French fell. In this manner the fight lasted until evening, when the lower part of the town was abandoned by both parties. The British maintained the chapel and crags, the French retired a cannon shot from the stream.

After the action a brigade of the light division

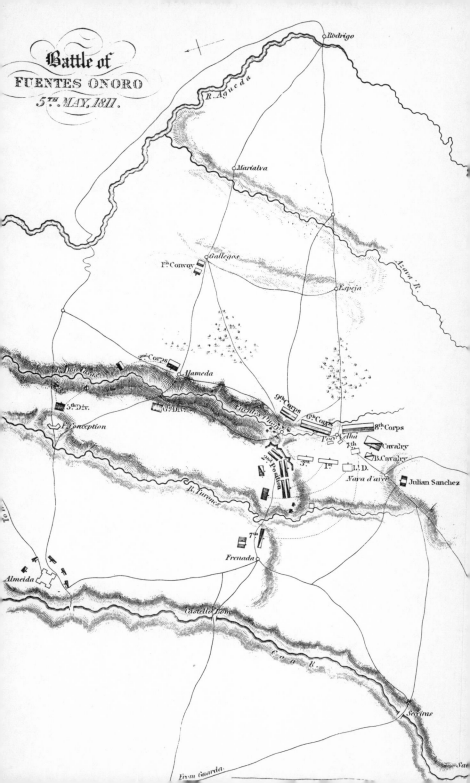

Battle of
FUENTES ONORO
5TH MAY, 1811.

Rodrigo

R. Agueda

Marialva

Azava R.

Gallegos

Ft. Convoy

Espeja

2nd Corps

Alameda

5th Div.

6th Div.

9th Corps

6th Corps

8th Corps

Conception

2nd Position

Poço Velho

7th

Cavalry

B. Cavalry

3rd.

1st.

L. D.

Nava d'aver

Julian Sanchez

R. Turones

7th

Frenada

To Ni

Almeida

Castello bom

Coa R.

To

Sexmes

From Guarda.

Sa

relieved the regiments in the village, a slight demonstration by the second corps near Fort Conception, was checked by a battalion of the Lusitanian legion, and both armies remained in observation. Fifteen hundred men and officers, of which three hundred were, prisoners, constituted the loss of the allies. That of the enemy was estimated at the time to be near five thousand, but this exaggerated calculation was founded upon the erroneous supposition, that four hundred dead, were lying about Fuentes Onoro. All armies make rash estimates on such occasions. Having had charge to bury the carcasses at that point, I can affirm that, immediately about the village, not more than one hundred and thirty bodies were to be found, one-third of which were British.

During the battle, the French convoy for the supply of Almeida was kept at Gallegos, in readiness to move, and lord Wellington now sent Julian Sanchez from Frenada, to menace it, and to disturb the communication with Ciudad Rodrigo. This produced no effect, and a more decisive battle being expected on the 6th, the light division made breast-works amongst the crags of Fuentes Onoro. Lord Wellington also entrenched that part of the position, which was immediately behind this village, so that the carrying of it would have scarcely benefitted the enemy. Fuentes Onoro, strictly speaking, was not tenable. There · was a wooded tongue of land on the British right, that overlooked, at half-cannon shot, all the upper as well as the lower part of the village both in flank and rear, yet was too distant from the position to be occupied by the allies: had Ney been at the head of the sixth corps, he would have quickly crowned this ridge, and then Fuentes could only have been maintained by submitting to a butchery.

On the 6th the enemy sent his wounded to the rear, making no demonstration of attack, and as the 7th passed in a like inaction, the British entrenchments were perfected. The 8th Massena withdrew his main body to the woods leading upon Espeja and Gallegos, but still maintained posts at Alameda and Fuentes. On the 10th, without being in any manner molested, he retired across the Agueda, the sixth and eighth corps, and the cavalry, passing at Ciudad Rodrigo, the second corps at the bridge of Barba del Puerco. Bessieres then carried off the imperial guards, Massena was recalled to France, and Marmont assumed the command of the army of Portugal.

Both sides claimed the victory. The French, because they won the passage at Poço Velho, cleared the wood, turned our right flank, obliged the cavalry to retire, and forced lord Wellington to relinquish three miles of ground, and to change his front. The English, because the village of Fuentes so often attacked, was successfully defended, and because the principal object (the covering the blockade of Almeida) was attained.

Certain it is, that Massena at first gained great advantages. Napoleon would have made them fatal! but it is also certain that, with an overwhelming cavalry, on ground particularly suitable to that arm, the prince of Esling having, as it were, indicated all the errors of the English general's position, stopped short at the very moment when he should have sprung forward. By some this has been attributed to extreme negligence, by others to disgust at being superseded by Marmont; but the true reason seems to be, that discord in his army had arisen to actual insubordination. The imperial guards would not charge at his order— Junot did not second him cordially—Loison disregarded his instructions—Drouet sought to spare his own divisions in the fight, and Reynier remained perfectly inactive. Thus the machinery of battle was shaken, and would not work.

General Pelet censures lord Wellington for not sending his cavalry against Reynier after the second position was taken up. He asserts that any danger, on that side, would have forced the French to retreat. This criticism is, however, unsustainable, being based on the notion that the allies had fifty thousand men in the field, whereas, including Sanchez' Partida, they had not thirty-five thousand. It may be, with more justice, objected to Massena that he did not launch some of his numerous horsemen, by the bridge of Seceiras, or Sabugal, against Guarda and Celerico, to destroy the magazines, cut the communication, and capture the mules and other means of transport belonging to the allied army. The vice of the English general's position would then have been clearly exposed, for, although the second regiment of German hussars was on the march from Lisbon, it had not passed Coimbra at this period, and could not have protected the depôts. But it can never be too often repeated that war, however adorned by splendid strokes of skill, is commonly a series of errors and accidents. All the operations, on both sides, for six weeks, furnished illustrations of this truth.

Ney's opposition had prevented Massena's march upon Coria, which would have secured Badajos and Campo Mayor, and, probably, added Elvas to them.

Appendix,
No. I.
Section 8.

Latour Maubourg's tardiness had like to have cost Mortier a rear guard and a battering-train. Beresford's blunder at Campo Mayor, and his refusing of the line of Merida, enabled the French to secure Badajos. At Sabugal, the petulance of a staff-officer marred an admirable combination, and produced a dangerous combat. Drouet's negligence placed Almeida at the mercy of the allies, and a mistaken notion of Massena's sufferings during the retreat, induced lord Wellington to undertake two great operations at the same time, which were above his strength. In the battle of Fuentes Onoro, more errors than skill were observable on both sides, and the train of accidents did not stop there. The prize contended for was still to present another example of the uncertainty of war.

EVACUATION OF ALMEIDA.

General Brennier, made prisoner at Vimiero, but afterwards exchanged, was governor of this fortress. During the battle of Fuentes Onoro, his garrison, consisting of fifteen hundred men, skirmished boldly with the blockading force, and loud explosions, supposed to be signals of communication with the relieving army, were frequent in the place. When all hopes of succour had vanished, a soldier, named Tillet, contrived, with extraordinary courage and presence of mind, to penetrate, although in uniform, through the posts of blockade. He carried an order for Brennier to evacuate the fortress.

Meanwhile Massena, by crossing the Agueda, abandoned Almeida to its fate, and the British general placed the light division in its old position on the Azava with cavalry-posts on the Lower Agueda.

He also desired sir William Erskine to send CHAP.
the fourth regiment to Barba del Puerco, and ___V.___
he directed general Alexander Campbell to con- 1811.
tinue the blockade with the sixth division and May.
with general Pack's brigade. But Campbell's dispositions were either negligently made, or negligently executed, and Erskine never transmitted
the orders to the fourth regiment, and it was under
these circumstances that Brennier, undismayed by
the retreat of the French army, resolved, like Julian
Estrada, at Hostalrich, to force his way through the
blockading troops. An open country and a double
line of posts greatly enhanced the difficulty, yet
Brennier was resolute not only to cut his own passage
but to render the fortress useless to the allies. To
effect this, he ruined all the principal bastions, and
kept up a constant fire of his artillery in a singular
manner; for always he fired several guns at one
moment with very heavy charges, placing one
across the muzzle of another, so that, while some
shots flew towards the besiegers and a loud explosion was heard, others destroyed pieces without
attracting notice.

At midnight of the 10th, all being ready, he
sprung his mines, sallied forth in a compact column, broke through the piquets, and passed between the quarters of the reserves, with a nicety
that proved at once his talent of observation and
his coolness. General Pack following, with a few
men collected on the instant, plied him with a
constant fire, yet nothing could shake or retard his
column, which in silence, and without returning
a shot, gained the rough country leading upon
Barba del Puerco. Here it halted for a moment,
just as daylight broke, and Pack, who was at hand,

hearing that some English dragoons were in a village, a short distance to the right, sent an officer to bring them out upon the French flank, thus occasioning a slight skirmish and consequent delay. The troops of blockade had paid little attention at first to the explosion of the mines, thinking them a repetition of Brennier's previous practice, but Pack's fire having roused them, the thirty-sixth regiment was now close at hand, and the fourth, also, having heard the firing at Valde Mula, was rapidly gaining the right flank of the enemy. Brennier, having driven off the cavalry, was again in march, but the British regiments, throwing off their knapsacks, followed at such a pace, that they overtook the rear of his column in the act of descending the deep chasm of Barba del Puerco. Many were killed and wounded, and three hundred were taken; but the pursuers having rashly passed the bridge in pursuit, the second corps, which was in order of battle, awaiting Brennier's approach, repulsed them with a loss of thirty or forty men. Had sir William Erskine given the fourth regiment its orders, the French column would have been lost.

Lord Wellington, stung by this event, and irritated by several previous examples of undisciplined valour, issued a remonstrance to the army. It was strong, and the following remarks are as applicable to some writers as to soldiers :—" *The officers of the army may depend upon it that the enemy to whom they are opposed is not less prudent than powerful. Notwithstanding what has been printed in gazettes and newspapers, we have never seen small bodies, unsupported, successfully opposed to large ; nor has the experience of any officer realized the stories which all have read of whole armies being driven by a handful of light infantry and dragoons.*"

CHAPTER VI.

WHEN Marmont had thus recovered the garrison of Almeida, he withdrew the greatest part of his army towards Salamanca. Lord Wellington then leaving the first, fifth, sixth, and light divisions, on the Azava, under general Spencer, directed the third and seventh divisions and the second German hussars upon Badajos. On the 15th, hearing that Soult, although hitherto reported, by Beresford, to be entirely on the defensive, was actually marching into Estremadura, he set out himself for that province; but, ere he could arrive, a great and bloody battle had terminated the operations.

While awaiting the Spanish generals' accession to lord Wellington's plan, Beresford had fixed his head-quarters at Almendralejos; but Latour Maubourg remained at Guadalcanal, whence his parties foraged the most fertile tracts between the armies. Penne Villamur was, therefore, reinforced with five squadrons; and colonel John Colborne was detached with a brigade of the second division, two Spanish guns, and two squadrons of cavalry, to curb the French inroads, and to raise the confidence of the people. Colborne, a man of singular talent for war, by rapid marches and sudden changes of direction, in concert with Villamur, created great confusion amongst the enemy's parties. He intercepted several convoys, and obliged the French troops to quit Fuente Ovejuna, La

See notice
at the be-
ginning of
this vol.

Granja, Azuaga, and most of the other frontier
towns; and he imposed upon Latour Maubourg with
so much address, that the latter, imagining a great
force was at hand, abandoned Guadalcanal also and
fell back to Constantino.

Having cleared the country on that side, Colborne
attempted to surprise the fortified post of Benel-
cazar, and, by a hardy attempt, was like to
have carried it. Riding on to the drawbridge
with a few officers in the grey of the morning, he
summoned the commandant to surrender, as the
only means of saving himself from the Spanish
army which was close at hand and would give
no quarter. The French officer, although amazed
at the appearance of the party, was however too
resolute to yield, and Colborne, quick to perceive
the attempt had failed, galloped off under a few
straggling shot. After this, taking to the mountains,
he rejoined the army without any loss. During his
absence, the Spanish generals had acceded to lord
Wellington's proposition; Blake was in march for
Xeres Caballeros, and Ballasteros was at Burgillos.
The waters of the Guadiana had also subsided, the
bridge under Jerumenha was restored, and the preparations completed for the

FIRST ENGLISH SIEGE OF BADAJOS.

The 5th of May, general William Stewart invested the place, on the left bank of the Guadiana,
with two squadrons of horse, six field-pieces, and
three brigades of infantry, and the formation of
the depôt of the siege was commenced by the engineers and artillery.

On the 7th the remainder of the infantry, reinforced by two thousand Spaniards under Carlos
d'España, encamped in the woods near the fortress;
Madden's Portuguese remained in observation near
Merida, and a troop of horse-artillery arriving
from Lisbon was attached to the English cavalry,
which was still near Los Santos and Zafra. The
flying bridge was at first brought up from Jerumenha,
and re-established near the mouth of the Caya,
but was again drawn over, because the right bank
of the Guadiana being still open, some French
horse had come down the river.

The 8th general Lumley invested Christoval on
the right bank, with a brigade of the second division, four light Spanish guns, the seventeenth
Portuguese infantry, and two squadrons of horse
drafted from the garrison of Elvas. These troops
did not arrive simultaneously at the point of assembly, which delayed the operation, and sixty
French dragoons moving under the fire of the
place maintained a sharp skirmish beyond the
walls.

Thus the first serious siege undertaken by the
British army in the Peninsula was commenced,
and, to the discredit of the English government,
no army was ever so ill provided with the means
of prosecuting such an enterprise. The engineer
officers were exceedingly zealous, and, notwithstanding some defects in the constitution and
customs of their corps, tending rather to make
regimental than practical scientific officers, many
of them were very well versed in the theory of
their business. But the ablest trembled when reflecting on their utter destitution of all that belonged to real service. Without a corps of sappers

and miners, without a single private who knew how to carry on an approach under fire, they were compelled to attack fortresses defended by the most warlike, practised, and scientific troops of the age : the best officers and the finest soldiers were obliged to sacrifice themselves in a lamentable manner, to compensate for the negligence and incapacity of a government, always ready to plunge the nation into war, without the slightest care of what was necessary to obtain success. The sieges carried on by the British in Spain were a succession of butcheries, because the commonest materials and the means necessary for their art were denied to the engineers.

Colonel Fletcher's plan was to breach the castle of Badajos, while batteries established on the right bank of the Guadiana should take the defence in reverse, and false attacks against the Pardaleras and Picurina were also to be commenced by re-opening the French trenches. It was, however, necessary to reduce the fort of Christoval ere the batteries for ruining the defences of the castle could be erected. In double operations, whether of the field or of siege, it is essential to move with an exact concert, lest the enemy should crush each in detail; but neither in the investment nor in the attack was this maxim regarded. Captain Squire, although ill provided with tools, was directed to commence a battery against Christoval on the night of the 8th, under a bright moon, and at the distance of only four hundred yards from the rampart. Exposed to a destructive fire of musketry from the fort, and of shot and shells from the town, he continued to work, with great loss, until the 10th, when the enemy, making a furious sally, carried his battery;

Appendix,
No. X.
Section 3
and 4.

the French were, indeed, immediately driven back, but the allies pursuing too hotly, were taken in front and flank with grape, and lost four hundred men. Thus five engineer and seven hundred officers and soldiers of the line were already on the long and bloody list of victims offered to this Moloch, and only one small battery against a small outwork was completed! On the 11th it opened, and before sunset the fire of the enemy had disabled four of its five guns, and killed many more of the besiegers. Nor could any other result be expected, seeing that this single work was exposed to the undivided fire of the fortress, for the approaches against the castle were not yet commenced, and two distant batteries on the false attacks scarcely attracted the notice of the enemy.

To check future sallies, a second battery was erected against the bridge-head, but this was also overmatched, and meanwhile Beresford, having received intelligence that the French army was again in movement, arrested the progress of all the works. On the 12th, believing this information premature, he resumed the labour, directing the trenches to be opened against the castle. The intelligence was, however, true, and being confirmed at twelve o'clock in the night, the working parties were again drawn off, and measures taken to raise the siege.

SOULT'S SECOND EXPEDITION TO ESTREMADURA.

The duke of Dalmatia resolved to succour Badajos the moment he heard of Beresford's being in Estremadura, and the tardiness of the latter had not only

given the garrison time to organize a defence, but had permitted the French general to tranquillise his province and arrange a system of resistance to the allied army in the Isla. With that view, Soult had commenced additional fortifications at Seville, and
renewed the construction of those which had been suspended in other places by the battle of Barosa. He thus deceived Beresford, who believed that, far from thinking to relieve Badajos, he was trembling for his own province. Nothing could be more fallacious. There were seventy thousand fighting men in Andalusia, and Drouet, who had quitted Massena immediately after the battle of Fuentes Onoro, was likewise in march for that province by the way of Avila and Toledo, bringing with him eleven thousand men.

All things being ready, Soult quitted Seville the 10th, with three thousand heavy dragoons, thirty guns, and two strong brigades of infantry under the command of general Werlé and general Godinot. This force, which was composed of troops drawn from the first and fourth corps and from the reserve of Dessolles, entered Olalla the 11th, and was there joined by general Maransin ; but Godinot marched by Constantino to reinforce the fifth corps, which was falling back from Guadalcanal in consequence of Colborne's operations. The 13th the junction was effected with Latour Maubourg, who assumed the command of the heavy cavalry, while Girard taking that of the fifth corps, advanced to Los Santos. The 14th the French head-quarters reached Villa Franca. Being then within thirty miles of Badajos, Soult caused his heaviest guns to fire salvos during the night, to give notice of

his approach to the garrison, but the expedient
failed of success, and the 15th, in the evening,
his army was concentrated at Santa Marta.

Beresford, as I have before said, remained in a
state of uncertainty until the night of the 12th,
when he commenced raising the siege, contrary to
the earnest representations of the engineers, who
promised to put him in possession of the place in
three days, if he would persevere. This promise
was ill-founded, and, if it had been otherwise,
Soult would have surprised him in the trenches:
his firmness, therefore, saved the army, and his
arrangements for carrying off the stores were admirably executed. The artillery and the platforms
were removed in the night of the 13th, and, at
twelve o'clock, on the 15th, all the guns and stores on
the left bank, having been passed over the Guadiana,
the gabions and fascines were burnt, and the flying-
bridge removed. These transactions were completely masked by the fourth division, which, with
the Spaniards, continued to maintain the investment; it was not until the rear guard was ready to
draw off, that the French, in a sally, after severely
handling the piquets of Harvey's Portuguese brigade, learned that the siege was raised, but of the
cause they were still ignorant.

Beresford held a conference with the Spanish
generals at Valverde, on the 13th, when it was
agreed to receive battle at the village of Albuera.
Ballasteros' and Blake's corps having already formed
a junction at Baracotta, were then falling back
upon Almendral, and Blake engaged to bring them
into line at Albuera, before twelve o'clock, on the
15th. Meanwhile, as Badajos was the centre of an
arc, sweeping through Valverde, Albuera, and

Talavera Real, it was arranged that Blake's army should watch the roads on the right, the British and the fifth Spanish army those leading upon the centre ; and that Madden's Portuguese cavalry should observe those on the left, conducting through Talavera Real.   The main body of the British being in the woods near Valverde, could reach Albuera by a half march, and no part of the arc was more than four leagues from Badajos, but the enemy being, on the 14th, still at Los Santos, was eight leagues distant from Albuera; hence, Beresford, thinking that he could not be forstalled on any point, of importance to the allies, continued to keep the fourth division in the trenches.   Colborne's moveable column joined the army on the 14th, Madden then retired to Talavera Real, and Blake's army reached Almendral.   Meanwhile the allied cavalry, under general Long, had fallen back before the enemy from Zafra and Los Santos, to Santa Marta, and was there joined by the dragoons of the fourth army.

In the morning of the 15th, the British occupied the left of the position of Albuera, which was a ridge about four miles long, having the Aroya Val de Sevilla in rear and the Albuera river in front. The right of the army was prolonged towards Almendral, the left towards Badajos, and the ascent from the river was easy, the ground being in all parts practicable for cavalry and artillery.   Somewhat in advance of the centre were the bridge and village of Albuera, the former commanded by a battery, the latter occupied by Alten's brigade.   The second division, under general William Stewart, was drawn up in one line, the right on a commanding hill over which the Valverde road passed ; the left on the road of Badajos, beyond which the order of battle was continued in two lines, by the Portuguese troops under general Hamilton and colonel Collins.

The right of the position, which was stronger, and higher, and broader than any other part, was left open for Blake's army, because Beresford, thinking the hill on the Valverde road to be the key of the position, as protecting his only line of retreat, was desirous to secure it with the best troops. The fourth division and the infantry of the fifth army were still before Badajos. General Cole had orders to send the seventeenth Portuguese regiment to Elvas, and to throw a battalion of Spaniards into Olivenza; to bring his second brigade, which was before Christoval, over the Guadiana, by a ford above Badajos, if practicable, and to be in readiness to march at the first notice.

In this posture of affairs, about three o'clock in the evening of the 15th, while Beresford was at some distance on the left, the whole mass of the allied cavalry, closely followed by the French light horsemen, came in from Santa Marta, and as no infantry were posted beyond the Albuera to support them, they passed that river. Thus the wooded heights on the right bank were abandoned to the enemy, and his force and dispositions being thereby effectually concealed, the strength of the allies' position was already sapped. Beresford immediately formed a temporary right wing with the cavalry and artillery, stretching his picquets along the road to Almendral, and sending officers to hasten Blake's movements; but that general, who had only a few miles of good road to march, and who had promised to be in line at noon, did not reach the ground before eleven at night, and his rear was not there before three o'clock in the morning of the 16th ; meanwhile, as the enemy was evidently in force on the Albuera road, Cole and Madden were ordered up.   The orders failed to reach the latter, but, at six o'clock in the morning, the former arrived on the position with the infantry of the fifth army, two squadrons of Portuguese cavalry, and two brigades of the fourth division ; the third brigade, under colonel Kemmis, being unable to cross the Guadiana, above Badajos, was in march by Jerumenha.   The Spanish troops immediately joined Blake on the right, the two brigades of the fourth division, were drawn up in columns behind the second division, and the Portuguese squadrons reinforced colonel Otway, whose horsemen, of the same nation, were pushed forward in front of the left wing.   The mass of the cavalry was concentrated behind the centre, and Beresford, dissatisfied with general Long, ordered general Lumley to assume the chief command.

The position was now occupied by thirty thousand infantry, above two thousand cavalry, and thirty-eight pieces of artillery, of which eighteen were nine-pounders ; but, the brigade of the fourth division being still absent, the British infantry, the pith and strength of battle, did not exceed seven thousand, and already Blake's arrogance was shaking Beresford's authority.   The French had fifty guns, and above four thousand veteran cavalry, but only nineteen thousand chosen infantry ; yet being of one nation, obedient to one discipline, and animated by one spirit, their excellent composition amply compensated for the inferiority of numbers, and their general's talent was immeasurably greater than his adversary's.

Soult examined Beresford's position, without CHAP.
hindrance, on the evening of the 15th, and having
heard that the fourth division was left before
Badajos, and that Blake would not arrive before
the 17th, he resolved to attack the next morning,
for he had detected all the weakness of the English
general's position of battle.

The hill in the centre, commanding the Valverde road, was undoubtedly the key of the position
if an attack was made parallel to the front. But the
heights on the right presented a rough sort of broken table-land, trending backwards towards the
Valverde road, and looking into the rear of the line
of battle; hence it was evident that, if a mass of
troops could be placed there, they must be beaten,
or the right wing of the allied army would be rolled
up on the centre and pushed into the narrow valley
of the Aroya: the Valverde road could then be
seized, the retreat cut, and the powerful cavalry
of the French would complete the victory. Now
the right of the allies and the left of the French
approximated to each other, being only divided by
a hill, about cannon-shot distance from either but
separated from the allies by the Albuera, and from
the French by a rivulet called the Feria. This
height, neglected by Beresford, was ably made use
of by Soult. During the night he placed behind
it, the artillery under general Ruty, the fifth corps
under Girard, and the heavy dragoons under Latour
Maubourg. He thus concentrated fifteen thousand
men and forty guns within ten minutes' march of
Beresford's right wing, and yet that general could
neither see a man nor draw a sound conclusion as
to the real plan of attack.

The light cavalry, the brigades of Godinot and

Werlé, and ten guns, still remained at the French marshal's disposal. These he formed in the woods, extending along the banks of the Feria towards its confluence with the Albuera. Werlé was to keep in reserve; but Godinot was to attack the village and bridge, and to bear strongly against the centre of the position, with a view to attract Beresford's attention, to separate his wings, and to double up his right at the moment when the principal attack should be developed.

BATTLE OF ALBUERA.

During the night, Blake and Cole, as we have seen, arrived with above sixteen thousand men, but so defective was the occupation of the ground, that Soult had no change to make in his plans from this circumstance, and, a little before nine o'clock in the morning, Godinot's division issued from the woods in one heavy column of attack, preceded by ten guns. He was flanked by the light cavalry, and followed by Werlé's division of reserve, and, making straight towards the bridge, commenced a sharp cannonade, attempting to force the passage; at the same time Briché, with two regiments of hussars, drew further down the river to observe colonel Otway's horse.

Dickson's guns posted on the rising ground above the village answered the fire of the French, and ploughed through their columns, which were crowding without judgement towards the bridge, although the stream was passable above and below. Beresford observing that Werlé's division did not follow closely, was soon convinced that the

principal effort would be on the right, and he, therefore, ordered Blake to form a part of the first and
all the second line of the Spanish army, on the
broad part of the hills, at right angles to their
actual front. Then drawing the Portuguese infantry of the left wing to the centre, he sent one
brigade down to support Alten, and directed
general Hamilton to hold the remainder in columns
of battalions, ready to move to any part of the
field. The thirteenth dragoons were posted near
the edge of the river, above the bridge, and, meanwhile, the second division marched to support
Blake. The horse-artillery, the heavy dragoons,
and the fourth division also took ground to the
right, and were posted, the cavalry and guns on a
small plain behind the Aroya, and the fourth division in an oblique line about half musket shot
behind them. This done, Beresford galloped to
Blake, for that general had refused to change his
front, and, with great heat, told colonel Hardinge,
the bearer of the order, that the real attack was at
the village and bridge. Beresford had sent again
to entreat that he would obey, but this message
was as fruitless as the former, and, when the marshal arrived, nothing had been done. The enemy's
columns were, however, now beginning to appear on
the right, and Blake yielding to this evidence, proceeded to make the evolution, yet with such pedan-
tic slowness, that Beresford, impatient of his folly,
took the direction in person.

Great was the confusion and the delay thus
occasioned, and ere the troops were completely
formed the French were amongst them. For
scarcely had Godinot engaged Alten's brigade, when
Werlé, leaving only a battalion of grenadiers and

some squadrons to watch the thirteenth dragoons and to connect the attacks, countermarched with the remainder of his division, and rapidly gained the rear of the fifth corps as it was mounting the hills on the right of the allies. At the same time the mass of light cavalry suddenly quitted Godinot's column, and crossing the river Albuera above the bridge, ascended the left bank at a gallop, and, sweeping round the rear of the fifth corps, joined Latour Maubourg, who was already in face of Lumley's squadrons. Thus half an hour had sufficed to render Beresford's position nearly desperate. Two-thirds of the French were in a compact order of battle on a line perpendicular to his right, and his army, disordered and composed of different nations, was still in the difficult act of changing its front. It was in vain that he endeavoured to keep the Spanish line sufficiently in advance to give room on the summit of the hill for the second division to support it; the French guns opened, their infantry threw out a heavy musketry fire, and their cavalry, outflanking the front, and menacing to charge here and there, put the Spaniards in disorder at all points, they fell fast, and they gave back. Soult, thinking the whole army was yielding, then pushed forward his columns, his reserves mounted the hill behind him, and general Ruty placed all the batteries in position.

At this critical moment general William Stewart arrived at the foot of the height, with colonel Colborne's brigade, which formed the head, and was the most advanced part of the second division. The colonel, seeing the confusion above, desired to form in order of battle previous to mounting the ascent, but Stewart, whose boiling courage overlaid

his judgement, led up, without hesitation, in column
of companies, and having passed the Spanish right,
attempted to open out his line in succession as the
battalions arrived at the summit. Being under a
destructive fire the foremost troops charged, but a
heavy rain prevented any object from being distinctly
seen, and four regiments of hussars and lancers,
which had turned the right flank in the obscurity,
came galloping in upon the rear of the line at the
instant of its developement, and slew or took two-
thirds of the brigade. One battalion only (the
thirty-first) being still in column, escaped the storm
and maintained its ground, while the French horsemen, riding violently over every thing else, penetrated to all parts, and captured six guns. In the
tumult, a lancer fell upon Beresford, the marshal,
a man of great strength, putting his spear aside
cast him from his saddle, and a shift of wind
blowing aside the mist and smoke, the mischief was
perceived from the plains by general Lumley, who
sent four squadrons out upon the lancers and cut
many of them off. Penne Villemur's cavalry were
also directed to charge, and galloped forward, but Appendix,
No. IX.
Section 4.
when within a few yards wheeled round and fled.

During this first unhappy effort of the second
division, so great was the disorder, that the Spanish
line continued to fire without cessation, although
the British were before them. Beresford, finding his exhortations to advance, fruitless, seized
an ensign and bore him and his colours, by main
force, to the front, yet the troops would not follow,
and the man went back again on being released.
In this crisis, the weather, which had ruined Colborne's brigade, also prevented Soult from seeing
the whole extent of the field of battle, and he still

kept his heavy columns together. His cavalry, indeed, began to hem in that of the allies, but the fire of the horse-artillery enabled Lumley, covered as he was by the bed of the Aroya and supported by the fourth division, to check them on the plain, Colborne still remained on the height with the thirty-first regiment, the British artillery, under major Julius Hartman, was coming fast into action, and William Stewart, who had escaped the charge of the lancers, was again mounting the hill with general Houghton's brigade, which he brought on with the same vehemence, but, instructed by his previous misfortune, in a juster order of battle. The weather now cleared, and a dreadful fire poured into the thickest of the French columns convinced Soult that the day was yet to be won.

Houghton's regiments reached the height under a very heavy cannonade, and the twenty-ninth regiment was charged on the flank by the lancers, but major Way, wheeling back two companies, foiled their attack with a sharp fire. The remaining brigade of the second division then came up on the left, and the Spanish corps of Zayas and Ballasteros at last moved forward. Hartman's artillery was now in full play, and the enemy's infantry recoiled, but soon recovering, renewed the fight with greater violence than before. The cannon on both sides discharged showers of grape at half range, the peals of musketry were incessant, and often within pistol-shot, but the close formation of the French embarrassed their battle, and the British line would not yield them one inch of ground, nor a moment of time to open their ranks. Their fighting was, however, fierce and dangerous. Stewart was twice wounded, colonel Duckworth, of the forty-eighth, was slain, and the gallant Houghton, who had received many wounds without shrinking, fell and died in the act of cheering his men. Still the struggle continued with unabated fury. Colonel Inglis, twenty-two officers, and more than four hundred men, out of five hundred and seventy that had mounted the hill, fell in the fifty-seventh alone, and the other regiments were scarcely better off; not one-third were standing in any, their ammunition failed, and as the English fire slackened, the enemy established a column in advance upon the right flank. The play of the artillery indeed checked them a moment, but in this dreadful crisis Beresford wavered! Destruction stared him in the face, his personal resources were exhausted, and the unhappy thought of a retreat rose in his agitated mind. He had before brought Hamilton's Portuguese into a situation to cover a retrograde movement, and he now sent orders to general Alten to abandon the bridge and village of Albuera, and to assemble with the Portuguese artillery, in such a position as would cover a retreat by the Valverde road. But while the marshal was thus preparing to resign the contest, colonel Hardinge boldly ordered general Cole to advance with the fourth division, and then riding to that brigade of the second division which was under the command of colonel Abercrombie, and which had been only slightly engaged, directed him also to push forward into the fight. The die being thus cast, Beresford acquiesced, Alten received orders to retake the village, and this terrible battle was continued.

The fourth division was composed of two brigades, the one of Portuguese under general

Harvey, the other commanded by sir William Myers, consisted of the seventh and twenty-third regiments, and was called the fuzileer brigade. Harvey's Portuguese being immediately pushed in between Lumley's dragoons and the hill, were charged by some French cavalry, whom they beat off, and meanwhile general Cole led the fuzileers up the contested height. At this time six guns were in the enemy's possession, the whole of Werlé's reserves were coming forward to reinforce the front column of the French, the remnant of Houghton's brigade could no longer maintain its ground, the field was heaped with carcasses, the lancers were riding furiously about the captured artillery on the upper parts of the hill, and behind all, Hamilton's Portuguese and Alten's Germans, withdrawing from the bridge, seemed to be in full retreat. Cole's fuzileers, flanked by a battalion of the Lusitanian legion under colonel Hawkshawe, soon mounted the hill, drove off the lancers, recovered five of the captured guns and one colour, and appeared on the right of Houghton's brigade precisely as Abercrombie passed it on the left.

Such a gallant line, issuing from the midst of the smoke, and rapidly separating itself from the confused and broken multitude, startled the enemy's heavy masses, which were increasing and pressing onwards as to an assured victory : they wavered, hesitated, and then vomiting forth a storm of fire, hastily endeavoured to enlarge their front, while a fearful discharge of grape from all their artillery whistled through the British ranks. Myers was killed, Cole, the three colonels, Ellis, Blakeney, and Hawkshawe, fell wounded, and the fuzileer battalions, struck by the iron tempest, reeled, and stag-

Campo Maior

Caya R.

Guadiana R.

Elvas

Christoval

Badajos

Talavera Real

Montigo

umena

R.

Merida

Valverde

Olivenza

Albuera

Sotano

Almendral

S. Marta

Almendralejo

Villa franca

Baracotta

Xerez Cavalhero

Burgillo

Zafra

Los Santos

Fregenal

Fuente Cantos

Lerena

Siera Morena

Monasterio

TTLE of ALBUERA
16ᵀᴴ MAY, 1811.

Lumley

Valverde Road

4ᵗ Divⁿ

Harvey

Aroya R.

Fuzileers

Houghton

5ᵗʰ Corps

Spaniards

2ⁿᵈ Divⁿ

Portuguese

Werle

Abercrombie

Colborne

13ᵗʰ Drⁿ

G. Alten

Albuera

Ferdia R.

Godinot

Albuera R.

gered like sinking ships. But suddenly and sternly recovering, they closed on their terrible enemies, and then was seen with what a strength and majesty the British soldier fights. In vain did Soult, by voice and gesture, animate his Frenchmen; in vain did the hardiest veterans, extricating themselves from the crowded columns, sacrifice their lives to gain time for the mass to open out on such a fair field; in vain did the mass itself bear up, and fiercely striving, fire indiscriminately upon friends and foes while the horsemen hovering on the flank threatened to charge the advancing line. Nothing could stop that astonishing infantry. No sudden burst of undisciplined valour, no nervous enthusiasm, weakened the stability of their order, their flashing eyes were bent on the dark columns in their front, their measured tread shook the ground, their dreadful volleys swept away the head of every formation, their deafening shouts overpowered the dissonant cries that broke from all parts of the tumultuous crowd, as slowly and with a horrid carnage, it was pushed by the incessant vigour of the attack to the farthest edge of the height. There, the French reserve, mixing with the struggling multitude, endeavoured to sustain the fight, but the effort only increased the irremediable confusion, the mighty mass gave way and like a loosened cliff went headlong down the steep. The rain flowed after in streams discoloured with blood, and fifteen hundred unwounded men, the remnant of six thousand unconquerable British soldiers, stood triumphant on the fatal hill!

CHAPTER VII.

WHILE the fuzileers were striving on the height, the cavalry and Harvey's brigade continually advanced, and Latour Maubourg's dragoons, battered by Lefebre's guns, retired before them, yet still threatening the fuzileers with their right, while with their left they prevented Lumley's horsemen from falling on the defeated infantry. Beresford, seeing that colonel Hardinge's decision had brought on the critical moment of the battle, then endeavoured to secure a favourable result. Alten's Germans were ordered to retake the village, which they effected with some loss. Blake's first line, which had not been at all engaged, was directed to support them, and Hamilton's and Collins's Portuguese, forming a mass of ten thousand fresh men, were brought up to support the attack of the fuzileers and Abercrombie's brigade; and at the same time the Spanish divisions of Zayas, Ballasteros, and España advanced. Nevertheless, so rapid was the execution of the fuzileers, that the enemy's infantry were never attained by these reserves, which yet suffered severely; for general Ruty got the French guns altogether, and worked them with prodigious activity, while the fifth corps still made head; and when the day was irrevocably lost, he regained the other side of the Albuera, and protected the passage of the broken infantry.

Beresford, being too hardly handled to pursue,

formed a fresh line with his Portuguese, parallel
to the hill from whence Soult had advanced to
the attack in the morning, and where the French
troops were now rallying with their usual celerity.
Meanwhile the fight continued at the bridge,
but Godinot's division and the connecting battalion
of grenadiers on that side were soon afterwards
withdrawn, and the action terminated before three
o'clock.

The serious fighting had endured only four hours,
and in that space of time, nearly seven thousand of
the allies and above eight thousand of their adversaries were struck down. Three French generals
were wounded, two slain, and eight hundred soldiers so badly hurt as to be left on the field. On
Beresford's side only two thousand Spaniards, and
six hundred Germans and Portuguese, were killed
or wounded, and hence it is plain with what a resolution the pure British fought, for they had only
fifteen hundred men left standing! The laurel is
nobly won when the exhausted victor reels as he
places it on his bleeding front.

The trophies of the French were five hundred
unwounded prisoners, a howitzer, and several
stand of colours. The British had nothing of that
kind to boast of, but the horrid piles of carcasses
within their lines told, with dreadful eloquence,
who were the conquerors; and all the night the
rain poured down, and the river and the hills and
the woods on each side, resounded with the dismal
clamour and groans of dying men. Beresford,
obliged to place his Portuguese in the front line,
was oppressed with the number of his wounded;
they far exceeded that of the sound amongst the
British soldiers, and when the latter's piquets

were established, few men remained to help the sufferers. In this cruel situation he sent colonel Hardinge to demand assistance from Blake; but wrath and mortified pride were predominant in that general's breast, and he refused, saying, it was customary with allied armies, for each to take care of its own men.

Morning came, and both sides remained in their respective situations, the wounded still covering the field of battle, the hostile lines still menacing and dangerous. The greater multitude had fallen on the French part, but the best soldiers on that of the allies, and the dark masses of Soult's powerful cavalry and artillery, as they covered all his front, seemed alone able to contend again for the victory: the right of the French also appeared to threaten the Badajos road, and Beresford, in gloom and doubt, awaited another attack. On the 17th, however, the third brigade of the fourth division came up by a forced march from Jerumenha, and enabled the second division to retake their former ground between the Valverde and the Badajos roads. On the 18th, Soult retreated.

He left to the generosity of the English general several hundred men too deeply wounded to be removed, but all that could travel he had, in the night of the 17th, sent towards Seville, by the royal road, through Santa Marta, Los Santos, and Monasterio. Protecting his movements with all his horsemen and six battalions of infantry, he filed the army, in the morning, to its right, and gained the road of Solano. When this flank march was completed, Latour Maubourg covered the rear with the heavy dragoons, and Briché protected the march of the wounded men by the royal road.

The duke of Dalmatia remained the 19th at Solano. His intention was to hold a position in Estremadura until he could receive reinforcements from Andalusia; for he judged truly that, although Beresford was in no condition to hurt Badajos, lord Wellington would come down, and that fresh combats would be required to save that fortress. On the 14th he had commenced repairing the castle of Villalba, a large structure between Almendralejos and Santa Marta, and he now continued this work, designing to form a head of cantonments, that the allies would be unable to take before the French army could be reinforced.

When Beresford discovered the enemy's retreat, he despatched general Hamilton to make a show of re-investing Badajos, which was effected at day-break the 19th, but on the left bank only. Meanwhile the allied cavalry, supported by Alten's Germans, followed the French line of retreat. Soult then transferred his head-quarters to Fuente del Maestre, and the Spanish cavalry, cutting off some of his men, menaced Villalba. Lord Wellington reached the field of battle the same day, and, after examining the state of affairs, desired the marshal to follow the enemy cautiously; then returning to Elvas himself, he directed the third and seventh divisions, which were already at Campo Mayor, to complete the re-investment of Badajos on the right bank.

Meanwhile Beresford advanced by the Solano road to Almendralejos, where he found some more wounded men. His further progress was not opposed. The number of officers who had fallen in the French army, together with the privations endured, had produced despondence and discontent;

the garrison at Villalba was not disposed to maintain the castle, and under these circumstances, the
duke of Dalmatia evacuated it, and continued his
own retreat in the direction of Llerena, where he assumed a position on the 23d, and placed his cavalry
near Usagre. This abandonment of the royal road
to Seville was a well-considered movement. The
country through which Soult passed being more
fruitful and open, he could draw greater advantage
from his superior cavalry, the mountains behind
him were so strong he had nothing to fear from an
attack, and by Belalcazar and Almaden, he could
maintain a communication with La Mancha, from
whence he expected Drouet's division. The road of
Guadalcanal was in his rear, by which he could draw
reinforcements from Cordoba and from the fourth
corps, and meanwhile the allies durst not venture
to expose their left-flank by marching on Monasterio.

From Llerena, a detachment was sent to drive
away a Spanish Partida corps which had cut his
communications with Guadalcanal, and at the same
time Latour Maubourg was directed to scour the
country beyond Usagre; this led to an action.
The town, built upon a hill, and covered towards
Los Santos by a river with steep and rugged banks,
had only the one outlet by the bridge on that side,
and when Latour Maubourg approached, Lumley
retired across the river. The French light cavalry
then marched along the right bank, with the intention of crossing lower down and thus covering the
passage of the heavy horsemen; but before they
could effect this object, general Bron rashly passed
the river with two regiments of dragoons, and drew
up in line just beyond the bridge. Lumley was,
however, lying close behind a rising ground, and

when the French regiments had advanced a sufficient
distance, Lefebre's guns opened on them, and the third, and fourth dragoon guards, charged them
in front while Madden's Portuguese fell on their flank. They were overthrown at the first shock, and fled towards the bridge, which being choked with the remainder of the cavalry advancing to their support, the fugitives turned to the right and left, and endeavoured to save themselves amongst some gardens situated on the banks of the river ; they were, however, pursued and sabred until the French on the opposite side, seeing their distress, checked the attack by a fire of carbines and artillery. Some wounded prisoners were taken, but a Guerilla party which had not joined in the attack suddenly massacred them. However above forty killed in fair fight, and more than a hundred wounded, attested the vigour of Lumley's conduct in this affair, which terminated Beresford's operations, for the miserable
state to which the Regency had reduced the Portuguese army, imperatively called for the marshal's presence elsewhere. General Hill, who had returned to Portugal, then re-assumed the command of the second division, amidst the eager rejoicings of the troops, and lord Wellington directed the renewed siege of Badajos in person.

OBSERVATIONS.

No general ever gained a great battle with so little increase of military reputation as marshal Beresford. His personal intrepidity and strength, qualities so attractive for the multitude, were conspicuously displayed, yet the breath of his own army

withered his laurels, and his triumph was disputed
by the very soldiers who followed his car. Their
censures have been reiterated, without change and
without abatement, even to this hour ; and a close
examination of his operations, while it detects
many ill-founded objections, and others tainted
with malice, leaves little doubt that the general
feeling was right.

When he had passed the Guadiana and driven
the fifth corps upon Guadalcanal, the delay that
intervened, before he invested Badajos, was unjustly
attributed to him : it was lord Wellington's order,
resulting from the tardiness of the Spanish generals,
that paralyzed his operations. But when the time
for action arrived, the want of concert in the investment, and the ill-matured attack on San Christoval
belonged to Beresford's arrangements ; and he is
especially responsible in reputation for the latter,
because captain Squire earnestly warned him of
the inevitable result, and his words were unheeded.

During the progress of the siege, either the
want of correct intelligence, or a blunted judgement,
misled the marshal. It was remarked that, at all
times, he too readily believed the idle tales of
distress and difficulties in the French armies, with
which the spies generally, and the deserters always,
interlarded their information : thus he was incre-
dulous of Soult's enterprise, and that officer was
actually over the Morena before the orders were
given to commence the main attack of the castle of
Badajos. However, the firmness with which Beresford resisted the importunities of the engineers to
continue the siege, and the quick and orderly removal of the stores and battering-train, were alike

Appendix,
No. X.

remarkable and praiseworthy. It would have been happy if he had shewn as much magnanimity in what followed.

When he met Blake and Castaños at Valverde, the alternative of fighting or retiring behind the Guadiana was the subject of consideration. The Spanish generals were both in favour of giving battle. Blake, who could not retire the way he had arrived, without danger of having his march intercepted, was particularly earnest to fight, affirming that his troops, who were already in a miserable state, would disperse entirely if they were obliged to enter Portugal. Castaños was of the same opinion. Beresford also argued that it was unwise to relinquish the hope of taking Badajos, and ungenerous to desert the people of Estremadura; that a retreat would endanger Elvas, lay open the Alemtejo, and encourage the enemy to push his incursions further, which he could safely do, having such a fortress as Badajos with its bridge over the Guadiana, in his rear. A battle must then be fought in the Alemtejo with fewer troops and after a dispiriting retreat; there was also a greater scarcity of food in the Portuguese than in the Spanish province, and, finally, as the weather was menacing, the Guadiana might again rise before the stores were carried over, when the latter must be abandoned, or the army endangered to protect their passage.

But these plausible reasons were but a mask. The true cause why the English general adopted Blake's proposals was the impatient temper of the British troops. None of them had been engaged in the late battles under lord Wellington. At Busaco the regiments of the fourth division were idle

spectators on the left, as those of the second division were on the right, while the action was in the
centre.   During Massena's retreat they had not
been employed under fire, and the combats of
Sabugal and Fuentes Onoro had been fought without them.   Thus a burning thirst for battle was
general, and Beresford had not the art either of
conciliating or of exacting the confidence of his
troops.   It is certain that if he had retreated, a
very violent and unjust clamour would have been
raised against him, and this was so strongly and
unceremoniously represented to him, by an officer
on his own staff, that he gave way.   These are
what may be termed the moral obstacles of war.
Such men as lord Wellington or sir John Moore
can stride over them, but to second-rate minds they
are insuperable.   Practice and study may make
a good general as far as the handling of troops
and the designing of a campaign, but that ascendancy of spirit which leads the wise, and con-
trols the insolence of folly, is a rare gift of
nature.

Beresford yielded with an unhappy flexibility
to the clamour of the army and the representations
of Blake, for it is unquestionable that the resolution to fight was unwarrantable on any sound
military principle.   We may pass over the argument founded upon the taking of Badajos, because
neither the measures nor the means of the English
general promised the slightest chance of success;
the siege would have died away of itself in default of
resources to carry it on.   The true question to consider was, not whether Estremadura should be
deserted or Badajos abandoned, but whether lord
Wellington's combinations and his great and well

considered design for the deliverance of the Peninsula, should be ruined and defaced at a blow. To
say that the Alemtejo could not have been defended
until the commander-in-chief arrived from the
north with reinforcements was mere trifling. Soult,
with twenty or even thirty thousand men, dared not
have attempted the siege of Elvas in the face of
twenty-four thousand men such as Beresford commanded. The result of the battle of Fuentes Onoro
was known in the English and in the French camps,
before Beresford broke up from Badajos, hence he
was certain that additional troops would soon be
brought down to the Guadiana; indeed, the third
and seventh divisions were actually at Campo Mayor
the 23d of May. The danger to the Alemtejo was,
therefore, slight, and the necessity of a battle
being by no means apparent, it remains to analyze
the chances of success.

Soult's numbers were not accurately known, but
it was ascertained that he had not less than twenty
thousand veteran troops; he had also a great
superiority of cavalry and artillery, and the country
was peculiarly suitable for these arms. The martial character of the man was also known. Now
the allies could bring into the field more of infantry
by ten thousand than the French, but they were of
various tongues, and the Spanish part, ill armed,
starving, and worn out with fatigue, had been
repeatedly and recently defeated by the very troops
they were going to engage. The French were
compact, swift of movement, inured to war, used
to act together, and under the command of one
able and experienced general. The allied army
was unwieldy, each nation mistrusting the other,
and the whole without unity of spirit, or of dis-

cipline, or of command. On what, then, could
marshal Beresford found his hopes of success?
The British troops. The latter were therefore to
be freely used. But was it a time to risk the total
destruction of two superb divisions and to encounter
a certain and heavy loss of men, whose value he
knew so well when he calculated upon them alone
for victory in such circumstances?

To resolve on battle was, however, easier than
to prepare for it with skill. Albuera, we have
seen, was the point of concentration. Colonel
Colborne's brigade did not arrive until the 14th,
and there was no certainty that it could arrive
before the enemy did. Blake did not arrive until
three in the morning of the 16th. The fourth division not until six o'clock. Kemmis with three fine
British regiments, and Madden's cavalry, did not
come at all. These facts prove that the whole plan
was faulty, it was mere accident that a sufficient
force to give battle was concentrated. Beresford
was too late, and the keeping up the investment
of Badajos, although laudable in one sense, was a
great error; it was only an accessory, and yet the
success of the principal object was made subservient to it. If Soult, instead of passing by Villa
Franca, in his advance, had pushed straight on
from Los Santos to Albuera, he would have arrived
the 15th, when Beresford had not much more than
half his force in position; the point of concentration would then have been lost, and the allies
scattered in all directions. If the French had even
continued their march by Solano instead of turning
upon Albuera, they must inevitably have communicated with Badajos, unless Beresford had fought
without waiting for Blake, and without Kemmis's

brigade. Why, then, did the French marshal turn out of the way to seek a battle, in preference to attaining his object without one? and why did he neglect to operate by his right or left until the unwieldy allied army should separate or get into confusion, as it inevitably would have done? Because the English general's dispositions were so faulty that no worse error could well be expected from him, and Soult had every reason to hope for a great and decided victory; a victory which would have more than counterbalanced Massena's failure. He knew that only one-half of the allied force was at Albuera on the 15th, and when he examined the ground, every thing promised the most complete success.

Marshal Beresford had fixed upon and studied his own field of battle above a month before the action took place, and yet occupied it in such a manner as to render defeat almost certain; his infantry were not held in hand, and his inferiority in guns and cavalry was not compensated for by entrenchments. But were any other proofs of error wanting, this fact would suffice, he had a greater strength of infantry on a field of battle scarcely three miles long, ten thousand of his troops never fired a shot, and three times the day was lost and won, the allies being always fewest in number at the decisive point. It is true that Blake's conduct was very perplexing; it is true that general William Stewart's error cost one brigade, and thus annihilated the command of colonel Colborne, a man capable of turning the fate of a battle even with fewer troops than those swept away from him by the French cavalry: but the neglect of the hill beyond the Albuera, fronting the right of the

position, was Beresford's own error and a most
serious one; so also were the successive attacks of
the brigades, and the hesitation about the fourth
division. And where are we to look for that
promptness in critical moments which marks the
great commander? It was colonel Hardinge that
gave the fourth division and Abercrombie's brigade,
orders to advance, and it was their astounding
valour in attack, and the astonishing firmness of
Houghton's brigade in defence that saved the day.
The person of the general-in-chief was indeed seen
every where, a gallant soldier! but the mind of the
great commander was seen no where.

Beresford remained master of the field of battle,
but he could not take Badajos, that prize was the
result of many great efforts, and many deep combinations by a far greater man; neither did he clear
Estremadura, for Soult maintained positions from
Llerena to Usagre. What then did he gain? The
power of simulating a renewal of the siege, and
holding his own cantonments on the left bank of
the Guadiana; I say simulating, for, if the third
and seventh divisions had not arrived from Beira,
even the investment could not have been completed.
These illusive advantages he purchased at the price
of seven thousand men. With a smaller loss lord
Wellington had fought two general and several
minor actions, had baffled Massena and turned
seventy thousand men out of Portugal!

Such being the fruit of victory, what would have
been the result of defeat? There was no retreat,
save by the temporary bridge of Jerumenha, and
had the hill on the right been carried in the battle,
the Valverde road would have been in Soult's possession, and the line of retreat cut; had it even been

otherwise, Beresford, with four thousand victorious
French cavalry at his heels, could never have passed
the river. Back, then, must have come the army
from the north, the Lines of Lisbon would have been
once more occupied—a French force fixed on the
south of the Tagus—Spain ruined—Portugal laid
prostrate—England in dismay. Could even the
genius of lord Wellington have recovered such a
state of affairs? And yet, with these results,
the terrible balance hung for two hours, and twice
trembling to the sinister side, only yielded at last to
the superlative vigour of the fuzileers. The battle
should never have been fought. The siege of Badajos could not have been renewed without reinforcements, and, with them, it could have been
renewed without an action, or at least without
risking an unequal one.

But would even the bravery of British soldiers
have saved the day, at Albuera, if the French
general had not also committed great errors. His
plan of attack and his execution of it, up to the
moment when the Spanish line fell back in disorder,
cannot be too much admired; after that, the great
error of fighting in dense columns being persisted
in beyond reason, lost the fairest field ever offered
to the arms of France. Had the fifth corps opened
out while there was time to do so, that is, between
the falling back of the Spaniards and the advance
of Houghton's brigade, what on earth could have
saved Beresford from a total defeat? The fire of
the enemy's columns alone destroyed two-thirds of
his British troops; the fire of their lines would
have swept away all!

It has been said that Latour Maubourg and Godinot did not second Soult with sufficient vigour,

the latter certainly did not display any great energy,
but the village was maintained by Alten's Germans,
who were good and hardy troops, and well backed
up by a great body of Portuguese. Latour Maubourg's movements seem to have been objected
to without reason. He took six guns, sabred many
Spaniards, and overthrew a whole brigade of the
British, without ceasing to keep in check their
cavalry. He was, undoubtedly, greatly superior in
numbers, but general Lumley handled the allied
squadrons with skill and courage, and drew all the
advantage possible from his situation, and, in the
choice of that situation, none can deny ability to
marshal Beresford. The rising ground behind the
horsemen, the bed of the Aroya in their front, the
aid of the horse-artillery, and the support of the
fourth division, were all circumstances of strength
so well combined that nothing could be better, and
they dictated Latour Maubourg's proceedings,
which seem consonant to true principles. If he had
charged in mass, under the fire of Lefebre's guns,
he must have been thrown into confusion in passing
the bed of the Aroya at the moment when the fourth
division, advancing along the slopes, would have
opened a musketry on his right flank; Lumley
could then have charged, or retired up the hill, according to circumstances. In this case, great loss
might have been sustained, and nothing very decisive could have accrued to the advantage of the
French, because no number of cavalry, if unsus-
tained by infantry and artillery, can make a serious
impression against the three arms united. It was
therefore another error in Soult not to have joined
some guns and infantry to his cavalry, when he
perceived that his enemy had done so on the other

part. Ten guns and half the infantry, uselessly slaughtered in columns on the height above, would have turned the scale of battle below, for it is certain that when the fuzileers came up the hill, Houghton's brigade was quite exhausted, and the few men standing were without ammunition; but if a French battery and a body of infantry had been joined to the French cavalry the fuzileers could not have moved.

On the other hand, seeing that he was not so strengthened, a repulse might have been fatal not only to himself but to the French infantry on the hill, as their left would have been open to the enterprises of the allied cavalry. If Latour Maubourg had stretched away to his own left, he would, in like manner, have exposed the flank of Soult's infantry, and his movements would have been eccentric, and contrary to sound principles; and, (in the event of a disaster to the corps on the hill, as really happened,) destructive to the safety of the retreating army. By keeping in mass on the plain, and detaching squadrons from time to time, as favourable opportunities offered for partial charges, he gained, as we have seen, great advantages during the action, and kept his troopers well in hand for the decisive moment; finally, he covered the retreat of the beaten infantry. Still it may be admitted that, with such superior numbers, he should have more closely pressed Lumley.

When Soult had regained the hills at the other side of the Albuera, the battle ceased, each side being, as we have seen, so hardly handled that neither offered to renew the fight. Here was the greatest failure of the French commander; he had lost eight thousand men, but he had still fifteen thousand under arms, his artillery and his cavalry being, comparatively, untouched. On the side of the allies, only eighteen hundred British infantry were left standing, and the troops were suffering greatly from famine; the Spaniards had been feeding on horse-flesh, and were so extenuated by continual fatigue and misery, that, for several days previous to the battle, they had deserted in considerable numbers even to the French, hoping thus to get food : these circumstances should be borne in mind, when reflecting on their conduct in the battle ; under such a commander as Blake, and, while enduring such heavy privations, it was a great effort of resolution, and honourable to them that they fought at all. Their resistance feeble, when compared to the desperate valour of the British, was by no means weak in itself or infirm; nor is it to be wondered at that men so exhausted and so ill-managed should have been deaf to the call of Beresford, a strange general, whose exhortations they probably did not understand. When the fortune of the day changed they followed the fuzileers with alacrity, and at no period did they give way with dishonour.

Nevertheless, all circumstances considered, they were not and could not be equal to a second desperate struggle ; a renewed attack on the 17th, would have certainly ended in favour of the French, and so conscious was Beresford of this, that, on the evening of the 16th, he wrote to lord Wellington, avowing that he anticipated a certain and ruinous defeat the next day. The resolution with which he maintained the position notwithstanding, was the strongest indication of military talent he gave during the whole of his operations ; had Soult

only persisted in holding his position with equal
pertinacity, Beresford must have retired. It was a
great and decided mistake of the French marshal
not to have done so. There is nothing more essential in war than a confident front ; a general should
never acknowledge himself vanquished, for the front
line of an army always looks formidable, and the
adversary can seldom see the real state of what is
behind. The importance of this maxim is finely
indicated in Livy, where he relates that, after a
drawn battle, a god called out in the night, the
Etruscans had lost one man more than the Romans !
Hereupon the former retired, and the latter, remaining on the field, gathered all the fruits of a
real victory.

PAPERS RELATING TO THE FORMER VOLUMES.

Letter from major-general F. Ponsonby to colonel Napier.

AFTER the very handsome manner in which you have mentioned my name, in your account of the battle of Talavera, it may appear extraordinary that I should trouble you with this letter; but my silence might be interpreted into the wish of taking praise to myself which I do not deserve.

The whole of your account of the charge made by general Anson's brigade is substantially correct; you have given the reason for it, and the result; but there are two points, in the detail, which are inaccurate. The first affecting the German hussars; the other respecting myself.

The Germans, on the left of the twenty-third, could not reach the French columns, from the impracticability of the ravine where they charged; this I ascertained, by personal observation, the following day; the obstacle was much less serious where the twenty-third attacked, headed by general Anson and colonel Seymour. The mountain torrent, which gradually decreased as it descended into the plain, was about thirty yards in front of the enemy, and the twenty-third, though much broken in passing this obstacle, charged up to the columns, and was repulsed, no rally could be attempted; but the right squadron, under captain Drake, having an easier passage of the ravine, and no French column immediately in front, passed through the intervals, and caused much confusion, which, together with the delay occasioned by the charge, prevented the masses of infantry which were in readiness on the French right flank, from joining in the general attack on our line.

You will perceive that this account, which I believe to be the exact truth, does not, in the slightest degree, affect the accuracy of your description of the movement; but, if I am correct, it proves that the Germans were obliged to halt by an insuperable difficulty, and that I had no particular merit in the execution of the charge of the twenty-third.

Believe me
Very sincerely yours,
F. PONSONBY.

Malta, Dec. 30, 1829.

Note sur la Situation actuelle de l'Espagne.

Rochefort, le Août, 1808.

1°. Les évènemens inattendus du général Dupont sont une preuve de plus que le succés de la guerre dépend de la prudence, de la bonne conduite, et de l'experience du général.

2°. A la seule lecture du rapport du colonel d'Affry, on avoit diviné tous les évènemens ; après une perte aussi considérable, on ne peut être surpris que le roi et les généraux jugent convenable de concentrer l'armée et d'évacuer Madrid.

En examinant avec attention, non les rapports mensongers des individus qui parlent dans leur sens, mais les faits tels qu'ils se sont passés, on est convaincu : premièrement, que le général Castaños n'avoit pas plus de vingt-cinq mille hommes de troupe de ligne et de quinze mille paysans ; un jour on sera à même de vérifier ce qui sera avancé ici. Secondement, que si le général Dupont les eut attaqués, ou se fut battû avec tout son corps réuni, il les eut complétement défaits.

3°. On pense qu'on aura tout le tems d'évacuer les blessés de Madrid qui arrivent à Aranda ; il faudra occuper aussi longtems qu'il sera possible les hauteurs de Buitrago, afin de donner le temps au maréchal Bessières de revenir de son mouvement de Gallice ; qu'il faut reorganiser la province de Burgos, les trois Biscayes, et la province de Navarre ; elles comprendront facilement que, dans ce moment plus que jamais, elles doivent rester fidèles et se bien conduire sous peine d'être traitées avec toute la rigueur de la guerre.

4°. On pense que l'armée doit être divisée en trois corps, *le corps principal*, ou de centre, où commande le roi, qu'on porteroit à 30,000 hommes campé à Aranda ; le corps de droite, du maréchal Bessières, d'environ 15 mille hommes faisant face à ce qui pourroit arriver de Gallice ou d'Estramadure, occupant Valladolid par une division, ayant une autre division intermédiaire avec le corps du centre, et une troisième division de plus sur sa droite, selon les circonstances ; enfin le *corps de gauche*, ou d'Arragon, destiné à maintenir la Navarre et le pays environnant, occupant Logrono et Tudela, et liant sa droite en corps du centre, par une division qui au besoin renforceroit ce corps et devra maintenir Soria par un corps volant.

Le corps du centre, et le corps de droite doivent s'appuyer sur Burgos, et le corps d'Arragon doit avoir son appui sur Pampelune.

5°. Pour organiser le corps du centre dans ce but, on croit

qu'on doit le renforcer de la brigade du 14me et 44me de ligne, 200 chevaux et 8 pièces de canon, qu'on tireroit du corps devant Saragosse ; de la brigade du général Mouton composée du 4me legère, 15me legère, du bataillon de Paris, et de huit pièces de canon ; de la brigade commandée par le maréchal Ney, et qui est déjà à une marche en avant de Bayonne, composée du 43me, et du 51me de ligne, du 26me de chasseurs, et de 6 pièces de canon ; enfin de 4 escadrons de marche de dragons et d'une régiment Polonais de la garde ; on réuniroit le 3me bataillon aux deux premiers de tous les régimens d'infantérie, et on méleroit les jeunes soldats aux anciens.

On évalue à environ dix mille hommes de renfort que recevroit le corps du centre, qui seroit alors composé : savoir des 18,000 qui le forment à présent··················· 18,000

Du renfort évalué à ·························· 10,000

Le détachement du dépôt du 4me legère, 15me legère.

14me, 44me, 43me, et 51me de ligne, le 2me et 12me legère rejoindront insensiblement et porteront ce corps à ·· 30,000 hommes.

Ces trente mille hommes ne sauroient être en meilleures mains, que sous les ordres du maréchal Ney, hormis une réserve de 4 à 5 mille hommes destinés à la garde du roi, et que le roi conserveroit auprès de sa personne et feroit marcher avec le général Saligny, ou avec le général Savary quand il le jugeroit nécessaire.

Le corps du centre ce tiendrait à la hauteur d'Aranda, ses communications bien assurées avec le maréchal Bessières à Valladolid, des têtes de pont bien établies à Aranda et à Valladolid. Ce corps se nourrira par Burgos, et devra non seulement maintenir la tranquillité dans cette province, mais encore assurer ses communications avec le corps de Saragosse qui occupera Tudela et Logrono.

Le corps du maréchal Bessières, fort de quinze mille hommes, devra occuper Valladolid en faisant face à ce qui arrivera d'Estramadure et de Castille, ayant ses trois divisions en échellons, et se nourrissant de la province de Valladolid, Placentia, et Leon.

On enverra le maréchal Moncey pour commander le corps du général Verdier, et on chargera le maréchal du commandement de le Biscaye et de tous les derrières.

On estime qu'on peut retirer du camp sous Saragosse le 14me et 44me de ligne, 200 chevaux, et 8 pièces de canon, le reste doit être formé en trois divisions, et destiné à maintenir la Navarre. La position de Logrono est trop près, il faut occuper au moins jusqu'à Tudela pour soumettre la Navarre, et tout ce qui bougeroit. Dans

l'ordre offensif, deux divisions peuvent se porter en marche forcée
sur l'armée.

6°. Il ne faut point faire une guerre timide, ni souffrir aucun
rassemblement armé à deux marches d'aucun corps d'armée. Si
l'ennemi s'approche, il ne faut point se laisser décourager par ce
qui s'est passé, se confier dans sa supériorité, marcher à lui et le
battre.   L'ennemi prendra lui même probablement une marche très
circonspecte : il y sera reduit du moment qu'il aura eu quelque
example.

Dans cette situation de choses, toutes les fois qu'on seroit
sérieusement attaqué par l'ennemi, on pourra lui opposer le corps
du roi, qui doit toujours être ensemble, et les deux tiers du corps
du maréchal Bessières.   Ce maréchal doit toujours tenir un tiers
de son corps, à une demi journée, un tiers à une journée du
corps du centre, et un tiers sur la droite, suivant les circonstances,
également, un tiers du corps du général Verdier doit se tenir à la
gauche du roi, pour le joindre si cela étoit nécessaire, de sorte
que dans un jour la roi puisse réunir 40 mille hommes.

7°. Il faut débuter par des coups d'éclat, qui rélèvent le moral du
soldat et qui fassent comprendre à l'habitant qu'il doit rester tranquille ; un des premiers coups le plus important à porter, et qui seroit
utile pour rélever l'opinion et compenser l'évacuation de Madrid,
seroit que la brigade du 14me et 44me qu'on rappelle de Saragosse,
aidée d'une detachement du corps du centre, soumette Soria, le
désarme, et le fasse rester tranquille.   Attaquer et culbuter tout
ce qui se présentera doit être l'instruction générale, donnée au
maréchal Bessières, au maréchal Ney, et au général Verdier, de
sorte qu'à une marche, ou à une marche et demie du corps
François, il n'y ait aucun rassemblement d'insurgés ; on est d'opinion
que si l'avant garde du général Castaños s'avance sur l'Aranda et
dépasse les montagnes de Buitrago, il faut, avec tout ce qu'on
réunira dans un jour, marcher à lui sans lui donner le tems de s'y
établir sérieusement, le culbuter, le jetter au delà des montagnes,
et si l'affaire est décisive, se reporter sur Madrid.   L'ennemi doit
essayer de déloger l'armée Française de cette position, par trois
points, par la Gallice et l'Estramadure, par la droite d'Aranda, et
enfin par les rassemblemens des provinces d'Arragon, de Valence,
et autres de Castille.   Toutes ces combinaisons sont difficiles à
l'ennemi, et si on dissipe ces rassemblemens à mesure qu'ils se
formeront sur tous les points et qu'on les tienne à distance d'une
ou deux marches du cantonnement François, si alternativement

les François prennent l'offensive, tantôt à leur droite, en renforçant
le maréchal Bessières, pendant que le centre se tiendra dans une
bonne position derrière la rivière, et à l'abri de toute attaque;
tantôt au centre avec le corps du roi, les deux tiers du corps
de droite, et un tiers du corps de gauche, l'ennemi sera bientôt
obligé à la plus grande circonspection.

8°. On auroit pu aussi conserver Madrid en renforçant le
corps qui s'y trouve, du 14me et 44me de ligne, de la brigade du
général Mouton, de celle du général Le Fevbre, qui en dernier
lieu a été renvoyée au maréchal Bessières, et enfin du renfort
qu' amène le maréchal Ney. On auroit ainsi renforcé le corps
de Madrid de plus de 14 mille hommes, et il est douteux que
l'ennemi eut voulu se mesurer avec des forces aussi considérables
et s'exposer à une perte certaine.

9°. Si de fortes raisons obligoient d'évacuer Aranda, on per-
droit l'espoir de rétablir ses communications avec le Portugal.
Dans le cas où un évènement quelconque porteroit à évacuer le
Duero et à se concentrer sur Burgos pour se réunir là avec
le maréchal Bessières, le corps du général Verdier peut
communiquer par l'Ebre, et avoir toujours son mouvement
isolé pour maintenir la Navarre, contenir l'Arragon, tous les
rassemblemens de ce côté, et protéger la route principale. Pendant
cet intervalle des renforts journaliers arriveront à l'armée, jusqu'
à ce qu'enfin les divisions de la grande armée qui sont en marche,
soient sur les Pyrenées.

On a recommandé de tous tems le petit fort de Pancorvo.
Il est necessaire de l'occuper, même quand on ne garderoit pas
la ligne de l'Ebre, c'est une vedette d'autant plus utile qu'elle
domine la plaine, et seroit un obstacle si jamais l'ennemi s'en
emparoit.*

10°. La troisième position qui se présente à l'armée, c'est la
gauche à Pampelune, et la droite sur Vittoria, maintenant ainsi
ses communications avec les places importantes de St. Sebastien
et de Pampelune. Au reste toutes ces notes peuvent difficilement
être de quelque utilité, les évènemens modifient nécessairement
les dispositions, tout dépend d'ailleurs de saisir un moment.

11°. Résumé. Le premier but est de se maintenir à Madrid
si cela est possible.

---

* [Note in Napoleon's own hand.] On ne doit pas oublier qu'en approchant
de France tout favourise la desertion.

Le second, de maintenir ses communications avec le Portugal en occupant la ligne du Duero.

Le troisième, de conserver l'Ebre.

Le quatrième de conserver ses communications avec Pampelune et St. Sebastien afin que la grande armée arrivant, on puisse en peu de tems culbuter et anéantir tous les révoltés.

LIEUT.-GEN. BERTRAND.

Rochefort, 6 *Août,* 1808.

APPENDIX.

APPENDIX.

No. 1.

SECTION 1.—GENERAL STATE OF THE FRENCH ARMY IN THE PENINSULA, EXTRACTED FROM THE IMPERIAL MUSTER ROLLS.

King Joseph commanding, 1st Oct. 1809.

Present under arms.		Detached.		Absent.		Effective.	Horses.	
Men.	Horses.	Men.	Horses.	Hospital.	Prison.	Men.	Cavalry.	Draught.
180,814	28,091	10,407	3,165	46,109	4,124	237,330	23,196	8,060
				Deduct for the governments....		10,407	3,165	
				Real total....		226,927	28,091	

15th July, 1810.

273,403	52,336	29,462	7,846	47,107	4,915	349,972	41,848	18,334
		In march to join						
6,121	736	,,	,,	636	,,	6,757		736
279,524	53,072	29,462	7,846	47,743	4,915	356,729		60,918

15th August, 1810.

279,639	52,063	25,340	6,017	46,982	5,995	351,961	41,446	16,634
In march to join						1,957	681	511
Total effective in Spain......353,918							43,127	17,145
Troops destined for Spain, quartered on the frontier................................ 16,006							1,447	,,
Grand total.................... 369,924							43,574	17,145

Note.—By this state it appears that allowance being made for casualties, the re-inforcements for Spain, in consequence of the peace with Austria, were not less than one hundred and fifty thousand men.

15th Jan. 1811.

Present under arms.		Detached.		Absent.	Effective.	Horses.	
Men.	Horses.	Men.	Horses.	Hospital.	Men.	Cavalry.	Draught.
295,227	52,462	17,780	4,714	48,831	361,838	41,189	15,987

15th April, 1811.

276,575	46,990	15,121	2,166	40,079	331,776	37,855	11,301

These states shew a decrease of nearly thirty thousand men in three months. During this period the siege of Badajos, the retreat of Massena, the battles of the Gebora, Barrosa, and Fuentes Onoro took place. Hence, if the deaths in hospital be added to the losses sustained in those operations we shall find that, at the period of its greatest activity, the Guerilla system was more harassing than destructive to the French army.

SECTION 2.—STATE OF THE ARMY OF PORTUGAL.

April, 1810.—Head-quarter Caceres. Massena, Prince of Esling, commanding.

	Under arms.		Detached.		Hospital.	Prisoners.	Effective.	Horses.	
	Men.	Horses.	Men.	Horses.	Men.	Men.	Men.	Cavalry.	Draught.
2d corps d'armee	18,372	4,449	1,119	132	1,628	7	21,126	3,520	1,061
6th Ditto	33,759	10,159	496	110	5,086	349	39,690	3,140	3,129
8th Ditto	28,045	7,070	25	,,	5,976	99	34,145	5,312	1,758
Total active army	80,176	21,678	1,640	242	12,690	455	94,961	15,972	5,948
Imperial guards	17,380	3,800	174	15	733	,,	18,287	2,831	954
Province of St. Ander	13,464	752	276	,,	1,774	377	15,891	15,752	,,
Province of Valladolid	4,509	124	123	,,	859	145	6,136	,,	126
Total under Massena's command	116,029	26,254	2,213	257	16,056	977	135,275	19,555	7,056

15th May, 1810.

	Under arms.		Detached.		Hospital.	Prisoners.	Effective.	Horses.	
Etat major et gens-d'arme	229	241	,,	,,	,,	,,	229	241	,,
2d corps Reynier	16,903	2,921	992	231	1,337	42	19,232	2,186	966
6th do. Ney	28,883	5,421	1,224	964	4,940	357	35,067	2,152	4,233
8th do. Junot	30,782	4,228	7	30	5,642	75	2,643	2,142	2,116
Reserve of cavalry. Montbrun	4,776	4,851	246	189	95	,,	5,117	5,040	11
Total active army	71,573	17,662	2,489	1,414	12,014	474	86,076	11,761	7,315

15th August, 1810.

	Under arms.		Detached.		Hospital.	Prisoners.	Effective.	Horses.	
Etat major, &c.	199	222	,,	,,	3	,,	202	222	,,
2d corps	16,418	2,894	2,494	397	3,006	,,	21,918	1,969	1,304
6th corps	23,456	2,496	1,865	577	5,541	193	30,862	1,701	1,372
8th corps	18,803	1,959	436	169	4,996	98	24,235	2,016	1,112
Reserve of cavalry	4,146	4,322	1,138	831	157	31	5,441	4,907	246
Artillerie et genie et du siege	2,724	2,969	206	159	409	,,	3,339	108	3,128
Total active army	65,746	15,862	6,139	2,119	14,112	302	85,997	10,815	7,162
6th Government Valladolid. Division Serras	12,693	3,045	639	20	1,775	641	15,107	2,931	134
Asturias et St. Ander. Bonet	12,913	,,	1,394	15	1,578	107	14,885	434	,,
Total under Massena	91,352	18,907	8,172	2,154	17,465	1,050	115,989	13,746	7,296
9th corps, Drouet Comte D'Erlon	19,144	2,436	24	,,	3,147	,,	22,315	2,436	,,
General Total	110,496	21,343	8,196	2,154	20,612	1,050	138,304	16,616	7,296

Army of Portugal, 27th September, 1810. The 9th corps to the 15th October.

The reserve of cavalry, and the artillery of siege to the 1st September only.

	Under arms.		Detached.		Hospital.	Effective.	Horses.	
	Men.	Horses.	Men.	Horses.	Men.	Men.	Cavalry.	Draught.
Etat major	192	219	,,	,,	4	196	219	,,
2d corps	16,575	2,921	2,397	287	2,214	21,186	1,872	1,336
6th do.	23,224	2,478	1,708	600	5,418	30,350	1,730	1,348
8th do.	18,807	2,958	663	140	4,656	24,126	2,027	1,071
Reserve of cavalry	4,146	4,322	1,138	831	157	5,441	4,907	246
Artilleries of siege	3,022	3,115	206	159	409	3,637	146	3,128
Battalion of march which quitted Bayonne the 22 of October	,,	,,	474	16	,,	474	16	,,
Total	65,966	16,013	6,586	2,033	12,858	85,410	10,917	7,129
9th corps	19,062	2,072	413	,,	3,516	22,991	1,755	317
Division Serras	8,586	1,015	269	35	1,750	10,605	1,050	,,
Grand Total	93,614	19,100	7,268	2,068	18,124	119,006	13,722	7,446

Army of Portugal—1st January, 1811.

Head-quarters, Torres Novas.

2d Corps, Head-quarters, Santarem.

	Under Arms.		Detached.		Hospital.	Effective.	Horses.	
	Men.	Horses.	Men.	Horses.	Men.	Men.	Cavalry.	Draught.
Merle's division, 9 battalions.........	4,368	,,	150	,,	1,549	6,067	,,	,,
Heudelet's do. 12 do.	5,718	,,	451	,,	2,646	8,815	,,	,,
Lt. cavalry, Soult, 15 squadrons......	1,146	993	523	537	231	1,900	1,530	,,
Artillery and engineers	1,284	1,121	52	9	189	1,425	112	1,018
Total	12,516	2,114	1,176	546	4,515	18,207	1,642	1,018

6th Corps, Thomar.

	Under Arms.		Detached.		Hospital.	Effective.	Horses.	
	Men.	Horses.	Men.	Horses.	Men.	Men.	Cavalry.	Draught.
Marchand, 11 battalions	4,987	28	529	,,	1,121	6,637	28	,,
Mermet's 11 do.	6,252	,,	743	,,	1,077	8,104	,,	,,
Loison, 12 do.	4,589	,,	1,037	,,	3,291	8,917	,,	,,
Light cavalry, Lamotte, 7 squadrons...............	652	651	663	663	117	1,432	1,314	,,
Artillery and engineers, 28 companies	1.769	1,372	47	78	165	1,981	52	1,398
Total	18,272	2,051	3,019	741	5,771	27,094	1,394	1,398

8th Corps, Pernes.

	Under Arms.		Detached.		Hospital.	Effective.	Horses.	
	Men.	Horses.	Men.	Horses.	Men.	Men.	Cavalry.	Draught.
Clausel, 11 battalions	4,007	18	484	,,	3,989	8,627	18	,,
Solignac, 14 do.	4,997	,,	1,953	,,	3,337	10,346	,,	,,
St.Croix'sdragoons, 12 squadrons......	981	1,024	698	698	238	1,917	1,722	,,
Artillery and engineers	1,106	859	24	4	359	1,522	151	712
On leave..............	,,	,,	,,	,,	,,	206	,,	,,
Total.............	11,108	1,901	3,159	702	7,956	22,605	1,191	712

Montbrun, Ourem.

	Under Arms.		Detached.		Hospital.	Effective.	Horses.	
	Men.	Horses.	Men.	Horses.	Men.	Men.	Cavalry.	Draught.
Reserve of cavalry 24 squadrons with artillery	2,729	2,871	1,486	1,466	178	4,533	4,337	
Artillery, engineers, and equipage of the army	1,546	614	,,	,,	283	2,090	614	

9th Corps, Leiria.

	Under Arms.		Detached.		Hospital.	Effective.	Horses.	
	Men.	Horses.	Men.	Horses.	Men.	Men.	Cavalry.	Draught.
Claparede, 15 battalions, Almeida	7,863	11	369	,,	482	8,714	,,	
Couroux, 12 battalions, Leiria. ..	7,592	27	447	,,	1,299	9,338	27	
Fournier's cavalry, 7 squadrons at Toro...............	1,698	1,591	60	67	114	1,872	1,658	
Artillery and engineers, Ciudad Rodrigo............	670	464	,,	72	742	,,	464	
Total	17,823	2,093	876	139	2,637	19,924	2,149	

Note.—Salamanca constituted a government containing the towns of Alba de Tormes, Penaranda, and Salamanca, in which were deposited the sick men, stragglers, equipages, and depôts, of the army of Portugal. The total amounting to 2,354 men and 1,102 horses.

	Present under arms.	
	Men.	Horses.
General Total of the army of Portugal in the position of Santarem	46,171	9,551
9th Corps	17,823	2,093
	63,994	11,644
Deduct troops of the 9th corps not in Portugal ..	10,231	2,066
Real number under Massena..........	53,763	9,578

Army of Portugal—1st April, 1811.

	Under arms.		Detached.		Hospital.	Effective.	Horses.
	Men.	Horses.	Men.	Horses.	Men.	Men.	
8th corps, Junot...............	13,448	,,	992	,,	5,719	20,159	,,
6th do. Marmont...............	13,984	,,	1,374	,,	1,576	16,934	,,
2d corps, Reynier	10,837	,,	1,350	,,	4,318	16,505	,,
Mont- Dragoon, 23 squadrons	4,173	4,404	,,	,,	,,	4,173	4,404
brun. Light cavalry, 14 squadrons..........	3,636	3,906	,,	,,	38	3,636	3,906
1 squadron of gens-d'armes	190	72	,,	,,	5	102	72

	Under arms.		Detached.		Hospital.	Effective.	Horses.
	Men.	Horses.	Men.	Horses.	Men.	Men.	
Artil. Foot artillery. {Almeida & Rodrigo.}	956	,,	,,	,,	88	1,055	,,
lery Horse artillery............	410	425	,,	,,	23	453	425
and Artillery of the train	2,181	2,378	,,	,,	237	2,448	2,378
Engi- Workmen	259	,,	,,	,,	25	295	,,
neers. Engineers................	1,448	60	,,	,,	140	1,623	,,
Military equipage........	596	897	,,	,,	60	668	897
Total artilleries, engineers &c...	5,969	3,395	,,	,,	573	6,542	2,760
Total of infantry 37,269		,,	3,716	,,	11,613	53,598	,,
Total of cavalry	7,999	8,382	,,	,,	43	7,911	8,382
General Total............... 51,237		11,717	3,716	,,	12,229	68,051	11,142

Note.—In the imperial rolls there was no state of the army of Portugal for May. Two divisions of the 9th corps, directed to be added to the army of Portugal, are included in the state for April, and the prince of Esling was empowered to distribute the cavalry as he pleased, provided the brigade of general Fournier, from the 9th corps, was kept in the reserve. The detached men were in the government of Salamanca. On the 1st of June, however, the army of Portugal is returned as present under arms 44,548 men, 7,253 horses, and 4,620 men detached. Hence, I have estimated the number of fighting men and officers, including the imperial guards, at Fuentes Onoro at 45,000, a number, perhaps, too great, when the artificers, engineers, &c. are deducted.

SECTION 3.—ARMY OF THE SOUTH—SOULT, DUKE OF DALMATIA, COMMANDING.

	Under arms.		Detached.		Hospital.	Effective.	Horses.	
	Men.	Horses.	Men.	Horses.	Men.	Men.	Cavalry.	Draught.
1st of January........	55,602	12,092	5,744	1,999	6,412	67,758	10,868	3,223
15th of May..........	75,133	13,124	3,915	1,336	11,420	90,468	12,156	2,304
Deduct the troops of the 9th corps in march from the north........	11,917	1,619	,,	,,	,,	13,310	1,220	399
Real total of the army of the South ..	63,216	11,505	3,915	1,336	11,420	77,158	10,936	1,905

SECTION 4.

5th Corps, 15th January.

Under arms.		Detached.	
Men.	Horses.	Men.	Horses.
18,766	**6,158**	**3,035**	**640**

16th December, 1810, le Duc de Dalmatie va faire le siège de Badajos, avec tout le 5ᵉᵐ corps d'armée, 8 regimens de cavalerie, formant 2,600 chevaux pris dans les 1ᵉʳᵉ et 5ᵉᵐ corps d'armée sous les ordres de général Latour Maubourg, 900 hommes du 63ᵉᵐ regiment de ligne, 2 compagnies d'artillerie légère, 4 compagnies de sappeurs, 1 compagnie de mineurs, et trois escadrons de cavalerie Espagnol.

SECTION 5.

1st Corps before Cadiz.

	Under arms.		Detached.		Hospital.	Effective.	Horses.	
	Men.	Horses.	Men.	Horses.	Men.	Men.	Cavalry.	Train.
15th February, 1811 ..	20,572	1,886	1,331	681	1,254	23,457	1,495	1,072
Reinforcement on the march from the Governments	5,209	775	,,	,,	743	5,952	712	62
Total	25,781	2,661	1,331	681	1,997	29,409	2,207	1,035
4th corps, 15th Feb. ..	16,703	4,007	741	397	1,699	19,143	3,612	792
Reinforcement on the march from the Governments............	6,620	1,457	,,	,,	878	6,854	1,451	,,
Total............	22,723	5,464	741	397	2,577	25,993	5,069	793

Note.—A reinforcement of more than one thousand men likewise joined the 5th corps while in front of Badajos.

SECTION 6.—ARMY OF THE NORTH—BESSIERES, DUKE OF ISTRIA, COMMANDING.

	Under arms.		Detached.	Hospital.	Effective.	Horses.	
	Men.	Horses.	Men.	Men.	Men.	Cavalry.	Train.
1st February, 1811	58,515	8,874	1,992	6,860	67,767	7,979	1,073
15th April, 1811..........	53,148	6,930	2,221	5,350	60,719	6,065	879

SECTION 7.—ARMÉE IMPÉRIALE DU MIDI DE L'ESPAGNE 1me CORPS.

Situation des présens sous les armes à l'époque du 22d Mars 1811.

Designation des Regimens, Division.	Etat des presens sous les armes.	Dans les Forts et Redoutes.	Emplacement des Troupes dans les Forts et Redoutes.	Disposables.	
1	9me Infantrie ligne	1,000		....	1,000	Sta Maria.
	24me do. do.	800	400	Depuis et compris le Fort St. Catherine jusqu'au Rio St. Petro.....	400	Do,
	96me do. do.	1,100		....	1,100	Do. San Lucar, Esta, Chipiona [la Viala Atta.
	16me do. do.	350	350	Xeres et la Cartuxa............	....	
2	8me do. do.	713		....	713	Port Reale au Trocadero.
	45me do. do.	1,072	744	Depuis et compris le Fort Napoleon jusqu'à Chiese fe	328	Port Reale.
	54me do. do.	820		....	820	Chiclana.
	Bataillon d'Elite	236		....	236	Do.
3	27me Infantrie ligne	1,400		....	1,400	Do.
	63me do. do.	845		....	845	Porte Reale.
	94me do. do.	1,500	650	Depuis et compris la Redoute jusqu'à cette de Vellati...........	850	Chiclana.
Régiment de Marine	95me do. do.	1,414	472	Arcos, Medina, Vejer, et Conil	942	Do.
	43me Battalions de marine	900	900	Au Trocadero		
	2e do. d'Ouvriers do.	615	615	Do.		
Cavalerie.	5e Chasseurs	320		....	320	Vejer et Conil.
	1e de Dragoons	230	50	De Montesa, Alcazar de Xeres	180	Xeres.
	2e do. do.	218	72	Do. et à la Cartuxa	146	Arcos.
	à pied à Cheval	678	500	Sur la ligne du Blocus........	178	Santa Maria, Puerto Reale, et [Chiclana.
Artillerie.	Sapeurs	323	323	Au Trocadero		
	Mineurs	77	77	Do.		
		14,611	5,153		9,458	

By this return, which is not extracted from the imperial rolls, but was found amongst colonel Lejeune's intercepted papers, it appears that Victor had above nine thousand disposable troops seventeen days after the battle of Barosa. He must, therefore, have had about eleven thousand disposable before that action, and Cassagne's detachment being deducted leaves about nine thousand disposable for the battle.

SECTION 8.—STATE OF THE BRITISH AND GERMAN TROOPS ON THE COA, 25TH APRIL, 1811, EXTRACTED FROM THE ADJUTANT-GENERAL'S RETURNS.

	Under arms. Men.	Sick. Men.	Detached. Men.
Cavalry 4 regiments............	1,525	274	542
Infantry 41 battalions	20,700	8,880	3,214
Artillery....................	1,378	144	1,156
Total of all arms......	23,613	9,298	4,912

Guns....24 British, 18 Portuguese ......Total 42

Note.—There are no separate returns of the army engaged in the battle of Fuentes Onoro. Hence, the above is only an approximation to the numbers of British and German troops; but if the Portuguese and the Partida of Julian Sanchez be added, the whole number in line will be about thirty-five thousand men of all arms.

No. II.

EXTRACTS OF LETTERS FROM LORD WELLINGTON TO LORD LIVERPOOL.

SECTION 1.

" *November* 30, 1809.

" I enclose copies and extracts of a correspondence which I have had with Mr. Frere on the subject of the co-operation of the British army with the corps of the duke of Albuquerque and the duke Del Parque in this plan of diversion.

" Adverting to the opinion which I have given to his majesty's ministers and the ambassador at Seville, it will not be supposed that I could have encouraged the advance of general Areizaga, or could have held out the prospect of any co-operation by the British army.

" The first official information which I had from the government of the movement of general Areizaga was on the 18th, the day before his defeat, and I gave the answer on the 19th regarding the plan of which I now enclose a copy.

" I was at Seville, however, when the general commenced his march from the Sierra Morena, and in more than one conversation

with the Spanish ministers and members of the Junta, I communicated to them my conviction that general Areizaga would be defeated. The expectation, however, of success from this large army, stated to consist of fifty thousand men, was so general and so sanguine that the possibility of disappointment was not even contemplated, and, accordingly, your lordship will find that, on the 10th only, the government began to think it necessary to endeavour to make a diversion in favour of general Areizaga, and it is probable that it was thought expedient to make this diversion only in consequence of the fall of the general's own hopes, after his first trial with the enemy on the night of the 10th instant."—
" I am anxious to cross the Tagus with the British army and to station it on the frontiers of Old Castile, from thinking that the point in which I can be of most use in preventing the enemy from effecting any important object, and which best answers for my future operations in the defence of Portugal. With this view, I have requested Mr. Frere to urge the government to reinforce the duke D'Albuquerque's corps, in order to secure the passage of the lower part of the Tagus. And, although the state of the season would render it desirable that I should make the movement at an early period, I do not propose to make it till I shall see most clearly the consequences of that defeat, and some prospect that the city of Seville will be secure after I shall move."

SECTION 2.

" *December* 7, 1809.
" ——— I had urged the Spanish government to augment the army of the duke D'Albuquerque to twenty thousand men, in order that it might occupy, in a sufficient manner, the passage of the Tagus at Almaraz and the passes through the mountains leading from Arzobispo to Truxillo, in which position they would have covered effectually the province of Estremadura, during the winter at least, and would have afforded time and leisure for preparations for farther opposition to the enemy, and I delayed the movement, which I have long been desirous of making, to the northward of the Tagus, till the reinforcements could be sent to the duke D'Albuquerque which I had lately recommended should be drawn from the army of the duke Del Parque. During the discussions upon the subject, the government have given orders to the duke D'Albuquerque to retire with his corps behind the Guadiana, to a

position which he cannot maintain, thus leaving open the road into Estremadura, and incurring the risk of the loss of that province whenever the enemy choose to take possession of it."

SECTION 3.

"*January* 31, 1810.

" ———— There is no doubt that, if the enemy's reinforcements have not yet entered Spain, and are not considerably advanced within the Spanish frontiers, the operation which they have undertaken is one of some risk, and I have maturely considered of the means of making a diversion in favour of the allies, which might oblige the enemy to reduce his force in Andalusia, and would expose him to risk and loss in this quarter. But the circumstances, which are detailed in the enclosed copy of a letter to Mr. Frere, have obliged me to refrain from attempting this operation at present. I have not, however, given up all thoughts of it, and I propose to carry it into execution hereafter, if circumstances will permit."

SECTION 4.

"*January* 12, 1811.

" My former despatch will have informed your lordship that I was apprehensive that the Spanish troops in Estremadura would not make any serious opposition to the progress which it was my opinion the enemy would attempt to make in that province; but as they had been directed to destroy the bridges on the Guadiana, at Merida and Medellin, and preparations had been ordered for that purpose, and to defend the passage of the Guadiana as long as was practicable, I was in hopes that the enemy would have been delayed at least for some days before he should be allowed to pass that river. But I have been disappointed in that expectation, and the town and bridge of Merida appear to have been given up to an advanced guard of cavalry."

SECTION 5.

"*January* 19, 1811.

" At the moment when the enemy entered Estremadura from

Seville general Ballasteros received an order from the Regency, dated the 21st December last, directing him to proceed with the troops under his command into the Condada de Niebla. The force in Estremadura was thus diminished by one-half, and the remainder are considered insufficient to attempt the relief of the troops in Olivenza."

" The circumstances which I have above related will show your lordship that the military system of the Spanish nation is not much improved, and that it is not very easy to combine or regulate operations with corps so ill organised, in possession of so little intelligence, and upon whose actions so little reliance can be placed. It will scarcely be credited that the first intelligence which general Mendizabal received of the assembly of the enemy's troops at Seville was from hence ; and if any combination was then made, either for retreat or defence, it was rendered useless, or destroyed by the orders from the Regency, to detach general Ballasteros into the Condado de Niebla, which were dated the 21st of December, the very day on which Soult broke up from Cadiz, with a detachment of infantry, and marched to Seville."

SECTION 6.

" *February* 2, 1811.

" The various events of the war will have shown your lordship that no calculation can be made on the result of any operation in which the Spanish troops are engaged. But if the same number of troops of any other nation (ten thousand) were to be employed on this operation, (the opening the communication with Badajos,) I should have no doubt of their success, or of their ability to prevent the French from attacking Badajos with the forces which they have now employed on this service."

SECTION 7.

" *February* 9, 1811.

" General Mendizabal has not adhered to the plan which was ordered by the late marquess De la Romana, which provided for the security of the communication with Elvas before the troops should be thrown to the left of the Guadiana. I don't believe that the strength of the enemy, on either side of the Guadiana, is accurately known, but if they should be in strength on the right of that river, it is to be apprehended that the whole of the troops will be shut up in Badajos, and I have reason to believe that this place is entirely unprovided with provisions, notwithstanding that the siege of it has been expected for the last year."

SECTION 8.

"*February* 23, 1811.

" Although experience has taught me to place no reliance upon the effect of the exertions of the Spanish troops, notwithstanding the frequent instances of their bravery, I acknowledge that this recent disaster has disappointed and grieved me much. The loss of this army and its probable consequences, the fall of Badajos, have materially altered the situation of the allies in this part of the Peninsula, and it will not be an easy task to place them in the situation in which they were, much less in that in which they would have been, if the misfortune had not occurred. I am concerned to add to this melancholy history, that the Portuguese brigade of cavalry did not behave much better than the other troops. Brigadier-general Madden did every thing in his power to induce them to charge, but in vain." " The operations of the Guerillas continue throughout the interior; and I have proofs that the political hostility of the people of Spain towards the enemy is increasing rather than diminishing. But I have not yet heard of any measure being adopted to supply the regular funds to pay and support an army, or to raise one."

SECTION 9.

"*March* 21, 1811.

" It (Campo Mayor) had been given over to the charge of the marquis of Romana, at his request, last year. But, lately, the Spanish garrison had been first weakened and then withdrawn, in a manner not very satisfactory to me, nor consistent with the honourable engagements to defend the place into which the marquis entered when it was delivered over to his charge. I am informed, however, that marshal Bessieres has collected at Zamora about seven thousand men, composed principally of the imperial guard, and of troops taken from all the garrisons in Castile. He

thus threatens an attack upon Gallicia, in which province there
are, I understand, sixteen thousand men under general Mahi;
but, from all I hear, I am apprehensive that that general will
make no defence, and that Gallicia will fall into the hands of the
enemy."

SECTION 10.

" *May* 7, 1811.

" Your lordship will have observed, in my recent reports of
the state of the Portuguese force, that their numbers are much
reduced, and I don't know what measure to recommend which
will have the effect of restoring them. All measures recommended
to the existing government in Portugal are either rejected, or are
neglected, or are so executed as to be of no use whatever; and
the countenance which the prince regent of Portugal has given to
the governors of the kingdom, who have uniformly manifested this
spirit of opposition to every thing proposed for the increase of the
resources of the government and the amelioration of their military
system, must tend to aggravate these evils. The radical defect,
both in Spain and Portugal, is want of money to carry on the
ordinary operations of the government, much more to defray the
expenses of such a war as that in which we are engaged."

" I have not received the consent of Castaños and Blake to
the plan of co-operation which I proposed for the siege of Badajos;
and I have been obliged to write to marshal Beresford to desire
him to delay the siege till they will positively promise to act as
therein specified, or till I can go to him with a reinforcement from
hence."

" Depend upon it that Portugal should be the foundation of all
your operations in the Peninsula, of whatever nature they may be,
upon which point I have never altered my opinion. If they are
to be offensive, and Spain is to be the theatre of them, your commander must be in a situation to be entirely independent of all
Spanish authorities; by which means alone he will be enabled to
draw some resources from the country and some assistance from
the Spanish armies."

*Extract of a Letter from Mr. Stuart to Lord Wellesley,
relative to Disputes with the Patriarch and Souza.*

" *Sept.* 8, 1810.

" I could have borne all this with patience, if not accompanied by a direct proposal that the fleet and transports should quit the Tagus, that the Regency should send an order to marshal Beresford to dismiss his quarter-master-general and military secretary, followed by a reflection on the persons composing the family of that officer, and by hints to the same purpose respecting the Portuguese who are attached to lord Wellington."

SECTION 12.

Letter from sir J. Moore to major-general M'Kenzie, commanding in Portugal.

Salamanca, 29*th November,* 1808.

SIR,

The armies of Spain, commanded by generals Castaños and Blake, the one in Biscay and the other in Arragon, have been beaten and dispersed. This renders my junction with sir David Baird's corps impracticable, but if it were, I cannot hope, with the British alone, to withstand the formidable force which France has brought against this country; and there is nothing else now in Spain to make head against it.

I have ordered sir David Baird to fall back on Coruña, re-embark, and proceed to the Tagus; I myself, with the corps which marched from Lisbon, mean to retire by Ciudad Rodrigo or Almeida, and, by taking up such positions as offer, endeavour to defend, for a time, the frontier of Portugal, and cover Lisbon. But, looking forward that this cannot be done for any considerable time against superior numbers, it becomes necessary for me to give you this notice, that you may embark the stores of the army, keeping on shore as little as possible that may impede a re-embarkation of the whole army both now with you and that which I am bringing.

We shall have great difficulties on the frontier for subsistence;

colonel Murray wrote on this subject to colonel Donkin yesterday, that supplies might be sent for us to Abrantes and Coimbra. Some are already at Oporto, and more may be sent. I have desired sir D. Baird, if he has with him a victualler, of small draft of water, to send her there. On the subject of provisions the commissary-general will write more in detail, and I hope you will use your influence with the government of Portugal to secure its aid and assistance. It will be right to consider with the Portuguese officers and engineers what points may be immediately strengthened and are most defensible, and what use you can make of the troops with you to support me in my defence of the frontiers, and I shall be glad to hear from you upon this subject. I cannot yet determine the line I shall take up, but generally it will be Almeida, Guarda, Belmonte, Baracal, Celerico, Viseu. The Portuguese, on their own mountains, can be of much use, and I should hope, at any rate, that they will defend the Tras os Montes. Mr. Kennedy will probably write to Mr. Erskine, who now had better remain at Lisbon; but, if he does not write to him, this, together with colonel Murray's letter to colonel Donkin, will be sufficient for you and Mr. Erskine to take means for securing to us not only a supply of biscuit and salt provisions, but the supplies of the country for ourselves and horses, &c. In order to alarm as little as possible, it may be said that more troops are expected from England, to join us through Portugal: this will do at first, but gradually the truth will, of course, be known. I am in great want of money, and nothing else will secure the aid of the country.

I have the honour to be, &c.

J. MOORE.

P.S. Elvas should be provisioned.

No. III.

EXTRACTS FROM THE CORRESPONDENCE OF VARIOUS PERSONS RELATIVE TO CADIZ.

SECTION 1.

Extract of a Letter from Mr. C. B. Vaughan, Secretary of Legation at Cadiz, to Mr. C. Stuart.

" *March* 6, 1810.

" I received your letter of 22d February. It was indeed time that a little common sense should be substituted in that country (Portugal) for that supreme humbug with which the Portuguese have hitherto been treated."*

" When the French *passed the Morena*, 20th January, the Supreme Junta gave orders for the Provincial Juntas to *provide for the defence of the provinces, and permitted the demolition of the forts commanding the bay of Cadiz ;* at the same time the Junta stole away from Seville for Isla de Leon. Romana and Bartholomew Frere remained till 24th January, Seville being in commotion, demanding that the Supreme Junta should be abolished. Montijo and Palafox released from prison,] and the former sent an order to Romana to appear before the revolutionary junta. He was desired to take the command of Seville ; according to B. Freres' account a most perilous post, as the people had no arms. Why was this fact not known after the defeat of Ocaña ? And why also were the immense stores of cannon, ammunition, &c. &c., accumulated at Seville, not moved to Cadiz. Romana, to avoid the defence of Seville, got appointed to bring down Del Parque's army to the defence of the city, and the people appointed a military junta, namely, Castaños, Montijo, Palafox, and Romana.

Frere set off for Cadiz, and at Xeres found the *president, vice-president*, and Cornel, imprisoned by order of the people of Seville. January 26th, the authority of the Supreme Junta of Seville was disavowed at Cadiz, and a junta of defence elected, and on the 30th the Supreme Junta assembled to nominate a

---

* This refers to Mr. Canning's system of diplomacy.

regency, namely, Castaños, Escano, Savaaedra, bishop of Orense, and Lardizabal, a deputy to the Cortes recently arrived from Mexico. 3d. Cadiz saved from being surprised by the French by the arrival of Albuquerque. 4th. The French appeared at the bridge of Zuazo."—" I never felt so little hope of Spanish independence as at this moment. It is not the rapid advance of the French into Andalusia that makes me despair, but *the manner in which they have been received by the people.* Seville, Cordoba, Jaen, Grenada, and Malaga surrendered to them without firing a shot, by the inhabitants, Joseph Buonaparte studiously endeavouring to profit from this dispirited state of the people to conciliate them. Three thousand Spaniards, well paid, well clothed, and well fed, *at this moment doing duty at Seville in his service;* while upon this last spot of ground that remains, a government has been established professing indeed to act upon very different principles to the last, but without having yet accomplished one single act that can tend to procure them the confidence of the people; protected by a Spanish force, wretchedly clothed, their pay in arrear to an immense amount, and by no means well fed. We now hear of disciplining an army, but very little has been done towards it since the arrival of the troops in the Sota. Depend upon it *Cadiz must be defended by the English.*"

SECTION 2.

Mr. C. B. Vaughan to Mr. C. Stuart.

" *Cadiz, March* 28, 1810.

" The quarrel between the duke of Albuquerque and the Junta has ended. The duke is going to England on a special mission, and Whittingham proposes to go with him. Depend upon it they will do their best to get out to South America. But the duke is so weak a man, so hasty, and so much the dupe of others, that I cannot think it prudent to give him any assistance in such views."

SECTION 3.

Mr. C. B. Vaughan to Mr. C. Stuart.

" The pontoon ran upon the French coast with 34 staff-officers, 337 officers, and 348 soldiers, French prisoners of war. The boats were under the *beastly* necessity of firing into her, while the poor devils were attempting to escape, and at last she was set fire to before all the prisoners had been able to get ashore. To me this is a most disgusting event in war; there were also eleven officers' wives on board !

General Graham to Mr. Stuart.

" *May* 18, 1810.

" You will hear of the escape of a great number of French officers by the pontoon. They were confined in going adrift in a gale the other night."—" The Spaniards are very angry, and *regret that this hulk was not set on fire before the prisoners got on shore.* I am afraid our gun-boats fired into her, but I was glad to hear that our officer of artillery at Puntales, who had the care of the upper batteries, (where the only two guns of the fort that could be brought to bear on the hulk were,) refused to fire on the poor devils, *many of them most unjustly confined since the battle of Baylen!*

Mr. Vaughan to Mr. Stuart.

" *June* 2, 1810.

" Another pontoon went on shore a few days ago, on the French side of the bay. It was the hospital-ship, and so severe a fire was kept up on it *by our boats* that few of the prisoners escaped, and many were burned to death when the hulk took fire. I like not such scenes, but we always continue to get the greatest possible share of odium for the least possible good!"

SECTION 4.

Extract from the Correspondence of an Officer of Engineers employed at Cadiz.

" *May* 7, 1810.

" We have at last broke ground for some works, but I am

almost at a loss to explain to you the cause of our delay. The
truth is, we left England so ill provided with tools and other
requisites for beginning works that till lately it has been positively
impossible to commence, even on a small scale, from our own
resources and number of men. These facts, with the backward-
ness of the Spaniards to contribute either stores or workmen to
the general cause, has kept us so long inactive. We have
now one thousand three hundred men at work, and the Board of
Ordnance has supplied us with more tools."

SECTION 5.

" *Isla, June* 1, 1810.

" We might defy the power of France to expel us by force
from hence if all were done that might be done, or even what is
projected, but we have only British troops at work on this important position, and our numbers will not permit the progress
which the exigency of affairs requires."—" We have in our
respected general (Graham) a confidence which is daily on the
increase. He has a mind and temper well adapted to encounter
difficulties which less favoured dispositions could not bear. We
may possibly maintain our ground. If we do, although our
success may have none of the brilliancy of victory, yet his merits,
who, by patience, prudence, and self-possession, shall have kept
all quiet within our lines, preserved tolerable harmony, and kept
an enterprizing enemy off with very inadequate means, should
be rewarded by his country's good opinion, although none but
those who have witnessed can fully estimate the value of his
exertions. On the whole, our situation may be said to inspire
hope, though not security : to animate resistance, though not to
promise victory."

SECTION 6.

" *June* 29, 1810.

" I have been attending a committee of Spanish engineers and
artillery-officers, to settle some determinate plan for taking up the
ground near the town of La Isla; but they will enter into no
views which include the destruction of a house or garden. They
continue to propose nothing but advanced batteries upon the marsh

in front of the town, the evident object of which is to keep the shells of the enemy rather farther from the houses. At a general attack, all this would be lost and carried, by small parties coming in on the flanks and gorges. Instead of deepening the ditches and constructing good redoubts at every seven hundred yards, this is what they propose, although we offer to perform the labour for them. On a barren spot they will agree to our working; but of what service is one redoubt, if unsupported by a collateral defence, and if a general system is not attended to? We have now been here three months, and although they have been constantly urged to construct something at that weak tongue of low land, St. Petri, still nothing of importance is begun upon, nor do I imagine they will agree to any work of strength at that point. I am almost in despair of seeing this place strongly fortified, so as to resist an army of from fifty to one hundred thousand men, which I am convinced it is capable of."—" We have now one thousand three hundred labourers of the line and eighty carpenters, but, for the latter, the timber we are supplied with from our ally is so bad that these artificers produce not more than one-fifth or one-sixth what they would be capable of if the materials were good. To judge from their conduct it is impossible to suppose them determined to oppose a vigorous resistance even in La Isla, and I have no idea of there ever being a siege of Cadiz itself."—" Of our seven subalterns of engineers, two are generally ill; we are obliged, therefore, to get assistance from the line. The consequence is that the work is neither so well nor so speedily executed. We ought to have many more (engineers). It is not economy in the governments; and with Lord Wellington they have hardly any with the army.

EXTRACTS FROM THE OFFICIAL ABSTRACT OF MILITARY REPORTS FROM THE BRITISH COMMANDERS AT CADIZ.

SECTION 6.

General William Stewart, March 13, 1810.
" The enemy's force was supposed to be diminished, but no advantage could be taken of it, on account of the inefficient state of the Spanish troops."

General Graham, March 26, 1810.

" The isle of Leon required for its defence a larger force than had been assigned. Its tenure was, in the then state of the defences, very precarious.

May, 1810.

" General Blake, appointed to command the Spanish forces, introduced some degree of activity and co-operation, in which the Spaniards had been very deficient."

October, 1810.

" The progress made by the enemy at the Trocadero assumed a very formidable character, while the Spaniards persisted in their apathy, and neglected to fortify the most vulnerable points of their line."

January 2, 1811.

" ———— As far as the exertions of the British engineers and soldiers under my command have been concerned, I have every reason to be satisfied. I can by no means say the same of the Spaniards, for, besides the reluctance with which some of the most essential measures of the defence were agreed to, our people were not permitted to carry into execution the plan for the intrenchment of the left part of the Cortadura de St. Fernado until after much delay and very unpleasant contests."

No. IV.

EXTRACTS FROM KING JOSEPH'S CORRESPONDENCE.

SECTION 1.

The duke of Santa Fé to the King, Paris, June 20, 1810.

(Translation from the Spanish.)

" Will your majesty believe that some politicians of Paris have arrived at saying, that in Spain there is preparing a new revolution, very dangerous for the French; and they assert that the

Spaniards attached to your majesty will rise against them. Let
your majesty consider if ever was heard a more absurd chimera,
and how prejudicial it might be to us if it succeeded in gaining
any credit. I hope that such an idea will not be believed by any
person of judgement, and that it will soon subside, being void of
probability."

SECTION 2.

Ministerial letter from the King to the marquis of Almenara.

(Translation from the Spanish.)

" *September* 21, 1810.

" The impolitic violence of the military governors has attacked
not only men, and fields, and animals, but even the most sacred
things in the nation, as the memorials and the actions of families,
in whose preservation those only are interested to whom they
belong, and from which strangers cannot reap the least fruit.
In this class are the general archives of the kingdom, called the
archives of Simancas, which are found in the province of Valladolid, the governor, Kellerman, has taken possession of them."
" Those archives, from the time of their institution, for centuries past, have contained the treaties of the kings since they
were known in Castile ; also, ancient manuscripts of the kindred
of the princes, the descents and titles of families, pleadings in the
tribunals, decisions of the Cortes ; in short, all that is publicly
interesting to the history of the nation, and privately to individuals."

SECTION 3.

The Spanish secretary of state to the duke of Santa Fé.

" *Madrid, September,* 12, 1812.

" ———— Si l'Andalusie n'est pas entièrement pacifiée ; si la
junte de Cadiz existe encore, et si les Anglais y exercent leur
fatale influence, on doit l'attribuer en grande partie aux machinations, et aux trames ourdies par la junte et l'Angleterre au
moment où parvint à leur connaissance le decret du 8 Febrier, qui

établit des gouvernemens militaires dans la Navarre, la Biscaye, l'Arragon, et la Catalogne. Quelques gouverneurs Francaises ayant traité ces provinces comme si elles étaient absolument détachées de la monarchie."

" ———— Mais combiens n'est il pas dementi par la conduite de certains gouverneurs qui paraissent s'obstiner à prolonger l'insurrection d'Espagne plutôt qu'a la soumettre ! Car dans plusieurs endroits on ne se contente pas d'exclure toute idée de l'autorité du roi, en faisant administrer la justice au nom de l'empereur, mais ce qui est pire, on a exigé que les tribunaux civils de Valladolid et de Palencia pretassent serment de fidelité et d'obeisance à sa majesté imperiale comme si la nation Espagnole n'avoit pas de roi."

SECTION 4.

Memorial from the duke of Santa Fé and marquis of Almenara to the prince of Wagram.

(Translation from the Spanish.)

" *Paris, September* 16, 1810.

" ———— The decrees of his majesty the emperor are the same for all the generals. The prince of Esling, who has traversed all the provinces to the borders of Portugal, who appears to be forming immense magazines, and has much greater necessities than the governors of provinces, has applied to the Spanish prefects, who have made the arrangements, and supplied him with even more than he required ; and this speaks in favour of the Spanish people, for the prince of Esling receives the blessings of the inhabitants of the provinces through which his troops pass. Such is the effect of good order and humanity amongst a people who know the rules of justice, and that war demands sacrifices, but who will not suffer dilapidations and useless vexations."

SECTION 5.

Intercepted letter of comte de Casa Valencia, counsellor of state, written to his wife, June 18, 1810.

" Il y a six mois que l'on ne nous paie point, et nous perissons.

" ——— Avant hier j'écrivis à Almenara lui peignant ma situation et le pryant de m'accorder quelque argent pour vivre ; de me secourir, si non comme ministre, du moins comme ami. Hier je restai trois heures dans son antichambre espérant un réponse, je le vis enfin et elle fut qu'il n'avait rien."

" ——— Rien que la faim m'attend aujourd'hui."

No. V.

EXTRACTS OF LETTERS FROM LORD WELLINGTON.

SECTION 1.

" *Celerico, May* 11, 1810.

" ——— I observe that the minister Don Miguel Forjas considers the inconvenience, on which I had the honour of addressing you, as of ordinary occurrence, and he entertains no doubt that inconveniences of this description will not induce me to desist from making the movements which I might think the defence of the country would require. It frequently happens that an army in operation cannot procure the number of carriages which it requires, either from the unwillingness of the inhabitants to supply them, or from the deficiency of the number of carriages in the country. But it has rarely happened that an army, thus unprovided with carriages, has been obliged to carry on its operations in a country in which there is literally no food, and in which, if there was food, there is no money to purchase it ; and, whenever that has been the case, the army has been obliged to withdraw to the magazines which the country had refused or been unable to remove to the army. This is precisely the case of the allied armies in this part of the country ; and, however trifling the difficulty may be deemed by the regency and the ministers, I consider a starving army to be so useless in any situation, that I shall certainly not pretend to hold a position or to make any movement in which the food of the troops is not secured. I have no doubt of the ability or the willingness of the country to do all that can be required of them, if the authority of the government is properly exerted to force individuals to attend to their public duties rather than to their private interests in this time of trial. I have written this same sentiment to the government so frequently, that they must be as tired of reading it as I am of writing it. But if they expect that individuals of the lower orders are to relinquish the pursuit of their private interests and business to serve the public, and mean to punish them for any omission in this important duty, they must begin with the higher classes of society. These must be forced to perform their duty, and no name, however illustrious, and no protection, however powerful, should shield from punishment those who neglect the performance of their duty to the public in these times. Unless these measures are strictly and invariably followed, it is vain to expect any serious or continued exertion in the country, and the regency ought to be aware, from the sentiments of his majesty's government, which I have communicated to them, that the continuance of his majesty's assistance depends not on the ability or the inclination, but on the actual effectual exertions of the people of Portugal in their own cause. I have thought it proper to trouble you so much at length upon this subject, in consequence of the light manner in which the difficulties which I had stated to exist were noticed by Monsieur de Forjas. I have to mention, however, that, since I wrote to you, although there exist several causes of complaint of different kinds, and that some examples must be made, we have received such assistance as has enabled me to continue till this time in our positions, and I hope to be able to continue as long as may be necessary. I concur entirely in the measure of appointing a special commission to attend the head quarters of the Portuguese army, and I hope that it will be adopted without delay. I enclose a proclamation which I have issued, which I hope will have some effect. It describes nearly the crimes, or rather the omissions, of which the people may be guilty in respect to the transport of the army; these may be as follow :—1st, refusing to supply carts, boats, or beasts of burthen, when required; 2dly, refusing to remove their articles or animals out of the reach of the enemy; 3dly, disobedience of the orders of the magistrate to proceed to and remain at any station

with carriages, boats, &c. ; 4th, desertion from the service either
with or without carriages, &c. ; 5th, embezzlement of provisions or stores which they may be employed to transport. The
crimes or omissions of the inferior magistrates may be classed
as follows :—1st, disobedience of the orders of their superiors;
2d, inactivity in the execution of them ; 3d, receiving bribes, to
excuse certain persons from the execution of requisitions upon
them."

SECTION 2.

Lord Wellington to M. Forjas.

Gouvea, September 6, 1810.

MOST ILLUSTRIOUS SIR,

I HAVE received your letter of the 1st of this month, inform-
ing me that you had placed before the government of this kingdom
my despatch of the 27th of August, announcing the melancholy
and unexpected news of the loss of Almeida, and that the government had learned with sorrow that an accident unforeseen had
prevented my moving to succour the place, hoping, at the same
time, that the depression of the people, caused by such an event,
will soon vanish, by the quick and great successes which they
expect with certainty from the efforts of the army. I have already made known to the government of the kingdom that the
fall of Almeida was unexpected by me, and that I deplored its loss
and that of my hopes, considering it likely to depress and afflict
the people of this kingdom. It was by no means my intention,
however, in that letter, to state whether it had or had not been
my intention to have succoured the place, and I now request
the permission of the government of the kingdom to say that,
much as I wish to remove the impression which this misfortune
has justly made on the public, I do not propose to alter the system and plan of operations which have been determined, after the
most serious deliberation, as best adequate to further the general
cause of the allies, and, consequently, Portugal. I request the
government to believe that I am not insensible to the value of their
confidence as well as that of the public ; as, also, that I am
highly interested in removing the anxiety of the public upon the
late misfortune ; but I should forget my duty to my sovereign, to
the prince regent, and to the cause in general, if I should permit

public clamour or panic to induce me to change, in the smallest
degree, the system and plan of operations which I have adopted,
after mature consideration, and which daily experience shews to
be the only one likely to produce a good end.

                              (Signed)   WELLINGTON.

SECTION 3.

Gouvea, September 7, 1810

——— In order to put an end at once to these miserable intrigues, I beg that you will inform the government that *I will
not stay* in the country, and that I will advise the king's government to withdraw the assistance which his majesty affords them,
if they interfere in any manner with the appointment of marshal
Beresford's staff, for which he is responsible, or with the operations of the army, or with any of the points which, with the
original arrangements with marshal Beresford, were referred exclusively to his management. I propose, also, to report to his
majesty's government, and refer to their consideration, what steps
ought to be taken, if the Portuguese government refuse or delay
to adopt the civil and political arrangements recommended by me,
and corresponding with the military operations which I am carrying on. The preparatory measures for the destruction of, or
rather rendering useless the mills, were suggested by me long
ago, and marshal Beresford did not write to government upon
them till I had reminded him a second time of my wishes on the
subject. I now beg leave to recommend that these preparatory
measures may be adopted not only in the country between the
Tagus and the Mondego, laying north of Torres Vedras, as originally proposed, but that they shall be forthwith adopted in all
parts of Portugal, and that the magistrates and others may be
directed to render useless the mills, upon receiving orders to do so
from the military officers. I have already adopted this measure
with success in this part of the country, and it must be adopted
in others in which it is probable that the enemy may endeavour to
penetrate ; and it must be obvious to any person who will reflect
upon the subject, that it is only consistent with all the other
measures which, for the last twelve months, I have recommended
to government to impede and make difficult, and if possible prevent, the advance and establishment of the enemy's force in the
country. But it appears that the government have lately dis-

covered that we are all wrong; they have become impatient for the defeat of the enemy, and, in imitation of the Central Junta, call out for a battle and early success. If I had had the power I would have prevented the Spanish armies from attending to this call; and if I had, the cause would now have been safe; and, having the power now in my hands, I will not lose the only chance which remains of saving the cause, by paying the smallest attention to the senseless suggestions of the Portuguese government. I acknowledge that I am much hurt at this change of conduct in the government; and, as I must attribute it to the persons recently introduced into the government, it affords additional reason with me for disapproving of their nomination, and I shall write upon the subject to the prince regent, if I should hear any more of this conduct. I leave you to communicate the whole or any part of this letter that you may think proper to the regency.   (Signed)   WELLINGTON.

SECTION 4.

Rio Mayor, October 6, 1810.
———— You will do me the favour to inform the regency, and above all the principal Souza, that his majesty and the prince regent having entrusted me with the command of their armies, and likewise with the conduct of the military operations, I will not suffer them, or any body else, to interfere with them. That I know best where to station my troops, and where to make a stand against the enemy, and I shall not alter a system formed upon mature consideration, upon any suggestion of theirs. I am responsible for what I do, and they are not; and I recommend to them to look to the measures for which they are responsible, which I long ago recommended to them, viz. to provide for the tranquillity of Lisbon, and for the food of the army and of the people, while the troops will be engaged with the enemy. As for principal Souza, I beg you to tell him, from me, that I have had no satisfaction in transacting the business of this country since he has been a member of the government; that, being embarked in a course of military operations, of which I hope to see the successful termination, I shall continue to carry them on to the end, but that no power on earth shall induce me to remain in the Peninsula for one moment after I shall have obtained his majesty's leave to resign my charge, if principal Souza is to remain either

a member of the government or to continue at Lisbon. Either
he must quit the country or I will : and, if I should be obliged to
go, I shall take care that the world, or Portugal at least, and the
prince regent shall be made acquainted with my reasons. From
the letter of the 3d, which I have received from Monsieur Forjas,
I had hoped that the government was satisfied with what I had
done, and intended to do, and that, instead of endeavouring to
render all further defence fruitless, by disturbing the minds of the
populace at Lisbon, they would have done their duty by adopting
measures to secure the tranquillity of the town ; but I suppose
that, like other weak individuals, they add duplicity to their
weakness, and that their expressions of approbation, and even
gratitude, were intended to convey censure.

WELLINGTON.

P.S.—All I ask from the Portuguese Regency is tranquillity in
the town of Lisbon, and provisions for their own troops while they
will be employed in this part of the country. I have but little
doubt of success ; but, as I have fought a sufficient number of
battles to know that the result of any one is not certain, even
with the best arrangements, I am anxious that the government
shoᵘˡd adopt preparatory arrangements, and take out of the
enemy's way those persons and their families who would suffer if
they were to fall into their hands.

SECTION 5.

Pero Negro, October 28, 1810.

The cattle, and other articles of supply, which the government have been informed have been removed from the island of
Lizirias, are still on the island, and most probably the secretary
of state, Don M. Forjas, who was at Alhandra yesterday, will
have seen them. I shall be glad to hear whether the government
propose to take any and what steps to punish the magistrates who
have disobeyed their orders and have deceived them by false reports. The officers and soldiers of the militia, absent from their
corps, are liable to penalties and punishments, some of a civil,
others of a military nature: first, they are liable to a forfeiture of
all their personal property, upon information that they are absent
from their corps without leave ; secondly, they are liable to be
transferred to serve as soldiers in the regiments of the line, upon

the same information; and, lastly, they are liable to the penalties of desertion inflicted by the military tribunals. The two first are penalties which depend upon the civil magistrate, and I should be very glad to have heard of one instance in which the magistrates of Lisbon, or in which the government had called upon the magistrates at Lisbon to carry into execution the law in either of these respects. I entreat them to call for the names of the officers and soldiers absent without leave from any one of the Lisbon regiments of militia, to disgrace any one or more of the principal officers, in a public manner, for their shameful desertion of their posts in the hour of danger, and to seize and dispose of the whole property of the militia soldiers absent without leave, and to send these men to serve with any of the regiments of the line. I entreat them to adopt these measures without favour or distinction of any individuals in respect to any one regiment, and to execute the laws *bonâ fide* upon the subject; and I shall be satisfied of their good intentions, and shall believe that they are sincerely desirous of saving the country; but, if we are to go on as we have hitherto, if Great Britain is to give large subsidies and to expend large sums in support of a cause in which those most interested sit by and take no part, and those at the head of the government, with laws and powers to force the people to exertion in the critical circumstances in which the country is placed, are aware of the evil but neglect their duty and omit to put the laws in execution, I must believe their professions to be false, that they look to little dirty popularity instead of to save their country; that they are unfaithful servants to their master, and persons in whom his allies can place no confidence. In respect to the military law, it may be depended upon that it will be carried into execution, and that the day will yet come on which those military persons who have deserted their duty in these critical times will be punished as they deserve. The governors of the kingdom forget the innumerable remonstrances which have been forwarded to them on the defects in the proceedings of courts martial, which, in times of active war, render them and their sentences entirely nugatory. As an additional instance of these defects, I mention that officers of the Olivera regiment of militia, who behaved ill in the action with the enemy at Villa Nova de Fosboa, in the beginning of August last, and a court martial was immediately assembled for this trial, are still, in the end of October, under trial, and the trial will, probably, not be concluded till Christmas. In like manner, the military trial of those deserters of the militia,

after assembling officers and soldiers at great inconvenience for
the purpose, cannot possibly be concluded till the period will have
gone by in which any benefit might be secured from the example
of the punishment of any one or number of them.   The defect
in the administration of the military law has been repeatedly
pointed out to the government, and a remedy for the evil has been
proposed to them, and has been approved of by the Prince
Regent.   But they will not adopt it; and it would be much better
if there was no law for the government of the army than that the
existing laws should continue without being executed."————

" WELLINGTON."

SECTION 6.

" October 29, 1810.

"   ———— In answer to lord Wellesley's queries respecting the
Portuguese Regency, my opinion is that the Regency ought to be
appointed by the Prince Regent, but during his pleasure; they
ought to have full power to act in every possible case, to make
appointments to offices, to dismiss from office, to make and alter
laws, in short, every power which the prince himself could
possess if he were on the spot.   They ought to report, in detail,
their proceedings on every subject, and their reasons for the
adoption of every measure.   The prince ought to decline to receive any application from any of his officers or subjects in Portugal not transmitted through the regular channels of the government here, and ought to adopt no measure respecting Portugal
not recommended by the Regency.   The smaller the number of
persons composing the Regency the better; but my opinion is
that it is not advisable to remove any of the persons now composing it excepting principal Souza, with whom I neither can nor
will have any official intercourse.   The patriarch is, in my
opinion, a necessary evil.   He has acquired a kind of popularity
and confidence through the country which would increase if he
was removed from office, and he is the kind of man to do much
mischief if he was not employed.   If we should succeed in removing the principal (which <i>must</i> be done), I think the patriarch
will take warning, and will behave better in future.   In respect to
military operations, there can be no interference on the part of
the Regency or any body else.   If there is I can no longer be
responsible.   If our own government choose to interfere themselves, or that the Prince Regent should interfere, they have only

to give me their orders in detail, and I will carry them strictly into execution, to the best of my abilities; and I will be responsible for nothing but the execution; but, if I am to be responsible, I must have full discretion and no interference on the part of the Regency or any body else. I should like to see principal Souza's detailed instructions for his " *embuscados*" on the left bank of the Tagus. If principal Souza does not go to England, or somewhere out of Portugal, the country will be lost. The time we lose in discussing matters which ought to be executed immediately, and in the wrong direction given to the deliberations of the government, is inconceivable. The gentlemen destined for the Alemtejo ought to have been in the province on the evening of the 24th, but, instead of that, three valuable days of fine weather will have been lost, because the government do not choose to take part in our arrangements, which, however undeniably beneficial, will not b much liked by those whom it will affect; although it is certain that, sooner or later, these persons must and will be ruined, by leaving behind them all their valuable property, and, as in the case of this part of the country, every thing which can enable the enemy to remain in the country. In answer to M. de Forjas' note of the 22d, enclosed in yours, (without date,) I have to say that I know of no carriages employed by the British army excepting by the commissary-general, and none are detained that I know of. I wish that the Portuguese government, or its officers, would state the names of those who have detained carriages, contrary to my repeated orders; or the regiment, or where they are stationed; but this they will never do. All that we do with the carriages is to send back sick in them, when there are any. It will not answer to make an engagement that the wheel-carriages from Lisbon shall not come farther than Bucellas, Montachique, &c. many articles required by the army cannot be carried by mules, and the carriages must come on with them here. In many cases the Portuguese troops in particular are ill provided with mules, therefore this must be left to the commissary-general of the army, under a recommendation to him, if possible, not to send the Lisbon wheel-carriages beyond the places above mentioned. I wish, in every case, that a regulation made should be observed, and the makers of regulations should take care always to frame them as that they can be observed, which is the reason of my entering so particularly into this point."

" WELLINGTON."

SECTION 7.

" *Pero Negro, October* 31, 1810.

" ——— I am glad that the gentlemen feel my letters, and I
hope that they will have the effect of inducing them to take some
decided steps as well regarding the provisions in the Alemtejo as
the desertion of the militia.   The *ordenanza* artillery now begin
to desert from the works, although they are fed by us with English
rations and taken care of in the same manner as our own troops.
Your note, No. —, of 29th, is strictly true in all its parts, the
French could not have staid here a week if all the provisions had
been removed, and the length of time they can now stay depends
upon the quantity remaining of what they have found in places
from which there existed means of removing every thing, if the
quantity had been ten times greater.   They are stopped effectually ; in front all the roads are occupied, and they can get
nothing from their rear ; but all the military arrangements which
have been made are useless if they can find subsistence on the
ground which they occupy.   For what I know to the contrary,
they may be able to maintain their position till the whole French
army is brought to their assistance.   It is heart-breaking to contemplate the chance of failure from such obstinacy and folly ! "

" WELLINGTON."

SECTION 8.

" *Pero Negro, November* 1, 1810.

" I have no doubt that the government can produce volumes of
papers to prove that they gave orders upon the several subjects to
which the enclosures relate, but it would be very desirable if they
would state whether any magistrate or other person has been
punished for not obeying those orders.   The fact is that the
government, after the appointment of principal Souza to be a
member of the Regency, conceived that the war could be maintained upon the frontier, contrary to the opinion of myself and
of every military officer in the country, and, instead of giving
positive orders preparatory to the event which was most likely
to occur, viz. that the allied army would retire, they spent much
valuable time in discussing, with me, the expediency of a measure which was quite impracticable, and omitted to give the orders
which were necessary for the evacuation of the country between

the Tagus and the Mondego by the inhabitants. Then, when convinced that the army would retire, they first imposed that duty on me, although they must have known that I was ignorant of the names, the nature of the offices, the places of abode of the different magistrates who were to superintend the execution of the measure, and, moreover, I have but one gentleman in my family to give me any assistance in writing the Portuguese language, and they afterwards issued the orders themselves, still making them referable to me, without my knowledge or consent, and still knowing that I had no means whatever of communicating with the country, and they issued them at the very period when the enemy was advancing from Almeida. If I had not been able to stop the enemy at Busaco he must have been in his present situation long before the order could have reached those to whom it was addressed. All this conduct was to be attributed to the same cause, a desire to avoid to adopt a measure which, however beneficial to the real interests of the country, was likely to disturb the habits of indolence and ease of the inhabitants, and to throw the odium of the measure upon me and upon the British government. I avowed, in my proclamation, that I was the author of that measure, and the government might have sheltered themselves under that authority, but the principle of the government has lately been to seek for popularity, and they will not aid in any measure, however beneficial to the real interests of the country, which may be unpopular with the mob of Lisbon. I cannot agree in the justice of the expression of the astonishment by the secretary of state that the measure should have been executed in this part of the country at all. The same measure was carried into complete execution in Upper Beira, notwithstanding that the army was in that province, and the means of transport were required for its service, not a soul remained, and, excepting at Coimbra, to which town my personal authority and influence did not reach, not an article of any description was left behind; and all the mills upon the Coa and Mondego, and their dependent streams, were rendered useless. But there were no discussions there upon the propriety of maintaining the war upon the frontier. The orders were given, and they were obeyed in time, and the enemy suffered accordingly. In this part of the country, notwithstanding the advantage of having a place of security to retire to, notwithstanding the advantage of water-carriage, notwithstanding that the Tagus was fordable in many places at the period when the inhabitants should have passed their property to the left of the river, and fortunately filled at the moment the enemy approached its banks; the inhabitants have fled from their habitations as they would have done under any circumstances, without waiting orders from me or from the government; but they have left behind them every thing that could be useful to the enemy, and could subsist their army, and all the mills untouched; accordingly, the enemy still remain in our front, notwithstanding that their communication is cut off with Spain and with every other military body; and if the provisions which they have found will last, of which I can have no knowledge, they may remain till they will be joined by the whole French army in Spain. I believe that in Santarem and Villa Franca alone, both towns upon the Tagus, and both having the advantage of water-carriage, the enemy found subsistence for their army for a considerable length of time. Thus will appear the difference of a measure adopted in time, and the delay of it till the last moment; and I only wish that the country and the allies may not experience the evil consequences of the ill-fated propensity of the existing Portuguese Regency to seek popularity. In the same manner the other measure since recommended, viz. the removal of the property of the inhabitants of Alemtejo to places of security has been delayed by every means in the power of the government, and has been adopted at last against their inclination: as usual, they commenced a discussion with me upon the expediency of preventing the enemy from crossing the Tagus, they then sent their civil officer to me to receive instructions, and afterwards they conveyed to him an instruction of the ————, to which I propose to draw the attention of his royal highness the prince Regent and of his majesty's government. His royal highness and his majesty's government will then see in what manner the existing regency are disposed to co-operate with me. The additional order of the 30th of October, marked 5 in the enclosures from M. Forjas, shew the sense, which the Regency themselves entertained of the insufficiency of their original instructions to the Disembargador Jacinto Paes de Matos. I may have mistaken the system of defence to be adopted for this country, and principal Souza and other members of the Regency may be better judges of the capacity of the troops and of the operations to be carried on than I am. In this case they should desire his majesty and the prince regent to remove me from the command of the army. But they cannot doubt my zeal for the cause in which we are engaged, and they know that not a moment of my time, nor a faculty of my mind, that is not devoted to promote it; and the records of this government will shew what I have done for them and their country. If, therefore, they do not manifest their dissatisfaction and want of confidence in the measures which I adopt by desiring that I should be removed, they are bound, as honest men and faithful servants to their prince, to co-operate with me by all means in their power, and thus should neither thwart them by opposition, nor render them nugatory by useless delays and discussions. Till lately I have had the satisfaction of receiving the support and co-operation of the government; and I regret that his royal highness the prince regent should have been induced to make a change which has operated so materially to the detriment of his people and of the allies. In respect to the operations on the left of the Tagus, I was always of opinion that the ordenança would be able to prevent the enemy from sending over any of their plundering parties; and I was unwilling to adopt any measure of greater solidity, from my knowledge, that, as soon as circumstances should render it expedient, on any account, to withdraw the troops, which I should have sent to the left of the Tagus, the ordenança would disperse. The truth is, that, notwithstanding the opinion of some of the government, every Portuguese, into whose hands a firelock is placed, does not become a soldier capable of meeting the enemy. Experience, which the members of the government have not had, has taught me this truth, and in what manner to make use of the different descriptions of troops in this country; and it would be very desirable, if the government would leave, exclusively, to marshal Beresford and me, the adoption of all military arrangements. The conduct of the governor of Setuval is, undoubtedly, the cause of the inconvenience now felt on the left of the Tagus. He brought forward his garrison to the river against orders, and did not reflect, and possibly was not aware as I am, that if they had been attacked in that situation, as they probably would have been, they would have dispersed; and thus Setuval, as well as the regiment, which was to have been its garrison, would have been lost. It was necessary, therefore, at all events, to prevent that misfortune, and to order the troops to retire to Setuval, and the ordenança as usual dispersed, and the government will lose their five hundred stand of new arms, and, if the enemy can cross the Tagus in time, their 3-pounders. These are the consequences of persons interfering in military operations, who have no knowledge of them, or of the nature of the troops which are

to carry them on.   I am now under the necessity, much to the
inconvenience of the army, of sending a detachment to the left
of the Tagus."

SECTION 9.

" *December* 5, 1810.

" All my proceedings have been founded on the following
principles : First, That, by my appointment of marshal-general
of the Portuguese army with the same powers as those vested in
the late duc de la Foéns, I hold the command of the army independent of the local government of Portugal.   Secondly, That,
by the arrangements made by the governors of the kingdom
with the king's government, when sir William Beresford was
asked for by the former to command the Portuguese army, it
was settled that the commander-in-chief of the British army
should direct the general operations of the combined force.
Thirdly, That, supposing that my appointment of marshal-general
did not give me the independent control over the operations of
the Portuguese army, or that, as commander-in-chief of the
British army, I did not possess the power of directing the operation of the whole under the arrangement above referred to; it
follows that either the operations of the two armies must have
been separated, or the Portuguese government must have had
the power of directing the operations of the British army.
Fourthly, It never was intended that both armies should be
exposed to the certain loss, which would have been the consequence of a disjointed operation; and, undoubtedly, his majesty's
government never intended to give over the British army to the
government of the kingdom, to make ducks and drakes of.   The
government of the kingdom must, in their reply to my letter,
either deny the truth of these principles, or they must prove
that my charge against them is without foundation, and that they
did not delay and omit to adopt various measures, recommended
by me and marshal Beresford, calculated to assist and correspond
with the operations of the armies, upon the proposition and under
the influence of principal Souza, under the pretence of discussing
with me the propriety of my military arrangements.

" WELLINGTON."

" *Cartaxo, January* 18, 1811.

" It is necessary that I should draw your attention, and that of the Portuguese government, upon the earliest occasion, to the sentiments which have dropped from the Patriarch, in recent discussions at the meeting of the Regency. It appears that his eminence has expatiated on the inutility of laying fresh burthens on the people, ' which were evidently for no other purpose than to nourish a war in the heart of the kingdom.' It must be recollected that these discussions are not those of a popular assembly, they can scarcely be deemed those of a ministerial council, but they are those of persons whom his royal highness the Prince Regent has called to govern his kingdom in the existing crisis of affairs. I have always been in the habit of considering his eminence the Patriarch as one of those in Portugal who are of opinion that all sacrifices are to be made, provided the kingdom could preserve its independence ; and, I think it most important that the British government, and the government of the Prince Regent, and the world, should be undeceived, if we have been mistaken hitherto. His eminence objects to the adoption of measures which have for their immediate object to procure funds for the maintenance of his royal highness's armies, because a war may exist in the heart of the kingdom, but I am apprehensive the Patriarch forgets the manner in which the common enemy first entered this kingdom, in the year 1807, that in which they were expelled from it, having had complete possession of it in 1808, and that they were again in possession of the city of Oporto, and of the two most valuable provinces of the kingdom in 1809, and the mode in which they were expelled from those provinces. He forgets that it was stated to him in the month of February, 1810, in the presence of the Marquis of Olhao, of Don M. Forjas, and of Don Joa Antonio Saltar de Mendoza, and Marshal Sir W. C. Beresford, that it was probable the enemy would invade this kingdom with such an army as that it would be necessary to concentrate all our forces to oppose him with any chance of success, and that this concentration could be made with safety in the neighbourhood of the capital only, and that the general plan of the campaign was communicated to him which went to bring the enemy into the heart of the kingdom ; and that he expressed before all these persons his high approbation of it. If he recollected these circumstances he would observe that nothing had occurred in this campaign that had not been foreseen and provided for by measures of which he had expressed his approbation, of whose consequences he now disapproves. The Portuguese nation are involved in a war not of aggression, or even defence on their parts, not of alliance, not in consequence of their adherence to any political system, for they adandoned all alliances and all political systems in order to propitiate the enemy. The inhabitants of Portugal made war purely and simply to get rid of the yoke of the tyrant whose government was established in Portugal, and to save their lives and properties; they chose this lot for themselves, principally at the instigation of his eminence the Patriarch, and they called upon his majesty, the ancient ally of Portugal, whose alliance had been relinquished at the requisition of the common enemy, to aid them in the glorious effort which they wished to make, and to restore the independence of their country, and to secure the lives and properties of its inhabitants. I will not state the manner in which his majesty has answered the call, or enumerate the services rendered to this nation by his army; whatever may be the result of the contest, nothing can make me believe that the Portuguese nation will ever forget them ; but when a nation has adopted the line of resistance to the tyrant under the circumstances under which it was unanimously adopted by the Portuguese nation in 1808, and has been persevered in, it cannot be believed that they intended to suffer none of the miseries of war, or that their government act inconsistently with their sentiments when they expatiate on ' the inutility of laying fresh burthens on the people, which were evidently for no other purpose than to nourish a war in the heart of the kingdom.' The patriarch in particular forgets his old principles, his own actions which have principally involved his country in the contest when he talks of discontinuing it, because, it has again, for the third time, been brought into ' the heart of the kingdom.' Although the patriarch, particularly, and the majority of the existing government approved of the plan which I explained to them in February, 1810, according to which it was probable that this kingdom would be made the seat of war which has since occurred, I admit that his eminence, or any of those members may fairly disapprove of the campaign and of the continuance of the enemy in Portugal. I have pointed out to the Portuguese government, in more than one despatch, the difficulties and risks which attended any attack upon the enemy's position in this country, and the probable success not only to ourselves but to our allies of our perseverance in the plan which I had adopted, and had hitherto followed so far successfully, as that the allies have literally sustained no loss of any description, and this army is, at this moment, more complete than it was at the opening of the campaign in April last. The inhabitants of one part of the country alone have suffered and are continuing to suffer. But without entering into discussions which I wish to avoid on this occasion, I repeat, that if my counsels had been followed these sufferings would at least have been alleviated, and I observe that is the first time I have heard that the sufferings of a part, and but a small part of any nation have been deemed a reason for refusing to adopt a measure which had for its object the deliverance of the whole. The patriarch may, however, disapprove of the system I have followed, and I conceive that he is fully justified in desiring his majesty and the prince regent to remove me from the command of these armies. This would be a measure consistent with his former conduct in this contest, under the circumstances of my having unfortunately fallen in his opinion, but this measure is entirely distinct from the refusal to concur in laying those burthens upon the people which are necessary to carry on and to secure the object of the war. It must be obvious to his eminence, and to every person acquainted with the real situation of the affairs of Portugal, unless a great effort is made to render the resources more adequate to the necessary expenditure all plans and systems of operation will be alike, for the Portuguese army will be able to carry on none. At this moment although all the corps are concentrated in the neighbourhood of their magazines, with means of transport, easy, by the Tagus the Portuguese troops are frequently in -want of provisions because there is no money to pay the expense of transport, and all the departments of the Portuguese army, including the hospitals, are equally destitute of funds to enable them to defray the necessary expenditure, and to perform their duty. The deficiencies and difficulties have existed ever since I have known the Portuguese army, and it is well known that it must have been disbanded more than once, if it had not been assisted by the provisions, stores, and funds, of the British army. It may likewise occur to his eminence that in proportion as the operations of the armies would be more extended, the expense would increase, and the necessity for providing adequate funds to support it would become more urgent, unless, indeed, the course of their operations should annihilate at one blow both army and expenditure. The objection then to adopt measures to improve the resources of the government, go to decide the question whether the war should be carried on or not in any manner. By desiring his majesty and the prince regent to remove me from the command of their armies, his eminence would endeavour to get rid of a person deemed incapable or unwilling to fulfil the duties of his situation. By objecting to improve the resources of the country he betrays an alteration of opinion respecting the contest, and a desire to forfeit its advantages, and to give up the independence of the country, and the security of the lives and properties of the Portuguese nation. In my opinion the Patriarch is in such a situation in this country that he ought to be called upon, on the part of his majesty, to state distinctly what he meant by refusing to concur in the measures which were necessary to insure the funds, to enable this country to carry on the war; at all events, I request that this letter may be communicated to him in the Regency, and that a copy of it may be forwarded to his royal highness the prince regent, in order that his royal highness may see that I have given his eminence an opportunity of explaining his motives either by stating his personal objections to me, or the alteration of his opinions, his sentiments, and his wishes, in respect to the independence of his country.

" WELLINGTON."

<hr/>

No. VI.

EXTRACT FROM A REPORT MADE BY THE DUKE OF DALMATIA TO THE PRINCE OF WAGRAM AND OF NEUFCHATEL.

SECTION I.

" *Seville, August 4th,* 1810.

" Par une décision de l'Empereur du mois de Fevrier dernier S. M. détermine qu'à compter du 1er Janvier toutes les dépenses d'administration générale du genie et de l'artillerie seraient au compte du gouvernement Espagnol; aussitôt que j'en fus instruit je sollicitai S. M. C. d'assigner à cet effet une somme; mais je ne pus obtenir que 2,000,000 de réaux (533,000 f.) et encore la Roi entendait il que les payements ne remontassent qu'au mois de Fevrier; cette somme était de beaucoup insuffisante. Je n'ai cessé d'en faire la representation, ainsi que Monsr. l'Intendant Général; nos demandes n'ont pas été accueillies, et pour couvrir autant que possible la différence j'ai dû avoir recours aux recettes extraordinaires faites sans la participation des ministres Espagnols.   J'espère que ce moyen réussira, déjà même il a produit quelques sommes.   L'état que je mets ci joint fait connaître les recouvremens qui ont été opérés sur les fonds de 533,000 f. du crédit mensuel à l'époque du 1er Août lesquels forment la somme de 3,731,000 f. mais indépendamment il y a eu des recettes extraordinaires pour au moins 500,000 f. qui ont reçu la même destination (les dépenses d'administration générale) anterieurement à cette époque.   J'avais fait mettre à la disposition de Monsr. l'Intendant Général des Valeurs pour plus d'un million qui devait servir à payer une partie de l'armée.   Mr. l'Intendant Général justifie de l'emploi de toutes ces sommes dans ses comptes généraux.   Les ministres de S. M. C. n'admettent pas les comptes que je presente; d'abord ils ne veulent pas allouer la somme de 500,000 f. qui a été reportée a l'article des dépenses d'administration générale, s'appuyant sur ce sujet sur la décision du roi qui ne fait remonter ces dépenses que jusqu'au mois de Fevrier, quoique l'empereur ait expressement entendu que le mois de Janvier devait aussi y être compris, ils ne veulent pas non plus reconnaître les recettes extraordinaires, où ils pretendent en précompter le produit sur le crédit mensuel de 533,000 f. il n'est pas dans mon pouvoir d'admettre leurs motifs, la décision de l'empereur est expresse, et tant que je serai dans la situation délicate ou je me trouve, mon devoir m'obligera de pourvoir aux besoins du service par tous les moyens praticables.   Les recettes qui ont eu lieu en Andalusie ont servi à toutes les dépenses de l'artillerie, du genie, des état majors et de l'administration générale qui sont vraiment immenses, et quoiqu'on ait absolument rien reçu de France ni de Madrid, j'ai en même temps pu faire payer trois mois de solde à l'armée, c'est sans doute bien peu quand il est du 8 à 10 mois d'arrière à la troupe et que l'insuffisance des moyens oblige à augmenter encore cet arrière, mais ne recevant rien je crois qu'il m'était impossible de mieux faire.   V. A. en sera elle même convaincue si elle veut s'arrêter un moment sur l'apperçu que je vais lui donner des charges que l' Andalusie supporte.   On consomme tous les jours près de 100,000 rations de vivres et 20,000 rations de fourrage; il y a 2000 malades aux hôpitaux. La forteresse de Jaen, le fort de Malaga, l'Alhambra de Grenade, au dessus duquel on a construit un grand camp retranché ; tous les châteaux sur les bords de la mer depuis le cap de Gata jusqu'à Fuengirola, le château d'Alcala la Réal, la place de Ronda, les anciens châteaux d'Olbera et de Moron, le château de Belalcazar, le château de Castillo de Los Guardias et plusieurs autres portes sur les frontières de l'Estremadura qu'on a dû aussi occuper. On a pourvu aux dépenses que les travaux devant Cadiz et la construction d'une flottille occasionment. On a établi à Grenade une poudrière et une fabrique d'armes, laquelle jusqu'à présent a peu donné, mais qui par la suite sera très utile. On a rétabli et mis dans une grande activité la fonderie et l'arsenal de Seville où journellement 1500 ouvriers sont employés. Nous manquions de poudre et de projectiles de feu et d'affuts. J'ai fait rétablir deux moulins à poudre à Seville et fait exploiter toutes les nitrières de l'Andalusie, à présent on compte aussi à Seville des projectiles de tous les calibres, jusqu'aux bombes de 12 pouces, tout le vieux fer a été ramassé, on a construit les affûts necessaires pour l'armement des batteries devant Cadiz. On a fait des requisitions en souliers et effets d'habillement dont la troupe a profité. J'ai fait lever dans le pays 2000 mules qui ont été données à l'artillerie, aux équipages militaires et au génie. J'ai fait construire et organiser un équipage de 36 pièces de montagnes, dont 12 obusiers, de 12 qui sont portés à dos de mulets et vont être repartis dans tous les corps d'armée. La totalité de ces dépenses ainsi qu'une infinité d'autres dont je ne fais pas l'énumeration sont au compte du gouvernement Espagnol, et le pays les supporte independamment du crédit mensuel de 533,000 f. et des recettes extraordinaires que je fais opérer lorsqu'il y a possibilité dont l'application a lieu en faveur de l'administration générale de l'armée, du genie, de l'artillerie, des états majors, des frais de courses et des dépenses secrètes. Ces charges sont immenses, et jamais le pays n'aurait pu les supporter si nous n'étions parvenus à mettre de l'ordre et la plus grande regularité dans les dépenses et consommations ; mais il serait difficile de les augmenter, peutêtre même y aurait il du danger de chercher à le faire ; c'est au point que malgré que nous soyons à la recolte il faut déjà penser à faire venir du bled des autres provinces, le produit de l'Andalusie étant insuffisant pour la consommation de ses habitans et celle de l'armée. Cependant S. M. C. et ses ministres qui sont parfaitement instruits de cette situation ont voulu attirer à Madrid les revenues de l'Andalusie : je dis les revenues, car leurs demandes dépassaient les recettes ; des ordres ont même été expédiés en consequence aux commissaires Royaux des Préfectures, et je me suis trouvé dans l'obligation de m'opposer ouvertement à l'effet de cette mesure dont l'exécution eut non seulement compromis tous les services de l'armée, mais occasionné peut-être des mouvemens séditieux; d'ailleurs il y avait impossibilité de la remplir, à ce sujet j'ai l'honneur de mettre sous les yeux de V. A. extrait d'une lettre que j'eus l'honneur d'écrire au roi le 13 Juillet dernier, et copie de celle que j'adressai à Monsieur le marquis d'Almenara, ministre des finances, le 30 du même mois pour répondre à une des siennes, où il me peignait l'étât désespérant des finances de S.M.C. Je supplie avec instance V. A. de vouloir bien rendre compte du contenu de ces lettres et du présent rapport à S. M. l'empereur.

" J'aurai voulu pour que S. M. fut mieux instruite de tout ce que s'est fait en Andalousie pouvoir entrer dans des détails plus étendus; mais j'ai dû me borner à traiter des points principaux, les détails se trouvent dans ma correspondance, et dans les rapports de Monsieur l'intendant général sur l'administration. Cependant d'après ce que j'ai dit S. M. aura une idée exacte des opérations administratives et autres qui ont eu lieu, ainsi que de l'étât de ses troupes et des embarras de ma situation: elle est telle aujourd'hui que je dois supplier avec la plus vive instance S. M. au nom même de son service de daigner la prendre en considération: j'ai des devoirs à remplir dont je sais toute l'étendue, je m'y livre sans reserve mais la responsabilité est trop forte pour que dans la position où je me trouve je puisse la soutenir; en effet j'ai à combattre des prétentions et des intérêts qui sont évidemment en opposition avec ceux de l'armée et par conséquent avec ceux de l'empereur; je suis forcé par mes propres devoirs de m'opposer à l'exécution des divers ordres que le roi donne et faire souvent le contraire. J'ai aussi constamment à lutter contre l'amour propre des chefs militaires, que souvent peuvent différer d'opinion avec moi et naturellement prétendent faire prévaloir leurs idées. Toutes ces considérations me font regarder la tâche qui m'est imposée comme au dessus de mes forces et me portent à desirer que S. M. l'empereur daigne me faire connaitre ses intentions ou pourvoir à mon remplacement et mettre à la tête de son armée dans le midi de l'Espagne, un chef plus capable que moi d'en diriger les opérations. Je me permettrai seulement de faire observer à ce sujet que le bien du service de l'empereur commande impérieusement que toutes les troupes qui sont dans le midi de l'Espagne depuis le Tage jusqu'aux deux mers suivent le même systême d'opérations, et soyent par conséquent commandés par un seul chef lequel doit être dans la pensée de l'empereur, et avoir ses instructions afin que le cas se présentant où il lui serait fait opposition d'une manière quelconque, il puisse se conduire en conséquence et parvenir au but qui lui sera indiqué ; tout autre systême retardera la marche des affaires et occasionera inévitablement des désagrémens qu'on peut autrement éviter.

" J'ai l'honneur, &c.

" (Signé)   LE MARECHAL DUC DE DALMATIE."

SECTION 2.

Intercepted Letter from marshal Mortier to the emperor,
13th July, 1810.

SIRE,

L'état de nullité où je suis depuis que Monsieur le duc de Dalmatie, major-général, a pris l'initiative de tous les mouvemens meme le plus minutieux de 5eme corps rend ici ma presence tout-à-fait inutile, il ne me reste que le chagrin de voir d'excellentes troupes animées du meilleur esprit, disséminées dans toute l'Andaluise et perdant tous les jours de braves gens sans but ni resultat. Dans cet état des choses je prie V.M. de vouloir bien me permettra de me retirer à Burgos pour y attendre des ordres s'il ne juge pas à propos de m'accorder un congé pour retourner en France, congé que reclame ma santé à la suite d'une maladie grave dont je suis à peine convalescent.

J'ai l'honneur, &c. &c.

LE MARECHAL DUC DE TREVISE.

No. VII.

SECTION 1.

Extract from an intercepted despatch of Massena, dated
July 10, 1810.

" Generals Romana and Carrera have gone to lord Wellington's head-quarters, but the latter has not abandoned his Lines."

General P. Boyer to S. Swartz, July 8, 1810.

" We are covering the siege of Ciudad Rodrigo, a place strong by its position and works, and which has been attacked with but little method. The English army is opposite ours, but, for good reasons, does not move: we compose the corps of observation; we are on the look out for them."

Extrait du Journal du C. de B. Pelet, premier aide-de-camp du maréchal prince d'Essling.

" 1810. 5 Août, à Ciudad Rodrigo.—Le capitaine du génie Boucherat arrive du 2ᵉ corps; il a fait la campagne du Portugal, 1807. Beaucoup causé avec lui sur ce pays. Il a fait la route de Lisbonne à Almeyda avec M. Mairet, et me remet un itinéraire qu'il en a dressé. Il prétend ces routes très difficiles; les rivières très encaissées, et inabordable sur les deux rives du Mondego. Celui-ci a peu d'eau, doit être guéable presque partout; et une partie de ses rives bien difficiles, et en certains endroits il n'y a pas plus de 20 toises de largeur; un seul pont sans chemin (je crois à Fornos;) mais la rivière n'est pas un obstacle aux communications des deux rives. La route d'Idanha, Castelbranco, &c. mauvaise, cependant non absolument impraticable à des pièces légères. Tage, très escarpé, rocailleux, profond jusqu'à Abrantes * * * * * Au dessus de cette ville, ou plutôt au confluent du Zezère, le pays devient plat; le lit du Tage s'élargit; il n'y a plus que des collines même éloignées, et tout est très praticable. Les montagnes de Santarem sont des collines peu élevées, praticables, accessibles sur leur sommet, peu propres à être défendues ce qui est commune jusqu'à la mer pour celles de Montachique, qui sont des plateaux arrondis, accessibles à toute les armes; et on pourrait marcher ou manœuvrer dans toutes les directions. J'ai fait copier cet itinéraire."

" 1810. 7 Octobre, à Leyria.—Causé avec le général Loison des position de Montachique, ensuite avec le prince."

" 1810. 9 Octobre, à Riomajor. On dit que l'ennemi se retranche à Alhandra et Bucellas. Les généraux Reynier et Foy ont une carte de Riomajor à Lisbonne; espèce de croquis fait à la hâte, d'après de bons matériaux, mais où la figure est très mauvaise. Je le fais copier."

SECTION 3.

A Monsieur le maréchal prince d'Essling.   Sur la hauteur en arrière de Moira, le 26 Septembre, 1810, à 10 heure ½.

J'ai l'honneur de vous adresser une lettre que je viens de recevoir du général Reynier et copie d'une réponse.

Vous trouverez également ci-joint une lettre du général Reynier adressée à votre excellence.

Je vous renouvelle, prince, l'assurance de ma haute consideration.

(Signé)   LE MARECHAL DUC D'ELCHINGEN.

A Monsieur le maréchal duc d'Elchingen.   St. Antonio, le 26 Septembre, à 8 heure du matin.

Depuis que le brouillard est dissipé, on apperçoit sur le Serra au delà de St. Antonio, cinq bataillons Portugais qui étoient à mi-côte et qui sont montés sur la crête à mesure que le brouillard s'est éclairci. Il y a de plus au col où passe le chemin, 6 pièces de canon et un détachement d'infantrie Anglaise, et à mi-côte une ligne de tirailleurs partie Anglais qui s'étend depuis le chemin qui monte du village de Carvailha à ma gauche, jusques vis-à-vis des postes du 6ᵉ corps, on voit des troupes sur les sommités qui font face au 6ᵉ corps ; mais comme on ne les apperçoit que de revers, ou ne peut juger de leur nombre.

On ne peut deviner s'il y a des troupes en arrière, mais d'après l'organisation de la montagne dont les crêtes sont étroites, et qui a des pentes rapides de chaque côte, il ne doit pas avoir de terrain pour y placer de fortes réserves et manœuvres. Cela me parait une arrière garde, mais la position est forte, et il faut faire des dispositions pour l'attaquer avec succès. J'attends des nouvelles de ce que l'ennemi fait devant vous pour faire aucun mouvement ; si vous jugez que c'est une arrière garde et que vous l'attaquiez, j'attaquerai aussi. Si vous jugez convenable d'attendre les ordres de Monsieur le maréchal prince d'Essling, j'attendrai aussi, comme je pense qu'il viendra vers votre corps, je vous prie de lui faire parvenir le rapport ci-joint avec les vôtres.

J'ai l'honneur de vous prier, Monsieur le maréchal, d'agréer l'hommage de mon respect.

(Signé)   REYNIER.

*A Monsieur le Général Reynier. Sur la hauteur en arrière
de Moira, le 26 Septembre* 1810, *à* 10 *heures* ½ *du matin.*

Je reçois à l'instant, mon cher général, votre lettre de ce jour.
Je pense qu'une grande partie de l'armée Anglo-Portugaise a
passé la nuit sur la crète des montagnes qui domine toute la
vallée de Moira. Un paysan dit qu'il existe de l'autre côté de ces
montagnes une plaine assez belle d'une demi-lieue d'étendue, et
très garnie d'Oliviers. Depuis ce matin, l'ennemi marche par
sa gauche, et semble diriger ses colonnes principales sur la route
d'Oporto ; cependant il tient encore assez de monde à la droite du
parc qui couvre le couvent des minimes nommé Sako ; et il montre
une 12ⁿᵉ de pièces d'artillerie. Le chemin de Coïmbre passe très
près de ce couvent.

J'ai envoyé ce matin un de mes aides-de-camp au prince
d'Essling pour lui dire que nous sommes en présence, et qu'il
serait nécessaire qu'il arrivât pour prendre un parti. Si j'avais le
commandement, j'attaquerais sans hésiter un seul instant ; mais je
crois, mon cher général, que vous ne pouvez rien compromettre
en vous échelonnant sur la droite de l'ennemi ; et en poussant ses
avant-postes, car c'est véritablement par ce point qu'il faudrait le
forcer à faire sa retraite.

Je vous renouvelle, &c.

(Signé) LE MARECHAL DUC D'ELCHINGEN.

SECTION 4.

*A Monsieur le maréchal prince d'Essling, Commandant-en-
chef, l'armée de Portugal, Paris, le* 4 *Decembre,* 1810.

Monsieur le prince d'Essling, le général Foy que vous avez
expédié est arrivé à Paris le 22 Novembre ; il a fait connâitre à
sa majesté et dans le plus grand détail ce qui s'est passé et votre
situation.

Dès le 4 Novembre le général Gardanne était en avant
d'Almeida avec un corps de 6,000 hommes. Le compte d'Erlon
avec les divisions Claparède, Conroux, et la division Fournier a
dû se trouver à Guarda vers le 20 Novembre.

L'Empereur, prince, a vu par les journaux Anglais, que vous
aviez établi des ponts sur le Tage et que vous en avez un sur le
Zézère, défendu sur les deux rives par de fortes têtes de pont.

Sa majesté pense que vous devez vous retrancher dans la position, que vous occupez devant l'ennemi; qu'Abrantés se trouvant à 800 toises du Tage, vous l'aurez isolé de son pont et bloqué pour en faire le siège. L'Empereur vous recommande d'établir deux ponts sur le Zézère, de défendre ces ponts par des ouvrages considérables, comme ceux du Spitz devant Vienne. Votre ligne d'opérations et de communications devant être établie par la route de Garda, partant du Zézère, passant par Cardigos, suivant la crète des montagnes par Campinha et Belmonte, vous aurez toujours la route de Castelbranco et Salvatera pour faire des vivres.

Je viens de donner de nouveau l'ordre déjà réitéré plusieurs fois au duc de Dalmatie, d'envoyer le 5me corps sur le Tage entre Montalveo et Villaflor, pour faire sa jonction avec vous. L'Empereur croit qu'il serait nécessaire de s'emparer d'Alcantara, de fortifier et de consolider tous les ponts sur le Zézère et sur le Tage, d'assurer toutes vos communications en saisissant les points favorables que peuvent offrir les localités pour fortifier de petites positions; des châteaux ou maisons qui, occupées par peu de troupes, soient à l'abri des incursions des milices.

Vous sentirez, Monsieur le Prince d'Essling, l'avantage de régulariser ainsi la guerre, ce qui vous mettra à même de profiter de la réunion de tous les corps qui vont vous renforcer, pour marcher sur lord Wellington et attaquer la gauche de sa position, soit pour l'obliger à se rembarquer en marchant sur la rive gauche du Tage, ou enfin, si tous ces moyens ne réussissaient pas, vous serez en mesure de rester en position pendant les mois de Décembre et de Janvier, en vous occupant d'organiser vos vivres et de bien établir vos communications avec Madrid et Almeyda.

L'armée du centre qui est à Madrid, ayant des détachements sur Placentia, vos communications avec cette capitale ne sont pas difficiles.

Deux millions 500 mille francs destinés à la solde de votre armée sont déjà à Valladolid; deux autre millions partent en ce moment de Bayonne. Ainsi votre armée sera dans une bonne situation.

Votre position deviendra très embarrassante pour les Anglais, qui, indépendamment d'une consommation énorme d'hommes et d'argent, se trouveront engagés dans une guerre de système, et ayant toujours une immensité de bâtimens à la mer pour leur rembarquement. Il faut donc, Prince, travailler sans cesse à

vous fortifier vis-à-vis de la position des ennemis, et pouvoir
garder la vôtre avec moins de monde ; ce qui rendra une partie
de votre armée mobile et vous mettra à même de faire des incursions dans le pays.

Vous trouverez ci-joint des moniteurs qui donnent des nouvelles
de Portugal, parvenues par la voie de l'Angleterre, datées du
12 Novembre.

Le Prince de Wagram et de Neuchâtel,

Major-Général,

(Signé) ALEXANDRE.

SECTION 5.

*A Monsieur le maréchal prince d'Essling, Commandant-en-
chef, l'armée de Portugal, Paris, le 22 Decembre, 1810.*

Je vous expédie, Prince, le général Foy que l'Empereur a
nommé général de division ; je vous envoie les moniteurs ; vous
y verrez que nous apprenons par les nouvelles d'Angleterre qu'au
1 Décembre, vous vous fortifiez dans votre position de Santarem.

L'Empereur met la plus grande importance à ce que vous
teniez constamment en échec les Anglais, à ce que vous ayez des
ponts sur le Zézère et sur le Tage ; la saison va devenir bonne
pour les opérations militaires, et vous aurez le moyen de harceler
les Anglais et de leur faire éprouver journellement des pertes.
Par les nouvelles des journaux Anglais, il parait qu'il y a beaucoup de malades dans leur armée, ils ne comptent que ————
27 à 28 mille hommes sous les armes et un effectif de 31 milles,
y compris la cavalerie et l'artillerie.   La situation de l'armée
Anglaise en Portugal tient Londres dans une angoise continuelle,
et l'Empereur regarde comme un grand avantage de tenir les
Anglais en échec, de les attirer et de leur faire perdre du monde
dans les affaires d'avant-gardes, jusqu'à ce que vous soyez à
même de les engager dans une affaire générale.   Je réitère encore
au maréchal duc de Trévise l'ordre de marcher sur le Tage avec
le 5ᵐᵉ corps.

Le comte d'Erlon, qui réunit son corps à Ciudad-Rodrigo,
va profiter de ce moment où les pluies cessent pour reprendre
l'offensive et battre tous ces corps de mauvaises troupes que se
trouvent sur vos communications et sur vos flancs.

Vos ponts étant bien assurés sur le Zézère, la ligne de vos

opérations la plus naturelle parait devoir être par la rive gauche de cette rivière.

Le général Foy, à qui l'Empereur a parlé longtems, vous donnera plus de détails.

Le Prince de Wagram et de Neuchâtel,

Major-Général,

(Signé)   ALEXANDRE.

SECTION 6.

A Monsieur le maréchal d'Essling, Commandant-en-chef, l'armée de Portugal, Paris, le 16 Janvier, 1811.

Je vous préviens, Prince, que par décret impérial, en date du 15 de ce mois, l'Empereur a formé une armée du Nord de l'Espagne, dont le commandement est confié à Monsieur le maréchal duc d'Istrie qui va établir son quartier général à Burgos.

L'arrondissement de l'armée du Nord de l'Espagne est composé : —

1°. De la Navarre formant le 3e gouvernement de l'Espagne.

2°. Des trois provinces de la Biscaye et de la province de Santander, formant le 4e gouvernement.

3°. De la province des Asturies.

4°. Des provinces de Burgos, Aranda, et Soria, formant le 5e gouvernement.

5°. Des provinces de Palencia, Valladolid, Leon, Benevente, Toro, et Zamore, formant le 6e gouvernement.

6°. De la province de Salamanque.

Ainsi cet arrondissement comprend tout le pays occupé par les troupes Françaises entre la mer, la France, le Portugal, et les limites de l'arrondissement des armées du centre et de l'Arragon.

Cette disposition, en centralisant le pourvoir, va donner de l'ensemble et une nouvelle impulsion d'activité aux opérations dans toutes les provinces du Nord de l'Espagne ; et Monsieur le maréchal duc d'Istrie mettra un soin particulier à maintenir les communications entre Valladolid, Salamanque, et Almeida.

Je vous engage, Prince, à correspondre avec Monsieur le maréchal duc d'Istrie toutes les fois que vous le jugerez utile au service.

D'après les ordres de l'Empereur je préviens Monsieur le duc

d'Istrie que dans des circonstances imprévues, il doit appuyer
l'armée de Portugal et lui porter du secours ; je le préviens aussi
que le 9ᵐᵉ corps d'armée serait sous ses ordres dans le cas où ce
corps rentrerait en Espagne.

Le Prince de Wagram et de Neuchâtel,
Major-Général,
(Signé)   ALEXANDRE.

SECTION 7.

*A Monsieur le maréchal duc de Dalmatie, Paris, le 24
Janvier, 1811.*

Vous verrez par le moniteur d'hier, Monsieur le duc de Dalmatie, que les armées de Portugal étaient à la fin de l'année der-
nière dans la même position.   L'Empereur me charge de vous
renouveller l'ordre de vous porter au secours du prince d'Essling,
qui est toujours à Santarem ; il a plusieurs ponts sur le Zézère,
et il attend que les eaux soient diminuées pour en jetter un sur le
Tage.   Il parait certain que le 9ᵐᵉ corps a opéré sa jonction avec
lui par le Nord, c'est-à-dire, par Almeyda.

L'Empereur *espère que le prince d'Essling aura jetté un pont
sur le Tage ;* ce que lui donnera des vivres.

Les corps insurgés de Valence et de Murcie vont se trouver
occupé par le corps du général Suchet, aussitôt que Tarragone
sera tombé entre nos mains, comme l'a fait la place de Tortose ;
alors Sa Majesté *pense que le 5ᵐᵉ corps* et une partie *du* 4ᵐᵉ
pourront se porter au *secours* du prince d'Essling.

Le Major-Général,
(Signé)   ALEXANDRE.

SECTION 8.

*A Monsieur le maréchal prince d'Essling, Paris, le 25 Janvier,
1811.*

Je vous préviens, prince, que Monsieur le maréchal duc de
Dalmatie s'est mis en marche dans les premiers jours de Janvier
avec le 5ᵐᵉ corps d'armée, un corps de cavalerie, et un équipage de
siège pour se porter sur Badajoz et faire le siège de cette place.
Ces troupes ont dû arriver le 10 de ce mois devant Badajoz ; je
mande au duc de Dalmatie qu'après la prise de cette place il doit

se porter sans perdre de tems sur le Tage avec son équipage de siège pour vous donner les moyens d'assiéger et de prendre Abrantés.

Le Prince de Wagram et de Neuchâtel,
Major-Général,
(Signé) ALEXANDRE.

SECTION IX.

Au Prince de Wagram et de Neuchâtel, major-général, Paris, le 6 Fevrier, 1811.

Mon cousin, je pense que vous devez envoyer le moniteur d'aujourd'hui au duc de Dalmatie, au duc de Trévise, au général Belliard, au duc d'Istrie, aux commandans de Cuidad Rodrigo et d'Almeida, aux général Thiébaut, et aux généraux Dorsenne, Cafarelli, et Reille. Ecrivez au duc d'Istrie en lui envoyant le moniteur, pour lui annoncer qu'il y trouvera les dernières nouvelles du Portugal, qui paraissent être du 13 ; que tout parait prendre une couleur avantageuse ; que si Badajos a été pris dans le courant de Janvier, le duc *de Dalmatie a pû se porter sur le Tage, et faciliter l'établissement du pont au prince d'Essling ;* qu'il devient donc très important de faire toutes les dispositions que j'ai ordonnées afin que le général Drouet avec ses deux divisions puisse être tout entier à la disposition du prince d'Essling. Ecrivez en même tems au duc de Dalmatie pour lui faire connaître la situation du duc d'Istrie, et lui réitérer l'ordre *de favoriser le prince d'Essling* pour son passage du Tage ; que j'espère que Badajoz aura été pris dans le courant de Janvier ; et que vers le 20 *Janvier sa jonction aura eu lieu sur le Tage,* avec le prince d'Essling ; qu'il peut, si cela est nécessaire, retirer des troupes du 4me corps ; *qu'enfin tout est sur le Tage.* Sur ce je prie Dieu, mon cousin, qu'il vous ait dans sa sainte et digne garde.

(Signé) NAPOLEON.

P.S. Je vous renvoie votre lettre au duc d'Istrie, faites le partir.

*A Monsieur le maréchal prince d'Essling, Commandant-en-
chef l'armée de Portugal, Paris, le 7 Fevrier, 1811.*

Je vous envoie, prince, le moniteur du 6, vous y trouverez les
dernières nouvelles que nous avons du Portugal ; elles vont jusqu'
au 13 Janvier, et annoncent *que tout prend une tournure avantageuse. Si Badajoz a été pris dans le courant de Janvier,
comme cela est probable, le duc de Dalmatie aura pu faire
marcher des troupes sur le Tage, et vous faciliter l'établissement
d'un pont.* Je lui en ai donné et je lui en réitère l'ordre ; l'Empereur espère que la *jonction des troupes de ce maréchal a eu
lieu maintenant avec vous sur le Tage.*

Les deux divisions d'infanterie du corps du général Drouet,
vont rester entièrement à votre disposition d'après les ordres que
je donne à Monsieur le maréchal duc d'Istrie, commandant en
chef l'armée du nord de l'Espagne ; je lui mande de porter son
quartier général à Valladolid, d'établir des corps nombreux de
cavalerie dans la province de Salamanque afin d'assurer d'une
manière journalière sure et rapide la correspondance entre Almeyda,
Cuidad Rodrigo et Valladolid, et nous envoyer promptement toutes
les nouvelles qui pourront parvenir à l'armée de Portugal.

Je lui prescris de tenir à Ciudad Rodrigo, un corps de 6,000
hommes qui puisse éloigner toute espèce de troupe ennemie de
Ciudad Rodrigo et d'Almeida, faire même des incursions sur
Pinhel et Guarda, empêcher qu'il se forme aucun rassemblement
sur les derrières du 9me corps, et présenter des dispositions offensives
sur cette frontière du Portugal.

De réunir une forte brigade de la garde impériale vers Zamora
d'où elle sera à portée de soutenir le corps de Ciudad Rodrigo, et
où elle se trouvera d'ailleurs dans une position avancée pour agir
suivant les circonstances.

De réunir une autre forte brigade de la garde à Valladolid où
elle sera en mesure d'appuyer la première ; et de réunir le reste
de la garde dans le gouvernement de Burgos.

Par ces dispositions, prince, les deux divisions d'infanterie du
9me corps, seront entièrement à votre disposition, et avec ce secours
vous serez en mesure de tenir longtems la position que vous occupez ; de vous porter sur la rive gauche du Tage ; ou enfin d'agir
comme vous le jugerez convenable sans avoir aucune inquiétude
sur le nord de l'Espagne, puisque le duc d'Istrie sera à portée de

marcher sur Almeyda et Ciudad Rodrigo et même sur Madrid, si des circonstances inattendues le rendaient nécessaire.

Dès que le duc d'Istrie aura fait ses dispositions il enverra un officier au général Drouet, pour l'en instruire et lui faire connoître qu'il peut rester en entier pour vous renforcer.

Le général Foy a dû partir vers le 29 Janvier de Ciudad Rodrigo, avec 4 bataillons et 300 hommes de cavalerie pour vous rejoindre.

Le Prince de Wagram et de Neuchâtel,

Major Général,

(Signé)　　　　　　　ALEXANDRE.

SECTION 11.

A Monsieur le maréchal duc d'Istrie, Guarda, le 29 Mars, 1811.

Mon cher Maréchal, vous aurez appris notre arrivée aux frontières du Portugal, l'armée se trouve dans un pays absolument ruiné; et avec toute ma volonté et la patience de l'armée, je crains de n'y pouvoir tenir 8 jours, et je me verrai forcé de rentrer en Espagne.

J'écris à M. le Cte. d'Erlon pour qu'il fasse approvisionner Almeyda et Rodrigo; ces deux places n'auraient jamais dû cesser d'avoir pour 3 mois de vivres aux quels on n'aurait pas dû toucher sous aucun prétexte; et ma surprise est extrême d'apprendre qu'il n'y a que pour 10 jours de vivres à Almeyda. Je lui écris aussi de prendre une position entre Rodrigo et Almeyda, avec ses deux divisions; vous sentez combien il est nécessaire, qu'il se place à portée de marcher au secours d'Almeyda.

Si je trouvais des vivres, je ne quitterais pas les frontières d'Espagne et du Portugal, mais comme je vous l'ai dit, je ne vois guère la possibilité d'y rester. . . . .

. . . .

(Signé)　　　　　　　LE PRINCE D'ESSLING.

SECTION 12.

A Monsieur le maréchal duc d'Istrie, Alfayates, le 2 Avril, 1811.

Mon cher Maréchal, le pays que l'armée occupe ne pouvant en

aucune manière le faire vivre, je me vois forcé de la faire rentrer en Espagne. Voici les cantonnements que je lui ai assignés et l'itinéraire de marche de chaque corps d'armée. . . . . . .

. . . .

(Signé)   LE PRINCE D'ESSLING.

SECTION 13.

A Monsieur le maréchal duc d'Istrie, Rodrigo, le 5 Avril, 1811.

Mon cher Maréchal, je suis arrivé avec toute l'armée sur Ciudad Rodrigo, mes troupes depuis plusieurs jours sont sans pain ; et je suis obligé de faire prendre sur les approvisionnements de Rodrigo 200 mille rations de biscuit, que je vous prie d'ordonner de remplacer avec les ressources qui peuvent se trouver à Salamanque et Valladolid. Nous partirons ensuite pour les cantonnements que j'ai eu soin de vous faire connaître. J'espère que vous aurez bien voulu faire donner des ordres aux intendants de province, d'y faire préparer des vivres, seul moyen d'y faire maintenir l'ordre.

Je compte séjourner 3 à 4 jours ici pour voir si l'ennemi ne s'approcherait pas des places.

(Signé)   LE PRINCE D'ESSLING.

SECTION 14.

A Monsieur le maréchal duc d'Istrie, Salamanque, le 15 Avril, 1811.

Mon cher Maréchal, ma position devient toujours plus allarmante ; les places appellent des secours ; je ne reçois pas de réponses de vous à aucune de mes demandes ; et si cet état de chose se prolonge, je serai forcé de faire prendre à l'armée des cantonnements où elle puisse vivre, et d'abandonner les places que je ne suis pas chargé de défendre et encore bien moins d'approvisionner, mes troupes manquant absolument de vivres.

(Signé)   LE PRINCE D'ESSLING.

SECTION 15.

A Monsieur la maréchal duc d'Istrie, Paris, le 3 Avril, 1811.

Le général Foy est arrivé, Monsieur le maréchal duc d'Istrie, ainsi que les deux aides-de-camp du maréchal prince d'Essling, le capitaine Porcher, et le chef d'escadron Pelet. Il parait que le prince d'Essling avec son corps d'armée prend position à Guarda, Belmonte, et Alfayates. Ainsi il protège Ciudad Rodrigo, Almeyda, Madrid et l'Andalousie. Ses communications doivent s'établir facilement avec l'armée du midi par Alcantara et Badajoz. Si ce qu'on ne prévoit pas, le prince d'Essling étoit vivement attaqué par l'armée Anglaise, l'empereur pense que *vous pourriez le soutenir avec une 15me de milles hommes.* L'armée du centre doit avoir poussé un corps sur Alcantara. L'armée du midi sera renforcée par ce que vous aurez déjà fait partir, et d'après le prince d'Essling, elle va se trouver assez forte pour ne rien craindre de l'ennemi. . . . .

(Le reste est sans interêt.)

Le Major-Général,
(Signé)   ALEXANDRE.

SECTION 16.

A Monsieur le maréchal duc d'Istrie, Salamanque, le 17 *Avril,* 1811.

MON CHER MARECHAL,

Le général Reynaud, commandant supérieur à Rodrigo, ainsi que le général Marchand, qui est avec sa division autour de cette place, me rendent compte que 2 divisions Portugaises avec une division Anglaise ont pris position aux environs d'Almeyda. Quoique cette place ait encore des vivres pour une 20ne de jours, et que les Anglais et les Portugais meurent de faim dans leurs positions, il faut faire des dispositions pour les chasser au delà de la Coa, et pour ravitailler cette place. Je vous propose en conséquence, mon cher maréchal, de mettre à ma disposition 12 à 1500 chevaux, ceux de l'armée de Portugal n'étant en état de rendre aucun service ; je vous demande de plus une division d'infanterie pour placer en réserve. Vers le 24 ou le 29, ces forces se joindront aux 6 divisions que je compte réunir de l'armée de Portugal pour attaquer l'ennemi, s'il nous attend dans ses positions et le chasser au delà de la Coa. Il est impossible de faire faire le moindre mouvement à toutes ces troupes, du moins à celles de l'armée de Portugal pour attaquer l'ennemi ; si on ne peut leur faire distribuer pour 10 jours de biscuit et avoir de l'eau de vie à la suite de l'armée. Je vous demande encore 15 à 18 pièces d'artillerie bien attelées, celles à mes ordres étant hors d'état de marcher. Avec ces moyens, nul doute que l'ennemi ne soit déposté et chassé hors des frontières de l'Espagne et au delà de la Coa. Mon cher maréchal, je vis ici au jour de jour ; je suis sans le sol, vous pouvez tout ; il faut donc nous envoyer du biscuit, de l'eau de vie, du pain et de l'orge. Ce sera avec ces moyens que nous pourrons manœuvrer. Il ne faut pas perdre un instant. Il est très urgent de marcher au secours d'Almeyda. C'est à vous à donner vos ordres ; et vous me trouverez porté de la meilleure volonté à faire tout ce qui sera convenable aux intérêts de S. M.

(Signé) LE PRINCE D'ESSLING.

SECTION 17.

A Monsieur le maréchal duc d'Istrie, Salamanque, le 22 Avril, 1811.

MON CHER MARÉCHAL,

J'ai reçu votre dépêche. Toutes vos promesses de vous réunir à moi s'évanouissent donc dans le moment où j'en ai besoin ; ravitailler Almeida et Rodrigo est la 1re opération et la seule qui peut nous donner la faculté de rendre l'armée de Portugal disponible, lorsqu'on n'aura plus rien à craindre sur le sort des places. En y jettant pour 3 à 4 mois de vivres, on peut ensuite établir plusieurs colonnes mobiles ; on peut envoyer des troupes à Avila et Ségovie ; on peut au besoin appuyer le mouvement de l'armée d'Andalousie. Mais ne serait il pas honteux de laisser rendre une place faute de vivres, en présence de deux maréchaux de l'Empire ? Je vous ai déjà prévenu de la nullité de ma cavalerie, de l'impossibilité où se trouvent les chevaux d'artillerie de rendre aucun service. Vous savez aussi que je dois envoyer le 9me corps en Andalousie ; je voulais aussi le faire concourir avant son départ au ravitaillement des places. Pouvez vous, mon cher maréchal, balancer un seul instant à m'envoyer de la cavalerie, et des attelages d'artillerie, si vous voulez garder votre matériel ? Ne vous ai-je pas prévenu que je commencerais mon mouvement le 26 ? et vous paraissez attendre le (22) une seconde demande de ma part. Vous le savez aussi bien que moi, perdre un ou deux jours à la guerre est beaucoup ; et ce délai peut avoir des suites fâcheuses qu'on ne répare plus.

Quand je vous ai dit que je ne réunerais que 6 divisions ; c'était pour ne pas tout dégarnir des points importans occupés par les corps d'armée ; mais de la cavalerie et de l'artillerie sont un secours dont je ne puis me passer.   Je vous prie en conséquence, mon cher maréchal, de me faire arriver de la cavalerie et des attelages d'artillerie à marches forcées.   Réflechissez qu'une fois les places réapprovisionnées, je pourrai disposer des $\frac{2}{3}$ de l'armée, et que cette opération passe avant tout.

En m'offrant de nous envoyer les attelages pour 16 pièces, vous aurez bien entendu, sans doute, mon cher maréchal y comprendre ceux nécessaires pour les caissons des pièces.

(Signé)   LE PRINCE D'ESSLING.

SECTION 18.

A Monsieur le maréchal duc d'Istrie, Salamanque, le 24 Avril, 1811.

MON CHER MARECHAL,

Je me rends demain à Ciudad Rodrigo, où toute l'armée sera réunie le 26.   Le ravitaillement de la place d'Almeida est du plus haut intérêt pour les armes de S. M. ; et il eut été bien à désirer que les secours que j'ai en l'honneur de vous demander nous eussent été envoyés.   L'ennemi parait avoir de 20 à 29 mille hommes autour de cette place.   Vous dire que je n'aurai en cavalerie que 15 à 1800 hommes, et seulement 20 pièces de canon pour toute l'armée, c'est vous faire sentir, mon cher maréchal, combien votre secours m'eut été nécessaire au moins sous deux rapports, pour votre armée même et pour la tranquillité du nord de l'Espagne.   Je n'ai pas ménagé mes instances auprès de vous.   Si mes efforts n'étaient pas heureux ; votre dévouement pour le service de l'Empereur, vous ferait certainement regretter de ne pas les avoir secondés avec les moyens que vous m'aviez fait espérer, avant que j'en eusse besoin.

(Signé)   LE PRINCE D'ESSLING.

SECTION 19.

A Monsieur le maréchal duc d'Istrie, Rodrigo, le 29 Avril, 1811.

MON CHER MARECHAL,

Vos lettres sont inconcevables.   Dans celle du 20, vous me dites que vous ne pouvez me donner aucun secours.   Par celle du 22, vous me dites que le 25 ou le 26 vous me joindrez partout où je serai, et que la tête de votre colonne arrivera à Salamanque le 26. Par celle que je reçois à l'instant, vous me dites, que votre cavalerie et votre artillerie se trouvent encore le 27 à une journée en arrière de Salamanque ; et vous concluez que mon mouvement doit être fini ; et vous me témoignez vos regrets de n'avoir pû y coopérer. Convenez, mon cher maréchal, que si l'armée de Portugal recevait un échec, vous auriez bien des reproches à vous faire. Je vous ai demandé de l'artillerie et des attelages et encore plus positivement de la cavalerie ; vous avez sous différens prétextes éludé ma demande. Toutes les troupes qui sont en Espagne, sont de la même famille. Vous êtes, jusques à ce qu'il y ait de nouveaux ordres, chargé de la défense et de l'approvisionnement des places d'Almeida et de Rodrigo. Je n'aurais pas mieux demandé que d'employer l'armée de Portugal sous mes ordres à défendre ces places, à marcher au secours de l'armée du midi ; mais comment puis-je le faire sans vivres ?

Je compte faire mon mouvement demain matin. J'ignore quelle pourra être l'issue de ce mouvement ; si ma lettre vous arrive dans la journée de demain ; votre cavalerie et votre artillerie pourraient toujours se mettre en mouvement dans la nuit pour arriver après demain 1er Mai à Cabrillas. Je vous prie de faire filer sans s'arrêter le biscuit, la farine, le grain que vous n'aurez pas manqué de réunir à la suite de vos troupes. Il est instant que ces ressources comme beaucoup d'autres, arrivent à Rodrigo ; cette place n'aura pas pour 15 jours de vivres. A mon départ d'ici, il faudra que des convois considerables y soient envoyés.

(Signé) LE PRINCE D'ESSLING.

SECTION 20.

A Monsieur le maréchal duc de Raguse, Paris, le 20 Avril, 1811.

MONSIEUR LE DUC DE RAGUSE,

Vous trouverez ci-joint l'ordre de l'Empereur qui vous donne le commandement de l'armée du Portugal. Je donne l'ordre au maréchal prince d'Essling de vous remettre le commandement de cette armée. Saisissez les rènes d'une main ferme ; faites dans l'armée les changemens qui deviendraient nécessaires. L'intention de l'Empereur est que le duc d'Abrantes et le général Reynier restent sous vos ordres. S. M.

compte assez sur le dévouement que lui portent ses géneraux, pour être persuadé qu'ils vous seconderont de tous leurs moyens.

L'Empereur ordonne, Monsieur le duc de Raguse, que le prince d'Essling en quittant l'armée n'emmène avec lui que son fils et un de ses aides-de-camp. Mais son chef d'état-major, le général Fririon, le colonel Pelet, ses autre aides-de-camp, tous les officiers de son état-major doivent rester avec vous.

Toutefois, Monsieur le duc, je vous le répète S. M. met en vous une confiance entière.

Le Major Général, &c.

(Signé)　　　　　　　　　　　Alexandre.

No. VIII.

Les Officiers Français Prisonniers de Guerre, déténus à la Maison, Rue S. Jean, à Monsieur le Général Trant, Gouverneur de la Ville et Province d'Oporto.

MONSIEUR LE GENERAL,

Chacun des officiers Français prisonniers de guerre, déténus à la maison rue S. Jean, pénétré des obligations qu'il vous a, desirerait vous offrir individuellement l'expression de sa reconnoisance. C'est nous que ces messieurs ont choisi pour être auprès de vous leur organes, et nous sommes d'autant plus flattés de cette commission agréable qu'il n'y en a pas un parmi nous qui dans son particulier n'ait reçu de vous des services importants. Nous osons nous flatter que vous agréerez favorablement ce foible témoignage de notre gratitude et les sincères remerciments que nous venons vous présenter pour toutes les bontés que vous avez eus pour nous. Ce n'est pas sans un vif regret que nous envisageons le moment de votre départ, mais ce que déjà vous avez fait pour nous, nous fait espérer que votre solicitude s'étendra au delà de votre séjour et que pendant votre absence nous continuerons à en éprouver les effets.

Ce n'est pas, monsieur le général, d'après l'étendue de notre lettre qu'il faudra mesurer celle de notre reconnoissance ; nous sommes mieux en état de sentir que d'exprimer ce que nous vous

devons et lorsque des circonstances plus heureuses nous raméne-
ront vers notre patrie, nous nous ferons un devoir et une satisfaction de faire connaître la manière dont nous avons été traités et
les peines que vous vous êtes donnés pour adoucir notre sort.
Nous nous recommandons à la continuation de votre bienveillance,
et nous vous prions d'agréer l'assurance de gratitude et de haute
considération avec lesquelles nous avons l'honneur d'être, monsieur
le général, vos très humbles et très obeissants serviteurs,

Au nom des officiers Français, prisonniers de guèrre,

FALLOT,

Docteur médecin des armées Françaises attaché au
grand quartier général des l'armée de Portugal.

Le colonel sous inspecteur aux revues des troupes Françaises,

CATELOT.

H. DELAHAYE,

C_{om}. de la marine.

No. IX.

SECTION 1.

*Letter from lieut.-general Graham to the right honourable
Henry Wellesley, Isla de Leon, 24th March, 1811.*

SIR,

You will do justice to my reluctance to enter into any contro-
versy for the purpose of counteracting the effects of that obloquy
which you yourself and many others assured me my conduct was
exposed to by the reports circulated, at Cadiz, relative to the issue
of the late expedition.

But a copy of a printed statement of general La Peña having
been shewn to me, which, by implication at least, leaves the
blame of the failure of the most brilliant prospects on me, it
becomes indispensably necessary that I should take up my pen in
self-defence.

Having already sent you a copy of my despatch to the earl of

Liverpool, with a report of thè action, 1 will not trouble you with a detail of the first movements of the army, nor with any other observation relative to them, than that the troops suffered much unnecessary fatigue by marching in the night, and without good guides.

Considering the nature of the service we were engaged in, I was most anxious that the army should not come into contest with the enemy in an exhausted state, nor be exposed to the attack of the enemy but when it was well collected; and, in consequence of representations to this effect, I understood that the march of the afternoon of the 4th was to be a short one, to take up for the night a position near Conil; to prepare which, staff-officers, of both nations, were sent forward with a proper escort.

The march was, nevertheless, continued through the night, with those frequent and harassing halts which the necessity of groping for the way occasioned.

When the British division began its march from the position of Barrosa to that of Bermeja, *I left the general on the Barrosa height, nor did I know of his intentions of quitting it;* and, when I ordered the division to countermarch in the wood, I did so to support the troops left for its defence, and believing the general to be there in person. In this belief I sent no report of the attack, which was made so near the spot where the general was supposed to be, and, though confident in the bravery of the British troops, I was not less so in the support I should receive from the Spanish army. The distance, however, to Bermeja is trifling, and no orders were given from head-quarters for the movement of any corps of the Spanish army to support the British division, to prevent its defeat in this unequal contest, or to profit of the success earned at so heavy expense. The voluntary zeal of the two small battalions, (Walloon guards and Ciudad Real,) which had been detached from my division, brought them alone back from the wood; but, notwithstanding their utmost efforts, they could only come at the close of the action.

Had the whole body of the Spanish cavalry, with the horse-artillery, been rapidly sent by the sea-beach to form in the plain, and to envelop the enemy's left; had the greatest part of the infantry been marched through the pine-wood, in our rear, to turn his right, what success might have been expected from such decisive movements? The enemy must either have retired instantly, and without occasioning any serious loss to the British division, or he would have exposed himself to absolute destruction, his cavalry greatly outnumbered, his artillery lost, his columns mixed and in confusion ; a general dispersion would have been the inevitable consequence of a close pursuit ; our wearied men would have found spirits to go on and would have done so trusting to finding refreshments and repose at Chiclana. This moment was lost. Within a quarter of an hour's ride of the scene of action, the general remained ignorant of what was passing, *and nothing was done !* Let not, then, this action of Barrosa form any part of the general result of the transactions of the day ; it was an accidental feature ; it was the result of no combination, it was equally unseen and unheeded by the Spanish staff; the British division, left alone, suffered the loss of more than one-fourth of its number, and became unfit for future exertion. Need I say more to justify my determination of declining any further co-operation in the field towards the prosecution of the object of the expedition ? I am, however, free to confess that, having thus placed myself and the British division under the direction of the Spanish commander-in-chief in the field, (contrary to my instructions,) I should not have thought myself justified to my king and country to risk the absolute destruction of this division in a second trial. But I have a right to claim credit for what would have been my conduct from what it was ; and I will ask if it can be doubted, after my zealous co-operation throughout, and the ready assistance afforded to the troops left on Barrosa height, that the same anxiety for the success of the cause would not have secured to the Spanish army the utmost efforts of the British division during the whole of the enterprise, *had we been supported as we had a right to expect ?*

There is not a man in the division who would not gladly have relinquished his claim to glory, acquired by the action of Barrosa, to have shared, with the Spaniards, the ultimate success that was within our grasp as it were.

The people of Spain, the brave and persevering people, are universally esteemed, respected, and admired by all who value liberty and independence ; the hearts and hands of British soldiers will ever be with them ; the cause of Spain is felt by all to be a common one.

I conclude with mentioning that the only request expressed to me, at head-quarters, on the morning of the 6th, on knowing

of my intention to send the British troops across the river St.
Petri, was *that the opportunity of withdrawing the Spanish
troops, during the night, was lost;* and on my observing that,
after such a defeat, there was no risk of attack from an enemy, a
very contrary opinion was maintained.

In point of fact, no enemy ever appeared during several days
employed in bringing off the wounded and burying the dead. It
may be proper to remark on the report published relative to the
enemy's number at St. Petri, (4500 men of Villat's division,) that,
by the concurrent testimony of all the French officers here, general
Villat's division had charge of the whole line,—what, then, must
be the strength of that division to have afforded 4500 men to
St. Petri alone? In order to establish, by authentic documents,
facts which may have been disputed, and to elucidate others, I
enclose, by way of appendix, the reports of various officers of
this division.

I have the honour to be, &c. &c. &c.

(Signed)   Thos. Graham,

Lt.-General.

P.S. I must add this postscript distinctly to deny my having
spoken, at head-quarters, in the evening of the 5th, of sending
for more troops, or for provisions from the Isla. My visit was a
very short one, of mere ceremony. I may have asked if the
Spanish troops expected were arrived. This error must have
arisen from the difficulty of conversing in a foreign language.

With this I send you a sketch of the ground, &c. of the
action of Barrosa; by which it will be seen how impossible,
according to my judgement, it would be for an enemy to expose
his left flank, by making a direct attack through the wood on the
Bermeja position, while that of Barrosa was occupied in force by
the allied army.

SECTION 2.

*Adjutant-general's state of the troops assembled at Tarifa,
under the command of lieut.-general Graham, 25th Feb.* 1810.

Designations.	Number of Bayonets.	Commanders.
Two squadrons of 2d German hussars.	,,	Major Busche.
Detachment of artillery. ··		Major Duncan. 10 guns.
Detachment of engineers ··	47	Captain Birch.
Brigade of guards, re-inforced by a detachment of the 2d battalion 95th rifles. ···············	1221	Brigadier-gen. Dilkes.
1st battalion 28th foot; 2d battalion 67th; 2d battalion 87th; re-inforced with 2 companies of the 20th Portuguese.	1764	Colonel Wheatley.
Flank battalion composed of detachments of the 3d battalion 95th rifles and two companies of the 47th foot ······	594	Lt.-col. A. Barnard, 95th regt.
Two companies of 2d battalion 9th regt.; two companies of 1st battalion 28th regt.; two companies of 2d battalion 82d regt. ······	475	Lt.-col. Brown, 28th regt.
One company of the royal staff corps ··········	33	Lieutenant Read.
Total number of bayonets ··	4114	
The hussars were about ··	180	
Total of sabres and bayonets	4294,	with 10 guns.

SECTION 3.—BATTLE OF BARROSA.

Extract from a letter of general Frederick Ponsonby.

" I proceeded rapidly towards the entrance of the wood, found the Germans, and conducted them along the right flank of our little army. We came in contact with the French dragoons, whom we found nearly abreast of our front line and about three hundred yards apart from it on our right flank, our line had just halted and the firing was gradually decreasing at the time we charged. I do not imagine the French dragoons much exceeded us in number, they behaved well, but if we had had half a dozen stout squadrons the mass of beaten infantry would not have returned to their camp."

SECTION 4.—BATTLE OF ALBUERA.

Extract of a letter from colonel Light, serving in the 4th Dragoons at the Battle of Albuera.

" After our brigade of infantry, first engaged, were repulsed, I was desired by General D'Urban to tell the Count de Penne Villamur, to charge the lancers, and we all started, as I thought, to do the thing well; but when within a few paces of the enemy the whole pulled up, and there was no getting them farther; and in a few moments after I was left alone to run the gauntlet as well as I could."

	Tués — Gén. de Brigade	Tués — Colonels	Tués — Chefs de Br. ou Escadron	Tués — Capitaines	Tués — Lieutenants	Tués — Sous Lieutenants	Tués — Sous Officiers et Soldats	Tués — Total	Blessés — Gén. de Division	Blessés — Colonels	Blessés — Chefs de Bat. ou Escadron	Blessés — Capitaines	Blessés — Lieutenants	Blessés — Sous Lieutenants	Blessés — Sous Officiers et Soldats	Blessés — Total	Restés — Gén. de Division	Restés — Colonels	Restés — Capitaines	Restés — Sous Lieutenants	Restés — Sous Officiers et Soldats	Restés — Total	Total général
St. Petri, 4 — 95 de Ligne	.	.	.	.	.	.	3	3	.	2	.	1	1	1	32	37	.	.	.	.	5	5	42
St. Petri, 4 — Etat Major	.	.	.	.	.	.	.	.	.	1	2	.	.	.	.	3	.	.	.	.	.	.	3
1 — Etat Major	1	1	.	.	.	.	.	2	.	.	.	.	.	.	.	.	1	.	.	.	.	1	3
1 — 9 Infr. Ligne	.	.	.	.	1	.	14	15	.	.	.	1	2	1	70	74	.	.	.	1	18	19	108
1 — 24 Ligne	.	.	.	1	1	.	33	35	.	.	.	3	3	1	214	221	.	.	2	1	21	24	280
1 — 96 Ligne	.	1	.	1	.	.	39	41	.	.	.	2	3	1	199	205	.	.	1	1	1	3	249
1 — 1 Br. Elite	.	.	.	1	.	.	1	2	.	.	.	2	2	1	136	141	.	.	.	1	59	60	203
2 (5 Mars) — Etat Major	.	.	.	.	.	.	.	.	.	.	1	1	.	.	.	2	.	.	.	.	.	.	2
2 — 45 Ligne	.	.	.	1	.	.	7	8	.	.	.	.	.	.	44	44	.	.	.	.	3	3	55
2 — 8 Ligne	.	.	2	3	3	3	63	74	.	.	1	4	5	1	622	633	.	.	.	.	19	19	726
3 — 54 Ligne	.	.	1	2	.	.	26	29	.	.	1	3	5	1	284	294	.	.	.	.	.	.	323
3 — Etat Major	.	.	.	.	.	.	.	.	1	.	.	.	.	.	.	1	.	.	.	.	.	.	1
3 — 27 Infr. Ligne	.	.	.	.	1	.	20	21	.	.	.	3	3	1	150	157	.	.	1	1	21	23	201
3 — 94 Ligne	.	.	.	1	.	.	9	10	.	.	.	1	1	1	49	52	.	.	.	.	.	.	62
3 — 95 Ligne	.	.	.	.	.	.	1	1	.	.	.	.	.	.	32	32	.	.	.	.	1	1	34
Dragoons — 1 Regt.	.	.	.	.	.	.	2	2	.	.	.	2	3	1	30	36	.	.	1	.	3	4	42
Dragoons — 2 Regt.	.	.	.	.	.	.	3	3	.	.	.	.	.	.	12	12	.	.	.	.	4	4	19
Dragoons — Artillerie	.	.	.	.	.	.	16	16	.	.	.	1	1	1	31	34	.	.	.	.	.	.	51
Puerte St. Maria — 45 Ligne	.	.	.	.	.	.	10	10	.	.	.	.	.	.	43	43	.	1	.	.	27	28	81
Puerte St. Maria — Artillerie	.	1	.	.	.	.	.	1	.	.	.	.	.	.	2	2	.	.	.	.	6	6	9
Médina, 9 Mars, 8 Dr. — 94	.	.	.	.	.	.	4	4	.	.	.	.	.	.	29	29	.	.	.	.	.	.	33
Médina, 9 Mars, 8 Dr. — 95	.	.	.	.	.	.	4	4	.	.	.	.	1	.	18	19	.	.	.	.	1	1	24
Total	1	3	3	9	6	3	255	281	1	3	5	23	27	12	1997	2068	1	1	5	6	189	202	2551

Note by the Editor.—Deduct affair of the 4th about Santa Petri 45
  ,,   ,,   at Puerta Santa Maria 81
  ,,   ,,   at Medina 64

Total 2551

```
2551
 190
————
2361
```

Remains loss at Barrosa....

SECTION 6.

Intercepted papers of colonel Lejeune..

ORDRE.

Il est ordonné à Monsieur le colonel baron le Jeune, mon A. D. C. de partir sur le champ en poste pour porter les ordres ci-joints et parcourir l'Andalousie et l'Estramadure.

Monsieur le colonel le Jeune se rendra d'abord à Grenade auprès de Monsieur le général Sebastiani, commandant du 4me corps d'armée, et il lui remettra les ordres qui le concernent.

De Grenade, Monsieur le Jeune se rendra par Séville devant Cadiz, et verra par lui-même la situation des choses, afin de pouvoir à son retour en rendre un compte détaillé à l'Empereur. Monsieur le Jeune remettra à Monsieur le maréchal duc de Dalmatie, les dépêches qui lui sont destinées, soit à Séville, soit à Cadiz, soit partout où il sera. Il se rendra ensuite au 5me corps d'armée commandé par Monsieur le maréchal duc de Trévise en Estremadure ; le corps doit être à Badajos, ou même sur le Tage.

Monsieur le Jeune prendra une connaissance exacte de sa position, et de celle des troupes de l'armée du centre commandée par le général   qui sont réunies sur le Tage. Il verra si ces corps sont en communication avec l'armée de Portugal, et recueillera les nouvelles que l'on pourrait avoir de cette armée de ce côté.

Monsieur le Jeune prendra tous les renseignemens nécessaires pour pouvoir répondre à toutes les questions de l'Empereur, sur la situation des choses en Andalousie, devant Cadiz, et en Estremadure, d'où il viendra me rendre compte de sa mission.

LE PRINCE DE WAGRAM ET DE NEUFCHATEL,
Major-général.

Paris, le 14 *Février*, 1811.

SECTION 7.

Extracts from Lejeune's reports.

CADIZ.

" Montagnes de Ronda foyer d'insurrection entre le 4me corps et le premier."

" Les obusiers à la villantrois portent à 2560 toises : l'obus doit peser 75 livres, et contient 11 à 12 onces de poudre : on charge l'obusier à poudre d'un $\frac{1}{3}$ du poids de l'obus pour obtenir cette distance. Il n'y en a que le 4 en batterie: à la redoute Napoléon on en a 12 en fondus: mais il manque de projectilles et de la poudre en suffisante quantité. Toutes les obus n'éclatent pas en ville."

" Le pont de St. Petri a été traversé le jour de l'affaire par un sergent du 24me qui est revenu avec les Espagnols que l'on a pris. Le moment eut été favorable pour s'emparer de l'Isle."

" Le duc de Bellune bien ennuyé, désire beaucoup retourner: bon général, mais voyant les choses trop en noir."

SECTION 8.

Puerto Real, 20 *Mars*, 1811.

MON CHER GENERAL,

Enfin après 15 jours des plus cruelles souffrances je me trouve en état de reprendre la plume et de continuer le récit que j'ai eu l'honneur de vous adresser dans ma lettre du 6 au 7 de ce mois.

L'une des choses qui mérite d'abord de fixer votre attention, est la composition de cette armée combinée dont nous avons été tout-à-coup assaillis. J'ai déjà dit que le 26 Février une flotte de 180 voiles était sortie de Cadiz portant 1500 hommes de débarquement, et que de ce nombre étaient environ 4000 Anglais et 1000 Portugais. Cette flotte se dirigea vers Tarifa où le débarquement se fit le lendemain sans aucun accident. Il parait que les Anglais en réunissant les garnisons d'Algéciras et de Gibraltar à quelques restes de troupes venues récemment de Sicile, avaient déjà formé à Tarifa un petit corps de 1000 Anglais et de 2000 Portugais commandé par le général Stuart, et qui forma avec 2 où 300 hommes de cavalerie, l'avant garde de l'expédition dirigée contre nous. Cette armée ainsi composée de 10 à 12,000 Espagnols bien où mal équipés, de 4 à 5000 Anglais et de 3000 Portugais se mit enfin en campagne, et vint nous attaquer le 5. Il parait que Monsieur le maréchal Victor ne fut instruit que tard de la vraie direction prise par l'armée ennemie. Il arriva à Chiclana le 5 entre 8 et 9 heures du matin, suivi des bataillons de la 1re et 2de division: le plan d'opérations auquel il s'arrêta fut d'envoyer sur le champ la division Villate avec un régiment de cavalerie aux lignes de St. Petri, avec ordre de laisser arriver l'ennemi, de lui résister foiblement pour l'engager à suivre notre mouvement de retraite et de l'attirer ainsi sous la position St. Anne, où il ne pouvait manquer de se trouver dans une situation extrêmement

desavantageuse. Pendant cette manœuvre Monsieur le maréchal
Victor s'était lui-même porté avec la 1re et 2de division entre Conil
et St. Petri, à peu près à la hauteur de la Torre Barrossa avec
l'intention de couper à l'ennemi la retraite des montagnes. Là,
rencontrant la queue de l'armée, qui finissait de se filer, il la fit
attaquer vigoureusement, culbuta tout ce qui se rencontra devant
lui et accula les Espagnols à la mer, mais les Anglais que cette
manœuvre hardie mettaient entre deux feux, et dans l'impossibilité
de regagner Conil, revinrent sur leurs pas, et attaquant avec la
rage du désespoir, ils forcèrent à la retraite nos deux divisions,
qui ne formaient pas ensemble 5000 hommes.

Cependant Monsieur le maréchal Victor se croyait si sur de la
victoire qu'avant d'attaquer il envoya ordre aux troupes qui étaient
à Médina, de se porter entre Veger et Conil, pour ramasser le
reste des trainards ; les bagages, et les trains de munitions qu'ils
pouvaient rencontrer.

Le projet d'attirer l'ennemi sur le feu de St. Anne n'avait pas
mieux réussi du côté de la division Villatte ; car si cette division
fut d'abord assaillie par presque toute l'armée combinée, les généraux Anglais et Espagnols, avertis de bonne heure que Monsieur
le maréchal les tournaient avec un corps de troupes, arrêterent
leurs colonnes sur la rive gauche du ruisseau qui touche au Moulin
d'Almanza, et là, naturellement retranchés derrière ce marais, ils
n'eurent à garder que le pont et le Moulin, les seuls endroits par
lesquels on pouvait les attaquer. Quelque chose de plus malheu-
reux, fut, que dès le commencement de l'action, nos lignes de St.
Petri n'étant pas défendues, il sortit par le pont de Radeaux 5000
hommes de troupes fraiches de la Isla, lesquels se plaçant en
bataille devant la division Villatte, et couverts par la ruisseau du
Moulin d'Almanza, laissèrent au reste de l'armée combinée la liberté
de se retourner tout entière contre l'attaque de Monsieur le maréchal Victor. Ainsi se termina la bataille du 5, l'ennemi coucha
sur son champ de battaille, sans poursuivre les divisions Laval et
Rufin dans leur retraite. Je vous ai déjà fait part de notre perte.
Le général Rufin que nous croyons tué par une balle, qui lui a
traversé la tête, a été porté par les Anglais à la Isla, ou après deux
jours de léthargie, il a donné signes de vie; on dit qu'il va mieux.

La perte de l'ennemi a été à peu près de 3000 Anglais ou
Portugais, et de 5 à 600 Espagnols, tués ou blessés ; les Anglais
ont eu beaucoup des officiers mis hors de combat, on croit les
généraux *Grâm* et Stuart ainsi que le général Pêna blessés.
Le 6 à la pointe du jour nous nous attendions bien à une attaque

générale qui pouvait nous-être très funeste ; mais l'ennemi se contenta d'occuper avec 2000 hommes le fort de Médina, que nous avions un peu imprudemment abandonnés : la flotille ennemie fit aussi des démonstrations d'attaque sur le Trocadero, mais sans effet. Elle débarqua 6 à 700 hommes entre le Port de St. Marie, et le fort St. Cataline, qui fût sommé de se rendre ; on répondit à coups de canons. Un officier Anglais vint chez le gouverneur de St. Marie le prévenir qu'il allait prendre possession de la ville, mais il avait laissé ses troupes à la porte. Elles courent faire une action d'éclat en brulant et réduisant la petite redoute St. Antoine, qui n'était point gardée ; enchantés de ce succès ils se rembarquèrent. M. le maréchal s'attendait bien à être attaqués le 6 à Chiclana, il avait donné des ordres en conséquence, ces ordres furent mal interprétés, et on endommagea mal-à-propos dans la nuit quelques uns de nos ouvrages, mais ils furent sur le champ réparés. Lui-même était venu à Puerto Réal avec la division Laval, et avait envoyé la 1re division à St. Marie pour reprendre la ligne de Blocus comme avant la bataille du 5. Le 5me regiment de chasseurs fut envoyé entre Puerto Real et Médina à la ferme de Guerra en reconnaissance ; il y rencontra une poste de cavalerie ennemie, et la tailla en pièces. Le 6 au soir, on essaya de reprendre le fort de Médina, mais sans succés. Le 7 il fallut y envoyer plus de monde, et les Espagnols l'évacuèrent sans opposer de résistance.

Dans la nuit du 5 les Espagnols avaient rasés nos lignes de St. Petri, ils employèrent pendant plusieurs jours et plusieurs nuits 6000 hommes, à transporter à la Isla, du bois, dont ils manquaient, quelques jours après, nous avons fait cesser ces approvisionnements, en reprenant la position de St. Petri, où on ne trouva personne ; les Espagnols craignant une répétition de l'affaire du 2 Mars, ont détruits eux-même de fort bonne grace leur tête de pont, et replié leur pont de Radeaux, dès ce moment chacun resta chez soi, comme avant les hostilités.

Du 21 *Mars*, 1811.

Il est surprenant que l'armée combinée ne nous ait pas poursuivis le 5, bien plus surprenant encore qu'elle ne nous ait point attaqués le 6 au matin ; on en conçoit plusieurs raisons. On conjecture d'abord que la principale perte de la bataille étant tombée sur les Anglais, qui ont eu un grand nombre d'officiers et même leurs généraux mis hors de combat, les Espagnols n'ont pas osé venir seuls nous attaquer. Le général *Grâm* voulait cependant les y contraindre le lendemain, mais sur leur refus formel, il les a traité de lâches, de gens indignes d'être secourus. Ils ont répondu qu'ils feraient une sortie de la Isla si l'on voulait mettre le tiers d'Anglais ou Portugais avec les deux tiers d'Espagnols, le général Anglais a répondu qu'il n'exposerait plus un seul de ses soldats avec des troupes de cette espèce, et sur le champ il a donné ordre aux Anglais et Portugais de se retirer, a Cadiz ou dans la ville de la Isla. Il parait même que le lendemain les Anglais se sont embarqués pour se rendre à Gibraltar ou peut-être à Lisbonne. Les gens du pays donnent pour certain que le général *Grâm*, en envoyant ces jours derniers à Londres trente-trois officiers des moins blessés, n'a pas dissimulé qu'il les chargeait d'exposer à son gouvernement quelle folie il y avait de sacrifier de braves gens pour soutenir en Espagne un parti sans moyens, sans bravoure et sans moralité. Si ce qui précède n'est pas vrai, au moins sommes nous certains qu'une grande mésintelligence règne entre les Espagnols et leurs alliés. Le 20, les Espagnols ont encore essayé une sortie de la Carraca mais sans succès; ils s'y prennent un peu tard. Nous sommes à présent très à mesure pour les recevoir. Ils font semblant d'embarquer continuellement des troupes qui n'agissent pas et qui ne peuvent plus nous nuire. Il est arrivé à Médina quelques bataillons du 4me corps, deux bataillons du soixante-trois sont aussi venus de Séville. Nous apprenons avec la prise de Badajos, que M. le maréchal Soult est à Séville. La blessure de M. le commandant Bompar et les miennes vont un peu mieux.

LEGENTIL.

Excusez les imperfections de cette longue lettre, j'écris de mon lit, dans une posture gênante.

Monsieur le général de division Lery, à Séville.

SECTION 9.

Extracts from the intercepted report of general Garbé, commanding the French engineers, at the blockade of Cadiz.

25 *Mars*, 1811.

" On avait apperçu le 26 de Février au matin un grand convoi partant de la baye de Cadiz, pour se diriger sur Tarifa. Ce convoi portait à peu près 6 ou 7000 hommes des troupes de débarquement, qui allait joindre celles qui étaient déja réunies sur la

Barbate et dans les environs de l'Alcala de los Gazules. Le 2
Mars à la pointe du jour, l'ennemi commença son opération sur
Caza Vieja, qui fut évacué, et en même temps, il éffectua vers
l'embouchure de St. Petri, un passage pour faciliter l'établissement d'un pont de radeaux et d'une tête de pont. Il fit aussi
débarquer des troupes dans l'Isletta del Coto, et s'occupa d'y
établir deux batteries. Le 3, on fit marcher la division du
général Rufin, qui prit position à moitié chemin de Puerto Real
à Médina Sidonia. Celle du général Laval, s'établit en avant de
Puerto Real, et le général Villatte garda ses positions auprès de
Chiclana. Ce jour on n'apperçut aucun mouvement de l'ennemi.
Tous les ouvrages de la ligne étaient gardés par les garnisons
qu'on avait designées auparavant. Santa Marie fut évacué et le
pont replié sur la rive gauche.

" Puerto Real était défendu par une compagnie de sapeurs,
deux du 45me regiment, et par tous les réfugiés Français qu'on
avoit armés.

" Le 4 Monsieur le maréchal fit attaquer à la pointe du jour
l'ennemi dans sa tête de pont de Santi Petri. Cette attaque se
fit par 4 compagnies du 95me régiment qui s'emparèrent de l'ou-
vrage, firent prisonniers 500 hommes, et enlevèrent un drapeau.
Il est certain que si on eut employé dans cette opération 2 ou 3000
hommes on enlevait le pont et l'Isle de Léon. L'ennemi fut si
disconcerté qu'il avait abandonné ses batteries et ses ouvrages
fermés. Un pareil résultât paraissait être d'un très bon augure
pour les grandes opérations. On fit partir le même jour de Médina
une reconnaissance sur Casa Vieja. Ou reçut avis dans la nuit que
cette reconnaissance n'avait rencontré personne, et que les colonnes
ennemies se dirigeant sur Conil, le mouvement ne pouvait avoir
pour but que d'opérer la jonction de ce corps d'armée, avec celui
qui était resté dans l'île. Le 5, avant le jour, on se mit en marche
de la position qu'on occupait à moitié chemin de Médina pour se
porter sur Chiclana. Arrivé dans cet endroit, Monsieur le maréchal donna l'ordre au général Villatte de rassembler toute sa division vers les flèches de St. Petri, pour y maintenir l'ennemi qui y
paraissait en force, pendant qu'il dirigeait sur la route de Conil,
les divisions de Laval et Rufin, et le peu de cavalerie qu'il avait
avec lui. Il se porta de ce côté, et ne tarda pas à rencontrer une
forte colonne, qui marchait le long de la mer entre St. Petri et
Conil, et se dirigeait sur le premier de ses endroits. Les troupes
arrivées à portée de canon se formèrent. Le général Rufin prit
la gauche pour aller occuper un mamelon où l'ennemi paraissait

s'établir. Quand les deux divisions furent formées, elle se trouvèrent en présence d'une armée, beaucoup plus nombreuse qu'on ne l'avait cru d'abord. L'artillerie n'était pas encore arrivée, et celle de l'ennemi commençait à jouer de toute parts. Le général Vilatte n'avait pu garder les flèches de St. Petri, qui étaient au moment d'être prises, n'étant alors défendues que par un seul bataillon du 27me d'infantrie legère.

Cette division fut obligée de se replier et de repasser le ravin dans lequel roulent les eaux du Moulin d'Almanza. Ce mouvement empêcha le général Vilatte de se réunir aux deux autres divisions, qui n'ayant en tout que dix bataillons, essuyaient un feu terrible de la part de l'ennemi. Nos pertes devenaient d'autant plus sensible que le nombre des combattans n'était que le tiers de celui de l'ennemi. Des corps entiers se trouvaient accablés avant qu'on eut pu entamer la ligne des Anglais. Il n'y avait point de réserve. Le deux mille hommes de Médina Sidonia étaient en marche pour Conil. Il fallut penser à la retraite qui se fit en bon ordre, jusque sur les hauteurs en avant de Chiclana, où l'on fit camper une division pendant la nuit. Les Anglais firent leur jonction avec les troupes de l'île de Léon, et les Espagnols continuèrent d'occuper notre position du Moulin d'Almanza et de St. Petri. Si l'ennemi voulant continuer ses opérations offensives dans la journée du 6, se fut présenté de bonne heure, il est probable que dans la situation où nous nous trouvions après la journée du 5 nous étions obligés d'évacuer le terrain jusqu'à Puerto Réal, où on aurait pris la position dont j'ai parlé plus haut, pour y livrer une seconde bataille, mais les opérations ont manqué d'ensemble. Il s'est contenté de rentrer dans l'île et pendant ce temps un très petit corps de troupes Anglaises opéraient un débarquement entre St. Marie, et la pointe de St. Catherine, qui n'eut d'autre résultât que d'enlever une batterie défendue par quinze hommes et de se promener une ou deux heures dans les rues de St. Marie. Monsieur le maréchal ne voyait aucun mouvement offensif, ordonna de rétablir les grandes communications par St. Marie, chacun rentra dans ses portes et cette mesure produisit beaucoup plus d'effet, sur l'armée et les habitans du Pays, que les dispositions qu'on auraient pu prendre."

No. X.

EXTRACTS FROM THE CORRESPONDENCE OF CAPTAIN SQUIRE, OF THE ENGINEERS.

SECTION 1.

"*March* 1, 1811.

" I have been employed in constructing batteries, opposite the mouth of the Zezere, for twenty-five guns ! though we have only one brigade of nine pounders to arm them.

" Thank God, for my own credit, I protested against these batteries from the first, in my reports which were sent to lord Wellington, and now I verily believe the marshal himself is ashamed of their construction. Punhete, you know, is situated precisely at the confluence of the Zezere with the Tagus, the enemy's bridge is about half a mile from the mouth of the river, and one mile, by measurement, from the nearest of our heights, which we have crowned with an eight-gun battery."

SECTION 2.

" I was truly sorry to hear that the Spaniards were so thoroughly routed near Badajos, but Mendizabel was an idiot. On the 18th February, the enemy threw a bridge over the Guadiana, above Badajos. Don Carlos España, an active officer, whom I know very well, reconnoitred the bridge, and made his report to Mendizabel, who was playing at cards. Very well, said the chief, we'll go and look at it to-morrow! At day-break the Spanish army was surprised."

SECTION 3.

" May 17, 1811. I reconnoitred the ground in front of Cristoval, and was pressed, by Colonel Fletcher, who was on the other side of the Guadiana, to commence our operations that evening. The soil was hard and rocky, and our tools infamous. I made,

however, no difficulties, and we began our battery on the night of
the 8th, the moon being at the full: our work was barely four
hundred yards from Cristoval.   In spite, however, of a most
destructive fire of musketry, and shot, and shells, from various
parts of the body of the place, we succeeded in completing our
battery on the night of the 10th; and, on the morning of the
11th, at four a.m. its fire was opened.   The enemy's fire was,
however, very superior to our own, and, before sunset, the three
guns and one howitzer were disabled, for against our little attack
was the whole attention of the enemy directed.   On the other
side of the river the intended attack had not yet been begun,
and we sustained the almost undivided fire of Badajos !   I told
the marshal, when I saw him on the 11th, that to continue to
fight our battery was a positive sacrifice ; he did not, however,
order us to desist till our guns were silenced.   If doubt and in-
decision had not governed all our operations, and had we begun
even on the night of the 9th, I am satisfied that our plan of
attack was excellent, and that we should have entered the place
on the 15th.   It is true that two distant batteries were erected, on
the left bank of the river, against the place, but they scarcely
excited the enemy's attention, our little corps bore the brunt of
the enemy's exertions, which were great and spirited.   Including
those who fell in the sortie, our loss has been from six to seven
hundred men.   Both officers and men were exhausted, mind and
body ; they felt and saw that they were absurdly sacrificed."

SECTION 4.

Elvas, May 20, 1811.

" Had our operations been conducted with common activity
and common judgement, Badajos would have been in our hands
before the 15th of May.   But what has been the fact?   Our
little corps on the Cristoval side was absolutely sacrificed.   The
whole fire and attention of Badajos was directed against our unsupported attack, and our loss in consequence was severe." —" Our
operation before Cristoval was absurdly pressed forward *without
any co-operation on the left bank of the river.*   The marshal
hesitated—delayed, and at last withdrew his troops at such a moment that he was scarcely time enough to meet the enemy in the
field !"

No. XI.

EXTRACT OF A LETTER FROM GENERAL CAMPBELL
TO LORD LIVERPOOL.

" *Gibraltar, October* 23, 1810.

" The troops at Malaga, with the exception of three hundred men, moved upon Fuengirola, of which lord Blayney was apprised; but, in place of his lordship taking advantage of this fortunate event, he wasted two days in a fruitless attack on the fort of Fuengirola, cannonading it from twelve-pounders, although he perceived that no impression had been made on it by the fire of the shipping and gun-boats, the artillery of which were double the calibre. In this situation he was surprised by an inferior force, and, whilst he was on board of a gun-boat, his guns taken and the whole thrown into confusion; at this moment he was informed of the disaster, and, so far to his credit, he retook his guns, but, immediately after, conceiving a body of French cavalry to be Spaniards, he ordered the firing to cease, when he was surrounded and made prisoner; his men, losing confidence, gave way, and, hurrying to the beach, relinquished their honour and the field."

END OF VOL. III.